SEVENTH EDITION

FINANCIAL ACCOUNTING

FOR DECISION MAKERS

Peter Atrill
Eddie McLaney

PEARSON

Harlow, England • London • New York • Boston • San Francisco • Toronto • Sydney
Auckland • Singapore • Hong Kong • Tokyo • Seoul • Taipei • New Delhi
Cape Town • São Paulo • Mexico City • Madrid • Amsterdam • Munich • Paris • Milan

Pearson Education Limited
Edinburgh Gate
Harlow CM20 2JE
Tel: +44 (0)1279 623623
Fax: +44 (0)1279 431059
Website: www.pearson.com/uk

Second edition published 1999 by Prentice Hall Europe
Third edition published 2002 by Pearson Education Limited
Fourth edition 2005
Fifth edition 2008
Sixth edition 2011
Seventh edition 2013 (print)

© Prentice Hall Europe 1996 (print), 1998 (print)
© Pearson Education Limited 2002 (print), 2013 (print and electronic)

The Financial Times. With a worldwide network of highly respected journalists, *The Financial Times*
provides global business news, insightful opinion and expert analysis of business, finance and
politics. With over 500 journalists reporting from 50 countries worldwide, our in-depth coverage of
international news is objectively reported and analysed from an independent, global perspective.
To find out more, visit **www.ft.com/pearsonoffer**.

ISBN: 978-0-273-78563-7 (print)
      978-0-273-78569-9 (PDF)
      978-0-273-78574-3 (eText)

British Library Cataloguing-in-Publication Data
A catalogue record for the print edition is available from the British Library

Library of Congress Cataloging-in-Publication Data
A catalog record for the print edition is available from the Library of Congress

10 9 8 7 6 5 4
16 15

Print edition typeset in 9.25/13pt Helvetica Neue Pro by 35
Printed and bound in Slovakia by Neografia

NOTE THAT ANY PAGE CROSS REFERENCES REFER TO THE PRINT EDITION

Brief contents

FINANCIAL ACCOUNTING FOR DECISION MAKERS, 7th Edition, ONLINE

A wide range of supporting resources are available at:

MyAccountingLab

Register to create your own personal account using the access code supplied with your copy of the book,* and access the following teaching and learning resources:

Resources for students

- **A dynamic eText** of the book that you can search, bookmark, annotate and highlight as you please
- **Self-assessment questions** that identify your strengths before recommending a personalised study plan that points you to the resources which can help you achieve a better grade
- **Flashcards** to help your understanding of key terms
- **Links** to relevant sites on the web
- **Case studies**

Resources for instructors

- Instructor's manual with additional questions, and complete and fully worked solutions, as well as case study debriefs
- PowerPoint slides containing figures from the book

For more information please contact your local Pearson Education sales representative or visit www.myaccountinglab.com

* If you don't have an access code, you can still access the resources.
Visit www.myaccountinglab.com for details.

Contents

5 Accounting for limited companies (2) — 148

6 Measuring and reporting cash flows — 185

Preface

This text provides a comprehensive introduction to financial accounting. It is aimed both at students who are not majoring in accounting and at those who are. Those studying introductory-level financial accounting as part of their course in business, economics, hospitality management, tourism, engineering, or some other area, should find that the book provides complete coverage of the material at the level required. Students who are majoring in accounting should find the book a useful introduction to the main principles, which can serve as a foundation for further study.

The main focus of the text is on the ways in which financial statements and information can improve the quality of decision making. To ensure that readers understand the practical implications of the subject, there are, throughout the text, numerous illustrative extracts with commentary from company reports, survey data and other sources. Although some technical issues are dealt with in the text, the main emphasis throughout is on basic principles and underlying concepts.

In this seventh edition, we have taken the opportunity to make improvements that have been suggested by students and lecturers who used the previous edition. We have updated and expanded the number of examples from real life. We have also incorporated developments that have occurred with International Financial Reporting Standards, as well as developments that have arisen in the area of corporate governance. The most important change, however, is a new chapter dealing with key recognition and reporting issues. Chapter 7 examines provisions, contingent assets and liabilities, internally generated intangible assets, finance leases and the treatment of certain borrowing costs.

The text is written in an 'open-learning' style. This means that there are numerous integrated activities, worked examples and questions throughout the text to help you to understand the subject fully. You are encouraged to interact with the material and to check your progress continually. Irrespective of whether you are using the book as part of a taught course or for personal study, we have found that this approach is more 'user-friendly' and makes it easier for you to learn.

We recognise that most of you will not have studied financial accounting before, and, therefore, we have tried to write in a concise and accessible style, minimising the use of technical jargon. We have also tried to introduce topics gradually, explaining everything as we go. Where technical terminology is unavoidable we try to provide clear explanations. In addition, you will find all of the key terms highlighted in the text, and then listed at the end of each chapter with a page reference. All of these key terms are also listed alphabetically, with a concise definition, in the glossary given in Appendix B. This should provide a convenient point of reference from which to revise.

A further important consideration in helping you to understand and absorb the topics covered is the design of the text itself. The page layout and colour scheme have been carefully considered to allow for the easy navigation and digestion of material. The layout features a large page format, an open design, and clear signposting of the various features and assessment material. More detail about the nature and use of these features is given in the 'How to use this book' section; and the main points are also summarised, using example pages from the text, in the Guided tour.

We do hope that you will find the book both readable and helpful.

Peter Atrill
Eddie McLaney

How to use this book

We have organised the chapters to reflect what we consider to be a logical sequence and, for this reason, we suggest that you work through the text in the order in which it is presented. We have tried to ensure that earlier chapters do not refer to concepts or terms that are not explained until a later chapter. If you work through the chapters in the 'wrong' order, you will probably encounter concepts and terms that were explained previously.

Irrespective of whether you are using the book as part of a lecture/tutorial-based course or as the basis for a more independent mode of study, we advocate following broadly the same approach.

Integrated assessment material

Interspersed throughout each chapter are numerous **activities**. You are strongly advised to attempt all of these questions. They are designed to simulate the sort of quick-fire questions that your lecturer might throw at you during a lecture or tutorial. Activities serve two purposes:

■ to give you the opportunity to check that you understand what has been covered so far;
■ to encourage you to think about the topic just covered, either to see a link between that topic and others with which you are already familiar, or to link the topic just covered to the next.

The answer to each activity is provided immediately after the question. This answer should be covered up until you have deduced your solution, which can then be compared with the one given.

Towards the end of Chapters 2–12 there is a **self-assessment question**. This is more comprehensive and demanding than most of the activities, and is designed to give you an opportunity to check and apply your understanding of the core coverage of the chapter. The solution to each of these questions is provided in Appendix C. As with the activities, it is important that you attempt each question thoroughly before referring to the solution. If you have difficulty with a self-assessment question, you should go over the relevant chapter again.

End-of-chapter assessment material

At the end of each chapter there are four **review questions**. These are short questions requiring a narrative answer or discussion within a tutorial group. They are intended to help you assess how well you can recall and critically evaluate the core terms and concepts covered in each chapter. Answers to these questions are provided in Appendix D at the end of the book.

At the end of each chapter, except for Chapter 1, there is a set of **exercises**. These are mostly computational and are designed to reinforce your knowledge and understanding. Exercises are graded as 'basic' 'intermediate' or 'advanced' according to their level of difficulty. The basic-level questions are fairly straightforward; the more advanced ones can be quite demanding but can be successfully completed if you have worked conscientiously through the chapter and have attempted the basic exercises. Solutions to some of the exercises in each chapter are provided in Appendix E. A coloured exercise number identifies these questions. Here, too, a thorough attempt should be made to answer each exercise before referring to the solution.

Solutions to the other exercises are provided in a separate *Instructors' Manual*.

To familiarise yourself with the main features and how they will benefit your study from this text, an illustrated 'Guided tour' is provided (on pp. xviii–xix).

Content and structure

The text comprises twelve main chapters. The market research for this text revealed a divergence of opinions, given the target market, on whether or not to include material on double-entry bookkeeping techniques. So as to not interrupt the flow and approach of the main chapters, Appendix A on recording financial transactions (including activities and three exercise questions) has been placed after Chapter 12.

Guided tour of the book

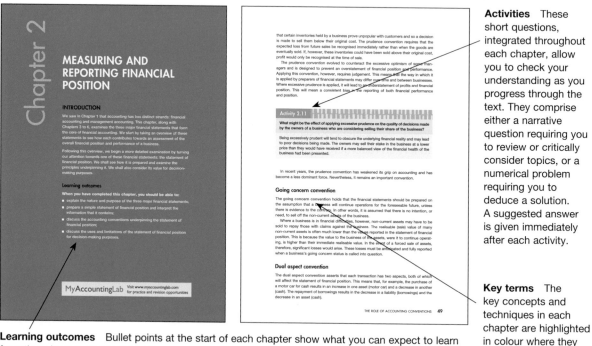

Learning outcomes   Bullet points at the start of each chapter show what you can expect to learn from that chapter, and highlight the core coverage.

Activities   These short questions, integrated throughout each chapter, allow you to check your understanding as you progress through the text. They comprise either a narrative question requiring you to review or critically consider topics, or a numerical problem requiring you to deduce a solution. A suggested answer is given immediately after each activity.

Key terms   The key concepts and techniques in each chapter are highlighted in colour where they are first introduced.

Examples   At frequent intervals throughout most chapters, there are numerical examples that give you step-by-step workings to follow through to the solution.

'Real World' illustrations   Integrated throughout the text, these illustrative examples highlight the practical application of accounting concepts and techniques by real businesses, including extracts from company reports and financial statements, survey data and other insights from business.

Self-assessment questions   Towards the end of most chapters you will encounter one of these questions, allowing you to attempt a comprehensive question before tackling the end-of-chapter assessment material. To check your understanding and progress, solutions are provided at the end of the book.

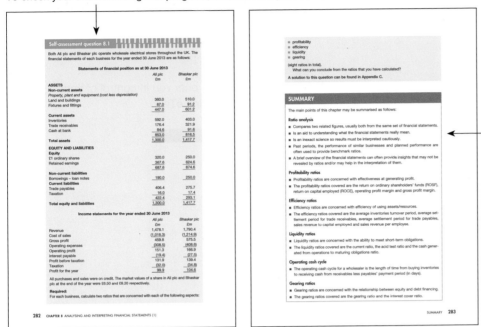

Bullet point chapter summary   Each chapter ends with a 'bullet-point' summary. This highlights the material covered in the chapter and can be used as a quick reminder of the main issues.

Key terms summary   At the end of each chapter, there is a listing (with page references) of all the key terms introduced in that chapter, allowing you to refer back easily to the most important points.

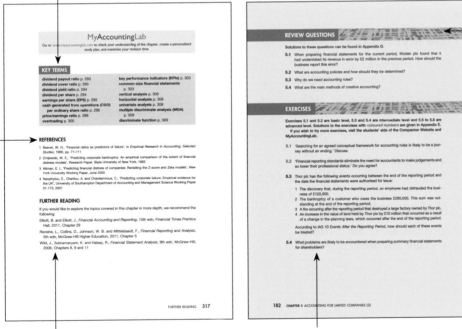

Review questions
These short questions encourage you to review and/or critically discuss your understanding of the main topics covered in each chapter, either individually or in a group. Solutions to these questions can be found at the back of the book.

Further reading   This section comprises a listing of relevant chapters in other textbooks that you might refer to in order to pursue a topic in more depth or gain an alternative perspective.

References   Provides full details of sources of information referred to in the chapter.

Exercises   These comprehensive questions at the end of most chapters. The more advanced questions are separately identified. Solutions to five of the questions (those with coloured numbers) are provided at the end of the book, enabling you to assess your progress. Solutions to the remaining questions are available online for lecturers only. Additional exercises can be found on the Companion Website at **www.pearsoned.co.uk/atrillmclaney**.

Guided tour of MyAccountingLab

MyAccountingLab is an online assessment and revision tool that puts you in control of your learning through a suite of study and practice tools tied to the online eText.

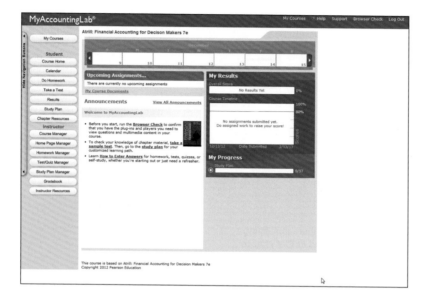

Why should I use MyAccountingLab?

With more than 300,000 registered students using MyAccountingLab each year, you can be confident that this is most effective and reliable learning solution for accounting available today.

We recently polled 10,000 student users of MyAccountingLab from around the globe:

- 92% of students said that MyAccountingLab learning aids helped them while completing homework and/or preparing for exams
- 89% of students said that MyAccountingLab helped them earn a higher grade.
- 92% of students would recommend MyAccountingLab for future courses.

How do I use MyAccountingLab?

Practice tests for each chapter of the textbook enable you to check your understanding and identify the areas in which you need to do further work.

Based on your test results, we create a personalised Study Plan. This highlights areas where you still need to revise, allowing you to focus on weaker areas and study more efficiently. It also links to the eText, so you can re-read sections in topics you have not yet mastered.

We also provide step-by-step solutions to exercises, so you can see how to get the right answer.

Lecturer training and support

Our dedicated team of Technology Specialists offer personalised training and support for **MyAccountingLab, ensuring that you can maximise the benefits of MyAccountingLab**. To make contact with your Technology Specialist please email feedback-cw@pearson.com. For a visual walkthrough of how to make the most of **MyAccountingLab**, visit www.myaccountinglab.com.

To find details of your local sales consultant, go to www.pearsoned.co.uk/replocator.

Acknowledgements

We are grateful to the following for permission to reproduce copyright material:

Figures

Figure 4.1 after information in Companies Register Activities 2011, Statistical Tables on Companies Registration Activities 2010/11, www.companieshouse.gov.uk, contains public sector information licenced under the Open Government Licence v.1.0; Figure 7.3 from UK Business and Enterprise Research and Development 2010, Office for National Statistics, www.ons.gov.uk, source: Office for National Statistics licensed under the Open Government Licence v.1.0; Figure 7.5 from Finance & Leasing Association Annual Review 2011, p. 10, www.fla.org.uk; Figure 8.2 after 'Profitability of UK companies Q4 2011', Office of National Statistics, 4 April 2012, www.statistics.gov.uk, adapted from data from the Office for National Statistics licenced under the Open Government Licence v.1.0; Figure 12.4 from a survey of annual reports of 84 companies from the FTSE 100 that were published between the beginning of November 2004 and the end of June 2005 in 'Audit Committee Reporting in 2005', Independent Audit Ltd; Figure 12.7 from Tesco plc Annual Report and Financial Statements 2011, p. 81, copyright Tesco Stores Ltd; Figure 12.8 adapted from 'Ownership of UK quoted shares 2010', Office for National Statistics (ONS), www.statistics.gov.uk, source: Office for National Statistics licenced under the Open Government Licence v.1.0.

Text

Box 1.1 from 'Morrison in uphill battle to integrate Safeway', *Financial Times*, 26/05/2005 (Rigby E), © The Financial Times Limited. All Rights Reserved; Box 1.2 from http://www.standardlife.com/about/index.html and http://www.standardlife.com/about/strategy.html, copyright Standard Life Employee Services Limited, www.standardlife.com, accessed 25 January 2012; Box 1.2 from www.elektron-technology.com; Box 1.3 from 'Fair shares?', *Financial Times*, 11/06/2005 (Skapinker M), © The Financial Times Limited. All Rights Reserved; Box 1.4 from 'How we've poisoned the well of wealth', *Financial Times*, 15/02/2009 (Goyder M), © The Financial Times Limited. All Rights Reserved; Box 2.1 from Brandz Top 100 Most Valuable Global Brands 2011, Millward Brown Optimor 2011, www.millwardbrown.com/Sites/Optimor; Box 2.2 from Tottenham Hotspur plc Annual Report 2011; Box 2.4 from Extracts from 'Swisscom takes 1.3 billion euro charge on Fastweb' (Simonian H) 14/12/11, www.ft.com, © The Financial Times Limited. All Rights Reserved; Box 2.5 from Amstrad (AMT), *Investors Chronicle* 7/10/2005, © The Financial Times Limited. All Rights Reserved; Box 2.6 from Ted Baker plc Annual Report and Accounts 2010/11, p. 51; Box 2.7 adapted from 'Balance sheets: the basics', www.businesslink.gov.uk; Box 3.2 from AMEC plc, Annual Report and Accounts 2011, Notes to Consolidated Accounts, p. 75; Box 3.3 After information in British Sky Broadcasting Group plc Annual Report and Accounts 2012; Box 3.4 from Carphone Warehouse Group plc Annual Report 2011, p. 53; Box 3.5 from British Airways Annual Report and Accounts 2008/09 Note 15, www.britishairways.com; Box 3.6 from Blacks Leisure Group plc Annual Report 2011 p. 39; Box 3.7 from EPI 2012 Industry White Paper, www.intrum.com, Intrum Justitia AB (publ); Box 4.1 from 'Monotub Industries in a spin as founder gets Titan for £1', *Financial Times*, 23/01/2003 (Urquhart L), © The Financial Times Limited. All Rights Reserved; Box 4.4 from Premier Oil plc letter from the chairman 15/04/2011, www.premier-oil.com; Box 4.5 from Ryanair Holdings plc Annual Report 2011 p. 128, copyright Ryanair Holdings plc; Box 4.6 adapted from Medusa Mining, 08/03/2010, www.medusamining.com.au; Box 4.7 from Rolls-Royce plc Annual Report and Accounts 2010, Note 14; Box 4.8 after Information taken from 'Peugeot launches 1 billion euro rights issue' (Reed J) 06/03/2012, www.ft.com, © The Financial Times Limited. All Rights Reserved; Article 4.9 from Extracts from 'Oxford Instruments to acquire two groups', Kavanagh M, 15/06/2011, www.ft.com, © The Financial Times Limited. All Rights Reserved; Box 4.10 from 'Eurotunnel pays first dividend since 1987 float' (King I) 04/03/2009, www.timesonline.co.uk; Box 4.11 from Ryanair Holdings plc Annual Report 2011, p. 7; Box 5.1 from International Accounting Standards Board, www.iasb.org.uk, Copyright © 2012 IFRS Foundation. All rights reserved. No permission granted to reproduce or distribute; Box 5.2 from

Tottenham Hotspur plc Annual Report 2011, p. 58; Box 5.3 from 'Battlelines are drawn up for fight on standards' (Bruce R) 07/01/2008, www.ft.com, © The Financial Times Limited. All Rights Reserved; Box 5.4 after Dirty laundry: how companies fudge the numbers, *The Times Business Section*, 22/09/2002; Box 5.5 from 'Dell to lower writedowns on restated earnings', *Financial Times*, 30/10/2007 (Allison K), © The Financial Times Limited. All Rights Reserved; Box 5.9 from 'Anglo Irish bank chief quits over hiding 87 million euro loan', 19/12/2008, www.belfasttelegraph.co.uk; Box 5.10 from quote from Alistair Hodgson 'It pays to read between the lines', *Financial Times*, 17/09/2005, © The Financial Times Limited. All Rights Reserved; Box 6.1 from 'Rations cut for army of buyers', *Financial Times*, 20/10/2008, © The Financial Times Limited. All Rights Reserved; Box 6.2 from The management column, *The Daily Telegraph Business*, 14/06/2010 (Timpson J), copyright © Telegraph Media Group Limited 2010; Box 6.3 from Tesco Annual Review 2011, p. 35, www.tescocorporate.com, Copyright Tesco Stores Ltd; Box 6.4 from LiDCO Group plc Annual Report 2011 and AIM company profile, www.londonstockexchange.com; Box 7.1 from 'BP plans $30 billion sales to meet spill costs' (Murphy P) 27/07/2010, www.ft.com, © The Financial Times Limited. All Rights Reserved; Box 7.2 from Interim results for the 26 weeks ended 31 July 2010, Kingfisher plc 16/09/2010, www.kingfisher.com; Box 7.3 from Astra Zeneca plc Annual Report and Form 20-F Information, p. 147; Boxs 7.6, 10.5 from British Sky Broadcasting Group plc Annual Report 2012; Box 8.4 adapted from 'Costs vibrate as VW accelerates' (Schafer D) 29 March 2010, www.ft.com, © The Financial Times Limited. All Rights Reserved; Box 8.5 adapted from 'Companies monitor suppliers' credit scores' (Moules J) 26 January 2012, www.ft.com, © The Financial Times Limited. All Rights Reserved; Box 8.7 from 'Gearing levels set to plummet', *Financial Times*, 10/02/2009 (Grant J), © The Financial Times Limited. All Rights Reserved; Box 9.1 from *Financial Times*, 14/02/2012, p. 28; Exercise 9.1 from *Financial Times*, 27/04/2012; Box 9.4 from easyjet plc Annual Report 2011, p. 103; Box 9.6 from 'New study re-writes the A to Z of value investing', *Financial Times*, 14/08/2009 (Mathurin P), © The Financial Times Limited. All Rights Reserved; Box 9.7 from *Arnold Weinstock and the Making of GEC*, published by Aurum Press (Aris S 1998), Thanks to the author, Stephen Aris, for permission to reproduce this extract; Box 10.1 after Associated British Foods plc Annual Report and Acccounts 2011, pp. 106–8; Box 10.2 after 'Glencore and Xstrata close to $88 billion deal', *Financial Times*, 02/02/2012 (Blas J and Pfeifer S), © The Financial Times Limited. All Rights Reserved; Box 11.1 from 'Multinationals face more tax audits' (Cohen N) 03/05/2011, www.ft.com, © The Financial Times Limited. All Rights Reserved; Boxs 11.2, 11.3, 11.4, 11.5, 11.6, 11.7 from Tesco plc Annual Report and Financial Statements 2011, Business Review, www.tesco.com, Copyright Tesco Stores Ltd; Box 11.8 from 'Regional, sub-regional and local Gross Value Added 2010', Office for National Statistics (ONS), 14/12/2011, www.statistics.gov.uk, source: Office for National Statistics licenced under the Open Government Licence v.1.0; Box 12.1 from www.frc.org.uk, © Financial Reporting Council (FRC). Adapted and reproduced with the kind permission of the Financial Reporting Council. All rights reserved. For further information, please visit www.frc.org.uk or call +44 (0)20 7492 2300; Box 12.2 after information in J Sainsbury plc Annual Report and Financial Statements 2011, p. 25, reproduced by kind permission of J Sainsbury plc; Box 12.3 from 'An expert hand behind the scenes', *Financial Times*, 30/09/2008 (Willman J), © The Financial Times Limited. All Rights Reserved; Box 12.4 from 'Report reveals sharp rise in non-exec fees' (Smith A and Hayes G) 29/04/2012, www.ft.com, © The Financial Times Limited. All Rights Reserved; Box 12.5 from 'Ineffective internal controls hurting GM', 23/03/2007, www.accountancyage.com, copyright Incisive Media; Box 12.6 from Marks and Spencer plc Annual Report 2011, p. 45; Box 12.7 adapted from Tesco plc Annual Report and Financial Statements 2011, p. 76, Copyright Tesco Stores Ltd; Box 12.8 from 'Top directors' total earnings rise 49%', Groom B, 27/10/2011, www.ft.com, © The Financial Times Limited. All Rights Reserved; Box 12.11 from Kingfisher plc Annual Report and Accounts 2011, Directors' Remuneration Report, www.kingfisher.com; Box 12.12 from 'Ebay seeks to alter terms of stock options', *Financial Times*, 11/03/2009 (Gelles D), © The Financial Times Limited. All Rights Reserved; Box 12.14 from 'Sly Bailey to leave Trinity Mirror' (Fenton B, Davoudi S and Burgess K) 03/05/2012, www.ft.com, © The Financial Times Limited. All Rights Reserved; Box 12.15 from Extracts taken from 'Corporate Governance, Stewardship' on website, www.fidelity.co.uk; Box 12.16 from 'UK Stewardship Code', p. 4, www.frc.org.uk, © Financial Reporting Council (FRC). Adapted and reproduced with the kind permission of the Financial Reporting Council. All rights reserved. For further information, please visit www.frc.org.uk or call +44 (0)20 7492 2300.

In some instances we have been unable to trace the owners of copyright material, and we would appreciate any information that would enable us to do so.

Chapter 1

INTRODUCTION TO ACCOUNTING

INTRODUCTION

In this opening chapter we consider the role of accounting. We shall see that it can be a valuable tool for decision making. We also identify the main users of accounting information and discuss how accounting information may improve the quality of their decisions. We then go on to consider the two main strands of accounting: financial accounting and management accounting. We shall discuss the key differences between the two main strands and why these differences arise.

Since this book is concerned with accounting and financial decision making for private-sector businesses, we shall review the main types of business enterprise that exist. We examine the form and structure of each and the factors that owners should take into account when deciding on which is most suitable. We end the chapter by discussing the key financial objective that all businesses are likely to pursue.

Learning outcomes

When you have completed this chapter, you should be able to:

■ explain the nature and roles of accounting;

■ identify the main users of financial information and discuss their needs;

■ distinguish between financial and management accounting;

■ explain the purpose of a business and describe how businesses are organised and structured.

MyAccountingLab   Visit **www.myaccountinglab.com** for practice and revision opportunities

WHAT IS ACCOUNTING?

Accounting is concerned with *collecting, analysing* and *communicating* financial information. The ultimate aim is to help those using this information to make more informed decisions. If the financial information that is communicated were not capable of improving the quality of decisions made, there would be no point in producing it.

Sometimes the impression is given that the purpose of accounting is simply to prepare financial (accounting) reports on a regular basis. While it is true that accountants undertake this kind of work, it does not represent an end in itself. As already mentioned, the ultimate aim of the accountant's work is to give people better financial information on which to base their decisions. This decision-making perspective of accounting fits in with the theme of this book and shapes the way in which we deal with each topic.

WHO ARE THE USERS OF ACCOUNTING INFORMATION?

For accounting information to be useful, the accountant must be clear *for whom* the information is being prepared and *for what purpose* the information will be used. There are likely to be various groups of people (known as 'user groups') with an interest in a particular organisation, in the sense of needing to make decisions about it. For the typical private-sector business, the more important of these groups are shown in Figure 1.1. Take a look at this figure and then try Activity 1.1.

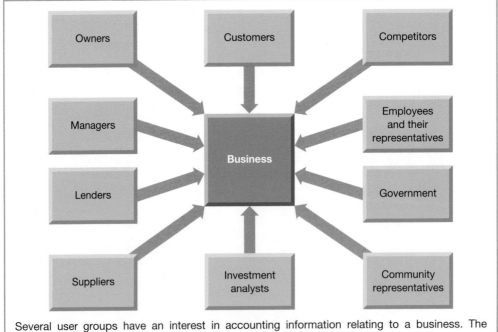

Several user groups have an interest in accounting information relating to a business. The majority of these are outside the business but, nevertheless, have a stake in it. This is not meant to be an exhaustive list of potential users; however, the groups identified are normally the most important.

Figure 1.1 Main users of financial information relating to a business

Ptarmigan Insurance plc (PI) is a large motor insurance business. Taking the user groups identified in Figure 1.1, suggest, for each group, the sorts of decisions likely to be made about PI and the factors to be taken into account when making these decisions.

Your answer may be along the following lines:

User group	Decision
Customers	Whether to take further motor policies with PI. This might involve an assessment of PI's ability to continue in business and to meet their needs, particularly in respect of any insurance claims made.
Competitors	How best to compete against PI or, perhaps, whether to leave the market on the grounds that it is not possible to compete profitably with PI. This might involve competitors using PI's performance in various respects as a 'benchmark' when evaluating their own performance. They might also try to assess PI's financial strength and to identify significant changes that may signal PI's future actions (for example, raising funds as a prelude to market expansion).
Employees	Whether to continue working for PI and, if so, whether to demand higher rewards for doing so. The future plans, profits and financial strength of the business are likely to be of particular interest when making these decisions.
Government	Whether PI should pay tax and, if so, how much; whether it complies with agreed pricing policies; whether financial support is needed and so on. In making these decisions an assessment of PI's profits, sales revenues and financial strength would be made.
Community representatives	Whether to allow PI to expand its premises and/or whether to provide economic support for the business. When making such decisions, PI's ability to continue to provide employment for the community and its willingness to use community resources and to fund environmental improvements are likely to be important considerations.
Investment analysts	Whether to advise clients to invest in PI. This would involve an assessment of the likely risks and future returns associated with PI.
Suppliers	Whether to continue to supply PI and, if so, whether to supply on credit. This would involve an assessment of PI's ability to pay for any goods and services supplied.
Lenders	Whether to lend money to PI and/or whether to require repayment of any existing loans. PI's ability to pay the interest and to repay the principal sum would be important factors in such decisions.
Managers	Whether the performance of the business needs to be improved. Performance to date would be compared with earlier plans or some other 'benchmark' to decide whether action needs to be taken. Managers may also wish to decide whether there should be a change in PI's future direction. This would involve looking at PI's ability to perform and at the opportunities available to it.
Owners	Whether to invest more in PI or to sell all, or part, of the investment currently held. This would involve an assessment of the likely risks and returns associated with PI. Owners may also be involved with decisions on rewarding senior managers. The financial performance of the business would normally be considered when making such a decision.

Although this answer covers many of the key points, you may have identified other decisions and/or other factors to be taken into account by each group.

THE CONFLICTING INTERESTS OF USERS

We have seen above that each user group will have its own particular interests. There is always a risk that the interests of the various user groups will collide. The distribution of business wealth provides the most likely area for a collision to take place. Let us take the example of owners and managers. Although managers are appointed to act in the best interests of the owners, they may not always do so. Instead, they may use the wealth of the business to award themselves large pay rises, to furnish large offices or to buy expensive cars for their own use. Accounting can play an important role in monitoring and reporting how various groups benefit from the business. Thus, owners may rely on accounting information to see whether pay and benefits received by managers are appropriate and accord with agreed policies.

There is also a potential collision of interest between lenders and owners. Funds loaned to a business, for example, may not be used for their agreed purpose. They may be withdrawn by the owners for their own use rather than used to expand the business as agreed. Lenders may, therefore, rely on accounting information to see whether the owners have kept to the terms of the loan agreement.

Activity 1.2

Can you think of other examples where accounting information may be relied on by a user group to see whether the distribution of business wealth is appropriate and/or in accordance with particular agreements?

Two possible examples that spring to mind are:

- employees wishing to check that they are receiving a 'fair share' of the wealth created by the business and that managers are complying with agreed profit-sharing schemes;
- governments wishing to check that the owners of a monopoly do not benefit from excessive profits and that any pricing rules concerning the monopoly's goods or services have not been broken.

You may have thought of other examples.

HOW USEFUL IS ACCOUNTING INFORMATION?

No one would seriously claim that accounting information fully meets all of the needs of each of the various user groups. Accounting is still a developing subject and we still have much to learn about user needs and the ways in which these needs should be met. Nevertheless, the information contained in accounting reports should help users make decisions relating to the business. The information should reduce uncertainty about the financial position and performance of the business. It should help to answer questions concerning the availability of funds to pay owners a return, to repay loans, to reward employees and so on.

Typically, there is no close substitute for the information provided by the financial statements. Thus, if users cannot glean the required information from the financial statements, it is often unavailable to them. Other sources of information concerning the financial health of a business are normally much less useful.

What other sources of information might, say, an investment analyst use in an attempt to gain an impression of the financial position and performance of a business? What kind of information might be gleaned from these sources?

Other sources of information available include:

- meetings with managers of the business;
- public announcements made by the business;
- newspaper and magazine articles;
- websites, including the website of the business;
- radio and TV reports;
- information-gathering agencies (for example, agencies that assess businesses' credit-worthiness or credit ratings);
- industry reports;
- economy-wide reports.

These sources can provide information on various aspects of the business, such as new products or services being offered, management changes, new contracts offered or awarded, the competitive environment within which the business operates, the impact of new technology, changes in legislation, changes in interest rates and future levels of inflation. However, this kind of information is not really a substitute for accounting information. Rather, it is best used in conjunction with accounting information to provide a clearer picture of the financial health of a business.

Evidence on the usefulness of accounting

There are arguments and convincing evidence that accounting information is at least *perceived* as being useful to users. Numerous research surveys have asked users to rank the importance of accounting information, in relation to other sources of information, for decision-making purposes. Generally, these studies have found that users rank accounting information very highly. There is also considerable evidence that businesses choose to produce accounting information that exceeds the minimum requirements imposed by accounting regulations. (For example, businesses often produce a considerable amount of accounting information for managers, which is not required by any regulations.) Presumably, the cost of producing this additional accounting information is justified on the grounds that users find it useful. Such arguments and evidence, however, leave unanswered the question of whether the information produced is actually used for decision-making purposes, that is: does it affect people's behaviour?

It is normally very difficult to assess the impact of accounting on decision making. One situation arises, however, where the impact of accounting information can be observed and measured. This is where the **shares** (portions of ownership of a business) are traded on a stock exchange. The evidence reveals that, when a business makes an announcement concerning its accounting profits, the prices at which shares are traded and the volume of shares traded often change significantly. This suggests that investors are changing their views about the future prospects of the business as a result of this new information becoming available to them and that this, in turn, leads them to make a decision either to buy or to sell shares in the business.

Although there is evidence that accounting reports are perceived as being useful and are used for decision-making purposes, it is impossible to measure just how useful accounting reports are to users. As a result we cannot say with certainty whether the cost of producing those reports represents value for money. Accounting information will usually represent only one input to a particular decision and so the precise weight attached to the accounting information by the decision maker and the resulting benefits cannot be accurately assessed.

It is possible, however, to identify the kinds of qualities which accounting information must possess in order to be useful. Where these qualities are lacking, the usefulness of the information will be diminished. This point is considered in the following section.

PROVIDING A SERVICE

One way of viewing accounting is as a form of service. The user groups identified in Figure 1.1 can be seen as the 'clients' and the accounting (financial) information produced can be seen as the service provided. The value of this service to the various 'clients' can be judged according to whether the accounting information meets their needs.

To be useful to users, the information provided must possess certain qualities. In particular, it must be relevant and it must faithfully represent what it is supposed to represent. These two qualities, **relevance** and **faithful representation**, are regarded as fundamental qualities of accounting information.

Relevance

Accounting information should make a difference. That is, it should be capable of influencing user decisions. To do this, it must help to *predict future events* (such as predicting next year's profit), or help to *confirm past events* (such as establishing last year's profit), or do both. By confirming past events, users can check on the accuracy of their earlier predictions. This can, in turn, help them to improve the ways in which they make predictions in the future.

To be relevant, accounting information must cross a threshold of **materiality**. An item of information is considered material, or significant, if its omission or misstatement would alter the decisions that users make. If the information is not material, it should not be included within the accounting reports. It will merely clutter them up and perhaps interfere with the users' ability to interpret them.

Activity 1.4

Do you think that what is material for one business will also be material for all other businesses?

No, it will normally vary from one business to the next. What is material will depend on factors such as the size of the business, the nature of the information and the amounts involved.

Faithful representation

Accounting information should represent what it is supposed to represent. This means that it should be *complete*, by providing all of the information needed to understand what is being portrayed. It should also be *neutral*, which means that the information should be presented and selected without bias. Finally, it should be *free from error*. This is not the same as saying that it must always be perfectly accurate; this is not really possible. Estimates may have to be made which eventually turn out to be inaccurate. It does mean, however, that there should be no errors in the way in which these estimates have been prepared and described. In practice, a piece of accounting information may not reflect perfectly these three aspects of faithful representation. It should try to do so, however, so far as possible.

Accounting information must contain *both* of these fundamental qualities if it is to be useful. There is little point in producing information that is relevant, but which lacks faithful representation, or producing information that is irrelevant, but which is faithfully represented.

Further qualities

Where accounting information is both relevant and faithfully represented, there are other qualities that, if present, can enhance its usefulness. These are **comparability**, **verifiability**, **timeliness** and **understandability**. Each of these qualities is now considered.

Comparability

Users of accounting information often want to make comparisons. They may want to compare performance of the business over time (for example, they may want to compare profit this year with that of last year). They may also want to compare certain aspects of business performance (such as the level of sales achieved during the year) to those of similar businesses. Better comparisons can be made where the accounting system treats items that are basically the same in the same way and where policies for measuring and presenting accounting information are made clear.

Verifiability

This quality provides assurance to users that the accounting information provided faithfully represents what it is supposed to represent. Accounting information is verifiable where different, independent experts would be able to agree that it provides a faithful portrayal. Verifiable information tends to be supported by evidence.

Timeliness

Accounting information should be produced in time for users to make their decisions. A lack of timeliness will undermine the usefulness of the information. Normally, the later accounting information is produced, the less useful it becomes.

Understandability

Accounting information should be set out as clearly and concisely as possible. It should also be understood by those at whom the information is aimed.

Activity 1.5

Do you think that accounting reports should be understandable to those who have not studied accounting?

It would be very useful if accounting reports could be understood by everyone. This, however, is unrealistic, as complex financial events and transactions cannot normally be expressed in simple terms.

It is probably best that we regard accounting reports in the same way that we regard a report written in a foreign language. To understand either of these, we need to have had some preparation. When producing accounting reports, it is normally assumed that the user not only has a reasonable knowledge of business and accounting but also is prepared to invest some time in studying the reports. Nevertheless, the onus is clearly on accountants to provide information in a way that makes it as understandable as possible to non-accountants.

It is worth emphasising that the four qualities just discussed cannot make accounting information useful. They can only enhance the usefulness of information that is already relevant and faithfully represented.

WEIGHING UP THE COSTS AND BENEFITS

Having read the previous sections you may feel that, when considering a piece of accounting information, provided the main qualities identified are present and it is material it should be gathered and made available to users. Unfortunately, there is one more hurdle to jump. Something may still exclude a piece of accounting information from the reports even when it is considered to be useful.

Activity 1.6

Suppose an item of information is capable of being provided. It is relevant to a particular decision and can be faithfully represented. It is also comparable, verifiable, timely and can be understood by the decision maker.

Can you think of the reason why, in practice, you might choose not to produce, or discover, the information?

The reason is that you judge the cost of doing so to be greater than the potential benefit of having the information. This cost–benefit issue will limit the amount of accounting information provided.

In theory, a particular item of accounting information should only be produced if the costs of providing it are less than the benefits, or value, to be derived from its use. Figure 1.2 shows the relationship between the costs and value of providing additional accounting information.

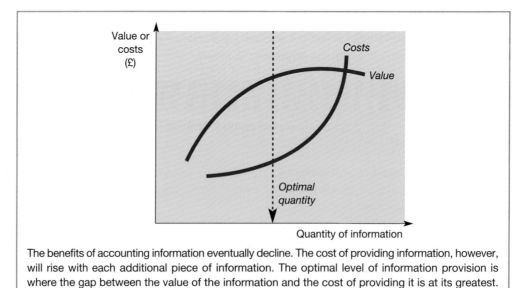

The benefits of accounting information eventually decline. The cost of providing information, however, will rise with each additional piece of information. The optimal level of information provision is where the gap between the value of the information and the cost of providing it is at its greatest.

Figure 1.2 Relationship between costs and the value of providing additional accounting information

The figure shows how the value of information received by the decision maker eventually begins to decline. This is, perhaps, because additional information becomes less relevant, or because of the problems that a decision maker may have in processing the sheer quantity of information provided. The costs of providing the information, however, will increase with each additional piece of information. The broken line indicates the point at which the gap between the value of information and the cost of providing that information is at its greatest. This represents the optimal amount of information that can be provided. This theoretical model, however, poses a number of problems in practice.

To illustrate the practical problems of establishing the value of information, let us assume that someone has collided with our car in a car park, dented one of the doors and scraped the paintwork. We want to have the dent taken out and the door resprayed at a local garage. We know that the nearest garage would charge £350 but we believe that other local garages may offer to do the job for a lower price. The only way of finding out the prices at other garages is to visit them, so that they can see the extent of the damage. Visiting the garages will involve using some petrol and will take up some of our time. Is it worth the cost of finding out the price for the job at the various local garages? The answer, as we have seen, is that if the cost of discovering the price is less than the potential benefit, it is worth having that information.

To identify the various prices for the job, there are several points to be considered, including:

- How many garages shall we visit?
- What is the cost of petrol to visit each garage?
- How long will it take to make all the garage visits?
- At what price do we value our time?

The economic benefit of having the information on the price of the job is probably even harder to assess. The following points need to be considered:

- What is the cheapest price that we might be quoted for the job?
- How likely is it that we shall be quoted a price cheaper than £350?

As we can imagine, the answers to these questions may be far from clear – remember that we have only contacted the local garage so far. When assessing the value of accounting information we are confronted with similar problems.

Producing accounting information can be very costly. The costs, however, are often difficult to quantify. Direct, out-of-pocket costs, such as salaries of accounting staff, are not usually a problem, but these are only part of the total costs involved. There are other costs such as the cost of users' time spent on analysing and interpreting the information provided.

Activity 1.7

What about the economic benefits of producing accounting information? Do you think it is easier, or harder, to assess the economic benefits of accounting information than to assess the costs of producing it?

It is normally much harder to assess the benefits. Even if we could accurately measure the economic benefits arising from a particular decision we must bear in mind that accounting information will be only one factor influencing that decision. Other factors will also be taken into account. The precise weight that has been attached to accounting information by the decision maker is often impossible to establish.

There are no easy answers to the problem of weighing costs and benefits. Although it is possible to apply some 'science' to the problem, a lot of subjective judgement is normally involved.

The qualities, or characteristics, influencing the usefulness of accounting information, which have been discussed above, are summarised in Figure 1.3.

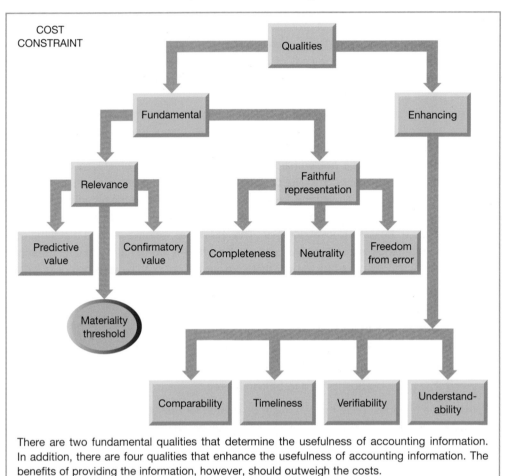

There are two fundamental qualities that determine the usefulness of accounting information. In addition, there are four qualities that enhance the usefulness of accounting information. The benefits of providing the information, however, should outweigh the costs.

Figure 1.3 The qualities that influence the usefulness of accounting information

ACCOUNTING AS AN INFORMATION SYSTEM

We have already seen that accounting can be viewed as the provision of a service to 'clients'. Another way of viewing accounting is as a part of the business's total information system. Users, both inside and outside the business, have to make decisions concerning the allocation of scarce resources. To ensure that these resources are efficiently allocated, users often need financial information on which to base decisions. It is the role of the accounting system to provide this information.

The **accounting information system** should have certain features that are common to all information systems within a business. These are:

■ identifying and capturing relevant information (in this case financial information);
■ recording, in a systematic way, the information collected;
■ analysing and interpreting the information collected; and
■ reporting the information in a manner that suits the needs of users.

The relationship between these features is set out in Figure 1.4.

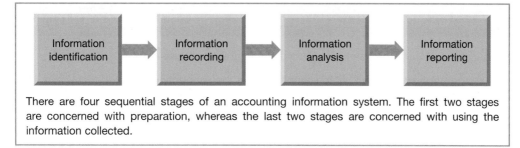

There are four sequential stages of an accounting information system. The first two stages are concerned with preparation, whereas the last two stages are concerned with using the information collected.

Figure 1.4 The accounting information system

Given the decision-making emphasis of this book, we shall be concerned primarily with the final two elements of the process: the analysis and reporting of financial information. We shall consider the way in which information is used by, and is useful to, users rather than the way in which it is identified and recorded.

Efficient accounting systems are an essential ingredient of an efficient business. When the accounting systems fail, the results can be disastrous. **Real World 1.1** provides an example of a systems failure when two businesses combined and then attempted to integrate their respective systems.

Real World 1.1

Blaming the system

When Sir Ken Morrison bought Safeway for £3.35bn in March 2004, he almost doubled the size of his supermarket chain overnight and went from being a regional operator to a national force. His plan was simple enough. He had to sell off some Safeway stores – Morrison has to date sold off 184 stores for an estimated £1.3bn – and convert the remaining 230 Safeway stores into Morrison's. Sir Ken has about another 50 to sell. But, nearly fifteen months on, and the integration process is proving harder in practice than it looked on paper. Morrison, once known for its robust performance, has issued four profit warnings in the past ten months. Each time the retailer has blamed Safeway. Last July, it was because of a faster-than-expected sales decline in Safeway stores. In March – there were two warnings that month – it was the fault of Safeway's accounting systems, which left Morrison with lower supplier incomes. This month's warning was put down to higher-than-expected costs from running parallel store systems. At the time of the first warning last July, Simon Procter, of the stockbrokers Charles Stanley, noted that the news 'has blown all profit forecasts out of the water and visibility is very poor from here on out'. But if it was difficult then to predict where Morrison's profits were heading, it is impossible now. Morrison itself cannot give guidance. 'No one envisaged this,' says Mr Procter. 'When I made that comment about visibility last July, I was thinking on a twelve-month time frame, not a two-year one.' Morrison says the complexity of the Safeway deal has put a 'significant strain' on its ability to cope with managing internal accounts. 'This is impacting the ability of the board to forecast likely trends in profitability and the directors are therefore not currently in a position to provide reliable guidance on the level of profitability as a whole,' admits the retailer.

FT *Source*: 'Morrison in uphill battle to integrate Safeway', (Rigby, E.), *Financial Times*, 26 May 2005, © The Financial Times Limited 2012. All rights reserved.

As a footnote to Real World 1.1, though Morrison had its problems, these were quickly overcome and the Safeway takeover has proved to be a success.

MANAGEMENT ACCOUNTING AND FINANCIAL ACCOUNTING

Accounting is usually seen as having two distinct strands. These are:

- **management accounting**, which seeks to meet the accounting needs of managers; and
- **financial accounting**, which seeks to meet those of all of the users identified earlier in the chapter, except for managers (see Figure 1.1).

The difference in their targeted user groups has led to each strand of accounting developing along different lines. The main areas of difference are as follows.

- *Nature of the reports produced*. Financial accounting reports tend to be general-purpose. Although they are aimed primarily at providers of finance such as owners and lenders, they contain financial information that will be useful for a broad range of users and decisions. Management accounting reports, on the other hand, are often specific-purpose reports. They are designed with a particular decision in mind and/or for a particular manager.
- *Level of detail*. Financial accounting reports provide users with a broad overview of the performance and position of the business for a period. As a result, information is aggregated and detail is often lost. Management accounting reports, however, often provide managers with considerable detail to help them with a particular operational decision.
- *Regulations*. Financial accounting reports, for many businesses, are subject to accounting regulations that try to ensure that they are produced with standard content and in a standard format. The law and accounting rule makers impose these regulations. As management accounting reports are for internal use only, there are no regulations from external sources concerning the form and content of the reports. They can be designed to meet the needs of particular managers.
- *Reporting interval*. For most businesses, financial accounting reports are produced on an annual basis, though some large businesses produce half-yearly reports and a few produce quarterly ones. Management accounting reports may be produced as frequently as required by managers. In many businesses, managers are provided with certain reports on a daily, weekly or monthly basis, which allows them to check progress frequently. In addition, special-purpose reports will be prepared when required (for example, to evaluate a proposal to purchase a piece of equipment).
- *Time orientation*. Financial accounting reports reflect the performance and position of the business for the past period. In essence, they are backward-looking. Management accounting reports, on the other hand, often provide information concerning future performance as well as past performance. It is an oversimplification, however, to suggest that financial accounting reports never incorporate expectations concerning the future. Occasionally, businesses will release projected information to other users in an attempt to raise capital or to fight off unwanted takeover bids. Even preparation of the routine financial accounting reports typically requires making some judgements about the future (as we shall see in Chapter 3).
- *Range and quality of information*. Financial accounting reports concentrate on information that can be quantified in monetary terms. Management accounting also produces such reports, but is also more likely to produce reports that contain information of a non-financial nature, such as physical volume of inventories, number of sales orders received, number of new products launched, physical output per employee and so on. Financial accounting places greater emphasis on the use of objective, verifiable evidence when preparing reports. Management accounting reports may use information that is less objective and verifiable, but nevertheless provide managers with the information they need.

We can see from this that management accounting is less constrained than financial account-ing. It may draw from a variety of sources and use information that has varying degrees of reliability. The only real test to be applied when assessing the value of the information produced for managers is whether or not it improves the quality of the decisions made.

The main differences between financial accounting and management accounting are summarised in Figure 1.5.

	Management accounting	Financial accounting
Nature of the reports produced	Tend to be specific-purpose	Tend to be general-purpose
Level of detail	Often very detailed	Usually broad overview
Regulations	Unregulated	Usually subject to accounting regulation
Reporting interval	As short as required by managers	Usually annual or bi-annual
Time orientation	Often based on projected future information as well as past information	Almost always historical
Range and quality of information	Tend to contain financial and non-financial information; often use information that cannot be verified	Focus on financial information; great emphasis on objective, verifiable evidence

Though management and financial accounting are closely linked and have broadly common objectives, they differ in emphasis in various aspects.

Figure 1.5 Management and financial accounting compared

The differences between management accounting and financial accounting suggest that there are differences in the information needs of managers and those of other users. While differences undoubtedly exist, there is also a good deal of overlap between these needs.

Activity 1.8

Can you think of any areas of overlap between the information needs of managers and those of other users? (Hint: Think about the time orientation and the level of detail of accounting information.)

Two points that spring to mind are:

- Managers will, at times, be interested in receiving a historical overview of business operations of the sort provided to other users.
- Other users would be interested in receiving detailed information relating to the future, such as the planned level of profits, and non-financial information, such as the state of the sales order book and the extent of product innovations.

To some extent, differences between the two strands of accounting reflect differences in access to financial information. Managers have much more control over the form and content of the information that they receive. Other users have to rely on what managers are prepared to provide or what financial reporting regulations insist must be provided. Although the scope of financial accounting reports has increased over time, fears concerning loss of competitive advantage and user ignorance about the reliability of forecast data have resulted in other users not receiving the same detailed and wide-ranging information as that available to managers.

In the past, accounting systems were biased in favour of providing information for external users. Financial accounting requirements were the main priority and management accounting suffered as a result. Survey evidence suggests, however, that this is no longer the case. Modern management accounting systems usually provide managers with information that is relevant to their needs rather than that determined by external reporting requirements. External reporting cycles, however, retain some influence over management accounting. Managers tend to be aware of external users' expectations (see reference 1 at the end of the chapter).

SCOPE OF THIS BOOK

This book is concerned with financial accounting rather than management accounting. In Chapter 2 we begin by introducing the three principal financial statements:

- the statement of financial position;
- the income statement; and
- the statement of cash flows.

These statements are briefly reviewed before we go on to consider the statement of financial position in more detail. We shall see that the statement of financial position provides information concerning the wealth held by a business at a particular point in time and the claims against this wealth. Included in our consideration of the statement of financial position will be an introduction to the **conventions of accounting**. These are generally-accepted rules that are followed when preparing financial statements.

Chapter 3 introduces the second of the major financial statements, the income statement. This provides information concerning the wealth (profit) created by a business during a period. In this chapter we shall be looking at such issues as how profit is measured, the point at which profit is recognised and the accounting conventions applied when preparing this statement.

In the UK and throughout much of the industrialised world, the limited company is the major form of business unit. In Chapter 4 we consider the accounting aspects of limited companies. Although these are, in essence, the same as for other types of business, there are some points of detail that we need to consider. In Chapter 5 we continue our examination of limited companies and, in particular, consider the framework of rules governing the presentation of accounting reports to owners and external users.

Chapter 6 deals with the last of the three principal financial statements, the statement of cash flows. This financial statement is important in identifying the financing and investing activities of the business over a period. It sets out how cash was generated and how cash was used during a period.

In Chapter 7 we shall see how financial reporting rules have developed to try to provide clear definitions and recognition criteria for key items appearing in the financial statements. The ultimate purpose of these rules is to enhance the comparability of financial statements between businesses. In an increasingly complex world, there is a need for rules to help both preparers and users of financial statements.

To gain a deeper understanding about the financial health of a business, the financial statements may be analysed using financial ratios and other techniques. Combining two figures in the financial statements in a ratio and comparing this with a similar ratio for, say, another business, can often tell us much more than just reading the figures themselves. Chapters 8 and 9 contain a discussion of various techniques for analysing financial statements.

The typical large business in the UK is a group of companies rather than just a single company. A group of companies will exist where one company controls one or more other companies. In Chapter 10 we consider the reasons why groups exist and explore the accounting issues raised by the combination of companies into groups.

In Chapter 11 we shall see how the focus of financial reporting has changed over time to become more decision-oriented. We shall also look at the ways in which the scope of financial reporting has increased in order to meet the needs of users.

Finally, in Chapter 12, we consider the way in which larger businesses are managed. We examine the reasons why conflicts of interests may arise between owners and managers and how the behaviour of managers may be monitored and controlled.

THE CHANGING FACE OF ACCOUNTING

Over the past four decades, the environment within which businesses operate has become increasingly turbulent and competitive. Various reasons have been identified to explain these changes, including:

- the increasing sophistication of customers;
- the development of a global economy where national frontiers become less important;
- rapid changes in technology;
- the deregulation of domestic markets (for example, electricity, water and gas);
- increasing pressure from owners (shareholders) for competitive economic returns; and
- the increasing volatility of financial markets.

This new, more complex, environment has brought new challenges for managers and other users of accounting information. Their needs have changed and both financial accounting and management accounting have had to respond. To meet the changing needs of users there has been a radical review of the kind of information to be reported.

The changing business environment has given added impetus to the search for a clear framework and principles upon which to base financial accounting reports. Various attempts have been made to clarify their purpose and to provide a more solid foundation for the development of accounting rules. The frameworks and principles that have been developed try to address fundamental questions such as:

- Who are the users of financial accounting information?
- What kinds of financial accounting reports should be prepared and what should they contain?
- How should items such as profit and asset values be measured?

In response to criticisms that the financial reports of some businesses are not clear enough to users, accounting rule makers have tried to improve reporting rules to ensure that the accounting policies of businesses are more comparable and more transparent and that they portray economic reality more faithfully.

The internationalisation of businesses has created a need for accounting rules to have an international reach. It can no longer be assumed that users of accounting information relating to a particular business are based in the country in which the business operates or are familiar with the accounting rules of that country. Thus, there has been increasing harmonisation of accounting rules across national frontiers.

Activity 1.9

How should the harmonisation of accounting rules benefit:

(a) an international investor
(b) an international business?

An international investor should benefit: because accounting definitions and policies that are used in preparing financial accounting reports will not vary across countries. This should make the comparison of performance between businesses operating in different countries much easier.

An international business should benefit because the cost of producing accounting reports in order to comply with the rules of different countries can be expensive. Harmonisation can, therefore, lead to significant cost savings.

Management accounting has also changed by becoming more outward-looking in its focus. In the past, information provided to managers has been largely restricted to that collected within the business. However, the attitude and behaviour of customers and rival businesses have now become the object of much information-gathering. Increasingly, successful businesses are those that are able to secure and maintain competitive advantage over their rivals.

To obtain this advantage, businesses have become more 'customer driven' (that is, concerned with satisfying customer needs). This has led to the production of management accounting information that provides details of customers and the market, such as customer evaluation of services provided and market share. In addition, information about the costs and profits of rival businesses, which can be used as 'benchmarks' by which to gauge competitiveness, is gathered and reported.

To compete successfully, businesses must also find ways of managing costs. The cost base of modern businesses is under continual review and this, in turn, has led to the development of more sophisticated methods of measuring and controlling costs.

WHAT KINDS OF BUSINESS OWNERSHIP EXIST?

The particular form of business ownership has certain implications for financial accounting and so it is useful to be clear about the main forms of ownership that can arise. There are basically three arrangements for private-sector businesses:

- sole proprietorships;
- partnerships; and
- limited companies.

We shall now consider these.

Sole proprietorship

Sole proprietorship, as the name suggests, is where an individual is the sole owner of a business. This type of business is often quite small in terms of size (as measured, for example, by sales revenue generated or number of staff employed); however, the number of such businesses is very large indeed. Examples of sole-proprietor businesses can be found in most industrial sectors but particularly within the service sector. Hence, services such as electrical repairs, picture framing, photography, driving instruction, retail shops and hotels have a large proportion of sole-proprietor businesses.

The sole-proprietor business is easy to set up. No formal procedures are required and operations can often commence immediately (unless special permission is required because of the nature of the trade or service, such as running licensed premises (a pub)). The owner can decide the way in which the business is to be conducted and has the flexibility to restructure or dissolve the business whenever it suits. The law does not recognise the sole-proprietor business as being separate from the owner, so the business will cease on the death of the owner.

Although the owner must produce accounting information to satisfy the taxation authorities, there is no legal requirement to produce accounting information relating to the business for other user groups. Some user groups, however, may demand accounting information about the business and may be in a position to enforce their demands (for example, a bank requiring accounting information on a regular basis as a condition of a loan). A sole proprietor has unlimited liability which means that no distinction is made between the proprietor's personal wealth and that of the business if there are business debts to be paid.

Partnership

A **partnership** exists where two or more individuals carry on a business together with the intention of making a profit. Partnerships have much in common with sole-proprietor businesses. They are usually quite small in size (although some, such as partnerships of accountants and solicitors, can be large). Partnerships are also easy to set up as no formal procedures are required (and it is not even necessary to have a written agreement between the partners). The partners can agree whatever arrangements suit them concerning the financial and management aspects of the business. Similarly, the partnership can be restructured or dissolved by agreement between the partners.

Partnerships are not recognised in law as separate entities and so contracts with third parties must be entered into in the name of individual partners. The partners of a business usually have unlimited liability.

Activity 1.10

What are the main advantages and disadvantages that should be considered when deciding between a sole proprietorship and a partnership?

The main advantages of a partnership over a sole-proprietor business are:

- sharing the burden of ownership;
- the opportunity to specialise rather than cover the whole range of services (for example, in a solicitors' practice each partner may specialise in a different aspect of the law);
- the ability to raise capital where this is beyond the capacity of a single individual.

The main disadvantages of a partnership compared with a sole proprietorship are:

- the risks of sharing ownership of a business with unsuitable individuals;
- the limits placed on individual decision making that a partnership will impose.

Limited company

Limited companies can range in size from quite small to very large. The number of individuals who subscribe capital and become the owners may be unlimited, which provides the opportunity to create a very large-scale business, though many are quite small. The liability of owners, however, is limited (hence 'limited' company), which means that those individuals subscribing capital to the company are liable only for debts incurred by the company up to the amount that they have invested or agreed to invest. This cap on the liability of the owners is designed to limit risk and to produce greater confidence to invest. Without such limits on owner liability, it is difficult to see how a modern capitalist economy could operate. In many cases, the owners of a limited company are not involved in the day-to-day running of the business and will, therefore, invest in a business only if there is a clear limit set on the level of investment risk.

The benefit of limited liability, however, imposes certain obligations on such companies. To start up a limited company, documents of incorporation must be prepared that set out, among other things, the objectives of the business. Furthermore, a framework of regulations exists that places obligations on limited companies concerning the way in which they conduct their affairs. Part of this regulatory framework requires annual financial reports to be made available to owners and lenders and usually an annual general meeting of the owners has to be held to approve the reports. In addition, a copy of the annual financial reports must be lodged with the Registrar of Companies for public inspection. In this way, the financial affairs of a limited company enter the public domain.

With the exception of small companies, there is also a requirement for the annual financial reports to be subject to an audit. This involves an independent firm of accountants examining the annual reports and underlying records to see whether the reports provide a true and fair view of the financial health of the company and whether they comply with the relevant accounting rules established by law and by accounting rule makers. Limited companies are considered in more detail later (in Chapters 4 and 5).

All of the large household-name UK businesses (Marks and Spencer, Tesco, Shell, BSkyB, Rolls-Royce, BT, easyJet and so on) are limited companies.

Activity 1.11

What are the main advantages of forming a partnership business rather than a limited liability company?

The main advantages are:

- the ease of setting up the business;
- the degree of flexibility concerning the way in which the business is conducted;
- the degree of flexibility concerning restructuring and dissolution of the business;
- freedom from administrative burdens imposed by law (for example, the annual general meeting and the need for an independent audit).

The main disadvantage of a partnership compared with a limited company is that it is not normally possible to limit the liability of all of the partners. There is, however, a hybrid form of business ownership that is referred to as a Limited Liability Partnership (LLP). This has many of the attributes of a normal partnership but is different insofar that the LLP, rather than the individual partners, is responsible for any debts incurred. Accountants and solicitors often use this type of partnership.

This text concentrates on the accounting aspects of limited liability companies because this type of business is by far the most important in economic terms. The early chapters will introduce accounting concepts through examples that do not draw a distinction between the different types of business. Once we have dealt with the basic accounting principles, which are the same for all three types of business, we can then go on to see how they are applied to limited companies. It must be emphasised that there are no differences in the way that these three forms of business keep their day-to-day accounting records. In preparing their periodic financial statements, there are certain differences that need to be considered. These differences are not ones of principle, however, but of detail.

HOW ARE BUSINESSES ORGANISED?

Nearly all businesses that involve more than a few owners and/or employees are set up as limited companies. Finance will come from the owners (shareholders) both in the form of a direct cash investment to buy shares (in the ownership of the business) and through the shareholders allowing past profits, which belong to them, to be reinvested in the business. Finance will also come from lenders (banks, for example), who earn interest on their loans. Further finance will be provided through suppliers of goods and services being prepared to supply on credit, with payment occurring a month or so after the date of supply, usually on an interest-free basis.

In larger limited companies, the owners (shareholders) tend not to be involved in the daily running of the business; instead they appoint a board of directors to manage the business on their behalf. The board is charged with three major tasks:

1 setting the overall direction and strategy for the business;
2 monitoring and controlling the activities of the business; and
3 communicating with shareholders and others connected with the business.

Each board has a chairman, elected by the directors, who is responsible for running the board in an efficient manner. In addition, each board has a chief executive officer (CEO) (managing director) who is responsible for running the business on a day-to-day basis. Occasionally, the roles of chairman and CEO are combined, although it is usually considered to be a good idea to separate them in order to prevent a single individual having excessive power. We shall come back to consider the relationship between directors and shareholders in more detail (in Chapters 4 and 12).

WHAT IS THE FINANCIAL OBJECTIVE OF A BUSINESS?

A business is normally created to enhance the wealth of its owners. Throughout this book we shall assume that this is its main objective. This may come as a surprise, as there are other objectives that a business may pursue that are related to the needs of others associated with the business. For example, a business may seek to provide good working conditions for its employees, or it may seek to conserve the environment for the local community. While a business may pursue these objectives, it is normally set up primarily with a view to increasing the wealth of its owners. In practice, the behaviour of businesses over time appears to be consistent with this objective.

Within a market economy there are strong competitive forces at work that ensure that failure to enhance owners' wealth will not be tolerated for long. Competition for the funds provided by the owners and competition for managers' jobs will normally mean that the owners' interests will prevail. If the managers do not provide the expected increase in ownership wealth, the owners have the power to replace the existing management team with a new team that is more responsive to owners' needs. Does this mean that the needs of other groups associated with the business (employees, customers, suppliers, the community and so on) are not really important? The answer to this question is certainly no, if the business wishes to survive and prosper over the longer term.

Satisfying the needs of other groups is usually consistent with increasing the wealth of the owners over the longer term. A business with disaffected customers, for example, may find that they turn to another supplier, resulting in a loss of shareholder wealth. **Real World 1.2** reveals how satisfying the needs of customer as a means to increase shareholder wealth is regarded by some businesses as their central purpose.

Real World 1.2

Standard practice

Standard Life, a leading long-term savings and investment business, states its purpose as follows:

> We will continue to drive shareholder value through being a leading, customer-centric business, focused on long-term savings and investment propositions. This means finding, acquiring and retaining valuable customers for mutual and sustained financial benefit.

Source: Standard Life plc, www.standardlife.com, accessed 25 January 2012.

On a mission

Elektron Technology plc, which operates in the fast-moving engineered products sector, states:

> Our mission is to deliver a highly competitive return to shareholders by using our technologies to create innovative solutions for our customers.

Source: Elektron Technology plc, www.elektron-technology.com, accessed 21 August 2011.

A dissatisfied workforce may result in low productivity, strikes and so forth, which will in turn have an adverse effect on owners' wealth. Similarly, a business that upsets the local community by unacceptable behaviour, such as polluting the environment, may attract bad publicity, resulting in a loss of customers and heavy fines. **Real World 1.3** provides an example of how two businesses responded to potentially damaging allegations.

Real World 1.3

The price of clothes

US clothing and sportswear manufacturers Gap and Nike have many of their clothes produced in Asia where labour tends to be cheap. However, some of the contractors that produce clothes on behalf of the two companies have been accused of unacceptable practices. Campaigners visited the factories and came up with damaging allegations. The factories were employing minors, they said, and managers were harassing female employees.

Nike and Gap reacted by allowing independent inspectors into the factories. They promised to ensure their contractors obeyed minimum standards of employment. Earlier this year, Nike took the extraordinary step of publishing the names and addresses of all its contractors' factories on the internet. The company said it could not be sure all the abuse had stopped. It said that if campaigners visited its contractors' factories and found examples of continued malpractice, it would take action.

Nike and Gap said the approach made business sense. They needed society's approval if they were to prosper. Nike said it was concerned about the reaction of potential US recruits to the campaigners' allegations. They would not want to work for a company that was constantly in the news because of the allegedly cruel treatment of those who made its products.

 Source: 'Fair shares?', (Skapinker, M.), *Financial Times*, 11 June 2005,
© The Financial Times Limited 2012. All rights reserved.

We should be clear that generating wealth for the owners is not the same as seeking to maximise the current year's profit. Wealth creation is concerned with the longer term. It relates not only to this year's profit but to that of future years as well. In the short term, corners can be cut and risks taken that improve current profit at the expense of future profit. **Real World 1.4** provides some examples of how emphasis on short-term profit can be damaging.

Real World 1.4

Short-term gains, long-term problems

For many years, under the guise of defending capitalism, we have been allowing ourselves to degrade it. We have been poisoning the well from which we have drawn wealth. We have misunderstood the importance of values to capitalism. We have surrendered to the idea that success is pursued by making as much money as the law allowed without regard to how it was made.

Thirty years ago, retailers would be quite content to source the shoes they wanted to sell as cheaply as possible. The working conditions of those who produced them was not their concern. Then headlines and protests developed. Society started to hold them responsible for previously invisible working conditions. Companies like Nike went through a transformation. They realised they were polluting their brand. Global sourcing became visible. It was no longer viable to define success simply in terms of buying at the lowest price and selling at the highest.

Financial services and investment are today where footwear was thirty years ago. Public anger at the crisis will make visible what was previously hidden. Take the building up of huge portfolios of loans to poor people on US trailer parks. These loans were authorised without proper scrutiny of the circumstances of the borrowers. Somebody else then deemed them fit to be securitised and so on through credit default swaps and the rest without anyone seeing the transaction in terms of its ultimate human origin.

Each of the decision makers thought it okay to act like the thoughtless footwear buyer of the 1970s. The price was attractive. There was money to make on the deal. Was it responsible? Irrelevant. It was legal, and others were making money that way. And the consequences for the banking system if everybody did it? Not our problem.

The consumer has had a profound shock. Surely we could have expected the clever and wise people who invested our money to be better at risk management than they have shown themselves to be in the present crisis? How could they have been so gullible in not

→

challenging the bankers whose lending proved so flaky? How could they have believed that the levels of bonuses that were, at least in part, coming out of their savings could have been justified in 'incentivising' a better performance? How could they have believed that a 'better' performance would be one that is achieved for one bank without regard to its effect on the whole banking system? Where was the stewardship from those exercising investment on their behalf?

The answer has been that very few of them do exercise that stewardship. Most have stood back and said it doesn't really pay them to do so. The failure of stewardship comes from the same mindset that created the irresponsible lending in the first place. We are back to the mindset that has allowed us to poison the well: never mind the health of the system as a whole, I'm making money out of it at the moment. Responsibility means awareness for the system consequences of our actions. It is not a luxury. It is the cornerstone of prudence.

FT *Source*: 'How we've poisoned the well of wealth', (Goyder, M.), *Financial Times*, 15 February 2009, © The Financial Times Limited 2012. All rights reserved.

BALANCING RISK AND RETURN

All decision making involves the future. Business decision making is no exception. The only thing certain about the future, however, is that we cannot be sure what will happen. Things may not turn out as planned and this risk should be carefully considered when making financial decisions.

As in other aspects of life, risk and return tend to be related. Evidence shows that returns relate to risk in something like the way shown in Figure 1.6.

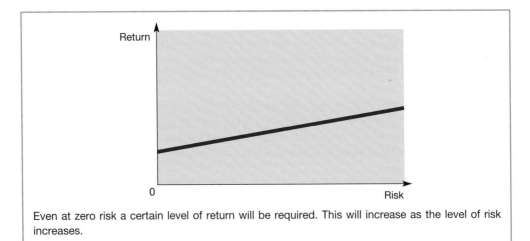

Even at zero risk a certain level of return will be required. This will increase as the level of risk increases.

Figure 1.6 Relationship between risk and return

Activity 1.12

Look at Figure 1.6 and state, in broad terms, where an investment in:

(a) a government savings account, and
(b) a lottery ticket

should be placed on the risk–return line.

A government savings account is normally a very safe investment. Even if a government is in financial difficulties, it may be able to print more money to repay investors. Returns from this form of investment, however, are normally very low. Investing in a lottery ticket runs a very high risk of losing the whole amount invested. This is because the probability of winning is normally very low. However, a winning ticket can produce enormous returns.

Thus, the government savings account should be placed towards the far left of the risk–return line and the lottery ticket towards the far right.

This relationship between risk and return has important implications for setting financial objectives for a business. The owners will require a minimum return to induce them to invest at all, but will require an additional return to compensate for taking risks; the higher the risk, the higher the required return. Managers must be aware of this and must strike the appropriate balance between risk and return when setting objectives and pursuing particular courses of action.

The recent turmoil in the banking sector has shown, however, that the right balance is not always struck. Some banks have taken excessive risks in pursuit of higher returns and, as a consequence, have incurred massive losses. They are now being kept afloat with taxpayers' money. **Real World 1.5** discusses the collapse of one leading bank, in which the UK government took a majority stake, and argues that the risk appetite of banks must now change.

Real World 1.5

Banking on change

The taxpayer has become the majority shareholder in the Royal Bank of Scotland (RBS). This change in ownership, resulting from the huge losses sustained by the bank, will shape the future decisions made by its managers. This does not simply mean that it will affect the amount that the bank lends to homeowners and businesses. Rather it is about the amount of risk that it will be prepared to take in pursuit of higher returns.

In the past, those managing banks such as RBS saw themselves as producers of financial products that enabled banks to grow faster than the economy as a whole. They did not want to be seen as simply part of the infrastructure of the economy. It was too dull. It was far more exciting to be seen as creators of financial products that created huge profits and, at the same time, benefited us all through unlimited credit at low rates of interest. These financial products, with exotic names such as 'collateralised debt obligations' and 'credit default swaps', ultimately led to huge losses that taxpayers had to absorb in order to prevent the banks from collapse.

Now that many banks throughout the world are in taxpayers' hands, they are destined to lead a much quieter life. They will have to focus more on the basics such as taking deposits, transferring funds and making simple loans to customers. Is that such a bad thing?

The history of banking has reflected a tension between carrying out their core functions and the quest for high returns through high risk strategies. It seems, however, that for some time to come they will have to concentrate on the former and will be unable to speculate with depositors' cash.

Source: Based on information in 'We own Royal Bank', Robert Peston, 28 November 2008, BBC News, www.bbc.co.uk.

NOT-FOR-PROFIT ORGANISATIONS

Though the focus of this book is accounting as it relates to private-sector businesses, there are many organisations that do not exist mainly for the pursuit of profit.

Activity 1.13

Can you think of at least four types of organisation that are not primarily concerned with making profits?

We thought of the following:

- charities
- clubs and associations
- universities
- local government authorities
- national government departments
- churches
- trade unions.

All of these organisations need to produce accounting information for decision-making purposes. Once again, various user groups need this information to help them to make decisions. These user groups are often the same as, or similar to, those identified for private-sector businesses. They may have a stake in the future viability of the organisation and may use accounting information to check that the wealth of the organisation is being properly controlled and used in a way that is consistent with its objectives.

Real World 1.6 provides an example of the importance of accounting to relief agencies, which are, of course, not-for-profit organisations.

Real World 1.6

Accounting for disasters

In the aftermath of the Asian tsunami more than £400 million was raised from charitable donations. It was important that this huge amount of money for aid and reconstruction was used as efficiently and effectively as possible. That did not just mean medical staff and engineers. It also meant accountants.

The charity that exerts financial control over aid donations is Mango: Management Accounting for Non-Governmental Organisations (NGOs). It provides accountants in the field and it provides the back-up, such as financial training and all the other services that should result in really robust financial management in a disaster area.

The world of aid has changed completely as a result of the tsunami. According to Mango's director, Alex Jacobs, 'Accounting is just as important as blankets. Agencies have been aware of this for years. But when you move on to a bigger scale there is more pressure to show the donations are being used appropriately.'

More recently, the earthquake in Haiti led to a call from Mango for French-speaking accountants to help support the relief programme and to help in the longer-term rebuilding of Haiti.

Source: Adapted from 'Tsunami: finding the right figures for disaster relief', Robert Bruce, FT.com, 7 March 2005; 'The work of Mango: coping with generous donations', Robert Bruce, FT.com, 27 February 2006; and 'Accountants needed in Haiti', Paul Grant, *Accountancy Age*, 5 February 2010.

SUMMARY

The main points of this chapter may be summarised as follows.

What is accounting?

■ Accounting provides financial information to help various user groups make better judgements and decisions.

Accounting and user needs

■ For accounting to be useful, it must be clear *for whom* and *for what purpose* the information will be used.

■ Conflicts of interest between users may arise over the ways in which business wealth is generated or distributed.

■ The evidence suggests that accounting is both used and useful for decision-making purposes.

Providing a service

■ Accounting can be viewed as a form of service as it involves providing financial information to various users.

■ To provide a useful service, accounting must possess certain qualities, or characteristics. The fundamental qualities are relevance and faithful representation. Other qualities that enhance the usefulness of accounting information are comparability, verifiability, timeliness and understandability.

■ Providing a service to users can be costly, and financial information should be produced only if the cost of providing the information is less than the benefits gained.

Accounting information

■ Accounting is part of the total information system within a business. It shares the features that are common to all information systems within a business, which are the identification, recording, analysis and reporting of information.

Management accounting and financial accounting

■ Accounting has two main strands – management accounting and financial accounting.

■ Management accounting seeks to meet the needs of the business's managers, and financial accounting seeks to meet the needs of providers of finance but will also be of use to other user groups.

■ These two strands differ in terms of the types of reports produced, the level of reporting detail, the time horizon, the degree of regulation and the range and quality of information provided.

The changing face of accounting

■ Changes in the economic environment have led to changes in the nature and scope of accounting.

■ Financial accounting has improved its framework of rules and there has been greater international harmonisation of accounting rules.

■ Management accounting has become more outward-looking, and new methods for managing costs have emerged.

→

What kinds of business ownership exist?

There are three main forms of business unit:

■ Sole proprietorship – easy to set up and flexible to operate but the owner has unlimited liability.

■ Partnership – easy to set up and spreads the burdens of ownership, but partners usually have unlimited liability and there are ownership risks if the partners are unsuitable.

■ Limited company – limited liability for owners but obligations imposed on the way a company conducts its affairs.

How are businesses organised and managed?

■ Most businesses of any size are set up as limited companies.

■ A board of directors is appointed by owners (shareholders) to oversee the running of the business.

What is the financial objective of a business?

■ The key financial objective is to enhance the wealth of the owners. To achieve this objective, the needs of other groups connected with the business, such as employees, cannot be ignored.

■ When setting financial objectives, the right balance must be struck between risk and return.

MyAccountingLab

Go to www.myaccountinglab.com to check your understanding of the chapter, create a personalised study plan, and maximise your revision time

KEY TERMS

accounting p. 1	understandability p. 7
shares p. 5	accounting information system p. 10
relevance p. 6	management accounting p. 12
faithful representation p. 6	financial accounting p. 12
materiality p. 6	conventions of accounting p. 14
comparability p. 7	sole proprietorship p. 16
verifiability p. 7	partnership p. 17
timeliness p. 7	limited companies p. 18

REFERENCE

1 Dugdale, D., Jones, C. and Green, S., *Contemporary Management Accounting Practices in UK Manufacturing*, CIMA Research Publication, vol. 1, no. 13, 2005

FURTHER READING

If you would like to explore the topics covered in this chapter in more depth, we recommend the following:

Alexander, D. and Nobes, C., *Financial Accounting: An International Introduction*, 4th edn, Financial Times Prentice Hall, 2010, Chapters 1 to 4

Drury, C., *Management and Cost Accounting,* 8th edn, Cengage Learning, 2012, Chapter 1

Elliot, B. and Elliot, J., *Financial Accounting and Reporting*, 15th edn, Financial Times Prentice Hall, 2011, Chapter 9

Godfrey, J., Hodgson, A., Tarca, A., Holmes, K. and Hamilton, J., *Accounting Theory*, 7th edn, John Wiley, 2010, Chapters 1 to 3

REVIEW QUESTIONS

Solutions to these questions can be found in Appendix D.

1.1 What is the purpose of producing accounting information?

1.2 Identify the main users of accounting information for a university. For what purposes would different user groups need information? Is there a major difference in the ways in which accounting information for a university would be used compared with that of a private-sector business?

1.3 What, in economic principle, should be the determinant of what accounting information is produced? Should economics be the only issue here? (Consider who are the users of accounting information.)

1.4 Financial accounting statements tend to reflect past events. In view of this, how can they be of any assistance to a user in making a decision when decisions, by their very nature, can only be made about future actions?

Chapter 2

MEASURING AND REPORTING FINANCIAL POSITION

INTRODUCTION

We saw in Chapter 1 that accounting has two distinct strands: financial accounting and management accounting. This chapter, along with Chapters 3 to 6, examines the three major financial statements that form the core of financial accounting. We start by taking an overview of these statements to see how each contributes towards an assessment of the overall financial position and performance of a business.

Following this overview, we begin a more detailed examination by turning our attention towards one of these financial statements: the statement of financial position. We shall see how it is prepared and examine the principles underpinning it. We shall also consider its value for decision-making purposes.

Learning outcomes

When you have completed this chapter, you should be able to:

- explain the nature and purpose of the three major financial statements;
- prepare a simple statement of financial position and interpret the information that it contains;
- discuss the accounting conventions underpinning the statement of financial position;
- discuss the uses and limitations of the statement of financial position for decision-making purposes.

THE MAJOR FINANCIAL STATEMENTS – AN OVERVIEW

The major financial accounting statements aim to provide a picture of the financial position and performance of a business. To achieve this, a business's accounting system will normally produce three financial statements on a regular, recurring basis. These three statements are concerned with answering the following questions relating to a particular period:

- What cash movements took place?
- How much wealth was generated?
- What is the accumulated wealth of the business at the end of the period and what form does it take?

To address each of the above questions, there is a separate financial statement. The financial statements are:

- the **statement of cash flows**;
- the **income statement** (also known as the profit and loss account); and
- the **statement of financial position** (also known as the balance sheet).

Together they provide an overall picture of the financial health of the business.

Perhaps the best way to introduce these financial statements is to look at an example of a very simple business. From this we shall be able to see the sort of information that each of the statements can usefully provide. It is, however, worth pointing out that, while a simple business is our starting point, the principles for preparing the financial statements apply equally to the largest and most complex businesses. This means that we shall frequently encounter these principles again in later chapters.

Example 2.1

Paul was unemployed and unable to find a job. He therefore decided to embark on a business venture. With Christmas approaching, he decided to buy gift-wrapping paper from a local supplier and to sell it on the corner of his local high street. He felt that the price of wrapping paper in the high street shops was unreasonably high. This provided him with a useful business opportunity.

He began the venture with £40 of his own money, in cash. On Monday, Paul's first day of trading, he bought wrapping paper for £40 and sold three-quarters of it for £45 cash.

What cash movements took place in Paul's business during Monday?

For Monday, a *statement of cash flows* showing the cash movements (that is, cash in and cash out) for the day can be prepared as follows:

Statement of cash flows for Monday

	£
Cash introduced (by Paul)	40
Cash from sales of wrapping paper	45
Cash paid to buy wrapping paper	(40)
Closing balance of cash	45

The statement shows that Paul placed £40 cash into the business. The business received £45 cash from customers, but paid £40 cash to buy the wrapping paper. This left £45 of cash by Monday evening. Note that we are taking the standard approach found in the financial statements of showing figures to be deducted (in this case the £40 paid out) in brackets. We shall take this approach consistently throughout the chapters dealing with financial statements.

How much wealth (that is, profit) was generated by the business during Monday?

An *income statement* can be prepared to show the wealth generated (profit) on Monday. The wealth generated arises from trading and will be the difference between the value of the sales made and the cost of the goods (that is, wrapping paper) sold:

Income statement for Monday

	£
Sales revenue	45
Cost of goods sold ($^3/_4$ of £40)	(30)
Profit	15

Note that it is only the cost of the wrapping paper *sold* that is matched against (and deducted from) the sales revenue in order to find the profit, not the whole of the cost of wrapping paper acquired. Any unsold inventories (also known as *stock*) will be charged against the future sales revenue that it generates. In this case the cost of the unsold inventories it is $^1/_4$ of £40 = £10.

What is the accumulated wealth on Monday evening and what form does it take?

To establish the accumulated wealth at the end of Monday's trading, we can draw up a *statement of financial position* for Paul's business. This statement will also list the forms of wealth held at the end of that day:

Statement of financial position as at Monday evening

	£
Cash (closing balance)	45
Inventories of goods for resale ($^1/_4$ of £40)	10
Total assets	55
Equity	55

Note the terms 'assets' and 'equity' that appear in this statement. 'Assets' are business resources (things of value to the business) and include cash and inventories. 'Equity' is the word used in accounting to describe the investment, or stake, of the owner(s) – in this case Paul – in the business. Both of these terms will be discussed in some detail a little later in this chapter. Note that the equity on Monday evening was £55. This represented the £40 that Paul put in to start the business, plus Monday's profit (£15) – profits belong to the owner(s).

We can see from the financial statements in Example 2.1 that each statement provides part of a picture of the financial performance and position of the business. We begin by showing the cash movements. Cash is a vital resource that is necessary for any business to function effectively. It is required to meet debts that become due and to acquire other resources (such as inventories). Cash has been described as the 'lifeblood' of a business.

Reporting cash movements alone, however, is not enough to portray the financial health of the business. To find out how much profit was generated, we need an income statement. It is important to recognise that cash and profits rarely move in unison. During Monday, for example, the cash balance increased by £5, but the profit generated, as shown in the income statement, was £15. The cash balance did not increase in line with profit because part of the wealth generated (£10) was held in the form of inventories.

The statement of financial position that was drawn up as at the end of Monday's trading provides an insight into the total wealth of the business. This wealth can be held in various forms. For Paul's business, wealth is held in the form of cash and inventories. This means that, when drawing up the statement of financial position, both forms will be listed. For a large business, many other forms of wealth may be held, such as property, equipment, motor vehicles and so on.

Let us now continue with our example.

Example 2.1 (continued)

On Tuesday, Paul bought more wrapping paper for £20 cash. He managed to sell all of the new inventories and all of the earlier inventories, for a total of £48.

The statement of cash flows for Tuesday will be as follows:

Statement of cash flows for Tuesday

	£
Opening balance (from Monday evening)	45
Cash from sales of wrapping paper	48
Cash paid to buy wrapping paper	(20)
Closing balance	73

The income statement for Tuesday will be as follows:

Income statement for Tuesday

	£
Sales revenue	48
Cost of goods sold (£20 + £10)	(30)
Profit	18

The statement of financial position as at Tuesday evening will be:

Statement of financial position as at Tuesday evening

	£
Cash (closing balance)	73
Inventories	–
Total assets	73
Equity	73

We can see that the total business wealth had increased to £73 by Tuesday evening. This represents an increase of £18 (that is, £73 – £55) over Monday's figure – which, of course, is the amount of profit made during Tuesday as shown on the income statement.

Activity 2.1

On Wednesday, Paul bought more wrapping paper for £46 cash. However, it was raining hard for much of the day and sales were slow. After Paul had sold half of his total inventories for £32, he decided to stop trading until Thursday morning.

Have a go at drawing up the three financial statements for Paul's business for Wednesday.

Statement of cash flows for Wednesday

	£
Opening balance (from the Tuesday evening)	73
Cash from sales of wrapping paper	32
Cash paid to buy wrapping paper	(46)
Closing balance	59

Income statement for Wednesday

	£
Sales revenue	32
Cost of goods sold ($\frac{1}{2}$ of £46)	(23)
Profit	9

Statement of financial position as at Wednesday evening

	£
Cash (closing balance)	59
Inventories ($\frac{1}{2}$ of £46)	23
Total assets	82
Equity	82

Note that the total business wealth has increased by £9 (that is, the amount of Wednesday's profit) even though the cash balance has declined. This is because the business is holding more of its wealth in the form of inventories rather than cash, compared with the position on Tuesday evening.

By Wednesday evening, the equity stood at £82. This arose from Paul's initial investment of £40, plus his profits for Monday (£15), Tuesday (£18) and Wednesday (£9). This represents Paul's total investment in his business at that time. The equity of most businesses will similarly be made up of injections of funds by the owner plus any accumulated profits.

We can see that the income statement and statement of cash flows are both concerned with measuring flows (of wealth and cash respectively) during a particular period. The statement of financial position, however, is concerned with the financial position at a particular moment in time. Figure 2.1 illustrates this point.

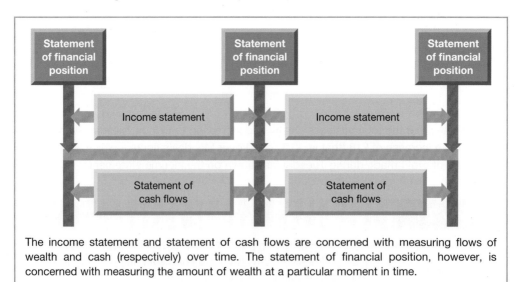

The income statement and statement of cash flows are concerned with measuring flows of wealth and cash (respectively) over time. The statement of financial position, however, is concerned with measuring the amount of wealth at a particular moment in time.

Figure 2.1 The relationship between the major financial statements

The three financial statements discussed are often referred to as the **final accounts** of the business.

For external users (that is, virtually all users except the managers of the business concerned), these statements are normally backward-looking because they are based on information concerning past events and transactions. This can be useful in providing feedback on past performance and in identifying trends that provide clues to future performance. However, the statements can also be prepared using projected data to help assess likely future profits, cash flows and so on. Normally, this is done only for management decision-making purposes.

Now that we have an overview of the financial statements, we shall consider each one in detail. The remainder of this chapter is devoted to the statement of financial position.

THE STATEMENT OF FINANCIAL POSITION

We saw a little earlier that this statement shows the forms in which the wealth of a business is held and how much wealth is held in each form. We can, however, be more specific about the nature of this statement by saying that it sets out the **assets** of a business, on the one hand, and the **claims** against the business, on the other. Before looking at the statement of financial position in more detail, we need to be clear about what these terms mean.

Assets

An asset is essentially a resource held by a business. For a particular item to be treated as an asset, for accounting purposes, it should have the following characteristics:

- *A probable future economic benefit must exist*. This simply means that the item must be expected to have some future monetary value. This value can arise through the asset's use within the business or through its hire or sale. This means that an obsolete piece of equipment that will be sold for scrap would still be considered an asset, whereas an obsolete piece of equipment that has no scrap value would not be regarded as one.
- *The benefit must arise from some past transaction or event*. In other words, the transaction (or other event) giving rise to a business's right to the benefit must have already occurred; it must not be one which will arise at some future date. For example, an agreement by a business to buy a piece of equipment at some future date would not mean the item is currently an asset of the business.
- *The business must have the right to control the resource*. Unless the business controls the resource, it cannot be regarded as an asset for accounting purposes. To a business offering holidays on barges, for example, the canal system may be a very valuable resource, but as the business will not be able to control the access of others to the canal system, it cannot be regarded as an asset of the business. (However, any barges owned by the business would be regarded as assets.)
- *The asset must be capable of measurement in monetary terms*. Unless the item can be measured in monetary terms, with a reasonable degree of reliability, it will not be regarded as an asset for inclusion on the statement of financial position. For instance, the title of a magazine (for example *Hello!* or *Vogue*) that was created by its publisher may be extremely valuable to that publishing business, but this value is difficult to quantify. It will not, therefore, be treated as an asset.

Note that all four of these conditions must apply. If one of them is missing, the item will not be treated as an asset for accounting purposes, and will not, therefore, appear on the statement of financial position. Figure 2.2 summarises the above discussion in the form of a decision chart.

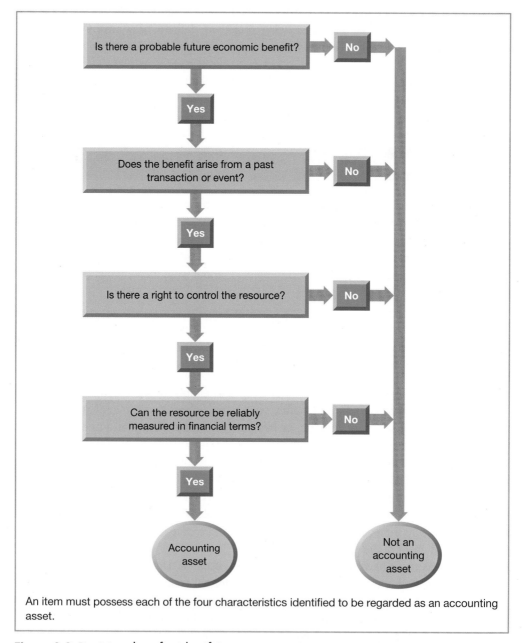

An item must possess each of the four characteristics identified to be regarded as an accounting asset.

Figure 2.2 Decision chart for identifying an accounting asset

We can see that these conditions will strictly limit the kind of resources that may be referred to as 'assets' in the statement of financial position. Some resources, like the canal system or the magazine title *Hello!*, may well be assets in a broader sense, but not for accounting purposes. Once an asset has been acquired by a business, it will continue to be considered an asset until the benefits are exhausted or the business disposes of it.

Indicate which of the following items could appear as an asset on the statement of financial position of a business. Explain your reasoning in each case.

1 £1,000 owed to the business by a credit customer who is unable to pay.
2 A patent, bought from an inventor, that gives the business the right to produce a new product. Production of the new product is expected to increase profits over the period during which the patent is held.
3 A recently hired new marketing director who is confidently expected to increase profits by over 30 per cent during the next three years.
4 A recently purchased machine that will save the business £10,000 each year. It is already being used by the business but it has been acquired on credit and is not yet paid for.

Your answer should be along the following lines.

1 Under normal circumstances, a business would expect a customer to pay the amount owed. Such an amount is therefore typically shown as an asset under the heading 'trade receivables' (or 'debtors'). However, in this particular case the customer is unable to pay. As a result, the item is incapable of providing future economic benefits and the £1,000 owing would not be regarded as an asset. Debts that are not paid are referred to as 'bad debts'.
2 The patent would meet all of the conditions set out above and would therefore be regarded as an asset.
3 The new marketing director would not be considered as an asset. One argument for this is that the business does not have exclusive rights of control over the director. (It may have an exclusive right to the services that the director provides, however.) Perhaps a stronger argument is that the value of the director cannot be measured in monetary terms with any degree of reliability.
4 The machine would be considered an asset even though it is not yet paid for. Once the business has agreed to buy the machine, and has accepted it, the machine represents an asset even though payment is still outstanding. (The amount outstanding would be shown as a claim, as we shall see shortly.)

The sorts of items that often appear as assets in the statement of financial position of a business include:

- property
- plant and equipment
- fixtures and fittings
- patents and trademarks
- trade receivables (debtors)
- investments outside the business.

Can you think of two additional items that might appear as assets in the statement of financial position of a typical business?

You may be able to think of a number of other items. Two that we have met so far, because they were held by Paul's wrapping paper business (in Example 2.1), are inventories and cash.

Note that an asset does not have to be a physical item – it may be a non-physical one that gives a right to certain benefits. Assets that have a physical substance and can be touched (such as inventories) are referred to as **tangible assets**. Assets that have no physical substance but which, nevertheless, provide expected future benefits (such as patents) are referred to as **intangible assets**.

Claims

A claim is an obligation of the business to provide cash, or some other form of benefit, to an outside party. It will normally arise as a result of the outside party providing assets for use by the business. There are essentially two types of claim against a business:

- **Equity**. This represents the claim of the owner(s) against the business. This claim is sometimes referred to as the *owner's capital*. Some find it hard to understand how the owner can have a claim against the business, particularly when we consider the example of a sole-proprietor-type business like Paul's, where the owner *is*, in effect, the business. For accounting purposes, however, a clear distinction is made between the business and the owner(s). The business is viewed as being quite separate from the owner. It is seen as a separate entity with its own separate existence. This means that, when financial statements are prepared, they relate to the business rather than to the owner(s). Viewed from this perspective, any funds contributed by the owner will be seen as coming from outside the business and will appear as a claim against the business in its statement of financial position.
- **Liabilities**. Liabilities represent the claims of all individuals and organisations, apart from the owner(s). They arise from past transactions or events such as supplying goods or lending money to the business. A liability will be settled through an outflow of assets (usually cash).

Once a claim from the owners or outsiders has been incurred by a business, it will remain as an obligation until it is settled.

Now that the meanings of the terms *assets*, *equity* and *liabilities* have been established, we can consider the relationship between them. This relationship is quite straightforward. If a business wishes to acquire assets, it must raise the necessary funds from somewhere. It may raise these funds from the owner(s), or from other outside parties, or from both. Example 2.2 illustrates this relationship.

Example 2.2

Jerry and Company is a new business that was created by depositing £20,000 in a bank account on 1 March. This amount was raised partly from the owner (£6,000) and partly from borrowing (£14,000). Raising funds in this way will give rise to a claim on the business by both the owner (equity) and the lender (liability). If a statement of financial position of Jerry and Company is prepared following the above transactions, it will appear as follows:

Jerry and Company
Statement of financial position as at 1 March

	£
ASSETS	
Cash at bank	20,000
Total assets	20,000
EQUITY AND LIABILITIES	
Equity	6,000
Liabilities – borrowing	14,000
Total equity and liabilities	20,000

We can see from the statement of financial position that the total claims (equity and liabilities) are the same as the total assets. Thus:

Assets = Equity + Liabilities

This equation – which we shall refer to as the *accounting equation* – will always hold true. Whatever changes may occur to the assets of the business or the claims against it, there will be compensating changes elsewhere that will ensure that the statement of financial position always 'balances'. By way of illustration, consider the following transactions for Jerry and Company:

2 March	Bought a motor van for £5,000, paying by cheque.
3 March	Bought inventories (that is, goods to be sold) on one month's credit for £3,000. (This means that the inventories were bought on 3 March, but payment will not be made to the supplier until 3 April.)
4 March	Repaid £2,000 of the amount borrowed to the lender, by cheque.
6 March	Owner introduced another £4,000 into the business bank account.

A statement of financial position may be drawn up after each day in which transactions have taken place. In this way, we can see the effect of each transaction on the assets and claims of the business. The statement of financial position as at 2 March will be:

Jerry and Company
Statement of financial position as at 2 March

	£
ASSETS	
Cash at bank (20,000 – 5,000)	15,000
Motor van	5,000
Total assets	20,000
EQUITY AND LIABILITIES	
Equity	6,000
Liabilities – borrowing	14,000
Total equity and liabilities	20,000

As we can see, the effect of buying the motor van is to decrease the balance at the bank by £5,000 and to introduce a new asset – a motor van – to the statement of financial position. The total assets remain unchanged. It is only the 'mix' of assets that has changed. The claims against the business remain the same because there has been no change in the way in which the business has been funded.

The statement of financial position as at 3 March, following the purchase of inventories, will be:

Jerry and Company
Statement of financial position as at 3 March

	£
ASSETS	
Cash at bank	15,000
Motor van	5,000
Inventories	3,000
Total assets	23,000
EQUITY AND LIABILITIES	
Equity	6,000
Liabilities – borrowing	14,000
Liabilities – trade payable	3,000
Total equity and liabilities	23,000

The effect of buying inventories has been to introduce another new asset (inventories) to the statement of financial position. Furthermore, the fact that the goods have not yet been paid for means that the claims against the business will be increased by the £3,000 owed to the supplier, who is referred to as a *trade payable* (or trade creditor) on the statement of financial position.

Activity 2.4

Try drawing up a statement of financial position for Jerry and Company as at 4 March.

The statement of financial postion as at 4 March, following the repayment of part of the borrowing, will be:

Jerry and Company
Statement of financial position as at 4 March

	£
ASSETS	
Cash at bank (15,000 – 2,000)	13,000
Motor van	5,000
Inventories	3,000
Total assets	21,000
EQUITY AND LIABILITIES	
Equity	6,000
Liabilities – borrowing (14,000 – 2,000)	12,000
Liabilities – trade payable	3,000
Total equity and liabilities	21,000

The repayment of £2,000 of the borrowing will result in a decrease in the balance at the bank of £2,000 and a decrease in the lender's claim against the business by the same amount.

Try drawing up a statement of financial position as at 6 March for Jerry and Company.

The statement of financial position as at 6 March, following the introduction of more funds, will be:

Jerry and Company
Statement of financial position as at 6 March

	£
ASSETS	
Cash at bank (13,000 + 4,000)	17,000
Motor van	5,000
Inventories	3,000
Total assets	25,000
EQUITY AND LIABILITIES	
Equity (6,000 + 4,000)	10,000
Liabilities – borrowing	12,000
Liabilities – trade payable	3,000
Total equity and liabilities	25,000

The introduction of more funds by the owner will result in an increase in the equity of £4,000 and an increase in the cash at bank by the same amount.

This example (Jerry and Company) illustrates the point that the accounting equation (assets equals equity plus liabilities) will always hold true, because it reflects the fact that, if a business wishes to acquire more assets, it must raise funds equal to the cost of those assets. The funds raised must be provided by the owners (equity) or by others (liabilities) or by a combination of the two. This means that the total cost of assets acquired should always equal the total equity plus liabilities.

It is worth pointing out that businesses do not normally draw up a statement of financial position after each day, as shown in the example. We have done this to illustrate the effect on the statement of financial position of each transaction. In practice, a statement of financial position for a business is usually prepared at the end of a defined reporting period.

Determining the length of the reporting period will involve weighing up the costs of producing the information against the perceived benefits of having that information for decision-making purposes. In practice, the reporting period will vary between businesses; it could be monthly, quarterly, half-yearly or annually. For external reporting purposes, an annual reporting period is the norm (although certain businesses, typically larger ones, report more frequently than this). For internal reporting purposes to managers, however, more frequent (perhaps monthly) financial statements may be prepared.

THE EFFECT OF TRADING TRANSACTIONS

In the example (Jerry and Company), we showed how various types of transactions affected the statement of financial position. However, one very important type of transaction – trading transactions – has yet to be considered. To show how this type of transaction affects the statement of financial position, let us return to Jerry and Company.

Example 2.2 (continued)

The statement of financial position that we drew up for Jerry and Company as at 6 March was as follows:

Jerry and Company
Statement of financial position as at 6 March

	£
ASSETS	
Cash at bank	17,000
Motor van	5,000
Inventories	3,000
Total assets	25,000
EQUITY AND LIABILITIES	
Equity	10,000
Liabilities – borrowing	12,000
Liabilities – trade payable	3,000
Total equity and liabilities	25,000

On 7 March, the business managed to sell all of the inventories for £5,000 and received a cheque immediately from the customer for this amount. The statement of financial position on 7 March, after this transaction has taken place, will be:

Jerry and Company
Statement of financial position as at 7 March

	£
ASSETS	
Cash at bank (17,000 + 5,000)	22,000
Motor van	5,000
Inventories (3,000 – 3,000)	–
Total assets	27,000
EQUITY AND LIABILITIES	
Equity (10,000 + (5,000 – 3,000))	12,000
Liabilities – borrowing	12,000
Liabilities – trade payable	3,000
Total equity and liabilities	27,000

We can see that the inventories (£3,000) have now disappeared from the statement of financial position, but the cash at bank has increased by the selling price of the inventories (£5,000). The net effect has therefore been to increase assets by £2,000 (that is, £5,000 less £3,000). This increase represents the net increase in wealth (the profit) that has arisen from trading. Also note that the equity of the business has increased by £2,000, in line with the increase in assets. This increase in equity reflects the fact that wealth generated, as a result of trading or other operations, will be to the benefit of the owners and will increase their stake in the business.

What would have been the effect on the statement of financial position if the inventories had been sold on 7 March for £1,000 rather than £5,000?

The statement of financial position on 7 March would then have been:

Jerry and Company
Statement of financial position as at 7 March

	£
ASSETS	
Cash at bank (17,000 + 1,000)	18,000
Motor van	5,000
Inventories (3,000 – 3,000)	–
Total assets	23,000
EQUITY AND LIABILITIES	
Equity (10,000 + (1,000 – 3,000))	8,000
Liabilities – borrowing	12,000
Liabilities – trade payable	3,000
Total equity and liabilities	23,000

As we can see, the inventories (£3,000) will disappear from the statement of financial position but the cash at bank will rise by only £1,000. This will mean a net reduction in assets of £2,000. This reduction represents a loss arising from trading and will be reflected in a reduction in the equity of the owners.

What we have just seen means that the accounting equation can be extended as follows:

Assets (at the end of the period) = Equity (amount at the start of the period
+ Profit (or – Loss) for the period)
+ Liabilities (at the end of the period)

(This is assuming that the owner makes no injections or withdrawals of equity during the period.)

Any funds introduced or withdrawn by the owners also affect equity. If the owners withdrew £1,500 for their own use, the equity of the owners would be reduced by £1,500. If these drawings were in cash, the cash balance would decrease by £1,500 in the statement of financial position.

Like all items in the statement of financial position, the amount of equity is cumulative. This means that any profit not taken out as drawings by the owner(s) remains in the business. These retained (or 'ploughed-back') earnings have the effect of expanding the business.

CLASSIFYING ASSETS

On the statement of financial position, assets and claims are usually grouped into categories. This is designed to help users, as a haphazard listing of these items could be confusing. Assets may be categorised as being either current or non-current.

Current assets

Current assets are basically assets that are held for the short term. To be more precise, they are assets that meet any of the following conditions:

- they are held for sale or consumption during the business's normal operating cycle;
- they are expected to be sold within the next year;
- they are held principally for trading;
- they are cash, or near cash such as easily marketable, short-term investments.

The operating cycle of a business, mentioned above, is the time between buying and/or creating a product or service and receiving the cash on its sale. For most businesses, this will be less than a year. (It is worth mentioning that sales made by most businesses are made on credit. The customer pays some time after the goods are received or the service is rendered.)

The most common current assets are inventories, trade receivables (customers who owe amounts for goods or services supplied on credit) and cash. For businesses that sell goods, rather than render a service, the current assets of inventories, trade receivables and cash are interrelated. They circulate within a business as shown in Figure 2.3. We can see that cash can be used to buy inventories, which are then sold on credit. When the credit customers (trade receivables) pay, the business receives an injection of cash and so on.

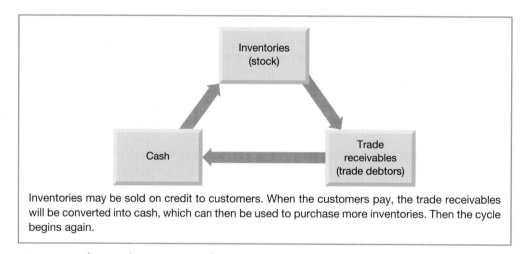

Inventories may be sold on credit to customers. When the customers pay, the trade receivables will be converted into cash, which can then be used to purchase more inventories. Then the cycle begins again.

Figure 2.3 The circulating nature of current assets

For purely service businesses, the situation is similar, except that inventories are not involved.

Non-current assets

Non-current assets (also called *fixed assets*) are simply assets that do not meet the definition of current assets. They tend to be held for long-term operations. Non-current assets may be either tangible or intangible. Tangible non-current assets normally consist of **property, plant and equipment**. We shall refer to them in this way from now on. This is a rather broad term that includes items such as land and buildings, motor vehicles and fixtures and fittings.

The distinction between assets that are continuously circulating within the business (current) and assets used for long-term operations (non-current) may be helpful when trying to assess the appropriateness of the mix of assets held. Most businesses will need a certain amount of both types of asset to operate effectively.

Activity 2.7

Can you think of two examples of assets that may be classified as non-current assets for an insurance business?

Examples of assets that may be defined as being non-current are:

- property
- furniture
- motor vehicles
- computers
- computer software
- reference books.

This is not an exhaustive list. You may have thought of others.

It is important to appreciate that how a particular asset is classified (that is, between current and non-current) may vary according to the nature of the business. This is because the *purpose* for which a particular type of asset is held may differ from business to business. For example, a motor vehicle manufacturer will normally hold inventories of the finished motor vehicles produced for resale; it would, therefore, classify them as part of the current assets. On the other hand, a business that uses motor vehicles for delivering its goods to customers (that is, as part of its long-term operations) would classify them as non-current assets.

Activity 2.8

The assets of Kunalun and Co., a large advertising agency, are as follows:

- cash at bank
- fixtures and fittings
- office equipment
- motor vehicles
- property
- computer equipment
- work in progress (that is, partly completed work for clients).

Which of these do you think should be defined as non-current assets and which should be defined as current assets?

Your answer should be as follows:

Non-current assets	*Current assets*
Fixtures and fittings	Cash at bank
Office equipment	Work in progress
Motor vehicles	
Property	
Computer equipment	

CLASSIFYING CLAIMS

As we have already seen, claims are normally classified into equity (owner's claim) and liabilities (claims of outsiders). Liabilities are further classified as either current or non-current.

Current liabilities

Current liabilities are basically amounts due for settlement in the short term. To be more precise, they are liabilities that meet any of the following conditions:

- they are expected to be settled within the business's normal operating cycle;
- they are held principally for trading purposes;
- they are due to be settled within a year after the date of the relevant statement of financial position;
- there is no right to defer settlement beyond a year after the date of the relevant statement of financial position.

Non-current liabilities

Non-current liabilities represent amounts due that do not meet the definition of current liabilities and so represent longer-term liabilities.

Activity 2.9

Can you think of one example of a current liability and one of a non-current liability?

An example of a current liability would be amounts owing to suppliers for goods supplied on credit (trade payables) or a bank overdraft (a form of short-term bank borrowing that is repayable on demand). An example of a non-current liability would be long-term borrowings.

It is quite common for non-current liabilities to become current liabilities. For example, borrowings to be repaid 18 months after the date of a particular statement of financial position will normally appear as a non-current liability. Those same borrowings will, however, appear as a current liability in the statement of financial position as at the end of the following year, by which time they would be due for repayment after six months.

This classification of liabilities between current and non-current helps to highlight those financial obligations that must shortly be met. The amount of current liabilities can be compared with the amount of current assets (that is, the assets that either are cash or will turn into cash within the normal operating cycle). This should reveal whether a business can cover its maturing obligations.

The classification of liabilities between current and non-current also helps to highlight the proportion of total long-term finance that is raised through borrowings rather than equity. Where a business relies on long-term borrowings, rather than relying solely on funds provided by the owner(s), the financial risks increase. This is because borrowing brings a commitment to make periodic interest payments and capital repayments. The business may be forced to stop trading if this commitment cannot be fulfilled. Thus, when raising long-term finance, the right balance must be struck between long-term borrowings and owners' equity. (We shall consider this issue in more detail in Chapter 8).

Having looked at the classification of assets and liabilities, we shall now consider the layout of the statement of financial position. Although there is an almost infinite number of ways in which the same information on assets and claims could be presented, we shall consider two basic layouts. The first of these follows the style that we adopted with Jerry and Company earlier. A more comprehensive example of this style is shown in Example 2.3.

Example 2.3

Brie Manufacturing
Statement of financial position as at 31 December 2012

	£000
ASSETS	
Non-current assets	
Property	45
Plant and equipment	30
Motor vans	19
	94
Current assets	
Inventories	23
Trade receivables	18
Cash at bank	12
	53
Total assets	147
EQUITY AND LIABILITIES	
Equity	60
Non-current liabilities	
Long-term borrowings	50
Current liabilities	
Trade payables	37
Total equity and liabilities	147

The non-current assets have a total of £94,000, which together with the current assets total of £53,000 gives a total of £147,000 for assets. Similarly, the equity totals £60,000, which together with the £50,000 for non-current liabilities and £37,000 for current liabilities gives a total for equity and liabilities of £147,000.

Within each category of asset (non-current and current) shown in Example 2.3, the items are listed in reverse order of liquidity (nearness to cash). Thus, the assets that are furthest from cash come first and the assets that are closest to cash come last. In the case of non-current assets, property is listed first as this asset is usually the most difficult to turn into cash, and motor vans are listed last as there is usually a ready market for them. In the case of current assets, we have already seen that inventories are converted to trade receivables and then trade receivables are converted to cash. As a result, under the heading of current assets, inventories are listed first, followed by trade receivables and finally cash itself. This ordering of assets will occur irrespective of the layout used.

Note that, in addition to a grand total for assets held, subtotals for non-current assets and current assets are shown. Subtotals are also used for non-current liabilities and current liabilities when more than one item appears within these categories.

A slight variation from the standard layout illustrated in Example 2.3 is as shown in Example 2.4.

Example 2.4

Brie Manufacturing
Statement of financial position as at 31 December 2012

	£000
ASSETS	
Non-current assets	
Property	45
Plant and equipment	30
Motor vans	19
	94
Current assets	
Inventories	23
Trade receivables	18
Cash at bank	12
	53
Total assets	147
LIABILITIES	
Non-current liabilities	
Long-term borrowings	(50)
Current liabilities	
Trade payables	(37)
Total liabilities	(87)
Net assets	60
EQUITY	60

We can see that the total liabilities are deducted from the total assets. This derives a figure for net assets – which is equal to equity. Using this format, the basic accounting equation is rearranged so that

Assets – Liabilities = Equity

This rearranged equation highlights the fact that equity represents the residual interest of the owner(s) after deducting all liabilities of the business.

The layout shown in Example 2.3 is the most popular in practice in the UK and will be used throughout the book.

CAPTURING A MOMENT IN TIME

As we have already seen, the statement of financial position reflects the assets, equity and liabilities of a business at *a specified point in time*. It has been compared to a photograph. A photograph 'freezes' a particular moment in time and will represent the situation only at that moment. Hence, events may be quite different immediately before and immediately after the photograph was taken. When examining a statement of financial position, therefore, it is important to establish the date for which it has been drawn up. This information should be prominently displayed in the heading to the statement, as shown above in Example 2.4. When we are trying to assess current financial position, the more recent the statement of financial position date, the better.

A business will normally prepare a statement of financial position as at the close of business on the last day of its annual reporting period. In the UK, businesses are free to choose their reporting period. When making a decision on which year-end date to choose, commercial convenience can often be a deciding factor. For example, a business operating in the retail trade may choose to have a year-end date early in the calendar year (for example, 31 January) because trade tends to be slack during that period and more staff time is available to help with the tasks involved in the preparation of the annual financial statements (such as checking the amount of inventories held). Since trade is slack, it is also a time when the amount of inventories held by the retail business is likely to be unusually low as compared with other times of the year. Thus the statement of financial position, though showing a fair view of what it purports to show, may not show a picture of what is more typically the position of the business over the rest of the year.

THE ROLE OF ACCOUNTING CONVENTIONS

Accounting has a number of rules or conventions that have evolved over time. They have evolved as attempts to deal with practical problems experienced by preparers and users of financial statements, rather than to reflect some theoretical ideal. In preparing the statements of financial position earlier, we have followed various accounting conventions, though they have not been explicitly mentioned. We shall now identify and discuss the major conventions that we have applied.

Business entity convention

For accounting purposes, the business and its owner(s) are treated as being quite separate and distinct. This is why owners are treated as being claimants against their own business in respect of their investment. The **business entity convention** must be distinguished from the legal position that may exist between businesses and their owners. For sole proprietorships and partnerships, the law does not make any distinction between the business and its owner(s). For limited companies, on the other hand, there is a clear legal distinction between the business and its owners. (As we shall see in Chapter 4, the limited company is regarded as having a separate legal existence.) For accounting purposes, these legal distinctions are irrelevant and the business entity convention applies to all businesses.

Historic cost convention

The **historic cost convention** holds that the value of assets shown on the statement of financial position should be based on their acquisition cost (that is, historic cost). Many argue, however, that historic costs soon become outdated and so are unlikely to help in the assessment of current financial position. Recording assets at their current value would provide a more realistic view of financial position and would be relevant for a wide range of decisions. A system of measurement based on current values can, however, present a number of problems.

The term 'current value' can be defined in different ways. It can be defined broadly as either the current replacement cost or the current realisable value (selling price) of an asset. These two types of valuation may result in quite different figures being produced to represent the current value of an item. Furthermore, the broad terms 'replacement cost' and 'realisable value' can be defined in different ways. We must therefore be clear about what kind of current value accounting we wish to use.

Current values, however defined, are often difficult to establish with any real degree of objectivity. Activity 2.10 illustrates the practical problems associated with current value accounting.

Activity 2.10

Plumber and Company has some motor vans that are used by staff when visiting customers' premises to carry out work. If it were decided to show these vans on the statement of financial position at a current value (rather than a value based on their historic cost), how might the business arrive at a suitable value and how reliable would this figure be?

Two ways of deriving a current value are to find out

- how much would have to be paid to buy vans of a similar type and condition (current replacement cost);
- how much a motor van dealer would pay for the vans, were the business to sell them (current realisable value).

Both options will normally rely on opinion and so a range of possible values could be produced for each. For example, both the cost to replace the vans and the proceeds of selling them is likely to vary from one dealer to another. Moreover, the range of values for each option could be significantly different from one option to the other. (The selling prices of the vans are likely to be lower than the amount required to replace them.) Thus, any value finally decided upon could arouse some debate.

Figures based on current values may be heavily dependent on the opinion of managers. Some form of independent verification is, therefore, normally required to ensure that the financial statements retain their credibility among users. The motor vans discussed in Activity 2.10 are less of a problem than many types of asset. There is a ready market for motor vans, which means that a value can be obtained by contacting a dealer. For a custom-built piece of equipment, however, identifying a replacement cost or (worse still) a selling price could be very difficult.

By reporting assets at their historic cost, more reliable information is provided. Subjective judgement is reduced as the amount paid for a particular asset is usually a matter of demonstrable fact. Information based on past costs, however, may not always be relevant to user needs.

Later in the chapter, we shall see that the historic cost convention is not always rigidly adhered to. Moreover, departures from this convention are becoming more frequent.

Prudence convention

The **prudence convention** holds that caution should be exercised when making accounting judgements. The application of this convention normally involves recording all losses at once and in full; this refers to both actual losses and expected losses. Profits, on the other hand, are recognised only when they actually arise. Greater emphasis is, therefore, placed on expected losses than on expected profits. To illustrate the application of this convention, let us assume that certain inventories held by a business prove unpopular with customers and so a decision is made to sell them below their original cost. The prudence convention requires that the expected loss from future sales be recognised immediately rather than when the goods are eventually sold. If, however, these inventories could have been sold above their original cost, profit would only be recognised at the time of sale.

The prudence convention evolved to counteract the excessive optimism of some managers and is designed to prevent an overstatement of financial position and performance. Applying this convention, however, requires judgement. This means that the way in which it is applied by preparers of financial statements may differ over time and between businesses. Where excessive prudence is applied, it will lead to an understatement of profits and financial position. This will mean a consistent bias in the reporting of both financial performance and position.

Activity 2.11

What might be the effect of applying excessive prudence on the quality of decisions made by the owners of a business who are considering selling their share of the business?

Being excessively prudent will tend to obscure the underlying financial reality and may lead to poor decisions being made. The owners may sell their stake in the business at a lower price than they would have received if a more balanced view of the financial health of the business had been presented.

In recent years, the prudence convention has weakened its grip on accounting and has become a less dominant force. Nevertheless, it remains an important convention.

Going concern convention

The **going concern convention** holds that the financial statements should be prepared on the assumption that a business will continue operations for the foreseeable future, unless there is evidence to the contrary. In other words, it is assumed that there is no intention, or need, to sell off the non-current assets of the business.

Where a business is in financial difficulties, however, non-current assets may have to be sold to repay those with claims against the business. The realisable (sale) value of many non-current assets is often much lower than the values reported in the statement of financial position. This is because the value to the business of the assets, were it to continue operating, is higher than their immediate realisable value. In the event of a forced sale of assets, therefore, significant losses would arise. These losses must be anticipated and fully reported when a business's going concern status is called into question.

Dual aspect convention

The **dual aspect convention** asserts that each transaction has two aspects, both of which will affect the statement of financial position. This means that, for example, the purchase of a motor car for cash results in an increase in one asset (motor car) and a decrease in another (cash). The repayment of borrowings results in the decrease in a liability (borrowings) and the decrease in an asset (cash).

Recording the dual aspect of each transaction ensures that the statement of financial position will continue to balance.

Figure 2.4 summarises the main accounting conventions that exert an influence on the construction of the statement of financial position.

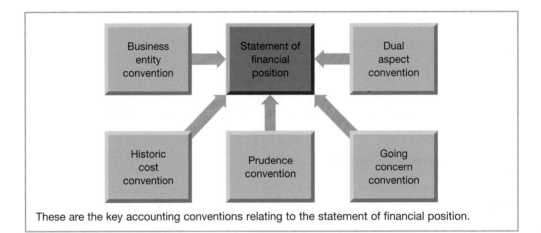

These are the key accounting conventions relating to the statement of financial position.

Figure 2.4 Accounting conventions influencing the statement of financial position

MONEY MEASUREMENT

We saw earlier that a resource will only be regarded as an asset and included on the statement of financial position if it can be measured in monetary terms, with a reasonable degree of reliability. Some resources of a business, however, do not meet this criterion and so are excluded from the statement of financial position. As a result, the scope of the statement of financial position is limited.

In answering this activity you may have thought of the following:

- the quality of the human resources of the business
- the reputation of the business's products
- the location of the business
- the relationship the business enjoys with its customers.

There have been occasional attempts to measure and report resources of a business that are normally excluded from the statement of financial position so as to provide a more complete picture of its financial position. These attempts, however, tend to fail the test of reliability. Unreliable measurement can lead to inconsistency in reporting and can create uncertainty among users of the financial statements. This, in turn, undermines the credibility of financial statements.

We shall now discuss some key resources of a business that normally defy reliable measurement.

Goodwill and brands

Some intangible non-current assets are similar to tangible non-current assets: they have a clear and separate identity and the cost of acquiring the asset can be reliably measured. Examples normally include patents, trademarks, copyrights and licences. Other intangible non-current assets, however, are quite different. They lack a clear and separate identity and reflect a hotchpotch of attributes, which are part of the essence of the business. Goodwill and product brands are often examples of assets that lack a clear and separate identity.

The term 'goodwill' is often used to cover various attributes such as the quality of the products, the skill of employees and the relationship with customers. The term 'product brands' is also used to cover various attributes, such as the brand image, the quality of the product, the trademark and so on. Where goodwill and product brands have been generated internally by the business, it is often difficult to determine their cost or to measure their current market value or even to be clear that they really exist. They are, therefore, excluded from the statement of financial position.

When they are acquired through an 'arm's-length transaction', however, the problems of uncertainty about their existence and measurement are resolved. (An arm's-length transaction is one that is undertaken between two unconnected parties.) If goodwill is acquired when taking over another business, or if a business acquires a particular product brand from another business, these items will be separately identified and a price agreed for them. Under these circumstances, they can be regarded as assets (for accounting purposes) by the business that acquired them and included on the statement of financial position.

To agree a price for acquiring goodwill or product brands means that some form of valuation must take place and this raises the question as to how it is done. Usually, the valuation will be based on estimates of future earnings from holding the asset – a process that is fraught with difficulties. Nevertheless, a number of specialist businesses now exist that are prepared to take on this challenge. **Real World 2.1** shows how one specialist business ranked and valued the top ten brands in the world for 2011.

Brand leaders

Millward Brown Optimor, part of the WPP marketing services group, produces an annual report which ranks and values the top world brands. For 2011, the top ten brands are as follows:

Ranking	Brand	Value ($m)
1	Apple	153,285
2	Google	111,498
3	IBM	100,849
4	McDonalds	81,016
5	Microsoft	78,243
6	Coca-Cola	73,752
7	AT&T	69,916
8	Marlboro	67,522
9	China Mobile	57,326
10	General Electric	50,318

We can see that the valuations placed on the brands owned are quite staggering.

Source: 'Brandz Top 100 Most Valuable Global Brands 2011', Millward Brown Optimor, www.millwardbrown.com, 2011.

Human resources

Attempts have been made to place a monetary measurement on the human resources of a business, but without any real success. There are, however, certain limited circumstances in which human resources are measured and reported in the statement of financial position. Professional football clubs provide an example of where these circumstances normally arise. While football clubs cannot own players, they can own the rights to the players' services. Where these rights are acquired by compensating other clubs for releasing the players from their contracts, an arm's-length transaction arises and the amounts paid provide a reliable basis for measurement. This means that the rights to services can be regarded as an asset of the club for accounting purposes (assuming, of course, that the player will bring benefits to the club).

Real World 2.2 describes how one leading club reports its investment in players on the statement of financial position.

Spurs players appear on the pitch and on the statement of financial position

Tottenham Hotspur Football Club (Spurs) has acquired several key players as a result of paying transfer fees to other clubs. In common with most UK football clubs, Spurs reports the cost of acquiring the rights to the players' services on its statement of financial position. The club's statement as at 30 June 2011 shows the total cost of registering its squad of players at about £227 million. The club treats a proportion of each player's transfer fee as an expense each year. The exact proportion depends on the length of the particular player's contract.

The £227 million does not include 'home-grown' players such as Ledley King, because Spurs did not pay a transfer fee for them and so no clear-cut value can be placed on their services. During the year to 30 June 2011, the club was active in the transfer market and spent around £27.5 million on acquiring new players, including Rafael van der Vaart, William Gallas and Steven Pienaar. Some players, including Jonathan Woodgate and Adel Taarabt, also left the club during the year.

The item of players' registrations is shown as an intangible asset in the statement of financial position as it is the rights to services, not the players, that are the assets. It is shown net of depreciation (or amortisation as it is usually termed for intangible non-current assets). The carrying amount at 30 June 2011 was £101 million and represented 35 per cent of Spurs' assets, as shown in the statement of financial position.

Source: Tottenham Hotspur plc Annual Report 2011.

Monetary stability

When using money as the unit of measurement, we normally fail to recognise the fact that it will change in value over time. In the UK and throughout much of the world, however, inflation has been a persistent problem. This has meant that the value of money has declined in relation to other assets. In past years, high rates of inflation have resulted in statements of financial position which were prepared on a historic cost basis reflecting figures for assets that were much lower than if current values were employed. Rates of inflation have been relatively low in recent years and so the disparity between historic cost values and current values has been less pronounced. Nevertheless, it can still be significant. Later we shall take a look at how businesses can try to prepare their financial statements in such a way as to make allowances for the effects of inflation (see Chapter 11).

The problem of inflation has added fuel to the more general debate concerning how to measure asset values on the statement of financial position. It is to the issue of valuing assets that we now turn.

VALUING ASSETS

We saw earlier that, when preparing the statement of financial position, the historic cost convention is normally applied for the reporting of assets. This point requires further explanation as, in practice, things are a little more complex than this. Large businesses throughout much of the world adhere to asset valuation rules set out in International Financial Reporting Standards. (These reporting standards will be discussed in detail in Chapters 5.) The key valuation rules are considered below.

Non-current assets

Non-current assets have lives that are either *finite* or *indefinite*. Those with a finite life provide benefits to a business for a limited period of time, whereas those with an indefinite life provide benefits without a foreseeable time limit. The distinction between the two types of non-current assets applies to both tangible and intangible assets.

Initially non-current assets are recorded at their historic cost, which will include any amounts spent on getting them ready for use.

Non-current assets with finite lives

Benefits from assets with finite lives will be used up over time as a result of market changes, wear and tear and so on. The amount used up, which is referred to as *depreciation* (or *amortisation*, in the case of intangible non-current assets), must be measured for each reporting period for which the assets are held. Although we shall leave a detailed examination of depreciation until Chapter 3, we need to know that when an asset has been depreciated, this must be reflected in the statement of financial position.

The total depreciation that has accumulated over the period since the asset was acquired must be deducted from its cost. This net figure (that is, the cost of the asset less the total depreciation to date) is referred to as the *carrying amount*. It is sometimes also known as *net book value* or *written-down value*. The procedure just described is not really a contravention of the historic cost convention. It is simply recognition of the fact that a proportion of the historic cost of the non-current asset has been consumed in the process of generating benefits for the business.

Activity 2.14

Can you think of a non-current asset that has a finite life and which can be classified as tangible, and one that has a finite life and can be classified as intangible?

Plant, equipment, motor vehicles and computers are examples of tangible assets that are normally considered to have a finite life. A patent, which gives the owner exclusive rights to use an invention, is an example of an intangible asset that has a finite life. (Many patents are granted for a period of 20 years.)

Non-current assets with indefinite lives

Benefits from assets with indefinite lives may or may not be used up over time. Property (real estate) is usually an example of a tangible non-current asset with an indefinite life. Purchased goodwill could be an example of an intangible one, though this is not always the case. These assets are not subject to routine annual depreciation over time.

Fair values

Although initially historic cost is the standard or 'benchmark' treatment for recording non-current assets of all types (tangible and intangible, with finite or indefinite lives), an alternative is allowed. Non-current assets may be recorded using **fair values** provided that these values can be measured reliably. The fair values, in this case, are the current market values (that is, the exchange values in an arm's-length transaction). The use of fair values, rather than cost figures, whether depreciated or not, can provide users with more up-to-date information, which may well be more relevant to their needs. It may also place the business in a better light, as assets such as property may have increased significantly in value over time. Of course, increasing the value of an asset on the statement of financial position does not make that asset more valuable. Perceptions of the business, however, may be altered by such a move.

One consequence of upwardly revaluing non-current assets with finite lives is that the depreciation charge will be increased. This is because the depreciation charge is based on the new (increased) value of the asset.

Real World 2.3 shows the effect of the revaluation of non-current assets on the financial position of one large business.

Rising asset levels

During the year to 31 March 2010, Veolia Water UK plc, which owns Thames Water, changed its policy on the valuation of certain types of non-current assets. These assets included land and buildings, infrastructure assets, and vehicles, plant and machinery. The business switched from the use of historic cost to the use of fair values and a revaluation exercise was carried out by independent qualified valuers.

The effect of this policy change was to report a revaluation gain of more than £436 million during the year. There was a 40 per cent increase in owners' (shareholders') equity, which was largely due to this gain.

Source: Veolia Water UK plc Annual Report 2009/10.

Activity 2.15

Refer to the statement of financial position of Brie Manufacturing shown earlier in Example 2.3 (page 45). What would be the effect of revaluing the property to a figure of £110,000 on the statement of financial position?

The effect on the statement of financial position would be to increase the property to £110,000 and the gain on revaluation (that is, £110,000 − £45,000 = £65,000) would be added to equity, as it is the owner(s) who will have benefited from the gain. The revised statement of financial position would therefore be as follows:

Brie Manufacturing
Statement of financial position as at 31 December 2012

	£000
ASSETS	
Non-current assets	
Property	110
Plant and equipment	30
Motor vans	19
	159
Current assets	
Inventories	23
Trade receivables	18
Cash at bank	12
	53
Total assets	212
EQUITY AND LIABILITIES	
Equity (60 + 65)	125
Non-current liabilities	
Long-term borrowings	50
Current liabilities	
Trade payables	37
Total equity and liabilities	212

Once non-current assets are revalued, the frequency of revaluation becomes an important issue. Reporting assets on the statement of financial position at out-of-date revaluations is the worst of both worlds. It lacks the objectivity and verifiability of historic cost; it also lacks the realism of current values. Thus, where fair values are used, revaluations should be frequent enough to ensure that the carrying amount of the revalued asset does not differ materially from its true fair value at the statement of financial position date.

When an item of property, plant or equipment (a tangible asset) is revalued on the basis of fair values, all assets within that particular group must be revalued. It is not acceptable to revalue some items of property but not others. Although this rule provides some degree of consistency within a particular group of assets, it does not prevent the statement of financial position from containing a mixture of valuations.

Intangible assets are not usually revalued to fair values. This is because revaluations can only occur where there is an active market, thereby permitting fair values to be properly determined. This kind of market rarely exists for intangible assets. There are, however, a few intangible assets such as transferable taxi licences, fishing licences and production quotas where an active market may exist.

The impairment of non-current assets

All types of non-current asset are at risk of suffering a significant fall in value. This may be caused by changes in market conditions, technological obsolescence and so on. In some cases, this fall in value may lead to the carrying amount of the asset being higher than the amount that could be recovered from the asset through its continued use or through its sale. When this occurs, the asset value is said to be impaired and the general rule is to reduce the value on the statement of financial position to the recoverable amount. Unless this is done, the asset value will be overstated. The amount by which the asset value is reduced is known as an **impairment loss**. (This type of impairment in value should not be confused with routine depreciation of assets with finite lives.)

Activity 2.16

With which one of the accounting conventions that we discussed earlier is this accounting treatment of impaired assets consistent?

The answer is the prudence convention, which states that actual or anticipated losses should be recognised in full.

Real World 2.4 provides an example of where impairment losses for one large business had a dramatic effect on profits and led to in huge write-downs in the value of goodwill.

Real World 2.4

Making the wrong call

Swisscom said on Wednesday that earnings for this year would be hit by a €1.3bn impairment charge on Fastweb, its ailing Italian business. The charge, which the Swiss telecommunications group attributed partly to the eurozone crisis, will lower net profits by SFr1.2bn this year ($1.3bn). Analysts had long expected a reduction in the goodwill carried for the Italian internet and telecommunications business. But Swisscom had always defended the valuation.

Swisscom bought Fastweb in stages, starting in early 2007, paying a total of €4.6bn in what it described as a high growth, high technology business in a big and flourishing market. Swisscom said the company had lived up to expectations in the corporate sector, with strong growth and earnings. 'With a market share of 20 per cent, Fastweb is the clear number two in the segment devoted to corporate customers, and is growing steadily,' it said. But sales to private customers had 'come under pressure in the last few quarters' after an initial growth phase because of intense and rising competition, pricing pressures and overall weakness in Italian private consumption.

Carsten Schloter, Swisscom chief executive, defended the Fastweb purchase price, which he said was in line with valuations of the time, although he recognised it appeared excessive in retrospect.

FT   *Source*: Extracts from 'Swisscom takes €1.3bn charge on Fastweb' (Simonian, H) FT.com, 14 December 2011, © The Financial Times Limited 2012, All rights reserved.

Intangible non-current assets with indefinite lives should be tested for impairment on an annual basis. Other non-current assets, however, must be also tested where events suggest that impairment has taken place.

We should bear in mind that impairment reviews involve making judgements about the appropriate value to place on assets. Employing independent valuers to make these judgements will normally give users greater confidence in the information reported. There is always a risk that managers will manipulate impairment values to portray a picture that they would like users to see.

Inventories

It is not only non-current assets that run the risk of a significant fall in value. The inventories of a business could also suffer this fate as a result of changes in market taste, obsolescence, deterioration, damage and so on. Where a fall in value means that the amount likely to be recovered from the sale of the inventories will be lower than their cost, this loss must be reflected in the statement of financial position. Thus, if the net realisable value (that is, selling price less any selling costs) falls below the historic cost of inventories held, the former should be used as the basis of valuation. This reflects, once again, the influence of the prudence convention on the statement of financial position.

Real World 2.5 reveals how one well-known business wrote down the inventories of one of its products following a sharp reduction in selling prices.

Real World 2.5

You're fired!

'You're fired!' is what some investors might like to tell Amstrad, run by *Apprentice* star Sir Alan Sugar. . . . Shares in the company fell nearly 10 per cent as it revealed that sales of its much-vaunted videophone have failed to take off.

Amstrad launched the E3, a phone allowing users to hold video calls with each other, in a blaze of publicity last year. But, after cutting the price from £99 to £49, Amstrad sold just 61,000 E3s in the year to June and has taken a £5.7m stock [inventories] write down.

    Source: 'Amstrad (AMT)', *Investors Chronicle*, 7 October 2005, © The Financial Times Limited. All rights reserved.

The published financial statements of large businesses will normally show the basis on which inventories are valued. **Real World 2.6** shows how one business reports this information.

MEETING USER NEEDS

The statement of financial position is the oldest of the three main financial statements and may help users in the following ways:

■ *It provides insights about how the business is financed and how its funds are deployed.* The statement of financial position shows how much finance is contributed by the owners and how much is contributed by outside lenders. It also shows the different kinds of assets acquired and how much is invested in each kind.

■ *It can provide a basis for assessing the value of the business*. Since the statement of financial position lists, and places a value on, the various assets and claims, it can provide a starting point for assessing the value of the business. We have seen earlier, however, that accounting rules may result in assets being shown at their historic cost and that the restrictive definition of assets may exclude certain business resources from the statement of financial position.

■ *Relationships between assets and claims can be assessed*. It can be useful to look at relationships between various items on the statement of financial position, for example the relationship between how much wealth is tied up in current assets and how much is owed in the short term (current liabilities). From this relationship, we can see whether the business has sufficient short-term assets to cover its maturing obligations. (We shall look at this and other relationships between items on the statement of financial position in some detail in Chapter 8.)

■ *Performance can be assessed*. The effectiveness of a business in generating wealth can usefully be assessed against the amount of investment that was involved. Thus, knowing the relationship between profit earned during a period and the value of the net assets invested can be helpful to many users, particularly owners and managers. (This and similar relationships will also be explored in detail in Chapter 8.)

Once armed with the insights that a statement of financial position can provide, users are better placed to make investment and other decisions. **Real World 2.7** shows how a small business was able to obtain a loan because its bank was impressed by its strong statement of financial position. Now check your progress in your personal Study Plan

Self-assessment question 2.1

The following information relates to Simonson Engineering as at 30 September 2012:

	£
Plant and equipment	25,000
Trade payables	18,000
Short-term borrowing	26,000
Inventories	45,000
Property	72,000
Long-term borrowing	51,000
Trade receivables	48,000
Equity at 1 October 2011	117,500
Cash in hand	1,500
Motor vehicles	15,000
Fixtures and fittings	9,000
Profit for the year to 30 September 2012	18,000
Drawings for the year to 30 September 2012	15,000

Required:

(a) Prepare a statement of financial position for the business as at 30 September 2012 using the standard layout illustrated in Example 2.3.

(b) Comment on the financial position of the business based on the statement prepared in (a) above.

(c) Show the effect on the statement of financial position shown in (a) above of a decision to revalue the property to £115,000 and to recognise that the net realisable value of inventories at the year end is £38,000.

A solution to this question can be found in Appendix C.

SUMMARY

The main points of this chapter may be summarised as follows.

The major financial statements

- There are three major financial statements: the statement of cash flows, the income statement and the statement of financial position.

- The statement of cash flows shows the cash movements over a particular period.

- The income statement shows the wealth (profit) generated over a particular period.

- The statement of financial position shows the accumulated wealth at a particular point in time.

The statement of financial position

- This sets out the assets of the business, on the one hand, and the claims against those assets, on the other.

- Assets are resources of the business that have certain characteristics, such as the ability to provide future economic benefits.

- Claims are obligations on the part of the business to provide cash, or some other benefit, to outside parties.

- Claims are of two types: equity and liabilities.

- Equity represents the claim(s) of the owner(s) and liabilities represent the claims of others.

- The statement of financial position reflects the accounting equation:

$$\text{Assets} = \text{Equity} + \text{Liabilities}$$

Classification of assets and liabilities

- Assets are normally categorised as being current or non-current.

- Current assets are cash or near cash or are held for sale or consumption in the normal course of business, or for trading, or for the short term.

- Non-current assets are assets that are not current assets. They are normally held for the long-term operations of the business.

- Liabilities are normally categorised as being current or non-current liabilities.

- Current liabilities represent amounts due in the normal course of the business's operating cycle, or are held for trading, or are to be settled within a year of, or cannot be deferred for at least a year after, the end of the reporting period.

- Non-current liabilities represent amounts due that are not current liabilities.

Statement of financial position layouts

- The standard layout begins with assets at the top of the statement of financial position and places equity and liabilities underneath.

- A variation of the standard layout begins with the assets at the top of the statement of financial position. From the total assets figure are deducted the non-current and current liabilities to arrive at a net assets figure. Equity is placed underneath.

Accounting conventions

■ Accounting conventions are the rules of accounting that have evolved to deal with practical problems experienced by those preparing financial statements.

■ The main conventions relating to the statement of financial position include business entity, historic cost, prudence, going concern and dual aspect.

Money measurement

■ Using money as the unit of measurement limits the scope of the statement of financial position.

■ Certain resources such as goodwill, product brands and human resources are difficult to measure. An 'arm's-length transaction' is normally required before such assets can be reliably measured and reported on the statement of financial position.

■ Money is not a stable unit of measurement – it changes in value over time.

Asset valuation

■ The 'benchmark treatment' is to show non-current assets at historic cost.

■ Fair values may be used rather than historic cost, provided that they can be reliably obtained. This is rarely possible, however, for intangible non-current assets.

■ Non-current assets with finite lives should be shown at cost (or fair value) less any accumulated depreciation (amortisation).

■ Where the value of a non-current asset is impaired, it should be written down to its recoverable amount.

■ Inventories are shown at the lower of cost or net realisable value.

The usefulness of the statement of financial position

■ It shows how finance has been raised and how it has been been deployed.

■ It provides a basis for valuing the business, though it can only be a starting point.

■ Relationships between various items on the statement of financial position can usefully be explored.

■ Relationships between wealth generated and wealth invested can be helpful indicators of business effectiveness.

MyAccountingLab

Go to www.myaccountinglab.com to check your understanding of the chapter, create a personalised study plan, and maximise your revision time

FURTHER READING

If you would like to explore the topics covered in this chapter in more depth, we recommend the following:

Elliott, B. and Elliott, J., *Financial Accounting and Reporting*, 15th edn, Financial Times Prentice Hall, 2011, Chapters 17 and 19

International Accounting Standards Board, *2011 International Financial Reporting Standards IFRS* (two-volume set), IASB, 2011

KPMG, *Insights into IFRS*, 8th edn, Sweet & Maxwell, 2011, Sections 3.2, 3.3, 3.8 and 3.10 (a summarised version of this is available free at www.kpmg.com)

Melville, A., *International Financial Reporting: A Practical Guide*, 3rd edn, Financial Times Prentice Hall, 2011, Chapters 5 to 8

REVIEW QUESTIONS

Solutions to these questions can be found in Appendix D.

2.1 An accountant prepared a statement of financial position for a business. In this statement, the equity of the owner was shown next to the liabilities. This confused the owner, who argued: 'My equity is my major asset and so should be shown as an asset on the statement of financial position.' How would you explain this misunderstanding to the owner?

2.2 'The statement of financial position shows how much a business is worth.' Do you agree with this statement? Explain the reasons for your response.

2.3 What is meant by the accounting equation? How does the form of this equation differ between the two statement of financial position layouts mentioned in the chapter?

2.4 In recent years there have been attempts to place a value on the 'human assets' of a business in order to derive a figure that can be included on the statement of financial position. Do you think humans should be treated as assets? Would 'human assets' meet the conventional definition of an asset for inclusion on the statement of financial position?

Exercises 2.1 and 2.2 are basic level, 2.3 to 2.6 are intermediate level and 2.7 and 2.8 are advanced level. Solutions to the exercises with **coloured numbers** are given in Appendix E.

If you wish to try more exercises, visit the students' side of the companion website and MyAccountingLab.

2.1 On Thursday, the fourth day of his business venture, Paul, the street trader in wrapping paper (see earlier in the chapter), bought more inventories for £53 cash. During the day he sold inventories that had cost £33 for a total of £47.

Required:
Draw up the three financial statements for Paul's business venture for Thursday.

2.2 The equity of Paul's business belongs to him because he is the sole owner of the business. Can you explain how the figure for equity by Thursday evening has arisen? You will need to look back at the events of Monday, Tuesday and Wednesday to do this.

2.3 While on holiday in Bridlington, Helen had her credit cards and purse stolen from the beach while she was swimming. She was left with only £40, which she had kept in her hotel room, but she had three days of her holiday remaining. She was determined to continue her holiday and decided to make some money to enable her to do so. She decided to sell orange juice to holidaymakers using the local beach. On the first day she bought 80 cartons of orange juice at £0.50 each for cash and sold 70 of these at £0.80 each. On the following day she bought 60 cartons at £0.50 each for cash and sold 65 at £0.80 each. On the third and final day she bought another 60 cartons at £0.50 each for cash. However, it rained and, as a result, business was poor. She managed to sell 20 at £0.80 each but sold off the rest of her inventories at £0.40 each.

Required:
Prepare an income statement and statement of cash flows for each day's trading and prepare a statement of financial position at the end of each day's trading.

2.4 On 1 March, Joe Conday started a new business. During March he carried out the following transactions:

1 March	Deposited £20,000 in a newly opened bank account.
2 March	Bought fixtures and fittings for £6,000 cash and inventories £8,000 on credit.
3 March	Borrowed £5,000 from a relative and deposited it in the bank.
4 March	Bought a motor car for £7,000 cash and withdrew £200 in cash for his own use.
5 March	A further motor car costing £9,000 was bought. The motor car bought on 4 March was given in part exchange at a value of £6,500. The balance of the purchase price for the new car was paid in cash.
6 March	Conday won £2,000 in a lottery and paid the amount into the business bank account. He also repaid £1,000 of the borrowings.

Required:
Draw up a statement of financial position for the business at the end of each day.

2.5 The following is a list of assets and claims of a manufacturing business at a particular point in time:

	£
Short-term borrowing	22,000
Property	245,000
Inventories of raw materials	18,000
Trade payables	23,000
Plant and equipment	127,000
Loan from Manufacturing Finance Co. (long-term borrowing)	100,000
Inventories of finished goods	28,000
Delivery vans	54,000
Trade receivables	34,000

Required:
Write out a statement of financial position in the standard format incorporating these figures. (*Hint*: There is a missing item that needs to be deduced and inserted.)

2.6 You have been talking to someone who had read a few chapters of an accounting text some years ago. During your conversation the person made the following statements:

(a) The income statement shows how much cash has come into and left the business during the accounting period and the resulting balance at the end of the period.
(b) In order to be included in the statement of financial position as an asset, an item must have a resale value – that is all.
(c) The accounting equation is:

Assets + Equity = Liabilities

(d) Non-current assets are things that cannot be moved.
(e) Goodwill has an indefinite life and so should not be amortised.

Required:
Comment critically on each of the above statements, going into as much detail as you can.

2.7 The following is a list of the assets and claims of Crafty Engineering Ltd at 30 June last year:

	£000
Trade payables	86
Motor vehicles	38
Long-term borrowing from Industrial Finance Co.	260
Equipment and tools	207
Short-term borrowings	116
Inventories	153
Property	320
Trade receivables	185

Required:
(a) Prepare the statement of financial position of the business as at 30 June last year from the above information using the standard layout. (*Hint*: There is a missing item that needs to be deduced and inserted.)
(b) Discuss the significant features revealed by this financial statement.

2.8 The statement of financial position of a business at the start of the week is as follows:

	£
ASSETS	
Property	145,000
Furniture and fittings	63,000
Inventories	28,000
Trade receivables	33,000
Total assets	269,000
EQUITY AND LIABILITIES	
Equity	203,000
Short-term borrowing (bank overdraft)	43,000
Trade payables	23,000
Total equity and liabilities	269,000

During the week the following transactions take place:

(a) Sold inventories for £11,000 cash; these inventories had cost £8,000.
(b) Sold inventories for £23,000 on credit; these inventories had cost £17,000.
(c) Received cash from trade receivables totalling £18,000.
(d) The owners of the business introduced £100,000 of their own money, which was placed in the business bank account.
(e) The owners brought a motor van, valued at £10,000, into the business.
(f) Bought inventories on credit for £14,000.
(g) Paid trade payables £13,000.

Required:
Show the statement of financial position after all of these transactions have been reflected.

Chapter 3

MEASURING AND REPORTING FINANCIAL PERFORMANCE

INTRODUCTION

In this chapter, we continue our examination of the major financial statements by looking at the income statement. This statement was briefly considered in Chapter 2, but we shall now look at it in some detail. We shall see how it is prepared and how it links with the statement of financial position. We shall also consider some of the key measurement problems to be faced when preparing the income statement.

Learning outcomes

When you have completed this chapter, you should be able to:

■ discuss the nature and purpose of the income statement;

■ prepare an income statement from relevant financial information and interpret the information that it contains;

■ discuss the main recognition and measurement issues that must be considered when preparing the income statement;

■ explain the main accounting conventions underpinning the income statement.

MyAccountingLab Visit **www.myaccountinglab.com** for practice and revision opportunities

Businesses exist for the primary purpose of generating wealth, or **profit**. The income statement – or profit and loss account, as it is sometimes called – measures and reports how much profit (wealth) a business has generated over a period. It is, therefore, an immensely important financial statement for many users.

To measure profit, the total revenue generated during a particular period must be identified. **Revenue** is simply a measure of the inflow of economic benefits arising from the ordinary operations of a business. These benefits will result in either an increase in assets (such as cash or amounts owed to the business by its customers) or a decrease in liabilities. Different forms of business enterprise will generate different forms of revenue. Some examples of the different forms that revenue can take are as follows:

- sales of goods (for example, by a manufacturer)
- fees for services (for example, of a solicitor)
- subscriptions (for example, of a club)
- interest received (for example, on an investment fund).

Real World 3.1 shows the various forms of revenue generated by a leading football club.

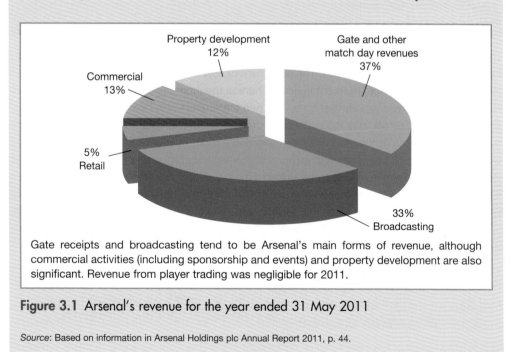

Real World 3.1

Gunning for revenue

Arsenal Football Club generated total revenue of almost £256 million for the year ended 31 May 2011. Like other leading clubs, it relies on various forms of revenue to sustain its success. Figure 3.1 shows the contribution of each form of revenue for the year.

Gate receipts and broadcasting tend to be Arsenal's main forms of revenue, although commercial activities (including sponsorship and events) and property development are also significant. Revenue from player trading was negligible for 2011.

Figure 3.1 Arsenal's revenue for the year ended 31 May 2011

Source: Based on information in Arsenal Holdings plc Annual Report 2011, p. 44.

The total expenses relating to each period must also be identified. **Expense** is really the opposite of revenue. It represents the outflow of economic benefits arising from the ordinary operations of a business. This loss of benefits will result in either a decrease in assets (such as cash) or an increase in liabilities (such as amounts owed to suppliers). Expenses are incurred in the process of generating, or attempting to generate, revenue. The nature of the business will again determine the type of expenses that will be incurred. Examples of some of the more common types of expense are:

■ the cost of buying or making the goods that are sold during the period concerned – known as *cost of sales* or *cost of goods sold*
■ salaries and wages
■ rent and rates
■ motor vehicle running expenses
■ insurance
■ printing and stationery
■ heat and light
■ telephone and postage.

The income statement simply shows the total revenue generated during a particular period and deducts from this the total expenses incurred in generating that revenue. The difference between the total revenue and total expenses will represent either profit (if revenue exceeds expenses) or loss (if expenses exceed revenue). Therefore:

> **Profit (or loss) for the period = Total revenue for the period**
> **– Total expenses incurred in generating that revenue**

The period over which profit or loss is normally measured is usually known as the **reporting period**, but it is sometimes called the 'accounting period' or 'financial period'.

DIFFERENT ROLES

The income statement and the statement of financial position are not substitutes for one another. Rather, they perform different roles. The statement of financial position sets out the wealth held by the business at a single moment in time, whereas the income statement is concerned with the *flow* of wealth over a period of time. The two statements are, however, closely related.

The income statement links the statements of financial position at the beginning and the end of a reporting period. At the start of a new reporting period, the statement of financial position shows the opening wealth position of the business. After an appropriate period, an income statement is prepared to show the wealth generated over that period. A statement of financial position is then prepared to reveal the new wealth position at the end of the period. It will reflect changes in wealth that have occurred since the previous statement of financial position was drawn up.

We saw in Chapter 2 that the effect on the statement of financial position of making a profit (or loss) means that the accounting equation can be extended as follows:

> **Assets (at the end of the period) = Equity (amount at the start of the period**
> **+ Profit (or – Loss) for the period)**
> **+ Liabilities (at the end of the period)**

(This is assuming that the owner makes no injections or withdrawals of equity during the period.)

Can you recall from Chapter 2 how a profit, or loss, for a period is shown in the statement of financial position?

It is shown as an adjustment to owners' equity. Profit is added and loss is subtracted.

The equation above can be extended to:

Assets (at the end of the period) = Equity (amount at the start of the period)
+ (Sales revenue – Expenses) (for the period)
+ Liabilities (at the end of the period)

In theory, it is possible to calculate the profit (or loss) for the period by making all adjustments for revenue and expenses through the equity section of the statement of financial position. However, this would be rather cumbersome. A better solution is to have an 'appendix' to the equity section, in the form of an income statement. By deducting expenses from revenue for the period, the income statement derives the profit (or loss) by which the equity figure in the statement of financial position needs to be adjusted. This profit (or loss) figure represents the net effect of trading for the period. This 'appendix' presents users with a detailed and more informative view of performance.

INCOME STATEMENT LAYOUT

The layout of the income statement will vary according to the type of business to which it relates. To illustrate an income statement, let us consider the case of a retail business (that is, a business that buys goods in their completed state and resells them).

Example 3.1 sets out a typical layout for the income statement of a retail business.

Example 3.1

Better-Price Stores
Income statement for the year ended 31 October 2012

	£
Sales revenue	232,000
Cost of sales	(154,000)
Gross profit	78,000
Salaries and wages	(24,500)
Rent and rates	(14,200)
Heat and light	(7,500)
Telephone and postage	(1,200)
Insurance	(1,000)
Motor vehicle running expenses	(3,400)
Depreciation – fixtures and fittings	(1,000)
Depreciation – motor van	(600)
Operating profit	24,600
Interest received from investments	2,000
Interest on borrowings	(1,100)
Profit for the period	25,500

We saw in Chapter 2 that brackets are used to denote when an item is to be deducted. This convention is used by accountants in preference to + or − signs and will be used throughout the text.

Gross profit

The first part of the income statement is concerned with calculating the **gross profit** for the period. We can see that revenue, which arises from selling the goods, is the first item to appear. Deducted from this item is the cost of sales (also called cost of goods sold) during the period. This gives the gross profit, which represents the profit from buying and selling goods, without taking into account any other revenues or expenses associated with the business.

Operating profit

Operating expenses (overheads) incurred in running the business (salaries and wages, rent and rates and so on) are deducted from the gross profit. The resulting figure is known as the **operating profit**. This represents the wealth generated during the period from the normal activities of the business. It does not take account of income from other activities. Better-Price Stores in Example 3.1 is a retailer, so interest received on some spare cash that the business has invested is not part of its operating profit. Costs of financing the business are also ignored in the calculation of the operating profit.

Profit for the period

Having established the operating profit, we add any non-operating income (such as interest receivable) and deduct any interest payable on borrowings to arrive at the **profit for the period** (or net profit). This final measure of wealth generated represents the amount attributable to the owner(s) and will be added to the equity figure in the statement of financial position. It is a residual: that is, the amount remaining after deducting all expenses incurred in generating the sales revenue and taking account of non-operating income.

FURTHER ISSUES

Having set out the main principles involved in preparing an income statement, we need to consider some further points.

Cost of sales

The **cost of sales** (or cost of goods sold) for a period can be identified in different ways. In some businesses, the cost of sales for each individual sale is identified at the time of the transaction. Each item of sales revenue is matched with the relevant cost of that sale. Many large retailers (for example, supermarkets) have point-of-sale (checkout) devices that not only record each sale but also simultaneously pick up the cost of the goods that are the subject of the particular sale. Businesses that sell a relatively small number of high-value items (for example, an engineering business that produces custom-made equipment) also tend to match sales revenue with the cost of the goods sold, at the time of sale. However, some businesses (for example, small retailers) may not find it practical to do this. Instead, they identify the cost of sales after the end of the reporting period.

To understand how this is done, we must remember that the cost of sales represents the cost of goods that were *sold* during the period rather than the cost of goods that were *bought* during the period. Part of the goods bought during the period may remain, as inventories, at the end of the period. These will normally be sold in the next period. To derive the cost of sales, we need to know the amount of opening and closing inventories for the period and the cost of goods bought during the period. Example 3.2 illustrates how the cost of sales is derived.

Example 3.2

Better-Price Stores, which we considered in Example 3.1, began the year with unsold inventories of £40,000 and during that year bought inventories at a cost of £189,000. At the end of the year, unsold inventories of £75,000 were still held by the business.

The opening inventories at the beginning of the year *plus* the goods bought during the year will represent the total goods available for resale, as follows:

	£
Opening inventories	40,000
Purchases (goods bought)	189,000
Goods available for resale	229,000

The closing inventories will represent that portion of the total goods available for resale that remains unsold at the end of the year. This means that the cost of goods actually sold during the year must be the total goods available for resale *less* the inventories remaining at the end of the year. That is:

	£
Goods available for resale	229,000
Closing inventories	(75,000)
Cost of sales (or cost of goods sold)	154,000

These calculations are sometimes shown on the face of the income statement as in Example 3.3.

Example 3.3

	£	£
Sales revenue		232,000
Cost of sales:		
Opening inventories	40,000	
Purchases (goods bought)	189,000	
Closing inventories	(75,000)	(154,000)
Gross profit		78,000

This is just an expanded version of the first section of the income statement for Better-Price Stores, as set out in Example 3.1. We have simply included the additional information concerning inventories balances and purchases for the year provided in Example 3.2.

Classifying expenses

The classification of expense items is often a matter of judgement. For example, the income statement set out in Example 3.1 could have included the insurance expense with the telephone and postage expense under a single heading – say, 'general expenses'. Such decisions are normally based on how useful a particular classification will be to users. This will usually mean that expense items of material size will be shown separately. For businesses that trade as limited companies, however, rules dictate the classification of expense items for external reporting purposes. (These rules will be discussed in Chapter 5.)

Activity 3.2

The following information relates to the activities of H & S Retailers for the year ended 30 April 2012:

	£
Motor vehicle running expenses	1,200
Closing inventories	3,000
Rent and rates payable	5,000
Motor vans – cost less depreciation	6,300
Annual depreciation – motor vans	1,500
Heat and light	900
Telephone and postage	450
Sales revenue	97,400
Goods purchased	68,350
Insurance	750
Loan interest payable	620
Balance at bank	4,780
Salaries and wages	10,400
Opening inventories	4,000

Prepare an income statement for the year ended 30 April 2012. (*Hint*: Not all items listed should appear on this statement.)

Your answer to this activity should be as follows:

H & S Retailers
Income statement for the year ended 30 April 2012

	£	£
Sales revenue		97,400
Cost of sales:		
Opening inventories	4,000	
Purchases	68,350	
Closing inventories	(3,000)	(69,350)
Gross profit		28,050
Salaries and wages		(10,400)
Rent and rates		(5,000)
Heat and light		(900)
Telephone and postage		(450)
Insurance		(750)
Motor vehicle running expenses		(1,200)
Depreciation – motor vans		(1,500)
Operating profit		7,850
Loan interest		(620)
Profit for the period		7,230

Note that neither the motor vans nor the bank balance are included in this statement, because they are both assets and so neither revenues nor expenses.

Figure 3.2 shows the layout of the income statement.

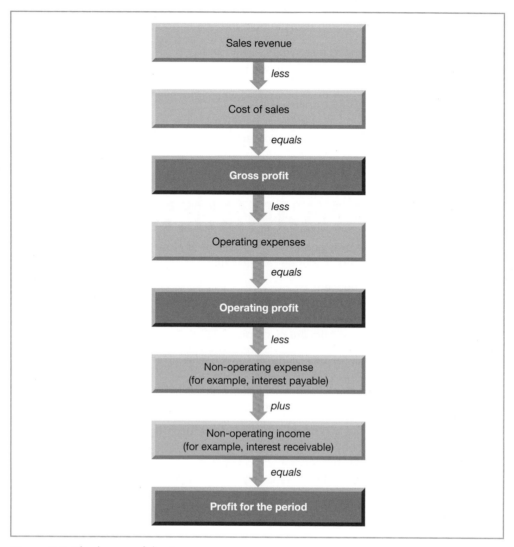

Figure 3.2 The layout of the income statement

RECOGNISING REVENUE

A key issue in the measurement of profit concerns the point at which revenue is recognised. Revenue arising from the sale of goods or provision of a service could be recognised at various points. Where, for example, a motor car dealer receives an order for a new car from one of its customers, the associated revenue could be recognised by the dealer

- at the time that the order is placed by the customer;
- at the time that the car is collected by the customer; or
- at the time that the customer pays the dealer.

These three points could be quite far apart, particularly where the order relates to a specialist car that is sold to the customer on credit.

The point chosen can have a profound impact on the total revenues reported for the reporting period. This, in turn, can have a profound effect on profit. If the sale transaction straddled the end of a reporting period, the point chosen for recognising revenue could determine whether it is included in an earlier reporting period or a later one.

The main criteria for recognising revenue from the sale of goods or services are that:

- the amount of revenue can be measured reliably; and
- it is probable that the economic benefits will be received.

An additional criterion, however, must be applied where the revenue comes from the sale of goods, which is that:

- ownership and control of the items should pass to the buyer.

Activity 3.3 provides an opportunity to apply these criteria to a practical problem.

Activity 3.3

A manufacturing business sells goods on credit. Below are four points in the production/selling cycle at which revenue might be recognised:

1 when the goods are produced;
2 when an order is received from the customer;
3 when the goods are delivered to, and accepted by, the customer;
4 when the cash is received from the customer.

At what point do you think the business should recognise revenue?

All of the three criteria mentioned above will usually be fulfilled at point 3: when the goods are passed to, and accepted by, the customer. This is because

- the selling price and the settlement terms will have been agreed and, therefore, the amount of revenue can be reliably measured;
- delivery and acceptance of the goods leads to ownership and control passing to the buyer;
- transferring ownership gives the seller legally enforceable rights that makes it probable that the buyer will pay.

We can see that the effect of applying these criteria is that a sale on credit is usually recognised *before* the cash is received. This means that the total sales revenue shown in the income statement may include sales transactions for which the cash has yet to be received. The total sales revenue will often, therefore, be different from the total cash received from sales during the period. For cash sales (that is, sales where cash is paid at the same time as the goods are transferred), there will be no difference in timing between reporting sales revenue and cash received.

Long-term contracts

Some contracts for goods or services may take more than one reporting period to complete. A misleading impression may be given, however, if a business waits until the completion of a long-term contract before recognising revenue. This is because all the revenue would be shown in the final reporting period and none in the preceding reporting periods when work was also carried out. In such a situation, it is possible to recognise revenue *before* the contract for the goods or services is completed, provided that the work can be broken down into a number of stages and each stage can be measured reliably.

Each stage can be awarded a separate price with the total for all the stages being equal to the total price for the entire contract. This means that, as each stage is completed, the supplier of the goods or services can recognise the price for that stage as revenue and bill the customer accordingly. This is provided that the outcome of the contract as a whole can be estimated reliably.

Construction contracts often extend over a long period of time and so this staged approach to recognising revenues tends to be applied. Suppose that a customer enters into a contract with a builder to have a new factory built that will take three years to complete. Let us assume that building the factory could be broken down into the following stages:

- Stage 1 – clearing and levelling the land and putting in the foundations;
- Stage 2 – building the walls;
- Stage 3 – putting on the roof;
- Stage 4 – putting in the windows and completing all the interior work.

As each stage is completed, the builder will bill the customer for the agreed price of that stage. The builder will treat the revenue for the stage as that of the reporting period in which the stage is completed. In this way, the revenue for each stage will appear in that reporting period's income statement as will the expenses incurred by the builder on that stage.

There are also certain kinds of service that may take years to complete. One example is where a consultancy business installs a new computer system for a client. If the contract can be broken down into stages, and each stage of completion measured reliably, a similar approach to that taken for construction contracts can be adopted. This would allow revenue to be recognised at each stage of completion.

This approach tends to be taken with any contract, either for goods and services, that takes a long time to complete.

Real World 3.2 sets out the revenue recognition criteria for one large business.

Real World 3.2

Subject to contract

Amec plc is an international business offering consultancy, engineering and project management services. The point at which revenue on long-term contracts is recognised by the business is as follows:

> As soon as the outcome of a long-term contract can be estimated reliably, contract revenue and expenses are recognised in the income statement in proportion to the stage of completion of the contract. The stage of completion is assessed by reference to surveys of work performed. When the outcome of a contract cannot be estimated reliably, revenue is recognised only to the extent of contract costs incurred that it is probable will be recoverable, and contract costs are expensed as incurred. An expected loss on a contract is recognised immediately in the income statement.

Source: AMEC plc, Annual Report and Accounts 2011, Notes to Consolidated Accounts, p. 75.

Continuous services

In some cases, a continuous service may be provided to customers. For example, a telecommunications business may provide open access to the internet for subscribers. Here, the benefits from providing the service are usually assumed to arise evenly over time and so revenue is recognised evenly over the subscription period.

Where it is not possible to break down a service into particular stages of completion, or to assume that benefits from providing the service accrue evenly over time, revenue is normally recognised after the service is completed. An example might be the work done by a solicitor on a house purchase for a client. **Real World 3.3** provides an example of how one major business recognises revenue from providing services.

Real World 3.3

Sky-high broadcasting revenue

British Sky Broadcasting Group plc is a major satellite broadcaster that generates various forms of revenue. Here are the ways in which some of its revenues are recognised:

■ pay-per-view revenues – when the event (movie or football match) is viewed
■ subscription services, including Sky TV and Sky Broadband – as the services are provided
■ advertising revenues – when the advertising is broadcast
■ installation, hardware and service revenue – when the goods and services are activated.

Source: Based on information in British Sky Broadcasting Group plc Annual Report and Accounts 2012, p. 77, http://annualreview2012.sky.com

Revenue for providing services is often recognised *before* the cash is received. There are occasions, however, when the business demands payment before providing the service.

Activity 3.4

Can you think of any examples where cash may be demanded in advance of a service being provided? (*Hint*: Try to think of services that you may use.)

Examples of cash being received in advance of the service being provided may include:

■ rent received from letting premises
■ telephone line rental charges
■ TV licence (BBC) or subscription fees (for example, Sky)
■ subscriptions received for the use of health clubs or golf clubs.

You may have thought of others.

RECOGNISING EXPENSES

Having considered the recognition of revenue, let us now turn to the recognition of expenses. The **matching convention** provides guidance on this. This convention states that expenses should be matched to the revenue that they helped to generate. In other words, the expenses associated with a particular item of revenue must be taken into account in the same reporting period as that in which the item of revenue is included. Applying this convention often means that an expense reported in the income statement for a period may not be the same as the cash paid for that item during the period. The expense reported might be either more or less than the cash paid during the period. Let us consider two examples that illustrate this point.

When the expense for the period is more than the cash paid during the period

Example 3.4

Domestic Ltd, a retailer, sells household electrical appliances. It pays its sales staff a commission of 2 per cent of sales revenue generated. Total sales revenue for last year amounted to £300,000. This means that the commission to be paid on sales for the year will be £6,000. However, by the end of the year, the amount of sales commission actually paid was only £5,000. If the business reported this amount, it would mean that the income statement would not reflect the full expense for the year. This would contravene the *matching convention* because not all of the expenses associated with the revenue of the year would have been matched in the income statement. This will be remedied as follows:

- Sales commission expense in the income statement will include the amount paid plus the amount outstanding (that is, £6,000 = £5,000 + £1,000).
- The amount outstanding (£1,000) represents an outstanding liability at the end of the year and will be included under the heading **accrued expenses**, or 'accruals', in the statement of financial position. As this item will have to be paid within twelve months of the year end, it will be treated as a current liability.
- The cash will already have been reduced to reflect the commission paid (£5,000) during the period.

These points are illustrated in Figure 3.3.

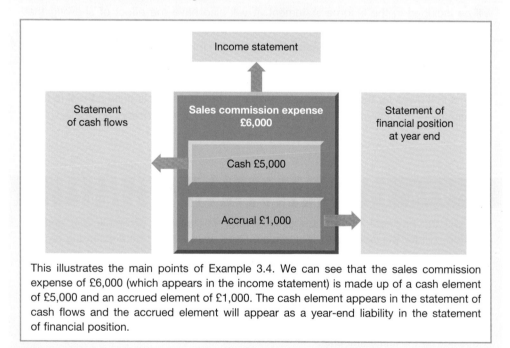

This illustrates the main points of Example 3.4. We can see that the sales commission expense of £6,000 (which appears in the income statement) is made up of a cash element of £5,000 and an accrued element of £1,000. The cash element appears in the statement of cash flows and the accrued element will appear as a year-end liability in the statement of financial position.

Figure 3.3 Accounting for sales commission

In principle, all expenses should be matched to the period in which the sales revenue to which they relate is reported. It is sometimes difficult, however, to match certain expenses to sales revenue in the same precise way that we have matched sales commission to sales revenue. For example, electricity charges incurred often cannot be linked directly to particular sales in this way. As a result, the electricity charges incurred by, say, a retailer would be matched to the *period* to which they relate. Example 3.5 illustrates this.

Example 3.5

Domestic Ltd has reached the end of its reporting period and has only paid for electricity for the first three quarters of the year (amounting to £1,900). This is simply because the electricity company has yet to send out bills for the quarter that ends on the same date as Domestic Ltd's year end. The amount of Domestic Ltd's bill for the last quarter of the year is £500. In this situation, the amount of the electricity expense outstanding is dealt with as follows:

- Electricity expense in the income statement will include the amount paid, plus the amount of the bill for the last quarter of the year (that is, £1,900 + £500 = £2,400) in order to cover the whole year.
- The amount of the outstanding bill (£500) represents a liability at the end of the year and will be included under the heading 'accruals' or 'accrued expenses' in the statement of financial position. This item would normally have to be paid within twelve months of the year end and will, therefore, be treated as a current liability.
- The cash will already have been reduced to reflect the amount (£1,900) paid for electricity during the period.

This treatment will mean that the correct figure for the electricity expense for the year will be included in the income statement. It will also have the effect of showing that, at the end of the reporting period, Domestic Ltd owed the amount of the last quarter's electricity bill. Dealing with the outstanding amount in this way reflects the dual aspect of the item and will ensure that the accounting equation is maintained.

Domestic Ltd may wish to draw up its income statement before it is able to discover how much it owes for the last quarter's electricity. In this case it is quite normal to make an estimate of the amount of the bill and to use this amount as described above.

Activity 3.5

How will the payment of the outstanding sales commission (Example 3.4) and the electricity bill for the last quarter (Example 3.5) be dealt with in the accounting records of Domestic Ltd?

When these amounts are eventually paid, they will be dealt with as follows:

- Reduce cash by the amounts paid.
- Reduce the amount of the accrued expense as shown on the statement of financial position by the same amounts.

Other expenses, apart from electricity charges, may also be matched to the period to which they relate.

Activity 3.6

Can you think of other expenses for a retailer that cannot be linked directly to sales revenue and for which matching will therefore be done on a time basis?

You may have thought of the following examples:

- rent and rates
- insurance
- interest payments
- licence fees payable.

This is not an exhaustive list. You may have thought of others.

When the amount paid during the period is more than the full expense for the period

It is not unusual for a business to be in a situation where it has paid more during the year than the full expense for that year. Example 3.6 illustrates how we deal with this.

Example 3.6

Images Ltd, an advertising agency, normally pays rent for its premises quarterly in advance (on 1 January, 1 April, 1 July and 1 October). On the last day of the last reporting period (31 December), it paid the next quarter's rent (£4,000) to the following 31 March, which was a day earlier than required. This would mean that a total of five quarters' rent was paid during the year. If Images Ltd reports all of the cash paid as an expense in the income statement, this would be more than the full expense for the year. This would contravene the matching convention because a higher figure than the expenses associated with the revenue of the year would appear in the income statement.

The problem is overcome by dealing with the rental payment as follows:

- Show the rent for four quarters as the appropriate expense in the income statement (that is, 4 × £4,000 = £16,000).
- The cash (that is, 5 × £4,000 = £20,000) would already have been paid during the year.
- Show the quarter's rent paid in advance (£4,000) as a prepaid expense under assets in the statement of financial position. (The rent paid in advance will appear as a current asset in the statement of financial position, under the heading **prepaid expenses** or 'prepayments'.)

In the next reporting period, this prepayment will cease to be an asset and will become an expense in the income statement of that period. This is because the rent prepaid relates to the next period during which it will be 'used up'.

$\rightarrow$

These points are illustrated in Figure 3.4.

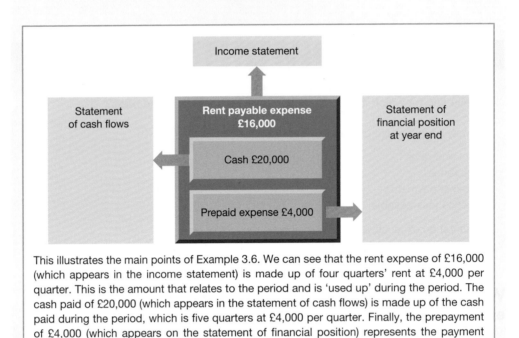

This illustrates the main points of Example 3.6. We can see that the rent expense of £16,000 (which appears in the income statement) is made up of four quarters' rent at £4,000 per quarter. This is the amount that relates to the period and is 'used up' during the period. The cash paid of £20,000 (which appears in the statement of cash flows) is made up of the cash paid during the period, which is five quarters at £4,000 per quarter. Finally, the prepayment of £4,000 (which appears on the statement of financial position) represents the payment made on 31 December and relates to the next reporting period.

Figure 3.4 Accounting for rent payable

In practice, the treatment of accruals and prepayments will be subject to the **materiality convention**. This convention states that, where the amounts involved are immaterial, we should consider only what is expedient. This will usually mean treating an item as an expense in the period in which it is acquired, rather than strictly matching it to the revenue to which it relates. For example, a business may find that, at the end of a reporting period, it holds £2 worth of unused stationery. The time and effort taken to record this as a prepayment would outweigh the negligible effect on the measurement of profit or financial position. As a result, it would be treated as an expense of the current period and ignored in the following period.

PROFIT, CASH AND ACCRUALS ACCOUNTING

We have seen that it is normally the case that, for a particular reporting period, total revenue is not the same as total cash received, and total expenses are not the same as total cash paid. As a result, the profit for the period (that is, total revenue minus total expenses) will not normally represent the net cash generated during that period. This reflects the difference between profit and liquidity. Profit is a measure of achievement, or productive effort, rather than a measure of cash generated. Although making a profit increases wealth, cash is only one possible form in which that wealth may be held.

These points are reflected in the **accruals convention**, which asserts that profit is the excess of revenue over expenses for a period, not the excess of cash receipts over cash payments. Leading on from this, the approach to accounting that is based on the accruals convention is frequently referred to as **accruals accounting**. The statement of financial position and the income statement are both prepared on the basis of accruals accounting.

DEPRECIATION

The expense of **depreciation**, which we have already come across, requires further examination. Most non-current assets do not have a perpetual existence, but have finite, or limited, lives. They are eventually 'used up' in the process of generating revenue for the business. This 'using up' may relate to physical deterioration (as with a motor vehicle). It may, however, be linked to obsolescence (as with some IT software that is no longer useful) or the mere passage of time (as with a purchased patent, which has a limited period of validity).

In essence, depreciation is an attempt to measure that portion of the cost (or fair value) of a non-current asset that has been depleted in generating the revenue recognised during a particular period. In the case of intangibles, we usually refer to the expense as **amortisation** rather than depreciation. In the interests of brevity, we shall use the word depreciation for both tangibles and intangibles.

Calculating the depreciation expense

To calculate a depreciation expense for a period, four factors have to be considered:

- the cost (or fair value) of the asset;
- the useful life of the asset;
- the residual value of the asset; and
- the depreciation method.

The cost (or fair value) of the asset

The cost of an asset will include all costs incurred by the business to bring the asset to its required location and to make it ready for use. This means that, in addition to the cost of acquiring the asset, any delivery costs, installation costs (for example, setting up a new machine) and legal costs incurred in the transfer of legal title (for example, in purchasing a lease on property) will be included as part of the total cost of the asset. Similarly, any costs incurred in improving or altering an asset to make it suitable for use will also be included as part of the total cost.

Andrew Wu (Engineering) Ltd bought a new motor car for its marketing director. The invoice received from the motor car supplier showed the following:

	£
New BMW 325i	26,350
Delivery charge	80
Alloy wheels	660
Sun roof	200
Petrol	30
Number plates	130
Road fund licence	120
	27,570
Part exchange – Reliant Robin	(1,000)
Amount outstanding	26,570

What is the total cost of the new car to be treated as part of the business's property, plant and equipment?

The cost of the new car will be as follows:

	£
New BMW 325i	26,350
Delivery charge	80
Alloy wheels	660
Sun roof	200
Number plates	130
	27,420

This cost includes delivery charges, which are necessary to bring the asset into use, and it includes number plates, as they are a necessary and integral part of the asset. Improvements (alloy wheels and sun roof) are also regarded as part of the total cost of the motor car. The petrol and road fund licence, however, are costs of operating the asset. These amounts will, therefore, be treated as an expense in the period incurred (although part of the cost of the licence may be regarded as a prepaid expense in the period incurred).

The part-exchange figure shown is part payment of the total amount outstanding and so is not relevant to a consideration of the total cost.

The fair value of an asset was defined in Chapter 2 as the exchange value that could be obtained in an arm's-length transaction. As we saw, assets may be revalued to fair value only if this can be measured reliably. Where fair values have been applied, the depreciation expense should be based on those fair values, rather than on the historic costs.

The useful life of the asset

A non-current asset has both a *physical life* and an *economic life*. The physical life will be exhausted through the effects of wear and tear and/or the passage of time. The economic life is decided by the effects of technological progress, by changes in demand or changes in the way that the business operates. The benefits provided by the asset are eventually outweighed by the costs as it becomes unable to compete with newer assets, or becomes irrelevant to the needs of the business. The economic life of an asset may be much shorter than its physical life. For example, a computer may have a physical life of eight years and an economic life of three years.

The economic life determines the expected useful life of an asset for depreciation purposes. It is often difficult to estimate, however, as technological progress and shifts in consumer tastes can be swift and unpredictable.

Residual value (disposal value)

When a business disposes of a non-current asset that may still be of value to others, some payment may be received. This payment will represent the **residual value**, or *disposal value*, of the asset. To calculate the total amount to be depreciated, the residual value must be deducted from the cost (or fair value) of the asset. The likely amount to be received on disposal can, once again, be difficult to predict. The best guide is often past experience of similar assets sold.

Depreciation methods

Once the amount to be depreciated (that is, the cost, or fair value, of the asset less any residual value) has been estimated, the business must select a method of allocating this depreciable amount between the reporting periods covering the asset's useful life. Although there are various ways in which this may be done, there are really only two methods that are commonly used in practice.

The first of these is known as the **straight-line method**. This method simply allocates the amount to be depreciated evenly over the useful life of the asset. In other words, there is an equal depreciation expense for each year that the asset is held.

Example 3.7

To illustrate this method, consider the following information:

Cost of machine	£78,124
Estimated residual value at the end of its useful life	£2,000
Estimated useful life	4 years

To calculate the depreciation expense for each year, the total amount to be depreciated must be calculated. This will be the total cost less the estimated residual value: that is, £78,124 − £2,000 = £76,124. Having done this, the annual depreciation expense can be derived by dividing the amount to be depreciated by the estimated useful life of the asset of four years. The calculation is therefore

$$\frac{£76,124}{4} = £19,031$$

This means that the annual depreciation expense that appears in the income statement in relation to this asset will be £19,031 for each of the four years of the asset's life.

The amount of depreciation relating to the asset will be accumulated for as long as the asset continues to be owned by the business or until the accumulated depreciation amounts to the cost less residual value. This accumulated depreciation figure will increase each year as a result of the annual depreciation expense in the income statement. This accumulated amount will be deducted from the cost of the asset on the statement of financial position. At the end of the second year, for example, the accumulated depreciation will be £19,031 × 2 = £38,062. The asset details will appear on the statement of financial position as follows:

	£
Machine at cost	78,124
Accumulated depreciation	(38,062)
	40,062

As we saw in Chapter 2, this balance of £40,062 is referred to as the **carrying amount** (sometimes also known as the **written-down value** or **net book value**) of the asset. It represents that portion of the cost (or fair value) of the asset that has still to be treated as an expense (written off) in future years plus the residual value. This carrying-amount figure does not, except by coincidence, represent the current market value, which may be quite different. The only point at which the carrying amount is intended to represent the market value of the asset is at the time of its disposal. In Example 3.7, at the end of the four-year life of the machine, the carrying amount would be £2,000 – its estimated disposal value.

The straight-line method derives its name from the fact that the carrying amount of the asset at the end of each year, when plotted against time, will result in a straight line, as shown in Figure 3.5.

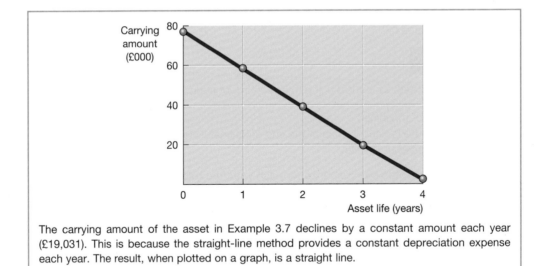

The carrying amount of the asset in Example 3.7 declines by a constant amount each year (£19,031). This is because the straight-line method provides a constant depreciation expense each year. The result, when plotted on a graph, is a straight line.

Figure 3.5 Graph of carrying amount against time using the straight-line method

The second approach to calculating the depreciation expense for a period is referred to as the **reducing-balance method**. This method applies a fixed percentage rate of depreciation to the carrying amount of the asset each year. The effect of this will be high annual depreciation expenses in the early years and lower expenses in the later years. To illustrate this method, let us take the same information that was used in Example 3.7. By using a fixed percentage of 60 per cent of the carrying amount to determine the annual depreciation expense, the effect will be to reduce the carrying amount to £2,000 after four years.

The calculations will be as follows:

	£
Cost of machine	78,124
Year 1 depreciation expense (60%* of cost)	(46,874)
Carrying amount	31,250
Year 2 depreciation expense (60% of carrying amount)	(18,750)
Carrying amount	12,500
Year 3 depreciation expense (60% of carrying amount)	(7,500)
Carrying amount	5,000
Year 4 depreciation expense (60% of carrying amount)	(3,000)
Residual value	2,000

* See the box below for an explanation of how to derive the fixed percentage.

Deriving the fixed percentage

Deriving the fixed percentage to be applied requires the use of the following formula:

$$P = (1 - \sqrt[n]{R/C} \times 100\%)$$

where: P = the depreciation percentage
  n = the useful life of the asset (in years)
  R = the residual value of the asset
  C = the cost, or fair value, of the asset.

The fixed percentage rate will, however, be given in all examples used in this book.

We can see that the pattern of depreciation is quite different between the two methods. If we plot the carrying amount of the asset, which has been derived using the reducing-balance method, against time, the result will be as shown in Figure 3.6.

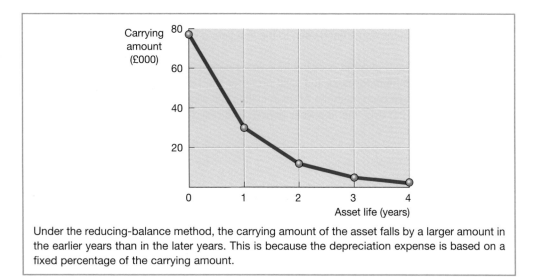

Under the reducing-balance method, the carrying amount of the asset falls by a larger amount in the earlier years than in the later years. This is because the depreciation expense is based on a fixed percentage of the carrying amount.

Figure 3.6 Graph of carrying amount against time using the reducing-balance method

Activity 3.9

Assume that the machine used in Example 3.7 was owned by a business that made a profit before depreciation of £40,000 for each of the four years in which the asset was held.

Calculate the profit for the business for each year under each depreciation method, and comment on your findings.

Your answer should be as follows:

Straight-line method

	(a) Profit before depreciation £	(b) Depreciation £	(a – b) Profit £
Year 1	40,000	19,031	20,969
Year 2	40,000	19,031	20,969
Year 3	40,000	19,031	20,969
Year 4	40,000	19,031	20,969

Reducing-balance method

	(a) Profit before depreciation £	(b) Depreciation £	(a – b) Profit/(loss) £
Year 1	40,000	46,874	(6,874)
Year 2	40,000	18,750	21,250
Year 3	40,000	7,500	32,500
Year 4	40,000	3,000	37,000

The straight-line method of depreciation results in the same profit figure for each year of the four-year period. This is because both the profit before depreciation and the depreciation expense are constant over the period. The reducing-balance method, however, results in very different profit figures for the four years, despite the fact that in this example the pre-depreciation profit is the same each year. In the first year a loss is reported and in the other years a rising profit.

Although the *pattern* of profit over the four-year period will be quite different depending on the depreciation method used, the *total* profit for the period (£83,876) will remain the same. This is because both methods of depreciating will allocate the same amount of total depreciation (£76,124) over the four-year period. It is only the amount allocated *between years* that will differ.

In practice, the use of different depreciation methods may not have such a dramatic effect on profits as suggested in Activity 3.9. This is because businesses typically have more than one depreciating non-current asset. Where a business replaces some of its assets each year, the total depreciation expense calculated under the reducing-balance method will reflect a range of expenses (from high through to low), as assets will be at different points in their economic lives. This could mean that each year's total depreciation expense may not be significantly different from that which would have been derived under the straight-line method.

Selecting a depreciation method

The appropriate depreciation method to choose is the one that reflects the consumption of economic benefits provided by an asset. Where the economic benefits are consumed evenly over time (for example, with buildings) the straight-line method is usually appropriate. Where the economic benefits consumed decline over time (for example, with certain types of machinery that lose their efficiency) the reducing-balance method may be more appropriate. Where the pattern of economic benefits consumed is uncertain, the straight-line method is normally chosen.

There is an international financial reporting standard (or international accounting standard) to deal with the depreciation of property, plant and equipment. (As we shall see in Chapter 5, the purpose of accounting standards is to narrow areas of accounting difference and to try to ensure that information provided to users is transparent and comparable.) The relevant standard endorses the view that the depreciation method chosen should reflect the pattern of consumption of economic benefits but does not specify particular methods to be used. It states that the useful life, depreciation method and residual values of non-current assets should be reviewed at least annually and adjustments made where appropriate.

Real World 3.4 sets out the depreciation policies of Carphone Warehouse Group plc, the mobile phone and PC retailer.

Real World 3.4

Communicating depreciation policies

Carphone Warehouse Group plc uses the straight-line method to depreciate all of its property, plant and equipment other than land and assets in the course of construction. The financial statements for the year ended 31 March 2011 show the annual rate at which different classes of assets are depreciated as follows:

Investment properties	2 per cent
Short leasehold costs	10 per cent or the lease term if less
Network equipment and computer hardware	12.5 to 50 per cent
Fixtures and fittings	20 to 25 per cent
Motor vehicles	25 per cent
Software and licences	At least 12.5 per cent

We can see that there are wide variations in the expected useful lives of the various assets held.

Source: Carphone Warehouse Group plc Annual Report 2011, p. 53.

Carphone Warehouse is typical of most UK businesses in that it uses the straight-line method. The reducing-balance method is much less popular.

The approach taken to calculating depreciation is summarised in Figure 3.7.

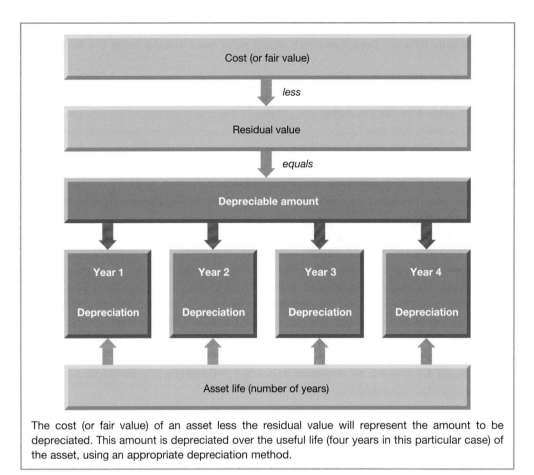

The cost (or fair value) of an asset less the residual value will represent the amount to be depreciated. This amount is depreciated over the useful life (four years in this particular case) of the asset, using an appropriate depreciation method.

Figure 3.7 Calculating the annual depreciation expense

Impairment and depreciation

We saw in Chapter 2 that all non-current assets could be subjected to an impairment test. Where a non-current asset with a finite life has its carrying amount reduced as a result of an impairment test, depreciation expenses for future reporting periods should be based on the impaired value of that asset.

Depreciation and asset replacement

Some people appear to believe that the purpose of depreciation is to provide the funds for the replacement of a non-current asset when it reaches the end of its useful life. However, this is not the case. It was mentioned earlier that depreciation represents an attempt to allocate the cost or fair value (less any residual value) of a non-current asset over its expected useful life. The depreciation expense for a particular reporting period is used in calculating profit for that period. If a depreciation charge is excluded from the income statement, we will not have a fair measure of financial performance. Whether or not the business intends to replace the asset in the future is irrelevant.

Where an asset is to be replaced, the depreciation expense in the income statement will not ensure that liquid funds are set aside specifically for this purpose. Although the depreciation expense will reduce profit, and therefore reduce the amount that the owners may decide to withdraw, the amounts retained within the business as a result may be invested in ways that are unrelated to the replacement of the asset.

Depreciation and judgement

From our discussions about depreciation, it is clear that accounting is not as precise and objective as it is sometimes portrayed as being. There are areas where subjective judgement is required.

Activity 3.10

What kinds of judgements must be made to calculate a depreciation expense for a period?

You may have thought of the following:

■ the expected residual or disposal value of the asset
■ the expected useful life of the asset
■ the choice of depreciation method.

Making different judgements on these matters would result in a different pattern of depreciation expenses over the life of the asset and, therefore, in a different pattern of reported profits. However, underestimations or overestimations that are made in relation to the above will be adjusted for in the final year of an asset's life. As a result, the total depreciation expense (and total profit) over the asset's life will not be affected by estimation errors.

Real World 3.5 describes the effect on annual performance of extending the useful life of a non-current asset held by a well-known business.

Real World 3.5

Engineering an improvement?

BA reported a loss of £358 million for the 2008/09 financial year. This loss, however, would have been significantly higher had the business not changed its depreciation policies. The 2008/09 annual report of the business states:

> During the prior year, the Group changed the depreciation period for the RB211 engine, used on Boeing 747 and 767 fleets, from 54 months to 78 months. The change resulted in a £33 million decrease in the annual depreciation charge for this engine type.

Source: British Airways Annual report and Accounts 2008/09, Note 15, www.britishairways.com.

Activity 3.11

Sally Dalton (Packaging) Ltd bought a machine for £40,000. At the end of its useful life of four years, the amount received on sale was £4,000. When the asset was bought the business received two estimates of the likely residual value of the asset, which were (a) £8,000 and (b) zero.

Show the pattern of annual depreciation expenses over the four years and the total depreciation expenses for the asset under each of the two estimates. The straight-line method should be used to calculate the annual depreciation expenses.

$\rightarrow$

The depreciation expense using estimate (a) will be £8,000 a year (that is, (£40,000 – £8,000)/4). The depreciation expense using estimate (b) will be £10,000 a year (that is, £40,000/4). As the actual residual value is £4,000, estimate (a) will lead to under-depreciation of £4,000 (that is, £8,000 – £4,000) over the life of the asset and estimate (b) will lead to over-depreciation of £4,000 (that is, £0 – £4,000). These under- and overestimations will be dealt with in year 4.

The pattern of depreciation and total depreciation expenses will therefore be:

| | | Estimate | |
| | | (a) | (b) |
Year		£	£
1	Annual depreciation	8,000	10,000
2	Annual depreciation	8,000	10,000
3	Annual depreciation	8,000	10,000
4	Annual depreciation	8,000	10,000
		32,000	40,000
4	Under/(over)depreciation	4,000	(4,000)
	Total depreciation	36,000	36,000

The final adjustment for under-depreciation of an asset is often referred to as 'loss (or deficit) on disposal of a non-current asset', as the amount actually received is less than the residual value. Similarly, the adjustment for over-depreciation is often referred to as 'profit (or surplus) on disposal of a non-current asset'. These final adjustments are normally made as an addition to the expense (or a reduction in the expense) for depreciation in the reporting period during which the asset is disposed of.

Activity 3.12

In practice, would you expect it to be more likely that the amount of depreciation would be overestimated or underestimated? Why?

We might expect there to be systematic overestimations of the annual depreciation expense. This is because the prudence convention tends to encourage a cautious approach to estimating the lives and residual values of assets.

COSTING INVENTORIES

The cost of inventories is important in determining financial performance and position. The cost of inventories sold during a reporting period will affect the calculation of profit, and the cost of inventories held at the end of the reporting period will affect the portrayal of assets held.

To calculate the cost of inventories, an assumption must be made about the physical flow of inventories through the business. This assumption need not have anything to do with how inventories *actually* flow through the business. It is concerned only with providing useful measures of performance and position.

Three common assumptions used are:

- **first in, first out (FIFO)**, in which it is assumed that the inventories acquired earliest are the first to be used;
- **last in, first out (LIFO)**, in which it is assumed that the inventories acquired latest are the first to be used; and
- **weighted average cost (AVCO)**, in which it is assumed that inventories acquired lose their separate identity and go into a 'pool'. Any issues of inventories from this pool will reflect the weighted average cost of inventories held.

During a period of changing prices, the choice of assumption used in costing inventories can be important. Example 3.8 provides an illustration of how each assumption is applied and the effect of each on financial performance and position.

Example 3.8

A business which supplies grass seed to farmers and horticulturalists has the following transactions during a period:

		Tonnes	Cost/tonne £
1 May	Opening inventories	100	100
2 May	Bought	500	110
3 May	Bought	800	120
		1,400	
6 May	Sold	(900)	
	Closing inventories	500	

First in, first out (FIFO)

Using the FIFO approach, the first 900 tonnes of seed bought are treated as if these are the ones that are sold. This will consist of the opening inventories (100 tonnes), the purchases made on 2 May (500 tonnes) and some of the purchases made on 3 May (300 tonnes). The remainder of the 3 May purchases (500 tonnes) will comprise the closing inventories. This means that we have:

	Cost of sales			Closing inventories		
	Tonnes	Cost/tonne £	Total £000	Tonnes	Cost/tonne £	Total £000
1 May	100	100	10.0			
2 May	500	110	55.0			
3 May	300	120	36.0	500	120	60.0
Cost of sales			101.0	Closing inventories		60.0

Last in, first out (LIFO)

Using the LIFO assumption, the later purchases will be treated as if these were the first to be sold. This is the 3 May purchases (800 tonnes) and some of the 2 May purchases (100 tonnes). The earlier purchases (the rest of the 2 May purchase and the opening inventories) will comprise the closing inventories. This can be set out as follows:

→

	Cost of sales			Closing inventories		
	Tonnes	*Cost/tonne* £	*Total* £000	*Tonnes*	*Cost/tonne* £	*Total* £000
3 May	800	120	96.0			
2 May	100	110	11.0	400	110	44.0
1 May				100	100	10.0
Cost of sales			107.0	Closing inventories		54.0

Figure 3.8 contrasts LIFO and FIFO.

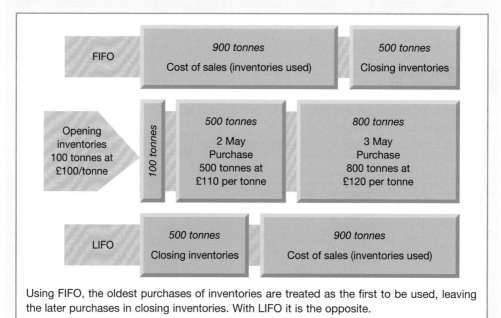

Using FIFO, the oldest purchases of inventories are treated as the first to be used, leaving the later purchases in closing inventories. With LIFO it is the opposite.

Figure 3.8 FIFO and LIFO treatment of the inventories in Example 3.8

Weighted average cost (AVCO)

Using the AVCO assumption, a weighted average cost will be determined that will be used to derive both the cost of goods sold and the cost of the remaining inventories held. This simply means that the total cost of the opening inventories, the 2 May and 3 May purchases, are added together and divided by the total number of tonnes to obtain the weighted average cost per tonne. Both the cost of sales and closing inventories values are based on that average cost per tonne. This means that we have:

	Purchases		
	Tonnes	*Cost/tonne* £	*Total* £000
1 May	100	100	10.0
2 May	500	110	55.0
3 May	800	120	96.0
	1,400		161.0

Average cost = £161,000/1,400 = £115 per tonne.

Cost of sales			Closing inventories		
Tonnes	Cost/tonne £	Total £000	Tonnes	Cost/tonne £	Total £000
900	115	103.5	500	115	57.5

Activity 3.13

Suppose the 900 tonnes of inventories in Example 3.8 were sold for £150 per tonne.

(a) Calculate the gross profit for this sale under each of the three methods.
(b) What observations concerning the portrayal of financial position and performance can you make about each method when prices are rising?

Your answer should be along the following lines:

(a) Gross profit calculation:

	FIFO £000	LIFO £000	AVCO £000
Sales revenue (900 @ £150)	135.0	135.0	135.0
Cost of sales	(101.0)	(107.0)	(103.5)
Gross profit	34.0	28.0	31.5
Closing inventories figure	60.0	54.0	57.5

(b) These figures reveal that FIFO will give the highest gross profit during a period of rising prices. This is because sales revenue is matched with the earlier (and cheaper) purchases. LIFO will give the lowest gross profit because sales revenue is matched against the more recent (and dearer) purchases. The AVCO method will normally give a figure that is between these two extremes.

  The closing inventories figure in the statement of financial position will be highest with the FIFO method. This is because the cost of goods still held will be based on the more recent (and dearer) purchases. LIFO will give the lowest closing inventories figure as the goods held will be based on the earlier (and cheaper) purchases. Once again, the AVCO method will normally give a figure that is between these two extremes.

Activity 3.14

Assume that prices in Activity 3.13 are falling rather than rising. How would your observations concerning the portrayal of financial performance and position be different for the various costing methods?

When prices are falling, the positions of FIFO and LIFO are reversed. FIFO will give the lowest gross profit as sales revenue is matched against the earlier (and dearer) goods bought. LIFO will give the highest gross profit as sales revenue is matched against the more recent (and cheaper) goods bought. AVCO will give a cost of sales figure between these two extremes. The closing inventories figure in the statement of financial position will be lowest under FIFO as the cost of inventories will be based on the more recent (and cheaper) purchases. LIFO will provide the highest closing inventories figure and AVCO will provide a figure between the two extremes.

RISEHOLME CAMPUS

The different costing assumptions only have an effect on reported profit from one reporting period to the next. The figure derived for closing inventories will be carried forward and matched with sales revenue in a later period. If the cheaper purchases of inventories are matched to sales revenue in the current period, it will mean that the dearer purchases will be matched to sales revenue in a later period. Over the life of the business, therefore, total profit will be the same either way.

Inventories – some further issues

We saw in Chapter 2 that the convention of prudence requires that inventories be valued at the lower of cost and net realisable value. (The net realisable value of inventories is the estimated selling price less any further costs necessary to complete the goods and any costs involved in selling and distributing them.) In theory, this means that the valuation method applied to inventories could switch each year, depending on which of cost and net realisable value is the lower. In practice, however, the cost of the inventories held is usually below the current net realisable value – particularly during a period of rising prices. It is, therefore, the cost figure that will normally appear in the statement of financial position.

Activity 3.15

Can you think of any circumstances where the net realisable value will be lower than the cost of inventories held, even during a period of generally rising prices?

The net realisable value may be lower where:

- goods have deteriorated or become obsolete;
- there has been a fall in the market price of the goods;
- the goods are being used as a 'loss leader';
- bad buying decisions have been made.

There is an International Financial Reporting Standard that deals with inventories. It states that, when preparing financial statements for external reporting, the cost of inventories should normally be determined using either FIFO or AVCO. The LIFO assumption is not acceptable for external reporting. The standard also requires the 'lower of cost and net realisable value' rule to be used and so endorses the application of the prudence convention.

Real World 3.6 sets out the inventories costing approach of one well-known high street retail business.

Real World 3.6

Costing inventories at leisure

Blacks Leisure Group plc, the leisure clothes and accessories business (Blacks, Millets, O'Neill and so on), uses the weighted average basis of inventories valuation. The business reports:

> Inventories are stated at the lower of cost and net realisable value. The cost includes all costs in bringing each product into the business. Inventories are valued on a weighted average basis and this is not deemed to be materially different to that which would be calculated on a 'first in, first out' basis. Net realisable value is defined as the estimated selling price less any direct costs of disposal.

Source: Blacks Leisure Group plc Annual Report 2011, p. 39.

Costing inventories and depreciation provide two examples where the **consistency convention** should be applied. This convention holds that once a particular method of accounting is selected, it should be applied consistently over time. It would not be acceptable to switch from, say, FIFO to AVCO between periods (unless exceptional circumstances make it appropriate). The purpose of this convention is to help users make valid comparisons of performance and position from one period to the next.

TRADE RECEIVABLES PROBLEMS

We have seen that, when businesses sell goods or services on credit, revenue will usually be recognised before the customer pays the amounts owing. Recording the dual aspect of a credit sale will involve increasing sales revenue and increasing trade receivables by the amount of the revenue from the credit sale.

With this type of sale there is always the risk that the customer will not pay the amount due. Where it becomes reasonably certain that the customer will not pay, the amount owed is considered to be a **bad debt**, which must be taken into account when preparing the financial statements.

To provide a more realistic picture of financial performance and position, the bad debt must be 'written off'. This will involve reducing the trade receivables and increasing expenses (by creating an expense known as 'bad debts written off') by the amount of the bad debt. The matching convention requires that the bad debt is written off in the same period as the sale that gave rise to the debt is recognised.

Note that, when a debt is bad, the accounting response is not simply to cancel the original sale. If this were done, the income statement would not be so informative. Reporting the bad debts as an expense can be extremely useful in assessing management performance.

Real World 3.7 describes the level of bad debts in different industry sectors.

Doubtful debts

At the end of a reporting period, it may not be possible to identify, with certainty, all bad debts incurred during the period. Doubts may surround certain trade receivables but it may only be at a later date that the true position will become clear. Nevertheless, the possibility that some trade receivables will not pay should not be ignored. It would not be prudent, nor would it comply with the need to match expenses to the period in which the associated sale is recognised.

The business must try to determine the amount of trade receivables that, at the end of the period, are doubtful (that is, there is a possibility that they may eventually prove to be bad). This amount may be derived by examining individual trade receivables' accounts or by taking a proportion of the total trade receivables outstanding based on past experience.

Once a figure has been derived, an expense known as an **allowance for trade receivables** should be recognised. This will be shown as an expense in the income statement and deducted from the total trade receivables figure in the statement of financial position. In this way, full account is taken, in the appropriate reporting period, of those trade receivables where there is a risk of non-payment. This accounting treatment of these 'doubtful' trade receivables will be in addition to the treatment of the 'more definite' bad debts described above.

Example 3.9 illustrates the reporting of bad debts and allowances for trade receivables.

Example 3.9

Desai Enterprises had trade receivables of £350,000 outstanding at the end of the reporting period to 30 June 2012. Investigation of these trade receivables revealed that £10,000 would probably be irrecoverable and that a further £30,000 were doubtful of being recoverable. Relevant extracts from the income statement and the statement of financial position would be as follows:

Income statement (extracts) for the year ended 30 June 2012

	£
Bad debts written off	10,000
Allowances for trade receivables	30,000

Statement of financial position (extracts) as at 30 June 2012

	£
Trade receivables	340,000*
Allowances for trade receivables	(30,000)
	310,000

* That is, £350,000 less £10,000 irrecoverable trade receivables.

The allowances for trade receivables figure is, of course, an estimate; it is quite likely that the actual amount of trade receivables that prove to be bad will be different from the estimate. Let us say that, during the next reporting period, it was discovered that, in fact, £26,000 of the trade receivables considered doubtful proved to be irrecoverable. These trade receivables must now be written off as follows:

- reduce trade receivables by £26,000; and
- reduce allowances for trade receivables by £26,000.

However, allowances for trade receivables of £4,000 will remain. This amount represents an overestimate made when creating the allowance as at 30 June 2012. As the allowance is no longer needed, it should be eliminated. Remember that the allowance was made by creating an expense in the income statement for the year to 30 June 2012. As the expense was too high, the amount of the overestimate should be 'written back' in the next reporting period. In other words, it will be treated as revenue for the year to 30 June 2013. This will mean:

- reducing the allowances for trade receivables by £4,000; and
- increasing revenue by £4,000.

Ideally, of course, the amount should be written back to the 2012 income statement; however, it is too late to do this. At the end of the year to 30 June 2013, not only will 2012's overestimate be written back but a new allowance should be created to take account of the trade receivables arising from 2013's credit sales that are considered doubtful.

Activity 3.18

Clayton Conglomerates had trade receivables of £870,000 outstanding at the end of the reporting period to 31 March 2011. The chief accountant believed that £40,000 of those trade receivables were irrecoverable and that a further £60,000 were doubtful of being recoverable. In the subsequent year, it was found that an over-pessimistic estimate of those trade receivables considered doubtful had been made and that only a further £45,000 of trade receivables had actually proved to be bad.

Show the relevant income statement extracts for both 2011 and 2012 to report the bad debts written off and the allowances for trade receivables. Also show the relevant statement of financial position extract as at 31 March 2011.

Your answer should be as follows:

Income statement (extract) for the year ended 31 March 2011

	£
Bad debts written off	40,000
Allowances for trade receivables	60,000

Income statement (extract) for the year ended 31 March 2012

	£
Allowances for trade receivables written back (revenue)	15,000

(*Note*: This figure will usually be netted off against any allowances for trade receivables created in respect of 2012.)

Statement of financial position (extract) as at 31 March 2011

	£
Trade receivables	830,000
Allowances for trade receivables	(60,000)
	770,000

Activity 3.19

The accounting treatment of bad debts and allowances for trade receivables are two further examples where judgement is needed to derive an appropriate expense figure.

What will be the effect of different judgements concerning the appropriate amount of bad debts expense and allowances for trade receivables expense on the profit for a particular period and on the total profit reported over the life of the business?

The judgement concerning whether to write off a debt as bad will affect the expenses for the period and, therefore, the reported profit. Over the life of the business, however, total reported profit would not be affected, as incorrect judgements made in one period will be adjusted for in a later period.

Suppose that a debt of £100 was written off in a period and that, in a later period, the amount owing was actually received. The increase in expenses of £100 in the period in which the bad debt was written off would be compensated for by an increase in revenue of £100 when the amount outstanding was finally received (bad debt recovered). If, on the other hand, the amount owing of £100 was never written off in the first place, the profit for the two periods would not be affected by the bad debt adjustment and would, therefore, be different – but the total profit for the two periods would be the same.

A similar situation would apply where there are differences in judgements concerning allowances for trade receivables.

USES AND USEFULNESS OF THE INCOME STATEMENT

The income statement may help in providing information on:

- *How effective the business has been in generating wealth.* Since wealth generation is the primary reason for most businesses to exist, assessing how much wealth has been created is an important issue. The income statement reveals the profit for the period, or bottom line as it is sometimes called. This provides a measure of the wealth created for the owners. Gross profit and operating profit are also useful measures of wealth creation.
- *How profit was derived.* In addition to providing various measures of profit, the income statement provides other information needed for a proper understanding of business performance. It reveals the level of sales revenue and the nature and amount of expenses incurred, which can help in understanding how profit was derived. (The analysis of financial performance will be considered in detail in Chapters 8 and 9.)

Self-assessment question 3.1

TT and Co. is a new business that started trading on 1 January 2011. The following is a summary of transactions that occurred during the first year of trading:

1 The owners introduced £50,000 of equity, which was paid into a bank account opened in the name of the business.
2 Premises were rented from 1 January 2011 at an annual rental of £20,000. During the year, rent of £25,000 was paid to the owner of the premises.
3 Rates (a tax on business premises) were paid during the year as follows:

For the period 1 January 2011 to 31 March 2011	£500
For the period 1 April 2011 to 31 March 2012	£1,200

4 A delivery van was bought on 1 January 2011 for £12,000. This is expected to be used in the business for four years and then to be sold for £2,000.
5 Wages totalling £33,500 were paid during the year. At the end of the year, the business owed £630 of wages for the last week of the year.
6 Electricity bills for the first three quarters of the year were paid totalling £1,650. After 31 December 2011, but before the financial statements had been finalised for the year, the bill for the last quarter arrived showing a charge of £620.
7 Inventories totalling £143,000 were bought on credit.
8 Inventories totalling £12,000 were bought for cash.
9 Sales revenue on credit totalled £152,000 (cost of sales £74,000).
10 Cash sales revenue totalled £35,000 (cost of sales £16,000).
11 Receipts from trade receivables totalled £132,000.
12 Payments to trade payables totalled £121,000.
13 Van running expenses paid totalled £9,400.

At the end of the year it was clear that a credit customer (trade receivable) who owed £400 would not be able to pay any part of the debt. All of the other trade receivables were expected to settle in full.

The business uses the straight-line method for depreciating non-current assets.

Required:
Prepare a statement of financial position as at 31 December 2011 and an income statement for the year to that date.

A solution to this question can be found in Appendix C.

SUMMARY

The main points of this chapter may be summarised as follows:

The income statement (profit and loss account)

- The income statement reveals how much profit (or loss) has been generated over a period and links the statements of financial position at the beginning and end of a reporting period.
- Profit (or loss) is the difference between total revenue and total expenses for a period.
- There are three main measures of profit:
  - gross profit – which is calculated by deducting the cost of sales from the sales revenue;
  - operating profit – which is calculated by deducting overheads from the gross profit;
  - profit for the period – which is calculated by adding non-operating income and deducting finance costs from the operating profit.

Expenses and revenue

- Cost of sales may be identified by matching the cost of each sale to the particular sale or by adjusting the goods bought during a period by the opening and closing inventories.
- Classifying expenses is often a matter of judgement, although there are rules for businesses that trade as limited companies.
- Revenue is recognised when the amount of revenue can be measured reliably and it is probable that the economic benefits will be received.
- Where there is a sale of goods, there is an additional criterion that ownership and control must pass to the buyer before revenue can be recognised.
- Revenue can be recognised after partial completion provided that a particular stage of completion can be measured reliably.
- The matching convention states that expenses should be matched to the revenue that they help generate.
- A particular expense reported in the income statement may not be the same as the cash paid. This will result in accruals or prepayments appearing in the statement of financial position.
- The materiality convention states that where the amounts are immaterial, we should consider only what is expedient.
- The accruals convention states that profit = revenue – expenses (not cash receipts – cash payments).

Depreciation of non-current assets

- Depreciation requires a consideration of the cost (or fair value), useful life and residual value of an asset. It also requires a consideration of the method of depreciation.
- The straight-line method of depreciation allocates the amount to be depreciated evenly over the useful life of the asset.
- The reducing-balance method applies a fixed percentage rate of depreciation to the carrying amount of an asset each year.
- The depreciation method chosen should reflect the pattern of consumption of economic benefits of an asset.
- Depreciation is an attempt to allocate the cost (or fair value), less the residual value, of an asset over its useful life. It does not provide funds for replacement of the asset.

Costing inventories

- The way in which we derive the cost of inventories is important in the calculation of profit and the presentation of financial position.
- The first in, first out (FIFO) assumption is that the earliest inventories held are the first to be used.
- The last in, first out (LIFO) assumption is that the latest inventories are the first to be used.
- The weighted average cost (AVCO) assumption applies an average cost to all inventories used.
- When prices are rising, FIFO gives the lowest cost of sales figure and highest closing inventories figure and for LIFO it is the other way around. AVCO gives figures for cost of sales and closing inventories that lie between FIFO and LIFO.
- When prices are falling, the positions of FIFO and LIFO are reversed.
- Inventories are shown at the lower of cost and net realisable value.
- When a particular method of accounting, such as a depreciation method, is selected, it should be applied consistently over time.

Bad debts

- Where it is reasonably certain that a credit customer will not pay, the debt is regarded as 'bad' and written off.
- Where it is doubtful that a credit customer will pay, an allowance for trade receivables expense should be created.

Uses of the income statement

- It provides measures of profit generated during a period.
- It provides information on how the profit was derived.

MyAccountingLab

Go to www.myaccountinglab.com to check your understanding of the chapter, create a personalised study plan, and maximise your revision time

KEY TERMS

profit p. 67	**depreciation** p. 81
revenue p. 67	**amortisation** p. 81
expense p. 68	**residual value** p. 83
reporting period p. 68	**straight-line method** p. 83
gross profit p. 70	**carrying amount** p. 84
operating profit p. 70	**written-down value** p. 84
profit for the period p. 70	**net book value** p. 84
cost of sales p. 70	**reducing-balance method** p. 84
matching convention p. 76	**first in, first out (FIFO)** p. 91
accrued expenses p. 77	**last in, first out (LIFO)** p. 91
prepaid expenses p. 79	**weighted average cost (AVCO)** p. 91
materiality convention p. 80	**consistency convention** p. 95
accruals convention p. 81	**bad debt** p. 95
accruals accounting p. 81	**allowance for trade receivables** p. 97

FURTHER READING

If you would like to explore the topics covered in this chapter in more depth, we recommend the following:

Alexander, D. and Nobes, C., *Financial Accounting: An International Introduction*, 4th edn, Financial Times Prentice Hall, 2010, Chapters 2, 16, 19 and 20

Elliott, B. and Elliott, J., *Financial Accounting and Reporting*, 15th edn, Financial Times Prentice Hall, 2011, Chapters 2, 20 and 21

International Accounting Standards Board, *2011 International Financial Reporting Standards IFRS* (two-volume set), IASB, 2011

KPMG, *Insights into IFRS*, 8th edn, Sweet and Maxwell, 2011, Sections 3.2, 3.3, 3.8, 3.10 and 4.2 (a summarised version of this is available free at www.kpmg.com)

REVIEW QUESTIONS

Solutions to these questions can be found in Appendix D.

3.1 'Although the income statement is a record of past achievement, the calculations required for certain expenses involve estimates of the future.' What does this statement mean? Can you think of examples where estimates of the future are used?

3.2 'Depreciation is a process of allocation and not valuation.' What do you think is meant by this statement?

3.3 What is the convention of consistency? Does this convention help users in making a more valid comparison between businesses?

3.4 'An asset is similar to an expense.' Do you agree?

EXERCISES

Exercises 3.1 and 3.2 are basic level, 3.4 and 3.5 are intermediate level and 3.6 to 3.8 are advanced level. Solutions to the exercises with coloured numbers are given in Appendix E.

If you wish to try more exercises, visit the students' side of the Companion Website and MyAccountingLab.

3.1 You have heard the following statements made. Comment critically on them.

    (a) 'Equity only increases or decreases as a result of the owners putting more cash into the business or taking some out.'

    (b) 'An accrued expense is one that relates to next year.'

    (c) 'Unless we depreciate this asset we shall be unable to provide for its replacement.'

    (d) 'There is no point in depreciating the factory building. It is appreciating in value each year.'

3.2 Singh Enterprises, which started business on 1 January 2009, has a reporting period to 31 December and uses the straight-line method of depreciation. On 1 January 2009 the business bought a machine for £10,000. The machine had an expected useful life of four years and an estimated residual value of £2,000. On 1 January 2010 the business bought another machine for £15,000. This machine had an expected useful life of five years and an estimated residual value of £2,500. On 31 December 2011 the business sold the first machine bought for £3,000.

Required:
Show the relevant income statement extracts and statement of financial position extracts for the years 2009, 2010 and 2011.

3.3 The owner of a business is confused and comes to you for help. The financial statements for the business, prepared by an accountant, for the last reporting period revealed a profit of £50,000. However, during the reporting period the bank balance declined by £30,000. What reasons might explain this apparent discrepancy?

3.4 Fill in the values (a) to (f) in the following table on the assumption that there were no opening balances involved.

	Relating to period		At end of period	
	Paid/Received	Expense/revenue for period	Prepaid	Accruals/deferred revenues
	£	£	£	£
Rent payable	10,000	**(a)**	1,000	
Rates and insurance	5,000	**(b)**		1,000
General expenses	**(c)**	6,000	1,000	
Interest payable on borrowings	3,000	2,500	**(d)**	
Salaries	**(e)**	9,000		3,000
Rent receivable	**(f)**	1,500		1,500

3.5 Spratley Ltd is a builders' merchant. On 1 September the business had, as part of its inventories, 20 tonnes of sand at a cost of £18 per tonne and, therefore, at a total cost of £360. During the first week in September, the business bought the following amounts of sand:

	Tonnes	Cost per tonne £
2 September	48	20
4 September	15	24
6 September	10	25

On 7 September the business sold 60 tonnes of sand to a local builder.

Required:
Calculate the cost of goods sold and of the remaining inventories using the following costing methods:

(a) first in, first out
(b) last in, first out
(c) weighted average cost.

3.6 The following is the statement of financial position of TT and Co. (see Self-assessment question 3.1) at the end of its first year of trading:

Statement of financial position as at 31 December 2011

	£
ASSETS	
Non-current assets	
Property, plant and equipment	
Delivery van at cost	12,000
Depreciation	(2,500)
	9,500
Current assets	
Inventories	65,000
Trade receivables	19,600
Prepaid expenses*	5,300
Cash	750
	90,650
Total assets	100,150
EQUITY AND LIABILITIES	
Equity	
Original	50,000
Retained earnings	26,900
	76,900
Current liabilities	
Trade payables	22,000
Accrued expenses†	1,250
	23,250
Total equity and liabilities	100,150

* The prepaid expenses consisted of rates (£300) and rent (£5,000).

† The accrued expenses consisted of wages (£630) and electricity (£620).

During 2012, the following transactions took place:

1 The owners withdrew £20,000 of equity in cash.
2 Premises continued to be rented at an annual rental of £20,000. During the year, rent of £15,000 was paid to the owner of the premises.
3 Rates on the premises were paid during the year as follows: for the period 1 April 2012 to 31 March 2013, £1,300.
4 A second delivery van was bought on 1 January 2012 for £13,000. This is expected to be used in the business for four years and then to be sold for £3,000.
5 Wages totalling £36,700 were paid during the year. At the end of the year, the business owed £860 of wages for the last week of the year.
6 Electricity bills for the first three quarters of the year and £620 for the last quarter of the previous year were paid totalling £1,820. After 31 December 2012, but before the financial statements had been finalised for the year, the bill for the last quarter arrived showing a charge of £690.
7 Inventories totalling £67,000 were bought on credit.
8 Inventories totalling £8,000 were bought for cash.
9 Sales revenue on credit totalled £179,000 (cost £89,000).
10 Cash sales revenue totalled £54,000 (cost £25,000).
11 Receipts from trade receivables totalled £178,000.
12 Payments to trade payables totalled £71,000.
13 Van running expenses paid totalled £16,200.

The business uses the straight-line method for depreciating non-current assets.

Required:

Prepare a statement of financial position as at 31 December 2012 and an income statement for the year to that date.

3.7 The following is the statement of financial position of WW Associates as at 31 December 2011:

Statement of financial position as at 31 December 2011

	£
ASSETS	
Non-current assets	
Machinery	25,300
Current assets	
Inventories	12,200
Trade receivables	21,300
Prepaid expenses (rates)	400
Cash	8,300
	42,200
Total assets	67,500
EQUITY AND LIABILITIES	
Equity	
Original	25,000
Retained earnings	23,900
	48,900
Current liabilities	
Trade payables	16,900
Accrued expenses (wages)	1,700
	18,600
Total equity and liabilities	67,500

During 2012, the following transactions took place:

1. The owners withdrew £23,000 of equity in cash.
2. Premises were rented at an annual rental of £20,000. During the year, rent of £25,000 was paid to the owner of the premises.
3. Rates on the premises were paid during the year for the period 1 April 2012 to 31 March 2013 and amounted to £2,000.
4. Some machinery (a non-current asset), which was bought on 1 January 2011 for £13,000, has proved to be unsatisfactory. It was part-exchanged for some new machinery on 1 January 2012 and WW Associates paid a cash amount of £6,000. The new machinery would have cost £15,000 had the business bought it without the trade-in.
5. Wages totalling £23,800 were paid during the year. At the end of the year, the business owed £860 of wages.
6. Electricity bills for the four quarters of the year were paid totalling £2,700.
7. Inventories totalling £143,000 were bought on credit.
8. Inventories totalling £12,000 were bought for cash.
9. Sales revenue on credit totalled £211,000 (cost £127,000).
10. Cash sales revenue totalled £42,000 (cost £25,000).
11. Receipts from trade receivables totalled £198,000.
12. Payments to trade payables totalled £156,000.
13. Van running expenses paid totalled £17,500.

The business uses the reducing-balance method of depreciation for non-current assets at the rate of 30 per cent each year.

Required:
Prepare an income statement for the year ended 31 December 2012 and a statement of financial position as at that date.

3.8 The following is the income statement for Nikov and Co. for the year ended 31 December 2012, along with information relating to the preceding year.

Income statement for the year ended 31 December

	2012	2011
	£000	£000
Sales revenue	420.2	382.5
Cost of sales	(126.1)	(114.8)
Gross profit	294.1	267.7
Salaries and wages	(92.6)	(86.4)
Selling and distribution costs	(98.9)	(75.4)
Rent and rates	(22.0)	(22.0)
Bad debts written off	(19.7)	(4.0)
Telephone and postage	(4.8)	(4.4)
Insurance	(2.9)	(2.8)
Motor vehicle expenses	(10.3)	(8.6)
Depreciation – Delivery van	(3.1)	(3.3)
– Fixtures and fittings	(4.3)	(4.5)
Operating profit	35.5	56.3
Loan interest	(4.6)	(5.4)
Profit for the year	30.9	50.9

Required:

Analyse the performance of the business for the year to 31 December 2012 in so far as the information allows.

Chapter 4

ACCOUNTING FOR LIMITED COMPANIES (1)

INTRODUCTION

Most businesses in the UK, including some of the very smallest, operate in the form of limited companies. About two and a half million limited companies now exist and they account for the majority of UK business activity and employment. The economic significance of this type of business is not confined to the UK; it can be seen in many of the world's developed countries.

In this chapter we shall consider the nature of limited companies and how they differ from sole proprietorship businesses and partnerships. This expands the brief discussion of various business forms in Chapter 1. We shall examine the ways in which the owners provide finance as well as the rules governing the way in which limited companies must account to their owners and to other interested parties. We shall also see how the financial statements, which were discussed in the previous two chapters, are prepared for this type of business.

Learning outcomes

When you have completed this chapter, you should be able to:

- discuss the nature and financing of the limited company;
- describe the main features of the equity (owners' claim) in a limited company;
- discuss the framework of rules designed to safeguard the interests of shareholders;
- explain how the income statement and statement of financial position of a limited company differ in detail from those of sole proprietorships and partnerships.

MyAccountingLab   Visit www.myaccountinglab.com
for practice and revision opportunities

THE MAIN FEATURES OF LIMITED COMPANIES

Legal nature

Let us begin our examination of limited companies by discussing their legal nature. A *limited company* has been described as an artificial person that has been created by law. This means that a company has many of the rights and obligations that 'real' people have. It can, for example, enter into contracts in its own name. It can also sue other people (real or corporate) and it can be sued by them. This contrasts sharply with other types of businesses, such as sole proprietorships and partnerships (that is, unincorporated businesses), where it is the owner(s) rather than the business that must enter into contracts, sue and so on, because those businesses have no separate legal identity.

With the rare exceptions of those that are created by Act of Parliament or by Royal Charter, all UK companies are created (or *incorporated*) by registration. To create a company the person or persons wishing to create it (usually known as *promoters*) fill in a few simple forms and pay a modest registration fee. After having ensured that the necessary formalities have been met, the Registrar of Companies, a UK government official, enters the name of the new company on the Registry of Companies. Thus, in the UK, companies can be formed very easily and cheaply (for about £100).

A limited company may be owned by just one person, but most have more than one owner and some have many owners. The owners are usually known as *members* or *shareholders*. The ownership of a company is normally divided into a number of shares, each of equal size. Each owner, or shareholder, owns one or more shares in the company. Large companies typically have a very large number of shareholders. For example, at 31 March 2011, BT Group plc, the telecommunications business, had about 1.1 million different shareholders. These shareholders owned 8,151 million shares between them.

Since a limited company has its own legal identity, it is regarded as being quite separate from those that own and manage it. It is worth emphasising that this legal separateness of owners and the company has no connection with the business entity convention of accounting, which we discussed in Chapter 2. This accounting convention applies equally well to all business types, including sole proprietorships and partnerships where there is certainly no legal distinction between the owner(s) and the business.

The legal separateness of the limited company and its shareholders leads to two important features of the limited company: perpetual life and limited liability. These are now explained.

Perpetual life

A company is normally granted a perpetual existence and so will continue even where an owner of some, or even all, of the shares in the company dies. The shares of the deceased person will simply pass to the beneficiary of his or her estate. The granting of perpetual existence means that the life of a company is quite separate from the lives of those individuals who own or manage it. It is not, therefore, affected by changes in ownership that arise when individuals buy and sell shares in the company.

Though a company may be granted a perpetual existence when it is first formed, it is possible for either the shareholders or the courts to bring this existence to an end. When this is done, the assets of the company are usually sold to generate cash to meet the outstanding liabilities. Any surplus arising after all liabilities have been met will then be used to pay the shareholders. Shareholders may agree to end the life of a company where it has achieved the purpose for which it was formed or where they feel that the company has no real future. The courts may bring the life of a company to an end where creditors (those owed money by the company) have applied to the courts for this to be done because they have not been paid.

Where shareholders agree to end the life of a company, it is referred to as a 'voluntary liquidation'. **Real World 4.1** describes the demise of one company by this method.

Limited liability

Since the company is a legal person in its own right, it must take responsibility for its own debts and losses. This means that, once the shareholders have paid what they have agreed to pay for the shares, their obligation to the company, and to the company's creditors, is satisfied. Thus shareholders can limit their losses to the amount that they have paid, or agreed to pay, for their shares. This is of great practical importance to potential shareholders since they know that what they can lose, as part owners of the business, is limited.

Contrast this with the position of sole proprietors or partners. They cannot 'ring-fence' assets that they do not want to put into the business. If a sole proprietorship or partnership business finds itself in a position where liabilities exceed the business assets, the law gives unsatisfied creditors the right to demand payment out of what the sole proprietor or partner may have regarded as 'non-business' assets. Thus the sole proprietor or partner could lose everything – house, car, the lot. This is because the law sees Jill, the sole proprietor, as being the same as Jill the private individual. The shareholder, by contrast, can lose only the amount committed to that company. Legally, the business operating as a limited company, in which Jack owns shares, is not the same as Jack himself. This is true even if Jack were to own all of the shares in the company.

Real World 4.2 gives an example of a well-known case where the shareholders of a particular company were able to avoid any liability to those that had lost money as a result of dealing with the company.

Real World 4.2

Carlton and Granada 1 – Nationwide Football League 0

Two television broadcasting companies, Carlton and Granada, each owned 50 per cent of a separate company, ITV Digital (formerly ON Digital). ITV Digital signed a contract to pay the Nationwide Football League (in effect the three divisions of English football below the Premiership) more than £89 million on both 1 August 2002 and 1 August 2003 for the rights to broadcast football matches over three seasons. ITV Digital was unable to sell enough subscriptions for the broadcasts and so collapsed because it was unable to meet its liabilities. The Nationwide Football League tried to force Carlton and Granada (ITV Digital's only two shareholders) to meet ITV Digital's contractual obligations. It was unable to do so because the shareholders could not be held legally liable for the amounts owing.

Carlton and Granada subsequently merged into one business, but at the time of ITV Digital were two independent companies.

Activity 4.1

The fact that shareholders can limit their losses to that which they have paid, or have agreed to pay, for their shares is of great practical importance to potential shareholders.

Can you think of any practical benefit to a private-sector economy, in general, of this ability of shareholders to limit losses?

Business is a risky venture – in some cases very risky. People will usually be happier to invest money when they know the limit of their liability. If investors are given limited liability, new businesses are more likely to be formed and existing ones are likely to find it easier to raise more finance. This is good for the private-sector economy and may ultimately lead to the generation of greater wealth for society as a whole.

Although **limited liability** has this advantage to the providers of equity finance (the shareholders), it is not necessarily to the advantage of all of the others who have a stake in the business, as we saw in the case of the Nationwide Football League clubs in Real World 4.2. Limited liability is attractive to shareholders because they can, in effect, walk away from the unpaid debts of the company if their contribution has not been sufficient to meet those debts. This is likely to make any individual, or another business, wary of entering into a contract with a limited company. This can be a real problem for smaller, less established companies. Suppliers may insist on cash payment before delivery of goods or the rendering of a service. Alternatively, they may require a personal guarantee from a major shareholder that the debt will be paid before allowing trade credit. In the latter case, the supplier circumvents the company's limited liability status by demanding the personal liability of an individual. Larger, more established companies, on the other hand, tend to have built up the confidence of suppliers.

LEGAL SAFEGUARDS

Various safeguards exist to protect individuals and businesses contemplating dealing with a limited company. These include the requirement to indicate limited liability status in the name of the company. When this is done, a warning is issued to prospective suppliers and lenders.

A further safeguard is the restrictions placed on the ability of shareholders to withdraw their equity from the company. These restrictions are designed to prevent shareholders from protecting their own investment and, as a result, leaving lenders and suppliers in an exposed position. We shall consider this point in more detail later.

Finally, limited companies are required to produce annual financial statements (income statements, statements of financial position and statements of cash flows) and make these publicly available. This means that anyone interested can gain an impression of the financial performance and position of the company. The form and content of the first two of these statements are considered in some detail later in the chapter. Chapter 6 is devoted to the statement of cash flows.

PUBLIC AND PRIVATE COMPANIES

When a company is registered with the Registrar of Companies, it must be registered either as a public or as a private company. The main practical difference between these is that a **public limited company** can offer its shares for sale to the general public, but a **private limited company** is restricted from doing so. A public limited company must signal its status to all interested parties by having the words 'public limited company', or its abbreviation 'plc', in its name. For a private limited company, the word 'limited' or 'Ltd' must appear as part of its name.

Private limited companies tend to be smaller businesses where the ownership is divided among relatively few shareholders who are usually fairly close to one another – for example, a family company. Numerically, there are vastly more private limited companies in the UK than there are public ones. Of the 2.49 million UK limited companies now in existence, only 7,812 (representing 0.3 per cent of the total) are public limited companies. Figure 4.1 shows the trend in the numbers of public and private limited companies in recent years.

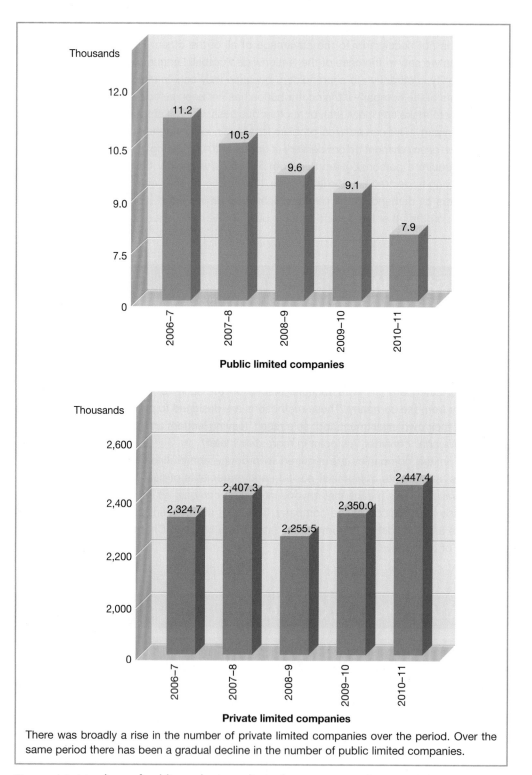

Thousands

12.0

11.2

10.5

10.5

9.6

9.1

9.0

7.9

7.5

0

2006–7   2007–8   2008–9   2009–10   2010–11

Public limited companies

Thousands

2,600

2,407.3

2,447.4

2,400

2,324.7

2,350.0

2,255.5

2,200

2,000

0

2006–7   2007–8   2008–9   2009–10   2010–11

Private limited companies

There was broadly a rise in the number of private limited companies over the period. Over the same period there has been a gradual decline in the number of public limited companies.

Figure 4.1 Numbers of public and private limited companies in the UK, 2006 to 2011

Source: After information in Companies Register Activities 2011, Statistical Tables on Companies Registration Activities 2010/11, www.companieshouse.gov.uk, contains public sector information licenced under the Open Government Licence v1.0.

Since individual public companies tend to be larger, they are often economically more important. In some industry sectors, such as banking, insurance, oil refining and grocery retailing, they are completely dominant. Although some large private limited companies exist, many private limited companies are little more than the vehicle through which one-person businesses operate.

Real World 4.3 shows the extent of the market dominance of public limited companies in one particular business sector.

A big slice of the market

The grocery sector is dominated by four large players: Tesco, Sainsbury, Morrison and Asda. The first three are public limited companies and the fourth, Asda, is owned by a large US public company, Wal-Mart Inc. Figure 4.2 shows the share of the grocery market enjoyed by each during the twelve-week period to 18 March 2012.

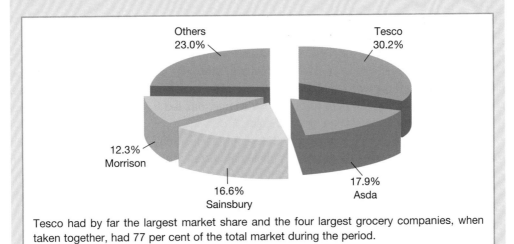

Tesco had by far the largest market share and the four largest grocery companies, when taken together, had 77 per cent of the total market during the period.

Figure 4.2 Market share of the four largest grocery companies: 12 weeks to 18 March 2012

Source: Compiled from information in 'Asda's UK grocery market share rises to 17.9%', *Dow Jones Newswires*, 2 April 2012.

TAXATION

Another consequence of the legal separation of the limited company from its owners is that companies must be accountable to the tax authorities for tax on their profits and gains. This leads to the reporting of tax in the financial statements of limited companies. The charge for tax is shown in the income statement. The tax charge for a particular year is based on that year's profit. Since only 50 per cent of a company's tax liability is due for payment during the year concerned, the other 50 per cent will appear on the end-of-year statement of financial position as a current liability. This will be illustrated a little later in the chapter. The tax position of companies contrasts with that of sole proprietorships and partnerships, where tax is levied not on the business but on the owner(s). Thus tax does not impact on the financial statements of unincorporated businesses, but is an individual matter between the owner(s) and the tax authorities.

Companies are charged **corporation tax** on their profits and gains and the percentage rate tends to vary over time. For 2013, the rates are 23 per cent for larger companies and 20 per cent for smaller ones. ('Larger' and 'smaller', in this context, relates to the size of the profit.) Corporation tax is levied on the company's taxable profit, which is not necessarily the same as the profit shown on the income statement. This is because tax law does not follow normal accounting rules in every respect. Generally, however, taxable profit and the company's accounting profit are pretty close to one another.

There can be tax advantages to trading as a limited company, rather than as a sole proprietor or partner. This may partly explain the rise in popularity of private limited companies over recent years.

THE ROLE OF THE STOCK EXCHANGE

The **London Stock Exchange** acts as both an important *primary* and *secondary* capital market for businesses. As a primary market, its function is to enable businesses to raise new finance. As a secondary market its function is to enable investors to sell their securities (including shares and loan notes) with ease. We have already seen that shares in a company may be transferred from one owner to another. The desire of some shareholders to sell their shares, coupled with the desire of others to buy those shares, has led to the existence of a formal market in which shares can be bought and sold.

Only the shares of certain companies (*listed* companies) may be traded on the London Stock Exchange. Just over 1,100 UK companies are listed. This represents only about 1 in 2,250 of all UK companies (public and private) and roughly one in seven public limited companies. However, many of these listed companies are massive. Nearly all of the UK businesses that are 'household names' (for example, Tesco, Next, BT, Vodafone, BP and so on) are listed companies.

Activity 4.2

If, as has been pointed out earlier, the change in ownership of shares does not directly affect the particular company, why do many public companies actively seek to have their shares traded in a recognised market?

The main reason is that investors are generally very reluctant to pledge their money unless they can see some way in which they can turn their investment back into cash. In theory, the shares of a particular company may be very valuable because the company has bright prospects. However, unless this value is capable of being turned into cash, the benefit to the shareholders is dubious. After all, we cannot spend shares; we normally need cash.

This means that potential shareholders are much more likely to be prepared to buy new shares from the company (thereby providing the company with new investment finance) where they can see a way of liquidating their investment (turning it into cash) as and when they wish. Stock Exchanges provide the means of liquidation.

Although the buying and selling of 'second-hand' shares does not provide the company with cash, the fact that the buying and selling facility exists will make it easier for the company to raise new share capital when it needs to do so.

Disadvantages of a listing

A Stock Exchange listing can have certain disadvantages for a business. These include the following:

■ Strict rules are imposed on listed businesses, including requirements for levels of financial disclosure additional to those already imposed by International Financial Reporting Standards (for example, the listing rules require that half-yearly financial reports are published).
■ Financial analysts, financial journalists and others tend to monitor closely the activities of listed businesses, particularly larger ones. Such scrutiny may not be welcome, particularly if the business is dealing with sensitive issues or is experiencing operational problems.
■ It is often suggested that listed businesses are under pressure to perform well over the short term. This pressure may detract from undertaking projects that will yield benefits only in the longer term. If the market becomes disenchanted with the business, and the price of its shares falls, this may make it vulnerable to a takeover bid from another business.
■ The costs of obtaining and retaining a listing are huge and this may be a real deterrent for some businesses.

Going private

Such are the disadvantages of a stock market listing that many businesses have 'delisted'. This has obviously denied them the advantages of a listing, but it has avoided the disadvantages.

CAPITAL MARKET EFFICIENCY

When share prices at all times rationally reflect all available, relevant information, the market in which they are traded is said to be an **efficient capital market**. This implies that any new information relating to a particular company and its share price will be taken into account quickly and rationally, in terms of size and direction of share price movement.

Activity 4.3

Can you suggest why a capital market like the Stock Exchange should be price efficient?

Many analysts study the performance of listed companies. Between them, they should make a valid assessment of the market value of those companies' shares.

Prices are set in capital markets by the forces of supply and demand. If the consensus view of those active in the market is that the shares of a particular business are underpriced, demand will force the price up.

In a secondary capital market such as the London Stock Exchange, share prices are observed by large numbers of people, many of them skilled and experienced. Nearly all of these people are moved to observe the market by that great motivator – financial gain. They glean information relating to the business from a variety of sources, including the business itself. This information may include published financial statements, press releases and company 'leaks' as well as industry and economy reports.

Where observers spot what they consider to be an irrational price, they try to take advantage of it, or advise others to do so. For example, an investment analyst employed by an insurance business might assess the worth of a share in Tesco plc at £5.00 while the current share price is only £4.00. The analyst may then contact the investment manager to recommend buying Tesco shares because they are underpriced and there are gains to be made. The increase in demand from large-scale buying tends to increase the share price.

Activity 4.4

If a capital market is price efficient, does this mean that the current market price of a share in a particular business is the correct price?

No. A share price is based on expectations concerning its future returns. No one can know for certain what those future returns will be.

Price efficiency does not imply perfect powers of prediction on the part of investors. All it means is that the current price of a share is the best estimate of its future returns on the basis of the available evidence.

The evidence on capital market efficiency

An enormous amount of research has been undertaken on the pricing efficiency of most of the world's capital markets. Although there are some relatively minor anomalies, the evidence on most capital markets (including the London Stock Exchange) is that

1 the price of a share in any particular business fully, rationally and very rapidly takes account of all relevant *publicly* available information that bears on that business and its shares; and
2 any information that is only *privately* available is not necessarily taken into account in the share price.

This means that it is not possible for investors to make systematic gains from trading on the basis of any information that is publicly available. On the other hand, relevant information that is known only, say, to a director of a particular business, but will become publicly known later, may enable that person to gain from trading in the shares.

Activity 4.5

If we look at a graph of the price of a share in a particular business plotted against time, we tend to find that it jumps up and down. This is similar to the effect that we get if we plot a graph of a series of random numbers.
 Does this mean that share prices are random and arbitrary?

No, it does not mean this. The share price movements mentioned above occur because new information does not arise in a gradual or systematic way but in a random, unexpected way. The share price movements will, however, be a rational and timely response to the new information coming to light.

MANAGING A COMPANY

A limited company may have legal personality, but it is not a human being capable of making decisions and plans about the business and exercising control over it. People must undertake these management tasks. The most senior level of management of a company is the board of directors.

The shareholders elect **directors** to manage the company on a day-to-day basis on behalf of those shareholders. By law there must be at least one director for a private limited company and two for a public limited company. In a small company, the board may be the only level of management and consist of all of the shareholders. In larger companies, the board may consist of ten or so directors out of many thousands of shareholders. Indeed, directors are not even required to be shareholders. Below the board of directors of the typical large company could be several layers of management comprising many thousands of people.

In recent years, the issue of **corporate governance** has generated much debate. The term is used to describe the ways in which companies are directed and controlled. The issue of corporate governance is important because, with larger companies, those who own the company (that is, the shareholders) are usually divorced from the day-to-day control of the business. The shareholders employ the directors to manage the company for them. Given this position, it may seem reasonable to assume that the best interests of shareholders will guide the directors' decisions. However, in practice this does not always seem to be the case. The directors may be more concerned with pursuing their own interests, such as increasing their pay and 'perks' (such as expensive motor cars, overseas visits and so on) and improving their job security and status. As a result, a conflict can occur between the interests of shareholders and the interests of directors.

(The problems and issues associated with corporate governance will be explored in detail in Chapter 12.)

FINANCING LIMITED COMPANIES

Equity (the owners' claim)

The equity of a sole proprietorship is normally encompassed in one figure on the statement of financial position. With companies, this is usually a little more complicated, although in essence the same broad principles apply. With a company, equity is divided between shares (for example, the original investment), on the one hand, and **reserves** (that is, profits and gains subsequently made), on the other. There is also the possibility that there will be more than one type of shares and of reserves. Thus, within the basic divisions of share capital and reserves, there might well be further subdivisions. This might seem quite complicated, but we shall shortly consider the reasons for these subdivisions and all should become clearer.

The basic division

When a company is first formed, those who take steps to form it (the promoters) will decide how much needs to be raised by the potential shareholders to set the company up with the necessary assets to operate. Example 4.1 illustrates this.

Example 4.1

Some friends decide to form a company to operate an office cleaning business. They estimate that the company will need £50,000 to obtain the necessary assets. Between them, they raise the cash, which they use to buy shares in the company, on 31 March 2011, with a **nominal value** (or **par value**) of £1 each.

At this point the statement of financial position of the company would be:

Statement of financial position as at 31 March 2011

	£
Net assets (all in cash)	50,000
Equity	
Share capital	
50,000 shares of £1 each	50,000

The company now buys the necessary non-current assets (vacuum cleaners and so on) and inventories (cleaning materials) and starts to trade. During the first year, the company makes a profit of £10,000. This, by definition, means that the equity expands by £10,000. During the year, the shareholders (owners) make no drawings of their equity, so at the end of the year the summarised statement of financial position looks like this:

Statement of financial position as at 31 March 2012

	£
Net assets (various assets less liabilities*)	60,000
Equity	
Share capital	
50,000 shares of £1 each	50,000
Reserves (revenue reserve)	10,000
Total equity	60,000

* We saw in Chapter 2 that Assets = Equity + Liabilities. We also saw that this can be rearranged so that Assets – Liabilities = Equity.

The profit is shown in a reserve, known as a **revenue reserve**, because it arises from generating revenue (making sales). Note that we do not simply merge the profit with the share capital: we must keep the two amounts separate (to satisfy company law). The reason for this is that there is a legal restriction on the maximum drawings of their equity (for example, as a **dividend**) that the shareholders can make. This is defined by the amount of revenue reserves and so it is helpful to show these separately. We shall look at why there is this restriction, and how it works, a little later in the chapter.

SHARE CAPITAL

Ordinary shares

Shares represent the basic units of ownership of a business. All companies issue **ordinary shares**. Ordinary shares are often known as *equities*. The nominal value of such shares is at the discretion of the people who start up the company. For example, if the initial share capital is to be £50,000, this could be two shares of £25,000 each, 5 million shares of one penny each or any other combination that gives a total of £50,000. All shares must have equal value.

In practice, £1 is the normal maximum nominal value for shares. Shares of 25 pence each and 50 pence each are probably the most common. BT's shares, which we mentioned earlier, have a nominal value of 5 pence each, though their market value is over £2 per share.

Altering the nominal value of shares

As we have already seen, the promoters of a new company may make their own choice of the nominal or par value of the shares. This value need not be permanent. At a later date the shareholders can decide to change it.

Suppose that a company has 1 million ordinary shares of £1 each and a decision is made to change the nominal value of the shares from £1 to £0.50, in other words to halve the value. This would lead the company to issue each shareholder exactly twice as many shares, each with half the nominal value. The result would be that each shareholder retains a holding of the same total nominal value. This process is known, not surprisingly, as **splitting** the shares. The opposite, reducing the number of shares and increasing their nominal value per share to compensate, is known as **consolidating**. Since each shareholder would be left, after a split or consolidation, with exactly the same proportion of ownership of the company's assets as before, the process should not increase the value of the total shares held.

Splitting is fairly common whereas consolidating is relatively rare. Both may be used to help make the shares more marketable. Splitting may help avoid share prices becoming too high and consolidating may help avoid share prices becoming too low. It seems that investors do not like either extreme. In addition, some Stock Exchanges do not allow shares to be traded at too low a price.

Real World 4.4 provides an example of a share split by one business.

Real World 4.4

Doing the splits

Premier Oil plc, the oil and gas exploration and production business, had a share split in May 2011, as announced by the business in a letter to its shareholders:

> The share split will result in shareholders holding four new ordinary shares of 12.5 pence each in the company for each existing ordinary share they held immediately prior to the share split. In recent months the price of the company's ordinary shares of 50 pence each has risen substantially to the point where the closing mid-market price on 1 April 2011 was £20.06. The board believes that the share split may improve the liquidity of the market in the company's shares and reduce the bid/offer spread of the company's shares.

Source: Premier Oil plc, Letter from the chairman, 15 April 2011, www.premier-oil.com.

Preference shares

Some companies issue other classes of shares in addition to ordinary shares, **preference shares** being the most common. Preference shares guarantee that *if a dividend is paid*, the preference shareholders will be entitled to the first part of it up to a maximum value. This maximum is normally defined as a fixed percentage of the nominal value of the preference shares. If, for example, a company issues one million preference shares of £1 each with a dividend rate of 6 per cent, this means that the preference shareholders are entitled to receive the first £60,000 (that is, 6 per cent of £1 million) of any dividend that is paid by the company for a particular year. The excess over £60,000 goes to the ordinary shareholders. Normally, any undistributed profits and gains also accrue to the ordinary shareholders.

The ordinary shareholders are the primary risk-takers as they are entitled to share in the profits of the company only after other claims have been satisfied. There are no upper limits, however, on the amount by which they may benefit. The potential rewards available to ordinary shareholders reflect the risks that they are prepared to take. Since ordinary shareholders take most of the risks, power normally rests in their hands. Usually, only the ordinary shareholders are able to vote on issues that affect the company, such as who the directors should be.

It is open to the company to issue shares of various classes – perhaps with some having unusual and exotic conditions – but in practice it is rare to find other than straightforward ordinary and preference shares. Even preference shares are not too common. Although a company may have different classes of shares whose holders have different rights, within each class all shares must be treated equally. The rights of the various classes of shareholders, as well as other matters relating to a particular company, are contained in that company's set of rules, known as the 'memorandum and articles of association'. A copy of these rules must be lodged with the Registrar of Companies, who makes it available for inspection by the general public.

RESERVES

As we have already seen, reserves are profits and gains that a company has made and which still form part of the shareholders' equity. One reason that past profits and gains may no longer continue to be part of equity is that they have been paid out to shareholders (as dividends and so on). Another reason is that reserves will be reduced by the amount of any losses that the company might suffer. In the same way that profits increase equity, losses reduce it. The shareholders' equity consists of share capital and reserves.

Activity 4.7

Are reserves amounts of cash? Can you think of a reason why this is an odd question?

To deal with the second point first, it is an odd question because reserves are a claim, or part of one, on the assets of the company, whereas cash is an asset. So reserves cannot be cash.

Reserves are classified as either revenue reserves or **capital reserves**. In Example 4.1 we came across a revenue reserve. We should recall that this reserve represents the company's retained trading profits and gains on the disposal of non-current assets. As we shall see later, retained earnings, as they are most often called, represent overwhelmingly the largest source of new finance for UK companies. For most companies they amount to more than share issues and borrowings combined.

Capital reserves arise for two main reasons:

- issuing shares at above their nominal value (for example, issuing £1 shares at £1.50);
- (upwards) revaluing of non-current assets.

Where a company issues shares at above their nominal value, UK law requires that the excess of the issue price over the nominal value be shown separately.

Activity 4.8

Can you think why shares might be issued at above their nominal value? (*Hint*: This would not usually happen when a company is first formed and the initial shares are being issued.)

Once a company has traded and has been successful, the shares would normally be worth more than the nominal value at which they were issued. If additional shares are to be issued to new shareholders to raise finance for further expansion, unless they are issued at a value higher than the nominal value, the new shareholders will be gaining at the expense of the original ones.

Example 4.2 shows how this works.

Example 4.2

Based on future prospects, the net assets of a company are worth £1.5 million. There are currently 1 million ordinary shares in the company, each with a nominal value of £1. The company wishes to raise an additional £0.6 million of cash for expansion and has decided to raise it by issuing new shares. If the shares are issued for £1 each (that is 600,000 shares), the total number of shares will be

$$1.0m + 0.6m = 1.6m$$

and their total value will be the value of the existing net assets plus the new injection of cash:

$$£1.5m + £0.6m = £2.1m.$$

This means that the value of each share after the new issue will be

$$£2.1m/1.6m = £1.3125.$$

The current value of each share is

$$£1.5m/1.0m = £1.50$$

so the original shareholders will lose

$$£1.50 - £1.3125 = £0.1875 \text{ a share}$$

and the new shareholders will gain

$$£1.3125 - £1.0 = £0.3125 \text{ a share.}$$

The new shareholders will, no doubt, be delighted with this outcome; the original ones will not.

Things could be made fair between the two sets of shareholders described in Example 4.2 by issuing the new shares at £1.50 each. In this case it would be necessary to issue 400,000 shares to raise the necessary £0.6 million. £1 a share of the £1.50 is the nominal value and will be included with share capital in the statement of financial position (£400,000 in total). The remaining £0.50 is a share premium, which will be shown as a capital reserve known as the **share premium account** (£200,000 in total).

It is not clear why UK company law insists on the distinction between nominal share values and the premium. In some other countries (for example, the United States) with similar laws governing the corporate sector, there is not this distinction. Instead, the total value at which shares are issued is shown as one comprehensive figure on the company's statement of financial position.

Real World 4.5 shows the equity of one very well-known business.

Real World 4.5

Flying funds

Ryanair Holdings plc, the no-frills airline, had the following share capital and reserves as at 31 March 2011:

	€ million
Share capital (10p ordinary shares)	9.5
Share premium	659.3
Retained earnings	1,967.6
Other reserves	317.5
Total equity	2,953.9

Note how the nominal share capital figure is only a small fraction of the share premium account figure. This implies that Ryanair has issued shares at much higher prices than the 10p a share nominal value. This reflects its trading success since the company was first formed. In 2011, retained earnings (profits) made up two-thirds of the total for share capital and reserves.

Source: Ryanair Holdings plc Annual Report 2011, p. 128.

BONUS SHARES

It is always open to a company to take reserves of any kind (irrespective of whether they are capital or revenue) and turn them into share capital. This will involve transferring the desired amount from the reserve concerned to share capital and then distributing the appropriate number of new shares to the existing shareholders. New shares arising from such a conversion are known as **bonus shares**. Issues of bonus shares used to be quite frequently encountered in practice, but more recently they are much less common. This may well be explained by the lack of business profitability during the current economic climate. Example 4.3 illustrates how bonus issues work.

Example 4.3

The summary statement of financial position of a company at a particular point in time is as follows:

Statement of financial position

	£
Net assets (various assets less liabilities)	128,000
Equity	
Share capital	
50,000 shares of £1 each	50,000
Reserves	78,000
Total equity	128,000

The directors decide that the company will issue existing shareholders with one new share for every share currently owned by each shareholder. The statement of financial position immediately following this will appear as follows:

Statement of financial position

	£
Net assets (various assets less liabilities)	128,000
Equity	
Share capital	
100,000 shares of £1 each (50,000 + 50,000)	100,000
Reserves (78,000 – 50,000)	28,000
Total equity	128,000

We can see that the reserves have decreased by £50,000 and share capital has increased by the same amount. Share certificates for the new 50,000 ordinary shares of £1 each, which have been created from reserves, will be issued to the existing shareholders to complete the transaction.

Activity 4.9

A shareholder of the company in Example 4.3 owned 100 shares before the bonus issue. How will things change for this shareholder as regards the number of shares owned and the value of the shareholding?

The answer should be that the number of shares would double, from 100 to 200. Now the shareholder owns one five-hundredth of the company (that is, 200/100,000). Before the bonus issue, the shareholder also owned one five-hundredth of the company (that is, 100/50,000). The company's assets and liabilities have not changed as a result of the bonus issue and so, logically, one five-hundredth of the value of the company should be identical to what it was before. Thus, each share is worth half as much as it used to be.

A bonus issue simply takes one part of the equity (a reserve) and puts it into another part (share capital). The transaction has no effect on the company's assets or liabilities, so there is no effect on shareholders' wealth.

Note that a bonus issue is not the same as a share split. A split does not affect the reserves.

Can you think of any reasons why a company might want to make a bonus issue if it has no economic consequence?

We think that there are three possible reasons:

- *Share price*. To lower the value of each share without reducing the shareholders' collective or individual wealth. This has a similar effect to share splitting.
- *Shareholder confidence*. To provide the shareholders with a 'feel-good factor'. It is believed that shareholders like bonus issues because they seem to make them better off, although in practice they should not affect their wealth.
- *Lender confidence*. Where reserves arising from operating profits and/or realised gains on the sale of non-current assets (revenue reserves) are used to make the bonus issue, it has the effect of taking part of that portion of the shareholders' equity that could be withdrawn by the shareholders, and locking it up. The amount transferred becomes part of the permanent equity base of the company. (We shall see a little later in this chapter that there are severe restrictions on the extent to which shareholders may make drawings from their equity.) An individual or business contemplating lending money to the company may insist that the extent to which shareholders can withdraw their funds is restricted as a condition of making the loan. This point will be explained shortly.

Real World 4.6 provides an example of a bonus share issue where it seemed that the main motive was to make the share price more manageable. The 'feel-good' factor also seems to be playing a part.

Real World 4.6

It's a bonus?

Medusa Mining is a gold producer that is listed on various international stock markets. In 2010, it announced a one-for-ten bonus issue of shares to all shareholders of the company.

In a statement, the company said it had achieved several significant milestones in the last calendar year and the bonus issue was in recognition of the invaluable support the company had received from its shareholders. The bonus issue was also designed to encourage greater liquidity in Medusa shares.

Geoff Davis, managing director of Medusa, said: 'The board is extremely pleased to be in a position to reward shareholders as a result of the company having rapidly expanded its production over the last 12 months and having met all targets on time.'

Source: Adapted from 'Medusa Mining', 8 March 2010, www.medusamining.com.au

SHARE CAPITAL JARGON

Before leaving our detailed discussion of share capital, it might be helpful to clarify some of the jargon relating to shares that is used in company financial statements.

Share capital that has been issued to shareholders is known as the **issued share capital** (or **allotted share capital**). Sometimes, but not very often, a company may not require shareholders to pay the whole amount that is due to be paid for the shares at the time of issue. This may happen where the company does not need the money all at once. Some money would normally be paid at the time of issue and the company would 'call' for further instalments until the shares were **fully paid shares**. That part of the total issue price that has been called is known as the **called-up share capital**. That part that has been called and paid is known as the **paid-up share capital**.

BORROWINGS

Most companies borrow money to supplement that raised from share issues and ploughed-back profits. Company borrowing is often on a long-term basis, perhaps on a ten-year contract. Lenders may be banks and other professional providers of loan finance. Many companies borrow in such a way that small investors, including private individuals, are able to lend small amounts. This is particularly the case with the larger Stock Exchange listed companies, and involves them making an issue of **loan notes**, which, though large in total, can be taken up in small slices by individual investors, both private individuals and investing institutions such as pension funds and insurance companies. In some cases, these slices of loans can be bought and sold through the Stock Exchange. This means that investors do not have to wait the full term of their loan to obtain repayment, but can sell their slice of it to another would-be lender at intermediate points in the term of the loan. Loan notes are often known as *loan stock* or *debentures*.

Some of the features of financing by loan notes, particularly the possibility that the loan notes may be traded on the Stock Exchange, can lead to confusing loan notes with shares. We should be clear that shares and loan notes are not the same thing. It is the shareholders who own the company and, therefore, who share in its losses and profits. Holders of loan notes lend money to the company under a legally binding contract that normally specifies the rate of interest, the interest payment dates and the date of repayment of the loan itself.

Usually, long-term loans are secured on assets of the company. This would give the lender the right to seize the assets concerned, sell them and satisfy the repayment obligation, should the company fail to settle either its interest payments or the repayment of the loan itself, on the dates specified in the contract between the company and the lender. A mortgage granted to a private individual buying a house or a flat is a very common example of a secured loan.

Long-term financing of companies can be depicted as in Figure 4.3.

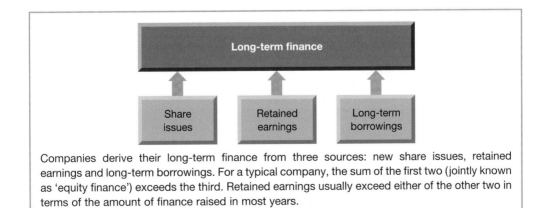

Companies derive their long-term finance from three sources: new share issues, retained earnings and long-term borrowings. For a typical company, the sum of the first two (jointly known as 'equity finance') exceeds the third. Retained earnings usually exceed either of the other two in terms of the amount of finance raised in most years.

Figure 4.3 Sources of long-term finance for a typical limited company

It is important to the prosperity and stability of a company that it strikes a suitable balance between finance provided by the shareholders (equity) and from borrowing. (This topic will be explored in Chapter 8.)

Real World 4.7 shows the long-term borrowings of Rolls-Royce plc, the engine-building business, at 31 December 2010.

Real World 4.7

Borrowing at Rolls-Royce

The following extract from the annual financial statements of Rolls-Royce plc sets out the sources of the company's long-term borrowings (non-current liabilities) as at 31 December 2010.

	£m
Unsecured	
Bank loans	206
7% notes 2016	200
6.38% notes 2013	162
6.55% notes 2015	60
6.75% notes 2019	506
Secured	
Obligations under finance leases payable after five years	1
	1,135

Source: Rolls-Royce plc Annual Report and Accounts 2010, Note 14.

Note the large number of sources of the company borrowings. This is typical of most large companies and probably reflects a desire to exploit all available means of raising finance, each of which may have some advantages and disadvantages. 'Secured' in this context means that the lender would have the right, should Rolls-Royce fail to meet its interest and/or capital repayment obligations, to seize a specified asset of the business (probably some land) and use it to raise the sums involved. Normally, a lender would accept a lower rate of interest where the loan is secured as there is less risk involved. It should be said that whether a loan to a company like Rolls-Royce is secured or unsecured is usually pretty academic. It is unlikely that such a large and profitable company would fail to meet its obligations.

RAISING SHARE CAPITAL

Once the company has made its initial share issue to start trading (usually soon after the company is first formed) it may decide to raise additional funds by making further issues of new shares. A business may issue shares in a number of ways. These may involve direct appeals to investors or the use of financial intermediaries. The most common methods of share issues are set out in Figure 4.4.

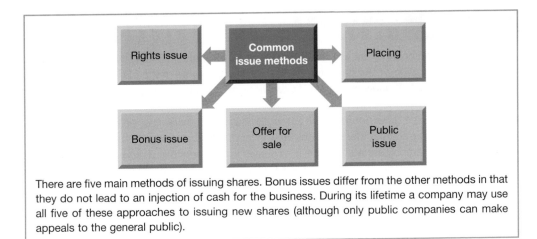

There are five main methods of issuing shares. Bonus issues differ from the other methods in that they do not lead to an injection of cash for the business. During its lifetime a company may use all five of these approaches to issuing new shares (although only public companies can make appeals to the general public).

Figure 4.4 Common methods of share issue

We shall now discuss each of the four methods of raising funds through a share issue, in turn.

Rights issues

Rights issues are made by established businesses that seek to raise additional funds by issuing new shares to their existing shareholders. Company law gives existing shareholders the first right of refusal to buy any new shares issued by a company, so the new shares would be offered to shareholders in proportion to their existing holding. Only where the existing shareholders agree to waive their right can the shares be offered to the investing public generally.

Rights issues have tended to be a popular form of share issue. During 2012, however, they accounted for only 17 per cent of all finance raised from share issues by UK businesses already listed on the London Stock Exchange (see reference 1 at the end of the chapter). This contrasts with 75 per cent in 2010 and an average of 55 per cent during the previous five years. The business (in effect, the existing shareholders) would typically prefer that existing shareholders buy the shares through a rights issue, irrespective of the legal position. This is for two reasons:

1 The ownership (and, therefore, control) of the business remains in the same hands; there is no 'dilution' of control.
2 The costs of making the issue (advertising, complying with various company law requirements) tend to be less if the shares are to be offered to existing shareholders. It is estimated that the average cost of making a rights issue is 5.8 per cent of the funds raised. Since a lot of the cost is fixed, this percentage will be greater or lesser for smaller and larger rights issues, respectively (see reference 2 at the end of the chapter). This compares with up to 11 per cent for an issue to the public (see reference 3 at the end of the chapter).

To encourage existing shareholders to take up their 'rights' to buy some new shares, those shares are always offered at a price below the current market price of the existing ones. The evidence shows that shares are typically offered at around 30 per cent below the current pre-rights price (see reference 2 at the end of the chapter).

Activity 4.11

Earlier in the chapter, the point was made that issuing new shares at below their current worth was to the advantage of the new shareholders at the expense of the old ones. In view of this, does it matter that rights issues are always made at below the current value of the shares?

The answer is that it does not matter *in these particular circumstances*, because, in a rights issue, the existing shareholders and the new shareholders are exactly the same people. Moreover, the shareholders will hold the new shares in the same proportion as they currently hold the existing shares. Thus, shareholders will gain on the new shares exactly as much as they lose on the existing ones. In the end, no one is better or worse off as a result of the rights issue being made at a discount.

Calculating the value of the rights offer received by shareholders is quite straightforward, as shown in Example 4.4.

Example 4.4

Shaw Holdings plc has 20 million ordinary shares of 50p in issue. These shares are currently valued on the Stock Exchange at £1.60 per share. The directors have decided to make a one-for-four issue (that is, one new share for every four shares held) at £1.30 per share.

The first step in the valuation process is to calculate the price of a share following the rights issue. This is known as the *ex-rights price* and is simply a weighted average of the price of shares before the issue of rights and the price of the rights shares. In this example, we have a one-for-four rights issue. The theoretical ex-rights price is therefore calculated as follows:

	£
Price of four shares before the rights issue (4 × £1.60)	6.40
Price of taking up one rights share	1.30
	7.70
Theoretical ex-rights price = £7.70/5	= £1.54

As the price of each share, in theory, should be £1.54 following the rights issue and the price of a rights share is £1.30, the value per share of the rights offer will be the difference between the two:

$$£1.54 - £1.30 = £0.24 \text{ per share}$$

Market forces will usually ensure that the actual and theoretical price of rights shares will be fairly close.

Activity 4.12

An investor with 2,000 shares in Shaw Holdings plc (see Example 4.4) has contacted you for investment advice. She is undecided whether to take up the rights issue, sell the rights or allow the rights offer to lapse.

Calculate the effect on the net wealth of the investor of each of the options being considered.

Before the rights issue the position of the investor was:

	£
Current value of shares (2,000 × £1.60)	3,200

If she takes up the rights issue, she will be in the following position:

	£
Value of holding after the rights issue ((2,000 + 500) × £1.54)	3,850
Cost of buying the rights shares (500 × £1.30)	(650)
	3,200

If the investor sells the rights, she will be in the following position:

	£
Value of holding after the rights issue (2,000 × £1.54)	3,080
Sale of the rights (500 × £0.24)	120
	3,200

If the investor lets the rights offer lapse, she will be in the following position:

	£
Value of holding after rights issue (2,000 × £1.54)	3,080

As we can see, the first two options should leave her in the same position concerning net wealth as before the rights issue. Before the rights issue she had 2,000 shares worth £1.60 each, or £3,200 in total. However, she will be worse off if she allows the rights offer to lapse than under the other two options.

In practice, businesses will typically sell the rights on behalf of those investors who seem to be allowing them to lapse. The businesses will then pass on the proceeds in order to ensure that they are not worse off as a result of the issue.

When considering a rights issue, the directors must first consider the amount of funds needing to be raised. This will depend on the future plans and needs of the business. The directors must then decide on the issue price of the rights shares. Normally, this decision is not critical. In Example 4.4, the business made a one-for-four issue with the price of the rights shares set at £1.30. However, it could have raised the same amount by making a one-for-two issue and setting the rights price at £0.65, a one-for-one issue and setting the price at £0.325, and so on. The issue price that is finally decided upon will not affect the value of the underlying assets of the business or the proportion of the underlying assets and earnings to which each shareholder is entitled. The directors must ensure that the issue price is not above the current market price of the shares, however, or the issue will be unsuccessful.

Real World 4.8 describes how a major car manufacturer has used a rights issue to help to fund the development of a new low-emissions car.

Real World 4.8

Driving through a rights issue

Peugeot Citroen, the France-based car maker, made a successful 16-for-31 rights issue in March 2012. It raised €1 billion. The offer price was €8.27 compared with a pre-rights share price of just over €14, a discount of about 41 per cent.

Source: Information taken from 'Peugeot launches €1bn rights issue' (Reed, J) FT.com, 6 March 2012.
© The Financial Times Limited 2012. All rights reserved.

Offers for sale and public issues

When a business wishes to sell new shares to the general investing public, it may make an **offer for sale** or a **public issue**. In the case of the former, the shares are sold to an *issuing house* (in effect, a wholesaler of new shares), which then sells them on to potential investors. With the latter, the shares are sold by the business making the share issue direct to potential investors. The advantage of an offer for sale, from the business's viewpoint, is that the sale proceeds of the shares are certain.

In practical terms, the net effect on the business is much the same whether there is an offer for sale or a public issue. As we have seen, the administrative costs of a public issue can be very large. Some share issues by Stock Exchange listed businesses arise from the initial listing of the business, often known as an *initial public offering (IPO)*. Other share issues are under-taken by businesses that are already listed and that are seeking additional finance from investors; usually such an issue is known as a *seasoned equity offering (SEO)*. IPOs are very popular, but SEOs are rather less so.

Private placings

A **private placing** does not involve an invitation to the public to subscribe for shares. Instead the shares are 'placed' with selected investors, such as large financial institutions. This can be a quick and relatively cheap form of raising funds, because savings can be made in advertising and legal costs. However, it can result in the ownership of the business being concentrated in a few hands. Sometimes, unlisted businesses seeking relatively small amounts of cash will make this form of issue.

Real World 4.9 describes how a placing was used by a high technology business to fund the acquisition of other businesses.

Real World 4.9

Well placed

Oxford Instruments, the provider of high technology tools and systems for industrial and academic research, has placed shares worth nearly £40 million ($65 million) to fund the acquisition of two businesses which extends its involvement in the nanotechnology market.

Jonathan Flint, chief executive, said the purchase of Frankfurt-based Omicron for €32 million ($46 million) in cash and Dallas-based Omniprobe for $19 million would strengthen Oxford Instruments' position as the leading supplier of capital equipment for those involved in nanotechnology research.

 Source: Extracts from: 'Oxford Instruments to acquire two groups' (Kavanagh, M) FT.com, 15 June 2011.

Placings are a popular way of issuing new shares for both newly listed and more seasoned listed businesses. During 2011, they accounted for more than 50 per cent of the total finance raised from shares issued by UK companies that were newly listed on the London Stock Exchange (see reference 1 at the end of the chapter). Placings also accounted for well over half of new finance raised by established listed UK companies. During 2011 they seemed to have taken over much of the territory previously occupied by rights issues.

WITHDRAWING EQUITY

Companies, as we have seen, are legally obliged to distinguish, on the statement of financial position, between that part of the shareholders' equity which may be withdrawn and that part which may not. The withdrawable part consists of profits arising from trading and from the disposal of non-current assets. It is represented in the statement of financial position by *revenue reserves*. The company paying dividends to all of its shareholders is the most usual way of enabling shareholders to withdraw part of their equity. An alternative is for the company to buy its own shares from those of its shareholders who may wish to sell them. This is usually known as a 'share repurchase'. The company would then usually cancel the shares concerned. Share repurchases usually involve only a small proportion of the shareholders, unlike a dividend which involves them all.

It is important to appreciate that the total of revenue reserves appearing in the statement of financial position is rarely the total of all trading profits and profits on disposals of non-current assets generated by the company. This total will normally have been reduced by at least one of the following three factors:

- corporation tax paid on those profits
- any dividends paid or amounts paid to purchase the company's own shares
- any losses from trading and from the disposal of non-current assets.

The non-withdrawable part consists of share capital plus profits arising from shareholders buying shares in the company and from upward revaluations of assets still held. It is represented in the statement of financial position by *share capital* and *capital reserves*.

Figure 4.5 shows the important division between the part of the shareholders' equity that can be withdrawn and the part that cannot.

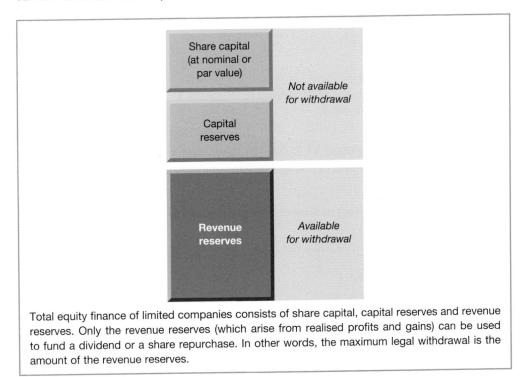

Total equity finance of limited companies consists of share capital, capital reserves and revenue reserves. Only the revenue reserves (which arise from realised profits and gains) can be used to fund a dividend or a share repurchase. In other words, the maximum legal withdrawal is the amount of the revenue reserves.

Figure 4.5 Availability for withdrawal of various parts of the shareholders' equity

The law does not specify how large the non-withdrawable part of a particular company's shareholders' equity should be. However, when seeking to impress prospective lenders and credit suppliers, the larger this part, the better. Those considering doing business with the company must be able to see from the company's statement of financial position how large it is.

Activity 4.13

Why are limited companies required to distinguish different parts of their shareholders' equity, whereas sole proprietorship and partnership businesses are not?

The reason stems from the limited liability that company shareholders enjoy but which owners of unincorporated businesses do not. If a sole proprietor or partner withdraws all of the equity, or even an amount in excess of this, the position of the lenders and credit suppliers of the business is not weakened since they can legally enforce their claims against the sole proprietor or partner as an individual. With a limited company, however, the business and the owners are legally separated and so such a right to enforce claims against individuals does not exist. To protect the company's lenders and credit suppliers, however, the law insists that the shareholders cannot normally withdraw a specific part of their equity.

Let us now look at an example that illustrates how this protection of creditors works.

Example 4.5

The summary statement of financial position of a company at a particular date is as follows:

Statement of financial position

	£
Total assets	43,000
Equity	
Share capital	
20,000 shares of £1 each	20,000
Reserves (revenue)	23,000
Total equity	43,000

A bank has been asked to make a £25,000 long-term loan to the company. If the loan were to be made, the statement of financial position immediately following would appear as follows:

Statement of financial position (after the loan)

	£
Total assets (£43,000 + £25,000)	68,000
Equity	
Share capital	
20,000 shares of £1 each	20,000
Reserves (revenue)	23,000
	43,000
Non-current liability	
Borrowings – loan	25,000
Total equity and liabilities	68,000

As things stand, there are assets with a total carrying amount of £68,000 to meet the bank's claim of £25,000. It would be possible and perfectly legal, however, for the company to withdraw part of the shareholders' equity (dividend or share repurchase) equal to the total revenue reserves (£23,000). The statement of financial position would then appear as follows:

Statement of financial position

	£
Total assets (£68,000 – £23,000)	45,000
Equity	
Share capital	
20,000 shares of £1 each	20,000
Reserves [revenue (£23,000 – £23,000)]	–
	20,000
Non-current liabilities	
Borrowings – bank loan	25,000
Total equity and liabilities	45,000

This leaves the bank in a very much weaker position, in that there are now total assets with a carrying amount of £45,000 to meet a claim of £25,000. Note that the difference between the amount of the borrowings (bank loan) and the total assets equals the equity (share capital and reserves) total. Thus, the equity represents a margin of safety for lenders and suppliers. The larger the amount of the equity withdrawable by the shareholders, the smaller is the potential margin of safety for lenders and suppliers.

Activity 4.14

Can you remember the circumstances in which the non-withdrawable part of a company's capital could be reduced, without contravening the law? (This was mentioned earlier in the chapter.)

It can be reduced as a result of the company sustaining trading losses, or losses on disposal of non-current assets, which exceed the withdrawable amount of shareholders' equity. It cannot legally be reduced by shareholders making withdrawals.

THE MAIN FINANCIAL STATEMENTS

As we might expect, the financial statements of a limited company are, in essence, the same as those of a sole proprietor or partnership. There are, however, some differences of detail. We shall now consider these. Example 4.6 sets out the income statement and statement of financial position of a limited company.

Example 4.6

Da Silva plc
Income statement for the year ended 31 December 2012

	£m
Revenue	840
Cost of sales	(520)
Gross profit	320
Wages and salaries	(98)
Heat and light	(18)
Rent and rates	(24)
Motor vehicle expenses	(20)
Insurance	(4)
Printing and stationery	(12)
Depreciation	(45)
Audit fee	(4)
Operating profit	95
Interest payable	(10)
Profit before taxation	85
Taxation	(24)
Profit for the year	61

Statement of financial position as at 31 December 2012

	£m
ASSETS	
Non-current assets	
Property, plant and equipment	203
Intangible assets	100
	303
Current assets	
Inventories	65
Trade receivables	112
Cash	36
	213
Total assets	516
EQUITY AND LIABILITIES	
Equity	
Ordinary shares of £0.50 each	200
Share premium account	30
Other reserves	50
Retained earnings	25
	305
Non-current liabilities	
Borrowings	100
Current liabilities	
Trade payables	99
Taxation	12
	111
Total equity and liabilities	516

Let us now go through these statements and pick up those aspects that are unique to limited companies.

The income statement

The main points for consideration in the income statement are as follows:

Profit

We can see that, following the calculation of operating profit, two further measures of profit are shown.

- The first of these is the **profit before taxation**. Interest charges are deducted from the operating profit to derive this figure. In the case of a sole proprietor or partnership business, the income statement would end here.
- The second measure of profit is the *profit for the period* (usually a year). As the company is a separate legal entity, it is liable to pay tax (known as corporation tax) on the profits generated. (This contrasts with the sole-proprietor business where it is the owner rather than the business that is liable for the tax on profits, as we saw earlier in the chapter.) This measure of profit represents the amount that is available for the shareholders.

Audit fee

Companies beyond a certain size are required to have their financial statements audited by an independent firm of accountants, for which a fee is charged. The purpose of the audit is to lend credibility to the financial statements (as we shall see in Chapter 5). Although it is also open to sole proprietorships and partnerships to have their financial statements audited, relatively few do so. Audit fee is, therefore, an expense that is most often seen in the income statement of a company.

The statement of financial position

The main points for consideration in the statement of financial position are as follows:

Taxation

The amount that appears as part of the current liabilities represents 50 per cent of the tax on the profit for the year 2012. It is, therefore, 50 per cent (£12 million) of the charge that appears in the income statement (£24 million); the other 50 per cent (£12 million) will already have been paid. The unpaid 50 per cent will be paid shortly after the statement of financial position date. These payment dates are set down by law.

Other reserves

This will include any reserves that are not separately identified on the face of the statement of financial position. It may include a *general reserve*, which normally consists of trading profits that have been transferred to this separate reserve for reinvestment ('ploughing back') into the operations of the company. It is not at all necessary to set up a separate reserve for this purpose. The trading profits could remain unallocated and still swell the retained earnings of the company. It is not entirely clear why directors decide to make transfers to general reserves, since the profits concerned remain part of the revenue reserves, and as such they still remain available for dividend. The most plausible explanation seems to be that directors feel that placing profits in a separate reserve indicates an intention to invest the funds, represented by the reserve, permanently in the company and, therefore, not to use them to pay a dividend or to fund a share repurchase. Of course, the retained earnings appearing on the statement of financial position are also a reserve, but that fact is not indicated in their title.

DIVIDENDS

We have already seen that dividends represent drawings by the shareholders of the company. Dividends are paid out of the revenue reserves and should be deducted from these reserves (usually retained earnings) when preparing the statement of financial position. Shareholders are often paid an annual dividend, which may be in two parts, with an 'interim' dividend being paid part way through the year and a 'final' dividend shortly after the year end.

Dividends declared by the directors during the year but still unpaid at the year end *may* appear as a liability in the statement of financial position. To be recognised as a liability, however, they must be properly authorised before the year-end date. This normally means that the shareholders must approve the dividend by that date.

Large companies tend to have a clear and consistent policy towards the payment of dividends. Any change in the policy provokes considerable interest and is usually interpreted by shareholders as a signal of the directors' views concerning the future. For example, an increase in dividends may be taken as a signal from the directors that future prospects are bright: a higher dividend is seen as tangible evidence of their confidence.

Real World 4.10 provides an example of one well-known business that paid a dividend after more than twenty years of trading.

Real World 4.10

At last!

Eurotunnel is to pay its first-ever dividend to its long-suffering shareholders, it revealed today. The Channel tunnel operator announced the €0.04-a-share payout (3.56p) as it reported net profits for the year of €40 million (£35.6 million), compared with a loss for 2007 of €12 million.

Eurotunnel floated on the London stock market in November 1987 when it raised £770 million from investors. This included some 574,000 small shareholders, who, if they invested more than £500 worth of shares at 350p each, were offered perks including free travel and discounts on hotels and car hire provided they held their shares beyond 1993, when the tunnel was expected to open.

However, as the project over-ran more cash was required on top of the company's credit facilities, leading to a £532 million rights issue in December 1990.

Commenting on today's results, Jacques Gounon, the chairman and chief executive of Eurotunnel, said:

Despite the incident in September [following a fire in one of the tunnels], the year 2008 clearly marks the end of financial uncertainty for Eurotunnel. Through its efficiency and the control of its costs, the group has recorded a solid profit which, for the first time in our history, allows us to pay a dividend to our loyal shareholders.

Source: 'Eurotunnel pays first dividend since 1987 float', Ian King, 4 March 2009, www.timesonline.co.uk, nisyndication.com.

Figure 4.6 shows an outline of the income statement for a limited company.

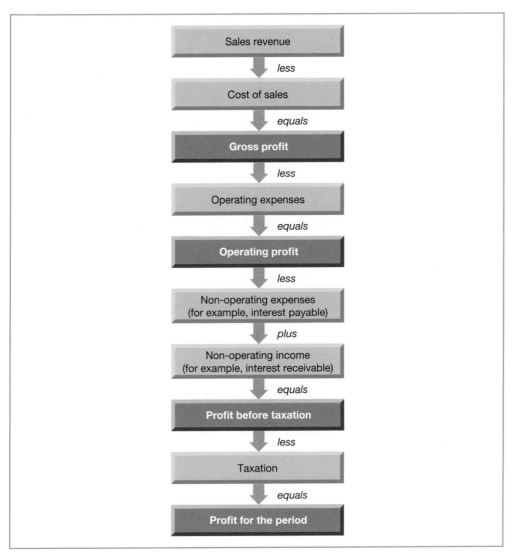

Figure 4.6 Outline of the income statement of a limited company

Dividend policy

The fact that directors of profitable businesses can decide the amount of dividends to be paid to shareholders raises the question of how large each year's dividend should be. The traditional view is that dividend payments should be maximised. The belief is that the higher the dividend payments, the more attractive the ordinary shares will become. This, in turn, will lead to higher share prices and more wealthy shareholders. Since the 1950s, however, this traditional view has been subject to increasing challenge.

The main thrust of the critics' argument is that, since the business is owned by the shareholders, why should transferring some of the business's assets to shareholders through a cash dividend make them better off? What shareholders are gaining, through the dividend, they are losing through their business being less well off. Funds handed to shareholders as dividends means less being retained within the business for investment in wealth-generating projects.

An alternative, more modern, view is that the interests of shareholders are best served by the directors retaining and investing such funds that would generate higher returns than the shareholders could earn from reinvesting dividends that they might otherwise receive. Where the directors cannot generate higher returns, however, the shareholders would be worse off. This means that the directors should only retain earnings where they can be invested at a rate at least as high as the shareholders' opportunity cost of funds. The residue should be paid as a dividend.

Not all businesses follow the modern view on dividend policy. One that does is Ryanair Holdings plc (the 'no-frills' airline). After never having paid a dividend, because it needed the funds to expand, the business eventually found itself with more funds than it could profitably invest. As a result it paid a dividend in 2010. The business made clear that further dividends should not necessarily be expected, as **Real World 4.11** shows.

Real World 4.11

No frills and probably no dividends

As a capital-intensive company, in a very cyclical industry, it would be wrong for shareholders to expect a continuous dividend stream. We intend to continue to build up cash, so that we can avail of opportunities including aircraft purchases, or acquisitions that will enhance Ryanair's profitability and our returns to shareholders.

Source: Ryanair Holdings plc Annual Report 2011, p. 7.

Self-assessment question 4.1

The summarised statement of financial position of Dev Ltd at a particular point in time is as follows:

Statement of financial position

	£
Net assets (various assets less liabilities)	235,000
Equity	
Share capital: 100,000 shares of £1 each	100,000
Share premium account	30,000
Revaluation reserve	37,000
Retained earnings	68,000
Total equity	235,000

Required:

(a) Without any other transactions occurring at the same time, the company made a one-for-five rights share issue at £2 per share payable in cash. This means that each shareholder was offered one share for every five already held. All shareholders took up their rights. Immediately afterwards, the company made a one-for-two bonus issue. Show the statement of financial position immediately following the bonus issue, assuming that the directors wanted to retain the maximum dividend payment potential for the future.

(b) Explain what external influence might cause the directors to choose not to retain the maximum dividend payment possibilities.

(c) Show the statement of financial position immediately following the bonus issue, assuming that the directors wanted to retain the *minimum* dividend payment potential for the future.

(d) What is the maximum dividend that could be paid before and after the events described in (a) if the minimum dividend payment potential is achieved?

(e) Lee owns 100 shares in Dev Ltd before the events described in (a). Assuming that the net assets of the company have a value equal to their carrying amount on the statement of financial position, show how these events will affect Lee's wealth.

(f) Looking at the original statement of financial position of Dev Ltd, shown above, what four things do we know about the company's status and history that are not specifically stated on the statement of financial position?

A solution to this question can be found in Appendix C.

SUMMARY

The main points of this chapter may be summarised as follows:

Main features of a limited company

- It is an artificial person that has been created by law.
- It has a life separate from its owners' and is granted a perpetual existence.
- It must take responsibility for its own debts and losses but its owners are granted limited liability.
- A public company can offer its shares for sale to the public; a private company cannot.
- It is governed by a board of directors, which is elected by the shareholders.
- Corporate governance is a major issue.

The Stock Exchange

- The Stock Exchange is an important primary and secondary market in capital for large businesses. However, obtaining a Stock Exchange listing can have certain drawbacks for a business.
- The Stock Exchange is broadly seen as an *efficient capital market*. This means that new information that becomes publicly available is quickly and rationally reflected in share prices. This leads to share prices always representing the best estimate of the 'true' value of shares, on the basis of publicly known information.

Reserves

- Reserves are of two types: revenue reserves and capital reserves.
- Revenue reserves arise from trading profits and from realised profits on the sale of non-current assets.
- Capital reserves arise from the issue of shares above their nominal value or from the upward revaluation of non-current assets.
- Revenue reserves can be withdrawn as dividends by the shareholders whereas capital reserves normally cannot.

Financing the limited company

- The share capital of a company can be of two main types: ordinary shares and preference shares.

→

- Holders of ordinary shares (equities) are the main risk-takers and are given voting rights; they form the backbone of the company.

- Holders of preference shares are given a right to a fixed dividend before ordinary shareholders receive a dividend.

- Reserves are profits and gains made by the company and form part of the ordinary shareholders' claim.

- Borrowings provide another major source of finance.

Share issues

- Share issues that involve the payment of cash by investors can take the form of a rights issue, public issue, offer for sale or a private placing.

- A rights issue is made to existing shareholders. Most share issues are of this type as the law requires that shares that are to be issued for cash must first be offered to existing shareholders. Rights issue costs are relatively low.

- A public issue involves a direct issue to the public and an offer for sale involves an indirect issue to the public.

- A private placing is an issue of shares to selected investors.

- A bonus issue of shares does not involve the receipt of cash in exchange for the shares issued.

Financial statements of limited companies

- The financial statements of limited companies are based on the same principles as those of sole-proprietorship and partnership businesses. However, there are some differences in detail.

- The income statement has three measures of profit displayed after the gross profit figure: operating profit, profit before taxation and profit for the year.

- The income statement also shows audit fees and tax on profits for the year.

- Any unpaid tax and unpaid, but authorised, dividends will appear in the statement of financial position as current liabilities.

- The share capital plus the reserves make up 'equity'.

MyAccountingLab

Go to www.myaccountinglab.com to check your understanding of the chapter, create a personalised study plan, and maximise your revision time

KEY TERMS

limited liability p. 111
public limited company p. 111
private limited company p. 111
corporation tax p. 114
Stock Exchange p. 114

London Stock Exchange p. 114
efficient capital market p. 115
directors p. 117
corporate governance p. 117
reserves p. 117

nominal value p. 118	**issued share capital** p. 124
par value p. 118	**allotted share capital** p. 124
revenue reserve p. 118	**fully paid shares** p. 125
dividend p. 118	**called-up share capital** p. 125
ordinary shares p. 118	**paid-up share capital** p. 125
splitting p. 119	**loan notes** p. 125
consolidating p. 119	**rights issues** p. 127
preference shares p. 120	**offer for sale** p. 130
capital reserves p. 120	**public issue** p. 130
share premium account p. 122	**private placing** p. 130
bonus shares p. 122	**profit before taxation** p. 135

REFERENCES

1 London Stock Exchange, *Market Statistics*, December 2011, Table 4.3

2 Armitage, S., 'The direct costs of UK rights issues and open offers', *European Financial Management*, March 2000

3 London Stock Exchange, *The Cost of Capital: An International Comparison*, 2006

FURTHER READING

If you would like to explore the topics covered in this chapter in more depth, we recommend the following:

Elliott, B. and Elliott, J., *Financial Accounting and Reporting*, 15th edn, Financial Times Prentice Hall, 2011, Chapter 10

Melville, A., *International Financial Reporting: A Practical Guide*, 3rd edn, Financial Times Prentice Hall, 2011, Chapters 1 and 18

Thomas, A. and Ward, A. M., *Introduction to Financial Accounting*, 6th edn, McGraw Hill, 2009, Chapter 29

REVIEW QUESTIONS

Solutions to these questions can be found in Appendix D.

4.1 How does the liability of a limited company differ from the liability of a real person, in respect of amounts owed to others?

4.2 Some people are about to form a company, as a vehicle through which to run a new business. What are the advantages to them of forming a private limited company rather than a public one?

4.3 What is a reserve? Distinguish between a revenue reserve and a capital reserve.

4.4 What is a preference share? Compare the main features of a preference share with those of

(a) an ordinary share; and
(b) loan notes.

Exercises 4.1 to 4.3 are basic level, 4.4 and 4.5 are intermediate level and 4.6 to 4.8 are advanced level. Solutions to the exercises with coloured numbers are given in Appendix E.

If you wish to try more exercises, visit the students' side of the Companion Website and MyAccountingLab.

4.1 Comment on the following quote:

'Limited companies can set a limit on the amount of debts that they will meet. They tend to have reserves of cash, as well as share capital and they can use these reserves to pay dividends to the share-holders. Many companies have preference as well as ordinary shares. The preference shares give a guaranteed dividend. The shares of many companies can be bought and sold on the Stock Exchange. Shareholders selling their shares can represent a useful source of new finance to the company.'

4.2 Comment on the following quotes:

(a) 'Bonus shares increase the shareholders' wealth because, after the issue, they have more shares, but each one of the same nominal value as they had before.'

(b) 'By law, once shares have been issued at a particular nominal value, they must always be issued at that value in any future share issues.'

(c) 'By law, companies can pay as much as they like by way of dividends on their shares, provided that they have sufficient cash to do so.'

(d) 'Companies do not have to pay tax on their profits because the shareholders have to pay tax on their dividends.'

4.3 Briefly explain each of the following expressions that you have seen in the financial statements of a limited company:

(a) dividend
(b) audit fee
(c) share premium account.

4.4 Iqbal Ltd started trading on 1 January 2008. During the first five years of trading, the following occurred:

Year ended 31 December	Trading profit/(loss) £	Profit/(loss) on sale of non-current assets £	Upward revaluation of non-current assets £
2008	(15,000)	–	–
2009	8,000	–	10,000
2010	15,000	5,000	–
2011	20,000	(6,000)	–
2012	22,000	–	–

Required:

Assume that the company paid the maximum legal dividend each year. Under normal circumstances, how much would each year's dividend be?

4.5 Hudson plc's outline statement of financial position as at a particular date was as follows:

	£m
Net assets (assets less liabilities)	72
Equity	
£1 ordinary shares	40
General reserve	32
Total equity	72

The directors made a one-for-four bonus issue, immediately followed by a one-for-four rights issue at a price of £1.80 per share.

Required:

Show the statement of financial position of Hudson plc immediately following the two share issues.

4.6 The following is a draft set of simplified financial statements for Pear Limited for the year ended 30 September 2012.

Income statement for the year ended 30 September 2012

	£000
Revenue	1,456
Cost of sales	(768)
Gross profit	688
Salaries	(220)
Depreciation	(249)
Other operating costs	(131)
Operating profit	88
Interest payable	(15)
Profit before taxation	73
Taxation at 30%	(22)
Profit for the year	51

Statement of financial position as at 30 September 2012

	£000
ASSETS	
Non-current assets	
Property, plant and equipment	
Cost	1,570
Depreciation	(690)
	880
Current assets	
Inventories	207
Trade receivables	182
Cash at bank	21
	410
Total assets	1,290
EQUITY AND LIABILITIES	
Equity	
Share capital	300
Share premium account	300
Retained earnings at beginning of year	104
Profit for year	51
	755
Non-current liabilities	
Borrowings (10% loan notes repayable 2015)	300
Current liabilities	
Trade payables	88
Other payables	20
Taxation	22
Borrowings (bank overdraft)	105
	235
Total equity and liabilities	1,290

The following information is available:

1 Depreciation has not been charged on office equipment with a carrying amount of £100,000. This class of assets is depreciated at 12 per cent a year using the reducing-balance method.

2 A new machine was purchased, on credit, for £30,000 and delivered on 29 September 2012 but has not been included in the financial statements. (Ignore depreciation.)

3 A sales invoice to the value of £18,000 for September 2012 has been omitted from the financial statements. (The cost of sales figure is stated correctly.)

4 A dividend of £25,000 had been approved by the shareholders before 30 September 2012, but was unpaid at that date. This is not reflected in the financial statements.

5 The interest payable on the loan notes for the second half-year was not paid until 1 October 2012 and has not been included in the financial statements.

6 An allowance for trade receivables is to be made at the level of 2 per cent of trade receivables.

7 An invoice for electricity to the value of £2,000 for the quarter ended 30 September 2012 arrived on 4 October and has not been included in the financial statements.

8 The charge for taxation will have to be amended to take account of the above information. Make the simplifying assumption that tax is payable shortly after the end of the year, at the rate of 30 per cent of the profit before tax.

Required:
Prepare a revised set of financial statements for the year ended 30 September 2012 incorporating the additional information in 1 to 8 above. (Work to the nearest £1,000.)

4.7 Presented below is a draft set of financial statements for Chips Limited.

Income statement for the year ended 30 June 2012

	£000
Revenue	1,850
Cost of sales	(1,040)
Gross profit	810
Depreciation	(220)
Other operating costs	(375)
Operating profit	215
Interest payable	(35)
Profit before taxation	180
Taxation	(60)
Profit for the year	120

Statement of financial position as at 30 June 2012

	Cost £000	Depreciation £000	£000
ASSETS			
Non-current assets			
Property, plant and equipment			
Buildings	800	(112)	688
Plant and equipment	650	(367)	283
Motor vehicles	102	(53)	49
	1,552	(532)	1,020
Current assets			
Inventories			950
Trade receivables			420
Cash at bank			16
			1,386
Total assets			2,406
EQUITY AND LIABILITIES			
Equity			
Ordinary shares of £1, fully paid			800
Reserves at beginning of the year			248
Profit for the year			120
			1,168
Non-current liabilities			
Borrowings (secured 10% loan notes)			700
Current liabilities			
Trade payables			361
Other payables			117
Taxation			60
			538
Total equity and liabilities			2,406

The following additional information is available:

1 Purchase invoices for goods received on 29 June 2012 amounting to £23,000 have not been included. This means that the cost of sales figure in the income statement has been understated.
2 A motor vehicle costing £8,000 with depreciation amounting to £5,000 was sold on 30 June 2012 for £2,000, paid by cheque. This transaction has not been included in the company's records.
3 No depreciation on motor vehicles has been charged. The annual rate is 20 per cent of cost at the year end.
4 A sale on credit for £16,000 made on 1 July 2012 has been included in the financial statements in error. The cost of sales figure is not affected.
5 A half-yearly payment of interest on the secured loan due on 30 June 2012 has not been paid.
6 The tax charge should be 30 per cent of the reported profit before taxation. Assume that it is payable, in full, shortly after the year end.

Required:
Prepare a revised set of financial statements incorporating the additional information in 1 to 6 above. (Work to the nearest £1,000.)

4.8 Rose Limited operates a small chain of retail shops that sell high-quality teas and coffees. Approximately half of sales are on credit. Abbreviated and unaudited financial statements are as follows:

Income statement for the year ended 31 March 2012

	£000
Revenue	12,080
Cost of sales	(6,282)
Gross profit	5,798
Labour costs	(2,658)
Depreciation	(625)
Other operating costs	(1,003)
Operating profit	1,512
Interest payable	(66)
Profit before taxation	1,446
Taxation	(434)
Profit for the year	1,012

Statement of financial position as at 31 March 2012

	£000
ASSETS	
Non-current assets	2,728
Current assets	
Inventories	1,583
Trade receivables	996
Cash	26
	2,605
Total assets	5,333
EQUITY AND LIABILITIES	
Equity	
Share capital (50p shares, fully paid)	750
Share premium	250
Retained earnings	1,468
	2,468
Non-current liabilities	
Borrowings – secured loan notes (2015)	300
Current liabilities	
Trade payables	1,118
Other payables	417
Tax	434
Borrowings – overdraft	596
	2,565
Total equity and liabilities	5,333

Since the unaudited financial statements for Rose Limited were prepared, the following information has become available:

1 An additional £74,000 of depreciation should have been charged on fixtures and fittings.

2 Invoices for credit sales on 31 March 2012 amounting to £34,000 have not been included; cost of sales is not affected.

3 Trade receivables totalling £21,000 are recognised as having gone bad, but they have not yet been written off.

4 Inventories which had been purchased for £2,000 have been damaged and are unsaleable. This is not reflected in the financial statements.

5 Fixtures and fittings to the value of £16,000 were delivered just before 31 March 2012, but these assets were not included in the financial statements and the purchase invoice had not been processed.

6 Wages for Saturday-only staff, amounting to £1,000, have not been paid for the final Saturday of the year. This is not reflected in the financial statements.

7 Tax is payable at 30 per cent of profit before taxation. Assume that it is payable shortly after the year end.

Required:

Prepare revised financial statements for Rose Limited for the year ended 31 March 2012, incorporating the information in 1 to 7 above. (Work to the nearest £1,000.)

Chapter 5

ACCOUNTING FOR LIMITED COMPANIES (2)

INTRODUCTION

This chapter continues our examination of the financial statements of limited companies. We begin by identifying the legal responsibilities of directors and then go on to discuss the main sources of accounting rules governing published financial statements. Although a detailed consideration of all of these accounting rules is beyond the scope of this book, the key rules that shape the form and content of the published financial statements are discussed. We also consider the efforts being made to ensure that these rules are underpinned by a coherent conceptual framework.

The established accounting rules enjoy widespread support and are generally considered to have had a beneficial effect on the quality of financial information provided to users. There are, however, potential problems with a rule-based approach. In this chapter, we shall consider these problems and their impact on the presentation of financial statements and on the future development of accounting.

Despite the proliferation of accounting rules and the increasing supply of financial information to users of financial reports, concerns have been expressed over the quality of some published reports. This chapter ends by considering some well-publicised accounting scandals and the problem of creative accounting.

Learning outcomes

When you have completed this chapter, you should be able to:

- describe the responsibilities of directors and auditors concerning the annual financial statements provided to shareholders and others;

- discuss both the framework of regulation and the conceptual framework that help to shape the form and content of annual financial statements;

- prepare a statement of financial position, statement of comprehensive income and statement of changes in equity in accordance with International Financial Reporting Standards;

- discuss the arguments for and against the use of accounting rules when preparing financial statements;

- discuss the threat posed by creative accounting and describe the main methods used to distort the fair presentation of position and performance.

MyAccountingLab   Visit www.myaccountinglab.com for practice and revision opportunities

THE DIRECTORS' DUTY TO ACCOUNT

For most large companies, it is not possible for all shareholders to be involved in the management of the company. Instead, they appoint directors to act on their behalf. This separation of ownership from day-to-day control creates a need for directors to be accountable for their stewardship (management) of the company's assets. To fulfil this need, the directors must prepare financial statements that provide a fair representation of the financial position and performance of the business. This means that they must select appropriate accounting policies, make reasonable accounting estimates and adhere to all relevant accounting rules when preparing the statements. To avoid misstatements on the financial statements, whether from fraud or error, the directors must also maintain appropriate internal control systems.

Each of the company's shareholders has the right to be sent a copy of the financial statements produced by the directors. These statements must also be made available to the general public. This is achieved by the company submitting a copy to the Registrar of Companies, which then allows anyone to inspect them. A London Stock Exchange listed company must also publish its financial statements on its website.

Activity 5.1

It can be argued that the publication of financial statements is vital to a well-functioning private sector. Why might this be the case?

There are at least two reasons:

- Unless shareholders receive regular information about the performance and position of a business they will have problems in appraising their investment. Under these circumstances, they would probably be reluctant to invest.
- Suppliers of labour, goods, services and finance, particularly those supplying credit (loans) or goods and services on credit, need information about the financial health of a business. They would be reluctant to engage in commercial relationships where a company does not provide information. The fact that a company has limited liability increases the risks involved in dealing with it.

In both cases, the functioning of the private sector of the economy would be adversely affected.

THE NEED FOR ACCOUNTING RULES

If we accept the need for directors to prepare and publish financial statements, we should also accept the need for a framework of rules concerning how these statements are prepared and presented. Without rules, there is a much greater risk that unscrupulous directors will adopt accounting policies and practices that portray an unrealistic view of financial health. There is also a much greater risk that the financial statements will not be comparable over time or with those of other businesses. Accounting rules can narrow areas of differences and reduce the variety of accounting methods. This should help ensure that businesses treat similar transactions in a similar way.

Example 5.1 illustrates the problems that may arise where businesses can exercise choice over the accounting policies used.

Example 5.1

Rila plc and Pirin plc are both wholesalers of electrical goods. Both commenced trading on 1 March 2012 with an identical share capital. Both acquired identical property, plant and equipment on 1 March and both achieved identical trading results during the first year of trading. The following financial information relating to both businesses is available:

	£m
Ordinary £1 shares fully paid on 1 March 2012	60
Non-current assets (at cost) acquired on 1 March 2012	40
Revenue for the year to 28 February 2013	100
Purchases of inventories during the year to 28 February 2013	70
Expenses for the year to 28 February 2013 (excluding depreciation)	20
Trade receivables as at 28 February 2013	37
Trade payables as at 28 February 2013	12
Cash as at 28 February 2013	5

The non-current assets held by both businesses are leasehold buildings that have five years left to run on the lease. Inventories for both businesses have been valued at the year end at £16 million on a FIFO basis and £12 million on a LIFO basis.

When preparing their financial statements for the first year of trading,

- Rila plc decided to write off the cost of the leasehold premises at the end of the lease period. Pirin plc adopted the straight-line basis of depreciation for the leasehold buildings.
- Rila plc adopted the FIFO method of inventories valuation and Pirin plc adopted the LIFO method.

The income statements and the statements of financial position for the two businesses, ignoring taxation, will be as follows:

Income statements for the year to 28 February 2013

	Rila plc £m	Pirin plc £m
Revenue	100	100
Cost of sales		
Rila plc (£70m – £16m)	(54)	
Pirin plc (£70m – £12m)		(58)
Gross profit	46	42
Expenses (excluding depreciation)	(20)	(20)
Depreciation		
Rila plc	(–)	
Pirin plc (£40m/5)		(8)
Profit for the year	26	14

Statements of financial position as at 28 February 2013

	Rila plc £m	Pirin plc £m
ASSETS		
Non-current assets		
Property, plant and equipment at cost	40	40
Accumulated depreciation	(–)	(8)
	40	32
Current assets		
Inventories	16	12
Trade receivables	37	37
Cash	5	5
	58	54
Total assets	98	86
EQUITY AND LIABILITIES		
Equity		
Share capital	60	60
Retained earnings	26	14
	86	74
Current liabilities		
Trade payables	12	12
Total equity and liabilities	98	86

Although the two businesses are identical in terms of funding and underlying trading performance, the financial statements create an impression that the financial health of each business is quite different. The accounting policies selected by Rila plc help to portray a much rosier picture. We can see that Rila plc reports a significantly higher profit for the year and higher assets at the year end.

Depreciation and inventories valuation are not the only areas where choices might be exercised. They nevertheless illustrate the potential impact of different accounting choices over the short term.

Accounting rules should help to provide greater confidence in the integrity of financial statements. This, in turn, may help a business to raise funds and to build stronger relationships with customers and suppliers. Users must be realistic, however, about what can be achieved through regulation. Problems of manipulation and of concealment can still occur even within a highly regulated environment and examples of both will be considered later in the chapter. The scale of these problems, however, should be reduced where there is a practical set of rules.

Even with a set of rules, problems of comparability can also still occur as accounting is not a precise science. Judgements and estimates must be made when preparing financial statements and these may hinder comparisons. Furthermore, no two businesses are identical (unlike the companies in Example 5.1) and accounting policies may vary between businesses for valid reasons.

SOURCES OF ACCOUNTING RULES

In recent years, there have been increasing trends towards the internationalisation of business and the integration of financial markets. These trends have helped to strengthen the case for the international harmonisation of accounting rules. When a common set of rules is followed, users of financial statements should be better placed to compare the financial health of companies based in different countries. The existence of such rules should also relieve international companies of some of the burden of preparing financial statements. Different financial statements will no longer have to be prepared to comply with the rules of the various countries in which a particular company operates.

The International Accounting Standards Board (IASB) is an independent body that is at the forefront of the move towards harmonisation. The Board, which is based in the UK, is dedicated to developing a single set of high-quality global accounting rules. These are designed to provide transparent and comparable information in financial statements. The rules, which are known as **International Accounting Standards** (IASs) or **International Financial Reporting Standards** (IFRSs), deal with key issues such as:

■ what information should be disclosed;
■ how information should be presented;
■ how assets should be valued; and
■ how profit should be measured.

Activity 5.2

We have already come across some IASs and IFRSs in earlier chapters. Try to recall at least two topics where financial reporting standards were mentioned.

We came across financial reporting standards when considering:

■ the valuation and impairment of assets (Chapter 2);
■ depreciation and impairment of non-current assets (Chapter 3); and
■ the valuation of inventories (Chapter 3).

The growing authority of the IASB

Several important developments have greatly increased the authority of the IASB in recent years. The first major boost came when the European Commission required nearly all companies listed on the stock exchanges of EU member states to adopt IFRSs for reporting periods commencing on or after 1 January 2005. As a result, nearly 7,000 companies in 25 different countries switched to IFRSs. This was followed in 2006 by the IASB and the US Financial Accounting Standards Board agreeing a roadmap for convergence between IFRSs and US accounting rules. In that same year, China closely aligned its financial reporting standards with IFRSs. In 2007, Brazil, Canada, Chile, India, Japan and Korea all announced their intention to adopt, or converge with, IFRSs. By 2010, the point was reached where all major economies either had adopted IFRSs or had set a timetable to adopt, or to converge with, IFRSs. This move towards international convergence is now supported by the Group of 20 Major Economies (G20).

Non-listed UK companies are not required to adopt IFRSs but have the option to do so. Some informed observers believe, however, that IFRSs may eventually become a requirement for all UK companies.

Adopting IFRSs

The EU requirement to adopt IFRSs, mentioned earlier, overrides any laws in force in member states that could either hinder or restrict compliance with them. The ultimate aim is to achieve a single framework of accounting rules for companies from all member states. The EU recognises that this will be achieved only if individual governments do not add to the requirements imposed by the various IFRSs. Thus, it seems that accounting rules developed within individual EU member countries will eventually disappear. For the time being, however, the EU accepts that the governments of member states may need to impose additional disclosures for some corporate governance matters and regulatory requirements.

In the UK, company law requires disclosure relating to various corporate governance issues. There is, for example, a requirement to disclose details of directors' remuneration in the published financial statements, which goes beyond anything required by IFRSs. Furthermore, the Financial Services Authority (FSA), in its role as the UK (Stock Exchange) listing authority, imposes rules on Stock Exchange listed companies. These include the requirement to publish a condensed set of interim (half-yearly) financial statements in addition to the annual financial statements. (These interim statements are not required by the IASB, although there is a standard providing guidance on their form and content. The statements and the standard will be considered in Chapter 11.)

Figure 5.1 sets out the main sources of accounting rules for Stock Exchange listed companies. While company law and the FSA still play an important role, in the longer term IFRSs seem set to become the sole source of company accounting rules.

International Financial Reporting Standards provide the basic framework of accounting rules for nearly all Stock Exchange listed companies. These rules are augmented by company law and by the Financial Services Authority (FSA) in its role as the UK listing authority.

Figure 5.1 Sources of external accounting rules for a UK public limited company listed on the London Stock Exchange

Real World 5.1 provides a list of IASB standards that were in force as at 1 April 2012. It gives some idea of the range of topics that are covered.

Real World 5.1

International standards

The following is a list of the International Accounting Standards (IASs) and International Financial Reporting Standards (IFRSs) in issue as at 1 April 2012. (The latter term is used for standards issued from 2003 onwards.) Several standards have been issued and subsequently withdrawn, which explains the gaps in the numerical sequence. In addition, several have been revised and reissued.

IAS 1	*Presentation of Financial Statements*
IAS 2	*Inventories*
IAS 7	*Statement of Cash Flows*
IAS 8	*Accounting Policies, Changes in Accounting Estimates and Errors*
IAS 10	*Events After the Reporting Period*
IAS 11	*Construction Contracts*
IAS 12	*Income Taxes*
IAS 16	*Property, Plant and Equipment*
IAS 17	*Leases*
IAS 18	*Revenue*
IAS 19	*Employee Benefits*
IAS 20	*Accounting for Government Grants and Disclosure of Government Assistance*
IAS 21	*The Effects of Changes in Foreign Exchange Rates*
IAS 23	*Borrowing Costs*
IAS 24	*Related Party Disclosures*
IAS 26	*Accounting and Reporting by Retirement Benefit Plans*
IAS 27	*Consolidated and Separate Financial Statements*
IAS 28	*Investments in Associates*
IAS 29	*Financial Reporting in Hyperinflationary Economies*
IAS 31	*Interests in Joint Ventures*
IAS 32	*Financial Instruments: Presentation*
IAS 33	*Earnings per Share*
IAS 34	*Interim Financial Reporting*
IAS 36	*Impairment of Assets*
IAS 37	*Provisions, Contingent Liabilities and Contingent Assets*
IAS 38	*Intangible Assets*
IAS 39	*Financial Instruments: Recognition and Measurement*
IAS 40	*Investment Property*
IAS 41	*Agriculture*
IFRS 1	*First-time Adoption of International Financial Reporting Standards*
IFRS 2	*Share-based Payment*
IFRS 3	*Business Combinations*
IFRS 4	*Insurance Contracts*
IFRS 5	*Non-current Assets Held for Sale and Discontinued Operations*
IFRS 6	*Exploration for and Evaluation of Mineral Resources*
IFRS 7	*Financial Instruments: Disclosures*
IFRS 8	*Operating Segments*
IFRS 9	*Financial Instruments*
IFRS 10	*Consolidated Financial Statements*
IFRS 11	*Joint Arrangements*
IFRs 12	*Disclosure of Interests in Other Entities*
IFRS 13	*Fair Value Measurement*

Source: International Accounting Standards Board, www.iasb.org.uk, IFRSs as issued at 1 April 2012.

The IASB has an ambitious agenda and so significant changes to this list are likely to occur in the future.

PRESENTING THE FINANCIAL STATEMENTS

Now that we have gained an impression of the sources of rules affecting limited companies, let us turn our attention to the main rules to be followed in the presentation of financial statements. We shall focus on the IASB rules and, in particular, those contained in IAS 1 *Presentation of Financial Statements*. This standard is very important as it sets out the structure and content of financial statements and the principles to be followed in preparing these statements.

It might be helpful to have a set of the most recent financial statements of a Stock Exchange listed company available as you work through this section. They should all be available on the internet. Select a listed company that interests you and go to its website.

The financial statements identified in IAS 1 are as set out in Figure 5.2.

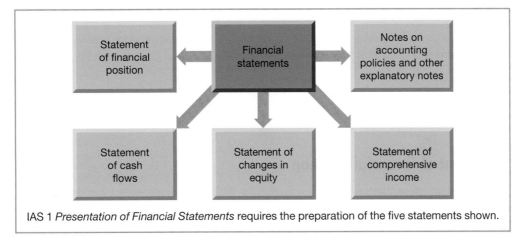

IAS 1 *Presentation of Financial Statements* requires the preparation of the five statements shown.

Figure 5.2 Financial statements required under IAS 1

The standard states that these financial statements should normally cover a one-year period and should be accompanied by comparative information for the previous year. Thus, at the end of each reporting period companies should normally produce two of each of the statements, plus the related notes. In practice, virtually all companies satisfy this requirement by showing the equivalent figures for the previous year in a separate column in the current year's statements.

Comparative narrative information should also be provided if needed for a better grasp of current period results – for example, as background to an ongoing legal dispute.

Fair representation

Before we consider the financial statements in detail, it is important to emphasise that the standard requires that they provide a fair representation of a company's financial position, financial performance and cash flows. There is a presumption that this will be achieved where they are drawn up in accordance with the various IASB standards that are currently in force. It is only in very rare circumstances that compliance with a standard would not result in a fair representation of the financial health of a company. Where the financial statements have been prepared in accordance with IASB standards, it should be clearly stated in the notes.

Activity 5.3

IAS 1 does not say that the requirement is for the financial statements to show a 'correct' or an 'accurate' representation of financial health. Why, in your opinion, does it not use those words? (*Hint*: Think of depreciation of non-current assets.)

Accounting can never really be said to be 'correct' or 'accurate' as these words imply that there is a precise value that an asset, claim, revenue or expense could have. This is simply not true in many, if not most, cases.

Depreciation provides a good example of where 'correct' or 'accurate' would not be appropriate. The annual depreciation expense is based on judgements about the future concerning the expected useful life and residual value of an asset. If all relevant factors are taken into account and reasonable judgements are applied, it may be possible to achieve a fair representation of the amount of the cost or fair value of the asset that is consumed for a particular period. However, a uniquely correct figure for depreciation for a period cannot be achieved.

Let us now consider each of the financial statements in turn.

Statement of financial position

IAS 1 does not prescribe the format (or layout) for this financial statement but does set out the *minimum* information that should be presented on the face of the statement of financial position. This includes the following:

- property, plant and equipment
- investment property
- intangible assets
- financial assets (such as shares and loan notes of other companies held as assets)
- inventories
- trade and other receivables
- cash and cash equivalents
- trade and other payables
- provisions (a provision is a liability that is of uncertain timing or amount – such as a possible obligation arising from a legal case against the company that has yet to be determined)
- financial liabilities (other than payables and provisions shown above)
- tax liabilities
- issued share capital and reserves (equity).

Additional information should be also shown where it is relevant to an understanding of the financial position of the business.

The standard requires that, on the statement of financial position, a distinction is normally made between current assets and non-current assets and between current liabilities and non-current liabilities. However, for certain types of business, such as financial institutions, the standard accepts that it may be more appropriate to order items according to their liquidity (that is, their nearness to cash).

Some of the assets and claims listed above may have to be sub-classified to comply with particular standards or because of their size or nature. Thus, sub-classifications are required for assets such as property, plant and equipment, receivables and inventories as well as for claims such as provisions and reserves. Certain details relating to share capital, such as the number of issued shares and their nominal value, must also be shown. To avoid cluttering up the statement of financial position, however, this additional information can be shown in the notes. In practice, most companies use notes for this purpose.

Statement of comprehensive income

This statement extends the conventional income statement to include certain other gains and losses that affect shareholders' equity. It may be presented either in the form of a single statement or as two separate statements, comprising an income statement and a **statement of comprehensive income**. This choice of presentation, however, seems to be a transitional arrangement as the IASB's clear preference is for a single statement.

Again the format of the statement of comprehensive income is not prescribed, but IAS 1 sets out the *minimum* information to be presented on the face of the statement. This includes:

- revenue
- finance costs
- profits or losses arising from discontinued operations
- tax expense
- profit or loss
- each component of other comprehensive income classified by its nature
- any share of the comprehensive income of associates or joint ventures
- total comprehensive income.

The standard makes it clear that further items should be shown on the face of the income statement where they are relevant to an understanding of performance. If, for example, a business is badly affected by flooding and inventories are destroyed as a result, the cost of the flood damage should be shown.

As a further aid to understanding, all material expenses should be separately disclosed. However, they need not be shown on the face of the income statement: they can appear in the notes to the financial statements. The kinds of material items that may require separate disclosure include:

- write-down of inventories to net realisable value
- write-down of property, plant and equipment
- disposals of investments
- restructuring costs
- discontinued operations
- litigation settlements.

This is not an exhaustive list and, in practice, other material expenses may require separate disclosure.

The standard suggests two possible ways in which expenses can be presented on the face of the income statement. Expenses can be presented either

- according to their nature, for example as depreciation, employee expenses and so on; or
- according to business functions, such as administrative activities and distribution.

The choice between the two possible ways of presenting expenses will depend on which one the directors believe will provide the more relevant and reliable information.

To understand what other information must be presented in this statement, apart from that already contained in a conventional income statement, we should remember that, broadly, the conventional income statement shows all *realised* gains and losses for the period. It also includes some unrealised losses (that is, losses relating to assets still held). However, unrealised gains, and some unrealised losses, do not pass through the income statement, but go directly to a reserve. We saw, in an earlier chapter, an example of an unrealised gain (which, therefore, would not have passed through the conventional income statement).

Activity 5.4

Can you think of this example?

The example that we met earlier is where a business revalues its land and buildings. The gain arising is not shown in the conventional income statement, but is transferred to a revaluation reserve, which forms part of the equity. (We met this example in Activity 2.15.) Land and buildings are not the only assets to which this rule relates, but these types of asset are, in practice, the most common examples of unrealised gains.

An example of an unrealised gain, or loss, that has not been mentioned so far, arises from exchange differences when the results of foreign operations are translated into UK currency. Any gain, or loss, usually bypasses the income statement and is taken directly to a currency translation reserve.

A weakness of conventional accounting is that there is no robust principle that we can apply to determine precisely what should, and what should not, be included in the income statement. For example, losses arising from the impairment of non-current assets normally appear in the income statement. On the other hand, losses arising from translating the carrying amount of assets expressed in an overseas currency (because they are owned by an overseas branch) do not. There is no real difference in principle between the two types of loss, but the difference in treatment is ingrained in conventional accounting practice.

The statement of comprehensive income includes *all* gains and losses for a period and so will also take into account unrealised gains and any remaining unrealised losses. It extends the conventional income statement by including these items immediately beneath the measure of profit for the year. An illustration of this statement is shown in Example 5.2. Here, expenses are presented according to business function, and comparative figures for the previous year are shown alongside the figures for the current year.

Example 5.2

Malik plc
Statement of comprehensive income for the year ended 31 December 2011

	2012	2011
	£m	£m
Revenue	100.6	97.2
Cost of sales	(60.4)	(59.1)
Gross profit	40.2	38.1
Other income	4.0	3.5
Distribution expenses	(18.2)	(16.5)
Administration expenses	(10.3)	(11.2)
Other expenses	(2.1)	(2.4)
Operating profit	13.6	11.5
Finance charges	(2.0)	(1.8)
Profit before tax	11.6	9.7
Tax	(2.9)	(2.4)
Profit for the year	8.7	7.3
Other comprehensive income		
Revaluation of property, plant and equipment	20.3	6.6
Foreign currency translation differences for foreign operations	12.5	4.0
Tax on other comprehensive income	(6.0)	(2.6)
Other comprehensive income for the year, net of tax	26.8	8.0
Total comprehensive income for the year	35.5	15.3

This example adopts a single-statement approach to presenting comprehensive income. The alternative two-statement approach simply divides the information shown into two separate parts. The income statement, which is the first statement, begins with the revenue for the reporting period and ends with the profit for the year. The statement of comprehensive income, which is the second statement, begins with the profit for the year and ends with the total comprehensive income.

Statement of changes in equity

The **statement of changes in equity** aims to help users to understand the changes in share capital and reserves that took place during the reporting period. It reconciles the figures for these items at the beginning of the period with those at the end. This is achieved by showing the effect on the share capital and reserves of total comprehensive income as well as the effect of share issues and purchases during the period. The effect of dividends during the period may also be shown in this statement, although dividends can be shown in the notes instead.

To see how a statement of changes in equity may be prepared, let us consider Example 5.3.

Example 5.3

At 1 January 2012 Miro plc had the following equity:

Miro plc

	£m
Share capital (£1 ordinary shares)	100
Revaluation reserve	20
Translation reserve	40
Retained earnings	150
Total equity	310

During 2012, the company made a profit for the year from normal business operations of £42 million and reported an upward revaluation of property, plant and equipment of £120 million (net of any tax that would be payable were the unrealised gains to be realised). A loss on exchange differences on translating the results of foreign operations of £10 million was also reported. To strengthen its financial position, the company issued 50 million ordinary shares during the year at a premium of £0.40. Dividends for the year were £27 million.

This information for 2012 can be set out in a statement of changes in equity as follows:

Statement of changes in equity for the year ended 31 December 2012

	Share capital	Share premium	Revaluation reserve	Translation reserve	Retained earnings	Total
	£m	£m	£m	£m	£m	£m
Balance at 1 January 2012	100	–	20	40	150	310
Changes in equity for 2012						
Issue of ordinary shares (Note 1)	50	20	–	–	–	70
Dividends (Note 2)	–	–	–	–	(27)	(27)
Total comprehensive income for the year (Note 3)	–	–	120	(10)	42	152
Balance at 31 December 2012	150	20	140	30	165	505

Notes:

1 The premium on the share price is transferred to a specific reserve.
2 We have chosen to show dividends in the statement of changes in equity rather than in the notes. They represent an appropriation of equity and are deducted from retained earnings.
3 The effect of each component of comprehensive income on the various elements of shareholders' equity must be separately disclosed. The revaluation gain and the loss on translating foreign operations are each allocated to a specific reserve. The profit for the year is added to retained earnings.

Statement of cash flows

The statement of cash flows should help users to assess the ability of a company to generate cash and to assess the company's need for cash. The presentation requirements for this statement are set out in IAS 7 *Statement of Cash Flows*, which we shall consider in some detail in the next chapter.

Notes

The notes play an important role in helping users to understand the financial statements. They will normally contain the following information:

■ a confirmation that the financial statements comply with relevant IFRSs;

■ a summary of the measurement bases used and other significant accounting policies applied (for example, the basis of inventories valuation);

■ supporting information relating to items appearing on the statement of financial position, statement of comprehensive income, statement of changes in equity and statement of cash flows; and

■ other significant disclosures such as future contractual commitments that have not been recognised and financial risk management objectives and policies.

General points

The standard provides support for three key accounting conventions when preparing the financial statements. These are:

■ the going concern convention;

■ the accruals convention (except for the statement of cash flows); and

■ the consistency convention.

These conventions were discussed in Chapters 2 and 3.

Finally, to improve the transparency of financial statements, the standard states that

■ offsetting liabilities against assets, or expenses against income, is not allowed. Thus it is not acceptable, for example, to offset a bank overdraft against a positive bank balance (where a company has both); and

■ material items must be shown separately.

SELECTED FINANCIAL REPORTING STANDARDS

If we look back at Real World 5.1, we can see that we have looked at a number of standards (for example IAS 1 and IAS 2). There are others (for example IAS 7 and IAS 27) that we shall consider in later chapters. There are also standards that deal with quite technical areas and which we need not concern ourselves with (for example, IAS 12 and IAS 19).

In this section we consider two important standards. They have a broad application and exert a significant influence over the way in which financial statements are prepared.

IAS 8 *Accounting Policies, Changes in Accounting Estimates and Errors*

IAS 8 sets out the criteria for selecting and changing accounting policies and the appropriate treatment for disclosing these policies. It also sets out the treatment for disclosing changes in accounting estimates and for the correction of errors. A key aim of the standard is to improve the comparability of financial statements both over time and between different businesses.

Accounting policies

Accounting policies are the principles, rules and conventions used to prepare the financial statements. Wherever possible, they should be determined by reference to an appropriate financial reporting standard. (The standard on inventories, for example, will provide policies to be adopted in this area.) In the absence of an appropriate standard, managers must make suitable judgements to ensure that users receive relevant and reliable information.

The general rule is that, once a particular policy has been selected and applied, it should not be changed. However, an accounting policy may be changed where

1 it is required by a new financial reporting standard; or
2 it will result in more relevant and reliable information being provided to users.

If a new financial reporting standard requires changes to be made, the name of the standard, and any transitional arrangements, should be disclosed. If it is a voluntary change, the reasons why it will result in more relevant and reliable information should be disclosed. In both cases, the nature of the change in policy and the amount of the adjustment on relevant items and on earnings per share for both the current and the prior period should be disclosed.

Changes in accounting estimates

Managers are normally required to make various estimates when preparing financial statements.

Activity 5.5

What estimates will normally be required? (*Hint*: Think back to Chapter 3.)

They will normally include estimates of:

- bad debts;
- the useful life of non-current assets;
- the net realisable value of inventories; and
- the fair value of non-current assets.

These estimates may need revision in the light of new information. If a revised estimate affects assets, liabilities or equity, it should be adjusted in the period of the change. If it affects profit, it should be revised in the period affected. This may be in the period of change and/or in future periods.

Activity 5.6

Try to think of an example of an estimate that will normally affect only the period of change and an example of one that will normally affect the period of change and future periods.

Normally, estimates of bad debts will only affect the period of change whereas a change in the estimated useful life of a non-current asset will affect the period of change and future periods.

Both the nature and amount of a change in estimate affecting the current period or future periods should be disclosed. If it is impracticable to estimate the amount, this fact must be disclosed.

Errors

Errors are omissions or misstatements in the financial statements. They may arise for a variety of reasons, which include mathematical mistakes, oversights, misinterpretation of facts and fraud. Sometimes these errors are significant in nature and/or size and are not discovered until a later period. In such a situation, the general rule is that the relevant figures for the earlier period(s) in which the errors occurred should be restated for comparison purposes. If the errors occurred before the prior periods presented for comparison, then the opening balances of assets, liabilities and equity for the earliest prior period presented should be restated. The nature of the errors and their effect on relevant items and on earnings per share for the current and the prior period(s) should also be disclosed.

IAS 10 *Events After the Reporting Period*

The main aim of IAS 10 is to clarify when financial statements should be adjusted for events that took place after the reporting period (or accounting period). The standard deals with events that occur between the end of the reporting period and the date when the financial statements are authorised to be issued both to the shareholders and to the general public. Two types of events are identified:

1 those providing evidence of conditions that existed before the end of the reporting period (adjusting events); and
2 those indicating conditions arising after the end of the reporting period (non-adjusting events).

The standard requires that financial statements should incorporate only the adjusting events.

Activity 5.7

Vorta plc received the following information between the end of the reporting period and the date at which the financial statements were authorised for issue:

1 Inventories which were reported in the statement of financial position at an estimated net realisable value of £250,000 were sold shortly after the year end for £200,000.
2 There was a decline of £150,000 in the market value of investments after the end of the reporting period.
3 An error was discovered which indicated that the trade receivables figure on the statement of financial position was understated by £220,000.

Which of the above are adjusting events?

Items 1 and 3 meet the definition of an adjusting event whereas item 2 meets the definition of a non-adjusting event. This is because, with items 1 and 3, we have received additional information on the position at the year end. With item 2, a change has occurred *after the* year end.

The standard clarifies two important points concerning events after the reporting period. First, if a dividend is declared for equity shareholders after the reporting period, it should not be treated as a liability in the financial statements. In the past it was normal practice to treat such dividends as liabilities. Secondly, if it becomes clear after the reporting period that the business will cease trading, the going concern assumption will not apply. As a result the financial statements must be prepared using a fundamentally different basis for valuation, meaning, for example, that assets will be shown at their estimated realisable values.

The date at which the financial statements were authorised for issue to shareholders and others must be disclosed as it is important to understanding what should and should not be included. There should also be disclosure of who authorised the issue.

Activity 5.8

Who do you think will normally authorise the issue of the financial statements?

It is normally the board of directors.

Where non-adjusting events are significant, they are capable of influencing users' decisions. The standard therefore requires significant non-adjusting events to be disclosed by way of a note. A major restructuring, a plan to discontinue an operation and the proposed purchase of a major asset are examples of non-adjusting events that might be disclosed. The standard requires the nature of the event and its likely financial effect be disclosed. If the financial effect cannot be reliably estimated, this fact should be disclosed.

Real World 5.2 is the note to the financial statements of Tottenham Hotspur plc that deals with non-adjusting events that occurred between the statement of financial position date (30 June 2011) and the date of issue of the financial statements (15 November 2011). They relate mainly to transfers of player during the Summer 2011 transfer window.

Real World 5.2

A window of opportunity for Spurs

Since the balance sheet [statement of financial position] date the following events have occurred:

  B Friedel joined on a free transfer
  C Ceballos joined on a free transfer
  S Coulibaly joined on a free transfer
  S Parker was bought from West Ham United
  J O'Hara was sold to Wolverhampton Wanderers
  E Adebayor joined on loan from Manchester City
  P-J M'Poku was sold to Standard Liege
  R Keane was sold to LA Galaxy
  A Hutton was sold to Aston Villa
  P Crouch was sold to Stoke City
  W Palacios was sold to Stoke City
  D Bentley was loaned to West Ham United
  J Jenas was loaned to Aston Villa

Including Football League levies, the net income of these transactions amounted to approximately £13,224,000.

Source: Tottenham Hotspur plc, 2011 Annual Report, p. 58.

Figure 5.3 summarises the main points to be considered when applying IAS 10.

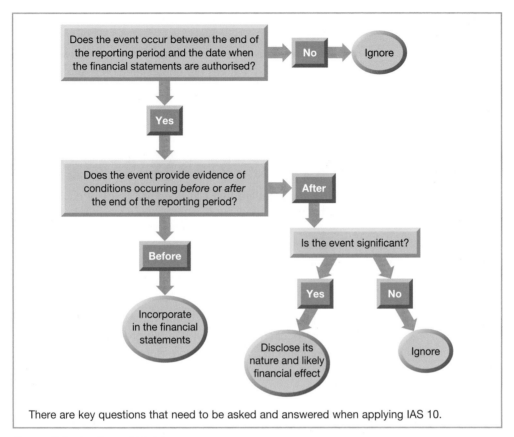

There are key questions that need to be asked and answered when applying IAS 10.

Figure 5.3 Applying IAS 10

PROBLEMS WITH STANDARDS

There is broad agreement that financial reporting standards have improved the quality of financial statements. Nevertheless, we should be alert to the potential problems associated with their use. These include the following:

Standards may inhibit change

By setting out rigid procedures to be followed, the development of new and better procedures may be stifled. Progress in financial reporting may require that businesses have the freedom to experiment and innovate. Unless they have this freedom, accounting practice may become ossified.

Although this problem cannot be easily dismissed, history has shown that financial reporting standards are changed when they prove to be ineffective or inadequate. Over the years, numerous standards have been either modified or withdrawn. Furthermore, developing a new standard involves wide consultation with interested parties and much debate about what constitutes best practice. Financial reporting standards can, therefore, provide the stimulus for new thinking.

Standards may impose false conformity

No two businesses are identical: each will have its own characteristics and operating methods. When common standards are insisted on, there is a danger that the unique aspects of each business will be obscured.

Although this argument has some merit, it can be taken too far. Differences between businesses can be overstated while their common features are understated. Furthermore, there is nothing to stop standards allowing a limited choice between accounting methods, which may help in reflecting individual characteristics.

Activity 5.9

Can you think of a financial reporting standard that allows some choice of accounting method? [*Hint*: Think back to Chapter 3].

The inventories standard permits some choice over inventories costing methods and the depreciation standard permits some choice over depreciation methods.

Finally, a business can, in exceptional circumstances, depart from a financial reporting standard where it conflicts with the requirement to provide a fair presentation of financial health. Businesses do not, therefore, have to comply with unreasonable rules.

Standards involve consensus seeking

Financial reporting standards affect certain groups who must be willing to accept them. Unless this happens, standards cannot be implemented effectively. The development of standards may, therefore, be influenced more by the need to achieve consensus than by technical considerations of what is the best approach to adopt. When this occurs, the quality of financial statements will suffer.

To date, there is no evidence to suggest that this has been a major problem. In order to command authority, standard setters must be responsive to the groups affected. In a democracy this is how authority is legitimised. The trick that they must achieve, however, is to make rules that are both technically sound and broadly acceptable.

Standards can be costly

There is now an intricate web of financial reporting standards surrounding large businesses. The costs of complying with these rules are high and are borne by shareholders. Each additional standard that incurs costs for businesses means that less is available for distribution to shareholders. There is an assumption that the benefits to shareholders of these standards outweigh their costs, but what if this is not the case? It is reasonable to expect standard setters to carry out an assessment of costs and benefits before adding to the burden of rules.

Standards can be complex

There is a growing concern that international financial reporting standards are making financial statements too complex to be useful to shareholders. This has led to calls for better regulation. International standards are meant to be based on principles rather than on legalistic rules, which should help to prevent excessive complexity. Many, however, question whether this principles-based approach is working effectively. **Real World 5.3** gives a flavour of the problem.

ACCOUNTING RULES OR ACCOUNTING CHOICE?

The alternative to a rule-based approach is to allow businesses freedom of choice in the accounting methods adopted. Instead of creating standards for all to follow, shareholders of each business should decide how much and what kind of information they require. It is argued that competitive forces should help to ensure that managers are responsive to shareholders' requirements.

Activity 5.10

What sort of competitive forces may encourage managers to be responsive?

They may include competition for funds and competition for managers' jobs.

It would be nice to think that the supply of financial information could be left to competitive forces. There are times, however, when these forces are weak. There are also times when managers have an incentive to conceal relevant information from shareholders.

Activity 5.11

What sort of information might managers have an incentive to conceal?

Managers may wish to conceal information that would cast doubt on their ability or integrity or might prevent the business from obtaining funds. This may include information relating to excessive management rewards, poor business performance or weak financial health.

Managers also have an incentive to select accounting methods and policies that enhance profits, particularly if they are linked to managerial rewards. This point will be considered further when we discuss creative accounting later in the chapter.

Given the management incentives described, there is always a risk that shareholders will not receive relevant and reliable information. Financial reporting standards combat this risk by imposing discipline on managers in financial reporting. This disciplinary role provided a major impetus for the creation of standards.

With freedom of choice comes the problem of comparability. Differences between businesses in terms of shareholder needs and in the strength of competitive forces will result in differences in the quantity and quality of information disclosed – which leads us back to one of the key aims of financial reporting standards.

THE NEED FOR A CONCEPTUAL FRAMEWORK

In Chapter 2 we came across various accounting conventions such as the prudence, historic cost and going concern conventions. These conventions were developed as a practical response to particular problems that were confronted when preparing financial statements.

They have stood the test of time and are still of value to preparers today. However, they do not provide, and were never designed to provide, a **conceptual framework**, or framework of principles, to guide the development of financial statements. As we grapple with increasingly complex financial reporting problems, the need to have a sound understanding of *why* we account for things in a particular way becomes more pressing. Knowing *why* we account, rather than simply *how* we account, is vital if we are to improve the quality of financial statements.

In recent years, much effort has been expended in various countries, including the UK, to develop a clear conceptual framework that will guide us in the development of accounting. Such a framework should provide clear answers to such fundamental questions as:

■ Who are the main users of financial statements?
■ What is the purpose of financial statements?
■ What qualities should financial information possess?
■ What are the main elements of financial statements?
■ How should these elements be defined, recognised and measured?

If these questions can be answered, accounting rule makers, such as the IASB, will be in a stronger position to identify best practice and to develop more coherent rules. This should, in turn, increase the credibility of financial reports in the eyes of users. It may even possibly help reduce the number of rules, because some issues may be resolved by reference to the application of general principles rather than by the generation of further rules.

THE IASB FRAMEWORK

The quest for a conceptual framework began in earnest in the 1970s when the Financial Accounting Standards Board (FASB) in the US devoted a large amount of time and resources to this task. It resulted in a broad framework, which other rule-making bodies, including the IASB, then drew upon to develop their own frameworks. The IASB Framework for the Preparation and Presentation of Financial Statements was produced in 1989 and has since provided guidance for the development of international financial reporting standards. Many of the standards that pre-dated the framework have now been replaced or revised. The IASB framework is itself, however, currently being revised.

The IASB and FASB have embarked on a joint project to produce a common conceptual framework that will underpin the financial reporting standards of both bodies. This project, which is ongoing, represents a major step towards convergence that will eventually lead to the replacement of the existing IASB framework. In 2010, the IASB and FASB announced completion of the first phase of the project, which deals with the objective and qualitative characteristics of financial reporting. Following this announcement, the IASB issued a document *Conceptual Framework for Financial Reporting 2010*, followed by its 2011 counterpart, which incorporate these revisions into its existing framework.

The revised IASB framework asserts that the objective of general-purpose financial reporting is 'to provide financial information about the reporting entity that is useful to existing and potential investors, lenders and other creditors in making decisions about providing resources to the entity'. Note that it is the providers of finance that are seen as the primary users of general-purpose financial reports. This is because investors, lenders and other creditors largely rely on these reports to make their investment decisions. Although other users may find general-purpose financial reports useful, the reports are not aimed at them.

The IASB framework also sets out the qualitative characteristics that make financial statements useful. The fundamental characteristics identified are relevance and faithful representation: it is these characteristics that make information useful. Characteristics that enhance the quality of financial reports are comparability, timeliness, verifiability and understandability. These are regarded as desirable, but not critical, characteristics. In the absence of relevance and faithful representation, they cannot make information useful. (All these characteristics were considered in some detail in Chapter 1.) The framework acknowledges that producing financial information incurs costs, which must be justified by the benefits provided.

The IASB framework identifies two important accounting conventions: going concern and accruals. It states that financial statements should normally be prepared on the assumption that a business is a going concern. If this assumption cannot be applied, a different basis of reporting will be required. This will affect the valuation of assets held. The framework supports the accruals convention, which is seen as a better means of assessing past and future performance than reliance on cash receipts and payments. Nevertheless, information on cash flows is also considered useful for assessing financing and investing activities, liquidity and solvency.

The IASB framework goes on to identify the main elements of financial statements. Those relating to the measurement of financial position are assets, liabilities and equity, and those relating to the measurement of performance are income and expense. Each of these elements is defined and the definitions provided are similar to those discussed in Chapters 2 and 3.

The IASB framework identifies different measurement bases, such as historic cost, current cost, and realisable value. There is no attempt, however, to support a particular measurement basis. The framework simply notes that historic cost is the most widely used basis but that it is often used with other measurement bases. To determine which measurement bases should be used for a particular situation, relevant financial reporting standards must be consulted.

The IASB framework does not have the same legal status as the IASB standards. Nevertheless, it offers guidance for dealing with accounting issues, particularly where no relevant financial reporting standard exists. Managers are required to consider the framework when dealing with issues that fall outside the scope of existing standards.

Overall, the IASB framework has provoked little controversy and the principles that it contains appear to enjoy widespread acceptance. There has been some criticism, mainly from academics, that the framework is really a descriptive document and does not provide theoretical underpinning to the financial statements. It has also been suggested that the framework is too broad in nature to provide useful guidance for developing financial reporting standards or to deal with emerging accounting issues. These criticisms have not, however, sparked any major debates.

THE AUDITORS' ROLE

Shareholders are required to elect a qualified and independent person or, more usually, a firm to act as **auditors**. The auditors' main duty is to report whether, in their opinion, the financial statements do what they are supposed to do, namely to show a true and fair view of the financial performance, position and cash flows of the company. To be able to form such an opinion, auditors must carefully scrutinise the financial statements and the underlying evidence upon which they are based. In particular, they will examine the accounting principles followed, the accounting estimates made and the robustness of the company's internal control systems. The auditors' opinion must be included with the financial statements sent to the shareholders and to the Registrar of Companies.

The relationship between the shareholders, the directors and the auditors is illustrated in Figure 5.4. This shows that the shareholders elect the directors to act on their behalf, in the day-to-day running of the company. The directors are then required to 'account' to the shareholders on the performance, position and cash flows of the company, on an annual basis. The shareholders also elect auditors, whose role it is to give the shareholders an independent view of the truth and fairness of the financial statements prepared by the directors.

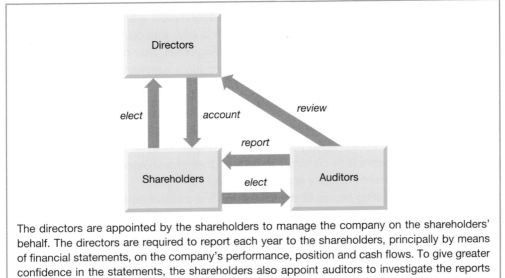

The directors are appointed by the shareholders to manage the company on the shareholders' behalf. The directors are required to report each year to the shareholders, principally by means of financial statements, on the company's performance, position and cash flows. To give greater confidence in the statements, the shareholders also appoint auditors to investigate the reports and to express an opinion on their reliability.

Figure 5.4 The relationship between the shareholders, the directors and the auditors

DIRECTORS' REPORT

In addition to preparing the financial statements, UK law requires the directors to prepare a report to shareholders and other interested parties relating to each reporting period. The **directors' report** will contain both financial and non-financial information, which goes beyond that contained in the financial statements. The information to be disclosed is diverse and will include the names of those who were directors during the reporting period, the principal activities of the company and any recommended dividend. The most important element of the report, however, is probably the **business review**. This is aimed at helping shareholders to assess how well the directors have performed. It should provide an analysis of financial performance and position and should also set out the principal risks and uncertainties facing the business. (We shall consider this review in some detail in Chapter 12.)

In addition to disclosing the information mentioned above, the directors' report must contain a declaration that the directors are not aware of any other information that the auditors might need in preparing their audit report. Furthermore, the report must declare that the directors have taken steps to ensure that the auditors are aware of all relevant information. The auditors do not carry out an audit of the directors' report. However, they will check to see that the information in the report is consistent with that contained in the audited financial statements.

For companies listed on the London Stock Exchange, the law also requires the publication of an annual directors' remuneration report. This should help shareholders to assess whether the rewards received by directors are appropriate.

SUMMARY FINANCIAL STATEMENTS

We saw earlier that the directors must provide each shareholder with a copy of the annual financial statements. For large businesses, these financial statements can be extremely detailed and complicated. Along with the accompanying notes, they may extend over many pages. It is possible, however, for the directors to provide a summarised version of the full financial statements as an alternative.

The main advantages of providing **summary financial statements** are that

- many shareholders do not wish to receive the full version because they may not have the time, interest or skill necessary to be able to gain much from it;
- directors could improve their communication with their shareholders by providing something closer to the needs of many shareholders; and
- reproducing and posting copies of the full version is expensive and a waste of resources where particular shareholders do not wish to receive it.

It has now become common practice for large businesses to send all of their shareholders who are private individuals a copy of the summary financial statements. These are accompanied with a clear message that a copy of the full version is available on request. Institutional investors (insurance companies, pension funds and so on) tend to receive a full version as a matter of routine.

Critics of summary financial statements, however, argue that it is dangerous for shareholders to receive financial reports that attempt to simplify complexity. Any attempt to do so runs the risk of discarding important information and distorting the message. If a shareholder is unwilling or unable to develop the necessary accounting skills, or to spend the necessary time to examine the full version of the financial statements, the proper solution is either to seek expert advice or to invest in mutual funds managed by experts. Viewed from this perspective, the best thing that a business can do to help less sophisticated shareholders is to provide more detailed information to experts such as investment analysts.

CREATIVE ACCOUNTING

Despite the proliferation of accounting rules and the independent checks that are imposed, concerns over the quality of published financial statements surface from time to time. There are occasions when directors apply particular accounting policies, or structure particular transactions, in such a way as to portray a picture of financial health that is in line with what they want users to see, rather than what is a true and fair view of financial position and performance. Misrepresenting the performance and position of a business in this way is often called **creative accounting**, and it poses a major problem for accounting rule makers and for society generally.

Activity 5.12

Why might the directors of a company engage in creative accounting?

There are many reasons including:

- to get around restrictions (for example, to report sufficient profit to pay a dividend);
- to avoid government action (for example, the taxation of excessive profits);
- to hide poor management decisions;
- to achieve sales revenue or profit targets, thereby ensuring that performance bonuses are paid to the directors;
- to attract new share capital or long-term borrowing by showing an apparently healthy financial position; and
- to satisfy the demands of major investors concerning levels of return.

Creative accounting methods

The ways in which unscrupulous directors can manipulate the financial statements are many and varied. However, they usually involve adopting novel or unorthodox practices for reporting key elements of the financial statements, such as revenue, expenses, assets and liabilities. They may also involve the use of complicated or obscure transactions in an attempt to hide the underlying economic reality. The manipulation carried out may be designed either to bend the rules or to break them.

We shall now consider some of the more important ways in which rules may be bent or broken.

Misstating revenue

Some creative accounting methods are designed to overstate the revenue for a period. These methods often involve the early recognition of sales revenue or the reporting of sales transactions that have no real substance. **Real World 5.4** provides examples of both types of revenue manipulation.

Real World 5.4

Overstating revenue

Early recognition of revenue: A business may report the sale of goods as soon as an order has been placed, rather than when the goods are delivered to, and accepted by, the customer. This will boost current revenues and profits and is known as 'pre-dispatching'.

Passing goods to distributors: A business may force its distributors to accept more goods than they can sell. This will again boost current revenues and profits and is known as 'channel stuffing' or 'trade loading'.

Artificial trading: This involves businesses in the same industry selling the same items between themselves to boost sales revenue. One example is where telecoms businesses sell unused fibre optic capacity to each other. This is known as 'hollow swaps'. Another example is where energy businesses sell energy between themselves for the same price and at the same time. This is known as 'round tripping' or 'in and out trading'.

→

Note that artificial trading between similar businesses will inflate the sales revenue for a period but will not inflate reported profits. Nevertheless, this may still benefit the business. Sales revenue growth has become an important yardstick of performance for some investors and can affect the value they place on the business.

Source: Based on information in 'Dirty laundry: how companies fudge the numbers', *The Times*, Business Section, 22 September 2002, nisyndication.com.

The manipulation of revenue has been at the heart of many of the accounting scandals recently exposed. Given its critical role in the measurement of performance, this is, perhaps, not surprising. **Real World 5.5** provides an example of how the financial results of one well-known business were distorted by the overstatement of sales revenues.

Real World 5.5

Recomputing the numbers

In August 2007, Dell (the computer manufacturer) admitted that some unnamed 'senior executives' had been involved in a scheme to overstate sales revenue figures during the period 2003 to 2007. This was done in an attempt to make it appear that quarterly sales targets had been met, when in fact this was not the case. The overstatement of sales revenue was estimated to amount to $92 million, about 1 per cent of total profit over the period concerned.

FT *Source*: 'Dell to lower writedowns on restated earnings' (Allison, K) *Financial Times*, 30 October 2007. © The Financial Times Limited 2012. All rights reserved.

Massaging expenses

Some creative accounting methods focus on the manipulation of expenses. Those expenses that rely on directors' estimates of the future or their choice of accounting policy are particularly vulnerable to manipulation.

Activity 5.13

Can you identify the kind of expenses where the directors make estimates or choices in the ways described?

These include certain expenses that we discussed in Chapter 3, such as

- depreciation of property, plant and equipment;
- amortisation of intangible assets, such as goodwill;
- inventories (cost of sales); and
- allowances for trade receivables.

By changing estimates about the future (for example, the useful life or residual value of an asset), or by changing accounting policies (for example, switching from FIFO to AVCO), it may be possible to derive an expense figure, and consequently a profit figure, that suits the directors.

The incorrect 'capitalisation' of expenses may also be used as a means of manipulation. This involves treating expenses as if they were amounts incurred to acquire or develop non-current assets, rather than amounts consumed during the period. The net effect of this is that the expenses will be unfairly understated and profit will, therefore, be unfairly boosted. Businesses that build their own assets are often best placed to undertake this form of malpractice.

Activity 5.14

What would be the effect on the profits and total assets of a business of incorrectly capitalising expenses?

Both would be artificially inflated. Reported profits would increase because expenses would be reduced. Total assets would be increased because the expenses would be incorrectly treated as non-current assets.

Real World 5.6 provides an example of one business that capitalised expenses on a huge scale.

Real World 5.6

Sorry – wrong numbers

One particularly notorious case of capitalising expenses is alleged to have occurred in the financial statements of WorldCom (now renamed MCI). This company, which is a large US telecommunications business, is alleged to have overstated profits by treating certain operating expenses, such as basic network maintenance, as capital expenditure. This happened over a fifteen-month period during 2001 and 2002. To correct for this overstatement, profits had to be reduced by a massive $3.8 billion.

FT *Source:* Based on two personal views on WorldCom posted on the FT.com site, 27 June 2002.

Concealing 'bad news'

Some creative accounting methods focus on the concealment of losses or liabilities. The financial statements can look much healthier if these can somehow be eliminated. One way of doing this is to create a 'separate' entity that will take over the losses or liabilities.

Real World 5.7 describes how one large business concealed losses and liabilities.

Real World 5.7

For a very special purpose

Perhaps the most well-known case of concealment of losses and liabilities concerned the Enron Corporation. This was a large US energy business that used 'special purpose entities' (SPEs) as a means of concealment. SPEs were used by Enron to rid itself of problem assets that were falling in value, such as its broadband operations. In addition, liabilities were

$\rightarrow$

transferred to these entities to help Enron's statement of financial position look healthier. The company had to keep its gearing ratios (the relationship between borrowing and equity) within particular limits to satisfy credit-rating agencies, and SPEs were used to achieve this. The SPEs used for concealment purposes were not independent of the company and should have been consolidated in the statement of financial position of Enron, along with their losses and liabilities.

When these, and other accounting irregularities, were discovered in 2001, there was a restatement of Enron's financial performance and position to reflect the consolidation of the SPEs, which had previously been omitted. As a result of this restatement, the company recognised $591 million in losses over the preceding four years and an additional $628 million worth of liabilities at the end of 2000.

The company collapsed at the end of 2001.

Source: 'The rise and fall of Enron', C. William Thomas, *Journal of Accountancy*, vol. 194, no. 3, 2002. This article represents the opinions of the author, which are not necessarily those of the Texas Society of Certified Public Accountants.

Misstating assets

There are various ways in which assets may be misstated. These include:

■ using asset values that are higher than their fair market values;
■ capitalising costs that should have been written off as expenses, as described earlier;
■ recording assets that are not owned or which do not exist.

Real World 5.8 describes how one large business reported an asset that did not exist.

Real World 5.8

When things go sour

Parmalat, a large Italian dairy and food business, announced in December 2003 that a bank account held in the Cayman Islands with the Bank of America did not have, as had been previously reported, a balance of €3.95 billion. The fake balance turned out to be part of a web of deception: it had simply been 'invented' in order to help offset more than €16 billion of outstanding borrowings. According to Italian prosecutors, the business had borrowed heavily on the strength of fictitious sales revenues.

A Cayman Islands subsidiary, which was supposed to hold the fake bank balance, engaged in fictitious trading in an attempt to conceal the true nature of the deception. This included the supply of 300,000 tons of milk powder from a fake Singapore-based business to a Cuban business through the subsidiary.

Source: Based on 'How it all went so sour', Peter Gumbel, *Time Europe Magazine*, 21 November 2004.

Inadequate disclosure

Directors may misrepresent or try to conceal certain information. This may relate to commitments made, key changes in accounting policies or estimates, significant events and so on. The information may also relate to financial transactions between the directors and the business. **Real World 5.9** provides such an example.

Figure 5.5 summarises the main methods of creative accounting.

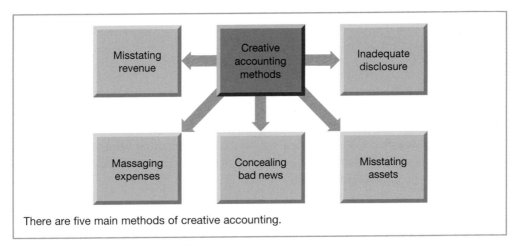

There are five main methods of creative accounting.

Figure 5.5 The main methods of creative accounting

Checking for creative accounting

When examining the financial statements of a business, a number of checks may be carried out on the financial statements to help gain a feel for their reliability. These can include checks to see whether

■ the reported profits are significantly higher than the operating cash flows for the period (as shown in the business's statement of cash flows), which may suggest that profits have been overstated;

- the tax charge is low in relation to reported profits, which may suggest, again, that profits are overstated, although there may be other, more innocent, explanations;
- the valuation methods used for assets held are based on historic cost or fair values and, if the latter approach has been used, why and how the fair values were determined;
- there have been changes in accounting policies over the period, particularly in key areas such as revenue recognition, inventories valuation and depreciation;
- the accounting policies adopted are in line with those adopted by the rest of the industry;
- the auditors' report gives a 'clean bill of health' to the financial statements; and
- the 'small print', that is the notes to the financial statements, is being used to hide significant events or changes.

Real World 5.10 describes the emphasis that one analyst places on this last check.

Real World 5.10

Taking note

Alistair Hodgson, investment manager at private client stockbroker Pilling and Co, says: 'I almost look at the notes more than I look at the main figures at first. The notes tend to hold the key to anything that looks strange. I look to pick out things that the auditor has told the company to declare – the kind of thing they might not want to declare, but they have got to do so in order to make the accounts honest.'

FT   *Source*: 'It pays to read between the lines', *Financial Times*, 17 September 2005.
© The Financial Times Limited 2012. All rights reserved.

Checks may also be carried out to provide confirmation of positive financial health. These may include checks to see whether the business is paying increased dividends, and whether the directors are buying shares in the business.

Although the various checks described are useful, they cannot be used to guarantee the reliability of the financial statements. Some creative accounting practices may be very deeply seated and may go undetected for years.

Creative accounting and economic growth

Some years ago there was a wave of creative accounting scandals, particularly in the US but also in Europe; however, it seems that this wave has now subsided. The quality of financial reporting is improving and, it is to be hoped, trust among investors and others is being restored. As a result of the actions taken by various regulatory bodies, and by accounting rule makers, creative accounting has become a more risky and difficult process for those who attempt it. However, it will never disappear completely and a further wave of creative accounting scandals may occur in the future.

The recent wave coincided with a period of strong economic growth and, during good economic times, investors and auditors become less vigilant, and thus it becomes easier to manipulate the figures. We must not, therefore, become too complacent. Things may change again when we next experience a period of strong growth.

You have overheard the following statements:

(a) 'Dividends announced between the end of the reporting period and the date at which the financial reports are authorised for publication, which relate to the reporting period just ended, should be treated as a liability in the statement of financial position at the end of that period.'
(b) 'IAS 1 provides support for three key accounting conventions – accruals, historic cost and consistency.'
(c) 'IAS 1 permits bank overdrafts to be offset against positive bank balances when preparing the statement of financial position.'
(d) 'Accounting policies can only be changed if it is required by a new financial reporting standard.'
(e) 'All non-adjusting events occurring between the end of the reporting period and the date at which the financial statements are authorised for issue should be ignored.'
(f) 'All companies must publish an annual directors' remuneration report.'

Required:
Critically comment on each of these statements.

A solution to this question can be found in Appendix C.

SUMMARY

The main points of this chapter may be summarised as follows:

Directors' duty

■ Separation of ownership from day-to-day control creates a need for directors to be accountable.

■ To fulfil this need, the directors have a duty to prepare and publish financial statements.

■ These financial statements must provide a fair representation of the financial health of the business.

The need for accounting rules

■ Accounting rules are necessary in order to avoid unacceptable accounting practices and to improve the comparability of financial statements.

■ This should give greater confidence in the integrity of financial statements.

Accounting rules

■ The International Accounting Standards Board (IASB) has become an important source of rules.

■ Company law and the London Stock Exchange are also sources of rules for UK companies.

Presenting financial statements

■ IAS 1 sets out the structure and content of financial statements.

- It requires preparation of a statement of financial position, a statement of comprehensive income, a statement of changes in equity and a statement of cash flows. In addition, explanatory notes are required.

- The financial statements must provide a fair representation of the financial health of a company and this will only normally be achieved by adherence to relevant IASB standards.

- IAS 1 sets out information to be shown in the various financial statements and some of the accounting conventions and principles to be followed in preparing the statements.

Selected financial reporting standards

- IAS 8 sets out the criteria for selecting and changing accounting policies.

- It also sets out the treatment for disclosing changes in accounting estimates and for the correction of errors.

- IAS 10 aims to clarify when financial statements should be adjusted for events that took place after the reporting period.

- Only events that provide evidence of conditions before the end of the reporting period lead to adjustments to the financial statements.

Problems with standards

- Various problems may arise from using financial reporting standards:
  - they may inhibit change
  - they may impose false conformity
  - they involve consensus seeking
  - they can be costly
  - they can introduce complexity.

- The alternative is to allow accounting choice. This, however, leads to the risk of manipulation, inadequate disclosure and lack of comparability.

Conceptual framework

- This helps to underpin financial reporting standards.

- The IASB framework sets out the objective and primary users of general-purpose financial reports, the qualitative characteristics and elements of financial statements and the different measurement bases that may be used.

- The IASB and FASB are working towards the development of a common conceptual framework.

Other statutory reports

- The auditors' report provides an opinion by an independent auditor concerning whether the financial statements provide a true and fair view of the financial health of a business.

- The directors' report contains information of a financial and a non-financial nature, which goes beyond that contained in the financial statements.

- For companies listed on the Stock Exchange, an annual directors' remuneration report must also be prepared.

$\rightarrow$

MyAccountingLab

Go to www.myaccountinglab.com to check your understanding of the chapter, create a personalised study plan, and maximise your revision time

KEY TERMS

International Accounting Standards
   p. 152
International Financial Reporting
   Standards p. 152
statement of comprehensive income
   p.157
statement of changes in equity p. 159

conceptual framework p. 169
auditors p. 170
directors' report p. 171
business review p. 171
summary financial statements p. 172
creative accounting p. 172

FURTHER READING

If you would like to explore the topics covered in this chapter in more depth, we recommend the following:

Alexander, D., Britton, A. and Jorissen, A. *International Financial Reporting and Analysis*, 5th edn, South-Western Cengage Learning, 2011, Chapters 2, 3, 8 and 9

Elliott, B. and Elliott, J., *Financial Accounting and Reporting*, 15th edn, Financial Times Prentice Hall, 2011, Chapters 9 and 10

International Accounting Standards Board, *The Conceptual Framework for Financial Reporting*, September 2010

International Accounting Standards Board, *2011 International Financial Reporting Standards IFRS* (two-volume set), IASB, 2011

Solutions to these questions can be found in Appendix D.

5.1 When preparing financial statements for the current period, Woden plc found that it had understated its revenue in error by £2 million in the previous period. How should the business report this error?

5.2 What are accounting policies and how should they be determined?

5.3 Why do we need accounting rules?

5.4 What are the main methods of creative accounting?

EXERCISES

Exercises 5.1 and 5.2 are basic level, 5.3 and 5.4 are intermediate level and 5.5 to 5.8 are advanced level. Solutions to the exercises with coloured numbers are given in Appendix E.

If you wish to try more exercises, visit the students' side of the Companion Website and MyAccountingLab.

5.1 'Searching for an agreed conceptual framework for accounting rules is likely to be a journey without an ending.' Discuss.

5.2 'Financial reporting standards eliminate the need for accountants to make judgements and so lower their professional status.' Do you agree?

5.3 Thor plc has the following events occurring between the end of the reporting period and the date the financial statements were authorised for issue:

1 The discovery that, during the reporting period, an employee had defrauded the business of £120,000.
2 The bankruptcy of a customer who owes the business £280,000. This sum was outstanding at the end of the reporting period.
3 A fire occurring after the reporting period that destroyed a large factory owned by Thor plc.
4 An increase in the value of land held by Thor plc by £10 million that occurred as a result of a change in the planning laws, which occurred after the end of the reporting period.

According to IAS 10 *Events After the Reporting Period*, how should each of these events be treated?

5.4 What problems are likely to be encountered when preparing summary financial statements for shareholders?

5.5 The following information was extracted from the financial statements of I. Ching (Booksellers) plc for the year to 31 December 2012:

	£000
Finance charges	40
Cost of sales	460
Distribution expenses	110
Revenue	943
Administration expenses	212
Other expenses	25
Gain on revaluation of property, plant and equipment	20
Loss on foreign currency translations on foreign operations	15
Tax on profit for the year	24
Tax on other components of comprehensive income	1

Required:

Prepare a statement of comprehensive income for the year ended 31 December 2012 that is set out in accordance with the requirements of IAS 1 *Presentation of Financial Statements*.

5.6 Manet plc had the following share capital and reserves as at 1 January 2012:

	£m
Share capital (£0.25 ordinary shares)	250
Share premium account	50
Revaluation reserve	120
Currency translation reserve	15
Retained earnings	380
Total equity	**815**

During the year to 31 December 2012, the company revalued property, plant and equipment upwards by £30 million and made a loss on foreign exchange translation of foreign operations of £5 million. The company made a profit for the year from normal operations of £160 million during the year and the dividend was £80 million.

Required:

Prepare a statement of changes in equity for the year ended 31 December 2012 in accordance with the requirements of IAS 1 *Presentation of Financial Statements*.

5.7 Professor Myddleton argues that financial reporting standards should be limited to disclosure requirements and should not impose rules on companies as to how to measure particular items in the financial statements. He states:

> The volume of accounting instructions is already high. If things go on like this, where will we be in 20 or 30 years' time? On balance I conclude we would be better off without any standards on accounting measurement. There could still be some disclosure requirements for listed companies, though probably less than now.

Do you agree with this idea? Discuss.

5.8 You have overheard the following statements:

(a) 'The role of independent auditors is to prepare the financial statements of the company.'

(b) 'International Accounting Standards (IASs) apply to all UK companies, but London Stock Exchange listed companies must also adhere to International Financial Reporting Standards (IFRSs).'

(c) 'All listed companies in European Union states must follow IASs and IFRSs.'

(d) 'According to IAS 1, companies' financial statements must show an "accurate representation" of what they purport to show.'

(e) 'IAS 1 leaves it to individual companies to decide the format that they use in the statement of financial position.'

(f) 'The statement of changes in equity deals with unrealised profits and gains, for example an upward revaluation of a non-current asset.'

(g) 'If a majority of the shareholders of a listed company agree, the company need not produce a full set of financial statements, but can just produce summary financial statements.'

Critically comment on each of these statements.

Chapter 6

MEASURING AND REPORTING CASH FLOWS

INTRODUCTION

This chapter is devoted to the third major financial statement identified in Chapter 2: the statement of cash flows. This statement reports the movements of cash over a period and the effect of these movements on the cash position of the business. It is an important financial statement because cash is vital to the survival of a business. Without cash, a business cannot operate.

In this chapter, we shall see how the statement of cash flows is prepared and how the information that it contains may be interpreted. We shall also see why the deficiencies of the income statement in identifying and explaining cash flows make a separate statement necessary.

The statement of cash flows is being considered after the chapters on limited companies because the format of the statement requires an understanding of this type of business. Most limited companies are required to provide a statement of cash flows for shareholders and other users as part of their annual financial reports.

Learning outcomes

When you have completed this chapter, you should be able to:

- discuss the crucial importance of cash to a business;
- explain the nature of the statement of cash flows and discuss how it can be helpful in identifying cash flow problems;
- prepare a statement of cash flows;
- interpret a statement of cash flows.

MyAccountingLab Visit **www.myaccountinglab.com** for practice and revision opportunities

THE STATEMENT OF CASH FLOWS

The statement of cash flows is a fairly recent addition to the annual published financial statements. Companies used only to be required to publish an income statement and a statement of financial position. The prevailing view seems to have been that all of the financial information needed by users would be contained within these two statements. This view may have been based partly on the assumption that if a business were profitable, it would also have plenty of cash. Although in the long run this is likely to be true, it is not necessarily true in the short to medium term.

We saw in Chapter 3 that the income statement sets out the revenue and expenses for the period, rather than the cash inflows and outflows. This means that the profit (or loss), which represents the difference between the revenue and expenses for the period, may have little or no relation to the cash generated for the period.

To illustrate this point, let us take the example of a business making a sale (generating revenue). This may well lead to an increase in wealth that will be reflected in the income statement. However, if the sale is made on credit, no cash changes hands – at least not at the time of sale. Instead, the increase in wealth is reflected in another asset: an increase in trade receivables. Furthermore, if an item of inventories is the subject of the sale, wealth is lost to the business through the reduction in inventories. This means that an expense is incurred in making the sale, which will also be shown in the income statement. Once again, however, no cash changes hands at the time of sale. For such reasons, the profit and the cash generated for a period will rarely go hand in hand.

Activity 6.1 should help to underline how profit and cash for a period may be affected differently by particular transactions or events.

Activity 6.1

The following is a list of business/accounting events. In each case, state the immediate effect (increase, decrease or none) on both profit and cash:

	Effect on profit	on cash
1 Repayment of borrowings	_____	_____
2 Making a profitable sale on credit	_____	_____
3 Buying a current asset on credit	_____	_____
4 Receiving cash from a credit customer (trade receivable)	_____	_____
5 Depreciating a non-current asset	_____	_____
6 Buying some inventories for cash	_____	_____
7 Making a share issue for cash	_____	_____

You should have come up with the following:

	Effect on profit	on cash
1 Repayment of borrowings	none	decrease
2 Making a profitable sale on credit	increase	none
3 Buying a non-current asset on credit	none	none
4 Receiving cash from a credit customer (trade receivable)	none	increase
5 Depreciating a non-current asset	decrease	none
6 Buying some inventories for cash	none	decrease
7 Making a share issue for cash	none	increase

The reasons for these answers are as follows:

1 Repaying borrowings requires that cash be paid to the lender. This means that two figures in the statement of financial position will be affected, but none in the income statement.
2 Making a profitable sale on credit will increase the sales revenue and profit figures. No cash will change hands at this point, however.
3 Buying a non-current asset on credit affects neither the cash balance nor the profit figure.
4 Receiving cash from a credit customer increases the cash balance and reduces the credit customer's balance. Both of these figures are on the statement of financial position. The income statement is unaffected.
5 Depreciating a non-current asset means that an expense is recognised. This causes a decrease in profit. No cash is paid or received.
6 Buying some inventories for cash means that the value of the inventories will increase and the cash balance will decrease by a similar amount. Profit is not affected.
7 Making a share issue for cash increases the shareholders' equity and increases the cash balance; profit is unaffected.

It is clear from the above that if we are to gain insights about cash movements over time, the income statement is not the place to look. Instead we need a separate financial statement. This fact has become widely recognised in recent years and in 1991 a UK financial reporting standard, FRS 1, emerged that required all but the smallest companies to produce and publish a statement of cash flows. This standard has been superseded for listed companies from 2005 by the international standard IAS 7. The two standards have broadly similar requirements. This chapter follows the provisions of IAS 7.

WHY IS CASH SO IMPORTANT?

It is worth asking why cash is so important. In one sense, it is just another asset that the business needs to enable it to function. Hence, it is no different from inventories or non-current assets.

The importance of cash lies in the fact that people will only normally accept cash in settlement of their claims. If a business wants to employ people, it must pay them in cash. If it wants to buy a new non-current asset, it must normally pay the seller in cash (perhaps after a short period of credit). When businesses fail, it is the lack of cash to pay amounts owed that really pushes them under. Cash generation is vital for businesses to survive and to be able to take advantage of commercial opportunities. These are the things that make cash the pre-eminent business asset.

During an economic downturn, the ability to generate cash takes on even greater importance. Banks become more cautious in their lending and businesses with weak cash flows often find it difficult to obtain finance. **Real World 6.1** describes how the recent financial crisis has led banks in China to place greater emphasis on cash flows when considering loan applications.

Cash flow is in top three places

'The banks are tightening the screws,' says K. B. Chan, chairman of Surface Mount Technology, which supplies consumer electronics companies. 'A lot of companies are strapped for cash.'

Stanley Wong, business development director at Man Yue Electronics, the world's fifth largest maker of aluminium capacitors, says: 'Banks don't even trust each other. They are being a lot more careful.' Mr Wong says that companies such as his, with strong cash flows, will still get working capital and other loans but bankers who used to lend to Man Yue and other manufacturers sight unseen are now tramping out to their factories for a closer look.

'The banks only look at cash flow – number one is cash flow, number two is cash flow and number three is cash flow,' says Mr Chan. 'Profit is only an accounting statement.'

Source: 'Rations cut for army of buyers', *Financial Times*, 20 October 2008.
© The Financial Times Limited 2012. All rights reserved.

Real World 6.2 is taken from a column written by John Timpson, which appeared in the *Daily Telegraph*. He is the chief executive of the successful high street shoe-repairing and key-cutting business that bears his name. In the column he highlights the importance of cash reporting in managing the business.

Cash is key

I look at our cash balance every day (not Saturdays and Sundays). It is the best way to test the financial temperature of our business. The trick is to compare with the same day last year, thus showing cash flow for the past 12 months.

It is not a perfect system (never forget that your finance department may secretly massage the cash by paying suppliers sooner or later than you anticipate) but a glance at the daily cash is more transparent than management accounts that are full of provisions and only appear once a month.

Finance and IT take a delight in producing a deluge of data. But being in possession of too many statistics is counterproductive. This daily cash report helps to clear the clutter created by computers – it's a simple report that helps you pose the right questions.

Why have things suddenly got worse? Are we in danger of breaking our bank borrowing limit? Why does the cash flow look so much better than in the management accounts? This cash report can also give you an early warning of changing financial circumstances.

It came to my rescue in 2004 when, through a major acquisition, the business doubled in size overnight and was going through a great deal of change. Our financial control suffered but I didn't realise how bad things were until I was waiting to board a plane to go on a Caribbean holiday. A quick look at my Blackberry (when my wife wasn't looking) showed an unexpected £500,000 deterioration in our overdraft. It wasn't a great start to the holiday and my wife was upset when I spent the first day on the telephone. However we were able to tackle the problem six weeks before it would have been revealed in the management accounts.

Source: 'The management column', John Timpson, *Daily Telegraph Business*, 14 June 2010.

THE MAIN FEATURES OF THE STATEMENT OF CASH FLOWS

The statement of cash flows summarises the inflows and outflows of cash (and cash equivalents) for a business over a period. To aid user understanding, these cash flows are divided into categories (for example, those relating to investments in non-current assets). Cash inflows and outflows falling within each category are added together to provide a total for that category. These totals are shown on the statement of cash flows and, when added together, reveal the net increase or decrease in cash (and cash equivalents) over the period.

When describing in detail how this statement is prepared and presented, as mentioned earlier, we shall follow the requirements of international accounting standard IAS 7 *Statement of Cash Flows*.

A DEFINITION OF CASH AND CASH EQUIVALENTS

IAS 7 defines cash as notes and coins in hand and deposits in banks and similar institutions that are accessible to the business on demand. Cash equivalents are short-term, highly liquid investments that are readily convertible to known amounts of cash and which are subject to an insignificant risk of changes of value. Figure 6.1 sets out this definition of cash equivalents in the form of a decision chart.

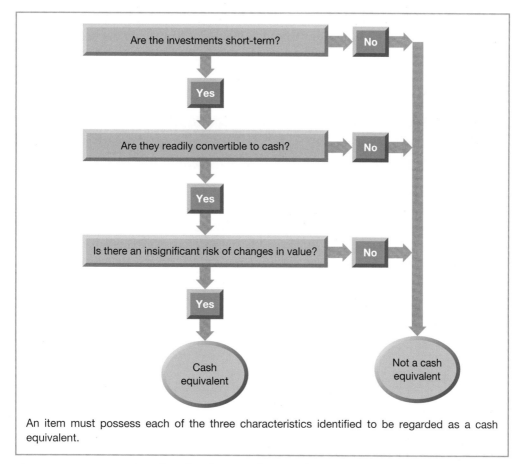

An item must possess each of the three characteristics identified to be regarded as a cash equivalent.

Figure 6.1 Decision chart for identifying cash equivalents

Activity 6.2 should clarify the types of items that fall within the definition of 'cash equivalents'.

Activity 6.2

At the end of its reporting period, Zeneb plc's statement of financial position included the following items:

1 A bank deposit account where one month's notice of withdrawal is required.
2 Ordinary shares in Jones plc (a Stock Exchange listed business).
3 A high-interest bank deposit account that requires six months' notice of withdrawal.
4 An overdraft on the business's bank current account.

Which (if any) of these four items would be included in the figure for cash and cash equivalents?

Your response should have been as follows:

1 A cash equivalent. It is readily withdrawable.
2 Not a cash equivalent. It can be converted into cash because it is Stock Exchange listed. There is, however, a significant risk that the amount expected (hoped for!) when the shares are sold may not actually be forthcoming.
3 Not a cash equivalent because it is not readily convertible into liquid cash.
4 This is cash itself, though a negative amount of it. The only exception to this classification would be where the business is financed in the longer term by an overdraft, when it would be part of the financing of the business, rather than negative cash.

THE RELATIONSHIP BETWEEN THE MAIN FINANCIAL STATEMENTS

The statement of cash flows is now accepted, along with the income statement and the statement of financial position, as a major financial statement. The relationship between the three statements is shown in Figure 6.2. The statement of financial position shows the various assets (including cash) and claims (including the shareholders' equity) of the business *at a particular point in time*. The statement of cash flows and the income statement explain the *changes over a period* to two of the items in the statement of financial position. The statement of cash flows explains the changes to cash. The income statement explains changes to equity arising from trading operations.

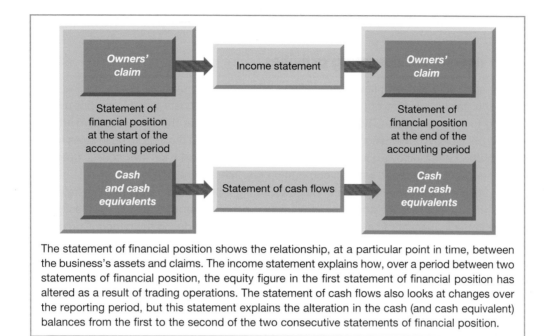

The statement of financial position shows the relationship, at a particular point in time, between the business's assets and claims. The income statement explains how, over a period between two statements of financial position, the equity figure in the first statement of financial position has altered as a result of trading operations. The statement of cash flows also looks at changes over the reporting period, but this statement explains the alteration in the cash (and cash equivalent) balances from the first to the second of the two consecutive statements of financial position.

Figure 6.2 The relationship between the statement of financial position, the income statement and the statement of cash flows

THE LAYOUT OF THE STATEMENT OF CASH FLOWS

As mentioned earlier, the cash flows of a business are divided into categories. The various categories and the way in which they are presented in the statement of cash flows are shown in Figure 6.3.

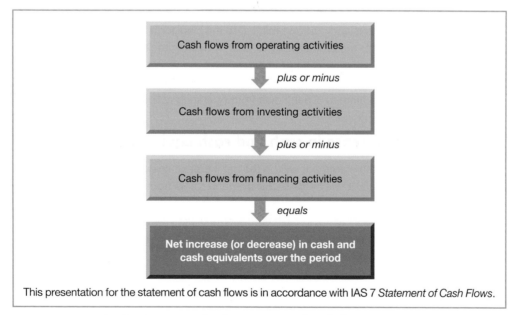

This presentation for the statement of cash flows is in accordance with IAS 7 *Statement of Cash Flows*.

Figure 6.3 Standard presentation for the statement of cash flows

Let us now consider each of the categories that has been identified.

Cash flows from operating activities

These represent the cash inflows and outflows arising from normal day-to-day trading activities, after taking account of the tax paid and the financing costs (equity and borrowings) relating to these activities. The cash inflows for the period are the amounts received from trade receivables (credit customers settling their accounts) and those from cash sales for the period. The cash outflows for the period are the amounts paid for inventories, operating expenses (such as rent and wages), corporation tax, interest and dividends.

Note that it is the cash inflows and outflows during a period that appear in the statement of cash flows, not revenue and expenses for that period. Similarly, tax and dividends that appear in the statement of cash flows are those actually paid during the period. Companies normally pay tax on their annual profits in four equal instalments. Two of these are paid during the year concerned and the other two are paid during the following year. Thus, by the end of each year, half of the tax will have been paid and the remaining half will still be outstanding, to be paid during the following year. This means that the tax payment during a year is normally equal to half of the previous year's tax charge and half of that of the current year.

Cash flows from investing activities

These include cash outflows to acquire non-current assets and cash inflows from the disposal of non-current assets. In addition to the normal items, such as buildings and machinery, non-current assets might include financial investments made in loans or shares in another company.

These cash flows also include cash inflows *arising from* financial investments (loans and shares). This means interest on loans made by the business and dividends from shares in other companies.

Cash flows from financing activities

These represent cash inflows and outflows relating to the long-term financing of the business. This part of the statement, therefore, includes cash movements relating to the raising and redemption of long-term borrowings and to shares.

Under IAS 7, it is permissible to include dividend payments made by the business here, as an alternative to including them in 'Cash flows from operating activities' (above).

Net increase or decrease in cash and cash equivalents

The final total shown on the statement will be the net increase or decrease in cash and cash equivalents over the period. It will be deduced from the totals from each of the three categories mentioned above.

The effect on a business's cash and cash equivalents of activities relating to each category is shown in Figure 6.4. The arrows show the *normal* direction of cash flow for the typical, profitable, business in a typical reporting period.

Various activities of the business each have their own effect on the total of the cash and cash equivalents, either positive (increasing the total) or negative (reducing it). The net increase or decrease in the cash and cash equivalents over a period will be the sum of these individual effects, taking account of the direction (cash in or cash out) of each activity.

Note that the direction of the arrow shows the *normal* direction of the cash flow in respect of each activity. In certain circumstances, each of these arrows could be reversed in direction.

Figure 6.4 Diagrammatical representation of the statement of cash flows

The normal direction of cash flows

Normally, 'operating activities' provide positive cash flows and therefore, increase the business's cash resources. For most UK businesses, cash generated from day-to-day trading, even after deducting tax, interest and dividends, is by far the most important source of new finance.

Activity 6.3

Last year's statement of cash flows for Angus plc showed a negative cash flow from operating activities. What could be the reason for this and should the business's management be alarmed by it? (*Hint*: We think that there are two broad possible reasons for a negative cash flow.)

The two possible reasons are:

1 The business is unprofitable. This leads to more cash being paid out to employees, to suppliers of goods and services, for interest and so on than is received from trade receivables in respect of sales. This would be alarming since a major expense for most businesses is depreciation. Depreciation does not lead to a cash flow. It is not, therefore, considered in 'net cash inflows from operating activities'. This means that a negative operating cash flow might well indicate a much larger trading loss – in other words, a significant loss of the business's wealth.
2 The business is expanding its activities (level of sales revenue). This may involve spending a lot of cash relative to the amount of cash coming in from sales. Cash will be spent on acquiring more assets (non-current and current) to accommodate the increased demand. For example, a business may need to have inventories in place before additional sales can be made. Similarly, staff will have to be employed and paid. Even when additional sales are made, they would normally be made on credit, with the cash inflow lagging behind the sales. This means that there would be no immediate cash benefit.

Expansion often causes cash flow strains for new businesses, which may be expanding inventories and other assets from zero. They would also need to employ and pay staff. To add to this problem, increased profitability may encourage a feeling of optimism, leading to a lack of attention being paid to the cash flows.

Investing activities typically cause net negative cash flows. This is because many non-current assets either wear out or become obsolete and need to be replaced. Businesses may also expand their asset base. Non-current assets may, of course, be sold, which would give rise to positive cash flows. In net terms, however, the cash flows are normally negative with cash spent on new assets outweighing that received from the sale of old ones.

Financing can go in either direction, depending on the financing strategy at the time. Since businesses seek to expand, there is a general tendency for this area to lead to cash coming into the business rather than leaving it.

Real World 6.3 shows the summarised statement of cash flows of Tesco plc, the UK-based supermarket company.

Real World 6.3

Cashing in

Like many larger companies, Tesco produces summary versions of its financial statements for users who do not want all of the detail. The summary statement of cash flows for the business for the year ended 26 February 2011 shows the cash flows of the business under each of the headings described above.

Summary group statement of cash flows
52 weeks ended 26 February 2011

	£m
Cash generated from operations	5,366
Interest paid	(614)
Corporation tax paid	(760)
Net cash from operating activities	3,992
Net cash used in investing activities	(1,859)
Cash flows from financing activities	
Dividends paid to equity owners	(1,081)
Other net cash flows from financing activities	(1,955)
Net cash from financing activities	(3,036)
Net decrease in cash and cash equivalents	(903)

Source: Tesco Annual Review 2011, p. 35, www.tescocorporate.com.

As we shall see shortly, more detailed information under each of the main headings is provided in the statement of cash flows presented to shareholders and other users.

Deducing net cash flows from operating activities

As we have seen, the first category within the statement of cash flows is the 'cash flows from operating activities'. There are two approaches that can be taken to deriving this figure: the direct method and the indirect method.

The direct method

The **direct method** involves an analysis of the cash records of the business for the period, picking out all payments and receipts relating to operating activities. These are summarised to give the total figures for inclusion in the statement of cash flows. Done on a computer, this is a simple matter, but hardly any businesses adopt the direct method.

The indirect method

The **indirect method** is much the more popular method. It relies on the fact that, sooner or later, sales revenue gives rise to cash inflows and expenses give rise to outflows. This means that the figure for profit for the year will be linked to the net cash flows from operating activities. Since businesses have to produce an income statement in any case, information from it can be used as a starting point to deduce the cash flows from operating activities.

Of course, profit for the period will not normally equal the net cash inflows from operating activities. When sales are made on credit, the cash receipt occurs some time after the sale. This means that sales revenues made towards the end of a reporting period will be included in that reporting period's income statement. However, most of the cash from those sales will flow into the business in the following period. That cash should, therefore, be included in the statement of cash flows of the following period. Fortunately it is easy to deduce the cash inflows from sales if we have the relevant income statement and statements of financial position, as we shall see in Activity 6.4.

Activity 6.4

How can we deduce the cash inflows from sales using the income statement and statement of financial position for the business?

The statement of financial position will tell us how much was owed in respect of credit sales at the beginning and end of the reporting period (trade receivables). The income statement tells us the sales revenue figure. If we adjust the sales revenue figure by the increase or decrease in trade receivables over the period, we deduce the cash from sales for the period.

Example 6.1

The sales revenue figure for a business for the year was £34 million. The trade receivables totalled £4 million at the beginning of the year, but had increased to £5 million by the end of the year.

Basically, the trade receivables figure is dictated by sales revenue and cash receipts. It is increased when a sale is made and decreased when cash is received from a credit customer. If, over the year, the sales revenue and the cash receipts had been equal, the beginning-of-year and end-of-year trade receivables figures would have been equal. Since the trade receivables figure increased, it must mean that less cash was received than sales revenues were made. In fact, the cash receipts from sales must have been £33 million (that is, 34 − (5 − 4)).

Put slightly differently, we can say that as a result of sales, assets of £34 million flowed into the business. If £1 million of this went to increasing the asset of trade receivables, this leaves only £33 million that went to increase cash.

The same general point is true in respect of nearly all of the other items that are taken into account in deducing the operating profit figure. The main exception is depreciation. The depreciation expense for a reporting period is not necessarily associated with any movement in cash during that same period.

All of this means that we can take the profit before taxation (that is, the profit after interest but before taxation) for the year, add back the depreciation and interest expense charged in arriving at that profit, and adjust this total by movements in inventories, trade (and other) receivables and payables. If we then go on to deduct payments made during the reporting period for taxation, interest on borrowings and dividends, we have the net cash from operating activities.

Example 6.2

The relevant information from the financial statements of Dido plc for last year is as follows:

	£m
Profit before taxation (after interest)	122
Depreciation charged in arriving at profit before taxation	34
Interest expense	6
At the beginning of the year:	
Inventories	15
Trade receivables	24
Trade payables	18
At the end of the year:	
Inventories	17
Trade receivables	21
Trade payables	19

The following further information is available about payments during last year:

	£m
Taxation paid	32
Interest paid	5
Dividends paid	9

The cash flow from operating activities is derived as follows:

	£m
Profit before taxation (after interest)	122
Depreciation	34
Interest expense	6
Increase in inventories (17 − 15)	(2)
Decrease in trade receivables (21 − 24)	3
Increase in trade payables (19 − 18)	1
Cash generated from operations	164
Interest paid	(5)
Taxation paid	(32)
Dividends paid	(9)
Net cash from operating activities	118

As we can see, the net increase in **working capital***(that is, current assets less current liabilities) as a result of trading was £162 million (that is, 122 + 34 + 6). Of this, £2 million went into increased inventories. More cash was received from trade receivables than sales revenue was made. Similarly, less cash was paid to trade payables than the amount spent on purchases of goods and services on credit. Both of these had a favourable effect on cash. Over the year, therefore, cash increased by £164 million. When account was taken of the payments for interest, tax and dividends, the net cash from operating activities was £118 million (inflow).

Note that we needed to adjust the profit before taxation (after interest) by the depreciation and interest expenses to derive the profit before depreciation, interest and taxation.

* Working capital is a term widely used in accounting and finance, not just in the context of the statement of cash flows. We shall encounter it several times in later chapters.

Activity 6.5

In deriving the cash generated from operations, we add the depreciation expense for the period to the profit before taxation. Does this mean that depreciation is a source of cash?

No, it does not mean that depreciation is a source of cash. The periodic depreciation expense is irrelevant to cash flow. Since the profit before taxation is derived *after* deducting the depreciation expense for the period, we need to eliminate the impact of depreciation by adding it back to the profit figure. This will give us the profit before tax *and before* depreciation, which is what we need.

We should be clear why we add back an amount for interest at the start of the derivation of cash flow from operating activities only to deduct an amount for interest further down. The reason is that the first is the interest expense for the reporting period, whereas the second is the amount of cash paid out for interest during that period. These may well be different amounts, as was the case in Example 6.2.

The indirect method of deducing the net cash flow from operating activities is summarised in Figure 6.5.

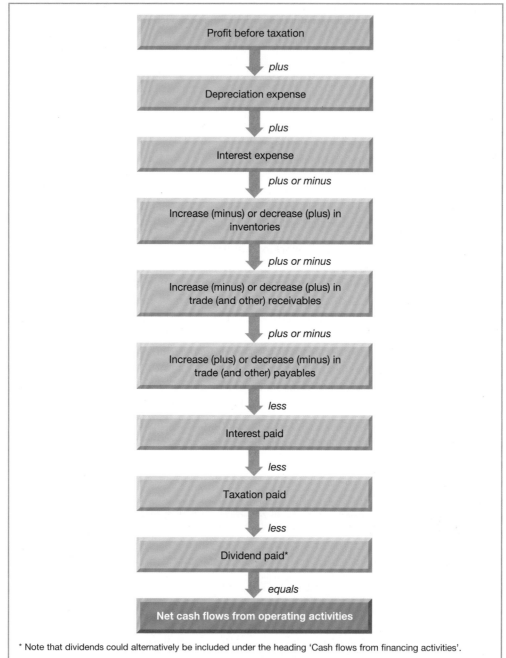

* Note that dividends could alternatively be included under the heading 'Cash flows from financing activities'.

Determining the net cash flows from operating activities first involves adding back the depreciation and the interest expense to the profit before taxation. Next, adjustment is made for increases or decreases in inventories, receivables and payables. Lastly, cash paid for interest, taxation and dividends is deducted.

Figure 6.5 The indirect method of deducing the net cash flows from operating activities

The relevant information from the financial statements of Pluto plc for last year is as follows:

	£m
Profit before taxation (after interest)	165
Depreciation charged in arriving at operating profit	41
Interest expense	21
At the beginning of the year:	
Inventories	22
Trade receivables	18
Trade payables	15
At the end of the year:	
Inventories	23
Trade receivables	21
Trade payables	17

The following further information is available about payments during last year:

	£m
Taxation paid	49
Interest paid	25
Dividends paid	28

What figure should appear in the statement of cash flows for 'Cash flows from operating activities'?

Net cash inflows from operating activities:

	£m
Profit before taxation (after interest)	165
Depreciation	41
Interest expense	21
Increase in inventories (23 – 22)	(1)
Increase in trade receivables (21 – 18)	(3)
Increase in trade payables (17 – 15)	2
Cash generated from operations	225
Interest paid	(25)
Taxation paid	(49)
Dividends paid	(28)
Net cash from operating activities	123

Deducing the other areas of the statement of cash flows

We can now go on to take a look at the preparation of a complete statement of cash flows through Example 6.3.

Example 6.3

Torbryan plc's income statement for the year ended 31 December 2012 and statements of financial position as at 31 December 2011 and 2012 are as follows:

Income statement for the year ended 31 December 2012

	£m
Revenue	576
Cost of sales	(307)
Gross profit	269
Distribution expenses	(65)
Administrative expenses	(26)
	178
Other operating income	21
Operating profit	199
Interest receivable	17
	216
Interest payable	(23)
Profit before taxation	193
Taxation	(46)
Profit for the year	147

Statements of financial position as at 31 December 2011 and 2012

	2011 £m	2012 £m
ASSETS		
Non-current assets		
Property, plant and equipment		
Land and buildings	241	241
Plant and machinery	309	325
	550	566
Current assets		
Inventories	44	41
Trade receivables	121	139
	165	180
Total assets	715	746
EQUITY AND LIABILITIES		
Equity		
Called-up ordinary share capital	150	200
Share premium account	–	40
Retained earnings	26	123
	176	363
Non-current liabilities		
Borrowings – loan notes	400	250
Current liabilities		
Borrowings (all bank overdraft)	68	56
Trade payables	55	54
Taxation	16	23
	139	133
Total equity and liabilities	715	746

During 2012, the business spent £95 million on additional plant and machinery. There were no other acquisitions or disposals of non-current assets. A dividend of £50 million was paid on ordinary shares during the year. The interest receivable revenue and the interest payable expense for the year were equal to the cash inflow and outflow respectively. £150,000 of loan notes were redeemed at their face (par) value.

The statement of cash flows would be as follows:

Torbryan plc
Statement of cash flows for the year ended 31 December 2012

	£m
Cash flows from operating activities	
Profit before taxation (after interest) (see Note 1 below)	193
Adjustments for:	
Depreciation (Note 2)	79
Interest receivable (Note 3)	(17)
Interest payable (Note 4)	23
Increase in trade receivables (139 – 121)	(18)
Decrease in trade payables (55 – 54)	(1)
Decrease in inventories (44 – 41)	3
Cash generated from operations	262
Interest paid	(23)
Taxation paid (Note 5)	(39)
Dividend paid	(50)
Net cash from operating activities	150
Cash flows from investing activities	
Payments to acquire tangible non-current assets	(95)
Interest received (Note 3)	17
Net cash used in investing activities	(78)
Cash flows from financing activities	
Repayments of loan notes	(150)
Issue of ordinary shares (Note 6)	90
Net cash used in financing activities	(60)
Net increase in cash and cash equivalents	12
Cash and cash equivalents at 1 January 2012 (Note 7)	(68)
Cash and cash equivalents at 31 December 2012	(56)

To see how this relates to the cash of the business at the beginning and end of the year it can be useful to provide a reconciliation as follows:

Analysis of cash and cash equivalents during the year ended 31 December 2012

	£m
Overdraft balance at 1 January 2012	(68)
Net cash inflow	12
Overdraft balance at 31 December 2012	(56)

Notes:
1 This is simply taken from the income statement for the year.
2 Since there were no disposals, the depreciation charges must be the difference between the start and end of the year's plant and machinery (non-current assets) values, adjusted by the cost of any additions.

	£m
Carrying amount at 1 January 2012	309
Additions	95
	404
Depreciation (balancing figure)	(79)
Carrying amount at 31 December 2012	325

3 Interest receivable must be deducted to work towards what the profit would have been before it was added in the income statement, because it is not part of operations but of investing activities. The cash inflow from this source appears under the 'Cash flows from investing activities' heading.

4 The interest payable expense must be taken out, by adding it back to the profit figure. We subsequently deduct the cash paid for interest payable during the year. In this case the two figures are identical.

5 Taxation is paid by companies 50 per cent during their reporting year and 50 per cent in the following year. As a result the 2012 payment would have been half the tax on the 2011 profit (that is, the figure that would have appeared in the current liabilities at the end of 2011), plus half of the 2012 taxation charge (that is, $16 + (\frac{1}{2} \times 46) = 39$). Probably the easiest way to deduce the amount paid during the year to 31 December 2012 is by following this approach:

	£m
Taxation owed at start of the year (from the statement of financial position as at 31 December 2011)	16
Taxation charge for the year (from the income statement)	46
	62
Taxation owed at the end of the year (from the statement of financial position as at 31 December 2012)	(23)
Taxation paid during the year	39

This follows the logic that if we start with what the business owed at the beginning of the year, add what was owed as a result of the current year's taxation charge and then deduct what was owed at the end, the resulting figure must be what was paid during the year.

6 The share issue raised £90 million, of which £50 million went into the share capital total on the statement of financial position and £40 million into share premium.

7 There were no 'cash equivalents', just cash (though negative).

WHAT DOES THE STATEMENT OF CASH FLOWS TELL US?

The statement of cash flows tells us how the business has generated cash during the period and where that cash has gone. This is potentially very useful information. Tracking the sources and uses of cash over several years could show financing trends that a reader of the statements could use to help to make judgements about the likely future behaviour of the business.

Looking specifically at the statement of cash flows for Torbryan plc in Example 6.3, we can see the following:

■ Net cash flow from operations seems strong, much larger than the profit for the year, after taking account of the dividend paid. This might be expected as depreciation is deducted in arriving at profit. Working capital has absorbed some cash, which may indicate an expansion of activity (sales revenue) over the year. As we have only one year's income statement, however, we cannot tell whether this has occurred.

■ There were net outflows of cash for investing activities, but this would not be unusual. Many types of non-current assets have limited lives and need to be replaced. Expenditure during the year was not out of line with the depreciation expense for the year, which is to be expected for a business with a regular replacement programme for its non-current assets.

■ There was a major outflow of cash to redeem borrowings, which was partly offset by the proceeds of a share issue. This may well represent a change of financing strategy. These financing changes, together with the retained profit for the year, have led to a significant shift in the equity/borrowings balance.

Real World 6.4 looks at the statement of cash flows of an emerging business, LiDCO Group plc, which is experiencing negative cash flows as it seeks to establish a profitable market for its products.

Real World 6.4

Not losing heart

LiDCO Group plc has its shares listed on the Alternative Investment Market (AIM). AIM is a junior market of the London Stock Exchange that specialises in the shares of smaller, up-and-coming businesses.

LiDCO makes highly sophisticated equipment for monitoring the hearts of cardiac patients, typically in hospitals and clinics. The business was started by doctors and scientists. It has spent £6.8 million over ten years developing its products, obtaining registration for their use from both the UK and US authorities and creating manufacturing facilities.

LiDCO's statement of cash flows for the year to 31 January 2011 was:

	£000
Net cash inflow from operating activities	115
Cash flows from investing activities	
Purchase of property, plant and equipment	(127)
Purchase of intangible assets	(429)
Interest received	8
Net cash used in investing activities	(548)
Cash flows from financing activities	
Repayment of finance lease	(10)
Issue of ordinary share capital	1
Net cash (outflow)/inflow from financing activities	(9)
Net (decrease)/increase in cash and cash equivalents	(442)

[Note that this was adapted from the statement that appeared in the business's annual report. Some more detail was supplied in the way of notes to the accounts.]

To put these figures into context, there was a loss before taxation for the year of £490,000 and the sales revenue for the year was £6.24 million. This means that the net cash inflow from operating activities was equal to 2 per cent of the revenue figure. This was an improvement, since there had been an outflow of 8 per cent in 2010, 27 per cent in 2009, 30 per cent in 2008, 40 per cent in 2007 and over 50 per cent in 2006.

2011 was the first year that the business had generated a positive net cash inflow from operating activities

Such cash flow profiles are fairly typical of 'high-tech' businesses that have enormous start-up costs to bring their products to the market in sufficient quantities to yield a profit. Of course, not all such businesses achieve this, but LiDCO seems to be turning into a profitable business.

Source: LiDCO Group plc Annual Report 2011 and AIM company profile, www.londonstockexchange.com.

PROBLEMS WITH IAS 7

IAS 7 *Statement of Cash Flows* does not enjoy universal acclaim. Its critics argue that the standard is too permissive in the description and classification of important items.

Some believe that the standard would inspire greater confidence among users if it insisted that only the direct method be used to calculate cash flows from operating activities. Supporters of the direct method argue that, being cash-based, it provides greater clarity by setting out operating cash receipts and payments. No accrual-based adjustments are made, and this makes it less susceptible to manipulation than the indirect approach, which has been described as 'a gift to dodgy companies' (see the reference at the end of the chapter). In its defence, however, it should be said that the indirect approach may help to shed light on the quality of reported profits by reconciling profit with the net cash from operating activities for a period. A business must demonstrate an ability to convert profits into cash and so revealing the link between profits and cash is important.

IAS 7 is also criticised for failing to require cash flows to be reconciled with movements in net debt, which may be defined as borrowings less any cash and cash equivalents. This reconciliation, so it is argued, would help users to gain a better understanding of movements in net debt and the management of cash flows. Net debt is often seen as a useful indicator of business solvency and so linking movements in this figure to the statement of cash flows may be important. Although not required to do so, many listed UK businesses provide this reconciliation as additional information. This is, at least partly, for historical reasons: the standard that preceded IAS 7 required this information.

Example 6.4 illustrates how this reconciliation may be carried out.

Example 6.4

Based on the information set out in the financial statements of Torbryan for the financial years ended 31 December 2011 and 2012 (see Example 6.3), the following reconciliation of net cash flow to movement in net debt for the year to 31 December 2012 can be carried out:

Reconciliation of net cash flow to movement in net debt for the year to 31 December 2012

	£m
Net increase in cash and cash equivalents during the year	12
Repayment of loan notes	150
Decrease in net debt during the year	162
Net debt at 1 January 2012 (400 + 68*)	468
Net debt at 31 December 2012 (250 + 56)	(306)
Decrease in net debt during the year	162

* We saw earlier that a bank overdraft is normally viewed as negative cash. An overdraft is added to other borrowings to derive the net debt, whereas a positive cash balance would be deducted.

We can see that the net debt has been reduced largely through the repayment of loan notes but partly through a reduction in the overdraft.

Touchstone plc's income statements for the years ended 31 December 2011 and 2012 and statements of financial position as at 31 December 2011 and 2012 are as follows:

Income statements for the years ended 31 December 2011 and 2012

	2011 £m	2012 £m
Revenue	173	207
Cost of sales	(96)	(101)
Gross profit	77	106
Distribution expenses	(18)	(20)
Administrative expenses	(24)	(26)
Other operating income	3	4
Operating profit	38	64
Interest payable	(2)	(4)
Profit before taxation	36	60
Taxation	(8)	(16)
Profit for the year	28	44

Statements of financial position as at 31 December 2011 and 2012

	2011 £m	2012 £m
ASSETS		
Non-current assets		
Property, plant and equipment		
Land and buildings	94	110
Plant and machinery	53	62
	147	172
Current assets		
Inventories	25	24
Treasury bills (short-term investments)	–	15
Trade receivables	16	26
Cash at bank and in hand	4	4
	45	69
Total assets	192	241
EQUITY AND LIABILITIES		
Equity		
Called-up ordinary share capital	100	100
Retained earnings	30	56
	130	156
Non-current liabilities		
Borrowings – loan notes (10%)	20	40
Current liabilities		
Trade payables	38	37
Taxation	4	8
	42	45
Total equity and liabilities	192	241

Included in 'cost of sales', 'distribution expenses' and 'administrative expenses', depreciation was as follows:

	2011 £m	2012 £m
Land and buildings	5	6
Plant and machinery	6	10

There were no non-current asset disposals in either year.

The interest payable expense equalled the cash payment made during each of the years.

The business paid dividends on ordinary shares of £14 million during 2011 and £18 million during 2012.

The Treasury bills represent a short-term investment of funds that will be used shortly in operations. There is insignificant risk that this investment will lose value.

Required:
Prepare a statement of cash flows for the business for 2012.

A solution to this question can be found in Appendix C.

SUMMARY

The main points of this chapter may be summarised as follows:

The need for a statement of cash flows

- Cash is important because no business can operate without it.

- The statement of cash flows is specifically designed to reveal movements in cash over a period.

- Cash movements cannot be readily detected from the income statement, which focuses on revenue and expenses rather than on cash inflows and outflows.

- Profit (or loss) and cash generated for the period are rarely equal.

- The statement of cash flows is a major financial statement, along with the income statement and the statement of financial position.

Preparing the statement of cash flows

- The cash flow statement has three major categories of cash flows: cash flows from operating activities, cash flows from investing activities and cash flows from financing activities.

- The total of the cash movements under these three categories will provide the net increase or decrease in cash and cash equivalents for the period.

- A reconciliation can be undertaken to check that the opening balance of cash and cash equivalents plus the net increase (or decrease) for the period equals the closing balance.

Calculating the cash generated from operations

- The net cash flows from operating activities can be derived by either the direct method or the indirect method.

- The direct method is based on an analysis of the cash records for the period, whereas the indirect method uses information contained within the income statement and statements of financial position.

- The indirect method takes the operating profit for the period, adds back any depreciation charge and then adjusts for changes in inventories, receivables and payables during the period.

Interpreting the statement of cash flows

- The statement of cash flows shows the main sources and uses of cash.

- Tracking the cash movements over several periods may reveal financing and investing patterns and may help predict future management action.

Problems with IAS 7

- IAS 7 has been criticised for being too permissive in the description and classification of important items and for allowing businesses to adopt the indirect method for determining net cash from operating activities.

- There have also been calls for movements in net debt to be reconciled with cash flows.

MyAccountingLab

Go to www.myaccountinglab.com to check your understanding of the chapter, create a personalised study plan, and maximise your revision time

KEY TERMS

direct method p. 195
indirect method p. 195

working capital p. 197

REFERENCE

1 'Cash flow statements', *Financial Times*, 25 August 2005, FT.com

FURTHER READING

If you would like to explore the topics covered in this chapter in more depth, we recommend the following:

Alexander, D. and Nobes, C., *Financial Accounting: An International Introduction*, 4th edn, Financial Times Prentice Hall, 2010, Chapter 13

Elliott, B. and Elliott, J., *Financial Accounting and Reporting*, 15th edn, Financial Times Prentice Hall, 2011, Chapter 5

International Accounting Standards Board, *2011 International Financial Reporting Standards IFRS* (two-volume set), IASB, 2011

KPMG, *Insights into IFRS*, 8th edn, Sweet and Maxwell, 2011, Section 2.3 (a summary of this book is available free at www.kpmg.com)

Solutions to these questions can be found in Appendix D.

6.1 The typical business outside the service sector has about 50 per cent more of its resources tied up in inventories than in cash, yet there is no call for a 'statement of inventories flows' to be prepared. Why is cash regarded as more important than inventories?

6.2 What is the difference between the direct and indirect methods of deducing cash generated from operations?

6.3 Taking each of the categories of the statement of cash flows in turn, in which direction would you normally expect the cash flow to be? Explain your answer.

(a) Cash flows from operating activities
(b) Cash flows from investing activities
(c) Cash flows from financing activities.

6.4 What causes the profit for the reporting period not to equal the net cash inflow?

Exercises 6.1 and 6.2 are basic level, 6.3 to 6.5 are intermediate level and 6.6 to 6.8 are advanced level. Solutions to the exercises with coloured numbers are given in Appendix E.

If you wish to try more exercises, visit the students' side of the Companion Website and MyAccountingLab.

6.1 How will each of the following events ultimately affect the amount of cash?

(a) An increase in the level of inventories
(b) A rights issue of ordinary shares
(c) A bonus issue of ordinary shares
(d) Writing off part of the value of some inventories
(e) The disposal of a large number of the business's shares by a major shareholder
(f) Depreciating a non-current asset.

6.2 The following information has been taken from the financial statements of Juno plc for last year and the year before last:

	Year before last £m	Last year £m
Operating profit	156	187
Depreciation charged in arriving at operating profit	47	55
Inventories held at end of year	27	31
Trade receivables at end of year	24	23
Trade payables at end of year	15	17

Required:
What is the figure for cash generated from the operations for Juno plc for last year?

6.3 Torrent plc's income statement for the year ended 31 December 2012 and the statements of financial position as at 31 December 2011 and 2012 are as follows:

Income statement for the year ended 31 December 2012

	£m
Revenue	623
Cost of sales	(353)
Gross profit	270
Distribution expenses	(71)
Administrative expenses	(30)
Rental income	27
Operating profit	196
Interest payable	(26)
Profit before taxation	170
Taxation	(36)
Profit for the year	134

Statements of financial position as at 31 December 2011 and 2012

	2011 £m	2012 £m
ASSETS		
Non-current assets		
Property, plant and equipment		
Land and buildings	310	310
Plant and machinery	325	314
	635	624
Current assets		
Inventories	41	35
Trade receivables	139	145
	180	180
Total assets	815	804
EQUITY AND LIABILITIES		
Equity		
Called-up ordinary share capital	200	300
Share premium account	40	–
Revaluation reserve	69	9
Retained earnings	123	197
	432	506
Non-current liabilities		
Borrowings – loan notes	250	150
Current liabilities		
Borrowings (all bank overdraft)	56	89
Trade payables	54	41
Taxation	23	18
	133	148
Total equity and liabilities	815	804

During 2012, the business spent £67 million on additional plant and machinery. There were no other non-current asset acquisitions or disposals.

There was no share issue for cash during the year. The interest payable expense was equal in amount to the cash outflow. A dividend of £60 million was paid.

Required:

Prepare the statement of cash flows for Torrent plc for the year ended 31 December 2012.

6.4 Chen plc's income statements for the years ended 31 December 2011 and 2012 and the statements of financial position as at 31 December 2011 and 2012 are as follows:

Income statements for the years ended 31 December 2011 and 2012

	2011 £m	2012 £m
Revenue	207	153
Cost of sales	(101)	(76)
Gross profit	106	77
Distribution expenses	(22)	(20)
Administrative expenses	(20)	(28)
Operating profit	64	29
Interest payable	(4)	(4)
Profit before taxation	60	25
Taxation	(16)	(6)
Profit for the year	44	19

Statements of financial position as at 31 December 2011 and 2012

	2011 £m	2012 £m
ASSETS		
Non-current assets		
Property, plant and equipment		
Land and buildings	110	130
Plant and machinery	62	56
	172	186
Current assets		
Inventories	24	25
Trade receivables	26	25
Cash at bank and in hand	19	–
	69	50
Total assets	241	236
EQUITY AND LIABILITIES		
Equity		
Called-up ordinary share capital	100	100
Retained earnings	56	57
	156	157
Non-current liabilities		
Borrowings – loan notes (10%)	40	40
Current liabilities		
Borrowings (all bank overdraft)	–	2
Trade payables	37	34
Taxation	8	3
	45	39
Total equity and liabilities	241	236

Included in 'cost of sales', 'distribution expenses' and 'administrative expenses', depreciation was as follows:

	2011 £m	2012 £m
Land and buildings	6	10
Plant and machinery	10	12

There were no non-current asset disposals in either year. The amount of cash paid for interest equalled the expense in each year. Dividends were paid totalling £18 million in each year.

Required:
Prepare a statement of cash flows for the business for 2012.

6.5 The following are the financial statements for Nailsea plc for the years ended 30 June 2011 and 2012:

Income statements for years ended 30 June

	2011 £m	2012 £m
Revenue	1,230	2,280
Operating expenses	(722)	(1,618)
Depreciation	(270)	(320)
Operating profit	238	342
Interest payable	–	(27)
Profit before taxation	238	315
Taxation	(110)	(140)
Profit for the year	128	175

Statements of financial position as at 30 June

	2011 £m	2012 £m
ASSETS		
Non-current assets		
Property, plant and equipment (at carrying amount)		
Land and buildings	1,500	1,900
Plant and machinery	810	740
	2,310	2,640
Current assets		
Inventories	275	450
Trade receivables	100	250
Bank	–	118
	375	818
Total assets	2,685	3,458
EQUITY AND LIABILITIES		
Equity		
Share capital (fully paid £1 shares)	1,400	1,600
Share premium account	200	300
Retained earnings	828	958
	2,428	2,858
Non-current liabilities		
Borrowings – 9% loan notes (repayable 2016)	–	300
Current liabilities		
Borrowings (all bank overdraft)	32	–
Trade payables	170	230
Taxation	55	70
	257	300
Total equity and liabilities	2,685	3,458

There were no disposals of non-current assets in either year. Dividends were paid in 2011 and 2012 of £40 million and £45 million, respectively.

Required:

Prepare a statement of cash flows for Nailsea plc for the year ended 30 June 2012.

6.6 The following financial statements for Blackstone plc are a slightly simplified set of published accounts. Blackstone plc is an engineering business that developed a new range of products in 2008. These products now account for 60 per cent of its sales revenue.

Income statements for the years ended 31 March

	Notes	2011 £m	2012 £m
Revenue		7,003	11,205
Cost of sales		(3,748)	(5,809)
Gross profit		3,255	5,396
Operating expenses		(2,205)	(3,087)
Operating profit		1,050	2,309
Interest payable	1	(216)	(456)
Profit before taxation		834	1,853
Taxation		(210)	(390)
Profit for the year		624	1,463

Statements of financial position as at 31 March

	Notes	2011 £m	2012 £m
ASSETS			
Non-current assets			
Property, plant and equipment	2	4,300	7,535
Intangible assets	3	–	700
		4,300	8,235
Current assets			
Inventories		1,209	2,410
Trade receivables		641	1,173
Cash at bank		123	–
		1,973	3,583
Total assets		6,273	11,818
EQUITY AND LIABILITIES			
Equity			
Share capital		1,800	1,800
Share premium		600	600
Capital reserves		352	352
Retained earnings		685	1,748
		3,437	4,500
Non-current liabilities			
Borrowings – bank loan (repayable 2015)		1,800	3,800
Current liabilities			
Trade payables		931	1,507
Taxation		105	195
Borrowings (all bank overdraft)		–	1,816
		1,036	3,518
Total equity and liabilities		6,273	11,818

Notes:

1 The expense and the cash outflow for interest payable are equal for each year.
2 The movements in property, plant and equipment during the year are:

	Land and buildings £m	Plant and machinery £m	Fixtures and fittings £m	Total £m
Cost				
At 1 April 2011	4,500	3,850	2,120	10,470
Additions	–	2,970	1,608	4,578
Disposals	–	(365)	(216)	(581)
At 31 March 2012	4,500	6,455	3,512	14,467
Depreciation				
At 1 April 2011	1,275	3,080	1,815	6,170
Charge for year	225	745	281	1,251
Disposals	–	(305)	(184)	(489)
At 31 March 2012	1,500	3,520	1,912	6,932
Carrying amount				
At 31 March 2012	3,000	2,935	1,600	7,535

3 Intangible assets represent the amounts paid for the goodwill of another engineering business acquired during the year.
4 Proceeds from the sale of non-current assets in the year ended 31 March 2012 amounted to £54 million.
5 Dividends were paid on ordinary shares of £300 million in 2011 and £400 million in 2012.

Required:

Prepare a statement of cash flows for Blackstone plc for the year ended 31 March 2012. (*Hint*: A loss (deficit) on disposal of non-current assets is simply an additional amount of depreciation and should be dealt with as such in preparing the statement of cash flows.)

6.7 Simplified financial statements for York plc are:

Income statement for the year ended 30 September 2012

	£m
Revenue	290.0
Cost of sales	(215.0)
Gross profit	75.0
Operating expenses (Note 1)	(62.0)
Operating profit	13.0
Interest payable (Note 2)	(3.0)
Profit before taxation	10.0
Taxation	(2.6)
Profit for the year	7.4

Statements of financial position as at 30 September

	2011 £m	2012 £m
ASSETS		
Non-current assets (Note 4)	80.0	85.0
Current assets		
Inventories and trade receivables	119.8	122.1
Cash at bank	9.2	16.6
	129.0	138.7
Total assets	209.0	223.7
EQUITY AND LIABILITIES		
Equity		
Share capital	35.0	40.0
Share premium account	30.0	30.0
Reserves	31.0	34.9
	96.0	104.9
Non-current liabilities		
Borrowings	32.0	35.0
Current liabilities		
Trade payables	80.0	82.5
Taxation	1.0	1.3
	81.0	83.8
Total equity and liabilities	209.0	223.7

Notes:

1 Operating expenses include depreciation of £13 million and a surplus of £3.2 million on the sale of non-current assets.

2 The expense and the cash outflow for interest payable are equal.

3 A dividend of £3.5 million was paid during 2012.

4 Non-current asset costs and depreciation:

	Cost £m	Accumulated depreciation £m	Carrying amount £m
At 1 October 2011	120.0	40.0	80.0
Disposals	(10.0)	(8.0)	(2.0)
Additions	20.0		20.0
Depreciation	–	13.0	(13.0)
At 30 September 2012	130.0	45.0	85.0

Required:

Prepare a statement of cash flows for York plc for the year ended 30 September 2012.

6.8 The statements of financial position of Axis plc as at 31 December 2011 and 2012 and the income statement for the year ended 31 December 2012 were as follows:

Statements of financial position as at 31 December

	2011		2012	
	£m	£m	£m	£m
ASSETS				
Non-current assets				
Property, plant and equipment				
Land and building at cost	130		130	
Accumulated depreciation	(30)	100	(32)	98
Plant and machinery at cost	70		80	
Accumulated depreciation	(17)	53	(23)	57
		153		155
Current assets				
Inventories		25		24
Trade receivables		16		26
Short-term investments		–		12
Cash at bank and in hand		–		7
		41		69
Total assets		194		224
EQUITY AND LIABILITIES				
Equity				
Share capital		100		100
Retained earnings		36		40
		136		140
Non-current liabilities				
Borrowings – 10% loan notes		20		40
Current liabilities				
Trade payables		31		36
Taxation		7		8
		38		44
Total equity and liabilities		194		224

Income statement for the year ended 31 December 2012

	£m
Revenue	173
Cost of sales	(96)
Gross profit	77
Sundry operating expenses	(24)
Deficit on sale of non-current asset	(1)
Depreciation – buildings	(2)
– plant	(16)
Operating profit	34
Interest receivable	2
Interest payable	(2)
Profit before taxation	34
Taxation	(16)
Profit for the year	18

During the year, plant (a non-current asset) costing £15 million and with accumulated depreciation of £10 million was sold.

The short-term investments were government securities, where there was little or no risk of loss of value.

The expense and the cash outflow for interest payable were equal.

During 2012 a dividend of £14 million was paid.

Required:

Prepare a statement of cash flows for Axis plc for the year ended 31 December 2012.

Chapter 7

RECOGNISING AND REPORTING ASSETS AND LIABILITIES

INTRODUCTION

In Chapter 2 we discussed the broad definitions and recognition criteria for assets and liabilities. These may, however, produce more questions than answers. In an increasingly complex world, the treatment of certain items in the financial statements can create headaches for both preparers and users. Various international accounting standards try to provide clear definitions and recognition criteria for these items, the ultimate purpose being to enhance the comparability of financial statements.

In this chapter, we consider the reporting rules set out in key international accounting standards. We shall see how certain items are defined and what recognition criteria are applied. We shall also see why some of these standards have attracted criticism.

The chapter contains a short appendix, which deals with the concept of present value. This is relevant to our examination of finance leases. Although you may already be familiar with this concept, the section within the appendix on the present value of lease payments should still be of value.

Learning outcomes

When you have completed this chapter, you should be able to:

- discuss the main recognition criteria for provisions, contingent liabilities and contingent assets and explain the main reporting requirements for each;

- discuss the main recognition criteria and reporting requirements for internally-generated intangible assets;

- distinguish between a finance lease and an operating lease and describe their treatment in the financial statements;

- explain the circumstances under which borrowing costs may be capitalised.

MyAccountingLab   Visit **www.myaccountinglab.com** for practice and revision opportunities

PROVISIONS, CONTINGENT LIABILITIES AND CONTINGENT ASSETS

In this first section, we examine the main features of IAS 37 *Provisions, Contingent Liabilities and Contingent Assets*. We begin by looking at the nature of provisions and the way in which they should be reported. We then go on to consider contingent liabilities and contingent assets. We shall see that uncertainty concerning future events provides a common thread for these items.

PROVISIONS

Businesses often report provisions in their financial statements. To understand what a **provision** is, let us begin by recalling how a liability is defined.

Activity 7.1

Can you recall (from Chapter 2) how we define a liability?

It is an obligation by a business to an outside party, which arises from past events and which is settled through an outflow of resources (usually cash).

A provision is simply a form of liability. To be more precise, it is a liability where the timing or amount involved is uncertain. Although other liabilities, such as accruals, may suffer from uncertainty, the degree of uncertainty is higher with a provision.

According to IAS 37, a provision should be recognised where *all* of the following criteria have been met:

- there is an obligation arising from a past event;
- an outflow of resources is probably needed to settle the obligation; and
- a reliable estimate of the obligation can be made.

The amount of the provision should be the best estimate of the sum needed to settle the obligation. A reliable estimate is assumed to be possible in all but exceptional cases.

A few points about the nature of the obligation which leads to the recognition of a provision should be noted. First, the obligation need not always arise from legal requirements. It may arise from particular business practices. (This is known as a *constructive obligation*.) This will occur where practices, or policies, lead others to form expectations as to how the business will discharge its responsibilities. Second, the obligation does not have to be established with perfect certainty. It is enough for the evidence to suggest that it probably exists (that there is a greater than 50 per cent chance that it exists). Finally, the obligation must be unavoidable. If a business can take action to avoid a future outflow of resources, the obligation cannot lead to the recognition of a provision.

The following activity should help to clarify the kind of situations where a provision should be recognised and reported in the financial statements.

Activity 7.2

Consider the following:

1 A coach operated by a transport business was involved in a major accident in which a number of people were seriously injured. The business is being sued for gross negligence and the court will soon make a decision on this matter. Lawyers for the business have advised that the business is unlikely (less than 50 per chance) to be found liable for the accident.
2 A travel business has expanded its operations and its current offices are no longer suitable for use. As a result, the business is relocating to larger offices on the opposite side of the city. The current offices are leased and another two years remain before the lease period ends. There is no real likelihood that these offices can be sub-let to another business and cancellation of the lease is not possible.
3 A retail business operates a well-established and well-known refunds policy. If a customer is unhappy with goods purchased for any reason, a full refund is provided. Past experience shows that 2 per cent of customers seek a refund.
4 A manufacturing business is expected to make a large operating loss next year as a result of a fall in demand for its goods.
5 A mining business has contaminated land over a number of years when carrying out its operations. New environmental legislation is about to be enacted that will create an obligation for businesses to undertake a clean-up of land already contaminated.

Which of the above should lead to the recognition of a provision? Give your reasons.

1 On the basis of the lawyers' opinion, there is no probable obligation arising from the accident. It therefore fails the first criterion and so a provision should not be recognised.
2 A provision should be recognised because:
   – there is an obligation under the lease;
   – the obligation will probably give rise to future outflows of resources.
3 A provision should normally be recognised because:
   – the sale of goods will result in a constructive obligation because of the refunds policy of the business;
   – a proportion of the goods sold will probably be returned (based on past experience), leading to an outflow of resources.
4 A provision should not be recognised. There is no obligation arising from a past event and so it fails to meet the first criterion.
5 A provision should be recognised because:
   – the contamination of the land will produce an obligation because of impending legislation;
   – an outflow of resources will probably be needed to decontaminate the land.

Where a provision is recognised, it has been assumed in each case that a reliable estimate of the outflow of resources can be made.

Provisions and business restructuring

An important form of provision is where a business decides to restructure its operations. Restructuring may involve selling a division, relocating business operations, changing the management hierarchy and so on. This can give rise to future outflows of resources and so a provision may be recognised.

IAS 37 states, however, that a constructive obligation will only exist where there is a formal, detailed restructuring plan. Furthermore, this plan must either have been communicated to those affected by it, or started to be implemented by the end of the reporting period. In these circumstances, the obligation to restructure is considered unavoidable. Where restructuring involves the sale of a business operation, an obligation arises only where there is a binding sale agreement.

Only the direct costs associated with restructuring must be included in the amount of the provision. These are the necessary costs of restructuring rather than those associated with ongoing business operations. Thus, costs incurred as a result of retraining employees, marketing and investment in new systems must not be included in any restructuring provision as they relate to future operations of the business.

Recognising and reporting provisions

Recognising a provision is fairly straightforward. The income statement is charged with the amount of the provision and this amount then appears as a liability in the statement of financial position. Thus, profit will decrease and liabilities will increase by the amount of the provision. Where costs relating to the provision are subsequently incurred, they will be charged against the provision rather than to the income statement.

A provision, once recognised, should be reviewed at the end of each reporting period and, if necessary, adjusted to reflect the current best estimate of the obligation. Where it is probable that an outflow of resources will no longer arise, the provision must be reversed. In other words, it must be added back to the income statement and eliminated from the liabilities.

IAS 37 sets out disclosure requirements for provisions. For each type of provision, the amounts at the beginning and end of the reporting period, increases or decreases in the provision and amounts charged against the provision during the period must be shown. In addition, the nature and timing of any obligation, the uncertainties surrounding the amount or timing of any outflow of resources and, where necessary, any major assumptions used concerning future events must be revealed.

Real World 7.1 reveals how the energy business BP was forced to create a huge provision for the damage caused by the oil spill in the Gulf of Mexico. It also indicates the enormous impact, including the devastating effect on profits, from the oil spill and subsequent recognition of the provision.

Real World 7.1

Pouring oil on troubled waters

BP moved to repair its image in the wake of the huge oil spill in the Gulf of Mexico as the energy group unveiled plans to sell $30bn of assets and confirmed the departure of its chief executive. The announcements came as BP reported one of the largest losses in British corporate history, losing $17bn after tax in the second quarter after a $32.2bn pre-tax provision to pay for cleaning up the spill and compensating its victims.

FT *Source:* 'BP plans $30bn sales to meet spill costs' (Murphy, P) FT.com, 27 July 2010.
© The Financial Times Limited 2012. All rights reserved.

Provisions and creative accounting

There is a risk that provisions will be misused by unscrupulous directors. Excessive provisions may be recognised in one period, only to be eliminated, or decreased, in subsequent periods. The aim may be to smooth profits from one year to the next. Investors are often assumed to prefer a smooth, upward trend in profits rather than an erratic pattern. By creating, and then reversing, provisions over time, it may be possible to produce such a trend. Before the regulators addressed this issue it was proving to be a real problem.

IAS 37 has made the misuse of provisions much more difficult. Various rules are now in place to restrict the opportunity for creative accounting. Three of these rules are:

- An obligation must be unavoidable before a provision can be recognised.
- A provision can only be used for the purpose for which it was created. Thus, unrelated expenditure cannot be offset against a provision.
- Excessive provisions cannot be created. Prudence must not be used as an excuse for treating an adverse future outcome as more probable than is likely to be the case.

CONTINGENT LIABILITIES

IAS 37 *Provisions, Contingent Liabilities and Contingent Assets* defines a **contingent liability** as

1 a possible obligation arising from past events, the existence of which will be only be confirmed by future events not wholly within the control of the business; or
2 a present obligation arising from past events, where either it is not probable that an outflow of resources is needed, or the amount of the obligation cannot be reliably measured.

Provisions and contingent liabilities are dealt with in the same standard because there is uncertainty surrounding the timing, or amount, of both. There is a difference, however, in the degree of uncertainty. Where, for example, a present obligation leads to a probable (more than 50 per cent chance) outflow of resources, a provision is normally recognised. Where a future outflow is possible, but not probable (less than 50 per cent chance), a contingent liability arises.

The following activity should help to identify the kind of situations where a contingent liability arises.

Activity 7.3

Consider the following:

1 A pharmaceutical business is being sued by a rival for infringement of patent rights. The court case has begun but a decision is not expected until after the end of the reporting period. Lawyers representing the business believe that it is probable that the court will find in favour of the rival.
2 A football club acquired a new player by a transfer from another club during its current reporting period. The terms of the transfer agreement state that, in addition to the £10 million fee already paid, a further £2 million will be paid if the player is selected for the national team within the next three years. It is possible that this will happen.
3 A manufacturer undertakes to guarantee the loan of £3 million taken out by a supplier, which provides vitally important raw materials. The supplier has experienced some financial difficulties lately, but it is not probable that it will default on its loan obligations.
4 A chemical business has accidentally contaminated a river following the release of dangerous chemicals. The business is legally obliged to pay to decontaminate the river and it will also be liable to pay fines. The accident occurred near the end of the reporting period and it is too early to derive a reliable estimate of the likely future costs incurred.

Which of the above should be regarded as a contingent liability? Give your reasons.

Your answers should be as follows:

1 As it is likely that the court will find in favour of the rival business, this should be regarded as a present obligation where an outflow of resources is probably needed. This meets the criteria for recognition of a provision (provided a reasonable estimate of the amount can be made). It is not, therefore, a contingent liability.
2 This is a possible obligation arising from past events that is not wholly within the control of the football club. It should, therefore, be regarded as a contingent liability.

Reporting contingent liabilities

A contingent liability is not recognised in the financial statements. Given the degree of uncertainty associated with such an item, this should not come as a surprise. We have seen that, for an item to be classified as a contingent liability, it must be less than probable that (1) a present obligation exists, or (2) an outflow of resources is required, or (3) the amount of the obligation can be reliably measured. Nevertheless, information concerning this type of liability may still be relevant to user needs.

IAS 37 states that contingent liabilities should be disclosed in the notes to the financial statements, unless the possibility of an outflow of resources is remote. For each class of contingent liability, there should be a brief description of its nature. Where practicable, there should also be some indication of its financial effect, the uncertainties surrounding the timing and amount of the outflow and the possibility of reimbursement.

Figure 7.1 summarises the recognition requirements for provisions and contingent liabilities.

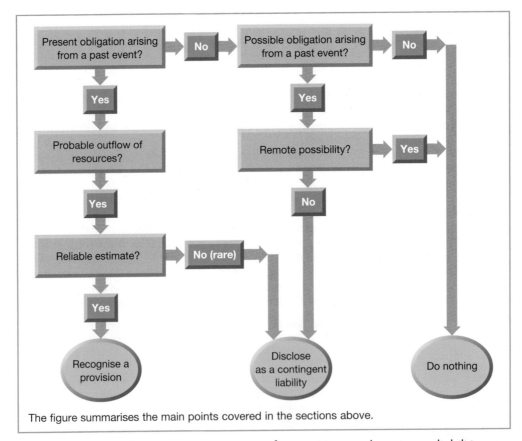

The figure summarises the main points covered in the sections above.

Figure 7.1 The main recognition requirements for provisions and contingent liabilities

Source: Adapted from diagram in IAS 37 *Provisions, Contingent Liabilities and Contingent Assets*, Appendix B.

CONTINGENT ASSETS

IAS 37 defines a **contingent asset** as a possible asset arising from past events, the existence of which will only be confirmed by future events not wholly within the control of the business.

Contingent assets are not recognised in the financial statements since they may not lead to an inflow of resources. Where, however, a future inflow of resources is probable, they should be disclosed by way of a note. This will involve a brief description of the nature of the contingent assets and, where practicable, an estimate of their financial effect.

Note the difference in disclosure requirements for a contingent liability and for a contingent asset. A contingent liability should be disclosed, unless the possibility of an outflow of resources is remote. A contingent asset, on the other hand, should only be disclosed where an inflow of resources is probable.

Activity 7.4

With which accounting convention is this difference in disclosure requirements consistent?

We saw in Chapter 2 that the prudence convention holds that caution should be exercised when making accounting judgements. Application of this convention normally requires recognition of anticipated losses and liabilities in the financial statements. Profits and assets, however, receive recognition only when they actually arise. A similarly cautious approach underpins these disclosure requirements.

Contingent assets should be reviewed continually to ensure that there has been no change in circumstances. Where it becomes virtually certain that the business will benefit from an inflow of resources, the asset is no longer treated as a contingent asset. It is recognised as an asset and will, therefore, be shown in the financial statements.

Figure 7.2 sets out the choices available where a contingent asset is being reviewed at the end of the reporting period.

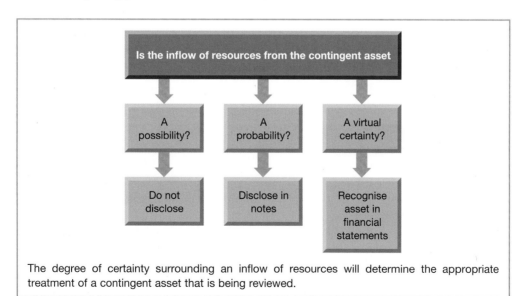

The degree of certainty surrounding an inflow of resources will determine the appropriate treatment of a contingent asset that is being reviewed.

Figure 7.2 Reviewing a contingent asset

The following activity should help to identify the kind of situations where a contingent asset arises.

Real World 7.2 provides an example of a contingent liability disclosed by the home improvement chain Kingfisher plc, which operates in Europe and Asia and which owns well-known brands such as B&Q.

INTERNALLY-GENERATED INTANGIBLE ASSETS

A business may spend large amounts in developing an intangible asset. Examples may include developing computer software, creating a patented product, producing a film and so on. In some cases, the intangible asset that has been developed may have a tangible element. An example would be a compact disc for storing computer software. Where, however, the intangible element is considered the more significant, the asset will be regarded as intangible.

Internally-generated intangible assets can create recognition problems. We saw in Chapter 2 that an asset must be capable of generating future economic benefits and its cost must be capable of reliable measurement. Where an intangible asset is internally generated, it can be difficult to demonstrate that these conditions have been met.

Research and development

To deal with the recognition problems, IAS 38 *Intangible Assets* classifies the generation of an intangible asset into two phases: a research phase and a development phase. The research phase precedes the development phase and may have no direct connection to the development of a particular product or service. It can cover activities such as:

- obtaining new knowledge;
- searching for, evaluating and applying research findings;
- searching for new materials, devices, processes and services;
- designing and evaluating new materials, devices, processes and services.

Amounts spent during the research phase are regarded as an expense when incurred and are, therefore, charged to the income statement. They are not treated as part of the cost of an intangible asset as they cannot be directly related to any future economic benefits.

The development phase is further advanced than the research phase and covers activities such as:

- the design, construction and testing of prototypes and models;
- the design of tools, jigs, moulds and dies;
- the design, construction and operation of a pilot plant to test the feasibility of commercial operations;
- the design, construction and testing of new materials, devices, processes and services.

For such activities, it may be possible to demonstrate that future economic benefits flow from any amounts spent.

IAS 38 requires the recognition of an intangible asset arising from the development phase, providing *all* of the following can be demonstrated:

- the technical feasibility of completing the intangible asset for use or sale;
- the intention to complete the intangible asset for use or sale;
- the ability to use or sell the intangible asset;
- how the intangible asset will generate probable future economic benefits;
- the availability of adequate technical, financial and other resources to complete the intangible asset for use or sale;
- the ability to measure reliably expenditure attributable to the intangible asset.

These tough conditions severely restrict the opportunities to carry forward development expenditure as an asset rather than to charge it as an expense. (This carrying forward of expenditure as an asset is referred to as **capitalisation**.)

Activity 7.6

Consider the conditions for capitalisation mentioned above. How might a business demonstrate

1 that the intangible asset will generate probable future economic benefits; and
2 its ability to measure reliably the expenditure attributable to the intangible asset?

Future benefits may be demonstrated by the existence of a market for whatever the asset produces. If the asset is used for internal purposes, its contribution to business processes must be demonstrated.

Reliable measurement of expenditure may be demonstrated by having efficient costing systems that capture the salaries, materials, services and fees that are incurred.

In some cases, it will not be possible to distinguish between a research phase and a development phase for expenditure on an intangible asset. Under these circumstances, all expenditure will be treated as though it were incurred during the research phase. That is, it will be charged to the income statement when incurred.

Capitalising development costs

Only development costs incurred after the intangible asset has met the conditions mentioned earlier should be capitalised. These costs, which are restricted to those directly attributable to producing the asset or getting it ready for use, may include:

■ materials and services consumed in creating the asset;
■ employee costs;
■ legal fees; and
■ depreciation (amortisation) of patents and licences.

They will not include selling, administrative or general overhead costs.

Research and development expenditure in practice

Many UK businesses spend considerable sums on researching and developing new products and services. During 2010, for example, the total came to £16.1 billion. In Figure 7.3, the amount spent, both in real terms (that is, after adjusting for inflation) and in cash terms, over the period 2003 to 2010 is shown.

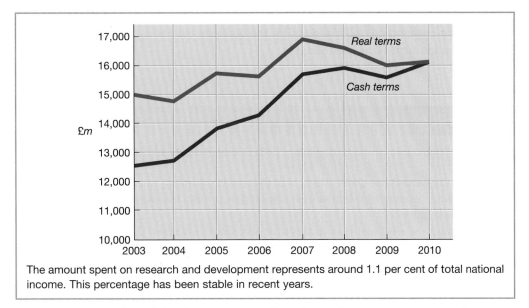

The amount spent on research and development represents around 1.1 per cent of total national income. This percentage has been stable in recent years.

Figure 7.3 Research and development expenditure by UK businesses 2003–2010

Source: UK Business Enterprise Research and Development 2010, Office for National Statistics, www.ons.gov.uk.

Expenditure on research and development (R&D) varies between industries. The pharmaceutical, aerospace and car manufacturing industries tend to be particularly heavy spenders. **Real World 7.3** below gives an insight into the R&D expenditure and policies of one large pharmaceutical business.

Real World 7.3

Hey big spender!

During 2011, AstraZeneca plc charged $5,523 million against revenue for research and development. In the preceding year, $5,318 million was charged against revenue. For both years, this represented around 16 per cent of annual revenue. Looking at Figure 7.3, it seems that, in 2010, AstraZeneca plc accounted for a large proportion of all R&D expenditure by UK businesses. (Information on total R&D expenditure is not available for 2011 but it is quite possible that the situation is similar.)

The accounting policies adopted by AstraZeneca plc for R&D expenditure are explained in its 2011 annual report as follows:

> Research expenditure is recognised in profit in the year in which it is incurred. Internal development expenditure is capitalised only if it meets the recognition criteria of IAS 38 'Intangible Assets'. Where regulatory and other uncertainties are such that the criteria are not met, the expenditure is recognised in profit and this is almost invariably the case prior to approval of the drug by the relevant regulatory authority. Where, however, recognition criteria are met, intangible assets are capitalised and amortised on a straight-line basis over their useful economic lives from product launch. At 31 December 2011, no amounts have met the recognition criteria.

Source: Annual Report and Form 20-F information 2011, AstraZeneca plc, p. 147.

The case of AstraZeneca plc provides an insight to the practical effect of IAS 38. Despite the huge amount spent on R&D during 2011, the business did not capitalise a single penny. This was also the case in the previous year.

Activity 7.7

Why might managers prefer to capitalise both research costs and development costs?

Managers may view these costs as a form of strategic investment, which is vital to the future survival and prosperity of the business. Capitalisation may, therefore, be considered the appropriate treatment.

They may, however, wish to capitalise for less worthy reasons. Capitalisation involves the transfer of costs incurred during a period to the statement of financial position rather than to the income statement. This will result in higher reported profit and asset figures. They may well prefer to report this rosier picture of financial health.

Recognition issues

IAS 38 specifically excludes certain types of internally-generated assets from recognition. Internally-generated brands, mastheads, publishing titles and customer lists cannot be recognised as intangible assets. The argument against their recognition is that it is not possible to distinguish the development of intangible assets from the development of the business as a whole. Internally-generated goodwill cannot be recognised as an intangible asset for a similar reason. It is not a separately identifiable resource.

Reporting internally-generated intangible assets

Internally-generated intangible assets are reported in the financial statements in the same way as other intangible assets. We saw in Chapter 2 that intangible assets are initially recognised at cost but, where there is an active market, may subsequently be shown at fair value. Where an intangible asset is shown at its fair value, other assets of the same class must also be shown at their fair value, unless there is no active market.

An intangible asset may have a finite or indefinite life. If it is the former, the asset must be depreciated (amortised) over its useful life. When calculating the depreciation charge, the residual value of the asset is normally assumed to be zero. The useful life and depreciation method must be reviewed at least annually and changes made where necessary. Where an intangible asset has an indefinite life, there is no depreciation charge but impairment tests must be carried out at least annually. There must also be an annual review to determine whether the asset still has an indefinite life.

IAS 38 requires that internally-generated intangible assets be disclosed separately from other intangible assets. The disclosure requirements for all intangible assets are extensive and require information relating to carrying amounts, revaluations, impairment losses, depreciation methods and useful life.

Finally, total research and development expenditure charged to the income statement for the period must be separately disclosed.

LEASES

When a business needs a particular asset, such as a piece of equipment, instead of buying it direct from a supplier, the business may arrange for a bank (or other business) to buy it and then lease it to the business. The lease arrangement will give the business the right to use the asset for a period in exchange for a payment or, more likely, a series of payments. The bank that owns the asset, and then leases it the business, is known as a 'lessor'. The business that leases the asset from the bank and then uses it is known as the 'lessee'.

A **finance lease**, as such an arrangement is known, is in essence a form of lending. This is because, had the lessee borrowed the funds and then used them to buy the asset itself, the effect would be much the same. The lessee would have use of the asset but would also have a financial obligation to the lender – just as with a leasing arrangement.

With finance leasing, legal ownership of the asset remains with the lessor but the lease agreement transfers to the lessee virtually all the rewards and risks associated with the leased item. The finance lease agreement will usually cover a substantial part of the life of the leased item and may not be capable of being cancelled.

Real World 7.4 gives an example of the use of finance leasing by a large international business.

Real World 7.4

Leased assets take off

Many airline businesses use finance leasing as a means of acquiring new aeroplanes. In July 2011 it was announced that Thai Airways had agreed to lease 22 aircraft from four different leasing companies. All were acquired under a standard 12-year leasing agreement with delivery of the new aircraft taking place between 2012 and 2017. The total value of the leased aircraft has been estimated at 69 billion baht (around £1.4 billion).

Source: Based on information in *Aviation News*, aviationnews-online.com, 6 July 2011.

A lease that does not fit the description of a finance lease is known as an **operating lease**. For such leases, the rewards and risks of ownership do not transfer to the lessee. In practice, the operating lease period tends to be short in relation to the life of the asset. An example of an operating lease is where a builder hires earth-moving equipment for three months to carry out a particular job.

Over the years, some important benefits associated with finance leasing have disappeared. Changes in the tax laws mean that it is no longer such a tax-efficient form of financing, and changes in disclosure requirements rule out concealing this form of 'borrowing' from investors. Nevertheless, the popularity of finance leases has continued. Other reasons must, therefore, exist for businesses to adopt this form of financing. These reasons are said to include the following:

■ *Ease of borrowing*. Leasing may be obtained more easily than other forms of long-term finance. Lenders normally require some form of security and a profitable track record before making advances to a business. However, a lessor may be prepared to lease assets to a new business without a track record and to use the leased assets as security for the amounts owing.

- *Cost*. Leasing agreements may be offered at reasonable cost. As the asset leased is used as security, standard lease arrangements can be applied and detailed credit checking of lessees may be unnecessary. This can reduce administration costs for the lessor and, thereby, help in providing competitive lease rentals.
- *Flexibility*. Leasing can help provide flexibility where there are rapid changes in technology. If an option to cancel can be incorporated into the lease, the business may be able to exercise this option and invest in new technology as it becomes available. This will help the business to avoid the risk of obsolescence.
- *Cash flows*. Leasing, rather than buying an asset outright, means that large cash outflows can be avoided. The leasing option allows cash outflows to be smoothed out over the asset's life. In some cases, it is possible to arrange for low lease payments to be made in the early years of the asset's life, when cash inflows may be low, and for these to increase over time as the asset generates positive cash flows.

These benefits are summarised in diagrammatic form in Figure 7.4.

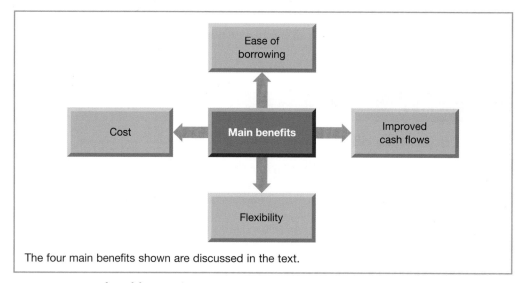

The four main benefits shown are discussed in the text.

Figure 7.4 Benefits of finance leasing

Real World 7.5 provides some impression of the importance of finance leasing over recent years.

Real World 7.5

Finance leasing in the UK

Figure 7.5 charts the changes in the value of finance leasing in the UK over the four years 2007 to 2010.

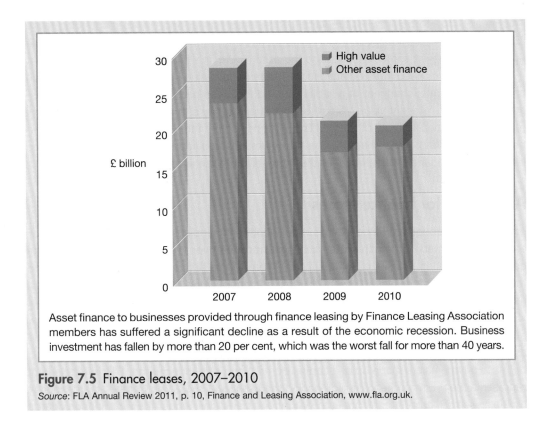

Asset finance to businesses provided through finance leasing by Finance Leasing Association members has suffered a significant decline as a result of the economic recession. Business investment has fallen by more than 20 per cent, which was the worst fall for more than 40 years.

Figure 7.5 Finance leases, 2007–2010

Source: FLA Annual Review 2011, p. 10, Finance and Leasing Association, www.fla.org.uk.

Recognising finance leases

Although a lessee is not granted legal ownership of the leased asset, it is granted the right to the economic benefits from using the asset. Furthermore, an obligation will be incurred to pay for that right. In substance, therefore, a finance lease gives rise to both an asset and a liability. It is this substance, rather than any legal form, that determines the accounting treatment of the lease in the financial statements of the lessee.

Activity 7.8

What problems arise by *not* treating an asset acquired through a finance lease in the way described?

If assets acquired through a finance lease are not dealt with as mentioned, the economic resources and the financial obligations of the business would be understated. Users of the lessee's financial statements could, therefore, be misled about the financial position of the business.

IAS 17 *Leases* states that, at the beginning of the finance lease, a lessee should recognise both an asset and a liability. These should be shown at:

1 the fair value of the leased asset, or, if lower,
2 the **present value** of the **minimum lease payments**.

This means that, to begin with, the value of the leased asset and the corresponding lease liability will usually be identical. Initial costs incurred in negotiating and securing the lease agreement, however, should be added to the asset figure, in which case the values will differ.

The above rules need further clarification. The term 'fair value' means the amount for which an asset could be exchanged, or a liability settled, between parties in an arm's-length transaction. The term 'present value' refers to the value in today's terms of the future lease payments using a specified rate of return. (This is explained in more detail in a short appendix to be found at the end of the chapter.) The 'minimum lease payments' are those payments the lessee can be required to make under the terms of the lease agreement.

Accounting for finance leases

An asset held through a finance lease is reported in the financial statements in the same way as if it were owned. Thus, where the asset depreciates over time, it will be subject to the normal depreciation policies of the business. There will be annual depreciation charges and the carrying value of the leased asset will reflect their cumulative effect. Where it is reasonably certain that the lessee will take ownership of the asset at the end of the lease term, the asset will be depreciated over its useful life. Otherwise, the depreciation period will be the shorter of the asset's useful life and the lease term. Impairment tests will also be carried out as if the asset were owned.

Lease payments are made up of a capital element and a finance charge. This latter element represents the return to the lessor for leasing the asset and should be treated as an expense by the lessee. To calculate the finance charge for a particular period, the total finance charge for the lease period is first calculated. This will be the difference between the total minimum lease payments and the fair value of the asset, or if lower, the present value of the lease payments. This total finance charge is then allocated between the relevant reporting periods.

The allocation method should aim to produce a constant rate of return on the outstanding lease payments. The finance charge will, therefore, be high at the beginning of the lease period, when the amount of outstanding lease payments is high, but will decrease over time as the liability for future lease payments decreases.

In practice, the **sum of the digits method** may be used to reflect the required pattern of finance charges over time. Although other methods are available, the sum of the digits method strikes a reasonable balance between simplicity and accuracy. To illustrate how this method is applied, let us take a look at Example 7.1.

Example 7.1

On 1 January 2013, Extravix plc takes out a finance lease for a helicopter. Details of the lease are as follows:

Annual lease payments	£1.5 million
Lease period	4 years
Lease payment date	31 December (in arrears)
Purchase cost (and fair value) of helicopter	£5 million

The business has a financial year end on 31 December.

To calculate the outstanding lease obligation for each year of the lease period, first the total finance charge is calculated as follows:

	£m
Total lease payments (4 × £1.5m)	6.0
Purchase cost of helicopter	5.0
Total finance charge	1.0

As the lease period is four years, with one instalment per year, there are four instalments. To allocate the finance charge between each year, the first instalment is assigned the digit 4, the second instalment is assigned the digit 3 and so on. The sum of the digits method then adds together the digits of the lease instalments as follows:

$$4 + 3 + 2 + 1 = 10.$$

(Where there are a large number of lease instalments, the formula $n(n + 1)/2$ may be used to derive the sum of the digits more quickly.)

The finance charge for each period is then calculated using the formula

(Relevant digit for the instalment/Sum of the digits) × Total finance charge.

The finance charge for each year is therefore:

Year to 31 December	Allocation	£m
2013	4/10 × £1.0m*	0.4
2014	3/10 × £1.0m	0.3
2015	2/10 × £1.0m	0.2
2016	1/10 × £1.0m	0.1
		1.0

* If the lease payments were in made in advance of the accounting period to which they relate, the sum of the digits would be 6 (3 + 2 + 1) and there would be no finance charge in the final year of the lease.

The split between the capital element and finance charge for each lease payment is therefore as follows:

| | 2013 | 2014 | 2015 | 2016 |
	£m	£m	£m	£m
Finance charge	0.4	0.3	0.2	0.1
Capital (balancing figure)	1.1	1.2	1.3	1.4
Total lease payment	1.5	1.5	1.5	1.5

The liability for lease payments will decrease each year as payments are made. At the inception of the lease, the finance lease liability will be £5 million (that is, the fair value of the asset). This amount will be reduced by any capital repayments made to date. In the statement of financial position it should be split between current and non-current liabilities.

For Extravix plc, the relevant calulations are as follows:

| | Inception of lease | 2013 | 2014 | 2015 | 2016 |
	£m	£m	£m	£m	£m
Lease liability	5.0	3.9	2.7	1.4	0.0
Allocated as follows:					
Non-current liabilities	3.9	2.7	1.4	0	0.0
Current liabilities	1.1	1.2	1.3	1.4	0.0
	5.0	3.9	2.7	1.4	0.0

Activity 7.9 should help to reinforce the points that have just been made.

Garadia plc took out a finance lease for a new machine on 1 January 2012. The purchase cost (and fair value) of the machine at this date was £12 million. The lease agreement is for three years and the annual lease payments, which are payable in arrears, are £5 million per year. The machine has a useful life of four years but the business intends to return the machine to the lessor at the end of the lease period. Garadia plc depreciates its property, plant and equipment using the straight-line method. The business has a financial year end on 31 December.

Show relevant extracts from the income statements and statements of financial position for each of the three years for which the machine is held.

The total finance charge is calculated as follows:

	£m
Total lease payments (3 × £5m)	15.0
Purchase cost of machine	12.0
Total finance charge	3.0

The finance charge for each year, using the sum of the digits method, is as follows:

Year to 31 December	Allocation	£m
2012	3/6 × £3m	1.5
2013	2/6 × £3m	1.0
2014	1/6 × £3m	0.5
		3.0

Income statement extracts for each year of the lease will be as follows:

	2012 £m	2013 £m	2014 £m
Depreciation (£12.0m/3)*	4.0	4.0	4.0
Finance charge	1.5	1.0	0.5

* Depreciation is allocated over the lease period as it is shorter than the useful life of the machine.

Before showing the statement of financial position extracts, we must calculate the capital element of each lease payment as follows:

	2012 £m	2013 £m	2014 £m
Finance charge	1.5	1.0	0.5
Capital (balancing figure)	3.5	4.0	4.5
Total lease payment	5.0	5.0	5.0

The statement of financial position extracts are as follows:

	Inception of lease £m	2012 £m	2013 £m	2014 £m
Non-current asset				
Machine	12.0	12.0	12.0	12.0
Accumulated depreciation	0.0	4.0	8.0	12.0
Carrying value	12.0	8.0	4.0	0.0
Non-current liabilities				
Lease payments	8.5	4.5	0.0	0
Current liabilities				
Lease payments	3.5	4.0	4.5	0

Operating leases

The accounting treatment of operating leases is more straightforward than for finance leases. No asset or liability will appear in the statement of financial position. This means that there is no need to calculate a depreciation charge or to split the lease instalments between a capital element and a finance charge. Instead, operating lease payments are simply recognised as an expense in the relevant reporting period.

Lease disclosure

Disclosure requirements for leases are extensive and are not considered in detail. For finance leases, they include:

- disclosure of the carrying value for each class of asset;
- total future minimum lease payments, and their present value, broken down into periods of less than one year, between two and five years and more than five years; and
- a general description of material leasing arrangements.

For operating leases, they include:

- total of future minimum lease payments under non-cancellable operating leases broken down into periods of less than one year, between two and five years and more than five years;
- lease payments recognised as an expense during the year; and
- a general description of material leasing arrangements.

Applying the standard

IAS 17 has been criticised for treating operating leases in a different way from finance leases. It has been suggested that operating leases also give rise to an asset and a liability and should, therefore, be capitalised in the same way as finance leases. The failure to capitalise means that users of the financial statements may be misled as to the financial position of the business. The IASB is aware of these concerns and a new standard, which will supersede IAS 17, may be introduced. There are, however, problems in dealing with operating leases in the same way as finance leases and it is not yet clear whether any new standard would go this far.

BORROWING COSTS

Suppose a business borrows money to finance the construction of an asset. The asset takes some time to complete and, during the construction period, the business pays interest on the amounts borrowed. A key question that arises is whether the interest payable should be charged against income in the period incurred or capitalised as part of the cost of the asset.

The general rule is that the cost of an asset should include all costs required to get it ready for use or for sale. The case for capitalisation is that borrowing costs, which include interest payable and also finance charges relating to finance leases, can be properly regarded as part of these costs. IAS 23 *Borrowing Costs* adopts this view. It argues that the cost of the asset will not be faithfully represented unless borrowing costs are included.

The core principle set out in IAS 23 is that borrowing costs which are directly attributable to the acquisition, production or construction of a qualifying asset should be included as part of its cost. All other borrowing costs are treated as an expense in the period incurred.

Two practical problems arise in applying this core principle. The first is that it is not always easy to identify a direct link between particular borrowings and a qualifying asset. It may be, for example, that a business borrows from various sources, at various rates of interest, and then creates a general pool of funds to finance the production of a qualifying asset. IAS 23 states that, in such a situation, a capitalisation rate based on the weighted average cost of the pool of borrowing should be applied.

The second problem concerns the definition of a 'qualifying asset'. IAS 23 states that it is an asset that takes a substantial period of time to get ready for use or for resale. It may include:

- inventories (excluding those taking a short period to produce)
- manufacturing plants
- power-generation facilities
- intangible assets
- investment properties.

This is a rather broad definition that could benefit from further clarification.

IAS 23 states that capitalisation of borrowing costs can begin only when:

1 borrowing costs are incurred;
2 expenditure for the asset is incurred; and
3 activities to prepare the asset for use or sale are in progress.

Capitalisation ends when active development of the asset is suspended or when the asset is substantially completed.

The disclosure requirements set out in the standard are quite straightforward. The borrowing costs capitalised during the period and the capitalisation rate used to determine any capitalised borrowing costs must be specified. **Real World 7.6** illustrates how one well-known business discloses this information.

> **Real World 7.6**
>
> ### Not much interest
>
> BSkyB, the satellite broadcaster, includes the following statement concerning capitalised borrowing costs in its 2011 annual report.
>
> > Borrowing costs included in the cost of qualifying assets during the year arose on the general borrowing pool and are calculated by applying a capitalisation rate of 5.4% (2010: 5.3%) to expenditure on such assets. The amount capitalised in the current year amounted to less than £1 million (2010: less than £1 million).
>
> *Source*: British Sky Broadcasting Group plc Annual Report 2012, p. 83, http://annualreview2012.sky.com.

Criticisms of IAS 23

The capitalisation of borrowing costs has attracted some criticism. It has been argued that measuring and monitoring capitalised borrowing costs is time-consuming, cumbersome and costly. It has also been argued that the benefits to users of capitalising interest are unclear. It has been claimed, for example, that, when examining the income statement to assess the degree of financial risks arising from interest charges, financial analysts reverse any capitalised interest. There is no strong evidence, however, of widespread dissatisfaction with the standard.

Some critics of IAS 23 would like businesses to be given a choice over whether to capitalise borrowing costs or to charge them to the period incurred. This choice was permitted in an earlier version of IAS 23.

Activity 7.10

What problems arise from giving businesses a choice over the treatment of borrowing costs?

One problem is that a quite different portrayal of financial performance and position may occur, according to whether interest charges are capitalised or whether they are charged to the current period. Providing a choice may, therefore, undermine comparability between different businesses or between different time periods.

A further problem is that, by offering a choice, the question as to what should be included in the cost of an asset is effectively avoided. This is an important question, to which the IASB should have a clear answer.

The following self-assessment question brings together some of the points contained within the chapter.

Self-assessment question 7.1

Prentaxia plc produced a draft income statement for the year just ended that reported a profit before tax of £87.2 million. An investigation of the underlying records produced the following information:

1 During the year, the business entered into a finance lease agreement to acquire a machine. The lease period is five years with an annual lease payment, payable in arrears, of £5 million. The first lease payment, which was paid at the end of the current year, was charged in full as an expense in the draft income statement. The purchase cost (and fair value) of the machine at the time of the lease agreement was £19 million.
2 Two years ago, the business began the construction of a new factory. Borrowing costs of £2 million relating to factory construction were incurred during the current year. These costs were charged to the draft income statement.
3 In the previous financial year, a provision was recognised for £10 million for cleaning up contaminated land near a factory owned by the business. The clean-up of the land is due to take place in two years' time. At the end of the current year, it was found that the contamination was more extensive than first estimated and that the total clean-up cost was now expected to be £12.6 million. No action has so far been taken.
4 One of the factories owned by the business has a large furnace. The lining of the furnace must be replaced every four years in order for it to remain in working order. A replacement lining is due next year. The existing lining, which cost £1.0 million, is being depreciated over its life. The directors decided to recognise a provision of £1.4 million during the current year to replace the lining.
5 During the year, a court case was brought against the business for infringement of patent rights. A rival business is claiming £4.5 million as compensation. The business

is defending the action but its lawyers believe that it will probably not succeed in its defence. A contingent liability for the full amount claimed has been disclosed in the draft financial statements.

6 During the year, the business spent £1.3 million in a search for new materials to replace materials that are currently used in its range of products. This amount was capitalised.

7 The law requires the business to fit smoke alarms throughout its offices and factories by next year. The estimated cost of doing so is £0.4 million. To date, no action has been taken in respect of this.

Required:

Show the revised profit before tax for the current year of Prentaxia plc after taking account of the above information, briefly stating the reasons for any adjustments that have been made.

A solution to this question can be found in Appendix C.

SUMMARY

The main points of this chapter may be summarised as follows:

Provisions, contingent liabilities and contingent assets (IAS 37)

■ A provision is a form of liability where the timing or amount involved is uncertain.

■ A provision is recognised where all of the following criteria are met:
  – there is an obligation arising from a past event;
  – an outflow of resources is probably needed to settle the obligation; and
  – a reliable estimate of the obligation can be made.

■ The amount of the provision should be the best estimate of the amount needed to settle the obligation.

■ A provision is created by charging the income statement with the amount of the provision. This amount then appears on the statement of financial position.

■ In the past, provisions have been used for creative accounting purposes.

■ A contingent liability is defined as:
  – a possible obligation arising from past events, the existence of which will only be confirmed by future events not wholly within the control of the business; or
  – a present obligation arising from past events, where it is either not probable that an outflow of resources is needed, or the amount of the obligation cannot be reliably measured.

■ Contingent liabilities are disclosed in the notes to financial statements, unless the possibility of an outflow of resources is remote.

■ A contingent asset is defined as a possible asset arising from past events, the existence of which will only be confirmed by future events not wholly within the control of the business.

■ Contingent assets are not recognised in the financial statements. Where, however, a future inflow of resources is probable, they should be disclosed by way of a note.

Internally-generated intangible assets (IAS 38)

- The generation process is divided into two phases: a research phase and a development phase.

- The research phase precedes the development phase and may have no direct connection to the development of a particular product or service.

- Research expenditure is regarded as an expense when incurred as it cannot be directly related to future economic benefits.

- The development phase is further advanced than the research phase and is related to the development of a product or service.

- Development expenditure should be capitalised provided it meets strict conditions including the ability to demonstrate probable future economic benefits.

- Only development costs arising after the internally-generated asset has been recognised and which are directly attributable to creating the asset or getting it ready for use can be capitalised.

- Certain internally-generated assets, such as goodwill, brands, mastheads, customer lists and publishing titles, cannot be recognised.

Leases (IAS 17)

- A finance lease transfers substantially all the risks and rewards of ownership of an asset to the lessee.

- The substance, rather than the legal form, of a finance lease agreement is that it gives rise to both an asset and a liability in the financial statements of the lessee.

- At the beginning of the lease term, the asset and liability should be reported at the fair value of the asset leased or, if lower, the present value of the minimum lease payments.

- An asset acquired through a finance lease is treated in the same way for depreciation purposes as if it were owned.

- The total finance charge for the lease will be allocated as an expense over the period of the lease.

- The allocated finance charge should decrease over time and the sum of the digits method may be used to calculate this decreasing charge.

- In the statement of financial position, the carrying value of the asset will reflect any depreciation to date. The liability for lease payments will reflect the total lease obligation at the inception of the lease, less any capital repayments to date.

- An operating lease is any lease that does not fit the description of a finance lease.

- Operating lease payments are charged as an expense in the relevant reporting period.

Borrowing costs (IAS 23)

- Borrowing costs that are directly attributable to the acquisition, production or construction of a qualifying asset form part of its cost.

- All other borrowing costs are treated as an expense in the period in which they are incurred.

- A qualifying asset is an asset that takes a substantial period of time to get ready for use or for resale.

KEY TERMS

provision p. 218
contingent liability p. 221
contingent asset p. 223
capitalisation p. 226
finance lease p. 229

operating lease p. 229
present value p. 231
minimum lease payments p. 231
sum of the digits method p. 232

FURTHER READING

If you would like to explore the topics covered in this chapter in more depth, try the following:

Alexander, D., Britton, A. and Jorissen, A., *International Financial Reporting and Analysis*, 5th edn, South–Western Cengage Learning, 2011, Chapters 13, 15 and 19

Elliott, B. and Elliott, J., *Financial Accounting and Reporting*, 15th edn, Financial Times Prentice Hall, 2011, Chapters 18 and 19

International Accounting Standards Board, *International Financial Reporting Standards 2012, IFRS Consolidated without Early Application (Blue Book)*, IASC Foundation Education, 2012, IAS 17, 23, 37 and 38

Melville, A., *International Financial Reporting: A Practical Guide*, 3rd edn, Financial Times Prentice Hall, 2011, Chapters 9 and 12

REVIEW QUESTIONS

Solutions to these questions can be found in Appendix D.

7.1 What is a contingent asset? How do the disclosure requirements for a contingent asset differ from those for a contingent liability?

7.2 What is a contingent liability? What are the key differences between a contingent liability and a provision?

7.3 'The treatment of research and development expenditure set out in IAS 38 *Intangible Assets* reflects the tension between the prudence convention and the accruals convention in accounting.' Explain.

7.4 In the past, finance lease payments were treated as an expense in the period incurred. Critics claimed, however, that this treatment could be used for creative accounting purposes. Explain how this could be the case.

Exercises 7.1 and 7.2 are basic level, 7.3 and 7.4 are intermediate level and 7.5 is advanced level. Solutions to the exercises with coloured numbers are given in Appendix E.

If you wish to try more exercises, visit the students' side of the Companion Website and MyAccountingLab.

7.1 Consider the following:

1 A motor car manufacturer offers a three-year warranty on all cars that it produces. The warranty undertakes to make good any defects arising from the manufacturing process. On past experience, 0.5 per cent of car owners make claims under the terms of the warranty.

2 A cruise ship suffered an outbreak of food poisoning that affected most of its passengers. Legal proceedings have been brought against the cruise ship company and a court case has just commenced. The lawyers for the company believe that it is probable that the cruise ship company will be found liable.

3 An airline company has just commenced operations and has acquired three new aircraft. The law requires that these aircraft be subject to a rigorous overhaul after two years of flying.

For which of the above should a provision be recognised? Give your reasons.

7.2 On 1 January 2012, Markon plc took out a finance lease for new plant. Details of the lease are as follows:

Annual lease payments	£2.0m
Lease period	4 years
Lease payment date	31 December (in arrears)

The business has a year end date of 31 December. The minimum lease payments are the four annual lease payments. The implicit interest rate in the lease is 12 per cent per year.

Required:

(a) Calculate the present value of the minimum lease payments as at the commencement of the lease. (Refer to the appendix to the chapter to answer this part of the question.)

(b) Explain why the lower, rather than the higher, of the fair value of the leased asset and the minimum lease payments should be used for initial recognition of the lease.

7.3 Consider the following:

1 Under new legislation, a retail business will be obliged to fit handrails to the staircases used in its stores. The law will come into force six months after the end of its current reporting period. So far the business has done nothing to respond to this change in the law. The cost of fitting the handrails is expected to be £2 million.

2 The board of directors of a manufacturing business has decided to close down its motor cycle division. The board has charged the chief executive with the task of drawing up a formal detailed plan for the closure. The costs of closure have been estimated as £4.5 million.

3 An energy business operates a nuclear power station. In fifty years' time, the power station will be decommissioned and the law requires the business to incur the costs of decommissioning. Decommissioning costs of £80 million are expected.

4 New health and safety rules have been introduced by the government, which apply to manufacturing businesses. A large manufacturer will need to retrain its managers to ensure compliance with the new rules. The cost of the retraining programme is estimated at £1 million. At the end of the reporting period, no retraining has taken place.

5 An energy business operates an oilfield in the North Sea. The licensing agreement with the UK government requires the business to remove the oil rig when oil production ceases and to restore the sea bed. It is estimated that 80 per cent of the restoration cost will arise from removal of the oil rig and 20 per cent from damage created from oil extraction. Total restoration costs are estimated to be £10 million. To date, the oil rig has not commenced operations and so no oil has been extracted.

For which of the above should a provision be recognised? Give your reasons.

7.4 Darco Instruments plc took out a finance lease for new plant on 1 June 2012. The lease period is four years and annual lease payments, which are payable in arrears, are for £3 million per year. The purchase cost of the plant would have been £10 million. The business has a financial year end on 31 May. The plant has a useful life of five years but the business intends to return the machine to the lessor at the end of the lease period.

Darco Instruments plc depreciates property, plant and equipment using the straight-line method.

Required:

(a) Show relevant extracts from the financial statements for each of the years for which the plant is leased.

(b) Show the relevant extracts from the financial statements for each year, assuming that it was an operating lease rather than a finance lease.

(c) Explain why finance charges for a finance lease are not normally charged in equal instalments to each reporting period.

7.5 The draft income statement for the most recent reporting period of Barchester United Football Club plc has reported a profit before tax of £48.8 million. An examination of the underlying records, however, shows that the following items need to be taken into account during the current period:

1 A provision for £15 million for restructuring the club was recognised in the preceding year. During the current year, the first phase of the restructuring was carried out and restructuring costs of £5.4 million were incurred. This amount has been charged to the current income statement.

2 A provision for a legal action against the club for unfair dismissal of the previous manager for £2.2 million was recognised in the preceding year. During the current year, the manager lost his case at an industrial tribunal and does not intend to appeal.

3 During the previous reporting period, a contingent asset was reported. This relates to an agreement to allow a television channel exclusive rights to televise reserve team matches. The agreement includes a formula for payment to Barchester United based on the number of television viewers (as measured by an independent body) per match. A dispute over the precise interpretation of this formula led Barchester United to sue the television channel for £2 million in underpaid income. The court case to decide the issue recently ended abruptly when the television channel finally accepted (on the advice of its lawyers) that its interpretation of the formula had been incorrect.

4 The club spent £1 million during the year to help fund research studies on the main causes of football injuries among professional football players. This amount was capitalised and shown on the statement of financial position.

5 The club is building new training facilities for its players. The facilities are currently being constructed and will take three years to complete. During the current year, the club incurred £3.3 million in interest charges on the construction of the facilities. These were charged to the current income statement.

6 At the beginning of the year, the club took out a finance lease to acquire a new type of plastic all-weather turf for its new training ground. The turf would have cost £4 million to purchase outright. Annual lease payments, which are payable in arrears, are £1.5 million per year in each of the four years. The finance charge appearing in the draft income statement has been calculated on the basis that the total finance charge for the lease is allocated evenly over the lease period.

Required:
Calculate a revised profit before tax for the current reporting period after taking account of the information shown above, and write brief notes to explain each adjustment that you have made to the draft profit before tax.

APPENDIX: TIME VALUE OF MONEY

We do not normally see an amount paid out today as being equivalent in value to the same amount being received in the future. Thus, if offered £1,000 in one year's time in exchange for £1,000 now, we would not normally be interested. This is because we are aware that, by being deprived of the opportunity to spend our money for a year, we are unable to invest it in a way that would earn interest. To put it another way, we are aware that money has a *time value*.

The time value of money can be seen from two perspectives: future value and present value. We shall now consider each of these in turn.

Future value

The *future value* of an investment is the amount to which its present value will grow in the future. Suppose that you want to invest £1,000 today at an interest rate of 20 per cent per year. Over a five-year period, the future value of your investment would build up as follows:

		Future value £
Initial investment	$£1,000 \times (1 + 0.20)^0$	1,000
One year's time	$£1,000 \times (1 + 0.20)^1$	1,200
Two years' time	$£1,000 \times (1 + 0.20)^2$	1,440
Three years' time	$£1,000 \times (1 + 0.20)^3$	1,728
Four years' time	$£1,000 \times (1 + 0.20)^4$	2,074
Five years' time	$£1.000 \times (1 + 0.20)^5$	2,488

The principles of compound interest are applied to determine the future value. Thus, interest earned is reinvested and then added to the initial investment to derive the future value. Reading from the table, we can see that the future value of the £1,000 investment, when invested at a compound interest rate of 20 per cent over five years, is £2,488.

The formula for deriving the future value of an investment for a given period is:

$$FV = PV(1 + r)^n$$

where: FV = Future value of the investment

PV = Initial sum invested (also known as the present value)

r = Rate of return per year from the investment (expressed as a proportion rather than a percentage)

n = Number of years of the investment.

This formula is being applied in the second column of the above table to reveal the future value of the investment in one year's time, two years' time and so on.

Present value

We have just seen that future value of an investment is the amount to which its present value will grow at some future point in time. As an alternative, we can take the future value of a sum of money and express it in terms of its present value. In other words, we can bring the future sum of money back to today's value.

Suppose that you are given an opportunity to receive £1,000 in one year's time by investing a sum of money today. You are told that similar investments provide a rate of return of 20 per cent. The maximum that you should be prepared to invest is the sum that would grow to £1,000 if invested at 20 per cent over one year. This maximum figure will represent the present value of the future sum of money.

Taking the example just mentioned, we can say of the present value (PV) figure that:

$$PV + (PV \times 20\%) = £1,000$$

or, to put it another way, that the amount plus income from investing the amount for the year must equal £1,000.

If we rearrange this equation, we find:

$$PV \times (1 + 0.20) = £1,000$$

Further rearranging gives

$$PV = £1,000/(1 + 0.20) = £833 \text{ (to nearest £1)}$$

The calculations shown immediately above can be expressed more formally as

$$PV = FV(1/1 + r)^n$$

Activity 7.11

Complete the table below to show the present value of £1,000 to be received in each year over a five-year period, assuming a rate of return of 20 per cent. (We already know the present value for today and for one year's time.)

		Present value £
Immediate receipt	$£1,000 \times 1/(1 + 0.20)^0$	1,000
One year's time	$£1,000 \times 1/(1 + 0.20)^1$	833
Two years' time	_____	____
Three years' time	_____	____
Four years' time	_____	____
Five years' time	_____	____

Your answer should be as follows:

		Present value £
Immediate receipt	$£1,000 \times 1/(1 + 0.20)^0$	1,000
One year's time	$£1,000 \times 1/(1 + 0.20)^1$	833
Two years' time	$£1,000 \times 1/(1 + 0.20)^2$	694
Three years' time	$£1,000 \times 1/(1 + 0.20)^3$	579
Four years' time	$£1,000 \times 1/(1 + 0.20)^4$	482
Five years' time	$£1.000 \times 1/(1 + 0.20)^5$	402

The rate of return that is used to determine the present value of future receipts is referred to as the *discount rate*.

The answer to Activity 7.11 shows how the value of £1,000 diminishes as its receipt, or payment, goes further into the future. This is shown in diagrammatic form in Figure 7.6.

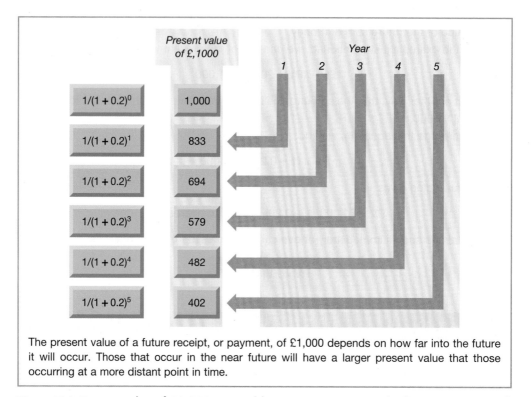

The present value of a future receipt, or payment, of £1,000 depends on how far into the future it will occur. Those that occur in the near future will have a larger present value that those occurring at a more distant point in time.

Figure 7.6 Present value of £1,000 receivable at various points in the future at an annual rate of return of 20 per cent

Lease payments and present value

Now that we have some idea of the concept of present value, let us return to the issue of lease payments. We should recall that, at the beginning of the finance lease, a lessee should recognise both an asset and a liability in the statement of financial position. These should be shown at:

1 the fair value of the leased asset: or, if lower,
2 the present value of the minimum lease payments.

To calculate (2) above, we simply calculate the present value figure for each of the future lease payments and add them together. The discount rate to be used when determining the present value of future lease payments is the interest rate implicit in the lease or, where this cannot be determined, the incremental borrowing rate of the business. One way to determine this latter figure is to use the rate of interest that the business would have to pay on a similar lease. Example 7.2 illustrates the calculation process.

Example 7.2

On 1 January 2013, Platina plc takes out a finance lease for robotic equipment. Details of the lease are as follows:

Annual lease payments	£1 million
Lease period	4 years
Lease payment date	31 December (in arrears)
Implicit interest rate	10 per cent per year

The minimum lease payments are the four annual lease payments.

At the commencement of the lease, the present value of the minimum lease payments is calculated as follows:

		Present value £000
One year's time	$£1,000 \times 1/(1 + 0.10)^1$	909
Two years' time	$£1,000 \times 1/(1 + 0.10)^2$	826
Three years' time	$£1,000 \times 1/(1 + 0.10)^3$	751
Four years' time	$£1,000 \times 1/(1 + 0.10)^4$	683
Total		3,169

Thus £3,169,000 should be compared to the fair value of the leased asset to determine the appropriate figure for initial recognition of the asset and liability.

Chapter 8

ANALYSING AND INTERPRETING FINANCIAL STATEMENTS (1)

INTRODUCTION

In this chapter we shall consider the analysis and interpretation of the financial statements that we discussed in Chapters 2, 3 and 6. We shall see how financial (or accounting) ratios can help in assessing the financial health of a business.

Financial ratios can be used to examine various aspects of financial position and performance and are widely used for planning and control purposes. They can be very helpful to managers in a wide variety of decision areas, such as profit planning, pricing, working-capital management and financial structure.

We shall continue our examination of the analysis and interpretation of financial statements in Chapter 9.

Learning outcomes

When you have completed this chapter, you should be able to:

- explain how ratios can be used to assess the position, performance and cash flows of a business;

- identify the major categories of ratios that can be used for analysing financial statements;

- calculate key ratios for assessing the profitability, efficiency, liquidity and gearing of a business;

- explain the significance of the ratios calculated.

FINANCIAL RATIOS

Financial ratios provide a quick and relatively simple means of assessing the financial health of a business. A ratio simply relates one figure appearing in the financial statements to another figure appearing there (for example operating profit in relation to sales revenue) or, perhaps, to some resource of the business (for example, operating profit per employee).

Ratios can be very helpful when comparing the financial health of different businesses. Differences may exist between businesses in the scale of operations. This means that a direct comparison of, say, the operating profit generated by each business may be misleading. By expressing operating profit in relation to some other measure (for example, capital employed), the problem of scale is eliminated. For example, a business with an operating profit of £10,000 and capital employed of £100,000 can be compared with a much larger business with an operating profit of £80,000 and capital employed of £1,000,000 by the use of a simple ratio. The operating profit to capital employed ratio for the smaller business is 10 per cent (that is, (10,000/100,000) × 100%) and the same ratio for the larger business is 8 per cent (that is, (80,000/1,000,000) × 100%). These ratios can be directly compared, whereas a comparison of the absolute operating profit figures might be much less meaningful. The need to eliminate differences in scale through the use of ratios can also apply when comparing the performance of the same business from one time period to another.

By calculating a small number of ratios it is often possible to build up a revealing picture of the position and performance of a business. It is not surprising, therefore, that ratios are widely used by those who have an interest in businesses and business performance. Although ratios are not difficult to calculate, they can be difficult to interpret. It is important to appreciate that the calculated ratios are really only the starting point for further analysis.

Ratios help to highlight the financial strengths and weaknesses of a business, but they cannot, by themselves, explain why those strengths or weaknesses exist or why certain changes have occurred. Only a detailed investigation will reveal these underlying reasons. Ratios tend to enable us to know which questions to ask, rather than provide the answers.

Ratios can be expressed in various forms, for example as a percentage or as a proportion. The way that a particular ratio is presented will depend on the needs of those who will use the information. Although it is possible to calculate a large number of ratios, only a few, based on key relationships, tend to be helpful to a particular user. Many ratios that could be calculated from the financial statements (for example, rent payable in relation to current assets) may not be considered because there is not usually any clear or meaningful relationship between the two items.

There is no generally accepted list of ratios that can be applied to the financial statements, nor is there a standard method of calculating many ratios. Variations in both the choice of ratios and their calculation will be found in practice. However, it is important to be consistent in the way in which ratios are calculated for comparison purposes. The ratios that we shall discuss are very popular – presumably because they are seen as useful for decision-making purposes.

FINANCIAL RATIO CLASSIFICATIONS

Ratios can be grouped into categories, with each category relating to a particular aspect of financial performance or position. The following broad categories provide a useful basis for explaining the nature of the financial ratios to be dealt with. There are five of them:

- *Profitability*. Businesses generally exist with the primary purpose of creating wealth for their owners. Profitability ratios provide insights relating to the degree of success in achieving this purpose. They express the profit made (or figures bearing on profit, such as sales revenue or overheads) in relation to other key figures in the financial statements or to some business resource.

- *Efficiency*. Ratios may be used to measure the efficiency with which particular resources have been used within the business. These ratios are also referred to as *activity* ratios.

- *Liquidity*. It is vital to the survival of a business that there are sufficient liquid resources available to meet maturing obligations (that is, amounts owing that must be paid in the near future). Some liquidity ratios examine the relationship between liquid resources held and amounts due for payment in the near future.

- *Financial gearing*. This is the relationship between the contribution to financing the business made by the owners of the business and the amount contributed by others, in the form of loans. The level of gearing has an important effect on the degree of risk associated with a business, as we shall see. Gearing ratios tend to highlight the extent to which the business uses borrowings.

- *Investment*. Certain ratios are concerned with assessing the returns and performance of shares in a particular business from the perspective of shareholders who are not involved with the management of the business.

These five key aspects of financial health that ratios seek to examine are summarised in Figure 8.1.

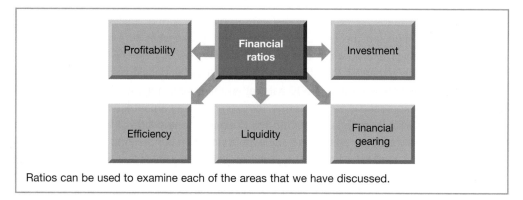

Ratios can be used to examine each of the areas that we have discussed.

Figure 8.1 The key aspects of financial health

The analyst must be clear *who* the target users are and *why* they need the information. Different users of financial information are likely to have different information needs, which will in turn determine the ratios that they find useful. For example, shareholders are likely to be particularly interested in their returns in relation to the level of risk associated with their investment. Profitability, investment and gearing ratios will, therefore, be of particular interest. Long-term lenders are concerned with the long-term viability of the business and, to help them to assess this, the profitability and gearing ratios of the business are also likely to be of particular interest. Short-term lenders, such as suppliers of goods and services on credit, may be interested in the ability of the business to repay the amounts owing in the short term. As a result, the liquidity ratios should be of interest.

We shall consider ratios falling into the first four of these five categories (profitability, efficiency, liquidity and gearing) a little later in the chapter. The remaining category (investment) takes a rather different perspective and will be considered in Chapter 9, along with other issues relating to ratios and their use.

THE NEED FOR COMPARISON

Merely calculating a ratio will not tell us very much about the position or performance of a business. For example, if a ratio revealed that a retail business was generating £100 in sales revenue per square metre of floor space, it would not be possible to deduce from this information alone whether this particular level of performance was good, bad or indifferent. It is only when we compare this ratio with some 'benchmark' that the information can be interpreted and evaluated.

Activity 8.1

Can you think of any bases that could be used to compare a ratio that you have calculated from the financial statements of your business for a particular period? (*Hint*: There are three main possibilities.)

You may have thought of the following bases:

■ past periods for the same business
■ similar businesses for the same or past periods
■ planned performance for the business.

We shall now take a closer look at these three in turn.

Past periods

By comparing the ratio that we have calculated with the same ratio, but for a previous period, it is possible to detect whether there has been an improvement or deterioration in performance. Indeed, it is often useful to track particular ratios over time (say, five or ten years) to see whether it is possible to detect trends. The comparison of ratios from different periods brings certain problems, however. In particular, there is always the possibility that trading conditions were quite different in the periods being compared. There is the further problem that, when comparing the performance of a single business over time, operating inefficiencies may not be clearly exposed. For example, the fact that sales revenue per employee has risen by 10 per cent over the previous period may at first sight appear to be satisfactory. This may not be the case, however, if similar businesses have shown an improvement of 50 per cent for the same period or had much better sales revenue per employee ratios to start with. Finally, there is the problem that inflation may have distorted the figures on which the ratios are based. Inflation can lead to an overstatement of profit and an understatement of asset values, as will be discussed later (in Chapters 9 and 11).

Similar businesses

In a competitive environment, a business must consider its performance in relation to that of other businesses operating in the same industry. Survival may depend on its ability to achieve comparable levels of performance. A useful basis for comparing a particular ratio, therefore, is the ratio achieved by similar businesses during the same period. This basis is not, however, without its problems. Competitors may have different year ends and so trading conditions may not be identical. They may also have different accounting policies (for example, different methods of calculating depreciation or valuing inventories), which can have a significant effect on reported profits and asset values. Finally, it may be difficult to obtain the financial statements of competitor businesses. Sole proprietorships and partnerships, for example, are not obliged to make their financial statements available to the public. In the case of limited companies, there is a legal obligation to do so. However, a diversified business may not provide a breakdown of activities that is sufficiently detailed to enable analysts to compare the activities with those of other businesses.

Planned performance

Ratios may be compared with targets that management have developed before the start of the period under review. The comparison of planned performance with actual performance may therefore be a useful way of assessing the level of achievement attained. However, the planned levels of performance must be based on realistic assumptions if they are to be useful for comparison purposes.

Planned performance is likely to be the most valuable benchmark against which managers may assess their own business. Businesses tend to develop planned ratios for each aspect of their activities. When formulating its plans, a business may usefully take account of its own past performance and the performance of other businesses. There is no reason, however, why a particular business should seek to achieve either its own previous level of performance or that of other businesses. Neither may be an appropriate target.

We should bear in mind that analysts outside the business do not normally have access to the business's plans. For these people, past performance and the performances of other, similar, businesses may provide the only practical benchmarks.

CALCULATING THE RATIOS

Probably the best way to explain financial ratios is through an example. Example 8.1 provides a set of financial statements from which we can calculate important ratios.

Example 8.1

The following financial statements relate to Alexis plc, which operates a wholesale carpet business:

Statements of financial position (balance sheets) as at 31 March

	2012 £m	2013 £m
ASSETS		
Non-current assets		
Property, plant and equipment (at cost less depreciation)		
Land and buildings	381	427
Fixtures and fittings	129	160
	510	587
Current assets		
Inventories	300	406
Trade receivables	240	273
Cash at bank	4	–
	544	679
Total assets	1,054	1,266
EQUITY AND LIABILITIES		
Equity		
£0.50 ordinary shares (Note 1)	300	300
Retained earnings	263	234
	563	534
Non-current liabilities		
Borrowings – 9% loan notes (secured)	200	300
Current liabilities		
Trade payables	261	354
Taxation	30	2
Short-term borrowings (all bank overdraft)	–	76
	291	432
Total equity and liabilities	1,054	1,266

Income statements for the years ended 31 March

	2012 £m	2013 £m
Revenue (Note 2)	2,240	2,681
Cost of sales (Note 3)	(1,745)	(2,272)
Gross profit	495	409
Operating expenses	(252)	(362)
Operating profit	243	47
Interest payable	(18)	(32)
Profit before taxation	225	15
Taxation	(60)	(4)
Profit for the year	165	11

Statements of cash flows for the years ended 31 March

	2012 £m	2013 £m
Cash flows from operating activities		
Profit, after interest, before taxation	225	15
Adjustments for:		
Depreciation	26	33
Interest expense	18	32
	269	80
Increase in inventories	(59)	(106)
Increase in trade receivables	(17)	(33)
Increase in trade payables	58	93
Cash generated from operations	251	34
Interest paid	(18)	(32)
Taxation paid	(63)	(32)
Dividend paid	(40)	(40)
Net cash from/(used in) operating activities	130	(70)
Cash flows from investing activities		
Payments to acquire property, plant and equipment	(77)	(110)
Net cash used in investing activities	(77)	(110)
Cash flows from financing activities		
Issue of loan notes	–	100
Net cash from financing activities	–	100
Net increase in cash and cash equivalents	53	(80)
Cash and cash equivalents at start of year		
Cash/(overdraft)	(49)	4
Cash and cash equivalents at end of year		
Cash/(overdraft)	4	(76)

Notes:

1. The market value of the shares of the business at the end of the reporting period was £2.50 for 2012 and £1.50 for 2013.
2. All sales and purchases are made on credit.
3. The cost of sales figure can be analysed as follows:

	2012 £m	2013 £m
Opening inventories	241	300
Purchases (Note 2)	1,804	2,378
	2,045	2,678
Closing inventories	(300)	(406)
Cost of sales	1,745	2,272

4. At 31 March 2011, the trade receivables stood at £223 million and the trade payables at £183 million.
5. A dividend of £40 million has been paid to the shareholders in respect of each of the years.
6. The business employed 13,995 staff at 31 March 2012 and 18,623 at 31 March 2013.
7. The business expanded its capacity during 2013 by setting up a new warehouse and distribution centre.
8. At 1 April 2011, the total of equity stood at £438 million and the total of equity and non-current liabilities stood at £638 million.

Before we start our detailed look at the ratios for Alexis plc (in Example 8.1), it is helpful to take a quick look at what information is obvious from the financial statements. This will usually pick up some issues that ratios may not be able to identify. It may also highlight some points that could help us in our interpretation of the ratios. Starting at the top of the statement of financial position, the following points can be noted:

- *Expansion of non-current assets.* These have increased by about 15 per cent (from £510 million to £587 million). Note 7 mentions a new warehouse and distribution centre, which may account for much of the additional investment in non-current assets. We are not told when this new facility was established, but it is quite possible that it was well into the year. This could mean that not much benefit was reflected in terms of additional sales revenue or cost saving during 2013. Sales revenue, in fact, expanded by about 20 per cent (from £2,240 million to £2,681 million); this is greater than the expansion in non-current assets.

- *Major expansion in the elements of working capital.* Inventories increased by about 35 per cent, trade receivables by about 14 per cent and trade payables by about 36 per cent between 2012 and 2013. These are major increases, particularly in inventories and payables (which are linked because the inventories are all bought on credit – see Note 2).

- *Reduction in the cash balance.* The cash balance fell from £4 million (in funds) to a £76 million overdraft between 2012 and 2013. The bank may be putting the business under pressure to reverse this, which could raise difficulties.

- *Apparent debt capacity.* Comparing the non-current assets with the long-term borrowings implies that the business may well be able to offer security on further borrowing. This is because potential lenders usually look at the value of assets that can be offered as security when assessing loan requests. Lenders seem particularly attracted to land and buildings as security. For example, at 31 March 2013, non-current assets had a carrying amount (the value at which they appeared in the statement of financial position) of £587 million, but long-term borrowing was only £300 million (though there was also an overdraft of £76 million). Carrying amounts are not normally, of course, market values. On the other hand, land and buildings tend to have a market value higher than their value as shown on the statement of financial position due a general tendency to inflation in property values.

- *Lower operating profit.* Though sales revenue expanded by 20 per cent between 2012 and 2013, both cost of sales and operating expenses rose by a greater percentage, leaving both gross profit and, particularly, operating profit massively reduced. The level of staffing, which increased by about 33 per cent (from 13,995 to 18,623 employees – see Note 6), may have greatly affected the operating expenses. (Without knowing when the additional employees were recruited during 2013, we cannot be sure of the effect on operating expenses.) Increasing staffing by 33 per cent must put an enormous strain on management, at least in the short term. It is not surprising, therefore, that 2013 was not successful for the business – not, at least, in profit terms.

Having had a quick look at what is fairly obvious, without calculating any financial ratios, we shall now go on to calculate and interpret those relating to profitability, efficiency, liquidity and gearing.

The following ratios may be used to evaluate the profitability of the business:

- return on ordinary shareholders' funds
- return on capital employed
- operating profit margin
- gross profit margin.

We shall now look at each of these in turn.

Return on ordinary shareholders' funds (ROSF)

The **return on ordinary shareholders' funds ratio** compares the amount of profit for the period available to the owners with the owners' average stake in the business during that same period. The ratio (which is normally expressed in percentage terms) is as follows:

$$\text{ROSF} = \frac{\text{Profit for the year (less any preference dividend)}}{\text{Ordinary share capital} + \text{Reserves}} \times 100$$

The profit for the year (less any preference dividend) is used in calculating the ratio, as this figure represents the amount of profit that is attributable to the owners.

In the case of Alexis plc, the ratio for the year ended 31 March 2012 is

$$\text{ROSF} = \frac{165}{(438 + 563)/2} \times 100 = 33.0\%$$

Note that, when calculating the ROSF, the average of the figures for ordinary shareholders' funds as at the beginning and at the end of the year has been used. This is because an average figure is normally more representative. The amount of shareholders' funds was not constant throughout the year, yet we want to compare it with the profit earned during the whole period. We know, from Note 8, that the amount of shareholders' funds at 1 April 2011 was £438 million. By a year later, however, it had risen to £563 million, according to the statement of financial position as at 31 March 2012.

The easiest approach to calculating the average amount of shareholders' funds is to take a simple average based on the opening and closing figures for the year. This is often the only information available, as is the case with Example 8.1. Averaging is normally appropriate for all ratios that combine a figure for a period (such as profit for the year) with one taken at a point in time (such as shareholders' funds).

Where not even the beginning-of-year figure is available, it will be necessary to rely on just the year-end figure. This is not ideal but, if this approach is consistently applied, it can produce ratios that are useful.

Activity 8.2

Calculate the ROSF for Alexis plc for the year to 31 March 2013.

The ratio for 2013 is:

$$\text{ROSF} = \frac{11}{(563 + 534)/2} \times 100 = 2.0\%$$

Broadly, businesses seek to generate as high a value as possible for this ratio. This is provided that it is not achieved at the expense of jeopardising future returns by, for example, taking on more risky activities. In view of this, the 2013 ratio is very poor by any standards; a bank deposit account will normally yield a better return than this. We need to try to find out why things went so badly wrong in 2013. As we look at other ratios, we should find some clues.

Return on capital employed (ROCE)

The **return on capital employed ratio** is a fundamental measure of business performance. This ratio expresses the relationship between the operating profit generated during a period and the average long-term capital invested in the business.

The ratio is expressed in percentage terms and is as follows:

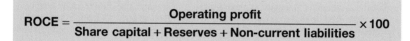

$$ROCE = \frac{Operating\ profit}{Share\ capital + Reserves + Non\text{-}current\ liabilities} \times 100$$

Note, in this case, that the profit figure used is the operating profit (that is, the profit *before* interest and taxation), because the ratio attempts to measure the returns to all suppliers of long-term finance before any deductions for interest payable on borrowings, or payments of dividends to shareholders, are made.

For the year to 31 March 2012, the ratio for Alexis plc is

$$ROCE = \frac{243}{(638 + 763)/2} \times 100 = 34.7\%$$

(The capital employed figure, which is the total equity plus non-current liabilities, at 1 April 2011 is given in Note 8.)

ROCE is considered by many to be a primary measure of profitability. It compares inputs (capital invested) with outputs (operating profit). This comparison is vital in assessing the effectiveness with which funds have been deployed. Once again, an average figure for capital employed should be used where the information is available.

Activity 8.3

Calculate the ROCE for Alexis plc for the year to 31 March 2013.

The ratio for 2013 is:

$$ROCE = \frac{47}{(763 + 834)/2} \times 100 = 5.9\%$$

This ratio tells much the same story as ROSF; namely a poor performance, with the return on the assets being less than the rate that the business has to pay for most of its borrowed funds (that is, 9 per cent for the loan notes).

Real World 8.1 shows how financial ratios are used by businesses as a basis for setting profitability targets.

Targeting profitability

The ROCE ratio is widely used by businesses when establishing targets for profitability. These targets are sometimes made public and here are some examples:

- Air France-KLM, the world's largest airline (on the basis of sales revenue), has set itself the target of achieving a ROCE of 7 per cent.
- BMW, the car maker, has a long-term target ROCE in excess of 26 per cent.
- Marks and Spencer plc, the retailer, announced in June 2011 a target return on capital employed for new capital invested of 12 to 15 per cent over three years.
- Tesco plc, the supermarket chain, aims to increase ROCE to 14.6 per cent by 2015. So far this has not been achieved and, in 2011, ROCE was 12.9 per cent.
- EasyJet, the budget airline, has a target ROCE of 12 per cent.

Source: Information taken from Air France-KLM press release, 14 February 2008; 'BMW adds to carmakers' gloom', FT.com, 1 August 2008; 'M&S to shake up executive pay to reflect Bolland plan', FT.com, 8 June 2011; 'Tesco looking afar for growth', FT.com, 19 April 2011; 'EasyJet faces debate on capital return', FT.com, 19 February 2012.

Real World 8.2 provides some indication of the levels of ROCE achieved by UK businesses.

Achieving profitability

ROCE ratios for UK manufacturing and service companies for each of the six years ending in 2011 are shown in Figure 8.2.

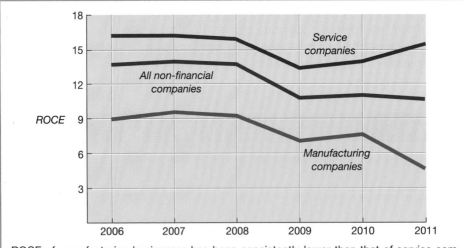

ROCE of manufacturing businesses has been consistently lower than that of service companies over the period. According to the Office of National Statistics, the difference in ROCE between the two sectors is accounted for by the higher capital intensity of manufacturing.

Figure 8.2 The ROCE of UK companies

Source: Figure compiled from information taken from 'Profitability of UK companies Q4 2011', Office of National Statistics, www.statistics.gov.uk, 4 April 2012.

Operating profit margin

The **operating profit margin ratio** relates the operating profit for the period to the sales revenue. The ratio is expressed as follows:

$$\text{Operating profit margin} = \frac{\text{Operating profit}}{\text{Sales revenue}} \times 100$$

The operating profit (that is, profit before interest and taxation) is used in this ratio as it represents the profit from trading operations before the interest payable expense is taken into account. This is often regarded as the most appropriate measure of operational performance when used as a basis of comparison, because differences arising from the way in which the business is financed will not influence the measure.

For the year ended 31 March 2012, Alexis plc's operating profit margin ratio is

$$\text{Operating profit margin} = \frac{243}{2,240} \times 100 = 10.8\%$$

This ratio compares one output of the business (operating profit) with another output (sales revenue). The ratio can vary considerably between types of business. For example, supermarkets tend to operate on low prices and, therefore, low operating profit margins. This is done in an attempt to stimulate sales and thereby increase the total amount of operating profit generated. Jewellers, on the other hand, tend to have high operating profit margins but have much lower levels of sales volume. Factors such as the degree of competition, the type of customer, the economic climate and industry characteristics (such as the level of risk) will influence the operating profit margin of a business. This point is picked up again later in the chapter.

Activity 8.4

Calculate the operating profit margin for Alexis plc for the year to 31 March 2013.

The ratio for 2013 is

$$\text{Operating profit margin} = \frac{47}{2,681} \times 100 = 1.8\%$$

Once again, this shows a very weak performance compared with that of 2012. In 2012 for every £1 of sales revenue an average of 10.8p (that is, 10.8 per cent) was left as operating profit, after paying the cost of the carpets sold and other expenses of operating the business. By 2013, however, this had fallen to only 1.8p for every £1. It seems that the reason for the poor ROSF and ROCE ratios was partially, perhaps wholly, a high level of other expenses relative to sales revenue. The next ratio should provide us with a clue as to how the sharp decline in this ratio occurred.

Real World 8.3 sets out the target operating profit margins for some well-known car manufacturers.

Profit driven

■ BMW set a target operating profit margin for 2011 of between 8 and 10 per cent, but achieved an 11.8 per cent return thanks to increasing sales to developing countries.

■ Daimler has set a target operating profit margin for its Mercedes unit of 10 per cent to be achieved by the second half of 2012.

■ Nissan has a target operating profit margin of 8 per cent and a target global market share of 8 per cent to be achieved by 2017. During the third quarter of 2011 the margin was just 5.1 per cent.

■ Toyota announced a medium-term target operating profit margin of 5 per cent in March 2011.

■ Opel, the European arm of General Motors, aims to achieve an operating profit margin of 4 to 5 per cent by 2013.

Premium car manufacturers, such as BMW and Mercedes, appear to have higher targets for their operating profit margin than mass-market car manufacturers, although the target periods often differ.

Source: 'BMW brings forward 2m car sales target', FT.com, 13 March 2012; 'Daimler has grand aims for small cars', FT.com, 14 June 2010; 'Nissan: Ghosn for broke', FT.com, 28 June 2011; 'Nissan: More China please', FT.com, 27 June 2011; 'Nissan Q3 operating profit sneaks up 3.5%', www.just-auto.com; 'Opel handed ambitious profit target', FT.com, 17 December 2009.

Gross profit margin

The **gross profit margin ratio** relates the gross profit of the business to the sales revenue generated for the same period. Gross profit represents the difference between sales revenue and the cost of sales. The ratio is therefore a measure of profitability in buying (or producing) and selling goods or services before any other expenses are taken into account. As cost of sales represents a major expense for many businesses, a change in this ratio can have a significant effect on the 'bottom line' (that is, the profit for the year). The gross profit margin ratio is calculated as follows:

$$\text{Gross profit margin} = \frac{\text{Gross profit}}{\text{Sales revenue}} \times 100$$

For the year to 31 March 2012, the ratio for Alexis plc is

$$\text{Gross profit margin} = \frac{495}{2,240} \times 100 = 22.1\%$$

 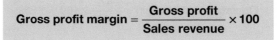
Calculate the gross profit margin for Alexis plc for the year to 31 March 2013.

The ratio for 2013 is

$$\text{Gross profit margin} = \frac{409}{2,681} \times 100 = 15.3\%$$

The decline in this ratio means that gross profit was lower *relative* to sales revenue in 2013 than it had been in 2012. Bearing in mind that

Gross profit = Sales revenue – Cost of sales (or cost of goods sold)

this means that cost of sales was higher *relative* to sales revenue in 2013 than in 2012. This could mean that sales prices were lower and/or that the purchase price of carpets had increased. It is possible that both sales prices and purchase prices had reduced, but the former at a greater rate than the latter. Similarly they may both have increased, but with sales prices having increased at a lesser rate than purchase prices.

Clearly, part of the decline in the operating profit margin ratio is linked to the dramatic decline in the gross profit margin ratio. Whereas, after paying for the carpets sold, for each £1 of sales revenue, 22.1p was left to cover other operating expenses in 2012, this was only 15.3p in 2013.

The profitability ratios for the business over the two years can be set out as follows:

	2012 %	2013 %
ROSF	33.0	2.0
ROCE	34.7	5.9
Operating profit margin	10.8	1.8
Gross profit margin	22.1	15.3

Activity 8.6

What do you deduce from a comparison of the declines in the operating profit and gross profit margin ratios?

We can see that the decline in the operating profit margin was 9 percentage points (from 10.8 per cent to 1.8 per cent), whereas that of the gross profit margin was only 6.8 percentage points (from 22.1 per cent to 15.3 per cent). This can only mean that operating expenses were greater, compared with sales revenue, in 2013 than they had been in 2012. The declines in both ROSF and ROCE were caused partly, therefore, by the business incurring higher inventories purchasing costs relative to sales revenue and partly through higher operating expenses compared with sales revenue. We should need to compare each of these ratios with their planned levels before we could usefully assess the business's success.

The analyst must now carry out some investigation to discover what caused the increases in both cost of sales and operating expenses, relative to sales revenue, from 2012 to 2013. This will involve checking on what has happened with sales and inventories prices over the two years. Similarly, it will involve looking at each of the individual areas that make up operating expenses to discover which ones were responsible for the increase, relative to sales revenue. Here, further ratios, for example staff expenses (wages and salaries) to sales revenue, could be calculated in an attempt to isolate the cause of the change from 2012 to 2013. In fact, as we discussed when we took an overview of the financial statements, the increase in staffing may well account for most of the increase in operating expenses.

Real World 8.4 discusses how high operating costs may adversely affect the future profitability of a leading car maker.

VW accelerates but costs vibrate

Volkswagen's fervent quest to overtake Japanese rival Toyota by 2018 threatens to exacerbate its already high cost structure and to hamper profitability in the coming years, analysts and industry executives have warned. The industry executives and analysts argue that VW's growth initiative – which involves a huge investment of €26.6 billion ($35.7 billion) in the next three years, the €16 billion takeovers of Porsche and its Salzburg dealership and a €1.7 billion stake in Japanese small car specialist Suzuki – will put the car maker back on a low-profit-margin track.

So far, Europe's largest car maker has been one of the most successful during the crisis. The Wolfsburg-based manufacturer posted a €911 million profit after tax and a 1.2 per cent profit margin in 2009 at a time when many others were making losses. VW is now aiming for an industry-leading pre-tax profit margin of more than 8 per cent in 2018, by which time it wants to become the world's leading car producer 'economically as well as ecologically', Martin Winterkorn, VW's chief executive, has said. The car maker wants to lift its sales from 6.3 million cars in the past year to more than 10 million by 2018.

While few dispute that VW could overtake Toyota – which sold almost 9 million cars in 2009 – in terms of sales, the profitability target remains in doubt. 'There should be more doubt in the market about the sustainability of VW's profits,' said Philippe Houchois, analyst at UBS.

In spite of its success, VW's cost structure is still in dire straits, particularly in Germany. With its 370,000 global workforce, the partly state-owned car maker trails almost all global rivals when it comes to statistics such as revenues or vehicles per employee. 'People forget that despite their large scale, VW has some of the worst cost structures in the industry. They have abysmal labour productivity and high plant costs,' said Max Warburton, analyst at research firm Sanford Bernstein.

Mr Warburton said that high margins have been the exception at VW. '2007 to 2008 represented a brief period of temporary profit maximisation delivered by a [now departed] temporary management team who made temporary, emergency cost cuts,' he said. VW disputes that it has taken its eye off cost-cutting. Hans Dieter Pötsch, the car maker's chief financial officer, said that 'by optimising our purchasing and increasing productivity . . . we have reached cost cuts of €1 billion throughout 2009'. In addition, he pointed to the carmaker's ongoing productivity improvement target of 10 per cent each year.

VW's profit figures for last year paint a dark picture of the car maker's cost structures. At least three of its nine brands – Seat, Bentley and Lamborghini, and probably also Bugatti whose results are not disclosed – were lossmaking, and are not expected to return to profit this year. VW's light truck operations only posted a profit after a one-off gain from the sale of its Brazil operations. Operating profit at the group's core brand, VW, was crimped by 79 per cent to €561 million, in spite of the marque benefiting hugely from European scrapping incentive programmes.

EFFICIENCY

Efficiency ratios are used to try to assess how successfully the various resources of the business are managed. The following ratios consider some of the more important aspects of resource management:

- average inventories turnover period
- average settlement period for trade receivables
- average settlement period for trade payables
- sales revenue to capital employed
- sales revenue per employee.

We shall now look at each of these in turn.

Average inventories turnover period

Inventories often represent a significant investment for a business. For some types of business (for example, manufacturers and certain retailers), inventories may account for a substantial proportion of the total assets held (see Real World 9.5). The **average inventories turnover period ratio** measures the average period for which inventories are being held. The ratio is calculated as follows:

$$\text{Average inventories turnover period} = \frac{\text{Average inventories held}}{\text{Cost of sales}} \times 365$$

The average inventories for the period can be calculated as a simple average of the opening and closing inventories levels for the year. However, in the case of a highly seasonal business, where inventories levels may vary considerably over the year, a monthly average may be more appropriate, should this information be available.

In the case of Alexis plc, the inventories turnover period for the year ended 31 March 2012 is

$$\text{Average inventories turnover period} = \frac{(241 + 300)/2}{1,745} \times 365 = 56.6 \text{ days}$$

(The opening inventories figure was taken from Note 3 to the financial statements.)

This means that, on average, the inventories held are being 'turned over' every 56.6 days. So, a carpet bought by the business on a particular day would, on average, have been sold about eight weeks later. A business will normally prefer a short inventories turnover period to a long one, because holding inventories has costs, for example the opportunity cost of the funds tied up. When judging the amount of inventories to carry, the business must consider such things as the likely demand for them, the possibility of supply shortages, the likelihood of price rises, the amount of storage space available and their perishability and/or susceptibility to obsolescence.

This ratio is sometimes expressed in terms of weeks or months rather than days. Multiplying by 52 or 12 rather than 365 will achieve this.

Activity 8.7

Calculate the average inventories turnover period for Alexis plc for the year ended 31 March 2013.

The ratio for 2013 is

$$\text{Average inventories turnover period} = \frac{(300 + 406)/2}{2,272} \times 365 = 56.7 \text{ days}$$

The inventories turnover period is virtually the same in both years.

Average settlement period for trade receivables

Selling on credit is the norm for most businesses, except for retailers. Trade receivables are a necessary evil. A business will naturally be concerned with the amount of funds tied up in trade receivables and try to keep this to a minimum. The speed of payment can have a significant effect on the business's cash flow. The **average settlement period for trade receivables ratio** calculates how long, on average, credit customers take to pay the amounts that they owe to the business. The ratio is as follows:

$$\text{Average settlement period for trade receivables} = \frac{\text{Average trade receivables}}{\text{Credit sales revenue}} \times 365$$

A business will normally prefer a shorter average settlement period to a longer one as, once again, funds are being tied up that may be used for more profitable purposes. Although this ratio can be useful, it is important to remember that it produces an *average* figure for the number of days for which debts are outstanding. This average may be badly distorted by, for example, a few large customers who are very slow or very fast payers.

Since all sales made by Alexis plc are on credit, the average settlement period for trade receivables for the year ended 31 March 2012 is

$$\text{Average settlement period for trade receivables} = \frac{(223 + 240)/2}{2{,}240} \times 365 = 37.7 \text{ days}$$

(The opening trade receivables figure was taken from Note 4 to the financial statements.)

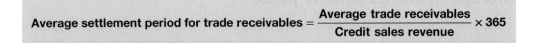

Activity 8.8

Calculate the average settlement period for Alexis plc's trade receivables for the year ended 31 March 2013.

The ratio for 2013 is

$$\text{Average settlement period for trade receivables} = \frac{(240 + 273)/2}{2{,}681} \times 365 = 34.9 \text{ days}$$

On the face of it, this reduction in the settlement period is welcome. It means that less cash was tied up in trade receivables for each £1 of sales revenue in 2013 than in 2012. Only if the reduction were achieved at the expense of customer goodwill or a high direct financial cost might the desirability of the reduction be questioned. For example, the reduction may have been due to chasing customers too vigorously or as a result of incurring higher expenses, such as discounts allowed to customers who pay quickly.

Average settlement period for trade payables

The **average settlement period for trade payables ratio** measures how long, on average, the business takes to pay those who have supplied goods and services on credit. The ratio is calculated as follows:

$$\text{Average settlement period for trade payables} = \frac{\text{Average trade payables}}{\text{Credit purchases}} \times 365$$

This ratio provides an average figure, which, like the average settlement period for trade receivables ratio, can be distorted by the payment period for one or two large suppliers.

As trade payables provide a free source of finance for the business, it is perhaps not surprising that some businesses attempt to increase their average settlement period for trade payables. However, such a policy can be taken too far and result in a loss of goodwill of suppliers.

For the year ended 31 March 2012, Alexis plc's average settlement period for trade payables is

$$\text{Average settlement period for trade payables} = \frac{(183 + 261)/2}{1,804} \times 365 = 44.9 \text{ days}$$

(The opening trade payables figure was taken from Note 4 to the financial statements and the purchases figure from Note 3.)

Activity 8.9

Calculate the average settlement period for trade payables for Alexis plc for the year ended 31 March 2013.

The ratio for 2013 is

$$\text{Average settlement period for trade payables} = \frac{(261 + 354)/2}{2,378} \times 365 = 47.2 \text{ days}$$

There was an increase between 2012 and 2013 in the average length of time that elapsed between buying inventories and services and paying for them. On the face of it, this is beneficial because the business is using free finance provided by suppliers. This is not necessarily advantageous, however, if it is leading to a loss of supplier goodwill that could have adverse consequences for Alexis plc.

Real World 8.5 reveals that paying promptly may also be desirable in order to keep small suppliers in business.

Real World 8.5

Feeling the squeeze

Large companies are increasingly monitoring the creditworthiness of their suppliers for fear that some of the smaller businesses may be at risk of collapse, according to Experian, the credit rating agency. Its claim, based on data and client feedback, suggests that large companies, previously criticised for unfairly squeezing smaller businesses by delaying payment to them, may now be realising that it is in their interests to look after these often vital elements of their supply chain.

This view is backed up by Experian's latest late payment figures. They show that the time companies took to settle supplier bills in the fourth quarter of 2012 shrank slightly compared with the previous three months despite the economy taking a turn for the worse. On average, companies took 25.84 days beyond the agreed date set out in their terms to pay their suppliers, compared with 26.17 in the third quarter of 2012, with the biggest improvements coming from the largest companies. This runs counter to previous experience,

→

when economic downturns have led to companies stretching out the time they take to pay suppliers in order to preserve some of the cash in their coffers.

Phil McCabe, FPB spokesman, said: 'Perhaps large companies are finally waking up to the fact that paying their suppliers late or imposing unfair changes to payment terms is damaging to their own businesses as well as small firms and the economy. Late payment forces businesses to close. Clearly, a smaller supplier base means less choice for these companies and, ultimately, their customers. Embracing prompt payment is simple commercial common sense.'

The improving payment times are not solely down to improved behaviour among large companies, because smaller businesses are also better at getting money owed to them in on time, according to Gareth Rumsey, research director at Experian. 'It is easy to bash the larger businesses that are paying late, but you cannot ignore the need for smaller businesses to get their own house in order,' he said.

Sales revenue to capital employed

The **sales revenue to capital employed ratio** (or net asset turnover ratio) examines how effectively the assets of the business are being used to generate sales revenue. It is calculated as follows:

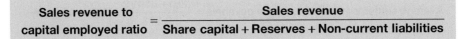

$$\text{Sales revenue to capital employed ratio} = \frac{\text{Sales revenue}}{\text{Share capital} + \text{Reserves} + \text{Non-current liabilities}}$$

Generally speaking, a higher sales revenue to capital employed ratio is preferred to a lower one. A higher ratio will normally suggest that assets are being used more productively in the generation of revenue. However, a very high ratio may suggest that the business is 'overtrading' on its assets, that is, it has insufficient assets to sustain the level of sales revenue achieved. We shall take a longer look at overtrading in Chapter 9.

When comparing the sales revenue to capital employed ratio for different businesses, factors such as the age and condition of assets held, the valuation bases for assets and whether assets are leased or owned outright can complicate interpretation.

A variation of this formula is to use the total assets less current liabilities (which is equivalent to long-term capital employed) in the denominator (lower part of the fraction). The same result is obtained.

For the year ended 31 March 2012 this ratio for Alexis plc is

$$\text{Sales revenue to capital employed} = \frac{2,240}{(638 + 763)/2} = 3.20 \text{ times}$$

Activity 8.10

Calculate the sales revenue to capital employed ratio for Alexis plc for the year ended 31 March 2013.

The ratio for 2013 is

$$\text{Sales revenue to capital employed} = \frac{2,681}{(763 + 834)/2} = 3.36 \text{ times}$$

This seems to be an improvement, since in 2013 more sales revenue was being generated for each £1 of capital employed (£3.36) than was the case in 2012 (£3.20). Provided that overtrading is not an issue, and that the additional sales are generating an acceptable profit, this is to be welcomed.

Sales revenue per employee

The **sales revenue per employee ratio** relates sales revenue generated during a reporting period to a particular business resource, that is, labour. It provides a measure of the productivity of the workforce. The ratio is

$$\text{Sales revenue per employee} = \frac{\text{Sales revenue}}{\text{Number of employees}}$$

Generally, businesses would prefer a high value for this ratio, implying that they are using their staff efficiently.

For the year ended 31 March 2012, the ratio for Alexis plc is

$$\text{Sales revenue per employee} = \frac{£2,240m}{13,995} = £160,057$$

Activity 8.11

Calculate the sales revenue per employee for Alexis plc for the year ended 31 March 2013.

The ratio for 2013 is

$$\text{Sales revenue per employee} = \frac{£2,681m}{18,623} = £143,962$$

This represents a fairly significant decline and probably one that merits further investigation. As we discussed previously, the number of employees had increased quite notably (by about 33 per cent) during 2013 and the analyst will probably try to discover why this had not generated sufficient additional sales revenue to maintain the ratio at its 2012 level. It could be that the additional employees were not appointed until late in the year ended 31 March 2013.

The efficiency, or activity, ratios may be summarised as follows:

	2012	2013
Average inventories turnover period	56.6 days	56.7 days
Average settlement period for trade receivables	37.7 days	34.9 days
Average settlement period for trade payables	44.9 days	47.2 days
Sales revenue to capital employed (net asset turnover)	3.20 times	3.36 times
Sales revenue per employee	£160,057	£143,962

What do you deduce from a comparison of the efficiency ratios over the two years?

Maintaining the inventories turnover period at the 2012 level might be reasonable, though whether this represents a satisfactory period can probably only be assessed by looking at the business's planned inventories period. The inventories turnover period for other businesses operating in carpet retailing, particularly those regarded as the market leaders, may have been helpful in formulating the plans. On the face of things, a shorter receivables collection period and a longer payables payment period are both desirable. On the other hand, these may have been achieved at the cost of a loss of the goodwill of customers and suppliers, respectively. The increased sales revenue to capital employed ratio seems beneficial, provided that the business can manage this increase. The decline in the sales revenue per employee ratio is undesirable but, as we have already seen, is probably related to the dramatic increase in the level of staffing. As with the inventories turnover period, these other ratios need to be compared with the planned standard of efficiency.

RELATIONSHIP BETWEEN PROFITABILITY AND EFFICIENCY

In our earlier discussions concerning profitability ratios, we saw that return on capital employed (ROCE) is regarded as a key ratio by many businesses. The ratio is

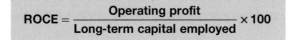

$$\text{ROCE} = \frac{\text{Operating profit}}{\text{Long-term capital employed}} \times 100$$

where long-term capital comprises share capital plus reserves plus long-term borrowings. This ratio can be broken down into two elements, as shown in Figure 8.3. The first ratio is the operating profit margin ratio and the second is the sales revenue to capital employed (net asset turnover) ratio, both of which we discussed earlier.

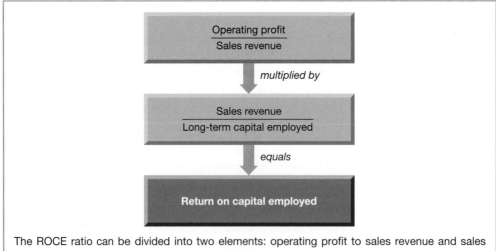

The ROCE ratio can be divided into two elements: operating profit to sales revenue and sales revenue to capital employed. By analysing ROCE in this way, we can see the influence of both profitability and efficiency on this important ratio.

Figure 8.3 The main elements of the ROCE ratio

By breaking down the ROCE ratio in this manner, we highlight the fact that the overall return on funds employed within the business will be determined both by the profitability of sales and by efficiency in the use of capital.

Example 8.2

Consider the following information, for last year, concerning two different businesses operating in the same industry:

	Antler plc £m	Baker plc £m
Operating profit	20	15
Average long-term capital employed	100	75
Sales revenue	200	300

The ROCE for each business is identical (20 per cent). However, the manner in which that return was achieved by each business was quite different. In the case of Antler plc, the operating profit margin is 10 per cent and the sales revenue to capital employed ratio is 2 times (so ROCE = 10% × 2 = 20%). In the case of Baker plc, the operating profit margin is 5 per cent and the sales revenue to capital employed ratio is 4 times (and so ROCE = 5% × 4 = 20%).

Example 8.2 demonstrates that a relatively high sales revenue to capital employed ratio can compensate for a relatively low operating profit margin. Similarly, a relatively low sales revenue to capital employed ratio can be overcome by a relatively high operating profit margin. In many areas of retail and distribution (for example, supermarkets and delivery services), operating profit margins are quite low but the ROCE can be high, provided that the assets are used productively (that is, low margin, high sales revenue to capital employed).

Activity 8.13

Show how the ROCE ratio for Alexis plc can be analysed into the two elements for each of the years 2012 and 2013. What conclusions can you draw from your figures?

	ROCE	=	Operating profit margin	×	Sales revenue to capital employed
2012	34.7%		10.8%		3.20
2013	5.9%		1.8%		3.36

As we can see, the relationship between the three ratios holds for Alexis plc for both years. The small apparent differences arise because the three ratios are stated here only to one or two decimal places.

Although the business was more effective at generating sales revenue (sales revenue to capital employed ratio increased) in 2013 than in 2012, in 2013 it fell well below the level necessary to compensate for the sharp decline in the effectiveness of each sale (operating profit margin). As a result, the 2013 ROCE was well below the 2012 value.

LIQUIDITY

Liquidity ratios are concerned with the ability of the business to meet its short-term financial obligations. The following ratios are widely used:

- current ratio
- acid test ratio
- cash generated from operations to maturing obligations.

These ratios will now be considered.

Current ratio

The **current ratio** compares the 'liquid' assets (that is, cash and those assets held that will soon be turned into cash) of the business with the current liabilities. The ratio is calculated as follows:

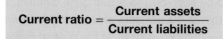

$$\text{Current ratio} = \frac{\text{Current assets}}{\text{Current liabilities}}$$

Some people seem to believe that there is an 'ideal' current ratio (usually 2 times or 2:1) for all businesses. However, this fails to take into account the fact that different types of business require different current ratios. For example, a manufacturing business will often have a relatively high current ratio because it has to hold inventories of finished goods, raw materials and work in progress. It will also normally sell goods on credit, thereby giving rise to trade receivables. A supermarket chain, on the other hand, will have a relatively low ratio, as it will hold only fast-moving inventories of finished goods and all of its sales will be made for cash (no credit sales) (see Real World 9.5).

The higher the ratio, the more liquid the business is considered to be. As liquidity is vital to the survival of a business, a higher current ratio might be thought to be preferable to a lower one. If a business has a very high ratio, however, it may be that excessive funds are tied up in cash or other liquid assets and are not, therefore, being used as productively as they might otherwise be.

As at 31 March 2012, the current ratio of Alexis plc is

$$\text{Current ratio} = \frac{544}{291} = 1.9 \text{ times (or 1.9:1)}$$

Activity 8.14

Calculate the current ratio for Alexis plc as at 31 March 2013.

The ratio as at 31 March 2013 is

$$\text{Current ratio} = \frac{679}{432} = 1.6 \text{ times (or 1.6:1)}$$

Although this is a decline from 2012 to 2013, it is not necessarily a matter of concern. The next ratio may provide a clue as to whether there seems to be a problem.

Acid test ratio

The **acid test ratio** is very similar to the current ratio, but it represents a more stringent test of liquidity in that it excludes inventories. For many businesses, inventories cannot be converted into cash quickly. (Note that, in the case of Alexis plc, the inventories turnover period was about 57 days in both years.) As a result, it may be better to exclude this particular asset from any measure of liquidity.

The minimum level for this ratio is often stated as 1.0 times (or 1:1; that is, current assets (excluding inventories) equal current liabilities). In many highly successful businesses that are regarded as having adequate liquidity, however, it is not unusual for the acid test ratio to be below 1.0 without causing particular liquidity problems.

The acid test ratio is calculated as follows:

$$\text{Acid test ratio} = \frac{\text{Current assets (excluding inventories)}}{\text{Current liabilities}}$$

The acid test ratio for Alexis plc as at 31 March 2012 is

$$\text{Acid test ratio} = \frac{544 - 300}{291} = 0.8 \text{ times (or 0.8:1)}$$

We can see that the 'liquid' current assets do not quite cover the current liabilities, so the business may be experiencing some liquidity problems.

Activity 8.15

Calculate the acid test ratio for Alexis plc as at 31 March 2013.

The ratio as at 31 March 2013 is

$$\text{Acid test ratio} = \frac{679 - 406}{432} = 0.6 \text{ times}$$

The 2013 ratio is significantly below that for 2012. The 2013 level may well be a cause for concern. The rapid decline in this ratio should lead to steps being taken, at least, to investigate the reason for this and, perhaps, to stop it falling further.

Cash generated from operations to maturing obligations

The **cash generated from operations to maturing obligations ratio** compares the cash generated from operations (taken from the statement of cash flows) with the current liabilities of the business. It provides a further indication of the ability of the business to meet its maturing obligations. The ratio is expressed as

$$\frac{\text{Cash generated from operations}}{\text{to maturing obligations}} = \frac{\text{Cash generated from operations}}{\text{Current liabilities}}$$

The higher this ratio is, the better the liquidity of the business. This ratio has the advantage over the current ratio that the operating cash flows for a period usually provide a more reliable guide to the liquidity of a business than do the current assets held at the statement of financial position date. Alexis plc's ratio for the year ended 31 March 2012 is

$$\text{Cash generated from operations to maturing obligations ratio} = \frac{251}{291} = 0.9 \text{ times}$$

This indicates that the operating cash flows for the year are not quite sufficient to cover the current liabilities at the end of the year.

Activity 8.16

Calculate the cash generated from operations to maturing obligations ratio for Alexis plc for the year ended 31 March 2013.

$$\text{Cash generated from operations to maturing obligations ratio} = \frac{34}{432} = 0.1 \text{ times}$$

This shows an alarming decline in the ability of the business to meet its maturing obligations from its operating cash flows. This confirms that liquidity is a real cause for concern for the business.

The liquidity ratios for the two-year period may be summarised as follows:

	2012	2013
Current ratio	1.9	1.6
Acid test ratio	0.8	0.6
Cash generated from operations to maturing obligations	0.9	0.1

Activity 8.17

What do you deduce from these liquidity ratios?

Although it is probably not really possible to make a totally valid judgement without knowing the planned ratios, there appears to have been a worrying decline in liquidity. This is indicated by all three of these ratios. The most worrying is in the last ratio because it shows that the ability of the business to generate cash from trading operations has declined, relative to the short-term debts, from 2012 to 2013. The apparent liquidity problem may, however, be planned, short-term and linked to the expansion in non-current assets and staffing. It may be that when the benefits of the expansion come on stream, liquidity will improve. On the other hand, short-term claimants may become anxious when they see signs of weak liquidity. This anxiety could lead to steps being taken to press for payment, which could cause problems for Alexis plc.

OPERATING CASH CYCLE

When assessing the liquidity of a business, it is important to be aware of the **operating cash cycle (OCC)** of the business. For a retailer, for example, this may be defined as the period between the outlay of cash necessary for the purchase of inventories and the ultimate receipt of cash from the sale of the goods. In the case of a business that purchases goods on credit for subsequent resale on credit, such as a wholesaler, the OCC is as shown in Figure 8.4.

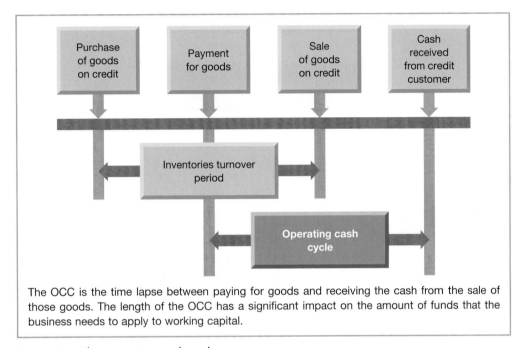

The OCC is the time lapse between paying for goods and receiving the cash from the sale of those goods. The length of the OCC has a significant impact on the amount of funds that the business needs to apply to working capital.

Figure 8.4 The operating cash cycle

Figure 8.4 shows that payment for inventories acquired on credit occurs some time after those inventories have been purchased. Therefore, no immediate cash outflow arises from the purchase. Similarly, cash receipts from credit customers will occur some time after the sale is made. There will be no immediate cash inflow as a result of the sale. The OCC is the period between the payment made to the supplier, for the goods concerned, and the cash received from the credit customer. Although Figure 8.4 depicts the position for a wholesaling business, the precise definition of the OCC can easily be adapted for other types of business.

The OCC is important because it has a significant influence on the financing requirements of the business. Broadly, the longer the cycle, the greater will be the financing requirements and the greater the financial risks. For this reason, the business is likely to want to reduce the OCC to the minimum possible period.

For the type of business mentioned above, which buys and sells on credit, the OCC can be calculated from the financial statements by the use of certain ratios. It is calculated as shown in Figure 8.5.

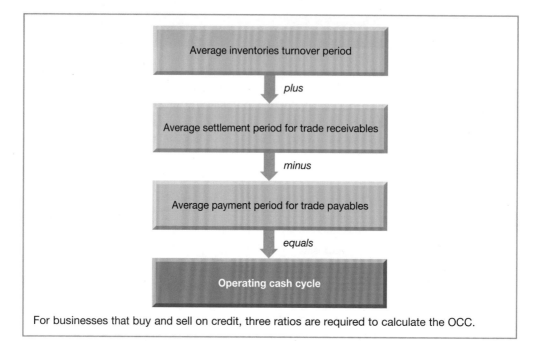

For businesses that buy and sell on credit, three ratios are required to calculate the OCC.

Figure 8.5 Calculating the operating cash cycle

Activity 8.18

The following figures are taken from the financial statements of Satview Ltd, a distributor of television satellite dishes, for the year ended 31 December last year:

	£000
Sales revenue	820
Cost of sales	544
Opening inventories	142
Closing inventories	166
Purchases	568
Inventories	166
Trade receivables	264
Trade payables	159

All purchases and sales are on credit. There has been no change in the level of trade receivables or payables over the period.

Calculate the length of the OCC for the business and go on to suggest how the business may seek to reduce this period.

The OCC may be calculated as follows:

	Number of days
Average inventories turnover period:	
$\dfrac{(\text{Opening inventories} + \text{Closing inventories})/2}{\text{Cost of sales}} \times 365 = \dfrac{(142 + 166)/2}{544} \times 365$	103
Average settlement period for trade receivables:	
$\dfrac{\text{Trade receivables}}{\text{Credit sales}} \times 365 = \dfrac{264}{820} \times 365$	118
Average settlement period for trade payables:	
$\dfrac{\text{Trade payables}}{\text{Credit purchases}} \times 365 = \dfrac{159}{568} \times 365$	(102)
OCC	119

The business can reduce the length of the OCC in a number of ways. The average inventories turnover period seems quite long. At present, average inventories held represent more than three months' sales requirements. Lowering the level of inventories held will reduce this. Similarly, the average settlement period for trade receivables seems long, at nearly four months' sales. Imposing tighter credit control, offering discounts, charging interest on overdue accounts and so on may reduce this. However, any policy decisions concerning inventories and trade receivables must take account of current trading conditions.

Extending the period of credit taken to pay suppliers could also reduce the OCC. However, for reasons that were explained earlier, this option must be approached with caution.

An objective of working capital management may be to maintain the OCC at a particular target level or within certain limits each side of the target. A problem with this objective is that not all days in the OCC are equally valuable. Take, for example, the information in Activity 8.18, where the operating cycle is 119 days. If both trade receivables and trade payables were increased by seven days (by allowing customers longer to pay and by Satview taking longer to pay suppliers), the OCC would be unchanged at 119 days. This would not, however, leave the amount tied up in working capital unchanged. Trade receivables would increase by £15,726 (that is, 7 × £820,000/365) whereas trade payables would increase by only £10,893 (that is, 7 × £568,000/365). This would mean a net increase of £4,833 in working capital.

Real World 8.6 shows the average operating cash cycle for large European businesses.

Cycling along

The average operating cycle reduced by 16 per cent between 2002 and 2010, with each element of working capital making a contribution to this improvement. Inventories fell by 9 per cent and trade receivables by 4 per cent, while trade payables increased by 8 per cent over the period.

A survey of working capital conducted by Ernst and Young calculates the average operating cash cycle for the top 1,000 European businesses (excluding financial and auto manufacturing businesses) (see Figure 8.6).

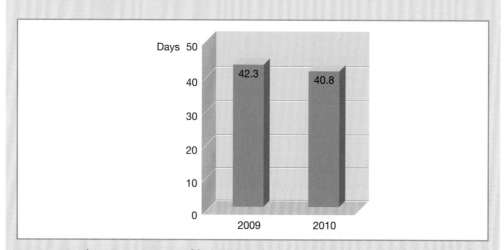

Figure 8.6 The average OCC of large European businesses for 2009 and 2010

The average OCC for 2009 was 42.3 days, and for 2010 was down to 40.8.

Source: Adapted from figure in *All Tied Up: Working Capital Management Survey 2011*, Ernst and Young, www.ey.com, p. 2.

FINANCIAL GEARING

Financial gearing occurs when a business is financed, at least in part, by borrowing instead of by finance provided by the owners (the shareholders) as equity. A business's level of gearing (that is, the extent to which it is financed from sources that require a fixed return) is an important factor in assessing risk. Where a business borrows, it takes on a commitment to pay interest charges and make capital repayments. Where the borrowing is heavy, this can be a significant financial burden; it can increase the risk of the business becoming insolvent. Nevertheless, most businesses are geared to some extent. (Costain Group plc, the builders and construction business, is a rare example of a UK business with no borrowings.)

Given the risks involved, we may wonder why a business would want to take on gearing (that is, to borrow). One reason may be that the owners have insufficient funds, so the only way to finance the business adequately is to borrow from others. Another reason is that gearing can be used to increase the returns to owners. This is possible provided that the returns generated from borrowed funds exceed the cost of paying interest. Example 8.3 illustrates this point.

Example 8.3

The long-term capital structures of two new businesses, Lee Ltd and Nova Ltd, are as follows:

	Lee Ltd £	Nova Ltd £
£1 ordinary shares	100,000	200,000
10% loan notes	200,000	100,000
	300,000	300,000

In their first year of operations, they each make an operating profit (that is, profit before interest and taxation) of £50,000. The tax rate is 30 per cent of the profit before taxation but after interest.

Lee Ltd would probably be considered relatively highly geared, as it has a high proportion of borrowed funds in its long-term capital structure. Nova Ltd is much less highly geared. The profit available to the shareholders of each business in the first year of operations will be:

	Lee Ltd £	Nova Ltd £
Operating profit	50,000	50,000
Interest payable	(20,000)	(10,000)
Profit before taxation	30,000	40,000
Taxation (30%)	(9,000)	(12,000)
Profit for the year (available to ordinary shareholders)	21,000	28,000

The return on ordinary shareholders' funds (ROSF) for each business will be:

Lee Ltd
$$\frac{21,000}{100,000} \times 100 = 21\%$$

Nova Ltd
$$\frac{28,000}{200,000} \times 100 = 14\%$$

We can see that Lee Ltd, the more highly geared business, has generated a better ROSF than Nova Ltd. This is despite the fact that the ROCE (return on capital employed) is identical for both businesses (that is, (£50,000/£300,000) × 100 = 16.7%).

Note that at the £50,000 level of operating profit, the shareholders of both Lee Ltd and Nova Ltd benefit from gearing, in terms of their returns. Were the two businesses totally reliant on equity financing, the profit for the year (profit after taxation) would be £35,000 (that is, £50,000 less 30 per cent taxation), giving an ROSF of 11.7 per cent (that is, £35,000/£300,000). Both businesses generate higher ROSFs than this as a result of financial gearing.

An effect of gearing is that returns to shareholders become more sensitive to changes in operating profits. For a highly geared business, a change in operating profits will lead to a proportionately greater change in the ROSF ratio.

Assume that the operating profit was 20 per cent higher for each business than stated above (that is, an operating profit of £60,000). What would be the effect of this on ROSF?

The revised profit available to the shareholders of each business in the first year of operations will be:

	Lee Ltd	Nova Ltd
	£	£
Operating profit	60,000	60,000
Interest payable	(20,000)	(10,000)
Profit before taxation	40,000	50,000
Taxation (30%)	(12,000)	(15,000)
Profit for the year (available to ordinary shareholders)	28,000	35,000

The ROSF for each business will now be:

Lee Ltd

$$\frac{28,000}{100,000} \times 100 = 28\%$$

Nova Ltd

$$\frac{35,000}{200,000} \times 100 = 17.5\%$$

We can see that for Lee Ltd, the higher-geared business, the returns to shareholders have increased by one-third (from 21 per cent to 28 per cent), whereas for the lower-geared business, Nova Ltd, the benefits of gearing are less pronounced, increasing by only one-quarter (from 14 per cent to 17.5 per cent). The effect of gearing can, of course, work in both directions. So, for a highly geared business, a small decline in operating profit will bring about a much greater decline in the returns to shareholders.

The reason that gearing seems to be beneficial to shareholders is that interest rates for borrowings are low by comparison with the returns that the typical business can earn. On top of this, interest expenses are tax-deductible, in the way shown in Example 8.3 and Activity 8.19. This makes the effective cost of borrowing quite cheap. It is debatable whether the apparent low interest rates really are beneficial to the shareholders. It is broadly accepted that since borrowing increases the risk to shareholders, there is a hidden cost of borrowing. In fact, many argue that this increased risk is precisely compensated by the higher returns, giving no net benefit to the shareholders. In other words, the apparent benefits of higher returns are illusory. What are not illusory, however, are the benefits to the shareholders of the tax-deductibility of interest on borrowings.

Activity 8.20

If shareholders gain from the tax-deductibility of interest on borrowings, who loses?

The loser is the tax authority – ultimately the government and other taxpayers.

The effect of gearing is like that of two intermeshing cogwheels of unequal size (see Figure 8.7). The movement in the larger cog (operating profit) causes a more than proportionate movement in the smaller cog (returns to ordinary shareholders).

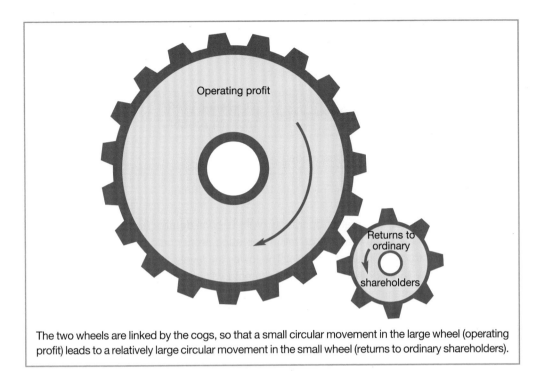

The two wheels are linked by the cogs, so that a small circular movement in the large wheel (operating profit) leads to a relatively large circular movement in the small wheel (returns to ordinary shareholders).

Figure 8.7 The effect of financial gearing

Two ratios are widely used to assess gearing:

- gearing ratio
- interest cover ratio.

Gearing ratio

The **gearing ratio** measures the contribution of long-term lenders to the long-term capital structure of a business:

$$\text{Gearing ratio} = \frac{\text{Long-term (non-current) liabilities}}{\text{Share capital} + \text{Reserves} + \text{Long-term (non-current) liabilities}} \times 100$$

The gearing ratio for Alexis plc, as at 31 March 2012, is

$$\text{Gearing ratio} = \frac{200}{(563 + 200)} \times 100 = 26.2\%$$

This is a level of gearing that would not normally be considered to be very high.

Activity 8.21

Calculate the gearing ratio of Alexis plc as at 31 March 2013.

The ratio as at 31 March 2013 is

$$\text{Gearing ratio} = \frac{300}{(534 + 300)} \times 100 = 36.0\%$$

This is a substantial increase in the level of gearing over the year.

Interest cover ratio

The **interest cover ratio** measures the amount of operating profit available to cover interest payable. The ratio may be calculated as follows:

$$\text{Interest cover ratio} = \frac{\text{Operating profit}}{\text{Interest payable}}$$

The ratio for Alexis plc for the year ended 31 March 2012 is

$$\text{Interest cover ratio} = \frac{243}{18} = 13.5 \text{ times}$$

This ratio shows that the level of operating profit is considerably higher than the level of interest payable. This means that a large fall in operating profit could occur before operating profit levels failed to cover interest payable. The lower the level of operating profit coverage, the greater the risk to lenders that interest payments will not be met. There will also be a greater risk to the shareholders that the lenders will take action against the business to recover the interest due.

Activity 8.22

Calculate the interest cover ratio of Alexis plc for the year ended 31 March 2013.

The ratio for the year ended 31 March 2013 is

$$\text{Interest cover ratio} = \frac{47}{32} = 1.5 \text{ times}$$

Alexis plc's gearing ratios are:

	2012	2013
Gearing ratio	26.2%	36.0%
Interest cover ratio	13.5 times	1.5 times

Activity 8.23

What do you deduce from a comparison of Alexis plc's gearing ratios over the two years?

The gearing ratio altered significantly. This is mainly due to the substantial increase in the contribution of long-term lenders to the financing of the business.

The interest cover ratio has declined dramatically from a position where operating profit covered interest 13.5 times in 2012, to one where operating profit covered interest only 1.5 times in 2013. This was partly caused by the increase in borrowings in 2013, but mainly caused by the dramatic decline in profitability in that year. The later situation looks hazardous; only a small decline in future profitability would leave the business with insufficient operating profit to cover the interest payments. The gearing ratio at 31 March 2013 would not necessarily be considered to be very high for a business that was trading successfully. It is the low profitability that is the problem.

Without knowing what the business planned these ratios to be, it is not possible to reach a valid conclusion on Alexis plc's gearing.

Real World 8.7 consists of extracts from an article that discusses the likely lowering of gearing levels in the face of the recession. It explains that many businesses are likely to issue additional ordinary shares (equity) to reduce borrowing as a means of reducing gearing. Note that the gearing ratio mentioned in the article differs slightly from the one discussed above.

Real World 8.7

Changing gear

With a wave of rights issues and other equity issuance now expected from the UK's non-financial companies – and with funds from these being used to pay down debt – the pendulum is rapidly swinging back in favour of more conservative balance sheet [statement of financial position] management. Gearing levels are set to fall dramatically, analysts say. 'There is going to be an appreciable and material drop in gearing, by about a quarter or a third over the next three years', predicts Mr Siddall, chief executive of the Association of Corporate Treasurers.

Historically, gearing levels – as measured by net debt as a proportion of shareholders' funds – have run at an average of about 30 per cent over the past 20 years. Peak levels (around 45 per cent) were reached in the past few years as companies took advantage of cheap credit. Current predictions see it coming down to about 20 per cent – and staying there for a good while to come. Graham Secker, managing director of equity research at Morgan Stanley, says: 'This is going to be a relatively long-term phenomenon.'

One of the most immediate concerns to heavily indebted companies is whether, in a recessionary environment, they will be able to generate the profit and cash flows to service their debts.

Gearing levels vary from sector to sector as well. Oil companies prefer low levels given their exposure to the volatility of oil prices. BP's net debt-shareholders' funds ratio of 21 per cent is at the low end of a 20 to 30 per cent range it considers prudent. Miners' gearing is on a clear downward trend already. Xstrata, the mining group, stressed last month that its £4.1 billion rights issue would cut gearing from 40 per cent to less than 30 per cent. A week later, BHP said its $13 billion of first-half cash flows had cut gearing to less than 10 per cent. Rio Tinto, which had gearing of 130 per cent at the last count in August 2008, is desperately trying to cut it by raising fresh equity.

Utilities tend to be highly geared because they can afford to borrow more against their typically reliable cash flows. But even here the trend is downwards. Severn Trent, the UK water group, says its appropriate long-term gearing level is 60 per cent. But 'given ongoing uncertainties . . . it is prudent in the near term to retain as much liquidity and flexibility as possible'. It does not expect to pursue that target until credit markets improve.

Reducing gearing is not easy, especially for the most indebted companies that need to the most: shareholders will be more reluctant to finance replacement equity in companies with highly leveraged balance sheets. The supply of fresh equity will also be constrained, not only by a glut of demand from companies but by the squeeze on investor money from a wave of government bond issuance.

Source: 'Gearing levels set to plummet' (Grant, J) *Financial Times*, 10 February 2009.

Both Ali plc and Bhaskar plc operate wholesale electrical stores throughout the UK. The financial statements of each business for the year ended 30 June 2013 are as follows:

Statements of financial position as at 30 June 2013

	Ali plc £m	Bhaskar plc £m
ASSETS		
Non-current assets		
Property, plant and equipment (cost less depreciation)		
Land and buildings	360.0	510.0
Fixtures and fittings	87.0	91.2
	447.0	601.2
Current assets		
Inventories	592.0	403.0
Trade receivables	176.4	321.9
Cash at bank	84.6	91.6
	853.0	816.5
Total assets	1,300.0	1,417.7
EQUITY AND LIABILITIES		
Equity		
£1 ordinary shares	320.0	250.0
Retained earnings	367.6	624.6
	687.6	874.6
Non-current liabilities		
Borrowings – loan notes	190.0	250.0
Current liabilities		
Trade payables	406.4	275.7
Taxation	16.0	17.4
	422.4	293.1
Total equity and liabilities	1,300.0	1,417.7

Income statements for the year ended 30 June 2013

	Ali plc £m	Bhaskar plc £m
Revenue	1,478.1	1,790.4
Cost of sales	(1,018.3)	(1,214.9)
Gross profit	459.8	575.5
Operating expenses	(308.5)	(408.6)
Operating profit	151.3	166.9
Interest payable	(19.4)	(27.5)
Profit before taxation	131.9	139.4
Taxation	(32.0)	(34.8)
Profit for the year	99.9	104.6

All purchases and sales were on credit. The market values of a share in Ali plc and Bhaskar plc at the end of the year were £6.50 and £8.20 respectively.

Required:
For each business, calculate two ratios that are concerned with each of the following aspects:

- profitability
- efficiency
- liquidity
- gearing

(eight ratios in total).

What can you conclude from the ratios that you have calculated?

A solution to this question can be found in Appendix C.

SUMMARY

The main points of this chapter may be summarised as follows:

Ratio analysis

- Compares two related figures, usually both from the same set of financial statements.
- Is an aid to understanding what the financial statements really mean.
- Is an inexact science so results must be interpreted cautiously.
- Past periods, the performance of similar businesses and planned performance are often used to provide benchmark ratios.
- A brief overview of the financial statements can often provide insights that may not be revealed by ratios and/or may help in the interpretation of them.

Profitability ratios

- Profitability ratios are concerned with effectiveness at generating profit.
- The profitability ratios covered are the return on ordinary shareholders' funds (ROSF), return on capital employed (ROCE), operating profit margin and gross profit margin.

Efficiency ratios

- Efficiency ratios are concerned with efficiency of using assets/resources.
- The efficiency ratios covered are the average inventories turnover period, average settlement period for trade receivables, average settlement period for trade payables, sales revenue to capital employed and sales revenue per employee.

Liquidity ratios

- Liquidity ratios are concerned with the ability to meet short-term obligations.
- The liquidity ratios covered are the current ratio, the acid test ratio and the cash generated from operations to maturing obligations ratio.

Operating cash cycle

- The operating cash cycle for a wholesaler is the length of time from buying inventories to receiving cash from receivables less payables' payment period (in days).

Gearing ratios

- Gearing ratios are concerned with the relationship between equity and debt financing.
- The gearing ratios covered are the gearing ratio and the interest cover ratio.

MyAccountingLab

KEY TERMS

return on ordinary shareholders' funds ratio (ROSF) p. 256

return on capital employed ratio (ROCE) p. 257

operating profit margin ratio p. 259

gross profit margin ratio p. 260

average inventories turnover period ratio p. 263

average settlement period for trade receivables ratio p. 264

average settlement period for trade payables ratio p. 264

sales revenue to capital employed ratio p. 266

sales revenue per employee ratio p. 267

current ratio p. 270

acid test ratio p. 271

cash generated from operations to maturing obligations ratio p. 271

operating cash cycle (OCC) p. 273

financial gearing p. 276

gearing ratio p. 279

interest cover ratio p. 280

FURTHER READING

If you would like to explore the topics covered in this chapter in more depth, try the following:

Elliott, B. and Elliott, J., *Financial Accounting and Reporting*, 15th edn, Financial Times Prentice Hall, 2011, Chapters 28 and 29

Fridson, M., and Alvarez, F., *Financial Statement Analysis: A Practitioner's Guide*, 4th edn, Wiley Finance, 2011, Chapters 13 and 14

Penman, S., *Financial Statement Analysis and Security Valuation*, 3rd edn, McGraw-Hill Irwin, 2012, Chapters 7 to 12

Schoenebeck, K. and Holtzman, M., *Interpreting and Analyzing Financial Statements*, 6th edn, Prentice Hall, 2012, Chapters 2 to 5

REVIEW QUESTIONS

Solutions to these questions can be found in Appendix D.

8.1 Some businesses (for example, supermarket chains) operate on a low operating profit margin. Does this mean that the return on capital employed from the business will also be low?

8.2 For the current year, the average settlement period for trade receivables at Arkle plc was 60 days. This figure is much higher than in previous years. What factors may have contributed to this change of ratio?

8.3 Two businesses operate in the same industry. One has an inventories turnover period that is longer than the industry average. The other has an inventories turnover period that is shorter than the industry average. Give three possible explanations for each business's inventories turnover period ratio.

8.4 In the text it was mentioned that ratios help to eliminate some of the problems of comparing businesses of different sizes. Does this mean that size is irrelevant when interpreting and analysing the position and performance of different businesses?

Exercises 8.1 to 8.3 are basic level, 8.4 and 8.5 are intermediate level and 8.6 to 8.8 are advanced level. Solutions to the exercises with **coloured numbers** are given in Appendix E.

If you wish to try more exercises, visit the students' side of the Companion Website and MyAccountingLab.

8.1 Set out below are ratios relating to three different businesses. Each business operates within a different industrial sector.

Ratio	A plc	B plc	C plc
Operating profit margin	3.6%	9.7%	6.8%
Sales to capital employed	2.4 times	3.1 times	1.7 times
Average inventories turnover period	18 days	N/A	44 days
Average settlement period for trade receivables	2 days	12 days	26 days
Current ratio	0.8 times	0.6 times	1.5 times

Required:
State, with reasons, which one of the three businesses is a holiday tour operator, which is a supermarket chain, and which is a food manufacturer.

8.2 I. Jiang (Western) Ltd has recently produced its financial statements for the current year. The directors are concerned that the return on capital employed (ROCE) has decreased from 14 per cent last year to 12 per cent for the current year.

The following reasons were suggested as to why this reduction in ROCE has occurred:

1 an increase in the gross profit margin;
2 a reduction in sales revenue;
3 an increase in overhead expenses;
4 an increase in amount of inventories held;
5 the repayment of some borrowings at the year end; and
6 an increase in the time taken for trade receivables (credit customers) to pay.

Required:
Taking each of these six suggested reasons in turn, state, with reasons, whether each of them could lead to a reduction in ROCE.

8.3 Amsterdam Ltd and Berlin Ltd are both engaged in retailing, but they seem to take a different approach to it according to the following information:

Ratio	Amsterdam Ltd	Berlin Ltd
Return on capital employed (ROCE)	20%	17%
Return on ordinary shareholders' funds (ROSF)	30%	18%
Average settlement period for trade receivables	63 days	21 days
Average settlement period for trade payables	50 days	45 days
Gross profit margin	40%	15%
Operating profit margin	10%	10%
Average inventories turnover period	52 days	25 days

Required:

Describe what this information indicates about the differences in approach between the two businesses. If one of them prides itself on personal service and one of them on competitive prices, which do you think is which and why?

8.4 The directors of Helena Beauty Products Ltd have been presented with the following abridged financial statements:

Helena Beauty Products Ltd
Income statements for the years ended 30 September

	2011		2012	
	£000	£000	£000	£000
Sales revenue		3,600		3,840
Cost of sales				
Opening inventories	320		400	
Purchases	2,240		2,350	
	2,560		2,750	
Closing inventories	(400)	(2,160)	(500)	(2,250)
Gross profit		1,440		1,590
Expenses		(1,360)		(1,500)
Profit		80		90

Statements of financial position as at 30 September

	2011	2012
	£000	£000
ASSETS		
Non-current assets		
Property, plant and equipment	1,900	1,860
Current assets		
Inventories	400	500
Trade receivables	750	960
Cash at bank	8	4
	1,158	1,464
Total assets	3,058	3,324
EQUITY AND LIABILITIES		
Equity		
£1 ordinary shares	1,650	1,766
Retained earnings	1,018	1,108
	2,668	2,874
Current liabilities	390	450
Total equity and liabilities	3,058	3,324

Required:

Using six ratios, comment on the profitability (three ratios) and efficiency (three ratios) of the business.

8.5 Conday and Co. Ltd has been in operation for three years and produces antique reproduction furniture for the export market. The most recent set of financial statements for the business is set out as follows:

Statement of financial position as at 30 November

	£000
ASSETS	
Non-current assets	
Property, plant and equipment (cost less depreciation)	
Land and buildings	228
Plant and machinery	762
	990
Current assets	
Inventories	600
Trade receivables	820
	1,420
Total assets	2,410
EQUITY AND LIABILITIES	
Equity	
Ordinary shares of £1 each	700
Retained earnings	365
	1,065
Non-current liabilities	
Borrowings – 9% loan notes (Note 1)	200
Current liabilities	
Trade payables	665
Taxation	48
Short-term borrowings (all bank overdraft)	432
	1,145
Total equity and liabilities	2,410

Income statement for the year ended 30 November

	£000
Revenue	2,600
Cost of sales	(1,620)
Gross profit	980
Selling and distribution expenses (Note 2)	(408)
Administration expenses	(194)
Operating profit	378
Finance expenses	(58)
Profit before taxation	320
Taxation	(95)
Profit for the year	225

Notes:

1. The loan notes are secured on the land and buildings.
2. Selling and distribution expenses include £170,000 in respect of bad debts.
3. A dividend of £160,000 was paid on the ordinary shares during the year.
4. The directors have invited an investor to take up a new issue of ordinary shares in the business at £6.40 each making a total investment of £200,000. The directors wish to use the funds to finance a programme of further expansion.

Required:

(a) Analyse the financial position and performance of the business and comment on any features that you consider significant.

(b) State, with reasons, whether or not the investor should invest in the business on the terms outlined.

8.6 Threads Limited manufactures nuts and bolts, which are sold to industrial users. The abbreviated financial statements for 2012 and 2013 are as follows:

Income statements for the years ended 30 June

	2012	2013
	£000	£000
Revenue	1,180	1,200
Cost of sales	(680)	(750)
Gross profit	500	450
Operating expenses	(200)	(208)
Depreciation	(66)	(75)
Operating profit	234	167
Interest	(–)	(8)
Profit before taxation	234	159
Taxation	(80)	(48)
Profit for the year	154	111

Statements of financial position as at 30 June

	2012	2013
	£000	£000
ASSETS		
Non-current assets		
Property, plant and equipment	702	687
Current assets		
Inventories	148	236
Trade receivables	102	156
Cash	3	4
	253	396
Total assets	955	1,083
EQUITY AND LIABILITIES		
Equity		
Ordinary share capital (£1 shares, fully paid)	500	500
Retained earnings	256	295
	756	795
Non-current liabilities		
Borrowings – bank loan	–	50
Current liabilities		
Trade payables	60	76
Other payables and accruals	18	16
Taxation	40	24
Short-term borrowings (all bank overdraft)	81	122
	199	238
Total equity and liabilities	955	1,083

Dividends were paid on ordinary shares of £70,000 and £72,000 in respect of 2012 and 2013, respectively.

Required:

(a) Calculate the following financial ratios for *both* 2012 and 2013 (using year-end figures for statement of financial position items):

1 return on capital employed
2 operating profit margin
3 gross profit margin
4 current ratio
5 acid test ratio
6 settlement period for trade receivables
7 settlement period for trade payables
8 inventories turnover period.

(b) Comment on the performance of Threads Limited from the viewpoint of a business considering supplying a substantial amount of goods to Threads Limited on usual trade credit terms.

8.7 Bradbury Ltd is a family-owned clothes manufacturer. For a number of years the chairman and managing director was David Bradbury. During his period of office, sales revenue had grown steadily at a rate of 2 to 3 per cent each year. David Bradbury retired on 30 November 2011 and was succeeded by his son Simon. Soon after taking office, Simon decided to expand the business. Within weeks he had successfully negotiated a five-year contract with a large clothes retailer to make a range of sports and leisurewear items. The contract will result in an additional £2 million in sales revenue during each year of the contract. To fulfil the contract, Bradbury Ltd acquired new equipment and premises.

Financial information concerning the business is given below:

Income statements for the years ended 30 November

	2011	2012
	£000	£000
Revenue	9,482	11,365
Operating profit	914	1,042
Interest charges	(22)	(81)
Profit before taxation	892	961
Taxation	(358)	(386)
Profit for the year	534	575

Statements of financial position as at 30 November

	2011 £000	2012 £000
ASSETS		
Non-current assets		
Property, plant and equipment		
Premises at cost	5,240	7,360
Plant and equipment (net)	2,375	4,057
	7,615	11,417
Current assets		
Inventories	2,386	3,420
Trade receivables	2,540	4,280
	4,926	7,700
Total assets	12,541	19,117
EQUITY AND LIABILITIES		
Equity		
Share capital	2,000	2,000
Reserves	7,813	8,268
	9,813	10,268
Non-current liabilities		
Borrowing – loans	1,220	3,675
Current liabilities		
Trade payables	1,157	2,245
Taxation	179	193
Short-term borrowings (all bank overdraft)	172	2,736
	1,508	5,174
Total equity and liabilities	12,541	19,117

Dividends of £120,000 were paid on ordinary shares in respect of each of the two years.

Required:

(a) Calculate, for each year (using year-end figures for statement of financial position items), the following ratios:

1 operating profit margin
2 return on capital employed
3 current ratio
4 gearing ratio
5 trade receivables settlement period
6 sales revenue to capital employed.

(b) Using the above ratios, and any other ratios or information you consider relevant, comment on the results of the expansion programme.

8.8 The financial statements for Harridges Ltd are given below for the two years ended 30 June 2012 and 2013. Harridges Limited operates a department store in the centre of a small town.

Income statements for the years ended 30 June

	2012 £000	2013 £000
Sales revenue	2,600	3,500
Cost of sales	(1,560)	(2,350)
Gross profit	1,040	1,150
Wages and salaries	(320)	(350)
Overheads	(260)	(200)
Depreciation	(150)	(250)
Operating profit	310	350
Interest payable	(50)	(50)
Profit before taxation	260	300
Taxation	(105)	(125)
Profit for the year	155	175

Statement of financial position as at 30 June

	2012 £000	2013 £000
ASSETS		
Non-current assets		
Property, plant and equipment	1,265	1,525
Current assets		
Inventories	250	400
Trade receivables	105	145
Cash at bank	380	115
	735	660
Total assets	2,000	2,185
EQUITY AND LIABILITIES		
Equity		
Share capital: £1 shares fully paid	490	490
Share premium	260	260
Retained earnings	350	450
	1,100	1,200
Non-current liabilities		
Borrowings – 10% loan notes	500	500
Current liabilities		
Trade payables	300	375
Other payables	100	110
	400	485
Total equity and liabilities	2,000	2,185

Dividends were paid on ordinary shares of £65,000 and £75,000 in respect of 2012 and 2013, respectively.

Required:
(a) Choose and calculate eight ratios that would be helpful in assessing the performance of Harridges Ltd. Use end-of-year values and calculate ratios for both 2012 and 2013.
(b) Using the ratios calculated in (a) and any others you consider helpful, comment on the business's performance from the viewpoint of a prospective purchaser of a majority of shares.

Chapter 9

ANALYSING AND INTERPRETING FINANCIAL STATEMENTS (2)

INTRODUCTION

In this chapter we shall continue our examination of the analysis and interpretation of financial statements. We begin by taking a detailed look at investment ratios. These ratios consider business performance from the perspective of a shareholder. We then go on to consider common-size financial statements. This technique presents the financial statements in the form of ratios and can offer useful insights into performance and position.

Decision making involves making predictions about the future. In this chapter we shall see how ratios may be of value in one important area, the prediction of financial collapse. Finally, we shall consider the problems encountered when undertaking ratio analysis. Although ratios can be very useful in assessing financial health, it is important to be aware of their limitations.

Learning outcomes

When you have completed this chapter, you should be able to:

- calculate and interpret key investment ratios;
- prepare and interpret common-size financial statements;
- evaluate the use of ratios in helping to predict financial failure;
- discuss the limitations of ratios as a tool of financial analysis.

To demonstrate how particular ratios are calculated and interpreted, we shall continue to refer to Alexis plc, whose financial statements and other information are set out in Example 8.1 (on pages 253 to 254).

INVESTMENT RATIOS

There are various ratios available that are designed to help shareholders assess the returns on their investment. The following are widely used:

- dividend payout ratio
- dividend yield ratio
- earnings per share
- cash generated from operations per share
- price/earnings ratio.

Dividend payout ratio

The **dividend payout ratio** measures the proportion of earnings that a business pays out to shareholders in the form of dividends. The ratio is calculated as follows:

$$\text{Dividend payout ratio} = \frac{\text{Dividends announced for the year}}{\text{Earnings for the year available for dividends}} \times 100$$

In the case of ordinary shares, the earnings available for dividend will normally be the profit for the year (that is, the profit after taxation) less any preference dividends relating to the year. This ratio is normally expressed as a percentage.

The dividend payout ratio for Alexis plc for the year ended 31 March 2012 is

$$\text{Dividend payout ratio} = \frac{40}{165} \times 100 = 24.2\%$$

The information provided by this ratio is often expressed slightly differently as the **dividend cover ratio**. Here the calculation is:

$$\text{Dividend cover ratio} = \frac{\text{Earnings for the year available for dividends}}{\text{Dividends announced for the year}}$$

In the case of Alexis plc (for 2012) it would be 165/40 = 4.1 times. That is to say, the earnings available for dividend cover the actual dividend paid by just over four times.

Activity 9.1

Calculate the dividend payout ratio of Alexis plc for the year ended 31 March 2013.

The ratio for 2013 is

$$\text{Dividend payout ratio} = \frac{40}{11} \times 100 = 363.6\%$$

This would normally be considered to be a very alarming increase in the ratio over the two years. Paying a dividend of £40 million in 2013 would probably be widely regarded as very imprudent.

Dividend yield ratio

The **dividend yield ratio** relates the cash return from a share to its current market value. This can help investors to assess the cash return on their investment in the business. The ratio, expressed as a percentage, is

$$\text{Dividend yield} = \frac{\text{Dividend per share}/(1 - t)}{\text{Market value per share}} \times 100$$

where t is the 'dividend tax credit' rate of income tax. This requires some explanation. In the UK, investors who receive a dividend from a business also receive a tax credit. As this tax credit can be offset against any tax liability arising from the dividends received, the dividends are effectively issued net of income tax, at the dividend tax credit rate.

Investors may wish to compare the returns from shares with the returns from other forms of investment. As these other forms of investment are usually quoted on a 'gross' (that is, pre-tax) basis it is useful to 'gross up' the dividend to make comparison easier. We can achieve this by dividing the **dividend per share** by $(1 - t)$, where t is the 'dividend tax credit' rate of income tax.

Using the 2011/2012 (and the 2012/13) dividend tax credit rate of 10 per cent, the dividend yield for Alexis plc for the year ended 31 March 2012 is

$$\text{Dividend yield} = \frac{0.067^*/(1 - 0.10)}{2.50} \times 100 = 3.0\%$$

* Dividend proposed/number of shares = 40/(300 × 2) = £0.067 dividend per share (the 300 is multiplied by 2 because they are £0.50 shares). The shares' market value is given in Note 1 to Example 8.1.

Activity 9.2

Calculate the dividend yield for Alexis plc for the year ended 31 March 2013.

The ratio for 2013 is:

$$\text{Dividend yield} = \frac{0.067^*/(1 - 0.10)}{1.50} \times 100 = 5.0\%$$

* 40/(300 × 2) = £0.067.

Earnings per share

The **earnings per share (EPS)** ratio relates the earnings generated by the business, and available to shareholders, during a period to the number of shares in issue. For equity (ordinary) shareholders, the amount available will be represented by the profit for the year (profit after taxation), less any preference dividend where applicable. The ratio for equity shareholders is calculated as follows:

$$\text{Earnings per share} = \frac{\text{Earnings available to ordinary shareholders}}{\text{Number of ordinary shares in issue}}$$

In the case of Alexis plc, the earnings per share for the year ended 31 March 2012 is:

$$\text{EPS} = \frac{£165\,\text{m}}{600\,\text{m}} = 27.5\text{p}$$

Many investment analysts regard the EPS ratio as a fundamental measure of share performance. The trend in earnings per share over time is used to help assess the investment potential of a business's shares. Although it is possible to make total profit rise through ordinary shareholders investing more in the business, this will not necessarily mean that the profitability *per share* will rise as a result.

It is not usually very helpful to compare the EPS of one business with that of another. Differences in financing arrangements (for example, in the nominal value of shares issued) can render any such comparison meaningless. However, it can be very useful to monitor the changes that occur in this ratio for a particular business over time.

Activity 9.3

Calculate the earnings per share of Alexis plc for the year ended 31 March 2013.

The ratio for 2013 is

$$\text{EPS} = \frac{£11\,\text{m}}{600\,\text{m}} = 1.8\text{p}$$

Cash generated from operations per share

It can be argued that, in the short term at least, cash generated from operations (found in the statement of cash flows) provides a good guide to the ability of a business to pay dividends and to undertake planned expenditures. Many see a cash generation measure as more useful in this context than the earnings per share figure. The **cash generated from operations (CGO) per ordinary share ratio** is calculated as follows:

$$\text{Cash generated from operations per share} = \frac{\text{Cash generated from operations less preference dividend (if any)}}{\text{Number of ordinary shares in issue}}$$

The ratio for Alexis plc for the year ended 31 March 2012 is

$$\text{CGO per share} = \frac{£251m}{600m} = 41.8p$$

There has been a dramatic decrease in this ratio over the two-year period.

Note that, for both years, the CGO per share for Alexis plc is higher than the earnings per share. This is not unusual. The effect of adding back depreciation to derive the CGO figures will often ensure that a higher figure is derived.

Price/earnings (P/E) ratio

The **price/earnings ratio** relates the market value of a share to the earnings per share. This ratio can be calculated as follows:

$$\text{P/E ratio} = \frac{\textbf{Market value per share}}{\textbf{Earnings per share}}$$

The P/E ratio for Alexis plc as at 31 March 2012 is

$$\text{P/E ratio} = \frac{£2.50}{27.5p^*} = 9.1 \text{ times}$$

* The EPS figure (27.5p) has been calculated already.

This ratio indicates that the market value of the share is 9.1 times higher than its current level of earnings. The ratio is a measure of market confidence in the future of a business. The higher the P/E ratio, the greater the confidence in the future earning power of the business and, consequently, the more investors are prepared to pay in relation to the earnings stream of the business.

P/E ratios provide a useful guide to market confidence about the future and they can, therefore, be helpful when comparing different businesses. However, differences in accounting policies between businesses can lead to different profit and earnings per share figures. This can distort comparisons.

Calculate the P/E ratio of Alexis plc as at 31 March 2013.

The ratio for 2013 is

$$\text{P/E ratio} = \frac{£1.50}{1.8p} = 83.3 \text{ times}$$

The investment ratios for Alexis plc over the two-year period are as follows:

	2012	2013
Dividend payout ratio	24.2%	363.6%
Dividend yield ratio	3.0%	5.0%
Earnings per share	27.5p	1.8p
Cash generated from operations per share	41.8p	5.7p
P/E ratio	9.1 times	83.3 times

What do you deduce from the investment ratios set out above?
    Can you offer an explanation why the share price has not fallen as much as it might have done, bearing in mind the very poor (relative to 2012) trading performance in 2013?

Athough the EPS has fallen dramatically and the dividend payment for 2013 seems very imprudent, the share price seems to have held up remarkably well (fallen from £2.50 to £1.50). This means that dividend yield and P/E value for 2013 look better than those for 2012. This is an anomaly of these two ratios, which stems from using a forward-looking value (the share price) in conjunction with historic data (dividends and earnings). Share prices are based on investors' assessments of the business's future. It seems with Alexis plc that, at the end of 2013, the 'market' was not happy with the business, relative to 2012. This is evidenced by the fact that the share price had fallen by £1 a share. On the other hand, the share price has not fallen as much as profit for the year. It appears that investors believe that the business will perform better in the future than it did in 2013. This may well be because they believe that the large expansion in assets and employee numbers that occurred in 2013 will yield benefits in the future; benefits that the business was not able to generate during 2013.

Real World 9.1 provides information about the share performance of a selection of large, well-known UK businesses. This type of information is provided on a daily basis by several newspapers, notably the *Financial Times*.

Market statistics for some well-known businesses

The following data was extracted from the *Financial Times* of 14 February 2012, relating to the previous day's trading of the shares of some well-known businesses on the London Stock Exchange:

Share	Price (pence)	Change	52-week		Yield	P/E	Volume (000s)
			High	Low			
Marks and Spencer	348.80	−1.40	411.20	296.20	4.9	9.0	6,362
J D Wetherspoon	410	+1.80	473	370.60	2.9	10.4	92
National Express	227.30	+2.60	272.50	198.90	4.0	11.2	931
Tesco	319.40	−1.25	490.50	280.40	4.6	10.3	35,561
Rolls-Royce	779.50	+7	794	311.06	2.0	17.2	5,279
TUI Travel	207.50	+5.70	266.40	134.10	5.4	8.8	4,125

The column headings are as follows:

Price — Mid-market price in pence (that is, the price midway between buying and selling price) of the shares at the end of trading on 13 February 2012

Change — Gain or loss in the mid-market price during 13 February 2012

52-week high/low — Highest and lowest prices reached by the share during the 52 weeks ended on 13 February 2012

Yield — Gross dividend yield, based on the most recent year's dividend and the current share price

P/E — Price/earnings ratio, based on the most recent year's (after-tax) profit for the year and the current share price

Volume — The number of shares (in thousands) that were bought/sold on 13 February 2012

So, for example, for the retail business Marks and Spencer plc

- the shares had a mid-market price of 348.80p each at the close of Stock Exchange trading on 13 February 2012;
- the shares had decreased in price by 1.40 pence during trading on 13 February 2012;
- the shares had highest and lowest prices during the previous 52 weeks of 411.20p and 296.20p, respectively;
- the shares had a dividend yield, based on the 13 February 2012 price (and the dividend for the most recent year) of 4.9 per cent;
- the shares had a P/E ratio, based on the 13 February 2012 price (and the after-taxation earnings per share for the most recent year) of 9.0;
- during trading on 13 February 2012, 6,362,000 of the business's shares had changed hands between buyers and sellers.

Real World 9.2 shows how investment ratios can vary between different industry sectors.

Yielding dividends

Investment ratios can vary significantly between businesses and between industries. To give some indication of the range of variations that occur, the average dividend yield ratios and average P/E ratios for listed businesses in twelve different industries are shown in Figures 9.1 and 9.2, respectively.

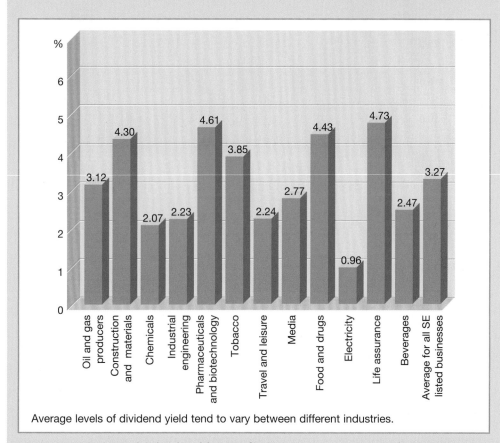

Average levels of dividend yield tend to vary between different industries.

Figure 9.1 Average dividend yield ratios for businesses in a range of industries

The dividend yield ratios are calculated from the current market value of the shares and the most recent year's dividend paid.

Some industries tend to pay out lower dividends than others, leading to lower dividend yield ratios. The average for all Stock Exchange listed businesses was 3.27 per cent (as is shown in Figure 9.1), but there is a wide variation, with electricity at 0.96 per cent and life assurance at 4.73 per cent.

Some types of businesses tend to invest heavily in developing new products, hence their tendency to pay low dividends compared with their share prices. Some of the inter-industry differences in the dividend yield ratio can be explained by the nature of the calculation of the ratio. The prices of shares at any given moment are based on expectations of their economic futures; dividends are actual past events. A business that had a good trading year recently may have paid a dividend that, in the light of investors' assessment of the business's economic future, may be high (a high dividend yield).

→

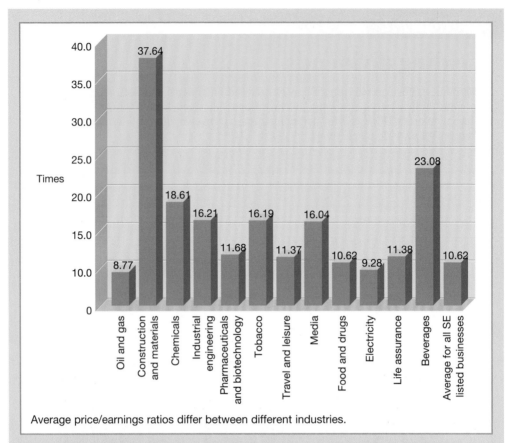

Average price/earnings ratios differ between different industries.

Figure 9.2 Average price/earnings ratios for businesses in a range of industries

The P/E ratios are calculated from the current market value of the shares and the most recent year's earnings per share (EPS).

Businesses that have a high share price relative to their recent historic earnings have high P/E ratios. This may be because their future is regarded as economically bright, which may be the result of investing heavily in the future at the expense of recent profits (earnings). On the other hand, high P/Es also arise where businesses have recent low earnings but investors believe that their future is brighter. The average P/E ratio for all Stock Exchange listed businesses was 10.62, but that for oil and gas producers was as low as 8.77 and that for construction and materials as high as 37.64.

FT *Source*: Both figures are constructed from data appearing in the *Financial Times*, 11/12 February 2012, p. 24.
© The Financial Times Limited 2012. All rights reserved.

FINANCIAL RATIOS AND THE PROBLEM OF OVERTRADING

In Chapter 8, we touched briefly on the topic of overtrading. We shall now look at it in rather more detail. **Overtrading** occurs where a business is operating at a level of activity that cannot be supported by the amount of finance that has been committed. For example, the business may have inadequate finance to fund the level of trade receivables and inventories necessary for the level of sales revenue that it is achieving. This situation usually reflects poor financial control over the business on the part of its management. The reasons for overtrading are varied. It may occur:

- in young, expanding businesses that fail to prepare adequately for the rapid increase in demand for their goods or services;
- in businesses where the managers may have misjudged the level of expected sales demand or have failed to control escalating project costs;
- as a result of a fall in the value of money (inflation), causing more finance to have to be committed to inventories and trade receivables, even where there is no expansion in the real volume of trade;
- where the owners are unable to inject further funds into the business themselves and/or they cannot persuade others to invest in the business.

Whatever the reason, the problems that it brings must be dealt with if the business is to survive over the longer term.

Overtrading results in liquidity problems such as exceeding borrowing limits, or slow repayment of borrowings and trade payables. It can also result in suppliers withholding supplies, thereby making it difficult to meet customer needs. The managers of the business might be forced to direct all of their efforts to dealing with immediate and pressing problems, such as finding cash to meet interest charges due or paying wages. Longer-term planning becomes difficult as managers spend their time going from crisis to crisis. Ultimately, the business may fail because it cannot meet its maturing obligations.

Activity 9.7

If a business is overtrading, do you think the following ratios would be higher or lower than normally expected?

1 Current ratio
2 Average inventories turnover period
3 Average settlement period for trade receivables
4 Average settlement period for trade payables.

Your answer should be as follows:

1 The current ratio would be lower than normally expected. This is a measure of liquidity, and lack of liquidity is a typical symptom of overtrading.
2 The average inventories turnover period would be lower than normally expected. Where a business is overtrading, the level of inventories held will be low because of the problems of financing them. In the short term, sales revenue may not be badly affected by the low inventories levels and therefore inventories will be turned over more quickly.
3 The average settlement period for trade receivables may be lower than normally expected. Where a business is suffering from liquidity problems it may chase credit customers more vigorously in an attempt to improve cash flows.
4 The average settlement period for trade payables may be higher than normally expected. The business may try to delay payments to its suppliers because of the liquidity problems arising.

To deal with the overtrading problem, a business must ensure that the finance available is consistent with the level of operations. Thus, if a business that is overtrading is unable to raise new finance, it should cut back its level of operations in line with the finance available. Although this may mean lost sales and lost profits in the short term, cutting back may be necessary to ensure survival over the longer term.

TREND ANALYSIS

It is often helpful to see whether ratios are indicating trends. Key ratios can be plotted on a graph to provide a simple visual display of changes occurring over time. The trends occurring within a business may, for example, be plotted against trends for rival businesses or for the industry as a whole for comparison purposes. An example of trend analysis is shown in **Real World 9.3**.

Real World 9.3

Trend setting

In Figure 9.3, the current ratio of three of the UK's leading supermarket businesses is plotted over time. We can see that the current ratios of the three businesses have tended to move closer. Tesco plc's current ratio was lower than those of its main rivals until 2005, when it overtook Morrison, and 2009, when it overtook Sainsbury. The current ratio of Sainsbury shows a fairly consistent downward path (although in 2010 it increased). With well-managed businesses like Sainsbury and Tesco, it seems highly probable that these changes are the result of deliberate policy.

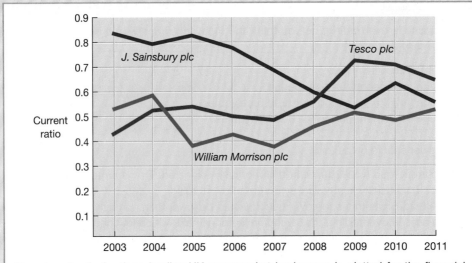

The current ratio for three leading UK supermarket businesses is plotted for the financial years ended during 2003 to 2011. This enables comparison to be made regarding the ratio, both for each of the three businesses over time and between the businesses.

Figure 9.3 Graph plotting current ratio against time

Source: Ratios calculated from information in the annual reports of the three businesses for each of the years 2003 to 2011.

KEY PERFORMANCE INDICATORS

Many businesses use **key performance indicators (KPIs)** to help measure the degree of success achieved in carrying out their operations. These KPIs often include financial ratios such as those that we have encountered. They may also, however, include other measures of performance. They may, for example, include ratios that compare a figure on the financial statements with a particular business resource. They may also include non-financial measures of performance.

Real World 9.4 shows extracts from the table of KPIs in the 2011 Annual Report of easy-Jet plc, the well-known budget airline operator. Results achieved over a five-year period are provided to enable users to assess progress over time.

Real World 9.4

Key performance measures of easyJet plc

	2011	2010	2009	2008	2007
Return on capital employed	12.7%	8.8%	3.6%	7.3%	11.7%
Gearing	28%	32%	38%	29%	20%
Profit before tax per seat (£)	3.97	2.75	1.04	2.12	4.54
Revenue per seat (£)	55.27	53.07	50.47	45.51	40.42
Cost per seat (£)	51.30	50.32	49.43	43.39	35.88
Cost per seat excluding fuel (£)	36.62	37.23	34.16	29.74	26.31
Seats flown (millions)	62.5	56.0	52.8	51.9	44.5

EasyJet's ROCE in 2011 was the best that it had been during the five years. Only in 2007 did it approach the 2011 level of achievement. This seems to reflect the highest profit per seat since 2007. From comments elsewhere in the annual report, it appears that management sees 2011 as having been a successful year for the airline, despite the economic recession.

Source: easyJet plc Annual Report 2011, p. 103.

COMMON-SIZE FINANCIAL STATEMENTS

Common-size financial statements are financial statements (such as the income statement, statement of financial position and statement of cash flows) that are expressed in terms of some base figure. The objective of presenting financial statements in this way is to make better comparisons. The detection of differences and trends is often more obvious than may be the case when examining the original statements, which are expressed in financial values.

Vertical analysis

One approach to common-size statements is to express all the figures in a particular statement in terms of one of the figures in that statement. This 'base' figure is typically one that is seen as a key figure in the statement, such as sales revenue in an income statement, total long-term funds in a statement of financial position and the cash flow from operating activities in the statement of cash flows.

Example 9.1 is a common-size income statement that uses sales revenue as the base figure. Note that the base figure is set at 100 and all other figures are expressed as a percentage of this.

Example 9.1

The common-size income statement of Alexis plc (see Example 8.1 on pages 253 to 254) for 2012 in abbreviated form, and using revenue as the base figure, will be as follows:

Common-size income statement for the year ended 31 March 2012

		Calculation of figures
Revenue	100.0	Base figure
Cost of sales	(77.9)	$(1,745/2,240) \times 100\%$
Gross profit	22.1	$(495/2,240) \times 100\%$
Operating expenses	(11.3)	$(252/2,240) \times 100\%$
Operating profit	10.8	$(243/2,240) \times 100\%$
Interest payable	(0.8)	$(18/2,240) \times 100\%$
Profit before taxation	10.0	$(225/2,240) \times 100\%$
Taxation	(2.7)	$(60/2,240) \times 100\%$
Profit for the year	7.3	$(165/2,240) \times 100\%$

Each of the figures in the income statement is simply the original financial figure divided by the revenue figure and then expressed as a percentage. Since the revised values have been expressed to only one decimal place, it was necessary to adjust to make the income statement add up despite rounding errors.

Not much, of course, can be discerned from looking at just one common-size statement. We need some benchmark for comparison. This could be other accounting periods for the same business.

Activity 9.8

The following is a set of common-size income statements for a major high street department store for five consecutive accounting periods:

	Year 1	*Year 2*	*Year 3*	*Year 4*	*Year 5*
Revenue	100.0	100.0	100.0	100.0	100.0
Cost of sales	(68.9)	(68.5)	(67.2)	(66.5)	(66.3)
Gross profit	31.1	31.5	32.8	33.5	33.7
Operating expenses	(28.1)	(28.4)	(27.6)	(29.2)	(30.2)
Operating profit	3.0	3.1	5.2	4.3	3.5
Interest payable	(1.1)	(1.2)	(1.6)	(2.1)	(1.3)
Profit before taxation	1.9	1.9	3.6	2.2	2.2

What significant features are revealed by the common-size income statements?

Operating profit, relative to revenue, rose in Year 3 but fell back again in Years 4 and 5 to end the five-year period at a higher level than it had been in Years 1 and 2. Although the gross profit margin rose steadily over the five-year period, so did the operating expenses, with the exception of Year 3. Clearly, the fall in operating expenses relative to revenue in Year 3 led to the improvement in operating profit relative to revenue.

The common-size financial statements being compared do not have to be for the same business. They can be for different businesses. **Real World 9.5** sets out common-size statements of financial position for five UK businesses that are either very well known by name, or whose products are everyday commodities for most of us. These businesses were randomly selected, except that each one has a high profile and each is from a different industry. For each business, the items from the statement of financial position are expressed as a percentage of the total investment by the providers of long-term finance (equity and non-current liabilities).

A summary of the statements of financial position of five UK businesses

Business:	Next plc	easyJet plc	Babcock International Group plc	Tesco plc	Severn Trent plc
Statement of financial position date	29.1.11	30.9.11	31.3.11	26.2.11	31.3.11
ASSETS					
Non-current assets	76	83	110	120	95
Current assets					
Inventories	38	–	4	11	–
Trade and other receivables	67	5	24	8	7
Other current assets	–	3	–	–	–
Cash and near cash	6	45	5	20	4
	111	53	33	39	11
Total assets	187	136	143	159	106
EQUITY AND LIABILITIES					
Equity and non-current liabilities	100	100	100	100	100
Current liabilities					
Trade and other payables	57	28	39	35	5
Taxation	11	3	1	1	1
Other short-term liabilities	6	–	1	18	–
Overdrafts and short-term borrowings	13	5	2	5	–
	87	36	43	59	6
Total equity and liabilities	187	136	143	159	106

The non-current assets, current assets and current liabilities are expressed as a percentage of the total net long-term investment (equity plus non-current liabilities) of the business concerned. Next plc is a major retail and home shopping business, easyJet plc is a leading airline, Babcock International Group plc is a large engineering and support business, Tesco plc is one of the UK's leading supermarkets, and Severn Trent plc is an important supplier of water, sewerage services and waste management, mainly in the UK.

Source: Table constructed from information appearing in the financial statements for the year ended during 2011 for each of the five businesses concerned.

Real World 9.5 reveals quite striking differences in the make-up of the statement of financial position from one business to the next. Take, for example, the current assets and current liabilities. Although the totals for current assets are pretty large when compared with the total long-term investment, these percentages vary considerably between businesses. When looking at the mix of current assets, we can see that Next, Babcock and Tesco, which produce and/or sell goods, are the only ones that hold significant amounts of inventories. The other two businesses are service providers and so inventories are not a significant item. We can also see that little of Tesco's, easyJet's or Severn Trent's sales are on credit, as these businesses have relatively small trade receivables.

Note that Tesco's trade payables are much higher than its trade receivables. They are also high compared to its inventories. Since trade payables mainly represent amounts due to suppliers of inventories, it means that Tesco receives the cash for a typical trolleyload of shopping well in advance of paying for those goods.

So far we have been considering what is known as **vertical analysis**. That is, we have been treating all of the figures in each statement as a percentage of a figure in that statement. This 'baseline' figure has been the sales revenue figure, in the case of the income statement, and the total long-term investment, with the statement of financial position. Note that common-size statements do not have to be expressed in terms of any particular factor; it is up to the individual carrying out or using the analysis.

Horizontal analysis

Horizontal analysis is an alternative to the vertical analysis that we have seen so far. Here the figures appearing in a particular financial statement are expressed as a base figure (such as 100) and the equivalent figures appearing in similar statements are expressed as a percentage of this base figure. So, for example, the inventories figure appearing in a particular statement of financial position may be set as the base figure (that is, set at 100) and then the inventories figures appearing in successive statements of financial position could each be expressed as a percentage of this base inventories figure. The 'base' statement would normally be the earliest (or latest) of a set of statements for the same business. Where the analysis was between businesses, as in Real World 9.5, selecting which business should be the base one is not so obvious, unless one of the businesses is the one of most interest, perhaps because the objective is to compare a particular business with each of the others in turn.

Example 9.2 shows a horizontally analysed common-size income statement for the business, a department store, which was the subject of Activity 9.8.

Example 9.2

The following is a set of common-size income statements for a major high street department store for five consecutive accounting periods, using horizontal analysis and making Year 1 the base year:

	Year 1	Year 2	Year 3	Year 4	Year 5
Revenue	100.0	104.3	108.4	106.5	108.9
Cost of sales	(100.0)	(103.7)	(105.7)	(102.9)	(104.8)
Gross profit	100.0	105.5	114.4	114.5	118.0
Operating expenses	(100.0)	(105.4)	(106.7)	(110.4)	(117.2)
Operating profit	100.0	106.6	105.9	113.3	125.6
Interest payable	(100.0)	(111.9)	(157.1)	(202.4)	(127.4)
Profit before taxation	100.0	103.5	102.8	104.5	124.5

Year 1 is the base year so all of the figures in the Year 1 income statement are 100.0. All of the figures for the other years are that year's figure divided by the Year 1 figure for the same item and then expressed as a percentage. For example, the Year 4 profit before taxation divided by the profit before taxation for Year 1 was 104.5. This tells us that the profit was 4.5 per cent greater in Year 4 than it had been for Year 1.

What are the significant features revealed by the common-size income statements in Example 9.2?

Revenue did not show much of an increase over the five years, particularly if these figures are not adjusted for inflation. Years 2 and 3 saw increases, but Years 4 and 5 were less impressive. The rate of increase in the cost of sales was less than that for revenue and, therefore, the gross profit growth was greater than the rate of increase of revenue. Operating expenses showed growth over the years. Interest payable increased strongly during the first four years of the period, but then fell back significantly in Year 5.

Activity 9.10

The vertical approach to common-size financial statements has the advantage of enabling the analyst to see each figure within a financial statement expressed in terms of the same item (revenue, long-term finance and so on).

- What are the limitations of this approach?
- How do horizontally analysed common-size statements overcome any limitations?
- What problems do horizontally analysed statements bring?

The problem with the vertical approach is that it is not possible to see, for example, that revenue values are different from one year or business to the next. Normally a vertically analysed common-size income statement shows the revenue figure as 100 for all years or businesses.

Horizontally analysed common-size statements overcome this problem because, for example, revenue figures are expressed in terms of one particular year or one particular business. This makes differences in revenue levels crystal clear. Unfortunately, such an approach makes comparison within a particular year's, or within a particular business's, statement rather difficult.

Perhaps the answer is to produce two sets of common-size statements, one analysed vertically and the other horizontally.

USING RATIOS TO PREDICT FINANCIAL FAILURE

Financial ratios, based on current or past performance, are often used to help predict the future. However, both the choice of ratios and the interpretation of results are normally dependent on the judgement and opinion of the analyst. In recent years, however, attempts have been made to develop a more rigorous and systematic approach to the use of ratios for prediction purposes. In particular, researchers have shown an interest in the ability of ratios to predict the financial failure of a business.

By financial failure, we mean a business either being forced out of business or being severely adversely affected by its inability to meet its financial obligations. It is often referred to as 'going bust' or 'going bankrupt'. This is, of course, a likely area of concern for all those connected with the business.

Using single ratios

Many approaches that attempt to use ratios to predict financial failure have been developed. Early research focused on the examination of individual ratios to see whether any particular ratios were good predictors of financial failure. Here, a particular ratio (for example, the current ratio) for a business that had failed was tracked over several years leading up to the date of the failure. The aim was to see whether the ratio had shown a trend that could have been taken as a warning sign.

Beaver (see reference 1 at the end of the chapter) carried out the first research in this area. He identified 79 businesses that had failed. He then calculated the average (mean) of various ratios for these 79 businesses, going back over the financial statements of each business for each of the ten years leading up to each business's failure. Beaver then compared these average ratios with similarly derived ratios for a sample of 79 businesses that did not fail over this period. (The research used a matched-pair design, where each failed business was matched with a non-failed business of similar size and industry type.) Beaver found that certain ratios exhibited a marked difference between the failed and non-failed businesses for up to five years prior to failure. These ratios were:

■ Cash flow/Total debt
■ Net income (profit)/Total assets
■ Total debt/Total assets
■ Working capital/Total assets
■ Current ratio
■ No credit interval (that is, cash generated from operations to maturing obligations).

To illustrate Beaver's findings the average current ratio of failed businesses for five years prior to failure, along with the average current ratio of non-failed businesses for the same period, is shown in Figure 9.4.

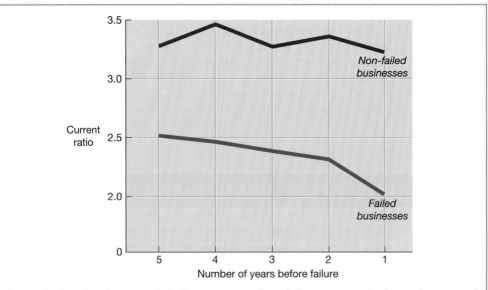

The vertical scale of the graph is the average value of the current ratio for each group of businesses (failed and non-failed). The horizontal axis is the number of years before failure. Thus, Year 1 is the most recent year and Year 5 the least recent year. We can see that a clear difference between the average for the failed and non-failed businesses can be detected five years prior to the failure of the former group.

Figure 9.4 Average (mean) current ratio of failed and non-failed businesses

Similar research by Zmijewski (see reference 2 at the end of the chapter), using a sample of 72 failed and 3,573 non-failed businesses over a six-year period, found that businesses that ultimately went on to fail were characterised by lower rates of return, higher levels of gearing, lower levels of coverage for their fixed interest payments and more variable returns on shares. While we may not find these results very surprising, it is interesting to note that Zmijewski, like a number of other researchers in this area, did not find liquidity ratios particularly useful in predicting financial failure. As mentioned, however, Beaver found the current ratio to be a useful predictor.

The approach adopted by Beaver and Zmijewski is referred to as **univariate analysis** because it looks at one ratio at a time. It can produce interesting results but there are practical problems with its use. For example, past research may have identified two ratios as being good predictors of financial failure. When applied to a particular business, however, one ratio predicts financial failure but the other does not. Given these conflicting signals, how should we interpret the results?

Using combinations of ratios

The weaknesses of univariate analysis have led researchers to develop models that combine ratios in such a way as to produce a single index that can be interpreted more clearly. One approach to model development, much favoured by researchers, applies **multiple discriminate analysis** (MDA). This is, in essence, a statistical technique that is similar to regression analysis and which can be used to draw a boundary between those businesses that fail and those businesses that do not. This boundary is referred to as the **discriminate function**. In this context, MDA attempts to identify those factors likely to influence financial failure. However, unlike regression analysis, MDA assumes that the observations come from two different populations (for example, failed and non-failed businesses) rather than from a single population.

To illustrate this approach, let us assume that we wish to test whether two ratios (say, the current ratio and the return on capital employed) can help to predict failure. To do this, we can calculate these ratios, first for a sample of failed businesses and then for a matched sample of non-failed ones. From these two sets of data we can produce a scatter diagram that plots each business according to these two ratios to produce a single coordinate. Figure 9.5 illustrates this approach.

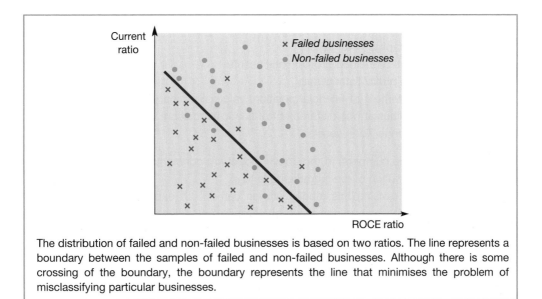

The distribution of failed and non-failed businesses is based on two ratios. The line represents a boundary between the samples of failed and non-failed businesses. Although there is some crossing of the boundary, the boundary represents the line that minimises the problem of misclassifying particular businesses.

Figure 9.5 Scatter diagram showing the distribution of failed and non-failed businesses

Using the observations plotted on the diagram, we try to identify the boundary between the failed and the non-failed businesses. This is the diagonal line in Figure 9.5.

We can see that those businesses that fall below and to the left of the line are predominantly failed ones and those that fall to the right are predominantly non-failed ones. Note that there is some overlap between the two populations. In practice, the boundary produced is unlikely, therefore, to eliminate all errors. Some businesses that fail may fall on the non-failed businesses side of the boundary. The opposite also happens. However, the analysis will tend to *minimise* the misclassification errors.

The boundary shown in Figure 9.5 can be expressed in the form

$$Z = a + (b \times \text{Current ratio}) + (c \times \text{ROCE})$$

where *a*, *b* and *c* are all constants and *b* and *c* are weights to be attached to each ratio. A weighted average or total score (Z) is then derived. By 'constants' we mean that the same values are used for assessing each individual business. The weights given to the two ratios will depend on the slope of the line and its absolute position (that is, they will depend on the values of *a*, *b* and *c*). Using this model to assess a particular business's health, we would deduce the current and ROCE ratios for that business and use them in the equation above. If the resulting Z-score were to come out below a certain value, we should view that business as being at risk.

Note that this example, using the current and ROCE ratios, is purely hypothetical and only intended to illustrate the approach.

Z-score models

Altman (see reference 3 at the end of the chapter) was the first to develop a model (in 1968), using financial ratios, that was able to predict financial failure in practice. In 2000 he revised the model. In fact, the revisions necessary to make the model effective in more modern times were quite minor. Altman's revised model, the Z-score model, is based on five financial ratios and is as follows:

$$Z = 0.717a + 0.847b + 3.107c + 0.420d + 0.998e$$

where   *a* = Working capital/Total assets
       b = Accumulated retained profits/Total assets
       c = Operating profit/Total assets
       d = Book (statement of financial position) value of ordinary and preference shares/ Total liabilities at book (statement of financial position) value
       e = Sales revenue/Total assets.

The coefficients (the numbers) in the above model are constants that reflect the importance to the Z-score of each of the ingredients (*a* to *e*).

In developing and revising this model, Altman carried out experiments using a paired sample of failed businesses and non-failed businesses and collected relevant data for each business for five years prior to failure. He found that the model represented by the formula above was able to predict failure for up to two years before it occurred. However, the predictive accuracy of the model became weaker the longer the time before the date of the actual failure.

The ratios used in this model were identified by Altman through a process of trial and error, as there is no underlying theory of financial failure to help guide researchers in their selection of appropriate ratios. According to Altman, those businesses with a Z-score of less than 1.23 tend to fail. The lower the score the greater is the probability of failure. Those with a Z-score greater than 4.14 tend not to fail. Those businesses with a Z-score between 1.23 and 4.14 occupied a 'zone of ignorance' and were difficult to classify. However, the model was able overall to classify 91 per cent of the businesses correctly; only 9 per cent fell into the 'zone of ignorance'. Altman based his model on US businesses.

In recent years, other models, using a similar approach, have been developed throughout the world. In the UK, Taffler has developed separate Z-score models for different types of business. (See reference 4 at the end of the chapter for a discussion of the work of Taffler and others.)

The prediction of financial failure is not the only area where research into the predictive ability of ratios has taken place. Researchers have also developed ratio-based models that claim to assess the vulnerability of a business to takeover by another. This is another area that is of vital importance to all those connected with the business.

Real World 9.6 discusses some research that showed that investing in shares in businesses with very low Z-scores is unsuccessful compared with investing in businesses with higher Z-scores. This is what we might expect to happen and provides support for the use of Z-scores in assessing the health of businesses. The research did not show, however, that the higher the Z-score, the more successful the investment.

Real World 9.6

From A to Z

Investors looking to profit during a recession should be targeting stocks [shares] with strong fundamentals, according to research by Morgan Stanley. This 'value investing' approach – buying into companies where fundamental measures, such as book value and earnings, are not yet reflected in their share prices – is not new. But Morgan Stanley's analysis has found that the ability of this approach to deliver returns in downturns depends on the financial strength of the companies – in particular, the importance attached to the balance sheet [statement of financial position] by investors. 'If a stock's balance sheet is weak, the valuation multiple will be of little importance at this stage in the economic cycle,' says Graham Secker, Morgan Stanley strategy analyst.

He ranked a basket of European companies by their Altman Z-score – a measure of financial strength devised by US academic Edward Altman. A Z-score can be calculated for all non-financial companies and the lower the score, the greater the risk of the company falling into financial distress. When Secker compared the companies' Z-scores with their share price movements, he discovered that the companies with weaker balance sheets underperformed the market more than two thirds of the time.

Morgan Stanley also found that a company with an Altman Z-score of less than 1 tends to underperform the wider market by more than 4 per cent over the year with an associated probability of 72 per cent. 'Given the poor performance over the last year by stocks with a low Altman Z-score, the results of our backtest are now even more compelling than they were 12 months ago,' argues Secker. 'We calculate that the median stock with an Altman Z-score of 1 or less has underperformed the wider market by 5–6 per cent per annum between 1990 and 2008.'

Secker sees this as logical. In a recession, companies with balance sheets that are perceived to be weak are deemed a higher risk by lenders and face a higher cost of capital. This turns market sentiment against them and will generally lead to their share prices falling below their peers.

→

In 2008, the share price performance for stocks with an Altman Z-score of less than 1 was the worst since Morgan Stanley's analysis began in 1991. Under the Morgan Stanley methodology, the 2008 score is calculated using 2007 company financials. Of all the companies with a 2008 Z-score of less than 1, the median share price performance was a loss of 49 per cent, compared with a wider market fall of 42 per cent.

When compound annual growth rates since 1991 are analysed, the results are more dramatic. On average, companies with Z-scores of less than 1 saw their shares fall 4.4 per cent, compared with an average rise of 1.3 per cent for their peers. In only five of the last 18 years has a stock with an Altman score of 1 or less outperformed the market. These were generally years of strong economic growth. However, companies with the highest Z-scores aren't necessarily the best performers. During the bear market of 2000 to 2002, companies that had a Z-score above 3 fell almost twice as much as the market.

Analysts say the 2009 Z-scores, based on 2008 balance sheets, are far lower than in previous years as companies absorb the strain of the downturn in their accounts. 'There's been a lot of change between 2007 and 2008 [accounting years], tightening of credit and a vast deterioration in corporate balance sheets,' says Secker. 'I'd expect 2009 [Z-scores] to be much worse.'

Analysis by the Financial Times and Capital IQ, the data provider, corroborates this – showing that the 2009 scores have been badly affected by the crisis. Some 8 per cent of global companies with a market capitalisation of more than $500 million have Altman scores below 1 for 2009 – based on 2008 company financials. This is the highest percentage since 2002 and the largest annual increase since 2001 – showing the impact of the recession on the balance sheets of even the largest companies. If smaller companies were included, the results would be worse – as their earnings and market capitalisations have been affected far more.

European balance sheets were hit the hardest, with companies averaging a Z-score of 2.8, compared with 4.0 for Asia and the US, according to Capital IQ. This suggests the scores are not due to chance. A similar differential was recorded in 2001 during the last recession. On this evidence, US companies appear more resilient than their global peers in a downturn.

On a sector basis, healthcare and IT companies have the highest Z-scores. In 2008, their scores were more than three times higher than the average for the lowest scoring sector: utilities. A similar pattern was found in 2001 – suggesting that investors may want to think twice before buying into 'defensive' utilities in a downturn.

LIMITATIONS OF RATIO ANALYSIS

Although ratios offer a quick and useful method of analysing the position and performance of a business, they are not without their problems and limitations. We shall now review some of the shortcomings of financial ratio analysis.

Quality of financial statements

It must always be remembered that ratios are based on financial statements. The results of ratio analysis are, therefore, dependent on the quality of these underlying statements. Ratios will inherit the limitations of the financial statements on which they are based. In Chapter 2 we saw that one important limitation of financial statements is their failure to include all resources controlled by the business. Internally generated goodwill and brands, for example, are excluded from the statement of financial position because they fail to meet the strict definition of an asset. This means that, even though these resources may be of considerable value, key ratios such as ROSF, ROCE and the gearing ratio will fail to acknowledge their presence.

There is also the problem of deliberate attempts to make the financial statements misleading. We discussed this problem of 'creative accounting' in Chapter 5.

Inflation

A persistent, though recently less severe, problem, in most countries is that the financial results of businesses can be distorted as a result of inflation. One effect of inflation is that the reported value of assets held for any length of time may bear little relation to current values. Generally speaking, the reported value of assets will be understated in current terms during a period of inflation as they are usually reported at their original cost (less any amounts written off for depreciation). This means that comparisons, either between businesses or between periods, will be hindered. A difference in, say, ROCE may simply be owing to the fact that assets shown in one of the statements of financial position being compared were acquired more recently (ignoring the effect of depreciation on the asset values). Another effect of inflation is to distort the measurement of profit. In the calculation of profit, sales revenue is often matched with costs incurred at an earlier time. This is because there is often a time lag between acquiring a particular resource and using it to help generate sales revenue. For example, inventories may well be acquired several months before they are sold. During a period of inflation, this will mean that the expense does not reflect prices that are current at the time of the sale. The cost of sales figure is usually based on the historic cost of the inventories concerned. As a result, expenses will be understated in the income statement and this, in turn, means that profit will be overstated. One effect of this will be to distort the profitability ratios discussed earlier. We shall take a look at attempts to correct for inflation in financial statements in Chapter 11.

The restricted view of ratios

It is important not to rely exclusively on ratios, thereby losing sight of information contained in the underlying financial statements. As we saw in Chapter 8, and earlier in this chapter, some items reported in these statements can be vital in assessing position and performance. For example, the total sales revenue, capital employed and profit figures may be useful in assessing changes in absolute size that occur over time, or in assessing differences in scale between businesses. Ratios do not provide such information. When comparing one figure with another, ratios measure *relative* performance and position and, therefore, provide only part of the picture. When comparing two businesses, therefore, it will often be useful to assess the absolute size of profits, as well as the relative profitability of each business. For example, Business A may generate £1 million operating profit and have a ROCE of 15 per cent and Business B may generate £100,000 operating profit and have a ROCE of 20 per cent. Although Business B has a higher level of *profitability*, as measured by ROCE, it generates lower total operating profits.

The basis for comparison

We saw earlier that if ratios are to be useful they require a basis for comparison. Moreover, it is important that the analyst compares like with like. Where the comparison is with another business, there can be difficulties. No two businesses are identical: the greater the differences between the businesses being compared, the greater are the limitations of ratio analysis. Furthermore, any differences in accounting policies, financing methods (gearing levels) and financial year ends will add to the problems of making comparisons between businesses.

Ratios relating to the statement of financial position

Because the statement of financial position is only a 'snapshot' of the business at a particular moment in time, any ratios based on figures, such as the liquidity ratios, from the statement of financial position may not be representative of the financial position of the business for the year as a whole. For example, it is common for a seasonal business to have a financial year end that coincides with a low point in business activity. As a result, inventories and trade receivables may be low at the year end. This means that the liquidity ratios may also be low. A more representative picture of liquidity can only really be gained by taking additional measurements at other points in the year.

Real World 9.7 points out another way in which ratios are limited.

Real World 9.7

Remember, it's people that really count . . .

Lord Weinstock (1924–2002) was an influential industrialist whose management style and philosophy helped to shape management practice in many UK businesses. During his long and successful reign at GEC plc, a major engineering business, Lord Weinstock relied heavily on financial ratios to assess performance and to exercise control. In particular, he relied on ratios relating to sales revenue, expenses, trade receivables, profit margins and inventories turnover. However, he was keenly aware of the limitations of ratios and recognised that, ultimately, people produce profits.

In a memo written to GEC managers he pointed out that ratios are an aid to good management rather than a substitute for it. He wrote:

> The operating ratios are of great value as measures of efficiency but they are only the measures and not efficiency itself. Statistics will not design a product better, make it for a lower cost or increase sales. If ill-used, they may so guide action as to diminish resources for the sake of apparent but false signs of improvement.
>
> Management remains a matter of judgement, of knowledge of products and processes and of understanding and skill in dealing with people. The ratios will indicate how well all these things are being done and will show comparison with how they are done elsewhere. But they will tell us nothing about how to do them. That is what you are meant to do.

Source: Extract from *Arnold Weinstock and the Making of GEC*, published by Aurum Press (Aris, S. 1998). Thanks to the author, Stephen Aris, for permission to reproduce this extract. Published in *The Sunday Times*, 22 February, 1998, p. 3.

The income statement and statement of financial position of Achilles plc are as follows:

Income statement for the year ended 31 December 2012

	£ million
Revenue	701
Cost of sales	(394)
Gross profit	307
Distribution costs	(106)
Administrative expenses	(104)
Operating profit	97
Interest payable	(33)
Profit before taxation	64
Taxation	(18)
Profit for the year	46

Statement of financial position as at 31 December 2012

	£ million
ASSETS	
Non-current assets	
Land and buildings	550
Plant and machinery	34
Motor vehicles	69
	653
Current assets	
Inventories	41
Trade receivables	108
Prepaid expenses	10
	159
Total assets	812
EQUITY AND LIABILITIES	
Equity	
Ordinary share capital	
200 million shares of £1 each	200
Retained earnings	151
	351
Non-current liabilities	
10% secured loan notes	300
Current liabilities	
Bank overdraft	86
Trade payables	43
Accrued expenses	14
Taxation	18
	161
Total equity and liabilities	812

The market price of the ordinary £1 shares was £3.49 at 31 December 2012. During 2012 the company paid a dividend on the ordinary shares totalling £15 million.

→

Required:

(a) Calculate the following ratios for Achilles plc for 2012:

- Dividend payout ratio;
- Dividend yield ratio;
- Earnings per share;
- P/E ratio.

(The dividend income tax credit rate can be taken to be 10 per cent.)

What can you conclude from the ratios that you have calculated?

(b) Calculate the Z-score for Achilles plc (using the equation given in the text) and comment on it.

A solution to this question can be found in Appendix C.

SUMMARY

The main points of this chapter may be summarised as follows:

Investment ratios

- Investment ratios are concerned with returns to shareholders.
- The investment ratios covered are the dividend payout ratio, the dividend yield ratio, earnings per share (EPS), cash generated from operations per share, and the price/earnings ratio.

Uses of ratios

- Individual ratios can be tracked to detect trends, for example by plotting them on a graph.
- Ratios can be used to predict financial failure.
- Univariate analysis looks at just one ratio over time in an attempt to predict financial failure.
- Multiple discriminate analysis (that is, looking at several ratios, put together in a model) can produce Z-scores that can also be used to predict financial failure.

Limitations of ratio analysis

- Ratios are only as reliable as the financial statements from which they derive.
- Inflation can distort the information.
- Ratios give a restricted view.
- It can be difficult to find a suitable benchmark (for example, another business) to compare with.
- Some ratios could mislead due to the 'snapshot' nature of the statement of financial position.

MyAccountingLab

Go to www.myaccountinglab.com to check your understanding of the chapter, create a personalised study plan, and maximise your revision time

KEY TERMS

dividend payout ratio p. 293
dividend cover ratio p. 293
dividend yield ratio p. 294
dividend per share p. 294
earnings per share (EPS) p. 295
cash generated from operations (CGO)
    per ordinary share ratio p. 295
price/earnings ratio p. 296
overtrading p. 300

key performance indicators (KPIs) p. 303
common-size financial statements
    p. 303
vertical analysis p. 306
horizontal analysis p. 306
univariate analysis p. 309
multiple discriminate analysis (MDA)
    p. 309
discriminate function p. 309

REFERENCES

1 Beaver, W. H., 'Financial ratios as predictors of failure', in *Empirical Research in Accounting: Selected Studies*, 1966, pp. 71–111

2 Zmijewski, M. E., 'Predicting corporate bankruptcy: An empirical comparison of the extent of financial distress models', Research Paper, State University of New York, 1983

3 Altman, E. I., 'Predicting financial distress of companies: Revisiting the Z-score and Zeta models', New York University Working Paper, June 2000

4 Neophytou, E., Charitou, A. and Charalamnous, C., 'Predicting corporate failure: Empirical evidence for the UK', University of Southampton Department of Accounting and Management Science Working Paper 01-173, 2001

FURTHER READING

If you would like to explore the topics covered in this chapter in more depth, we recommend the following:

Elliott, B. and Elliott, J., *Financial Accounting and Reporting*, 15th edn, Financial Times Prentice Hall, 2011, Chapter 29

Revsine, L., Collins, D., Johnson, W. B. and Mittelstaedt, F., *Financial Reporting and Analysis*, 5th edn, McGraw-Hill Higher Education, 2011, Chapter 5

Wild, J., Subramanyam, K. and Halsey, R., *Financial Statement Analysis*, 9th edn, McGraw-Hill, 2006, Chapters 8, 9 and 11

Solutions to these questions can be found in Appendix D.

9.1 What potential problems arise particularly for the external analyst from the use of statement of financial position figures in the calculation of financial ratios?

9.2 Identify and discuss three factors that might influence the level of dividend per share a company decides to pay.

9.3 Identify and discuss three reasons why the P/E ratio of two businesses operating within the same industry may differ.

9.4 Identify and discuss three ratios that are likely to be affected by a business overtrading.

EXERCISES

Exercises 9.1 and 9.2 are basic level, 9.3 to 9.5 are intermediate level and 9.6 to 9.8 are advanced level. Solutions to the exercises with coloured numbers are given in Appendix E.

If you wish to try more exercises, visit the students' side of the Companion Website and MyAccountingLab.

9.1 At the close of share trading on 27 April 2012, investment ratios for Next plc, the UK fashion and textiles retailer, and the averages for the 'general retailers' section, were as follows:

	Next plc	General retailers section
Dividend yield (%)	3.0	3.7
P/E ratio (times)	11.3	10.9
Dividend cover (times)	3.2	2.5

Source: *Financial Times*, 27 April 2012.

Required:
Comment on what can be deduced about Next plc, relative to the general retailers sector, from an equity investor's point of view.

9.2 Telford Industrial Services plc is a medium-sized business. Extracts from the business's financial statements appear below.

Summary of statements of financial position at 31 December

	2009 £m	2010 £m	2011 £m	2012 £m
ASSETS				
Non-current assets	48	51	65	64
Current assets				
Inventories	21	22	23	26
Trade receivables	34	42	34	29
Cash	–	3	–	–
	55	67	57	55
Total assets	103	118	122	119
EQUITY AND LIABILITIES				
Equity	48	61	61	63
Non-current liabilities	30	30	30	30
Current liabilities				
Trade payables	20	27	25	18
Short-term borrowings	5	–	6	8
	25	27	31	26
Total equity and liabilities	103	118	122	119

Summary of income statements for years ended 31 December

	2009 £m	2010 £m	2011 £m	2012 £m
Sales revenue	152	170	110	145
Operating profit	28	40	7	15
Interest payable	(4)	(3)	(4)	(5)
Profit before taxation	24	37	3	10
Taxation	(12)	(16)	–	(4)
Profit for the year	12	21	3	6

Required:
Prepare a set of common-size statements of financial position and common-size income statements, on a vertical basis, using equity as the base figure for the statements of financial position and sales revenue as the base figure for the income statements.

9.3 Ali plc and Bhaskar plc both operate electrical stores throughout the UK. The financial statements of each business for the year ended 30 June 2013 are as follows:

Statements of financial position as at 30 June 2013

	Ali plc £m	Bhaskar plc £m
ASSETS		
Non-current assets		
Property, plant and equipment (cost less depreciation)		
Land and buildings	360.0	510.0
Fixtures and fittings	87.0	91.2
	447.0	601.2
Current assets		
Inventories	592.0	403.0
Trade receivables	176.4	321.9
Cash at bank	84.6	91.6
	853.0	816.5
Total assets	1,300.0	1,417.7
EQUITY AND LIABILITIES		
Equity		
£1 ordinary shares	320.0	250.0
Retained earnings	367.6	624.6
	687.6	874.6
Non-current liabilities		
Borrowings – loan notes	190.0	250.0
Current liabilities		
Trade payables	406.4	275.7
Taxation	16.0	17.4
	422.4	293.1
Total equity and liabilities	1,300.0	1,417.7

Income statements for the year ended 30 June 2013

	Ali plc £m	Bhaskar plc £m
Revenue	1,478.1	1,790.4
Cost of sales	(1,018.3)	(1,214.9)
Gross profit	459.8	575.5
Operating expenses	(308.5)	(408.6)
Operating profit	151.3	166.9
Interest payable	(19.4)	(27.5)
Profit before taxation	131.9	139.4
Taxation	(32.0)	(34.8)
Profit for the year	99.9	104.6

Ali plc paid a dividend of £135 million and Bhaskar plc £95 million during the year. The market values of a share in Ali plc and Bhaskar plc at the end of the year were £6.50 and £8.20 respectively. The dividend income tax credit rate can be taken to be 10 per cent.

Required:

(a) Calculate the Z-scores for Ali plc and Bhaskar plc using the Altman model given in the text.

(b) Comment on the Z-scores for the two businesses and on the validity of using this particular model to assess these businesses.

9.4 Diversified Industries plc (DI) is a business that has interests in engineering, caravan manufacturing and a chain of shops selling car accessories. DI has recently been approached by the directors of Automobile Care plc (AC), a smaller chain of accessory shops, who wish to negotiate the sale of their business to DI. The following information, which has been extracted from AC's financial statements, is available:

	Years ended 31 December		
	2010	2011	2012
	£m	£m	£m
Revenue	18.1	28.2	36.9
Profit before taxation	3.2	4.1	7.3
Taxation	(1.0)	(1.7)	(3.1)
Profit for the year	2.2	2.4	4.2
Dividend paid for the year	0.9	1.1	1.3
Issued share capital			
16 million shares of 25p each	4.0	4.0	4.0
Reserves	8.0	9.3	12.2

AC's market price per share at 31 December 2012 was £3.15.

Required:

(a) Calculate the following items for AC for 2012 and explain the use of each one:

1 earnings per share
2 price/earnings ratio
3 dividend yield (assuming a 10 per cent dividend income tax credit rate)
4 dividend payout ratio.

(b) Write some short notes on the factors the directors of DI should take into account when considering the possible purchase of AC. You should use the income statement details together with the figures that you calculated in your answer to part (a).

9.5 One of the main suppliers to your business is Green Ltd, a family-owned business. It is the only available supplier of certain products and your business buys 60 per cent of Green Ltd's output. Recently, Green Ltd has run into a severe cash shortage and it requires extra finance to re-equip its factory with modern machinery that is expected to cost £8 million. The machinery's life is expected to be ten years and savings, before depreciation, arising from its installation are expected to be £1 million a year. Green Ltd has approached your business to see if you are able to help with finance. The directors of Green Ltd have pointed out that, if it could acquire the new machinery, your business will be able to share in the benefits through reduced prices for supplies.

Extracts from Green Ltd's recent financial statements are as follows:

Income statement data for years ended 31 December

	2010	2011	2012
	£m	£m	£m
Revenue	11.5	8.0	9.5
Operating profit (loss)	(0.2)	(2.0)	1.9
Interest payable	(1.2)	(2.4)	(1.5)
Profit (loss) before taxation	(1.4)	(4.4)	0.4

There was no charge for taxation and no dividends were paid in respect of any of these three years.

Statements of financial position as at 31 December

	2010 £m	2011 £m	2012 £m
ASSETS			
Non-current assets			
Property, plant and equipment, at cost	22.1	23.9	24.0
Depreciation	(10.2)	(12.0)	(14.0)
	11.9	11.9	10.0
Current assets			
Inventories	4.3	3.5	3.8
Trade receivables	2.8	2.6	4.1
	7.1	6.1	7.9
Total assets	19.0	18.0	17.9
EQUITY AND LIABILITIES			
Equity			
Ordinary shares	1.0	1.0	1.0
Reserves	7.4	3.0	3.4
	8.4	4.0	4.4
Non-current liabilities			
Borrowings – loan notes	6.5	8.2	7.4
Current liabilities			
Trade payables	1.4	1.7	1.9
Short-term borrowings (all bank overdraft)	2.7	4.1	4.2
	4.1	5.8	6.1
Total equity and liabilities	19.0	18.0	17.9

Required:

(a) Calculate for each year, and comment on each, the following ratios for Green Ltd:
  1 return on capital employed ratio
  2 acid test ratio
  3 trade receivables settlement period ratio (in months)
  4 interest cover ratio
  5 gearing ratio.

(b) Write some short notes suggesting the level and nature of the financial assistance that your business might be prepared to provide for Green Ltd. Your notes should also suggest what terms and conditions you would seek to impose.

9.6 Russell Ltd installs and services heating and ventilation systems for commercial premises. The business's most recent statement of financial position and income statement are as follows:

Statement of financial position

	£000	£000
ASSETS		
Non-current assets		
Property, plant and equipment		
Machinery and equipment at cost	883.6	
Accumulated depreciation	(328.4)	555.2
Motor vehicles at cost	268.8	
Accumulated depreciation	(82.2)	186.6
		741.8
Current assets		
Inventories		293.2
Trade receivables		510.3
		803.5
Total assets		1,545.3
EQUITY AND LIABILITIES		
Equity		
£1 ordinary shares		400.0
General reserve		52.2
Retained earnings		380.2
		832.4
Non-current liabilities		
12% loan notes		250.0
Current liabilities		
Trade payables		199.7
Taxation		128.0
Short-term borrowings (bank overdraft)		135.2
		462.9
Total equity and liabilities		1,545.3

Income statement for the year

	£000
Revenue	5,207.8
Operating profit	542.0
Interest payable	(30.0)
Profit before taxation	512.0
Taxation (25%)	(128.0)
Profit for the year	384.0
Dividend paid during the year	153.6

The business wishes to invest in more machinery and equipment in order to cope with an upsurge in demand for its services. An additional operating profit of £120,000 a year is expected if £600,000 is invested in more machinery.

The directors are considering an offer from a private equity firm to finance the expansion programme. The finance will be made available immediately through either

1 an issue of £1 ordinary shares at a premium of £3 a share; or
2 an issue of £600,000 10 per cent loan notes at nominal value.

The directors wish to maintain the same dividend payout ratio in future years as in past years whichever method of finance is chosen.

Required:

(a) For each of the financing schemes:
  1 prepare a projected income statement for next year;
  2 calculate the projected earnings per share for next year;
  3 calculate the projected level of gearing as at the end of next year.

(b) Briefly assess both of the financing schemes under consideration from the viewpoint of the existing shareholders.

9.7 The following is the statement of financial position (in abbreviated form) of Projections Ltd as at the end of this year:

Statement of financial position as at 31 December

	£000
ASSETS	
Non-current assets	
Cost	290
Accumulated depreciation	(110)
	180
Current assets	
Inventories	26
Trade receivables	35
Cash	5
	66
Total assets	246
EQUITY AND LIABILITIES	
Equity	
Share capital	150
Retained earnings	48
	198
Current liabilities	
Trade payables	21
Taxation (payable during next year)	27
	48
Total equity and liabilities	246

The following plans have been made for next year:

1 Revenue is expected to total £350,000, all on credit. Sales will be made at a steady rate over the year and two months' credit will be allowed to customers.

2 £200,000 worth of inventories will be bought during the year, all on credit. Purchases will be made at a steady rate over the year and suppliers will allow one month's credit.

3 New non-current assets will be bought, and paid for, during the year at a cost of £30,000. No disposals of non-current assets are planned. The depreciation expense for the year will be 10 per cent of the cost of the non-current assets owned at the end of the year.

4 Inventories at the end of the year are expected to have a value double that which applied at the beginning of the year.

5 Operating expenses, other than depreciation, are expected to total £52,000, of which £5,000 will remain unpaid at the end of the year.

6 During the year, the tax noted in the start of the year statement of financial position will be paid.

7 The tax rate can be assumed to be 25 per cent of operating profit. The tax will not be paid during the year.

8 A dividend of £10,000 will be paid during the year.

Required:

Prepare a projected income statement for next year and a statement of financial position as at the end of next year, to the nearest £1,000.

9.8 Genesis Ltd was incorporated three years ago and has grown rapidly since then. The rapid rate of growth has created problems for the business, which the directors have found difficult to deal with. Recently, a firm of management consultants has been asked to help the directors to overcome these problems.

In a preliminary report to the board of directors, the management consultants state: 'Most of the difficulties faced by the business are symptoms of an underlying problem of overtrading.'

The most recent financial statements of the business are set out below.

Statement of financial position as at 31 October

	£000	£000
ASSETS		
Non-current assets		
Property, plant and equipment		
Land and buildings at cost	530	
Accumulated depreciation	(88)	442
Fixtures and fittings at cost	168	
Accumulated depreciation	(52)	116
Motor vans at cost	118	
Accumulated depreciation	(54)	64
		622
Current assets		
Inventories		128
Trade receivables		104
		232
Total assets		854
EQUITY AND LIABILITIES		
Equity		
Ordinary £0.50 shares		60
General reserve		50
Retained earnings		74
		184
Non-current liabilities		
Borrowings – 10% loan notes (secured)		120
Current liabilities		
Trade payables		184
Taxation		8
Short-term borrowings (all bank overdraft)		358
		550
Total equity and liabilities		854

Income statement for the year ended 31 October

	£000	£000
Revenue		1,640
Cost of sales		
Opening inventories	116	
Purchases	1,260	
	1,376	
Closing inventories	(128)	(1,248)
Gross profit		392
Selling and distribution expenses		(204)
Administration expenses		(92)
Operating profit		96
Interest payable		(44)
Profit before taxation		52
Taxation		(16)
Profit for the year		36

All purchases and sales were on credit.

A dividend was paid during the year on ordinary shares of £4,000.

Required:

(a) Calculate and discuss five financial ratios that might be used to establish whether the business is overtrading. Do these five ratios suggest that the business is overtrading?

(b) State the ways in which a business may overcome the problem of overtrading.

Chapter 10

REPORTING THE FINANCIAL RESULTS OF GROUPS OF COMPANIES

INTRODUCTION

Many larger businesses, including virtually all of those that are household names in the UK, consist of a group of companies rather than just a single company. Here one company (the parent company) controls one or more other companies (the subsidiary companies). This usually arises because the parent company owns more than 50 per cent of the shares of the subsidiary companies.

In this chapter we shall look at the accounting treatment of groups of companies. This will draw heavily on what we have covered so far, particularly in Chapters 2 to 6. We shall also consider the accounting treatment of associate companies. An associate company relationship exists where one company has a substantial but not a controlling influence in another company.

Learning outcomes

When you have completed this chapter, you should be able to:

- discuss the nature of groups, and explain why they exist and how they are formed;
- prepare a group statement of financial position (balance sheet) and income statement;
- explain the nature of associate company status and its accounting implications;
- explain and interpret the contents of a set of group financial statements.

MyAccountingLab   Visit **www.myaccountinglab.com** for practice and revision opportunities

WHAT IS A GROUP OF COMPANIES?

It is quite common for one company to be able to exercise control over the activities of another. Control typically arises because the first company (the **parent company**) owns more than 50 per cent of the ordinary (voting) shares of the second company (the **subsidiary company**). This leads to the directors of the parent company being able to appoint the directors of the subsidiary company and, therefore, being able to dictate its policies. Where this relationship arises, a **group (of companies)** is said to exist. Where there is a group, the relevant International Financial Reporting Standards (IAS 27 *Consolidated and Separate Financial Statements* and IFRS 3 *Business Combinations*) normally require that a set of financial statements is drawn up annually not only for each individual company, but also for the group taken as a whole. Before we go on to consider how the **group financial statements** (that is, the financial statements of a group of companies) are prepared, we shall look at the reasons why groups exist at all and at the types of group relationships that can exist.

WHY DO GROUPS EXIST?

Companies have subsidiaries where:

1 The parent company creates a new company to operate some part of its business, perhaps a new activity.
2 The parent company buys a majority, or perhaps all, of the shares of an existing company – that is, a **takeover**.

Many companies have subsidiaries as a result of both of these reasons.

Newly created companies

It is very common for large businesses to be made up of a number of individual companies. These companies are controlled by a parent company, sometimes known as the **holding company**. In some cases, the only assets of the parent company are the shares that it owns in the subsidiary companies. Although the subsidiary companies own the land, buildings, machinery, inventories and so on, since the parent owns the subsidiaries, it effectively controls the productive assets of those companies. **Real World 10.1** looks at Associated British Foods plc, the major UK food manufacturer and retailer.

Real World 10.1

Food for thought

Under the heading 'Non-current assets' in the statement of financial position of Associated British Foods plc, there is no property, plant and equipment, just 'goodwill' and 'investment in subsidiaries'. The productive assets of the group are owned by more than eighty subsidiary companies. These include such well-known names as

- British Sugar plc
- R. Twining and Company Limited (tea producers)
- Primark Stores Limited.

Source: Associated British Foods plc Annual Report and Accounts 2011, pp. 106–108.

An obvious question to ask is: why do businesses operate through subsidiaries? To put it another way, why do the parent companies not own all of the assets of the business directly, instead of them being owned by the subsidiaries? The answers to these questions are probably:

- *Limited liability*. Each individual company has limited liability. This means that if there is a financial failure of one subsidiary, neither the assets of other subsidiaries nor those of the parent could be legally demanded by any unsatisfied claimants (lenders, trade payables and so on) against the failed company. Thus the group can 'ring-fence' each part of the business by having separate companies, each with its own limited liability.
- *Individual identity*. A sense of independence and autonomy may be created that could, in turn, increase levels of commitment among staff. It may also help to develop, or perpetuate, a market image of a smaller, independent business. Customers, as well as staff, may prefer to deal with what they see as a smaller, specialist business than with a division of a large diversified business.

To create a subsidiary, the would-be parent may simply form a new company in the normal way. The new company would then issue shares to the parent, in exchange for some asset or assets of the parent. Where the new subsidiary has been formed to undertake a completely new activity, the asset may well be cash. If the subsidiary is to carry on some activity which the parent had undertaken directly up to that point, the assets are likely to be such things as the non-current and current assets associated with the particular activity.

Example 10.1

The summarised statement of financial position of Baxter plc is as follows:

Statement of financial position

	£m
ASSETS	
Non-current assets	
Property, plant and equipment	
Land	43
Plant	15
Vehicles	8
	66
Current assets	
Inventories	15
Trade receivables	23
Cash	13
	51
Total assets	117
EQUITY AND LIABILITIES	
Equity	
Called-up share capital: ordinary shares of £1 each, fully paid	50
Retained earnings	16
	66
Non-current liabilities	
Borrowings – loan notes	40
Current liabilities	
Trade payables	11
Total equity and liabilities	117

Baxter plc has recently formed a new company, Nova Ltd, which is to undertake the work that has previously been done by the industrial fibres division of Baxter plc. The following assets are to be transferred to Nova Ltd at the values that currently are shown in the statement of financial position of Baxter plc:

	£m
Land	10
Plant	5
Vehicles	3
Inventories	6
Cash	3
	27

Nova Ltd is to issue £1 ordinary shares at their nominal value to Baxter plc in exchange for these assets.

Baxter plc's statement of financial position immediately after these transfers will be:

Statement of financial position

	£m
ASSETS	
Non-current assets	
Property, plant and equipment	
Land (43 – 10)	33
Plant (15 – 5)	10
Vehicles (8 – 3)	5
	48
Investments	
27 million ordinary £1 shares of Nova Ltd	27
	75
Current assets	
Inventories (15 – 6)	9
Trade receivables	23
Cash (13 – 3)	10
	42
Total assets	117
EQUITY AND LIABILITIES	
Equity	
Called-up share capital: ordinary shares of £1 each, fully paid	50
Retained earnings	16
	66
Non-current liabilities	
Borrowings – loan notes	40
Current liabilities	
Trade payables	11
Total equity and liabilities	117

As you have probably noted, the individual productive assets have simply been replaced by the asset of shares in Nova Ltd.

Try to prepare the statement of financial position of Nova Ltd, immediately following the transfers of the assets and the shares being issued.

It should look something like this:

Statement of financial position

ASSETS	£m
Non-current assets	
Property, plant and equipment (at transfer value)	
Land	10
Plant	5
Vehicles	3
	18
Current assets	
Inventories	6
Cash	3
	9
Total assets	27
EQUITY AND LIABILITIES	
Equity	
Called-up share capital: ordinary shares of £1 each, fully paid	27

Takeovers

A would-be parent company may also create a subsidiary by taking over an existing company. Here it acquires more than 50 per cent of the shares of a **target company** to enable it to exercise control, thereby making the target company a subsidiary. The shares are, of course, acquired from the existing shareholders of the target company.

The bid consideration in a takeover will normally take the form of cash, or shares in the parent company, or a combination of the two. Where shares are offered as all or part of the bid consideration, the target company shareholders who accept the offer will exchange their shares for shares in the parent company. They therefore cease to be shareholders of the target company and become shareholders in the parent.

Real World 10.2 outlines a recent 'share-for-share' takeover involving two businesses listed on the London Stock Exchange.

Real World 10.2

Banking on shares

When Glencore International plc took over Xstrata plc during 2012, shareholders of the latter business were given shares in the former in exchange for their Xstrata shares. The deal valued Xstrata at around $40 billion. The value of the entire business is estimated at around $90 billion.

Both businesses are involved in mining. Glencore was primarily a metals trader and Xstrata was a mining business.

Example 10.2 below illustrates the effect of a takeover involving a share-for-share exchange on the statement of financial position of the parent company.

Example 10.2

The summarised statement of financial position of Adams plc is as follows:

Statement of financial position

	£m
ASSETS	
Non-current assets	
Property, plant and equipment	
Land	35
Plant	21
Vehicles	12
	68
Current assets	
Inventories	25
Trade receivables	28
Cash	22
	75
Total assets	143
EQUITY AND LIABILITIES	
Equity	
Called-up share capital: ordinary shares of £1 each, fully paid	60
Share premium account	5
Retained earnings	5
	70
Non-current liabilities	
Borrowings – loan notes	50
Current liabilities	
Trade payables	23
Total equity and liabilities	143

Adams plc has recently made an offer of £1 a share for all the share capital of Beta Ltd. Beta Ltd's issued share capital is 20 million shares of 50p each. Adams plc will 'pay' for this by issuing the appropriate number of new ordinary shares of Adams plc at an issue value of £2 a share.

All the Beta Ltd shareholders accepted the offer. This means that Adams plc will need to issue shares to the value of £20 million (that is, 20 million × £1). Since the Adams plc shares are to be issued at £2 each, 10 million shares will need to be issued, at a share premium of £1 each.

Following the takeover, the statement of financial position of Adams plc will look as follows:

Statement of financial position

	£m
ASSETS	
Non-current assets	
Property, plant and equipment	
Land	35
Plant	21
Vehicles	12
	68
Investments	
Shares in Beta Ltd	20
	88
Current assets	
Inventories	25
Trade receivables	28
Cash	22
	75
Total assets	163
EQUITY AND LIABILITIES	
Equity	
Called-up share capital: ordinary shares of £1 each, fully paid (60 + 10)	70
Share premium account (5 + 10)	15
Retained earnings	5
	90
Non-current liabilities	
Borrowings – loan notes	50
Current liabilities	
Trade payables	23
Total equity and liabilities	163

Note that the assets have increased by £20 million and that this is balanced by the value of the shares issued (£10 million share capital and £10 million share premium).

Activity 10.2

If, instead of the consideration offered being all in shares, the offer had been 50 per cent in cash and 50 per cent in Adams plc shares, what would the statement of financial position of Adams plc have looked like after the takeover?

The total offer value would still be £20 million, but this would be met by paying cash totalling £10 million and issuing shares worth £10 million (£5 million share capital and £5 million share premium). So the statement of financial position would be:

→

Statement of financial position

	£m
ASSETS	
Non-current assets	
Property, plant and equipment	
Land	35
Plant	21
Vehicles	12
	68
Investments	
Shares in Beta Ltd	20
	88
Current assets	
Inventories	25
Trade receivables	28
Cash (22 − 10)	12
	65
Total assets	153
EQUITY AND LIABILITIES	
Equity	
Called-up share capital: ordinary shares of £1 each, fully paid (60 + 5)	65
Share premium account (5 + 5)	10
Retained earnings	5
	80
Non-current liabilities	
Borrowings – loan notes	50
Current liabilities	
Trade payables	23
Total equity and liabilities	153

Activity 10.3

How would the takeover affect the statement of financial position of Beta Ltd?

The statement of financial position of Beta Ltd would not be affected at all. A change of shareholders does not affect the financial statements of a company.

It is not necessary that the parent company should retain the target/subsidiary as a separate company, following the takeover. The subsidiary could be wound up and its assets owned directly by the parent. Normally this would not happen, however, for the reasons that we considered above, namely limited liability and individual identity. The latter may be particularly important in the case of a takeover. The new parent company may be very keen to retain the name and identity of its new subsidiary, where the subsidiary has a good marketing image.

TYPES OF GROUP RELATIONSHIP

So far we have considered a situation where there is a simple relationship between a parent and its subsidiary or subsidiaries such as that shown in Figure 10.1.

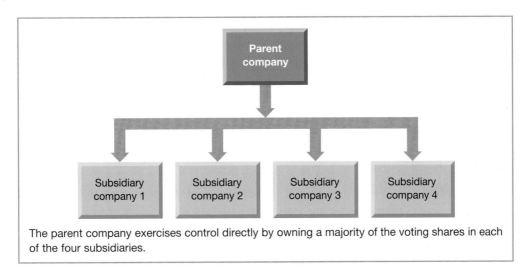

The parent company exercises control directly by owning a majority of the voting shares in each of the four subsidiaries.

Figure 10.1 A simple parent/subsidiaries relationship

A slightly more complex relationship is shown in Figure 10.2.

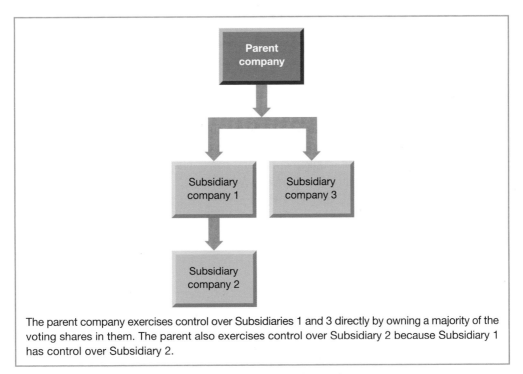

The parent company exercises control over Subsidiaries 1 and 3 directly by owning a majority of the voting shares in them. The parent also exercises control over Subsidiary 2 because Subsidiary 1 has control over Subsidiary 2.

Figure 10.2 A more complex parent/subsidiaries relationship

Here Subsidiary 2 is a subsidiary by virtue of being controlled by another company (Subsidiary 1) that is, in turn, a subsidiary of the parent. In these circumstances, Subsidiary 2 is usually called a 'sub-subsidiary' of the parent. The parent company here is sometimes known as the 'ultimate' parent company of Subsidiary 2. Subsidiary 3 is a straightforward subsidiary.

Earlier, it was pointed out that one company is a subsidiary of another because the latter *controls* the former. This is usually as a result of the parent owning a majority, or all, of the voting shares of the other, but this does not need to be the case. Consider Figure 10.2 and suppose that the parent owns 60 per cent of the voting shares of Subsidiary 1 and that Subsidiary 1 owns 60 per cent of the shares of Subsidiary 2. In effect, the parent only owns 36 per cent of the shares of Subsidiary 2 (that is, 60 per cent of 60 per cent), yet the latter is a subsidiary of the former. This is because the parent has complete control over (though not total ownership of) Subsidiary 1, which in turn has complete control over (though again not total ownership of) Subsidiary 2.

Activity 10.4

Company A owns 40 per cent of the voting shares of both Company B and Company C. The other 60 per cent of the voting shares of Company C are owned by Company B.
  Is Company C a subsidiary of Company A?

The answer is no. This is despite the fact that Company A can be seen to own 64 per cent of the shares of Company C; 40 per cent directly and 24 per cent (that is, 40 per cent × 60 per cent) through Company B. Since A does not control B, it cannot control B's shares in C.

Though ownership and control do not necessarily go hand-in-hand, in practice they tend to do so.

The reason that we are concerned as to whether one company is a subsidiary of another is, of course, that group financial statements must be prepared where there is a parent/subsidiary relationship, but not otherwise.

Real World 10.3 shows the subsidiaries of the Go-Ahead Group plc. Most of us in the UK use the services of at least one of the subsidiaries, many of us on a daily basis. Most of the productive assets of the group are owned by the subsidiaries, rather than directly by the parent company. Note that Go-Ahead uses the word 'group' in its official name. Although this is not unusual, it is not a legal requirement. Many companies that operate mainly through subsidiaries do not indicate this in the company name.

Going ahead with subsidiaries

Go-Ahead Group plc: Principal subsidiaries

Name	Percentage of shares owned
Brighton & Hove Bus and Coach Company Limited	100
City of Oxford Motor Services Limited	100
Go North East Limited	100
London Central Bus Company Limited	100
London General Transport Services Limited	100
Docklands Buses Limited	100
Blue Triangle Buses Limited	100
Plymouth Citibus Limited	100
Metrobus Limited	100
New Southern Railway Limited	65
London and South Eastern Railway Limited	65
Govia Limited	65
Abingdon Bus Company Limited	100
Aviance UK Limited	100
Reed Aviation Limited	100
Meteor Parking Limited	100
Konectbus Limited	100
Nicaro Limited	100
Thames Travel (Wallingford) Limited	100
Southern Railway Limited	65
Go South Coast Limited	100
Go-Ahead Leasing Limited	100
London and Birmingham Railway Limited	65
Go-Ahead Holding LLC	100

Source: Go-Ahead Group plc Annual Report 2011, p. 128.

PREPARING A GROUP STATEMENT OF FINANCIAL POSITION

We are now going to look at the preparation of a **group statement of financial position**. We shall do this by considering a series of examples, starting with the simplest possible case and gradually building in more and more of the complexities found in real life.

Each company within the group will prepare its own statement of financial position. In addition, however, the parent company will produce a statement of financial position that reflects the assets and claims of the group as a whole. In effect, the group statement of financial position looks at the group as if the parent company owns the assets and is, therefore, responsible for the outside liabilities of all the group members. This means, among other things, that whereas the *parent company* statement of financial position will include the assets of investments in the shares of the subsidiary companies, in the *group* statement of financial position, this will be replaced by the net assets (assets less non-group liabilities). In other words, the group statement of financial position looks behind the subsidiary company shares to see what they represent, in terms of assets and liabilities. The assets and liabilities of subsidiaries are **consolidated** into the statement of financial position of the parent company. This point should become clearer as we look at some examples.

Example 10.3

The statements of financial position of Parent plc and of Subsidiary Ltd, on the date that the former bought all the shares in the latter, were as follows:

Statements of financial position

	Parent plc £m	Subsidiary Ltd £m
ASSETS		
Non-current assets		
Property, plant and equipment		
Land	40	5
Plant	30	2
Vehicles	20	2
	90	9
Investment		
5 million shares of Subsidiary Ltd	10	–
	100	9
Current assets		
Inventories	20	3
Trade receivables	30	2
Cash	10	2
	60	7
Total assets	160	16
EQUITY AND LIABILITIES		
Equity		
Called-up share capital: ordinary shares of £1 each, fully paid	70	5
Share premium account	10	–
Retained earnings	30	5
	110	10
Non-current liabilities		
Borrowings – loan notes	30	–
Current liabilities		
Trade payables	20	6
Total equity and liabilities	160	16

To derive the group statement of financial position, we simply combine each of the like items by adding them together. For example, the group investment in land is £45 million, representing £40 million invested by Parent plc and £5 million invested by Subsidiary Ltd.

The only exceptions to the rule that we simply add like items together lies with the investment in the shares of Subsidiary Ltd in the statement of financial position of Parent plc, and with the equity (share capital plus reserves) in the statement of financial position of Subsidiary Ltd. In effect, these are two sides of the same coin, since Parent plc is the owner of Subsidiary Ltd. For this reason, it is logical simply to add these two items together and since one is an asset and the other is a claim and they are equal in amount, they will cancel each other out.

The group statement of financial position will be as follows:

Statement of financial position

	£m
ASSETS	
Non-current assets	
Property, plant and equipment	
Land (40 + 5)	45
Plant (30 + 2)	32
Vehicles (20 + 2)	22
	99
Current assets	
Inventories (20 + 3)	23
Trade receivables (30 + 2)	32
Cash (10 + 2)	12
	67
Total assets	166
EQUITY AND LIABILITIES	
Equity	
Called-up share capital: ordinary	
shares of £1 each, fully paid	70
Share premium account	10
Retained earnings	30
	110
Non-current liabilities	
Borrowings – loan notes (30 + 0)	30
Current liabilities	
Trade payables (20 + 6)	26
Total equity and liabilities	166

The 'Equity' section of the group statement of financial position is simply that of Parent plc. The £10 million equity for Subsidiary Ltd cancels out with the £10 million that relates to '5 million shares of Subsidiary Ltd' in the non-current assets section of the parent company's statement of financial position. Since Parent owns all of Subsidiary's shares, all of Subsidiary's equity is attributable to Parent.

The statements of financial position of Large plc and of Small plc, on the date that Large plc bought all the shares in Small plc, were as follows:

Statements of financial position

	Large plc £m	Small plc £m
ASSETS		
Non-current assets		
Property, plant and equipment		
Land	55	–
Plant	43	21
Vehicles	25	17
	123	38
Investment		
20 million shares of Small plc	32	–
	155	38
Current assets		
Inventories	42	18
Trade receivables	18	13
Cash	24	13
	84	44
Total assets	239	82
EQUITY AND LIABILITIES		
Equity		
Called-up share capital:		
ordinary shares of £1 each, fully paid	100	20
Share premium account	–	5
Retained earnings	64	7
	164	32
Non-current liabilities		
Borrowings – loan notes	50	30
Current liabilities		
Trade payables	25	20
Total equity and liabilities	239	82

Have a try at deducing the group statement of financial position.

The group statement of financial position will be as follows:

Statement of financial position

	£m
ASSETS	
Non-current assets	
Property, plant and equipment	
Land (55 + 0)	55
Plant (43 + 21)	64
Vehicles (25 + 17)	42
	161
Current assets	
Inventories (42 + 18)	60
Trade receivables (18 + 13)	31
Cash (24 + 13)	37
	128
Total assets	289
EQUITY AND LIABILITIES	
Equity	
Called-up share capital: ordinary	
shares of £1 each, fully paid	100
Retained earnings	64
	164
Non-current liabilities	
Borrowings – loan notes (50 + 30)	80
Current liabilities	
Trade payables (25 + 20)	45
Total equity and liabilities	289

The 'equity' section of the group statement of financial position is simply that of Large plc. The £32 million for the equity (share capital and reserves) of Small plc cancels out with the £32 million relating to 'Investment in 20 million shares of Small plc' in the non-current assets section of the statement of financial position of Large plc.

The example and the activity represent the simplest case because

1 the parent owns all of the shares of the subsidiary;
2 the price paid for the shares (£10 million and £32 million, respectively) exactly equals the 'carrying amount', or 'book value', of the net assets of the subsidiary (that is the values at which they appear in the subsidiary's statement of financial position); and
3 no trading has taken place since the shares were acquired.

In practice, things are usually more complex. We shall now look at various 'complications' that may arise, both one by one and together.

Complication 1: Less than 100 per cent ownership of the subsidiary by the parent

The problem here is that when setting the asset of 'shares of subsidiary', in the statement of financial position of the parent, against the 'equity' (owners' claim) in the statement of financial position of the subsidiary, they do not completely cancel one another out.

Example 10.4

The statements of financial position of Parent plc and of Subsidiary Ltd, on the date that the former bought the shares in the latter, are the same as in the previous example (Example 10.3) except that Parent plc owns only 4 million (of the 5 million) shares of Subsidiary Ltd. Thus the investment is only £8 million, instead of £10 million. As a result, Parent plc's cash balance is £2 million greater than in the previous example.

The two statements of financial position were as follows:

Statements of financial position

	Parent plc £m	Subsidiary Ltd £m
ASSETS		
Non-current assets		
Property, plant and equipment		
Land	40	5
Plant	30	2
Vehicles	20	2
	90	9
Investment		
4 million shares of Subsidiary Ltd	8	–
	98	9
Current assets		
Inventories	20	3
Trade receivables	30	2
Cash	12	2
	62	7
Total assets	160	16
EQUITY AND LIABILITIES		
Equity		
Called-up share capital: ordinary shares of £1 each, fully paid	70	5
Share premium account	10	–
Retained earnings	30	5
	110	10
Non-current liabilities		
Borrowings – loan notes	30	–
Current liabilities		
Trade payables	20	6
Total equity and liabilities	160	16

As before, to prepare the group statement of financial position, we simply add like items together. The problem is that when we come to set the £8 million investment made by Parent plc against the £10 million equity of Subsidiary Ltd, they do not cancel. There is an owners' claim of £2 million in the statement of financial position of Subsidiary Ltd that has not been cancelled out.

Can you puzzle out what the £2 million represents?

It represents the extent to which Parent plc does not own all of the shares of Subsidiary Ltd. Parent plc only owns 80 per cent of the shares and, therefore, other investors must own the rest. Since we are including all of the assets and liabilities of Subsidiary Ltd as being those of the group, the group statement of financial position needs to acknowledge that there is another source of equity finance, as well as Parent plc.

This £2 million owners' claim is known as **non-controlling interests** (or **minority interests**). It is shown in the group statement of financial position as an addition to, but not part of, the equity.

The group statement of financial position will be as follows:

Statement of financial position

	£m
ASSETS	
Non-current assets	
Property, plant and equipment	
Land (40 + 5)	45
Plant (30 + 2)	32
Vehicles (20 + 2)	22
	99
Current assets	
Inventories (20 + 3)	23
Trade receivables (30 + 2)	32
Cash (12 + 2)	14
	69
Total assets	168
EQUITY AND LIABILITIES	
Equity	
Called-up share capital: ordinary	
shares of £1 each, fully paid	70
Share premium account	10
Retained earnings	30
	110
Non-controlling interests	2
	112
Non-current liabilities	
Borrowings – loan notes (30 + 0)	30
Current liabilities	
Trade payables (20 + 6)	26
Total equity and liabilities	168

This statement of financial position reflects the fact that the group has control over net assets totalling £112 million (at statement of financial position values). Of this amount, £110 million is financed by shareholders of the parent company and £2 million by others.

It may have occurred to you that an alternative approach to dealing with less than 100 per cent ownership is to scale down the assets and liabilities to reflect this, before carrying out the consolidation of the two sets of financial statements. Since Parent plc only owns 80 per cent of Subsidiary Ltd, we could multiply all of the figures in Subsidiary Ltd's statement of financial position by 0.8 before preparing the group financial statements. If we did this, the owners' claim would be reduced to £8 million, which would exactly cancel with the asset (shares of Subsidiary Ltd) in the statement of financial position of Parent plc.

Activity 10.7

Can you think of the (logical) reason why we do not 'scale down' for less than 100 per cent owned subsidiaries when preparing the group statement of financial position?

The reason that all of the assets and liabilities of the subsidiary are included in the group statement of financial position in these circumstances is that the parent company *controls* all of the subsidiaries' assets, even though it may not strictly own them all. Control is the key issue in group financial statements.

Activity 10.8

The statements of financial position of Large plc and of Small plc, on the date that Large plc bought the shares in Small plc, were as follows:

Statements of financial position

	Large plc £m	Small plc £m
ASSETS		
Non-current assets		
Property, plant and equipment		
Land	55	–
Plant	43	21
Vehicles	25	17
	123	38
Investment		
15 million shares of Small plc	24	–
	147	38
Current assets		
Inventories	42	18
Trade receivables	18	13
Cash	32	13
	92	44
Total assets	239	82
EQUITY AND LIABILITIES		
Equity		
Called-up share capital: ordinary shares of £1 each, fully paid	100	20
Share premium account	–	5
Retained earnings	64	7
	164	32
Non-current liabilities		
Borrowings – loan notes	50	30
Current liabilities		
Trade payables	25	20
Total equity and liabilities	239	82

Have a go at preparing the group statement of financial position.

The group statement of financial position will be as follows:

Statement of financial position

	£m
ASSETS	
Non-current assets	
Property, plant and equipment	
Land (55 + 0)	55
Plant (43 + 21)	64
Vehicles (25 + 17)	42
	161
Current assets	
Inventories (42 + 18)	60
Trade receivables (18 + 13)	31
Cash (32 + 13)	45
	136
Total assets	297
EQUITY AND LIABILITIES	
Equity	
Called-up share capital: ordinary shares of £1 each, fully paid	100
Retained earnings	64
	164
Non-controlling interests	8
	172
Non-current liabilities	
Borrowings – loan notes (50 + 30)	80
Current liabilities	
Trade payables (25 + 20)	45
Total equity and liabilities	297

Large plc owns 75 per cent of the shares, costing £24 million. The £8 million for non-controlling interests represents the remaining 25 per cent of the Small plc shares owned by the 'outside' shareholders (that is, 25 per cent of £32 million).

Complication 2: Paying more or less than the underlying net asset value for the shares

Here the problem is that, even where the subsidiary is 100 per cent owned, the asset of 'shares of the subsidiary', in the statement of financial position of the parent, will not exactly cancel against the equity figure in the statement of financial position of the subsidiary. Anything paid in excess of the underlying net asset value of the subsidiary's shares must represent an undisclosed asset, which is normally referred to as **goodwill arising on consolidation**. Any amount paid below the underlying net asset value is normally referred to as **negative goodwill arising on consolidation**. This situation tends only to arise where there is a takeover of an existing business. Where a would-be parent creates a new subsidiary, goodwill (positive or negative) will not usually arise.

For the sake of simplicity, we shall assume that the statement of financial position of a subsidiary reflects all of its assets and liabilities and that these are recorded at their fair values. We shall, however, later consider the situation where this is not the case.

Example 10.5

We are returning to the original statements of financial position of Parent plc and Subsidiary Ltd as shown in Example 10.3, on the date that Parent plc bought the shares in Subsidiary Ltd. So Parent plc owns all of the shares in Subsidiary Ltd, but we shall assume that they were bought for £15 million rather than £10 million. Parent plc's cash balance reflects the higher amount paid. The statements of financial position are as follows:

Statements of financial position

	Parent plc £m	Subsidiary Ltd £m
ASSETS		
Non-current assets		
Property, plant and equipment		
Land	40	5
Plant	30	2
Vehicles	20	2
	90	9
Investment		
5 million shares of Subsidiary Ltd	15	–
	105	9
Current assets		
Inventories	20	3
Trade receivables	30	2
Cash	5	2
	55	7
Total assets	160	16
EQUITY AND LIABILITIES		
Equity		
Called-up share capital: ordinary shares of £1 each, fully paid	70	5
Share premium account	10	–
Retained earnings	30	5
	110	10
Non-current liabilities		
Borrowings – loan notes	30	–
Current liabilities		
Trade payables	20	6
Total equity and liabilities	160	16

The normal routine of adding like items together and cancelling the investment in Subsidiary Ltd shares against the equity of that company is followed, except that the last two do not exactly cancel. The difference is, of course, goodwill arising on consolidation.

The group statement of financial position will be as follows:

Statement of financial position

	£m
Non-current assets	
Property, plant and equipment	
Land (40 + 5)	45
Plant (30 + 2)	32
Vehicles (20 + 2)	22
	99
Intangible assets	
Goodwill arising on consolidation (15 – 10)	5
	104
Current assets	
Inventories (20 + 3)	23
Trade receivables (30 + 2)	32
Cash (5 + 2)	7
	62
Total assets	166
EQUITY AND LIABILITIES	
Equity	
Called-up share capital: ordinary shares of £1 each, fully paid	70
Share premium account	10
Retained earnings	30
	110
Non-current liabilities	
Borrowings – loan notes (30 + 0)	30
Current liabilities	
Trade payables (20 + 6)	26
Total equity and liabilities	166

The goodwill represents the excess of what was paid by Parent plc for the shares over the fair value of their underlying net assets, at the time of the takeover.

The statements of financial position of Large plc and of Small plc, on the date that Large plc bought all the shares in Small plc, were as follows:

Statements of financial position

	Large plc £m	Small plc £m
ASSETS		
Non-current assets		
Property, plant and equipment		
Land	48	–
Plant	43	21
Vehicles	25	17
	116	38
Investment		
20 million shares of Small plc	35	–
	151	38
Current assets		
Inventories	42	18
Trade receivables	18	13
Cash	28	13
	88	44
Total assets	239	82
EQUITY AND LIABILITIES		
Equity		
Called-up share capital: ordinary shares of £1 each, fully paid	100	20
Share premium account	–	5
Retained earnings	64	7
	164	32
Non-current liabilities		
Borrowings – loan notes	50	30
Current liabilities		
Trade payables	25	20
Total equity and liabilities	239	82

Have a go at preparing the group statement of financial position.

The group statement of financial position will be as follows:

Statement of financial position

	£m
ASSETS	
Non-current assets	
Property, plant and equipment	
Land (48 + 0)	48
Plant (43 + 21)	64
Vehicles (25 + 17)	42
	154
Intangible asset	
Goodwill arising on consolidation (35 − 32)	3
	157
Current assets	
Inventories (42 + 18)	60
Trade receivables (18 + 13)	31
Cash (28 + 13)	41
	132
Total assets	289
EQUITY AND LIABILITIES	
Equity	
Called-up share capital: ordinary shares of £1 each, fully paid	100
Retained earnings	64
	164
Non-current liabilities	
Borrowings – loan notes (50 + 30)	80
Current liabilities	
Trade payables (25 + 20)	45
Total equity and liabilities	289

A little later we shall see that there is a slightly different approach that can be taken in the valuation of goodwill arising on consolidation in the group statement of financial position. In practice, however, most businesses take the approach that we have just explored.

Complications 1 and 2 taken together

We shall now take a look at how we cope with a situation where the parent owns less than all of the shares of its subsidiary, *and* it has paid more or less than the underlying net asset value of the shares.

Example 10.6

Again we shall look at the statements of financial position of Parent plc and Subsidiary Ltd, on the date that the former bought the shares in the latter. This time we shall combine both of the 'complications' that we have already met. Here, Parent plc now only owns 80 per cent of the shares of Subsidiary Ltd, for which it paid £3 a share, that is, £1 above their underlying net asset value.

Statements of financial position

	Parent plc £m	Subsidiary Ltd £m
ASSETS		
Non-current assets		
Property, plant and equipment		
Land	40	5
Plant	30	2
Vehicles	20	2
	90	9
Investment		
4 million shares of Subsidiary Ltd	12	–
	102	9
Current assets		
Inventories	20	3
Trade receivables	30	2
Cash	8	2
	58	7
Total assets	160	16
EQUITY AND LIABILITIES		
Equity		
Called-up share capital: ordinary shares of £1 each, fully paid	70	5
Share premium account	10	–
Retained earnings	30	5
	110	10
Non-current liabilities		
Borrowings – loan notes	30	–
Current liabilities		
Trade payables	20	6
Total equity and liabilities	160	16

The normal routine still applies. This means adding like items together and cancelling the investment in Subsidiary Ltd shares against the equity of that company. Again they will not cancel, but this time for a combination of two reasons; non-controlling interests *and* goodwill arising on consolidation.

We need to separate out these two issues before we go on to prepare the group financial statements.

To establish the non-controlling interests element, we need simply to calculate the part of the owners' claim of Subsidiary Ltd that is not owned by Parent plc. Parent plc owns 80 per cent of the shares, so others own the remaining 20 per cent. Twenty per cent of the equity of Subsidiary Ltd is £2 million (that is, 20 per cent × £10 million).

To discover the appropriate goodwill figure, we need to compare what Parent plc paid and what it got, in terms of the fair values reflected in the statement of financial position. It paid £12 million and got net assets with a fair value of £8 million (that is, 80 per cent × £10 million). Thus, goodwill is £4 million (that is, 12 − 8).

The group statement of financial position will be as follows:

Statement of financial position

	£m
ASSETS	
Non-current assets	
Property, plant and equipment	
Land (40 + 5)	45
Plant (30 + 2)	32
Vehicles (20 + 2)	22
	99
Intangible assets	
Goodwill arising on consolidation	
(12 − (80% × 10))	4
	103
Current assets	
Inventories (20 + 3)	23
Trade receivables (30 + 2)	32
Cash (8 + 2)	10
	65
Total assets	168
EQUITY AND LIABILITIES	
Equity	
Called-up share capital: ordinary	
shares of £1 each, fully paid	70
Share premium account	10
Retained earnings	30
	110
Non-controlling interests	2
	112
Non-current liabilities	
Borrowings – loan notes (30 + 0)	30
Current liabilities	
Trade payables (20 + 6)	26
Total equity and liabilities	168

The statements of financial position of Large plc and Small plc, on the date that Large plc bought the shares in Small plc, were as follows:

Statements of financial position

	Large plc £m	Small plc £m
ASSETS		
Non-current assets		
Property, plant and equipment		
Land	49	–
Plant	43	21
Vehicles	25	17
	117	38
Investment		
15 million shares of Small plc	27	–
	144	38
Current assets		
Inventories	42	18
Trade receivables	18	13
Cash	35	13
	95	44
Total assets	239	82
EQUITY AND LIABILITIES		
Equity		
Called-up share capital: ordinary shares of £1 each, fully paid	100	20
Share premium account	–	5
Retained earnings	64	7
	164	32
Non-current liabilities		
Borrowings – loan notes	50	30
Current liabilities		
Trade payables	25	20
Total equity and liabilities	239	82

Have a try at preparing the group statement of financial position.

The non-controlling interests will be £8 million (that is, 25 per cent of £32 million).

To determine goodwill, we need to compare what was paid (£27 million) with what was obtained (75 per cent of £32 million = £24 million). Thus, we have goodwill of £3 million.

The group statement of financial position will be as follows:

Statement of financial position

	£m
ASSETS	
Non-current assets	
Property, plant and equipment	
Land (49 + 0)	49
Plant (43 + 21)	64
Vehicles (25 + 17)	42
	155
Intangible assets	
Goodwill arising on consolidation	3
	158
Current assets	
Inventories (42 + 18)	60
Trade receivables (18 + 13)	31
Cash (35 + 13)	48
	139
Total assets	297
EQUITY AND LIABILITIES	
Equity	
Called-up share capital: ordinary shares of £1 each, fully paid	100
Retained earnings	64
	164
Non-controlling interests (25% × 32)	8
	172
Non-current liabilities	
Borrowings – loan notes (50 + 30)	80
Current liabilities	
Trade payables (25 + 20)	45
Total equity and liabilities	297

Complication 3: Trading has taken place since the shares were acquired

Except very rarely, most group statements of financial position will be prepared after some time has elapsed from the date that the parent company acquired the shares in the subsidiary. This does not in any way raise major difficulties, but we need to backtrack to the position at the time of the acquisition to establish the goodwill figure.

We shall look at another example. All three of our 'complications' exist here.

The statements of financial position of Mega plc and Micro plc, as at 31 December, are set out below. Mega plc bought its shares in Micro plc some time ago, at a time at which the latter's share capital was exactly as shown below and the retained earnings balance stood at £30 million.

Statements of financial position as at 31 December

	Mega plc £m	Micro plc £m
ASSETS		
Non-current assets		
Property, plant and equipment		
Land	53	18
Plant	34	11
Vehicles	24	9
	111	38
Investment		
6 million shares of Micro plc	33	–
	144	38
Current assets		
Inventories	27	10
Trade receivables	29	11
Cash	11	1
	67	22
Total assets	211	60
EQUITY AND LIABILITIES		
Equity		
Called-up share capital: ordinary shares of £1 each, fully paid	100	10
Retained earnings	38	35
	138	45
Non-current liabilities		
Borrowings – loan notes	50	10
Current liabilities		
Trade payables	23	5
Total equity and liabilities	211	60

We can see that the investment in the statement of financial position of Mega plc (£33 million) comes nowhere near cancelling with the £45 million owners' claim of Micro plc. We need to separate out the elements.

Let us start with non-controlling interests. Here we are not concerned at all with the position at the date of the takeover. If the equity of Micro plc totals £45 million at the statement of financial position date and the minorities own 4 million of the 10 million shares, their contribution to the financing of the group's assets must be £18 million (that is, 40 per cent × £45 million).

Next let us ask ourselves what Mega plc got when it paid £33 million for the shares. At that time, the equity part of Micro plc's statement of financial position looked like this:

	£m
Called-up share capital: ordinary shares of £1 each, fully paid	10
Retained earnings	30
	40

This means that the net assets of Micro plc must have also been worth (in terms of fair values reflected in the statement of financial position) £40 million; otherwise the statement of financial position would not have balanced. Since Mega plc bought 6 million of 10 million shares, it paid £33 million for net assets worth £24 million (that is, 60 per cent of £40 million). Thus, there is goodwill arising on consolidation of £9 million (that is, £33m – £24m).

We shall assume that no steps have been taken since the takeover to alter this goodwill figure. We shall consider why such steps may have been taken a little later.

In dealing with non-controlling interests and goodwill we have, in effect, picked up the following parts of the owners' claim of Micro plc at 31 December:

■ the minorities' share of the equity (as non-controlling interests);
■ Mega plc's share of the share capital and its share of the reserves as they stood at the date of the takeover (in the calculation of the goodwill figure).

The only remaining part of the owners' claim of Micro plc at 31 December is Mega plc's share of Micro plc's reserves that have built up since the takeover, that is, its share of (£35 million – £30 million =) £5 million. This share is £3 million (that is, 60 per cent of £5 million). This is Mega plc's share of the profits that have been earned by its subsidiary since the takeover, to the extent that profits have not already been paid out as dividends. As such, it is logical for this £3 million to be added to the retained earnings balance of the parent company in arriving at the group reserves.

This treatment of the equity of Micro plc can be represented in a tabular form as shown in Figure 10.3.

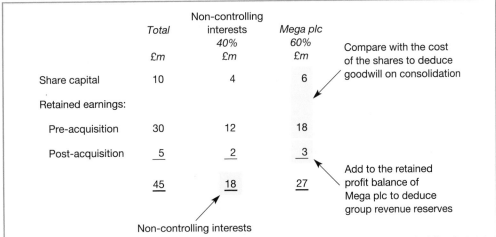

Figure 10.3 The treatment of the share equity of Micro plc in producing the group statement of financial position

The group statement of financial position will be as follows:

Statement of financial position as at 31 December

	£m
ASSETS	
Non-current assets	
Property, plant and equipment	
Land (53 + 18)	71
Plant (34 + 11)	45
Vehicles (24 + 9)	33
	149
Intangible assets	
Goodwill arising on consolidation (33 − (6 + 18))	9
	158
Current assets	
Inventories (27 + 10)	37
Trade receivables (29 + 11)	40
Cash (11 + 1)	12
	89
Total assets	247
EQUITY AND LIABILITIES	
Equity	
Called-up share capital: ordinary	
shares of £1 each, fully paid	100
Retained earnings (38 + 3)	41
	141
Non-controlling interests (40% × 45)	18
	159
Non-current liabilities	
Borrowings – loan notes (50 + 10)	60
Current liabilities	
Trade payables (23 + 5)	28
Total equity and liabilities	247

The statements of financial position of Grand plc and Petit Ltd, as at 30 June, are set out below. Grand plc bought its shares in Petit Ltd at a time when the latter's share capital was the same as it is currently and the retained earnings balance stood at £14 million.

Statements of financial position as at 30 June

	Grand plc £m	Petit Ltd £m
ASSETS		
Non-current assets		
Property, plant and equipment		
Land	12	10
Plant	14	8
Vehicles	3	6
	29	24
Investment		
7.5 million shares of Petit Ltd	21	–
	50	24
Current assets		
Inventories	10	5
Trade receivables	9	4
Cash	2	2
	21	11
Total assets	71	35
EQUITY AND LIABILITIES		
Equity		
Called-up share capital: ordinary shares of £1 each, fully paid	30	10
Retained earnings	14	22
	44	32
Non-current liabilities		
Borrowings – loan notes	20	–
Current liabilities		
Trade payables	7	3
Total equity and liabilities	71	35

Prepare the statement of financial position for the group as at 30 June.

Your answer should be something like this:

Non-controlling interests:

$$25\% \times £32 \text{ million} = £8 \text{ million}$$

Goodwill arising on consolidation:

$$£21 \text{ million} - (75\% \times (£10 \text{ million} + £14 \text{ million})) = £3 \text{ million}$$

Grand plc's share of Petit Ltd's post-acquisition reserves:

$$75\% \times (£22 \text{ million} - £14 \text{ million}) = £6 \text{ million}$$

Assuming that no steps have been taken since the takeover to alter the goodwill figure, the group statement of financial position will be as follows:

Statement of financial position as at 30 June

	£m
ASSETS	
Non-current assets	
Property, plant and equipment	
Land (12 + 10)	22
Plant (14 + 8)	22
Vehicles (3 + 6)	9
	53
Intangible assets	
Goodwill arising on consolidation	3
	56
Current assets	
Inventories (10 + 5)	15
Trade receivables (9 + 4)	13
Cash (2 + 2)	4
	32
Total assets	88
EQUITY AND LIABILITIES	
Equity	
Called-up share capital: ordinary shares of £1 each, fully paid	30
Retained earnings (14 + 6)	20
	50
Non-controlling interests	8
	58
Non-current liabilities	
Borrowings – loan notes (20 + 0)	20
Current liabilities	
Trade payables (7 + 3)	10
Total equity and liabilities	88

GOODWILL ARISING ON CONSOLIDATION AND ASSET CARRYING AMOUNTS

Goodwill arising on consolidation represents the difference between the cost of acquiring the shares in a subsidiary and the fair value of the net assets acquired. In the examples considered so far, we have assumed that the values at which a subsidiary's assets appear in the subsidiary's statement of financial position are the same as the fair values of those assets. Thus, it has been possible to deduce goodwill by making a comparison of the cost of acquiring the subsidiary with the values appearing in the subsidiary's statement of financial position. Unfortunately, things are not usually that simple!

Carrying amounts often differ from the fair values of assets. Generally speaking, the values at which assets are shown in the statement of financial position are lower because accounting conventions such as prudence and historic cost conspire to produce a conservative bias. As a result, not only do assets tend to be shown on the statement of financial position at less than their fair value, but some assets are completely omitted from the normal statement of financial position. This is particularly true of intangible assets, such as brand values. This means that, to calculate goodwill arising on consolidation, we cannot rely on statement of financial position values. We must find out what the fair values of the assets acquired really are. This must include both assets that appear on the statement of financial position of the subsidiary and those that do not (such as brand values).

Example 10.8 seeks to illustrate this point.

Example 10.8

The statements of financial position of Parent plc and of Subsidiary Ltd (which we last met in Example 10.6), on the date that the former bought the shares in the latter, were as follows:

Statements of financial position

	Parent plc £m	Subsidiary Ltd £m
ASSETS		
Non-current assets		
Property, plant and equipment		
Land	40	5
Plant	30	2
Vehicles	20	2
	90	9
Investment		
5 million shares of Subsidiary Ltd	15	–
	105	9
Current assets		
Inventories	20	3
Trade receivables	30	2
Cash	5	2
	55	7
Total assets	160	16
EQUITY AND LIABILITIES		
Equity		
Called-up share capital: ordinary		
shares of £1 each, fully paid	70	5
Share premium account	10	–
Retained earnings	30	5
	110	10
Non-current liabilities		
Borrowings – loan notes	30	–
Current liabilities		
Trade payables	20	6
Total equity and liabilities	160	16

When Parent plc was valuing the shares of Subsidiary Ltd, it was judged that most of the statement of financial position values were in line with the fair values, but that the following fair values should be applied to the three categories of property, plant and equipment of the subsidiary:

$\rightarrow$

	£m
Land	7
Plant	3
Vehicles	3

In addition it was recognised that the subsidiary has goodwill valued at £1 million. When these fair values are incorporated into the group statement of financial position, it will be as follows:

Statement of financial position

ASSETS	£m
Non-current assets	
Property, plant and equipment	
Land (40 + 7)	47
Plant (30 + 3)	33
Vehicles (20 + 3)	23
	103
Intangible assets	
Goodwill	1
	104
Current assets	
Inventories (20 + 3)	23
Trade receivables (30 + 2)	32
Cash (5 + 2)	7
	62
Total assets	166
EQUITY AND LIABILITIES	
Equity	
Called-up share capital: ordinary	
shares of £1 each, fully paid	70
Share premium account	10
Retained earnings	30
	110
Non-current liabilities	
Borrowings – loan notes (30 + 0)	30
Current liabilities	
Trade payables (20 + 6)	26
Total equity and liabilities	166

This example takes the simple case of no outside shareholdings in the subsidiary (that is, the subsidiary is 100 per cent owned by the parent) and no post-acquisition trading (the statements of financial position are at the date of acquisition), but these 'complications' would not alter the principles.

It should be noted that there is no need for the statement of financial position of the subsidiary to be adjusted for fair values, just the group statement of financial position. As far as the subsidiary is concerned, no change occurs with the takeover except a change in the names on the list of shareholders.

The financial reporting standard that deals with this area of group financial statements (IFRS 3) is clear that intangible assets of the subsidiary, at the date of the takeover, such as brand values and patent rights, must be separately identified at their fair value. These assets must then be incorporated at those values in the group statement of financial position.

The non-current assets of the subsidiary that have finite lives should have a depreciation (or amortisation) charge, based on their fair values, in the group income statement. This charge may well be different in amount to that which arises in the financial statements of the subsidiary.

Goodwill arising on consolidation is simply the excess of what the parent company paid for the subsidiary company's shares over their fair value, based on all of the identifiable assets (tangible and intangible) of the subsidiary. This means that what is identified as goodwill arising on consolidation tends to represent only the value of

- having a workforce in place;
- cost synergies – arising from the fact that the combined business can make cost savings by, say, having just one head office instead of two; and
- sales synergies – arising, for example, from group members trading with one another.

These attributes that represent goodwill could well be enduring, but they can also be lost, either partially or completely. IFRS 3 recognises this and states that the value of goodwill should be reviewed annually, or even more frequently if circumstances dictate. Where its value has been impaired, it must be reduced accordingly in the group financial statements. It should be noted that goodwill arising on consolidation does not appear in the statements of financial position either of the parent or the subsidiary. It only appears on the group statement of financial position.

Despite the requirement of IFRS 3 that all subsidiary company assets, whether they appear on the subsidiary's statement of financial position, whether they are tangible or intangible, should be reflected at their fair value in the group statement of financial position, this seems not always to happen in reality. **Real World 10.4** relates to an investigation into how some large, well-known businesses seem not to be following the spirit of IFRS 3.

Real World 10.4

Where there's goodwill . . .

During the first year that IFRS 3 applied (2005), the largest 100 businesses listed on the London Stock Exchange between them spent £40 billion on taking over other businesses. This acquisition cost was treated as follows in the subsequent group statements of financial position:

	£ billion	Percentage
Tangible assets	6.8	17
Intangible assets	12.0	30
Goodwill arising on consolidation	21.2	53

Thayne Forbes, concluded that this treatment was counter to the spirit of IFRS 3. It seemed implausible that such a large proportion of the total should be treated as goodwill, when IFRS 3 limits what should be treated as goodwill quite severely.

Forbes identified some examples. Included is the takeover of RAC plc (the UK motoring organisation) by Aviva plc (the UK-based insurance business) in March 2005. Aviva paid £1.1 billion, of which the majority was treated as goodwill. RAC had 7 million customers and is one of the most trusted brands in the UK, yet these were valued at only £260 million and £132 million respectively.

Forbes identified four possible reasons for these apparent misapplications of IFRS 3. These are:

1 *To reduce depreciation charges and increase profits*. Since goodwill cannot be depreciated and intangible assets with finite lives should be, reported profit will tend to be enhanced by treating as much of the purchase price as possible as goodwill.

→

2   *To minimise impairment charges.* Though both intangible assets without finite lives and goodwill are subject to tests of impairment of value and a possible accounting charge as a result, the tests for goodwill are less stringent. So another intangible asset is more likely to lead to an impairment charge than is goodwill.

3   *Lack of skills.* Having to value intangibles following a takeover is a new requirement, so the skills to do so may not be so readily available.

4   *Failure to see the big picture.* Businesses may get so bogged down with the regulations that they fail to consider the key issues and effects of the takeover.

Forbes went on to say:

> The implications of this inadequate reporting are far reaching. It renders annual reports more useless than they currently are, it makes a standard ineffective when applied and the financial bodies that govern them, it sets a dangerous precedent for future years and it opens a new era of creative accounting that distances shareholders and investors further from reality.

A year later, Forbes felt that the situation was improving, with more explanation and justification being given by businesses for the goodwill values included in group statements of financial position. He seemed not to believe, however, that practice was by that time totally satisfactory.

The position seemed not to have become satisfactory by 2009. The Financial Reporting Council looked at the financial reporting of twenty takeovers that had occurred in 2008 and were reported in the financial statements of the parent company concerned during 2009. The Council concluded that 'there is a need for improved compliance with the disclosure requirements of IFRS'.

Source: 'Technical update – inadequate IFRS 3', Thayne Forbes, *Finance Week*, 30 January 2007, www.financeweek.co.uk; 'Intangibles and IFRS 3: Seen but not heard', Thayne Forbes, www.intangiblebusiness.com, 8 February 2008; and *Accounting for Acquisitions*, Financial Reporting Council, January 2010, p. 3.

In the cases that we have considered so far, goodwill arising on consolidation has always been a positive value (that is, more was paid for the parent's share of the net assets of the subsidiary than their fair values). It is possible for goodwill to be negative. This is where the parent pays less than the fair values. Where negative goodwill on consolidation arises, IFRS 3 says that fair values of all assets and liabilities of the subsidiary concerned should be reassessed. This reassessment is to try to ensure that no assets have been overstated or liabilities understated or omitted. If this reassessment still results in negative goodwill, the amount of this negative goodwill should be treated as a gain and transferred immediately to the group income statement of the year of the acquisition of the subsidiary. In practice, negative goodwill is pretty rare.

Goodwill arising on consolidation: an alternative approach

IFRS 3 *Business Combinations* was revised with effect from 1 July 2009. Most of the changes brought in by the revised standard were fairly technical. One, however, was more fundamental and intended to correct an anomaly with the way that goodwill arising on consolidation is valued.

Activity 10.12

Can you puzzle out what the anomaly is? (*Hint*: It is concerned with the fact that goodwill arising on consolidation is treated differently from all other assets of the subsidiary that appear in the group statement of financial position.)

The anomaly is that goodwill is the only subsidiary company asset that is not shown in full; it is scaled down according to the proportion of the subsidiary's shares that are owned by the parent. All other assets of the subsidiary are included in full, irrespective of the parent's proportion of the ownership.

As we saw earlier, it is a basic principle of preparing group financial statements that if the parent controls the assets of the subsidiary, even if it does not own them 100 per cent, all of their value should be included. The revised IFRS 3 allows, though it does not require, that goodwill be shown in the statement of financial position at its full value.

Our Example 10.9 returns to Example 10.6, which included two of our 'complications' (the parent owning less than 100 per cent of the subsidiary and paying more than the fair value for them).

Example 10.9

The group statement of financial position for Parent plc and its subsidiary applying the 'old' IFRS 3 approach is as follows:

Statement of financial position

	£m
ASSETS	
Non-current assets	
Property, plant and equipment	
Land	45
Plant	32
Vehicles	22
	99
Intangible assets	
Goodwill arising on consolidation (12 − (80% × 10))	4
	103
Current assets	
Inventories	23
Trade receivables	32
Cash	10
	65
Total assets	168
EQUITY AND LIABILITIES	
Equity	
Called-up share capital: ordinary	
shares of £1 each, fully paid	70
Share premium account	10
Retained earnings	30
	110
Non-controlling interests	2
	112
Non-current liabilities	
Borrowings – loan notes	30
Current liabilities	
Trade payables	26
Total equity and liabilities	168

The goodwill (£4 million) represents the excess of what was paid by Parent plc for the shares (£12 million) over the fair value of its proportion of the underlying net assets at the time of the takeover (£8 million).

Logically, if Parent's share of the goodwill is £4 million, the total value of it is £5 million. Including this total value in the group statement of financial position would be more in line with the general approach to preparing group financial statements. The revised IFRS 3 permits this.

Activity 10.13

If the goodwill figure in the statement of financial position in Example 10.9 is to be increased by £1 million, something else on the statement will also need to be adjusted to maintain equality between total assets and total claims (equity and liabilities). What would this adjustment logically be?

The answer is that the figure for non-controlling interests will need to be increased by that amount. This is because £1 million of the value of the goodwill belongs to outside shareholders, which needs to be reflected in their claim as it appears in the group statement of financial position.

As mentioned above, groups may use this 'new' approach to the value of goodwill arising on consolidation if they wish. It is widely believed that relatively few groups will do so in practice. The new approach seems to be supported more by academics than by businesses.

In view of the likely limited take-up of the new approach in practice, we shall use the 'old' approach (that is, the one explored earlier in this chapter) in all subsequent examples and exercises.

INTER-COMPANY ASSETS AND CLAIMS

Though members of a group are separate legal entities, the element of control exercised by the parent, and generally close relations between group members, tend to lead to inter-company trading and other inter-company transactions. This, in turn, means that a particular asset in one company's statement of financial position could relate to an equal-sized liability in the statement of financial position of another member of the same group.

The principle underlying the group statement of financial position is that it should represent the situation as if all the assets and claims of individual group members were directly the assets and claims of the parent company. Since the parent company cannot owe itself money, where there are inter-company balances these must be eliminated when preparing the group statement of financial position.

Example 10.10

Delta plc and its subsidiary Gamma plc are the only members of a group. Delta plc sells goods on credit to Gamma plc. At the statement of financial position date the following balances existed in the books of the companies:

	Trade receivables £m	Trade payables £m
Delta plc	34	26
Gamma plc	23	18

Included in the trade receivables of Delta plc, and the trade payables of Gamma plc, is £5 million in respect of some recent inter-company trading.

In deducing the figures to be included in the group statement of financial position, we have to eliminate the inter-company balance, as follows:

$$\text{Trade receivables} = 34 - 5 + 23 = £52 \text{ million}$$
$$\text{Trade payables} = 26 + 18 - 5 = £39 \text{ million}$$

Note that these consolidated trade receivables and trade payables figures represent what is, respectively, owed by and owed to individuals and organisations outside of the group. This is what they are intended to represent, according to the principles of group accounting.

PREPARING A GROUP INCOME STATEMENT

The **group income statement** follows very similar principles to those that apply to the group statement of financial position. These are:

- Like items are added together. For example, the revenue of each subsidiary is added to that of the parent company to discover group revenue.
- All the amounts appearing under each heading in the income statements of subsidiaries are included in the total, even where they are not wholly owned subsidiaries. For example, the revenue of a subsidiary that is 60 per cent owned by the parent is included in full.
- The interests of outside shareholders (non-controlling interests) are separately identified towards the bottom of the income statement.

Example 10.11

Holder plc owns 75 per cent of the ordinary shares of Sub Ltd. The outline income statements of the two companies for the year ended on 31 December are as follows:

Income statements for the year ended 31 December

	Holder plc £m	Sub Ltd £m
Revenue	83	40
Cost of sales	(41)	(15)
Gross profit	42	25
Administration expenses	(16)	(9)
Distribution expenses	(6)	(3)
Operating profit	20	13
Interest payable	(2)	(1)
Profit before taxation	18	12
Taxation	(8)	(4)
Profit for the year	10	8

Preparing the group income statement is a very simple matter of adding like items together, except that not all of the profit for the year of the subsidiary 'belongs' to the group. Twenty-five per cent (£2 million) of it belongs to outside shareholders. We recognise this in the group income statement by deducting the 25 per cent of the subsidiary's profit for the year from the combined profit for the year.

The group income statement will be as follows:

Income statement for the year ended 31 December

	£m
Revenue (83 + 40)	123
Cost of sales (41 + 15)	(56)
Gross profit	67
Administration expenses (16 + 9)	(25)
Distribution expenses (6 + 3)	(9)
Operating profit	33
Interest payable (2 + 1)	(3)
Profit before taxation	30
Taxation (8 + 4)	(12)
Profit for the year	18
Attributable to non-controlling interests	(2)
Profit for the year attributable to Holder plc shareholders	16

This statement says that the assets under the control of the group generated profit for the year of £18 million. Of this, £2 million is the share of the 'outside' shareholders of Sub Ltd. This follows the normal approach of group financial statements of treating all assets, claims, revenues, expenses and cash flows of group companies as if they were those of the group. Where the subsidiaries are not 100 per cent owned by the parent, this fact is acknowledged by making an adjustment to reflect the non-controlling interests.

Ajax plc owns 60 per cent of the ordinary shares of Exeter plc. The outline income statements of the two companies for the year ended on 31 December are as follows:

Income statements for the year ended 31 December

	Ajax plc £m	Exeter plc £m
Revenue	120	80
Cost of sales	(60)	(40)
Gross profit	60	40
Administration expenses	(17)	(4)
Distribution expenses	(10)	(15)
Operating profit	33	21
Interest payable	(3)	(1)
Profit before taxation	30	20
Taxation	(12)	(10)
Profit for the year	18	10

Have a try at preparing a consolidated (group) income statement.

Your answer should look something like this:

Group income statement for the year ended 31 December

	£m
Revenue (120 + 80)	200
Cost of sales (60 + 40)	(100)
Gross profit	100
Administration expenses (17 + 4)	(21)
Distribution expenses (10 + 15)	(25)
Operating profit	54
Interest payable (3 + 1)	(4)
Profit before taxation	50
Taxation (12 + 10)	(22)
Profit for the year	28
Attributable to non-controlling interests (40% × 10)	(4)
Profit for the year attributable to Ajax plc shareholders	24

THE STATEMENT OF COMPREHENSIVE INCOME

As we saw in Chapter 5, IAS 1 *Presentation of Financial Statements* requires listed companies to provide a statement of comprehensive income, which extends the conventional income statement to include certain other gains and losses that affect shareholders' equity. It may be presented either as a single statement or as two separate statements, an income statement and a statement of comprehensive income. IAS 1 demands that in the group's statement of comprehensive income, both the profit (or loss) for the period and the comprehensive income for the period distinguish between that which is attributable to non-controlling interests and that attributable to the shareholders of the parent company.

INTER-COMPANY TRADING

As we saw earlier, it is common for members of the group to trade with one another. As far as each member of the group is concerned such trading should be dealt with in the accounting records, including the income statement, in exactly the same way as trading with any other party. When we come to the group income statement, however, trading between group members must be eliminated. It is in the spirit of group accounting that the group income statement should only recognise trading with parties outside of the group, as if the group were one single business.

GROUP STATEMENT OF CASH FLOWS

Groups must normally prepare a statement of cash flows that follows the same logic as the statement of financial position and income statement – that is, it has to show the movements in all of the cash that is in the control of the group, for the period under review.

The preparation of a **group statement of cash flows** follows the same rules as those that apply to the preparation of the statement for individual companies. In view of this we need not spend time looking separately at statements of cash flows in a group context.

Cash transfers between group members should not be reflected in the group statement of cash flows. It is only cash transfers with parties outside of the group that must be taken into account.

ACCOUNTING FOR LESS THAN A CONTROLLING INTEREST – ASSOCIATE COMPANIES

What happens when one company makes a substantial investment in another company but this does not provide the investing company with a controlling interest? In other words, the company whose shares have been acquired does not become a subsidiary of the investing company. One approach would simply include the investment of shares in the company at cost in the investing company's statement of financial position. Assuming that the shares are held on a long-term basis, they would be treated as a non-current asset. Any dividends received from the investment would be treated as income in the investing company's income statement.

The problem with this approach, however, is that companies normally pay dividends of much less than the profits earned for the period. The profits that are not distributed, but are ploughed back to help to generate more profits for the future, still belong to the shareholders. From the perspective of the investing company, the accounting treatment described would not, therefore, fully reflect the benefits from the investment made. Where the investment does not involve the purchase of a substantial shareholding in the company, this problem is overlooked and so the treatment of the investment described above (that is, showing the investment, at cost, as a non-current asset and taking account only of any dividends received) is applied. Where, however, the investment involves the purchase of a significant number of voting shares in the company, a different kind of accounting treatment seems more appropriate.

To deal with the problem identified above, a particular type of relationship between the two companies has been defined. An **associate company** is one in which an investing company or group has a substantial, but not controlling, interest. To be more precise, it is a company over which another company can exercise significant influence regarding its operating and financial policies. If a company holds 20 per cent or more of the voting shares of another company it is presumed to be able to exercise significant influence. This influence is usually demonstrated by the investing company being represented on the board of directors of the associate company or by participation in policy making. The relevant international accounting standard (IAS 28 *Investments in Associates*) provides the detailed guidelines concerning what constitutes an associate company.

The accounting treatment of an associate company falls somewhere between full consolidation, as with group financial statements, and the treatment of small share investments, as described at the beginning of this section. Let us assume that a company invests in another company, so that the latter becomes an associate of the former. The accounting treatment will be as follows:

- The investing company will be required to produce consolidated financial statements that reflect not only its own performance and position, but also those of its associate company.
- In the consolidated income statement, the investing company's share of the operating profit of the associate company will be shown and will be added to the operating profit of the investing company. As operating profit represents the profit before interest and taxation, the investing company's share of any interest payable and tax relating to the associate company will also be shown. These will be deducted in deriving the profit for the year for the investing company and its associate company.
- In the consolidated statement of financial position, the investment made in the associate company will be shown and the investing company's share of any post-acquisition reserves will be added to the investment. In this way profits of the associate which have not been paid to the investing company will be recognised in the investing company's statement of financial position. This will have the effect of showing more fully the investment in the associate company.
- Dividends received by the investing company from the associate company will not be included in the consolidated income statement. This is because the investing company's share of the associate company's profit will already be fully reflected in the consolidated income statement.
- If the investing company also has subsidiaries, their financial statements will also have to be incorporated, in the manner that we saw for groups earlier. Thus a company that has both subsidiary companies and associate companies will prepare just one set of consolidated financial statements reflecting all of these, irrespective of how many subsidiaries and associates it may have.

To illustrate these points, let us take a simple example.

Example 10.12

A plc owns 25 per cent of the ordinary shares of B plc. The price paid for the shares was £26 million. A plc bought its shares in B plc when the latter's reserves stood at £24 million. The reserves of B plc have increased to £40 million by 31 March last year.

The income statements for A plc and B plc for the year ended 31 March this year are as follows:

Income statements for the year ended 31 March this year

	A plc	B plc
	£m	£m
Revenues	800	100
Cost of sales	(500)	(60)
Gross profit	300	40
Operating expenses	(120)	(12)
Operating profit	180	28
Interest payable	(30)	(8)
Profit before taxation	150	20
Taxation	(40)	(4)
Profit for the year	110	16

To comply with the relevant standard (IAS 28), A plc's share of the operating profit of B plc, as well as its share of interest payable and taxation relating to B plc, will be incorporated within A plc's consolidated income statement. A plc's consolidated income statement will, therefore, be as follows:

A plc
Consolidated income statement

	£m	
Revenues	800	
Cost of sales	(500)	
Gross profit	300	
Operating expenses	(120)	
	180	
Share of operating profit of associate – B plc	7	(25% × £28m)
Operating profit	187	
Interest payable:		
A plc	(30)	
Associate – B plc	(2)	(25% × £8m)
Profit before taxation	155	
Taxation:		
A plc	(40)	
Associate – B plc	(1)	(25% × £4m)
Profit for the year	114	

The consolidated statement of financial position of A plc, treating B plc as an associate company, would include an amount for the investment in B plc that is calculated as follows:

Extract from A plc's consolidated statement of financial position
as at 31 March this year

	£m	
Cost of investment in associate company	26	
Share of post-acquisition reserves	4	(that is, 25% × (40 − 24))
	30	

What is the crucial difference between the approach taken when consolidating subsidiary company results and incorporating the results of associate companies, as far as the statement of financial position and income statement are concerned?

In preparing group financial statements, all of the items in the statements are added together, as if the parent owned them all, even when the subsidiary is less than 100 per cent owned. For example, the revenue figure in the consolidated income statement is the sum of all the revenues made by group companies; the inventories figure in the statement of financial position is the sum of all the inventories held by all members of the group.

When dealing with associate companies, we only deal with the shareholding company's share of the profit of the associate and its effect on the value of the shareholding.

Real World 10.5 looks at a well-known associate of British Sky Broadcasting Group plc ('Sky').

Real World 10.5

The last third

Sky owns a third of the shares in MUTV Limited, the subscription satellite television channel, which is dedicated to matters concerning Manchester United football club. The remaining two-thirds of the shares are owned by the club itself, Manchester United Ltd. MUTV's financial results are consolidated into Sky's annual financial statements, treating MUTV as an associate company.

Source: British Sky Broadcasting Group plc Annual Report 2012, p. 116, http://annualreview2012.sky.com

THE ARGUMENT AGAINST CONSOLIDATION

There seems to be a compelling logic for consolidating the results of subsidiaries controlled by a parent company, to reflect the fact that the shareholders of the parent company effectively control all of the assets of all of the companies in the group. There is also, however, a fairly strong argument against doing so.

Anyone reading the consolidated financial statements of a group of companies could be misled into believing that trading with any member of the group would, in effect, be the same as trading with the group as a whole. It might be imagined that all of the group's assets could be called upon to meet any amounts owed by any member of the group. This, however, is not the case. Only assets owned by the particular group member are available to creditors of that group member. The reason for this is, of course, the legal separateness of the limited company from its shareholder(s), which in turn leads to limited liability of individual group members. There is no legal obligation on a parent company, or a fellow subsidiary, to meet the financial obligations of a struggling subsidiary. In fact, this is why some businesses operate through a series of subsidiaries, as mentioned earlier.

Despite this criticism of consolidation, the requirement to prepare group financial statements is a very popular legal requirement throughout the world.

The statements of financial position, as at 31 December last year, and income statements, for the year ended last 31 December, of Great plc and Small plc are set out below. Great plc bought its shares in Small plc on 1 January last year at which time the latter's share capital was the same as it is currently and the retained earnings balance stood at £35 million.

At the time of the acquisition, the fair value of all the assets of Small plc was thought to be the same as that shown in their statement of financial position, except for land whose fair value was thought to be £5 million more than the statement of financial position value. It is believed that there has been no impairment in the value of the goodwill arising on consolidation since 1 January last year.

Statements of financial position as at 31 December last year

	Great plc £m	Small plc £m
ASSETS		
Non-current assets		
Property, plant and equipment		
Land	80	14
Plant	33	20
Vehicles	20	11
	133	45
Investment		
16 million shares of Small plc	53	–
	186	45
Current assets		
Inventories	20	9
Trade receivables	21	6
Cash	17	5
	58	20
Total assets	244	65
EQUITY AND LIABILITIES		
Equity		
Called-up share capital: ordinary shares of £1 each, fully paid	100	20
Retained earnings	77	40
	177	60
Non-current liabilities		
Borrowings – loan notes	50	–
Current liabilities		
Trade payables	17	5
Total equity and liabilities	244	65

Income statements for the year ended 31 December last year

	Great plc £m	Small plc £m
Revenue	91	27
Cost of sales	(46)	(13)
Gross profit	45	14
Administration expenses	(8)	(3)
Distribution expenses	(6)	(2)
Operating profit	31	9
Interest payable	(3)	–
Profit before taxation	28	9
Taxation	(12)	(4)
Profit for the year	16	5

Required:

Prepare the statement of financial position and income statement for the group.

A solution to this question can be found in Appendix C.

SUMMARY

The main points of this chapter may be summarised as follows:

Groups

- A group exists where one company (parent) can exercise control over another (subsidiary), usually by owning more than 50% of the voting shares.
- Groups arise by a parent setting up a new company or taking over an existing one.
- Businesses operate as groups in order to have limited liability for each part of the business, and to give each part of the business an individual identity.
- Normally parent companies are required to produce financial statements for the group as a whole, as if all of the group members' assets, liabilities, revenues, expenses and cash flows were those of the parent company directly.

Group statements of financial position

- Group statements of financial position are derived by adding like items (assets and liabilities) together and setting the equity of each subsidiary (in the subsidiary's statement of financial position) against the investment in subsidiary figure (in the parent's statement of financial position).
- Where the equity of the subsidiary does not cancel the investment in subsidiary it will be for three possible reasons:
  1 more (or less) was paid for the subsidiary shares than their fair value, leading to goodwill arising on consolidation (an intangible non-current asset), or negative goodwill arising on consolidation.
  2 the parent does not own all of the shares of the subsidiary, leading to non-controlling (or minority) interests (similar to equity in the group statement of financial position)

$\rightarrow$

RISEHOLME CAMPUS

reflecting the fact that the parent's shareholders do not supply all of the equity finance to fund the group's net assets;

3 the subsidiary has made profits or losses since it became a subsidiary.

■ 'Goodwill arising on consolidation' represents the value of the ability of the subsidiary to generate additional profits as a result of an established workforce, cost synergies or sales synergies.

■ Goodwill remains on the group statement of financial position, but is subject to an impairment review annually and will be written down in value if it is established that its value has diminished.

■ Negative goodwill should be immediately credited to the group income statement.

■ It is permissible for a company to show the entire value of the goodwill of its subsidiaries, not just the parent's share of that value.

■ Inter-group company balances (receivables and payables) must be eliminated from the group statement of financial position.

Group income statement

■ Group income statements are derived by adding like items (revenues and expenses).

■ The non-controlling (minority) shareholders' share of the after-tax profit is deducted from the group total to reflect the fact that not all of the subsidiary's profit belongs to the parent company's shareholders.

■ Inter-group company trading transactions (revenues and expenses) must be eliminated from the group income statement.

Group statement of comprehensive income

■ Group statements of comprehensive income are derived by adding like items.

■ The statement must distinguish between comprehensive income that is attributable to non-controlling interests and that which is attributable to the shareholders of the parent company.

Group statement of cash flows

■ Group statements of cash flows are derived by adding like items (cash flows).

■ Inter-group company cash transfers must be eliminated from the group statement of cash flows.

Associate companies

■ An 'associate company' is one in which a company has less than a controlling interest, but yet is able to exert significant influence over it, often indicated by representation on the board of directors.

■ The investing company will be required to produce consolidated financial statements that reflect not only its own performance and position, but those of its associate company as well.

■ In the consolidated income statement, the investing company's share of the operating profit of the associate company is added to the operating profit of the investing company. Any interest payable and tax relating to the associate company will also be shown.

- In the consolidated statement of financial position, the investment made in the associate company will be shown and the investing company's share of any post-acquisition reserves will be added to the investment.

- Dividends received by the investing company from the associate company are not included in the consolidated income statement.

MyAccountingLab

Go to www.myaccountinglab.com to check your understanding of the chapter, create a personalised study plan, and maximise your revision time

KEY TERMS

parent company p. 328
subsidiary company p. 328
group (of companies) p. 328
group financial statements p. 328
takeover p. 328
holding company p. 328
target company p. 331
group statement of financial
    position p. 337

consolidated financial statements p. 338
non-controlling interests p. 343
minority interests p. 343
goodwill arising on consolidation p. 345
negative goodwill arising on
    consolidation p. 345
group income statement p. 365
group statement of cash flows p. 368
associate company p. 369

FURTHER READING

If you would like to explore the topics covered in this chapter in more depth, we recommend the following:

Alexander, D., Britton, A. and Jorissen, A., *International Financial Reporting and Analysis*, 5th edn, South-Western Cengage Learning, 2011, Chapters 25 to 28

Elliott, B. and Elliott, J., *Financial Accounting and Reporting*, 15th edn, Financial Times Prentice Hall, 2011, Chapters 22 to 26

REVIEW QUESTIONS

Solutions to these questions can be found in Appendix D.

10.1 When does a group relationship arise and what are its consequences for accounting?

10.2 What does a group statement of financial position show?

10.3 Quite often, when an existing company wishes to start a new venture, perhaps to produce a new product or render a new service, it will form a subsidiary company as a vehicle for the new venture. Why would it choose not to have the new venture conducted by the original company?

10.4 What is an associate company and how should an associate company be recognised in the financial statements of a group of companies?

Exercises 10.1 and 10.2 are basic level, 10.3 to 10.5 are intermediate level and 10.6 to 10.8 are advanced level. Solutions to the exercises with coloured numbers are given in Appendix E.

If you wish to try more exercises, visit the students' side of the Companion Website and MyAccountingLab.

10.1 An abridged set of consolidated financial statements for Toggles plc is given below.

Toggles plc
Consolidated income statement for the year ended 30 June

	£m
Revenue	172.0
Operating profit	21.2
Taxation	(6.4)
Profit after taxation	14.8
Non-controlling interests	(2.4)
Profit for the year	12.4

Consolidated statement of financial position as at 30 June

ASSETS	£m
Non-current assets	
Property, plant and equipment	85.6
Intangible assets	
Goodwill arising on consolidation	7.2
	92.8
Current assets	
Inventories	21.8
Trade receivables	16.4
Cash	1.7
	39.9
Total assets	132.7
EQUITY AND LIABILITIES	
Equity	
Share capital	100.0
Retained earnings	16.1
	116.1
Non-controlling interests	1.3
	117.4
Current liabilities	
Trade payables	15.3
Total equity and liabilities	132.7

Required:

(a) Answer, briefly, the following questions:

1 What is meant by 'non-controlling interests' in both the income statement and the statement of financial position?

2 What is meant by 'goodwill arising on consolidation'?

3 Why will the 'retained earnings' figure on the consolidated statement of financial position usually be different from the 'retained earnings' as shown in the parent company's statement of financial position?

(b) Explain the purposes and advantages in preparing consolidated financial statements for the parent company's shareholders.

10.2 Arnold plc owns 75 per cent of the ordinary shares of Baker plc. The outline income statements of the two companies for the year ended on 31 December are as follows:

Income statements for the year ended 31 December

	Arnold plc £m	Baker plc £m
Revenue	83	47
Cost of sales	(36)	(19)
Gross profit	47	28
Administration expenses	(14)	(7)
Distribution expenses	(21)	(10)
Profit before taxation	12	11
Taxation	(4)	(3)
Profit for the year	8	8

Required:
Prepare the consolidated (group) income statement for Arnold plc and its subsidiary for the year ended 31 December.

10.3 Giant plc bought a majority shareholding in Jack Ltd, on 31 March. On that date the statements of financial position of the two companies were as follows:

Statements of financial position as at 31 March

	Giant plc £m	Jack Ltd £m
ASSETS		
Non-current assets		
Property, plant and equipment		
Land	27	12
Plant	55	8
Vehicles	18	7
	100	27
Investment		
10 million shares of Jack Ltd	30	–
	130	27
Current assets		
Inventories	33	13
Trade receivables	42	17
Cash	22	5
	97	35
Total assets	227	62
EQUITY AND LIABILITIES		
Equity		
Called-up share capital: ordinary shares of £1 each, fully paid	50	10
Share premium account	40	5
Revaluation reserve	–	8
Retained earnings	46	7
	136	30
Non-current liabilities		
Borrowings – loan notes	50	13
Current liabilities		
Trade payables	41	19
Total equity and liabilities	227	62

Required:

Assume that the statement of financial position values of Jack Ltd's assets represent 'fair' values. Prepare the group statement of financial position immediately following the takeover.

10.4 The statements of financial position of Jumbo plc and of Nipper plc, on the date that Jumbo plc bought the shares in Nipper plc, were as follows:

Statements of financial position as at 31 March

	Jumbo plc £m	Nipper plc £m
ASSETS		
Non-current assets		
Property, plant and equipment		
Land	84	18
Plant	34	33
Vehicles	45	12
	163	63
Investment		
12 million shares of Nipper plc	24	–
	187	63
Current assets		
Inventories	55	32
Trade receivables	26	44
Cash	14	10
	95	86
Total assets	282	149
EQUITY AND LIABILITIES		
Equity		
Called-up share capital: ordinary shares of £1 each, fully paid	100	20
Share premium account	–	12
Retained earnings	41	8
	141	40
Non-current assets		
Borrowings – loan notes	100	70
Current liabilities		
Trade payables	41	39
Total equity and liabilities	282	149

Required:

Assume that the statement of financial position values of Nipper plc's assets represent fair values. Prepare the group statement of financial position immediately following the share acquisition.

10.5 The summary statements of financial position for Apple Limited and Pear Limited are set out below.

Statements of financial position as at 30 September

	Apple Limited £000	Pear Limited £000
ASSETS		
Non-current assets		
Property, plant and equipment	950	320
Investment		
Shares in Pear Limited	240	–
	1,190	320
Current assets		
Inventories	320	160
Trade receivables	180	95
Cash at bank	41	15
	541	270
Total assets	1,731	590
EQUITY AND LIABILITIES		
Equity:		
£1 fully paid ordinary shares	700	200
Reserves	307	88
	1,007	288
Non-current liabilities		
Loan notes	500	160
Current assets		
Trade payables	170	87
Taxation	54	55
	224	142
Total equity and liabilities	1,731	590

Apple Ltd purchased 150,000 shares in Pear Ltd at a price of £1.60 per share on 30 September (the above statement of financial position date). The statement of financial position of Pear Ltd reflects all of the assets of the company, net of liabilities, stated at their fair values.

Required:

Prepare a consolidated statement of financial position for Apple Ltd as at 30 September.

10.6 Abridged financial statements for Harvest Limited and Wheat Limited as at 30 June this year are set out below. On 1 July last year Harvest Limited acquired 800,000 ordinary shares in Wheat Limited for a payment of £3,500,000. Wheat Ltd's share capital and share premium were each the same throughout. Similarly, the assets in the statement of financial position of Wheat Limited were shown at fair market values throughout.

Statements of financial position as at 30 June this year

	Harvest Limited £000	Wheat Limited £000
ASSETS		
Non-current assets		
Property, plant and equipment	10,850	4,375
Investment		
Shares of Wheat Limited	3,500	–
	14,350	4,375
Current assets	3,775	1,470
Total assets	18,125	5,845
EQUITY AND LIABILITIES		
Equity		
Share capital (£1 shares)	2,000	1,000
Share premium account	3,000	500
Revenue reserves at 1 July last year	2,800	375
Profit for the current year	399	75
	8,199	1,950
Non-current liabilities		
Bank loans	7,000	2,500
Current liabilities	2,926	1,395
Total equity and liabilities	18,125	5,845

Required:

Prepare the consolidated statement of financial position for Harvest Ltd as at 30 June this year, using the data given above.

10.7 A year ago Pod Limited bought 225,000 £1 fully paid ordinary shares of Pea Limited for a consideration of £500,000. Pea Limited's share capital and share premium were each the same as at today's date. Simplified statements of financial position for both companies as at today's date, after having traded as a group for a year, are set out below. The statement of financial position of Pea Ltd reflects all of the assets of the company, net of liabilities, stated at their fair values.

Statements of financial position as at today

	Pod Limited £	Pea Limited £
ASSETS		
Non-current assets		
Property, plant and equipment	1,104,570	982,769
Investment		
Shares in Pea Limited	500,000	–
	1,604,570	982,769
Current assets		
Inventories	672,471	294,713
Trade receivables	216,811	164,517
Amounts due from subsidiary company	76,000	–
Cash	2,412	1,361
	967,694	460,591
Total assets	2,572,264	1,443,360
EQUITY AND LIABILITIES		
Equity		
Share capital: £1 ordinary shares	750,000	300,000
Share premium	250,000	50,000
Reserves as at a year ago	449,612	86,220
Profit for year	69,504	17,532
	1,519,116	453,752
Non-current liabilities		
Bank loan	800,000	750,000
Current liabilities		
Trade payables	184,719	137,927
Amounts owing to holding company	–	76,000
Borrowings – overdraft	68,429	25,681
	253,148	239,608
Total equity and liabilities	2,572,264	1,443,360

Required:
Prepare a consolidated statement of financial position for Pod Ltd and its subsidiary company as at today's date.

10.8 The statements of financial position for Maxi Limited and Mini Limited are set out below.

Statements of financial position as at 31 March this year

	Maxi Limited £000	Mini Limited £000
ASSETS		
Non-current assets		
Property, plant and equipment	23,000	17,800
Investment		
1,500,000 shares in Mini Limited	5,000	–
	28,000	17,800
Current assets		
Inventories	5,000	2,400
Trade receivables	4,280	1,682
Amounts owed by Maxi Limited	–	390
Cash at bank	76	1,570
	9,356	6,042
Total assets	37,356	23,842
EQUITY AND LIABILITIES		
Equity		
10,000,000 £1 ordinary shares, fully paid	10,000	
2,000,000 50p ordinary shares, fully paid		1,000
Share premium account	3,000	2,000
Retained earnings at beginning of year	3,100	2,080
Profit for the year	713	400
	16,813	5,480
Non-current liabilities		
Bank loans	13,000	14,000
Current liabilities		
Trade payables	3,656	2,400
Other payables	1,047	1,962
Amounts owed to Mini Limited	390	–
Short-term borrowings – overdraft	2,450	–
	7,543	4,362
Total equity and liabilities	37,356	23,842

On 1 April last year, Maxi Limited bought 1,500,000 shares of Mini Limited for a total consideration of £5 million. At that date Mini Limited's share capital and share premium were each the same as shown above. The statement of financial position of Mini Ltd reflects all of the assets of the company, net of liabilities stated at their fair values.

Required:
Prepare a consolidated statement of financial position for Maxi Limited at 31 March this year.

Chapter 11

INCREASING THE SCOPE OF FINANCIAL REPORTING

INTRODUCTION

Over the years, there has been a trend towards greater disclosure of information regarding the performance and position of businesses. Various reasons can be suggested for this trend. They include the increasing complexity of business, the increasing sophistication of users and an increasing recognition that other groups, apart from shareholders, have a stake in the success of a business.

In this chapter we consider additional financial reports that may be provided by businesses. Some of these simply expand on the information contained within the annual financial report, while others offer a different perspective on how business success is defined and measured.

Learning outcomes

When you have completed this chapter, you should be able to:

■ explain the purpose of segmental reports and describe their main features;

■ discuss the benefits of narrative reporting and describe the main features of the business review;

■ discuss the role of interim financial statements and outline the key measurement and reporting requirements of IAS 34;

■ explain the purpose of the value added statement and prepare a simple value added statement from available information;

■ describe the impact of inflation on the measurement of financial position and performance and outline the two main approaches to dealing with inflation in financial statements.

MyAccountingLab Visit www.myaccountinglab.com for practice and revision opportunities

THE DEVELOPMENT OF FINANCIAL REPORTING

Let us begin by placing the additional financial reports in historical context. Financial reporting has been around for many hundreds of years. It seems to have emerged as a result of one or more persons having custody and management of assets belonging to one or more others. Examples might include a farm manager looking after land owned by another person, or a merchant ship's captain taking goods, owned by someone else, overseas and selling them. The owners would normally require that the steward (that is, the person looking after the assets) report on how the assets were deployed and how successfully. These reports were often expressed in financial terms and gave rise to what is known as 'stewardship accounting'.

Limited liability companies first came into being during the middle of the nineteenth century. Their advent gave added impetus to assets being owned by one group of people (the shareholders) and managed by another group (the directors). The creation of these new legal entities was not accompanied by stringent requirements either to publish financial statements or to have them audited. Nevertheless, many companies did so. This was largely in response to pressure from investors who were reluctant to part with their money without relevant feedback, in the form of periodic financial reports, from the directors.

These financial reports reduced uncertainty in the minds of investors, who then became more willing to provide funds and to scale down their expectations of financial returns. There is quite strong evidence to suggest that greater disclosure of financial information tends to lower a company's cost of capital (that is, the required rate of return for shareholders and other providers of finance), and, furthermore, that directors understand this relationship between disclosure and the cost of capital (see reference 1 at the end of the chapter). Thus directors may have an incentive to disclose financial information since this can lead to a lower cost of capital and, in turn, to greater wealth.

Relying on market forces to determine the form and content of financial reports is, however, a risky business. Directors control access to financial information and it is not always in their interests to ensure that the truth is revealed in a timely and accurate way. Furthermore, investors are often dispersed and find it difficult to act collectively. They are, therefore, in a weak position to exert pressure on the directors. Given these problems, it is not surprising that the 'market model' resulted in abuses and led, inevitably, to calls for regulation.

The past century and a half has been characterised by a movement away from market-led financial reporting towards a highly elaborate regulatory framework. The UK government started the ball rolling with the Companies Act 1862, which recommended the preparation of a rudimentary income statement and statement of financial position each year (as well as an audit of the latter). This was followed by a succession of Companies Acts, with each requiring greater financial disclosure. Since the 1970s accounting standard-setting bodies, and in particular the IASB, have become major forces in financial reporting regulation and have added considerably to the mountain of rules. The IASB, for example, has more than forty standards currently in existence.

The relentless increase in reporting requirements has created some disquiet. Doubts have been raised as to whether the increasing complexity of financial statements has led to an improvement in their usefulness. There is a concern that both accounting regulators and businesses have lost a sense of focus and forgotten the purpose for which financial statements are prepared. Thus, a major challenge for the future is to produce better regulation, rather than simply more of it. The quality of financial statements is dependent on regulators ensuring that rules are clearly targeted and are proportionate to the problems that they address. It is also dependent on businesses providing financial statements which are as clear, open and understandable as possible within the rules that exist.

As a footnote to this section, it is worth mentioning that financial reports of many businesses provide more information than required by the regulations. This is done, presumably, to make their activities more transparent and thereby reduce uncertainty.

FROM STEWARDSHIP TO DECISION MAKING

We have seen that, in the early days of financial reporting, stewardship was the key issue. It was concerned with recounting what had happened so as to make stewards (managers) accountable and perhaps, therefore, more careful in deploying the assets of the owner. Over time, however, the focus of interest among users has changed towards its decision-making potential. This has resulted in regulation becoming more targeted on making financial statements useful as decision-making tools.

Decision making involves making predictions about the future and it is argued that, to help users, financial reporting should have both a *predictive role* and a *confirmatory role*. That is to say, it should enable a user to make reliable predictions about future earnings and cash flows. It should also enable a user to confirm whether past predictions were reliable.

We shall now look at three relatively recent additions to the financial reports. They are segmental reports, business reviews and interim financial statements. Preparing these reports is obligatory for many larger and/or listed companies.

SEGMENTAL FINANCIAL REPORTS

Most large businesses are engaged in a number of different operations, with each having its own levels of risk, growth and profitability. Information relating to each type of business operation, however, is normally added together (aggregated) in the financial statements so as to provide an overall picture of financial performance and position. For example, the revenue figure at the top of the income statement represents all of the company's revenues added together. This will be true even where the revenues come from quite different activities. Although this aggregation of information can help to provide a clearer broad picture, it can make it difficult to undertake comparisons over time or between businesses. Some idea of the range and scale of the various types of operation must be gained for a proper assessment of financial health. Thus, to undertake any meaningful analysis of financial performance and position, it is usually necessary to disaggregate the information contained within the financial statements. This disaggregated information is disclosed in **segmental financial reports**.

By breaking down the financial information according to each type of business operation, or operating segment, we can evaluate the relative risks and profitability of each segment and make useful comparisons with other businesses or other business operating segments. We can also see the trend of performance for each operating segment over time and so determine more accurately the likely growth prospects for the business as a whole. We should also be able to assess more easily the impact on the overall business of changes in market conditions relating to particular operating segments.

Disclosure of information relating to the performance of each segment may also help to improve the efficiency of the business by keeping managers on their toes. Operating segments that are performing poorly will be revealed and this should put pressure on managers to take corrective action. Finally, where an operating segment has been sold, the shareholders will be better placed to assess the wisdom of the managers' decision to sell it.

Segmental reporting rules

An IASB standard (IFRS 8 *Operating Segments*) requires listed companies to disclose information about their various operating segments. Defining an operating segment, however, can be a tricky business. The IASB has opted for a 'management approach', which means that an operating segment is defined by reference to how management has segmented the business for internal reporting and monitoring purposes. An operating segment is, therefore, defined as a part of the business that

■ generates revenues and expenses,
■ has its own separate financial statements, and
■ has its results regularly reviewed for resource-allocation and assessment purposes.

Not all parts of the business will meet the criteria identified. The headquarters of the business ('head office'), for example, is unlikely to do so.

Activity 11.1

What do you think are the main advantages of adopting the management approach?

Under the management approach, shareholders will receive similar reports to the internal reports produced for management, which means that they can assess business performance from the same viewpoint as management. It should also mean that businesses will avoid additional, perhaps heavy, reporting costs as the information will already have been produced.

There are, of course, other ways of identifying an operating segment. One approach would be to define a segment according to the industry to which it relates. This, however, may lead to endless definition and classification problems.

To be reported separately, an operating segment must be of significant size. This normally means that it must account for 10 per cent or more of the combined revenue, profits or assets of all operating segments. A segment that does not meet this size threshold may be combined with other similar segments to produce a reportable segment, or separately reported despite its size, at the directors' discretion. If neither of these options is chosen, it should be reported with other segments under a separate category of 'all other segments'.

Segmental disclosure

Financial information to be disclosed includes some profit (/loss) measure (for example, operating profit) for each segment, along with the following income statement items, provided that they are regularly reported to management:

■ revenue, distinguishing between revenue from external customers and revenue from other segments of the business;
■ interest revenue and interest expense;
■ depreciation and other material non-cash items;

- material items of income and expense;
- any profit (loss) from associate companies or joint ventures;
- income tax (where it is separately reported for a segment).

The business must also disclose the total assets and the total liabilities for each segment, along with any additions to non-current assets during the period, if these are regularly reported to management. Where these items are not regularly reported to management, they need not be included in the segmental report that appears in the business's annual report.

Example 11.1 provides an illustrative segmental financial report for a business.

Example 11.1

Goya plc
Segmental report for the year ended 31 December 2012

	Publishing £m	Film-making £m	All other £m	Totals £m
Revenue from external customers	150	200	25	375
Inter-segment revenue	20	10	–	30
Interest revenue	10	–	–	10
Interest expense	–	15	–	15
Depreciation	40	20	5	65
Reportable segment profit	15	19	4	38
Other material non-cash items:				
Impairment of assets	–	10	–	10
Reportable segment assets	60	80	12	152
Expenditures for reportable segment non-current assets	12	18	2	32
Reportable segment liabilities	25	32	4	61

We can see that information relating to each segment as well as a combined total for all operating segments is shown.

Key items, which include revenues, profits, assets, and liabilities, must be reconciled with the corresponding amounts for the business as a whole. For example, Goya plc's income statement should show revenue of £375 million for the business as a whole. When carrying out a reconciliation, we should bear in mind that

- inter-segment revenues should be eliminated as no transaction with external parties occurs;
- any profit arising from inter-segment transfers should also be eliminated;
- assets and liabilities that have not been allocated to a particular segment should be taken into account.

The last item normally refers to assets and liabilities relating to business-wide activities. Thus, head office buildings may provide an example of unallocated assets, and staff pension liabilities may provide an example of unallocated liabilities.

IFRS 8 requires certain non-financial information concerning segments to be disclosed, including the basis for identifying operating segments and the types of products and services that each segment provides. It also requires business-wide information, such as geographical areas of operations and reliance on major customers, to be disclosed.

Segmental reporting problems

Various problems arise when preparing segmental reports, not least of which is that of identifying a segment. We have already seen that the relevant IFRS identifies operating segments according to the internal reporting and monitoring procedures of the business. While this may be the most sensible course of action, comparisons between segments in other businesses may be impossible because of the different ways in which they are defined.

Another problem may arise where there is a significant amount of sales between operating segments. Where this occurs, the **transfer price** of the goods or services between segments can have a substantial impact on the reported profits of each segment. (The transfer price is the price at which sales are made between different segments of the business.) A potential risk is that revenues and profits will be manipulated for each segment through the use of particular transfer pricing policies.

Activity 11.2

Why might a business wish to do this?

Where a business operates in different countries, it may try to report high profits in a country that has low tax rates and to report low profits (or even losses) in a country with high tax rates.

Real World 11.1 reveals how tax authorities around the world are taking an increasingly hard line towards the transfer pricing policies that businesses adopt.

Real World 11.1

A taxing issue

The drive by governments around the world to collect taxes from corporations as they attempt to close yawning budget deficits has sparked a rise in the number of tax authority audits of multinationals, research shows.

A survey by Taxand, a network of global tax professionals, found that 82 per cent of multinational companies saw a rise in the number of government audits they were subject to, and 84 per cent said that as a result they had experienced a rise in compliance costs.

The survey interviewed the chief financial officer or tax director at 52 multinational companies. It found that the single most challenging area for multinationals was transfer pricing – the price a multinational charges one part of its business for goods or services produced by another – and that this area was coming under most scrutiny from tax authorities.

'At the heart of this is the perception that multinationals may manipulate their transfer pricing strategies to create a significant tax advantage,' said Antoine Glaize, a specialist in transfer pricing at Taxand.

 Source: 'Multinationals face more tax audits' (Cohen, N) FT.com, 3 May 2011.

IFRS 8 recognises the impact of transfer pricing policies on segmental revenues and profit by stating that the basis for accounting for transactions between segments must be disclosed.

A third problem is that some expenses and assets may relate to more than one operating segment and their allocation between segments may vary between businesses. Again, this may hinder comparisons of segmental profits and profitability between businesses.

BUSINESS REVIEW

A business, particularly a large business, may have extremely complex organisational arrangements, financing methods and operating characteristics. The financial statements must, however, reflect this complexity if they are to provide a faithful portrayal of financial health. As a consequence, the statements can often be lengthy, detailed and difficult to understand.

To provide a clearer picture for users, a narrative report can be provided that reviews the business and its results. UK law now requires all except the smallest companies to include a business review in their annual financial report. This review, which is prepared by the directors, must provide a balanced and comprehensive analysis of the year's performance and of the position at the year end. The review must also set out information concerning

- the principal risks and uncertainties that are faced;
- key performance indicators;
- the main trends and factors likely to affect the future;
- the company's employees;
- environmental, social and community issues; and
- persons with whom the company has essential contractual or other arrangements, unless disclosure is prejudicial to the person or to the public interest.

Activity 11.3

What do you think are the main qualitative characteristics that information contained within the business review should possess? (*Hint*: Think back to Chapter 1.)

To be useful, the information should exhibit the characteristics for accounting information in general, which we identified in Chapter 1. Thus the information should be relevant, faithfully represented, comparable, verifiable, timely and understandable. The fact that we are dealing with narrative information does not alter the need for these characteristics to be present.

To be useful, the information provided must be complete. This means that it should include all significant information that will help assess business performance. Information that places the business in an unfavourable light must not be omitted.

The reporting framework

The particular form that a business review should take is left to the discretion of the directors. In searching for a suitable framework, the directors may look to the Reporting Standard RS 1 issued by the UK Accounting Standards Board (ASB). This statement precedes the legal requirement for a business review but, nevertheless, covers the same sort of ground. It is not mandatory; it simply aims to provide guidance on best practice.

The framework set out in RS 1 rests on the disclosure of information relating to four key elements of a business: the nature of the business; business performance; resources, risks and relationships; and financial position. Figure 11.1 shows these four key elements.

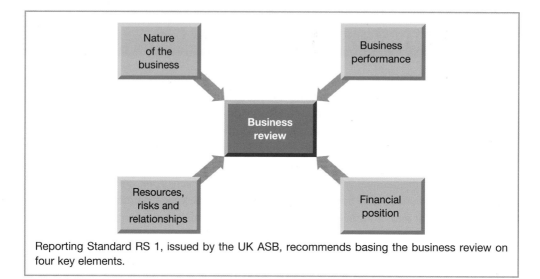

Reporting Standard RS 1, issued by the UK ASB, recommends basing the business review on four key elements.

Figure 11.1 The key elements of the business review

The information to be reported for each of these elements is discussed below.

The nature of the business

This part of the review should describe the environment within which the business operates. As might be imagined, this can cover a wide range and may include a commentary on key operational matters such as the products sold, business processes, business structure and competitive position. It can also include a commentary on the legal, economic and social environment.

This part should also describe the objectives of the business and the strategy adopted to achieve those objectives. **Real World 11.2** indicates how one well-known business deals with this topic in its business review.

Real World 11.2

Reviewing the situation

In its 2011 annual report, Tesco plc's business review discusses the business's strategy as follows:

> In 1997, Tesco set out a strategy to grow the core business and diversify with new products and services in existing and new markets. This strategy enabled us to deliver strong, sustained growth over the past 14 years. We've followed customers into large expanding markets in the UK – such as financial services, general merchandise and telecoms – and new markets abroad, initially in Europe and Asia and more recently in the United States.

> In order to reflect changing consumer needs and the increasingly global nature of our business we've evolved our strategy. The strategy now has seven parts and applies to our five business segments – the UK, Asia, Europe, the United States and Tesco Bank.

Some elements of the strategy remain unchanged. The goal 'to grow the core UK business' is as relevant today as it was in 1997. The UK is the largest business in the Group and a key driver of sales and profit. There are many opportunities for further growth and so we will continue **to grow the UK core.**

Another of our original goals was to be a 'successful international retailer'. In 1997, our international businesses generated 1.8% of the Group's profits. Today they represent 25% and we're now either number one or number two in eight of our 13 markets outside the UK. So we're already 'successful'. Our next step is **to be an outstanding international retailer in stores and online.**

In 1997, we were largely a food retailer so we set ourselves the challenge of becoming 'as strong in non-food as in food'. As our business has grown and we offer an ever wider variety of products to customers, the term non-food no longer does justice to all the products and services we sell. We now aim **to be as strong in everything we sell as we are in food.**

Our services businesses have come a long way since we first included in our strategy the desire 'to develop retailing services'. Today these parts of Tesco generate £583 million profit, representing 16% of the Group total. To date this has been largely UK-focused, but as many of our international businesses have now established well-known brands in their local market, it is time to expand our ambitions and aim **to grow retail services in all our markets.**

In 2007, we added a fifth element to our strategy to underpin our commitment to communities and the environment. We've updated this objective slightly by emphasising our responsibilities in these areas. Our goal is **to put our responsibilities to the communities we serve at the heart of what we do.**

There are two new strategic goals, both of which reflect the way that Tesco has developed over the last decade and our areas of emphasis for the future.

The first is **to be a creator of highly valued brands.** Our brand has evolved from a logo above a few stores in the UK to a multitude of store, product and service brands across the world. Building brands gives our business more meaning with our customers. On one level, this relates to our Retail brands such as the Tesco brand itself, but it also refers to our Product brands such as F&F and Technika and our Pillar brands such as Finest and Value.

Our final goal is **to build our team so that we create more value.** As our business continues to grow and diversify we need more leaders to run the many substantial business and support functions within the Group. Our leaders not only have an important role today, but also have a responsibility to help build a bigger and better team for the future.

Source: Tesco plc Annual Report and Financial Statements 2011, Business Review, www.Tesco.com.

Finally, this part of the business review should include a commentary on the key performance indicators (KPIs) used to assess the success of the business strategy. KPIs will vary between businesses but will normally comprise a combination of financial and non-financial measures. Key financial measures may be based upon sales revenue growth, profit, total shareholder return, dividends and so on. Key non-financial measures may relate to market share, employee satisfaction, product quality, supplier satisfaction and so on.

Business performance

This part of the review considers the development and performance of the business for the year and for the future. It should include comments on anything affecting performance, such as changes in market conditions or the launch of new products or services. It should also identify trends and anything else that may affect future prospects. **Real World 11.3** provides an extract from Tesco's business review which sets out details of new store openings and store extensions in its core UK business.

Real World 11.3

Extra growth

Quoting from the business review in Tesco plc's 2011 annual report:

> New space has continued to drive sales growth. We've opened over 200 new stores in 2010/11 and have a strong opening programme for the coming year.
>
> We have seen particularly strong growth in our convenience format, Tesco Express, with over 150 new stores and have achieved significant share gain in the convenience sector. This growth follows our work to tailor the range and promotions in Express to better suit the needs of our customers locally. Overall last year, we had 80 million more customer visits to our Express stores than in 2009/10.
>
> We have also refreshed or extended over 400 stores this year, receiving a great response from customers. For example, we've added 7,000 sq ft to Wembley Extra, expanding our World Foods offer to meet better the needs of customers in the local area – the store is outperforming by 16% and over three-quarters of customers have told us that it is greatly improved.

Source: Tesco plc Annual Report and Financial Statements 2011, Business Review, www.Tesco.com.

Resources, risks and relationships

This part should comment on the resources of the business and how they are managed. The resources discussed should not be confined to items shown in the statement of financial position and may include such things as corporate reputation, patents, trademarks, brand names, market position and the quality of employees.

This part should also include comments on the main risks and uncertainties facing the business and how they are managed. **Real World 11.4** shows how Tesco plc comments on one important risk in its business review.

Real World 11.4

A risky business

In its 2011 business review, Tesco plc identified well over twenty forms of risk that the business must consider. These cover a wide range and include competition, IT systems, reputational, environmental, fraud, terrorism and currency risks. The risk posed by product safety is described as follows:

> Failures could damage customer trust and confidence, impacting our customer base and therefore financial results.

Tesco then went on to describe the key controls and mitigating factors associated with product safety risk as follows:

- Detailed, established procedures to ensure product integrity
- Strict trading law and technical safety testing regime with regular reporting; Group Compliance Committee reviews compliance with laws and policies
- Partnering with suppliers for mutual understanding of required standards
- Monitoring of developments to respond to changing customer trends and legislation such as labelling and dietary responsibilities
- Clear crisis management processes

Source: Tesco plc Annual Report and Financial Statements 2011, Business Review, www.Tesco.com.

Finally, this part of the business review should include a commentary on key relationships with stakeholders, apart from shareholders, that may affect the business. The stakeholders may include customers, suppliers, employees, contractors, shareholders and lenders as well as other businesses with which the business has strategic alliances. **Real World 11.5** shows how, in its 2011 business review, Tesco plc describes feedback received from shareholders.

Real World 11.5

Every little helps

Tesco plc's 2011 business review:

> We are committed to having a constructive dialogue with stakeholders to ensure we understand what is important to them and allow ourselves the opportunity to present our position. Every year we carry out a survey of a cross section of shareholders in order to assess shareholder perceptions of the Company. The results of this survey are reviewed by the Board. Engagement helps us identify new risks and opportunities to ensure that our long-term strategy is sustainable. In some instances we find that working with stakeholders in partnership can help deliver shared goals. We might not be able to satisfy all stakeholder concerns all the time but through engagement we can do our best to balance competing demands. We know that customers need to be able to trust our business and they will only trust us if they believe that we are engaging on an appropriate basis with our stakeholders.

Source: Tesco plc Annual Report and Financial Statements 2011, Business Review, www.tesco.com.

Financial position

This final part of the of the business review should describe events that have influenced the financial position of the business during the year and those that are likely to affect the business in the future. It should also include a discussion of the capital (financial) structure, cash flows and liquidity of the company. **Real World 11.6** shows how, in its 2011 business review, Tesco plc comments on its funding.

Real World 11.6

Finding the funds

Tesco plc's 2011 business review:

> The Group finances its operations by a combination of retained profits, disposals of property assets, long and medium-term debt capital market issues, short-term commercial paper, bank borrowings and leases. The objective is to ensure continuity of funding. The policy is to smooth the debt maturity profile, to arrange funding ahead of requirements and to maintain sufficient undrawn committed bank facilities and a strong credit rating so that maturing debt may be refinanced as it falls due. Tesco Group has a long-term rating of A3 with a negative outlook by Moody's, A- (stable) with Fitch and A- (stable) by Standard & Poor's. New funding of £1.7 billion was arranged during the year, including a net £1.6 billion from property disposals and £0.1 billion from long-term debt. At the year end, net debt was £6.8 billion (2010 – £7.9 billion).

Source: Tesco plc Annual Report and Financial Statements 2011, Business Review, www.tesco.com.

This part of the business review should also comment on the treasury policy of the business, which is concerned with managing cash, obtaining finance and managing relationships with financial institutions. Possible areas for discussion can include major financing transactions and the effects of interest charges, or interest rate changes, on the business. **Real World 11.7** shows how, in its 2011 business review, Tesco plc comments on interest rates.

The quality of business reviews

Business reviews are still at an early stage of development and problems concerning their quality are, perhaps, to be expected. A major risk is that these reports will paint too rosy a picture. If they are to be useful, managers must resist this temptation and must be honest about any failings. However, in a world where there is no real incentive for managers to behave in this way and no independent scrutiny, we should not be surprised if this does not occur.

In 2006, the ASB carried out a survey of narrative reporting practice. It found that, generally, businesses provided a good account of the nature of the business and its markets as well as of their business strategy and objectives, but the reporting of principal risks, KPIs and the resources of the business needed improvement. The greatest problem area for businesses, however, was the reporting of forward-looking information. (See reference 2 at the end of the chapter.)

Activity 11.4

Why might the reporting of forward-looking information be a problem for the directors of a business?

The directors may be concerned that the information will be of use to competitors and so damage the competitive position of the business. There is also a risk that the information may turn out to be incorrect and users may then feel that they have been misled.

It seems that the business review will soon be superseded by a new form of narrative report. The government has recently announced plans to replace the business review with a concise, stand-alone, report which deals with the strategy and business model that a company follows. New legislation is planned to come into force in October 2013 to implement the change.

INTERIM FINANCIAL STATEMENTS

Interim financial statements were first published in the US at the turn of the last century and began to appear in the UK in the 1950s. The main impetus for their publication came from progressive managers who felt that the interval between annual financial statements is too long for users to be without information. Now, interim financial statements are an integral part of the financial reporting cycle of most large businesses. Regulatory authorities, particularly Stock Exchanges, have been the major reason for this. Producing half-yearly or quarterly interim financial statements is usually an important listing requirement.

Activity 11.5

The London Stock Exchange requires listed businesses to produce half-yearly interim financial statements. The US Securities and Exchange Commission (SEC), on the other hand, requires listed businesses to produce quarterly financial statements.

What are the advantages and disadvantages of producing interim financial statements on a quarterly, rather than a half-yearly, basis?

Quarterly statements will track more closely financial progress throughout the year and will provide more timely information to users than half-yearly statements. This may, however, be achieved at the expense of reliability. The shorter the reporting period, the greater the need for estimates as there is not enough time for events to unfold. This leads to a greater risk of inaccuracy and error. The costs of quarterly reporting will also be greater.

The precise role of interim financial statements has proved to be a source of contention. Some believe that they are simply a supplement to the annual financial statements, their purpose being to provide timely information that can help in predicting annual profits or losses. Others, however, believe that they should not focus simply on helping to predict the future. They should also help to confirm the results of earlier predictions. Like annual financial statements, they should have both a predictive and a confirmatory role and there is no reason why they should not. A year, after all, is an arbitrary reporting period and annual financial statements rarely cover the operational cycle of a business.

Measuring interim profit

The role of interim financial statements has important implications for the measurement of interim profit. Two methods of measuring interim profit have been proposed, with each reflecting one side of the debate. The **integral method** of profit measurement sees the interim period as being simply part of the annual reporting period. It seeks to provide a measure of interim profit that can be used to help predict the annual profit. To do this, annual expenses are predicted and then a proportion of these are allocated to the interim period based on the proportion of annual sales revenue generated in that period. Under this approach, interim and annual profit margins are maintained at a fairly consistent level. The **discrete method** of profit measurement, on the other hand, treats the interim period as quite separate and distinct from the annual period. It is not primarily concerned with predicting annual profit and adopts accounting methods and policies for measuring interim profit that are the same as those used to measure annual profit.

Example 11.2 should make the differences between the two methods clear.

Varna plc is a large retailer that produces interim financial statements on a half-yearly basis. The business has produced the following estimates for the forthcoming year:

1 Revenue will be £40 million for the first half-year and £100 million for the whole year.
2 Cost of sales will be 50 per cent of sales revenue.
3 Administration expenses will be fixed at £1.5 million per month for the first six months of the year and £2.5 million per month thereafter.
4 The business will sponsor a sports event at a total cost of £5 million in the first half year. The benefits from the sponsorship deal are expected to benefit the whole year.

The estimated interim profit for the first half year, calculated using the integral and discrete methods, will be as follows:

	Estimated interim profit	
	Integral	*Discrete*
	£m	*£m*
Revenue	40.0	40.0
Cost of sales (50%)	(20.0)	(20.0)
Administration – (40/100 × £24m)	(9.6)	
– (6 × £1.5m)		(9.0)
Sponsorship – (40/100 × £5m)	(2.0)	
		(5.0)
Interim profit	8.4	6.0

Notes

1 The discrete method uses the same approach to profit measurement as for the annual period. Expenses are assigned to the particular period in which they are incurred. The sponsorship cost will be written off in the first half year even though the benefits are expected to extend into the second half year. This cost does not meet the definition of an asset at the year end and so is not deferred at the end of an interim period.
2 The integral method 'smooths out' the total annual expenses between the two half-year periods based on the level of activity. Thus, the first half year is charged with 40% (that is, £40m/£100m) of the total expenses for the year.

Let us now calculate annual profit to see how interim profit, when derived using the integral method, may be helpful for prediction purposes.

	Estimated annual profit
	£m
Revenue	100.0
Cost of sales (50%)	(50.0)
Administration ((6 × £1.5m) + (6 × £2.5m))	(24.0)
Sponsorship	(5.0)
Profit for the year	21.0

Interim profit, based on the integral method, represents 40 per cent of the annual profit (£8.4m/£21m = 40%). This, of course, is the same as the percentage of interim sales to annual sales (£40m/£100m = 40%). In other words, (interim sales/annual sales)% = (interim profit/annual profit)%. (See reference 3 at the end of the chapter.) If users can predict sales for the second half of the year, this should provide a good basis for predicting profit. (Having ploughed through this example, you may wonder whether, instead of adopting the integral approach, it would be better simply to provide external users with a profit forecast for the year.)

The International Accounting Standards Board (IASB) has produced a standard for interim financial statements (IAS 34 *Interim Financial Reporting*). It applies to all businesses that either are required, or wish, to prepare these statements in line with international standards. The standard favours the discrete approach to income measurement and states that accounting policies and methods adopted at the interim stage should be in line with those adopted at the annual stage. One problem, however, is that certain items, such as tax, can only be considered in the context of the year as a whole. The standard deals with the tax problem by stating that the tax rate applied to interim profit should be based on the average effective tax rate for the year as a whole.

Interim financial disclosure

There is nothing to stop a business producing a comprehensive set of financial statements for the interim period, although considerations of cost and timeliness will normally make this impractical. IAS 34 recognises that a full reporting option is available to businesses and therefore sets out the *minimum* components of interim financial statements. The standard requires

- a condensed statement of financial position,
- a condensed statement of comprehensive income (either as a single statement or as a separate income statement plus a statement of comprehensive income),
- a condensed statement of changes in equity,
- a condensed statement of cash flows, and
- selected explanatory notes.

Headings and subtotals appearing in the condensed financial statements should be in line with those appearing in the most recent annual financial statements. This should help users to track events occurring since the annual statements were published.

Activity 11.6

What do you think is the main risk of preparing condensed interim financial statements? (*Hint*: Think back to Chapter 5 where we considered summary financial statements.)

The main risk is that, if an attempt is made to simplify complex reality, important information may be lost and the message may become distorted.

The standard assumes that users will have access to the most recent annual report and so explanatory notes focus on issues relating specifically to the interim reporting period. These include

- confirmation that the interim financial statements use the same accounting policies and methods as those used for the annual financial statements,
- suitable explanations concerning the seasonality and cyclicality of business operations,
- the nature and amount of any unusual items affecting assets, liabilities, income and cash flows,
- details of the issue/redemption of loans or share capital and dividends paid,
- information relating to business segments,
- details of significant events, including changes in the composition of the business, changes in contingent assets or liabilities, and material events affecting the business after the end of the interim period.

These disclosure requirements should enable users to glean a fair amount of information concerning the financial progress of the business.

We shall now consider two approaches to financial reporting that also go beyond the routine financial statements. These approaches are not mandatory, though they have been adopted by some businesses. They are the value added statement and accounting for inflation.

THE VALUE ADDED STATEMENT

The **value added statement (VAS)** came to prominence in the mid 1970s following publication of an influential discussion document entitled *The Corporate Report* (see reference 4 at the end of the chapter). This report argued for the inclusion of the VAS within the annual report. It regarded the VAS as an important financial statement and went so far as to suggest that the VAS might one day become more important than the income statement. Following publication of *The Corporate Report*, two government reports lent further support for the inclusion of the VAS within the annual reports of large businesses.

The VAS is similar to the income statement insofar that they are both concerned with measuring wealth created by a business over time. The key difference between the two, however, is the way in which wealth is defined and measured. The VAS measures *value added* whereas the income statement measures *profit earned*.

What is value added?

Value added is an alternative measure of the wealth generated by a business over time. A business can be seen as buying in goods and/or services to which it then 'adds value'. The amount of value added is derived by calculating the total output of the business and then deducting the cost of total inputs. This is shown diagrammatically in Figure 11.2.

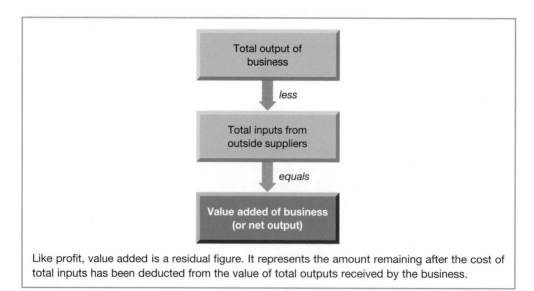

Like profit, value added is a residual figure. It represents the amount remaining after the cost of total inputs has been deducted from the value of total outputs received by the business.

Figure 11.2 Calculating value added by a business

The total output of the business will normally be the sales revenue for the period. The total inputs will be the bought-in materials and services such as the purchase of inventories, rent, rates, electricity, telephone, postage and so on. The difference between total output and total inputs, which is the value added, represents the wealth generated from the collective effort of those with a stake in the business – that is, employees, suppliers of capital and government.

Value added is a broader measure of wealth than profit. It recognises that various groups contribute to, and have a stake in, the wealth generated by a business and it seeks to measure how much wealth is attributable to these 'stakeholders'. This is in contrast to the measure of profit, which is concerned only with the wealth attributable to the owners (that is, the shareholders).

Preparing a value added statement

The VAS begins by measuring the value added by a business and then goes on to show how it is distributed among the key 'stakeholders'. Example 11.3 shows the layout for a value added statement.

Example 11.3

Value added statement for the year ended 30 June

	£m
Revenue	130.6
Bought-in materials and services	(88.4)
Value added	42.2
Applied in the following way:	
To employees	
Wages, pensions and fringe benefits	28.1
To suppliers of capital	
Interest payable on loans	2.6
Dividends to shareholders	3.8
	6.4
To pay government	
Tax payable	3.2
To provide for maintenance and expansion of assets	
Depreciation of non-current assets	3.0
Retained earnings	1.5
	4.5
	42.2

We can see that, in the first part of the VAS, valued added is derived by deducting the cost of bought-in materials and services from sales revenue. The second part then shows how much value added is divided between the various stakeholder groups and how much is retained within the business. (Depreciation and retained earnings represent amounts reinvested to maintain and expand the asset base.)

The VAS does not provide any information that is not already contained within the conventional income statement. It is, in fact, a rearrangement of the income statement. It is claimed, however, that through this rearrangement new insights concerning the performance of the business may be gained.

Ray Cathode (Lighting Supplies) plc has produced the following income statement for the year to 31 December:

Income statement for the year ended 31 December

	£m
Revenue	198
Cost of sales	(90)
Gross profit	108
Salaries and wages	(35)
Rent and rates	(18)
Insurance	(3)
Light and heat	(10)
Postage and stationery	(1)
Advertising	(4)
Depreciation	(19)
Operating profit	18
Interest payable	(6)
Profit before taxation	12
Taxation	(4)
Profit for the year	8

During the year a dividend of £3 million was announced and paid.

From the above information, see if you can produce a value added statement for the year to 31 December. (Use the format in Example 11.3 above to guide you.)

Your answer should be as follows:

Value added statement for the year ended 31 December

	£m
Revenue	198
Bought-in materials and services (90 + 18 + 3 + 10 + 1 + 4)	(126)
Value added	72
Applied in the following way:	
To employees	
Salaries and wages	35
To suppliers of capital	
Interest payable on loans	6
Dividends to shareholders	3
	9
To pay government	
Tax payable	4
To provide for maintenance and expansion of assets	
Depreciation of non-current assets	19
Retained profits (8 − 3)	5
	24
	72

What useful information can you glean from the VAS in Activity 11.7?

The VAS in Activity 11.7 reveals that nearly half of the value added generated by the business during the year was distributed to employees in the form of salaries and wages. This proportion is much higher than that distributed to suppliers of capital. A relatively high proportion of value added being distributed to employees is not unusual. The business retained one-third of the value added to replace and expand the assets. A high proportion of value added retained may suggest a concern for growth to be financed through internally generated sources. The proportion of value added required to pay tax is relatively small.

Benefits of the VAS

The VAS helps to promote the message that a business is a coalition of interests and that business success depends on co-operation between the various stakeholders. It may even foster better relations by encouraging a team spirit among those with a stake in the business. If employees are identified as important stakeholders, they may feel more part of the business team and respond by showing greater co-operation and commitment. The VAS may also help managers to appreciate that employees are team members and not simply an expense, as portrayed in the conventional income statement.

A further benefit claimed for the VAS is that some useful ratios can be derived from this statement. These include

- value added to sales revenue (per cent);
- value added per £1 of wages and salaries (£);
- dividends to value added (per cent);
- tax to value added (per cent);
- depreciation and retentions to value added (per cent);
- value added to capital employed (per cent).

Calculate each of the above ratios using the information contained in the solution to Activity 11.7 above. How could these ratios be useful? (For purposes of calculation, assume that the business's capital employed is £80 million.)

Your answer should be as follows:

$$\text{Value added to sales revenue} = \frac{72}{198} \times 100\% = 36.4\%$$

The lower this ratio is, the greater will be the reliance on outside sources of materials and services. For example, a wine retailer that purchases its wine from a wholesaler will have a lower ratio than a wine retailer that owns its own vineyards and bottling facilities. A low ratio may indicate vulnerability to difficulties caused by external suppliers.

$$\text{Value added per £1 of wages} = \frac{72}{35} = £2.06$$

→

This ratio is a measure of labour productivity. In this case, the employees are generating £2.06 of value added for every £1 of wages expended: the higher the ratio, the higher the level of productivity. Normally, the ratio would be higher than 1.0. A ratio of less than 1.0 would indicate that employees are being paid more than the value of their output.

$$\text{Dividends to value added} = \frac{3}{72} \times 100\% = 4.2\%$$

This ratio shows the portion of value added that will be received in cash, more or less immediately, by shareholders. The trend of this ratio may provide an insight into the distribution policy of the business over time. It is important to remember, however, that shareholders also benefit, in the form of capital growth, from amounts reinvested in the business. Thus, the ratio is only a partial measure of the benefits received by shareholders.

$$\text{Tax to value added} = \frac{4}{72} \times 100\% = 5.6\%$$

This ratio indicates that portion of the value added which is payable to government in the form of taxes. It may be useful in assessing whether or not the business has an unfair burden of taxation.

$$\text{Depreciation and retentions to value added} = \frac{24}{72} \times 100\% = 33.3\%$$

This ratio provides some indication of the way that finance is raised. A high ratio may indicate that finance for new investment tends to be raised from internal sources rather than from external sources, such as borrowing or new share issues.

$$\text{Value added to capital employed} = \frac{72}{80} \times 100\% = 90\%$$

This ratio is a measure of the productivity of capital employed. A high ratio is, therefore, normally preferred to a low ratio.

It is interesting to note that the UK government regards value added as an important measure of wealth creation. Each year, it produces an annual report of value added per head of population for the UK as a whole and for the regions. **Real World 11.8** discusses some of the recent findings.

Real World 11.8

Something of value

The average value added per head of population through productive activity for the UK as a whole during 2010 was £20,476. The highest figure was for London at £35,026 and the lowest was Wales at £15,145.

Source: Regional, sub-regional and local Gross Value Added 2010, Office of National Statistics, 14 December 2011, www.statistics.gov.uk.

Problems of the VAS

The proposal to include a VAS as part of the annual report was initially greeted with enthusiasm. At the peak of its popularity, it was included in the annual reports of almost one-third of the hundred largest listed businesses. This peak has long passed, however, and now the VAS has become a rare sighting in the financial reporting landscape.

Although the VAS simply rearranges information contained in the conventional income statement, the effect of this rearrangement is to raise a number of thorny theoretical and practical problems. Many of these problems remain unresolved, leaving doubts over its usefulness. The more important of these problems are:

- *The team concept*. Some dismiss the idea of a business being a team of stakeholders working together as no more than a public relations exercise. It is seen as a misguided attempt to obscure the underlying conflict between suppliers of capital and employees.
- *Team membership*. Even if the team concept is accepted, there is room for debate about the nature and composition of the team. Suppliers, for example, may work closely with a business to ensure the timely flow of goods and services, yet cannot be treated as team members because of the way in which value added is calculated. They may, however, have a stronger case for being considered team members than, say, government, which may have little contact with a business, apart from when collecting taxes.
- *The classification of items*. The VAS is beset with classification problems. For example, gross wages paid to employees (that is, wages before tax and national insurance payments are deducted) are normally shown under the heading 'To employees'. Yet it is the government that receives the taxation and National Insurance payments. Employees will receive their wages net of taxation and National Insurance, with the employer paying the deductions directly to the government.
- *The importance of profit*. Within a capitalist economy, profit will always be at the heart of financial reporting. Shareholders, who are the owners and principal risk takers, are concerned with the returns from their investment. If managers do not keep this firmly in mind and provide shareholders with acceptable returns, they are likely to be replaced by managers who will.
- *Loss of focus*. There is a danger that if managers become too concerned with increasing value added this may have an adverse effect on profit. To illustrate this point, consider Activity 11.10.

Activity 11.10

Ray Von plc is considering whether to make a particular component or to purchase the item from an outside supplier. The component can be sold by Ray Von for £40. Making the component would involve Ray Von in a labour cost of £12 a unit and a material cost of £18. The cost of buying the item from an outside supplier would be £26. Calculate both the value added and profit arising from one unit of the component under each option.

Your answer should be as follows:

	Buy-in £	Make £
Selling price	40	40
Bought-in materials	(26)	(18)
Value added	14	22
Labour costs	(–)	(12)
Profit	14	10

We can see that making the item will provide a higher value added but a lower profit than buying in. Thus, a decision to maximise value added would be at the expense of profit.

Finally, it is worth making the point that the profit generated by a business is likely to be important to various stakeholders and not simply to shareholders. Lenders will be interested in the profit generated to enable them to assess the riskiness of their loan; governments will be interested for taxation purposes; and employees will be interested for the assessment of likely future pay increases and job security. So far, there has been a failure to demonstrate that value added is as useful for decision-making purposes as profit.

Reporting value added

Although the VAS now rarely appears in the annual reports of UK businesses, some of them still use this statement when reporting business performance to employees. It may then be portrayed in diagrammatic form for ease of understanding. For example, the application of total value added of Ray Cathode (Lighting Supplies) plc that we met earlier in Activity 11.7 can be represented in the form of a pie chart, as in Figure 11.3.

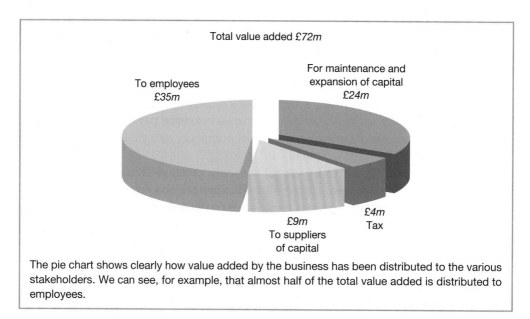

Total value added £72m

To employees £35m

For maintenance and expansion of capital £24m

£4m Tax

£9m To suppliers of capital

The pie chart shows clearly how value added by the business has been distributed to the various stakeholders. We can see, for example, that almost half of the total value added is distributed to employees.

Figure 11.3 Distribution of total value added by Ray Cathode (Lighting Supplies) plc

Reporting value added only to employees, however, raises an issue of credibility. Employees may well ask why a financial report that is not regarded as being important to other users is being provided to them. They may feel the major motivation is to demonstrate the extent to which value added is taken up in salaries and wages. As mentioned earlier, a sizeable proportion of total value added is usually distributed to employees.

As we saw above, few UK businesses include a VAS with their annual reports. In other countries they are rather more popular, however. **Real World 11.9** shows the VAS that was included in the 2010/11 annual report of John Keells Hotels plc, a Sri Lankan business. The business has a chain of resort hotels in Sri Lanka and the Maldives.

Consolidated value added statement

**Consolidated value added statement
for the year ended 31 March 2011**

In Rs. '000s

		%
Revenue	5,884,513	
Other operating income	188,212	
Total	6,072,725	
Less: Cost of materials and services	(3,565,043)	
Value added	2,507,682	
Distributed as follows:		%
To employees as salaries and other benefits	991,148	40
To the government as taxes	262,516	10
To the providers of capital		
Interest on borrowings	272,972	11
Minority interest	2,039	0
Retained within the business		
As depreciation	455,063	18
As reserves	523,944	21
Total	2,507,682	100

Source: Annual report of John Keells Hotels plc, 2010/11, p. 146.

INFLATION ACCOUNTING AND REPORTING

We saw in Chapter 2 that there is an assumption in accounting that money, which is the unit of measurement, will remain stable over time. This, however, is an unrealistic assumption as the value of money changes. Usually, it is inflation that is the culprit. This occurs when the general purchasing power of money is reduced because of a rise in prices. Occasionally, however, it is because of deflation, which occurs when the general purchasing power of money is increased because of a fall in prices.

The measurement of financial performance and position is complicated by changes in the value of money and this, in turn, can undermine the usefulness of financial statements. In the following sections, we focus on the distorting effect of inflation as it is this, rather than deflation, that has been the more persistent problem over the years. We shall see that inflation results in an overstatement of profit and an inadequate portrayal of financial position. We shall also consider two broad approaches that attempt to correct for the distorting effects of inflation in the financial statements.

Inflation and profit measurement

During a period of inflation, profit tends to be overstated. This is because time elapses between buying a particular resource and its subsequent use. Inventories are a good example of this problem, as illustrated in Example 11.4.

Example 11.4

Kostova Car Sales Ltd acquired a new Mercedes motor car for £25,000 as part of its show-room inventories. The car was held for three months before being sold to a customer for £30,000. The cost of replacing the vehicle from the manufacturer increased during the three-month inventories holding period to £26,250. This was in line with the general rate of inflation for that period. What is the profit made on the sale of the motor car?

The conventional approach to measuring profit is to match the selling price of the vehicle with the original cost of acquisition. Thus, the conventionally derived profit will be £5,000:

	£
Sale of motor car	30,000
Cost of acquisition	(25,000)
Profit	5,000

Where the value of money is constant, this approach can produce a valid result. Where, however, prices are rising, there is a problem. The original acquisition cost will understate the resources consumed. During the inventories holding period, the cost of replacing the car increased in line with the rate of inflation. (This is to say that the *average* purchasing power of money, as measured by the general rate of inflation, and the *specific* purchasing power of money, as measured by changes in the cost of the car, decreased by the same amount during the inventories holding period.) Given this loss of purchasing power, the original cost of the car is no longer a meaningful measure of the resources consumed during the period. It would be more realistic to calculate the profit for the period by taking the difference between the selling price and cost of the new car *expressed in current terms*.

This means the inflation-adjusted profit will be £3,750:

	£
Sale of motor car	30,000
Current purchase cost of car	(26,250)
Profit	3,750

We can see that, if the current purchase cost of the car is substituted for the original cost, the profit for the period is lower. It can be argued that, unless this is done, profits will be overstated.

The problem of time elapsing between the acquisition of a resource and its ultimate use is even more acute in the case of non-current assets. A non-current asset, such as a building, may be held for many years and the income statement for each of these years will be charged with its depreciation. Where this charge is based on the acquisition (historic) cost of the asset, it will become increasingly out of date and so will not reflect the resources consumed during the period. Unless revenues are matched with depreciation charges expressed in current terms, profits will be overstated.

Inflation and financial position

During a period of rising prices, financial statements based on historic cost do not adequately portray financial position. There are three potentially serious problems:

- an erosion of the equity base may not be clearly recognised;
- the assets of the business will tend to be understated; and
- any gains and losses from holding monetary items will not be recognised.

We shall now consider each of these problems.

Maintaining the equity base

If the owners are to maintain the purchasing power of their investment and the business is to maintain its scale of operations, the equity base of the business must be kept intact. There is a risk, however, that inflation will erode this base and that the statement of financial position will fail to indicate that this erosion has occurred. To illustrate this point, let us consider Example 11.5.

Example 11.5

Habbad Enterprises sells software packages to small businesses. The statement of financial position of the business at the beginning of a period is:

Statement of financial position at beginning of the period

	£
ASSETS	
Inventories (20 packages @ £100)	<u>2,000</u>
EQUITY	
Opening equity	<u>2,000</u>

During the period, the business managed to sell all of the software packages for cash for £150 each. The conventionally derived profit for the period would be £1,000 (that is, $20 \times £(150 - 100)$) and the statement of financial position at the end of the period would be:

Statement of financial position at the end of the period

	£
ASSETS	
Cash (20 × £150)	<u>3,000</u>
EQUITY	
Opening equity	2,000
Profit for the period	<u>1,000</u>
	<u>3,000</u>

When prices are constant, it would be possible for Habbad Enterprises to distribute the whole of the reported profit for the period to the owners and still retain the equity base intact. That is, the distribution would not have an adverse effect on the purchasing power of the owners' investment in the business, or the ability of the business to maintain its scale of operations. Following the distribution of profits, £2,000 would still remain, representing the equity at the start of the period.

Let us assume, however, that the general rate of inflation during the period was 10 per cent and the cost of the software packages increased in line with this rate. To ensure that the owners' investment in the business is kept intact and the business is able to continue its current scale of operations, it would not now be possible to distribute all of the profits as conventionally measured.

What amount of profit do you think could be distributed to the owners of Habbad Enterprises without any adverse effect on the equity base?

As the general rate of inflation was 10 per cent during the period, and the cost of software packages increased in line with this rate, the equity base must be increased by this amount to preserve the owners' investment and to ensure that the existing scale of operations can be maintained. The equity at the end of the period should, therefore, be

$$£2,000 + (10\% \times £2,000) = £2,200$$

As the equity at the end of the period is £3,000, the amount that can be distributed will be

$$£3,000 - £2,200 = £800$$

Calculating profit by matching revenue with the cost of purchases expressed in current terms will also provide a measure of the amount that can be safely distributed to owners. Hence:

	£
Sales revenue (20 @ £150)	3,000
Cost of packages in current terms (20 @ £110)	(2,200)
Profit	800

Maintaining the equity base and profit measurement are really two sides of the same coin. Profit can be defined as the amount that may be distributed to the owners without eroding the equity base.

Reporting assets

During a period of rising prices, the acquisition (historic) cost of assets acquired becomes outdated. Current values will be higher and so reporting assets using their original costs will tend to understate the financial position: the higher the rate of inflation, the greater this understatement.

It is worth remembering that assets held at the end of an accounting period will normally be acquired at different dates. Equipment (a non-current asset), for example, may be held at the end of an accounting period and acquired as follows:

Equipment at cost

	£
Acquired 31 March 2007	38,000
Acquired 30 June 2010	54,000
Acquired 20 September 2012	62,000
	154,000

During a period of inflation, the purchasing power of the pound will be quite different at each acquisition date. The total cost of this group of assets (£154,000) appearing on the statement of financial position will, therefore, be meaningless. In effect, the pounds spent at the various dates represent different currencies, each with different purchasing power.

Monetary items

Some items appearing on a statement of financial position have a fixed number of pounds assigned to them. The particular amount may be fixed by contract or by statute and will not change as a result of inflation. These are known as **monetary items**.

It is important to identify monetary items. This is because holding monetary assets during a period of inflation will result in a loss of purchasing power. Holding monetary liabilities, on the other hand, will lead to a gain. Example 11.6 illustrates this point.

Example 11.6

A business holds a constant £1,000 in cash during a year when inflation is at the rate of 20 per cent. As a result, the purchasing power of the cash held will be lower at the end of the year than at the beginning. Those goods and services which would have cost £1,000 at the beginning of the period would, on average, cost £1,200 by the end of the period. This represents a loss of purchasing power of £200 (in terms of end-of-period £s) over the period.

This loss of purchasing power will have a real effect on the business's ability to preserve the capital invested by the owners and on its ability to maintain its scale of operations.

The reverse situation will apply where a monetary liability is held during a period of inflation. The liability will be reduced, in real terms, and so the owners will make a gain at the expense of the lenders. These monetary gains and losses may be significant but will not be reported in the conventional financial statements. This is because money is the unit of measurement and it cannot measure changes in its own purchasing power.

Reporting the effects of inflation

The distorting effects of inflation on the conventional financial statements can be severe. Even relatively low inflation rates can have a significant cumulative effect over time. To combat the problem, various methods of accounting for inflation have been proposed and there has been much debate as to which should be adopted. At the heart of the debate lies the problem of equity maintenance and, in particular, how equity maintenance should be defined. If this problem is resolved, other problems, such as the way in which profit is measured and how assets should be reported, can then be resolved.

Approaches to equity maintenance

Two broad approaches to equity maintenance have competed for acceptance. We shall now discuss these.

Maintaining the owners' investment

The first approach is concerned with ensuring that the *general purchasing power of the owners' investment in the business* is maintained during a period of inflation. To do this, a general price index, such as the Retail Price Index (RPI), is used to measure changes in the purchasing power of the pound. (A general price index is constructed by taking a basket of goods and services at a particular point in time and expressing their total cost at a base value of 100. The prices of these goods and services are then measured regularly over time and any changes are expressed in relation to the base value.) A set of financial statements is then prepared using the price index measures for different dates.

Financial transactions occurring at different dates will be expressed in terms of their purchasing power at a single, common date – the end of the accounting period. This is done by adjusting for the change in the price index between the date of the transaction and the end of the accounting period. Profit available for distribution will be derived by expressing both the revenue received and the cost of the goods sold for the period in terms of their current (end-of-accounting-period) purchasing power. The cost of assets acquired will also be expressed in terms of their current purchasing power.

To illustrate how **current (or constant) purchasing power (CPP) accounting** works, let us look at Example 11.7.

Example 11.7

Konides and Co. commenced trading on 1 August when the RPI stood at 110. The conventional financial statements of the business showed the opening statement of financial position as follows:

Statement of financial position as at 1 August

ASSETS	£
Cash	280,000
EQUITY	
Opening equity	280,000

On 1 August, inventories were purchased for cash at a cost of £200,000 and land was acquired at a cost of £80,000. The inventories were sold on 31 August for £250,000 cash when the RPI stood at 121. No other transactions took place during the month.

The CPP profit for the period is calculated by matching revenues and costs of goods sold *after* the amounts have been expressed in terms of their purchasing power at the end of August. Thus, the CPP income statement will be as follows:

CPP income statement for the period to 31 August

	CPP £
Sales revenue (250,000 × 121/121) (Note 1)	250,000
Cost of sales (200,000 × 121/110) (Note 2)	(220,000)
Profit for the period	30,000

Notes:
1 The sales revenue is already expressed in terms of current purchasing power as the sale of inventories took place on the last day of the accounting period.
2 The cost of sales figure is adjusted as the inventories were acquired at an earlier date. [Note that where there are lots of sales and purchases that accrue evenly over the period, an average index for the period is used as the denominator (bottom figure) when making adjustments.]

The CPP statement of financial position at the end of August will be as follows:

CPP statement of financial position as at 31 August

	CPP £
ASSETS	
Non-current assets	
Land (£80,000 × 121/110) (Note 1)	88,000
Current assets	
Cash (Note 2)	250,000
Total assets	338,000
EQUITY	
Equity (£280,000 × 121/110) (Note 3)	308,000
Retained earnings	30,000
Total equity	338,000

Notes:
1 The value for land has been adjusted to reflect changes in the purchasing power of the pound since the date of acquisition.
2 Cash has not been adjusted as it is a monetary item that stays fixed irrespective of changes in the purchasing power of the pound. (There is no loss on holding cash during the period as it was received at the end of the month.)
3 To maintain the equity base, the opening equity will have to be increased by £280,000 × 121/110 = CPP£308,000. This has been achieved and so the owners' investment in the business has been maintained.

Activity 11.14

We have seen that maintaining the owners' investment relies on the use of a *general* price index. Can you think of a problem with this?

The main problem is that a general price index may not reflect the particular cost of goods and services for individual owners.

Maintaining business operations

The second approach to maintaining equity intact is concerned with ensuring that the business is able to maintain its scale of operations. To do this, the specific price changes that affect the business must be taken into account when preparing the financial statements. **Current cost accounting (CCA)** is an important method of accounting for specific price changes. It is mainly, but not exclusively, based on the current cost of replacing an item. In other words, the current costs rather than the historic costs of items are reported.

Under CCA, the profit available for distribution is normally calculated by matching revenue with the cost of replacing the goods that were sold. In many cases, price changes that affect a business will not correspond to general price changes occurring within the economy (although, for the sake of convenience, we assumed in earlier examples that the specific price of goods changed in line with the general rate of inflation).

Example 11.8

Referring to Konides and Co. (see Example 11.7), let us assume that the cost of replacing the inventories sold rose by 20 per cent and the value of the land rose by 5 per cent during August. Using the specific purchasing power approach to accounting for inflation, the profit for the period would be:

CCA income statement for the period to 31 August

	£
Sales revenue	250,000
Cost of sales (£200,000 + (20% × £200,000))	(240,000)
Profit for the period	10,000

We can see that the cost of sales is increased by 20 per cent to reflect the current replacement cost of the goods sold.

CCA statement of financial position as at 31 August

	£
ASSETS	
Non-current assets	
Land (£80,000 + (5% × £80,000) (Note 1)	84,000
Current assets	
Cash (Note 2)	250,000
Total assets	334,000
EQUITY	
Equity (£280,000 + £4,000 + £40,000) (Note 3)	324,000
Retained earnings	10,000
Total equity	334,000

Notes:
1   The value for land has been adjusted to reflect changes in replacement cost since the date of acquisition.
2   Cash has not been adjusted as it is already shown at replacement cost.
3   To maintain the equity base, the opening equity must be increased to reflect the increase in the replacement cost of the land (£4,000) and inventories (£40,000), giving (£280,000 + £4,000 + £40,000) = £324,000. This allows the business to maintain its scale of operations. Konides and Co. could pay out £10,000 to its owners and still be left with £240,000 to replace the inventories just sold. Thus it would be able to maintain the same level of operations.

We have seen that CCA regards maintaining the operating capacity of the business as important. Can you think of any circumstances where it would not be important?

There would be no point in maintaining operating capacity if demand for the goods or services produced by the business was falling.

Which method is better?

There is a clear philosophical divide between the two approaches regarding the issue of equity maintenance. We have seen that the CPP approach seeks to protect the general purchasing power of the owners' investment, so that the owners would still have the same command over goods and services generally. The CCA approach, on the other hand, seeks to maintain the scale of business operations, so that the business can continue operating at the same level. Choosing between the two approaches will inevitably involve a value judgement as to whether it is the owners' investment or the business entity that is of paramount importance.

It could be argued that the two approaches are not mutually exclusive and that annual financial reports could incorporate both. In other words, the business could produce CPP, CCA and historic cost financial statements. This would provide users with a fuller picture. This, however, ignores, or at least underplays, the reporting costs involved and the problems likely to be created for less sophisticated users of financial statements.

The two approaches (CPP and CCA) reflect, to some extent, the familiar tension in accounting between verifiability and relevance. The CPP approach is often commended for its verifiability. The historic cost of items is normally used as the basis for making adjustments and the adjustments are made using an objective index. The relevance of some of the CPP information produced, however, is questionable. In Example 11.7 above we saw that the value for land had been adjusted to take account of the general rise in prices. We also saw, however, that the current value (replacement cost) of the land did not rise in line with the general rate of inflation. We may well ask, therefore, what is the point of reporting the CPP figure relating to the land? How can it be used for decision-making purposes?

The CCA approach is often commended for its relevance. The current value of land appearing on the statement of financial position, for example, may help in decisions as to whether to hold or to sell this item. The verifiability of the information, however, may be an issue, particularly where assets are unique and where there is no market for them. Sometimes, the spectre is raised of unscrupulous directors manipulating CCA figures to portray a picture of financial health that they would like users to see. This risk, however, may be mitigated by hiring independent, professional valuers to provide the CCA information.

CPP and CCA differ in their choice of measurement unit. The CPP approach abandons money as the unit of measurement. Instead, items are expressed in terms of pounds of current purchasing power. Many users, however, may find this measurement unit difficult to understand and so may struggle to interpret the significance of CPP financial statements. The CCA approach, on the other hand, continues to use money as the unit of measurement. (A consequence of using different measurement units is that the profit calculated under each approach cannot be easily compared.)

The vital importance of money for business transactions, and for accounting measurement, cannot be overstated. It is, after all, money that is received from customers and that is used to pay dividends, suppliers, taxes and so on. This means that, if the CPP approach is adopted, it can only provide information in the form of supplementary reports. The conventional financial statements, on which the CPP adjustments are based, will remain the centrepiece of financial reporting. CCA financial statements, on the other hand, could replace, rather than be supplementary to, the conventional financial statements.

Activity 11.16

Now that we have considered the two broad approaches to dealing with inflation, can you think of any arguments for adopting neither and, instead, sticking with financial statements based on historic costs? Try to think of at least three arguments.

Various arguments exist, including the following:

- Historic cost accounting is a 'tried and tested' approach with which users are familiar.
- It provides objective, verifiable information that can help reassure users of the integrity of the financial statements.
- It is based on actual transactions that have been carried out.
- It avoids some of the key weaknesses of CPP and CCA. (For example, it uses money as the unit of measurement and does not rely on valuations that may prove to be incorrect.)
- There is a lack of unanimity concerning which of the two approaches to dealing with inflation should be adopted.

You may have thought of others.

The inflation accounting debate has lost its intensity in recent years as most of the industrialised world has enjoyed relatively low rates of inflation. Accounting regulators have therefore given the issue low priority and have, instead, grappled with more pressing issues.

The weaknesses of the historic cost approach, however, are widely recognised. Currently, a number of international accounting standards either allow or require current values to be used instead of historic costs. It is possible that further progress in developing a conceptual framework for accounting will see current values taking centre stage in the measurement of profit and the portrayal of financial position.

Self-assessment question 11.1

You have overheard the following comments:

(a) 'Stewardship accounting is concerned with determining the profit earned in the various bars on cruise ships.'
(b) 'The market model of financial reporting deals with the accounts of street traders.'
(c) 'IFRS 8 requires that businesses produce segmental accounts on a geographical basis, with each region being treated as a separate segment. Any segment with less than 10 per cent of a business's combined revenue can aggregate that segment's results with those of other, similar, segments.'
(d) 'In a segmental report, segmental revenues must not include revenues for transfers between segments.'
(e) 'The business review is an independent assessment of the business by its auditors.'

(f) 'Interim financial statements are the first draft of the annual financial statements which are adjusted for events that occur after the balance sheet date to derive the final version that is sent to the shareholders.'

(g) 'A business's value added is generally taken to be its sales revenue.'

(h) 'CPP financial statements are based on the historic cost statements.'

(i) 'In inflation accounting, monetary items are those aspects of the business that appear in the financial statements with a monetary value.'

(j) 'CCA is particularly concerned with maintaining the spending power of the shareholders' investment over a range of goods and services.'

Required:
Discuss each of the statements pointing out any errors and explaining them fully.

A solution to this question can be found in Appendix C.

SUMMARY

The main points of this chapter may be summarised as follows:

Developments in financial reporting

- Initially, financial reports were unregulated and were only prepared in response to investors' demands for information.

- Abuses arising from the provision of unregulated reports led to financial reporting regulation and the need for independent audit.

- Financial reporting regulation from government, and more recently from standard setters, has increased dramatically over the past 150 years.

- In the future the challenge is to provide better, rather than more, regulation.

Segmental reports

- Segmental reports disaggregate information on the financial statements to help users to achieve a better understanding of financial health.

- An operating segment is defined by the IASB using the 'management approach'.

- IFRS 8 requires certain information relating to each segment to be shown.

- The way in which an operating segment is defined can hinder comparisons of segments between businesses.

Business review

- A business review is a narrative report that requires the directors to provide a balanced and comprehensive analysis of the development and performance of the business. It should also set out the principal risks.

- In the UK, the ASB has issued a Reporting Standard (RS 1) that provides useful guidance when producing a business review.

Interim financial statements

- Interim financial statements may be viewed as supplements to the annual financial statements or as separate financial statements in their own right.

→

- The integral method of interim profit measurement reflects the predictive role of interim financial statements. It aims to smooth out annual expenses between interim periods in order to enhance the ability of interim statements to help users to predict annual profit.

- The discrete method of interim profit measurement reflects the role of interim financial statements in both confirming past predictions and predicting the future. It uses the same accounting policies and methods as those used for annual financial statements.

- IAS 34 favours the discrete method but requires the tax rate applied to interim profit to reflect the average effective tax rate for the year.

- IAS 34 sets out minimum disclosure requirements for interim reports. These consist of condensed financial statements and explanatory notes.

Value added statements

- Value added = total outputs less total inputs.

- The VAS consists of two parts: a calculation of value added and a description of how value added was applied.

- The VAS has a number of problems, including the team concept, team membership and the classification of items.

- Within a capitalist economy, value added has only limited usefulness as a measure of wealth creation.

Inflation accounting and reporting

- Inflation tends to lead to an overstatement of profit.

- Inflation undermines the portrayal of financial position. Problems include obscuring erosion of the equity base, understatement of asset values, and failure to show gains and losses on holding monetary items.

- Two broad approaches to accounting for inflation have been proposed. Each reflects a different view about how equity is maintained.

- Current purchasing power (CPP) accounting focuses on the general purchasing power of the owners' investment.

- Current cost accounting (CCA) focuses on maintaining a business's scale of operations.

MyAccountingLab

Go to www.myaccountinglab.com to check your understanding of the chapter, create a personalised study plan, and maximise your revision time

KEY TERMS

segmental financial reports p. 385
transfer price p. 388
integral method p. 395
discrete method p. 395
value added statement (VAS) p. 398

monetary items p. 409
current (or constant) purchasing power (CPP) accounting p. 410
current cost accounting (CCA) p. 412

REFERENCES

1 Armitage, S. and Marston, C., 'Corporate disclosure, cost of capital and reputation: Evidence from finance directors', *British Accounting Review*, December 2008, pp. 314–36.

2 Accounting Standards Board, *A Review of Narrative Reporting by UK Listed Companies in 2006*, January 2007.

3 Green, D., 'Towards a theory of interim reports', *Journal of Accounting Research*, Spring 1964, pp. 35–49. (Note: Variations to this integral model can be found in the literature.)

4 Accounting Standards Committee, *The Corporate Report*, ASC, 1975.

FURTHER READING

If you would like to explore the topics covered in this chapter in more depth, we recommend the following:

Accounting Standards Board, *Reporting Statement: Operating and Financial Review*, 2006.

Alexander, D., Britton, A. and Jorissen, A., *International Financial Reporting and Analysis*, 5th edn, South Western Cengage Learning, 2011, Chapters 4 to 7

Elliot, B. and Elliot, J., *Financial Accounting and Reporting*, 15th edn, Financial Times Prentice Hall, 2011, Chapters 4, 6 and 7

IASC Foundation Education, *A Guide through International Financial Reporting Standards*, 2012, IFRS 8 and IAS 34

Morley, M., *The Value Added Statement*, Gee Publishing, 1978

REVIEW QUESTIONS

Solutions to these questions can be found in Appendix D.

11.1 'Including a VAS as part of the annual financial reports will undermine their credibility.' What might be the basis for such criticism and do you think that it is valid?

11.2 'CCA is not a method of accounting for inflation. There is really only one method and that is CPP.' What might be the justification for such a statement?

11.3 Can you think of any drawbacks in providing interim financial statements for users?

11.4 What problems does a user of segmental financial statements face when seeking to make comparisons between businesses?

EXERCISES

Exercises 11.1 and 11.2 are basic level, 11.3 to 11.5 are intermediate level and 11.6 to 11.8 are advanced level. Solutions to the exercises with coloured numbers are given in Appendix E.

If you wish to try more exercises, visit the students' side of the Companion Website and MyAccountingLab.

11.1 It has been suggested that too much information might be as bad as too little information for users of annual reports. Explain.

11.2 'The value added statement simply rearranges information contained within the conventional income statement. As a result it is of little value to users.' Discuss the validity of this statement.

11.3 The following information has been taken from the accounts of Buttons Ltd for the year ended 30 September.

	£
Revenue	950,000
Materials	(220,000)
Wages and salaries	(160,000)
Other expenses	(95,000)
Depreciation	(80,000)
Operating profit	395,000
Interest	(45,000)
Profit before taxation	350,000
Taxation	(110,000)
Profit for the year	240,000

During the year a dividend of £120,000 was announced and paid.

Required:
(a) Prepare a value added statement for Buttons Ltd for the year ended 30 September.
(b) State and comment upon the reasons why a business may present a value added statement to its shareholders in addition to an income statement.

11.4 Refer to your answer to Exercise 11.3 above. Calculate ratios that you believe could be used to interpret the VAS for Buttons Ltd. Explain the purpose of each ratio.

11.5 Segmental information relating to Dali plc for the year to 31 December 2012 is shown below.

	Car parts £m	Aircraft parts £m	Boat parts £m	Total £m
Revenues from external customers	360	210	85	655
Inter-segment revenues	95	40	–	135
Interest revenue	34	–	–	34
Interest expense	–	28	8	36
Depreciation	80	55	15	150
Reportable segment profit	20	24	18	62
Other material non-cash items:				
Impairment of assets	–	39	–	39
Reportable segment assets	170	125	44	339
Expenditures for reportable segment:				
Non-current assets	28	23	26	77
Reportable segment liabilities	85	67	22	174

Required:
Analyse the performance of each of the three main business segments for the year and comment on your results.

11.6 Alkrom plc, an oil trader, commenced trading on 1 January and had the following opening statement of financial position.

Statement of financial position as at 1 January

	£m
ASSETS	
Cash	20.0
EQUITY	
Opening equity	20.0

On 1 January Alkrom plc acquired offices at a cost of £4m, and 320,000 barrels of oil at £50 per barrel; both acquisitions were paid for immediately. The company held on to the oil as oil prices were expected to rise in the following months. On 31 March all the oil was sold on credit for £60 per barrel.

The RPI stood at 115 on 1 January and 120 on 31 March.

Required:
Prepare a CPP income statement for the three-month period to 31 March and a CPP statement of financial position as at 31 March. (Ignore taxation and depreciation and work to one decimal place.)

11.7 Segmental information relating to Turner plc for the year to 30 April 2012 is shown below.

	Software £m	Electronics £m	Engineering £m	Totals £m
Revenues from external customers	250	230	52	532
Inter-segment revenues	45	25	–	70
Interest revenue	18	–	–	18
Interest expense	–	25	–	25
Depreciation	60	35	10	105
Reportable segment profit	10	34	12	56
Other material non-cash items:				
Impairment of assets	–	5	–	5
Reportable segment assets	140	90	34	264
Expenditures for reportable segment:				
Non-current assets	22	12	10	44
Reportable segment liabilities	55	38	4	97

Required:
Analyse the performance of each of the three main business segments for the year and comment on your results.

11.8 Obtain a copy of the business review for two separate companies within the same industry. Compare the usefulness of each. In answering this question, consider the extent to which each of the two business reviews incorporate the recommendations made by the Accounting Standards Board in RS 1.

Chapter 12

GOVERNING A COMPANY

INTRODUCTION

We saw in Chapter 4 that corporate governance, which concerns the way in which companies are directed and controlled, has become an important issue. Strenuous efforts have been made in recent years to improve standards of corporate governance, particularly for large listed companies. In this final chapter, we consider the framework of rules that has been created to try to protect the interests of shareholders. We also consider some of the key issues and problems associated with monitoring and controlling the behaviour of directors.

Learning outcomes

When you have completed this chapter, you should be able to:

- discuss the need for corporate governance rules and the principles upon which such rules should be based;

- explain the role and composition of the board of directors and discuss the issues and problems associated with the roles of chairman and non-executive director;

- describe the audit process and the contribution of the key players to this process;

- explain the main issues and problems associated with the remuneration of directors;

- discuss the importance of shareholder involvement in the corporate governance process and outline the different forms of shareholder involvement that may be found.

MyAccountingLab Visit www.myaccountinglab.com for practice and revision opportunities

CORPORATE GOVERNANCE

We saw in Chapter 4 that, with large companies, there tends to be a separation of ownership from day-to-day control of the business. A conflict of interest can, therefore, arise between directors and shareholders. There is a risk that directors will pursue their own interests rather than those of shareholders. If this occurs, it is clearly a problem for the shareholders; however, it may also be a problem for society as a whole. Where investors feel that their funds are likely to be mismanaged, they will be reluctant to invest. A shortage of funds will mean that companies can make fewer investments. Furthermore, the costs of finance will increase as companies compete for what funds are available. This means that a lack of concern for shareholders can have a profound effect on the performance of individual companies and, with this, the health of the economy. To avoid these problems, most competitive market economies have a framework of rules to help monitor and control the behaviour of directors.

These rules are usually based around three guiding principles:

- *Disclosure*. This lies at the heart of good corporate governance. An OECD report (see reference 1 at the end of the chapter) summed up the benefits of disclosure as follows:

  > Adequate and timely information about corporate performance enables investors to make informed buy-and-sell decisions and thereby helps the market reflect the value of a corporation (company) under present management. If the market determines that present management is not performing, a decrease in stock [share] price will sanction management's failure and open the way to management change.

- *Accountability*. This involves defining the roles and duties of the directors and establishing an adequate monitoring process. In the UK, company law requires that the directors of a company act in the best interests of the shareholders. This means, among other things, that they must not try to use their position and knowledge to make gains at the expense of the shareholders. The law also requires larger companies to have their annual financial statements independently audited (as we saw in Chapter 5). The purpose of an independent audit is to lend credibility to the financial statements prepared by the directors. We shall consider this point in more detail later.

- *Fairness*. Directors should not be able to benefit from access to 'inside' information that is not available to shareholders. As a result, both the law and the London Stock Exchange place restrictions on the ability of directors to buy and sell the shares of the company. One example of these restrictions is that the directors cannot buy or sell shares immediately before the announcement of the annual trading results of the company or before the announcement of a significant event, such as a planned merger or the loss of the chief executive.

These principles are set out in Figure 12.1.

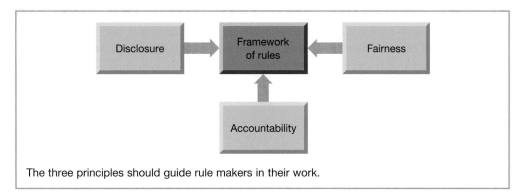

The three principles should guide rule makers in their work.

Figure 12.1 Principles underpinning a framework of rules

Strengthening the framework of rules

The number of rules designed to safeguard shareholders has increased considerably over the years. This has been in response to weaknesses in corporate governance procedures, which have been exposed through well-publicised business failures and frauds, excessive pay increases to directors and evidence that some financial reports were being 'massaged' so as to mislead shareholders. (This last point about 'creative accounting' was discussed in some detail in Chapter 5.)

Many believe, however, that the shareholders must bear some of the blame for any weaknesses. Not all shareholders in large companies are private individuals owning just a few shares each. In fact, ownership, by market value, of the shares listed on the London Stock Exchange is increasingly concentrated in the hands of investing institutions such as insurance businesses, banks, pension funds and so on (see Real World 12.13). These are often massive operations, owning large quantities of the shares of the companies in which they invest. These institutional investors employ specialist staff to manage their portfolios of shares in various companies. It has been argued that the large institutional shareholders, despite their size and relative expertise, have not been very active in corporate governance matters. As a result, there has been little monitoring of directors. We shall see in a later section, however, that things seem to be changing. There is increasing evidence that institutional investors are becoming more proactive in relation to the companies whose shares they hold.

THE BOARD OF DIRECTORS

Before we consider corporate governance issues in more detail, it might be helpful to clarify the role and composition of the board of directors. The board governs the company on behalf of the shareholders and is responsible for promoting their interests. It is led by a chairman and, for a listed public company, the board will normally include both executive and non-executive directors.

The chairman

The **chairman** is the senior director. This individual is elected by the other directors and chairs board meetings.

Executive directors

Executive directors are salaried employees with senior management responsibilities. The finance directors of most large companies, for example, are full-time employees. In addition to being a board member and taking part in board decisions, this individual is responsible for managing the finance function within the company.

Non-executive directors

Non-executive directors act purely as directors; they are not full-time employees of the company. They often have business experience gained from past or present activities concerned with businesses and/or administration, apart from the company concerned. Many non-executive directors are, at the same time, directors of other companies. The role of non-executive directors has taken on increasing significance in recent years and reflects the increased importance given to corporate governance issues.

The **UK Corporate Governance Code**, which we shall discuss very shortly, draws a distinction between non-executive directors and *independent* non-executive directors. The term 'independent' in this context implies freedom from other significant links to the company, to its directors and to major shareholders. According to the UK Code, for example, a non-executive director could not be regarded as independent if that person had been an employee of the company concerned in the previous five years.

Both types of non-executive, however, should need to take an independent attitude towards their roles. Independence of mind is vital for any non-executive director. They should be able to bring an objectivity of approach that can be difficult for executive directors whose working life is so bound up in the affairs of the company. Indeed, this is a major reason for having non-executive directors.

To try to ensure an effective presence of independent non-executive directors, the UK Code states that, for large listed companies, at least half the board, excluding the chairman, should consist of independent non-executive directors. The chairman should also be an independent non-executive director, at the time of being appointed. For smaller listed companies, at least two independent non-executive directors should be on the board.

Although executive directors are much more deeply involved in running a company than non-executive directors, both have the same legal obligations towards the shareholders of the company. The role of the non-executive directors will be discussed in more detail later.

THE UK CORPORATE GOVERNANCE CODE

During the 1990s there was a real effort by the accountancy profession and the London Stock Exchange to address the problems of poor corporate governance mentioned earlier. A Code of Best Practice on Corporate Governance emerged in 1992. This was concerned with accountability and financial reporting. In 1995, a separate code of practice emerged which dealt with directors' pay and conditions. These two codes were revised, 'fine tuned' and amalgamated to produce the Combined Code, which was issued in 1998. Every few years, the impact and effectiveness of the Code has been reviewed and this has led to revisions being made. In 2010, the Combined Code changed its name to the 'UK Corporate Governance Code'.

The UK Corporate Governance Code has the backing of the London Stock Exchange. This means that companies listed on the London Stock Exchange must 'comply or explain'. That is, they must comply with the requirements of the UK Code or must give their shareholders good reason why they do not. Failure to do one or other of these can lead to the company's shares being suspended from listing.

Activity 12.1

Why might this be an important sanction against a non-compliant company?

A major advantage of a Stock Exchange listing is that it enables investors to sell their shares whenever they wish. A company that is suspended from listing would find it hard and, therefore, expensive to raise funds from investors because there would be no ready market for the shares.

The UK Code sets out a number of principles relating to such matters as the role of the directors, their relations with shareholders, and their accountability. **Real World 12.1** outlines some of the more important of these.

The UK Corporate Governance Code

Key elements of the UK Code are as follows:

- Every listed company should have a board of directors that is collectively responsible for its success.
- There should be a clear division of responsibilities between the chairman and the chief executive officer of the company to try to ensure that a single person does not have unbridled power.
- As part of their role as members of a unitary board, non-executive directors should constructively challenge and help develop proposals on strategy.
- There should be an appropriate balance of skills, experience, independence and knowledge to enable the board to carry out its duties effectively.
- The board should receive timely information that is of sufficient quality to enable it to carry out its duties. All board members should refresh their skills regularly and new board members should receive induction.
- Appointments to the board should be the subject of rigorous, formal and transparent procedures and should be drawn from a broad talent pool.
- All directors should submit themselves for re-election at regular intervals, subject to satisfactory performance.
- Remuneration levels should be sufficient to attract, retain and motivate directors of the appropriate quality and should take account of both individual and company performance.
- There should be formal and transparent procedures for developing policy on directors' remuneration. No director should determine his or her own level of remuneration.
- The board should present a balanced and understandable assessment of the company's position and future prospects.
- The board should try to ensure that a satisfactory dialogue with shareholders occurs.
- Boards should use the annual general meeting to communicate with investors and encourage their participation.
- The board should define the company's risk appetite and tolerance and should maintain a sound risk management system.
- Formal and transparent arrangements for applying financial reporting and internal control principles and for maintaining an appropriate relationship with auditors should be in place.
- The board should undertake a formal and rigorous examination of its own performance each year, which will include its committees and individual directors.

Source: www.frc.org.uk.

Strengthening the framework of rules in this way has been generally agreed to have improved the quality of information available to shareholders, resulted in better checks on the powers of directors, and provided greater transparency in corporate affairs. However, rules can only be a partial answer. A balance must be struck between the need to protect shareholders and the need to encourage the entrepreneurial spirit of directors – which could be stifled under a welter of rules. This implies that rules should not be too tight, and so unscrupulous directors may still find ways around them.

Rules are not the only answer. What could shareholders do to try to ensure that the directors act in the shareholders' best interests?

Two ways are commonly used in practice:

- Shareholders may insist on monitoring closely the actions of the directors and the way in which they use the resources of the company.
- They may impose incentive schemes on directors, which link their pay to changes in shareholder wealth. In this way, the interests of the directors and shareholders will become more closely aligned.

Real World 12.2 provides some idea of the make-up of the board of directors of a major UK retail business, J Sainsbury plc. It is fairly typical for a large listed company.

Real World 12.2

The Sainsbury's board

Chairman

David Tyler	Former finance director of GUS plc (1997 to 2006)
	Non-executive chairman of Logica plc
	Non-executive director of Experian plc and Burberry Group plc

Chief executive officer (executive director)

Justin King	Non-executive director of Staples Inc
	Board member of London Organising Committee of the Olympic Games and Paralympic Games
	Formerly Director of Food at Marks and Spencer Group plc

Chief financial officer (executive director)

| John Rogers | Board member Sainsbury's Bank plc |
| | Formerly Group Finance Director of Hanover Acceptances |

Group commercial director (executive director)

| Mike Coupe | Formerly managing director of Iceland Food Stores and director of Big Food Group plc |

Group development director (executive director)

Darren Shapland	Chairman of Sainsbury's Bank plc
	Non-executive director of Ladbrokes plc
	Formerly Group Finance Director of Carpetright plc

Independent non-executive director

Val Gooding	Non-executive director of the Lawn Tennis Association
	Non-executive director of the BBC
	Non-executive director of Standard Chartered Bank plc
	Trustee of the British Museum and of the Rose Theatre
	Formerly chief executive of BUPA

→

Independent non-executive director

Gary Hughes	Chief financial officer of Gala Coral Group
	Director of Scottish Exhibition Centre Ltd
	Formerly chief executive of CMP Information Ltd

Independent non-executive director

Bob Stack	Trustee and non-executive director of Earthwatch International
	Non-executive director of IMI plc
	Formerly director of Cadbury plc

Senior independent non-executive director

John McAdam	Chairman of Rentokil Initial plc and United Utilities plc
	Non-executive director of Rolls-Royce Group plc and Sarah Lee Corporation

Independent non-executive director

Anna Ford	Former BBC newsreader
	Non-executive director of N Brown Group plc
	Trustee of Royal Botanical Gardens
	Chancellor of Manchester University

Independent non-executive director

Mary Harris	Member of supervisory board of TNT NV and Unibail-Rodamco S A
	Previously partner in McKinsey and Company

Independent non-executive director

Matt Britten	Managing Director of Google UK & Ireland
	Director of The Climate Group and The Media Trust charities

Note that of the twelve directors, four are executives each with his own clear role in the management of the company. All of the other eight (including the chairman) are independent non-executive directors. Most of the directors also hold directorships of other major companies. They also have experience of management/administration at a high level.

Source: Based on information in J. Sainsbury plc Annual Report and Financial Statements 2011, p. 25.

TASKS OF THE BOARD

To try to ensure that the company succeeds in its purpose, the board is charged with various tasks. The main tasks are to:

1 *Decide on the strategic direction of the company.* The degree of involvement in strategy setting tends to vary between boards. In some cases, the full board will establish the strategic aims but will delegate responsibility for developing a strategic plan to an **executive committee**. This is a committee made up of board members, which usually includes the **chief executive officer**, who leads the management team, and the other executive directors. Once the committee has developed a plan, it will be put before the full board for approval.

2 *Exercise control.* To try to ensure that things go according to plan and resources are properly allocated, the board must exercise control. This is often done through board committees. Each committee is made up of board members who report to the full board on their progress and findings. The key committees are mentioned below.

The main areas over which the board must exercise control include:

- *Carrying out the strategic plan.* Having developed a strategic plan, the executive committee will usually be charged with its successful implementation.
- *Checking the integrity of the financial statements.* The UK Corporate Governance Code states that a separate board committee, known as the **audit committee**, should be set up to promote the reliability of the financial reporting systems.
- *Evaluating and managing risk.* Although a separate **risk management committee** may be formed, the audit committee may take on this responsibility.
- *Nominating and remunerating directors.* The UK Corporate Governance Code states that a **nomination committee** and a **remuneration committee** should each be established to help provide formal and transparent procedures in these areas.
- *Assessing board performance.* Appraisals based on contributions made, or outcomes achieved, should be carried out on individual directors and on the board as a whole.

The control function of the board will be discussed in more detail in later sections.

3 *Maintain external relations.* The board is responsible for promoting the interests of the company and establishing good relationships with shareholders. Relationships with major shareholders are often helped through informal meetings involving key board members. These meetings, which usually involve a free exchange of views between board members and shareholders, may help the shareholders to adopt a long-term perspective on company performance. They may also help in securing support when the board has to make difficult decisions.

The main tasks discussed are summarised in Figure 12.2.

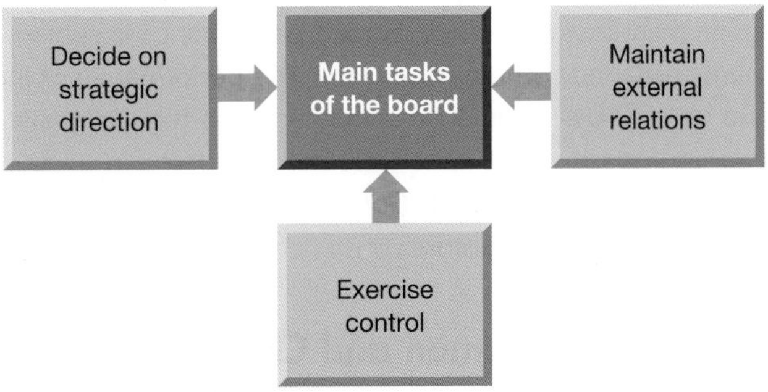

These three main tasks have been discussed above.

Figure 12.2 The main tasks of the board of directors

CHAIRING THE BOARD

We have seen that the role of chairman is to lead and manage the board of directors. The chairman should try to ensure that the board operates as an effective decision-making body and that board meetings are conducted in a business-like manner. To fulfil the role, the chairman will normally be expected to:

- hold frequent board meetings so that key issues and problems can be dealt with at the appropriate time;

- try to ensure that the board agenda properly reflects the key issues and problems confronting the company;
- provide board members with relevant, reliable and timely information to help in their deliberations;
- provide enough time at board meetings for key issues and problems to be discussed thoroughly;
- allow all directors the opportunity to voice their opinions at board meetings;
- guide discussions so that the focus does not deviate from key strategic issues and problems.

The chairman plays a crucial role in defining the culture of the board and, through this, the company as a whole. It is important, therefore, that the chairman tries to foster a good working relationship between board members by providing a supportive environment where directors feel valued and where a climate of trust prevails.

Activity 12.3

In trying to establish good working relations, should the chairman try to ensure that boardroom conflict is avoided?

No. There are occasions when conflict between board members is beneficial. It can help ensure that issues are thoroughly aired and that important proposals are given proper scrutiny.

The chairman will act as an important link between the board and the shareholders. When the board wishes to inform shareholders of its recent proposals and decisions, the chairman will normally take a lead role. Similarly, when shareholders wish to respond to board proposals and decisions, or to raise concerns, they will often relay their views to the board through the chairman. Good communication skills are, therefore, a vital ingredient of a successful chairman.

Finally, the chairman must try to ensure that board performance is subject to proper scrutiny and that improvements are made where necessary. The performance of individual directors, as well as the board as a whole, should be evaluated on a regular basis, at least annually. The criteria for assessing board performance will be considered in a later section. To try to ensure effective board performance, the UK Code requires the chairman to agree and review development needs with individual directors.

Separating the roles of chairman and CEO

We have seen that the role of the chairman is to lead the board of directors and the role of the chief executive officer (CEO) is to lead the management team. The UK Corporate Governance Code states that both roles should not be occupied by the same individual.

Activity 12.4

What risks are associated with a single individual occupying both roles?

Where the two roles are combined, too much power may be concentrated in the hands of a single individual. This power may be used to dominate the board and to marginalise the contribution of others. It may also be used to plunder the company's resources through excessive pay, bonuses and 'perks'. When the company is performing well these abuses of power may be overlooked, but when things turn sour, questions regarding accountability will inevitably surface. There is a need, therefore, to maintain appropriate checks and balances.

Having a separate chairman may provide a number of benefits. The chairman may be a useful source of support for the chief executive when the occasion demands. Where, for example, problems that create controversy among board members arise, they are more likely to be resolved when the chairman and chief executive adopt the same stance. A chairman can also act as a sounding board for new ideas and provide advice for the chief executive. In many cases, chairmen have occupied the position of chief executive at an earlier point in their careers and are older than the chief executive of the company. They are often, therefore, well placed to undertake these supportive roles.

Having a separate chairman may also help in smoothing the path of succession. Where a chief executive leaves the company, the continued presence of the chairman can help to 'steady the ship' and provide a sense of continuity during the period of transition. (See reference 2 at the end of the chapter.) The chairman can also help a newly-appointed chief executive to settle in and to become familiar with the issues and challenges to be faced.

Finally, a separate chairman may help the company to cope more effectively with the demands of modern business. The skills and time required to fulfil both roles are likely to be beyond the capacity of a single individual. It is argued that only by separating the roles can proper attention be given to corporate governance matters and to managing the company.

Is separation always the best solution?

There is little doubt that a powerful chairman/chief executive can create problems for a company. What is less certain, however, is whether a 'one size fits all' approach is the best solution for dealing with this issue. There may be circumstances where combining the roles may be appropriate. A company in difficulties, for example, may benefit from a single, strong leader who has a clear vision and who can act in a decisive and fairly unconstrained manner. A company that has just appointed a young and relatively inexperienced chief executive, on the other hand, may benefit from an experienced non-executive chairman who can support the new appointee.

Those in favour of separating the roles often ignore, or at least underplay, the potential problems of adopting this approach.

Activity 12.5

Can you think of potential problems that may arise from separating the two roles?

Responsibilities may become hazy and this, in turn, may result in a lack of clear direction. There is also a risk that the two individuals occupying the roles simply do not get on. They may have conflicting personalities. They may also have conflicting views over the way in which each role should be carried out and the general direction in which the company should be heading. A breakdown in relationships can lead to endless power struggles, which may badly affect the performance of the company.

Perhaps a clinching argument in favour of separating the two roles would be that it leads to superior shareholder returns. There is, however, no evidence to support this.

Making separation work

Separating the two roles will only be successful if the two individuals concerned strike up a good working relationship. To maximise the chances of success, the board should appoint to the roles individuals whose personalities appear to mesh. The board should also appoint two individuals with complementary skills and knowledge. (See reference 3 at the end of the chapter.) This will help to fill any gaps and should help to build mutual respect between the chairman and chief executive.

The board of directors should try to define the two roles and should make everyone aware of the responsibilities and duties associated with each role. Defining these roles, however, is easier said than done. It is impossible for all situations to be covered. Some overlaps are likely to occur and there is likely to be some uncertainty about who is responsible for certain tasks. This brings the inevitable risk of boundary disputes. Where the company operates in a highly dynamic environment, new tasks are continually emerging and so this will be a particular problem. In this situation, constant renegotiations of the two roles may have to occur. For any chance of success, both parties must enter into any renegotiations with mutual respect for each other's abilities and for the authority vested in each role.

To avoid misunderstanding and to build mutual trust, there should be frequent communications between the two parties. Important information should be shared and there should be no 'surprises'.

Activity 12.6

Will the chairman or the chief executive normally have the most information to share?

As the person responsible for leading the management team, the chief executive will normally have the most information to share. So, it is particularly important for this individual to be open and transparent.

Finally, the chairman, who is often a former chief executive, must resist any temptation to intervene in the management of the business. The role of chairman demands that a different approach be taken. It requires a willingness to operate in the background and to keep ego and ambition firmly in check.

Should the chief executive go on to become chairman?

The UK Corporate Governance Code recommends that the chief executive should not go on to become chairman of the same company.

Activity 12.7

Can you think of a potential problem that may arise from allowing the chief executive to relinquish this post and then become the chairman?

The main risk here is that the individual will be unable to give up the reins of management easily and will still become involved in operating decisions.

The chairman's involvement in day-to-day management issues can create disharmony and can have a detrimental effect on company performance. It can lead to confusion and divided loyalties among the management team and can also undermine the decisions of the current chief executive. There is also a risk, however, that the opposite may occur. The chairman may be too sensitive to the risk of intervening and so may withdraw too far. As a result, the new chief executive may be given too free a hand in managing the company. (See reference 4 at the end of the chapter.)

Allowing the chief executive to become chairman can also increase the risk of defensive behaviour. The new chief executive may feel that points can be scored by criticising the decisions made, and results achieved, when the former chief executive (and now chairman) was managing the company. This is likely to be more of a problem where the new chief executive has been recruited from outside the company and is keen to establish authority. The chairman, on the other hand, may seek to justify past decisions and actions. This may lead to criticism of the new chief executive and attempts to undermine any proposals for change.

Real World 12.3 provides the results of a survey of directors on their attitudes towards this issue.

Real World 12.3

The wrong move

A survey of 430 directors serving on more than 900 boards by Directorbank, a UK specialist recruitment agency, found that 58 per cent of respondents opposed the idea of the chief executive going on to take over the role of chairman.

One said there would be too much baggage, another that they would be too concerned to defend their past record. BA's Lord Marshall, chief executive before becoming chairman of the airline, says he would now come down marginally against making such a transition in the same company. He recognises that at times he has consciously not intervened to give the newcomer 'space', when with hindsight he should have done. 'I certainly found myself biting my tongue. I'd been CEO for thirteen years and a lot of staff continued to look to me as the leader.'

Steve Norris, Jarvis chairman, says moving from chief executive to chairman could be dangerous, especially in private companies. 'I can't tell you the number of people I know who decided they would like to take a "back seat" – that's the expression they use – and hired someone to be chief executive, but actually can never give up driving, and when that happens, that's just lethal; lethal for them and lethal for the business.'

Some of the directors doubted whether the chief executive role was good preparation for chairing the board, which required a 'completely different mindset' to be successful. 'There are a lot of very good chief executives who do make outstanding chairmen,' says Sir Rob Margetts of Legal & General. 'But unquestionably, chief executive-type behaviours, which tend to be control-type behaviours, are not the characteristics you need in a chairman. Or put the other way round, a chairman who has those characteristics and hasn't actually modified them is unlikely to get on very well with his chief executive. . . .'

It seems that few companies allow the chief executive to become chairman. Nevertheless, there may be disadvantages in not doing so.

Activity 12.8

Can you think what these disadvantages might be?

The most important is the loss to the company of the chief executive's expertise and experience. This loss can be particularly severe where the company's operations are unique or highly complex. In these circumstances, recruiting a suitable outside chairman may be extremely difficult. A further disadvantage of not allowing the chief executive to become chairman is that a sense of continuity may be lost.

THE ROLE OF NON-EXECUTIVE DIRECTORS

Not so long ago, the image of the non-executive director was that of an avuncular figure offering kindly guidance and advice to the board concerning the direction of the company. This was not seen as an unduly onerous role and any time spent on the company's affairs could be confined to board meetings and in perusing background documents for the various agenda items. Whatever truth such an image may have contained, it is not a faithful portrayal of the current role of the non-executive director of a UK listed public company. An important consequence of strengthening corporate governance standards, which was referred to earlier, has been to increase the demands placed on the non-executive directors.

Non-executive directors are expected to contribute towards each of the functions of the board mentioned above and the contribution they make will largely depend on their background, experience and personal qualities. As we have seen, often non-executive directors of a listed public company are, or have been, executive directors of another listed public company and so will usually have experience of the commercial world as well as expertise in a particular field, such as finance or marketing. As a result non-executive directors can often play a valuable role in discussions on strategy. They may make useful suggestions or may constructively challenge the assumptions and decisions of the executive directors.

Activity 12.9

How might the fact that non-executive directors are not engaged in the day-to-day running of the company help in board discussions?

They are more detached from company problems and this allows them to provide a more objective view. This may be of particular value during periods of change or crisis, when an objective view can help executive directors to maintain perspective.

Non-executive directors can also play an important role in monitoring and controlling the activities of the company. In working towards the strategic plan, control mechanisms involving plans, budgets, quality indicators and benchmarking may be used. The experience and skills of non-executive directors may enable them to identify weaknesses in the current control systems and to suggest ways of improving them. They may also be able to highlight areas of poor performance.

Non-executives have an important role in the various board committees that are set up to control the activities of the company. It was mentioned earlier that, to promote the integrity of financial information, an audit committee is usually set up. The UK Corporate Governance Code states that this committee should consist entirely of non-executive directors, the majority of whom should be independent non-executive directors. It was also mentioned earlier that listed companies normally have a remuneration committee that is charged with recommending to the board the remuneration of the executive directors and the chairman. The UK Code states that this committee should also consist of independent non-executive directors. This means that non-executives have enormous influence over the remuneration of executive directors, and, where there are performance-related elements, will be involved in setting targets and in monitoring the performance of the executive directors. The roles of both the audit committee and the remuneration committee will be considered in more detail later in the chapter.

Finally, we have seen that listed companies normally have a nomination committee. Its role is to lead the nomination process by identifying the skills, knowledge and experience required for the board and by preparing appropriate job specifications. The UK Code states that this committee should have a majority of independent non-executive directors as members.

The board and large shareholders often maintain a dialogue through informal meetings, which non-executives may attend. This can help them to appreciate the concerns of shareholders. At times, non-executives may become the shareholders' communications channel to the board of directors. Shareholders may be particularly reliant on this channel if they have already voiced concerns to the chairman, or to the executive directors, and have not received satisfactory replies.

Non-executive directors may help to raise the profile of the company. They often enjoy a good reputation within their particular field and may have strong links with a wide range of bodies, including government agencies and foreign companies. These links may be extremely valuable in developing new contacts and in promoting the company's interests.

Role conflict

The different roles that non-executives are expected to play provide potential for conflict. In developing strategy, co-operation between the executive and non-executive directors is essential. All directors are expected to work together as part of a team in pursuit of a common purpose. However, the monitoring role that non-executive directors also have means that they must assess the performance of executive directors. Disputes between executive and non-executive directors can easily arise over the company's financial systems, control systems and remuneration systems. Given this potential conflict, non-executive directors must tread carefully and should retain a certain distance from the executive directors to maintain their independence.

Relations with the executive directors

The potential for disputes may make the non-executive and executive directors wary of each other. Executive directors may resent the presence of non-executives on the board because they believe that the non-executives

■ are monitoring their behaviour and, effectively, acting as 'corporate police officers';
■ do not fully understand the nature of the company's business; and
■ do not devote enough time and effort in carrying out their duties.

Non-executives, on the other hand, may sense that executives are acting in an unhelpful or guarded manner towards them. They may feel that executive directors are seeking to undermine their position by:

- withholding key information or reports;
- failing to provide important information at the required time; and
- holding informal meetings on important matters to which the non-executives are not invited.

The chairman of the board can play an important part in overcoming these suspicions and problems.

Activity 12.10

What do you think the chairman could do? (Try to think of at least two possible initiatives the chairman could take.)

The chairman can take various initiatives, such as trying to ensure that the board's procedures are transparent and that informal meetings of cliques are discouraged. Where doubts exist over the competence of particular directors, the chairman should see that appropriate training and development opportunities are made available. To allow any suspicions and problems to be aired, the chairman should arrange meetings between executive and non-executive directors. Finally, the chairman should try to ensure that all directors receive timely and relevant information.

Maintaining independence

There is a danger that non-executive directors will not provide an independent voice. They may come under the influence of the executive directors and fail to challenge decisions and so promote proper accountability. The fact that non-executives are often executive directors of other companies may lead them to develop some empathy with the executive directors on the board.

Activity 12.11

How might shareholders intervene in an attempt to ensure that the risk of non-executive directors not being sufficiently independent is avoided, or at least reduced?

Shareholders could become involved in the appointment of the non-executive directors, perhaps by identifying and proposing suitable candidates. Once appointed, regular meetings with shareholders may help to strengthen their independence from the executive directors, as well as their commitment to the shareholders' interests.

The increasing burdens placed on non-executive directors mean that a lot of time must be spent in dealing with company affairs. Some, however, have been accused of accepting too many non-executive director appointments, which undermines their ability to devote sufficient time to increasingly complex board issues. The UK Code does not recommend any minimum time commitments for directors, but does state that *all* directors should allocate sufficient time to be able to carry out their duties effectively.

To encourage a diligent attitude, non-executives should be properly rewarded for the time spent on company business. There is a risk, however, of paying non-executives too handsomely for their efforts.

What problem may arise from paying non-executive directors large salaries?

It may compromise their independence. Where non-executives are paid fairly modest salaries, based on the time spent carrying out their duties, the amounts will usually form only a small proportion of their total income. This may help them retain a higher degree of independence when making decisions.

There is normally a large gulf between the total remuneration received by part-time, non-executive directors and that of full-time, executive directors. The 2011 annual report for Tesco plc showed that non-executive directors (excluding the chairman) were paid between £76,000 and £109,000 each and executive directors between £1.756 million and £4.223 million each. (These figures exclude those employed for part of the year only.) The chairman was paid £693,000.

Listed companies recognise the increasing burden placed on non-executives and in recent years their pay has been increasing. **Real World 12.4** reveals the rate of increase for those on the boards of the UK's largest companies.

Real World 12.4

Time to get on board

Chairmen at the UK's biggest quoted companies have received percentage fee increases higher than the rises for chief executives at those companies over the past five years, according to research. Fee levels for non-executive directors who serve on audit and remuneration committees have gone up even further since 2006 – doubling in some cases.

Increases for senior non-executive directors have not attracted the same investor and political attention as rises awarded to executive board members. The study by PwC, the professional services firm, found that fee levels for chairmen of the 100 largest quoted groups increased by 40 per cent between 2006 and 2011, while for chairmen of the next 250 largest companies they rose by 45 per cent. These compare with rises in total remuneration for chief executives of FTSE 100 companies of 37 per cent and for FTSE 250 groups of 39 per cent.

Across the five-year period, the median amount of time that FTSE 100 chairmen commit to their roles has remained broadly stable, rising just from 100 days a year in 2006 to 104 last year.

But Sean O'Hare, remuneration partner at PwC, says the chairman's position has become significantly more demanding. 'Changes to corporate governance standards and requirements have brought greater complexity and reputational risk to the role,' he says. 'The fee increase reflects that additional responsibility and risk.' The PwC research also highlights the higher fees paid to non-executive directors who sit on board committees.

Fees for audit and remuneration committee members at FTSE 100 companies have doubled over the five-year period, while the fees for chairing those committees have risen by four-fifths and one-half respectively. Mr O'Hare says that the work of the audit committee has come under intense scrutiny since the financial crisis. 'Audit committees have come to play a key part in ensuring that corporate risk is properly assessed and managed,' he says. 'Most non-executive directors we talked to considered that chairing these committees was the most challenging non-exec board role after the chairmanship.'

As part of the research, PwC surveyed non-executive directors and found that almost half of them considered their current fees were too low: for a non-executive at a FTSE 100 company the basic fee is £61,000. But three-quarters did not envisage a fee increase over the next financial year.

FT *Source*: 'Report reveals sharp rise in non-exec fees' (Smith, A and Hayes, G) FT.com, 29 April 2012.
© The Financial Times Limited 2012. All rights reserved.

THE AUDIT PROCESS

External audit

External audit forms an important element of corporate governance. To understand what it entails, we must first be clear about the roles and responsibilities of directors and auditors concerning the published financial statements.

Company law requires that the directors prepare annual financial statements that provide a true and fair view of the state of affairs of the company (as we saw in Chapter 5). This will involve:

- selecting suitable accounting policies and applying them consistently;
- making estimates and judgements that are prudent and practical;
- stating whether appropriate accounting standards have been adopted; and
- applying the going concern convention where it is appropriate to do so.

The annual financial statements must be published and made available to shareholders, lenders and others. In addition to preparing the annual financial statements, the law also obliges the directors to keep proper accounting records and to safeguard the assets of the company.

External auditors are appointed by, and report to, the shareholders. They are normally an independent firm of accountants and their role is to examine the annual financial statements prepared by the directors. They must assess the reliability of these statements by examining the underlying accounting records and by reviewing the key assumptions and estimates used in their preparation. Following this, the auditors will provide shareholders with an independent opinion as to whether the financial statements provide a true and fair view of the state of affairs of the company and comply with legal and other regulatory requirements. This opinion is contained within an audit report, which becomes part of the published annual report.

The external auditors must inform shareholders of any significant problems that have been unearthed during the audit process and so the audit report must include instances where:

- proper accounting records have not been kept;
- information and explanations required to undertake the audit have not been received;
- information specified by the law or by regulatory bodies, such as the UK listing authority, has not been disclosed; and
- the directors' report contains information that is inconsistent with the financial statements.

For companies listed on the London Stock Exchange, the auditors must also review the corporate governance statement, which is also prepared by the directors, to see whether it complies with the provisions of the UK Corporate Governance Code. Where the auditors have no concerns over the reliability and integrity of the financial statements, an 'unqualified' opinion is provided, which should lend credibility to the statements.

Internal audit

Many large companies have an **internal audit** function, although there is no legal requirement to have one. The main purpose of internal audit is to provide the directors with reassurance concerning the reliability of the company's control and financial reporting systems. Internal auditors are employees of the company and so do not have the same independence as external auditors. They will normally report to the directors, who will determine the nature and scope of the internal audit.

Although some variation will be found in practice, internal audit will usually involve a review of:

- the internal control systems to see whether they are effective in safeguarding the company's assets and in preventing errors and fraud;
- the accounting systems to see whether they provide reliable information, which meets the needs of management and complies with relevant regulations;
- internal operations and processes to see whether they are efficient and provide value for money.

Real World 12.5 reveals how serious failures in the internal control systems of one major car maker put its business plan at risk.

Real World 12.5

Losing control at GM

Struggling carmaker General Motors has warned that ineffective internal controls over financial reporting might make it difficult for it to execute on its business plan.

GM said weaknesses include poor 'maintenance of records that, in reasonable detail, accurately and fairly reflect the transactions and dispositions of the assets of the corporation', as well as failing to ensure that 'receipts and expenditures of the corporation are being made only in accordance with authorisations of management and directors of the corporation'.

GM said that its management recognised the problems and is taking steps to correct them – but declined to comment further on the matter.

Source: 'Ineffective internal controls hurting GM', www.accountancyage.com, 16 May 2007.

As internal auditors regularly review the reliability of the company's accounting and internal control systems, the external auditors are likely to take this into account when planning the scope and nature of the external audit work to be undertaken. Although the external auditors must retain full responsibility for the external audit, it may be possible to place confidence in certain work carried out by a well-resourced and competent internal audit team.

Risk management

In recent years, the risk management processes of a company have been identified as a further element of good corporate governance. An important consequence of this has been to widen the remit of the internal audit function to include a review of these processes. As a result, internal auditors are now often expected to provide assurances to the directors concerning the adequacy and effectiveness of the company's risk management procedures. They may also be involved in promoting a risk management philosophy within the company through employee risk awareness and risk management programmes.

Real World 12.6 sets out the risk management approach taken by Marks and Spencer plc, the retailer.

Real World 12.6

Risk on the radar

During 2011, the risk management approach taken by Marks and Spencer plc centred around three themes. The first was to ensure that each area of operations identified the key risks to the achievement of its three-year plan and business objectives. The second was to develop clearer descriptions of the risks that were faced and the third was to ensure that appropriate action plans were in place to address each risk.

When identifying the risks faced, Marks and Spencer plc distinguishes between those that:

- are external to the business;
- are core to day-to-day operations;
- are related to changes being undertaken by the business; and
- could emerge in the future.

The main risks within each of these categories are shown in the 'risk radar' map shown in Figure 12.3.

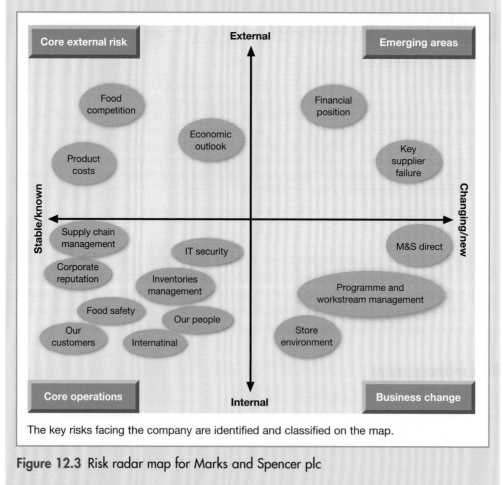

The key risks facing the company are identified and classified on the map.

Figure 12.3 Risk radar map for Marks and Spencer plc

Source: Marks and Spencer plc Annual Report 2011, p. 45.

Auditor independence

There is a danger that the role of the directors as preparers of the financial statements and the role of external auditor as 'watchdog' will not be properly carried out. We saw in Chapter 5 that there have been several accounting scandals involving directors preparing financial statements that portray a company's financial health in a way that bears little resemblance to economic reality (creative accounting). External auditors have sometimes failed to spot irregular accounting practices used by directors to obscure the true position. This has cast doubt over the quality of the audit process and, in some cases, over the independence of auditors.

Two key issues have surfaced concerning the independence of auditors: their period of tenure and their role in carrying out non-audit work. It has been pointed out that auditors appointed by the largest 100 UK listed companies are rarely replaced. They have an average tenure of 48 years and the auditor, or its predecessor firms, for Barclays Bank plc has been in place since 1896. (See reference 5 at the end of the chapter.) Such long tenures may create close relationships between auditors and directors, which may, in turn, work against the interests of shareholders. In many cases, an audit firm will carry out additional non-audit work for a client company. This may include tax advice, IT support, financial and management consultancy. It has been argued that such work, which is awarded by the directors, can undermine the ability to carry out audits on behalf of the shareholders.

Activity 12.13

Why might undertaking additional non-audit work undermine an audit firm's ability to carry out and audit?

Non-audit work is often very well paid and, as we have seen, awarded by the directors. The auditors may, therefore, wish to keep on good terms with the directors. There is a risk that this could lead to the interests of shareholders being compromised when carrying out an audit.

Audit committees

The UK Corporate Governance Code places audit committees at the heart of the financial reporting process and they are seen as vital to good corporate governance. The responsibilities of the audit committee have increased in recent years following the introduction of international financial reporting standards and tougher overseas corporate governance rules, such as the Sarbanes–Oxley Act in the US. This Act was introduced in the wake of accounting scandals and applies to a number of large UK listed companies that also list their shares in the US.

The role of the audit committee

The UK Corporate Governance Code recommends that an audit committee should have delegated authority for trying to ensure that financial reporting and internal control principles are properly applied and for maintaining an appropriate relationship with the external auditors. The committee should consist of at least three, or in the case of smaller companies, two, independent non-executive directors. The main role and responsibilities of the audit committee should be as follows:

- to monitor the integrity of the financial statements;
- to review the company's internal controls;
- to make recommendations concerning the appointment and removal of the external auditor and to approve the terms of engagement;
- to review and monitor the independence, objectivity and effectiveness of the external auditor; and
- to establish and implement policies concerning the supply of non-audit services by the external auditor.

In addition to these duties, the audit committee may also take responsibility for reviewing the risk management systems of the company where the board, or a separate risk committee, does not address this issue.

Fulfilling the role

The audit committee will receive its terms of reference from the board of directors. In practice, these terms are normally in line with the role and responsibilities set out above. The board of directors must also seek to ensure that the committee has the authority and resources to carry out its responsibilities: without these, the committee will have no real 'teeth'.

It is important to establish the right membership of the committee. It should consist of individuals with the integrity, judgement and strength of character to deal with difficult issues that may have to be confronted. They must be prepared to pursue enquiries, even when faced with determined opposition from senior managers or executive directors.

Activity 12.14

Do you think that members of the committee should all be qualified accountants?

There is a case for having qualified accountants on the committee as it will often have to grapple with complex accounting issues. The UK Corporate Governance Code, however, makes the fairly modest recommendation that at least one member should have 'recent and relevant financial experience'. It is worth stating that committee members may be put under enormous pressure to agree to controversial accounting policies. When faced with such pressure, the personal qualities mentioned above will be more important than formal accounting qualifications.

The audit committee should meet regularly and adequate time should be allocated to each meeting. Some meetings should be planned to coincide with important events such as the start of the annual audit, the publication of interim financial statements and the announcement of the preliminary results for the year. In practice, it seems that audit committees of most large UK listed companies meet at least four times a year. Those companies that are also registered with the US Securities and Exchange Commission (SEC) must comply with strict US requirements and are likely to meet more frequently. Figure 12.4 shows the frequency of meetings of SEC-registered and non-SEC-registered companies that are in the FTSE 100.

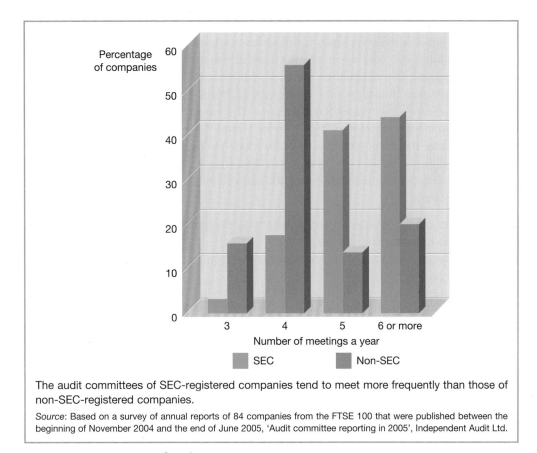

The audit committees of SEC-registered companies tend to meet more frequently than those of non-SEC-registered companies.

Source: Based on a survey of annual reports of 84 companies from the FTSE 100 that were published between the beginning of November 2004 and the end of June 2005, 'Audit committee reporting in 2005', Independent Audit Ltd.

Figure 12.4 Frequency of audit committee meetings

To be effective, the audit committee should have clear lines of communication with key individuals such as the chief executive, the finance director and the heads of the internal and external audit teams. These individuals should provide the audit committee with timely and relevant information and, where appropriate, attend meetings of the audit committee.

When reviewing internal controls, the audit committee should receive details of the effectiveness of the processes put in place by both the internal and external audit teams. The committee must be satisfied that the internal controls have operated satisfactorily during the year and that any recommendations for improvement were implemented. When reviewing the company's risk management systems, the committee will need to check that key risk areas are being monitored and that any control failures or emerging risks are quickly identified and dealt with. The committee must also be satisfied that risk management is not seen as simply a 'box-ticking' exercise and that everyone recognises its importance.

Internal auditors should help the audit committee by reporting on the effectiveness of internal control and risk management procedures. They can become the 'eyes and ears' of the audit committee and may be invaluable in providing necessary assurances. The internal auditors can benefit from a close relationship with the audit committee as it can strengthen their independence and status within the company. The audit committee can help foster greater independence through meetings with the internal auditors where management is excluded. The committee can also strengthen the authority of internal auditors by insisting that management co-operates with them. (See reference 6 at the end of the chapter.)

When reviewing the external audit process, the audit committee should consider the experience and expertise of the audit team. It should also review the audit plans and procedures and seek to ensure that they mesh with the work of the internal audit team. It will need to check that sufficient time is spent on the audit and that key risks are being addressed. To help monitor progress, meetings with the external auditor should be held to compare actual performance against earlier planned performance. The amount of non-audit services undertaken by the external auditors should also be monitored. To maintain a fresh perspective to the audit process, the committee may regularly rotate the head of external audit and/or the audit firm.

When reviewing the financial statements, the audit committee should pay particular attention to the following:

- the accounting policies adopted and whether they conform to the industry norm;
- any changes to accounting policies;
- the estimates and judgements made in key areas such as bad debts, provisions, depreciation and so on;
- any unusual items, such as large write-offs, or unusual relationships, such as a very high bad debts to sales revenue figure; and
- any unusual trends in financial performance or position.

This should help to identify irregular accounting practices or fraudulent behaviour. Any questions arising should be capable of being answered by the chief executive, finance director and external auditors.

The audit committee will normally produce a report for shareholders to be contained within the annual report. In practice, the quality of these reports varies considerably. In some cases, they simply describe the main features of the committee such as its constitution and membership, its role, the frequency of meetings and so on. This kind of information, however, offers little insight as to the way in which the committee has gone about its work. The audit committee report will be presented to the annual general meeting, which the chairman of the audit committee should attend. This will give shareholders the opportunity to question the chairman on any matters for which the committee has responsibility.

Are audit committees worthwhile?

Audit committees are fairly new and it is too early to judge just how effective they are in dealing with the problems discussed. It seems, however, that at least many audit committee members *believe* that these committees are effective. A survey by the Audit Committee Institute asked audit committee members of leading UK and US companies whether they believed that the high-profile financial reporting scandals of the last few years could have been avoided, or reduced, if there had been an effective audit committee in place. The results are shown in Figure 12.5.

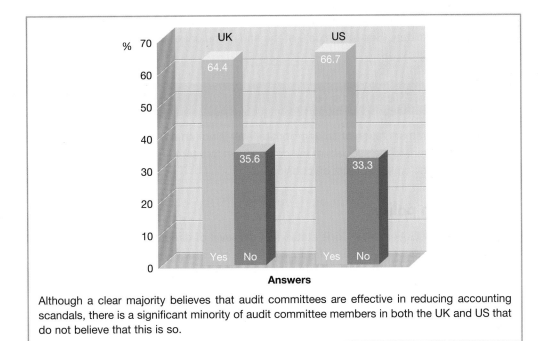

Although a clear majority believes that audit committees are effective in reducing accounting scandals, there is a significant minority of audit committee members in both the UK and US that do not believe that this is so.

Figure 12.5 Would effective audit committees have avoided or reduced the losses caused by accounting scandals?

We can see that roughly two-thirds of audit committee members believe that effective audit committees would have helped. There seems to be little difference between the responses of UK and US committee members. (See reference 7 at the end of the chapter.)

Activity 12.15

How might a sceptic respond to the above results? Why might the results give some cause for concern?

A sceptic might argue that the survey results provide little more than self-justification. To vote against the proposition would cast doubt over the effectiveness of a key function of the audit committee. The fact that roughly one-third of committee members voted against the proposition may be regarded as cause for concern.

It is also worth noting that empirical research studies suggest that audit committees can be effective in reducing **earnings management**. This term is used to describe a situation where a misleading impression of profit performance is provided to external users, normally to benefit directors.

There are potential costs in placing heavy responsibilities on the audit committee and in scrutinising its activities and decisions. There is always a risk that such pressure will cultivate an increasingly cautious approach among committee members. A 'compliance' mentality may inhibit creativity and risk taking, which are essential to long-term prosperity. (See reference 8 at the end of the chapter.)

The responsibilities placed on the audit committee, and the scrutiny to which its activities are subjected, may dissuade individuals from chairing, or even becoming a member of, the audit committee. A great deal of time and effort is normally required to carry out the committee's work and an individual's reputation may be damaged if things go wrong. One survey has shown that non-executive directors are increasingly reluctant to take on the role of chairing the audit committee. (See reference 9 at the end of the chapter.)

REMUNERATING DIRECTORS

Setting directors' remuneration at an appropriate level is not an easy task. Nevertheless, it is often vitally important to the success of the company. In this section we consider some of the key issues and problems that must be considered.

Remuneration policy

The UK Corporate Governance Code states that the level of directors' remuneration should be sufficient to attract, retain and motivate individuals of the right quality. The UK Code also states that remuneration should be linked to long-term performance and to the risk policy of the company. A significant proportion of the total remuneration awarded to executive directors should be based on company and individual performance.

If pay is linked to performance, some of the risks and rewards of being a shareholder are passed to the directors. If a particular course of action yields good returns, the directors will benefit; if it fails to make a return the directors will not. This may encourage them to think more like shareholders and to take tough decisions that are likely to benefit shareholders.

The remuneration package of an executive director of a large listed company is usually made up of two elements:

- a fixed element, which is largely in the form of a base salary but will also include benefits such as pension contributions, medical insurance, company car and so on; and
- a variable element, which rewards directors on the basis of both short-term and long-term performance.

The variable element is normally dependent on the executive directors achieving clear targets that reflect the goals of the company. The rewards for achieving these targets are usually taken in the form of cash and/or shares.

The main elements of the remuneration package for an executive director of a listed public company are shown in Figure 12.6.

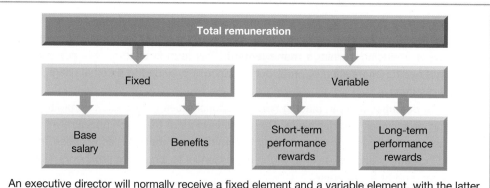

An executive director will normally receive a fixed element and a variable element, with the latter being performance-related.

Figure 12.6 The main elements of remuneration for an executive director of a listed public company

The UK Code discourages performance-related payments to non-executives.

Activity 12.16

Should non-executive directors, as well as executive directors, have a performance-related element to their remuneration?

In the UK, non-executive directors are rewarded on the basis of the time spent and responsibilities undertaken on behalf of the company. The view is that if performance-related remuneration is offered, there is a risk that their independence will be compromised. Not all countries, however, adopt this view.

In large listed businesses, performance-related awards often account for more than half the total rewards given to executive directors. **Real World 12.7** indicates the importance that Tesco plc places on performance when rewarding directors.

Real World 12.7

Tesco rewards

The executive directors of Tesco plc receive a fixed base salary (plus benefits) and a variable reward based on the achievement of performance targets. These targets reflect the responsibilities of individual directors and the objectives of the business.

The performance-related element of Tesco plc's executive directors represents a large proportion of total remuneration. Depending on individual incentive arrangements and performance, the base salary will represent between 14% and 40% and performance-related rewards will represent between 60% and 86% of total remuneration.

Source: Adapted from Tesco plc Annual Report and Financial Statements 2011, p. 76.

The targets and rewards that might be included in directors' incentive schemes will be discussed in more detail later.

Tenure and service contracts

The UK Corporate Governance Code recommends that all directors submit themselves for re-election, by shareholders, at regular intervals. For larger companies, it is recommended that all directors be subject to annual re-election. For smaller companies, re-elections should take place at least every three years. Non-executive directors who have served more than nine years, however, should be subject to annual re-election. The annual re-election of directors of larger companies is designed to ensure greater accountability. There are, however, concerns that it is potentially disruptive and may encourage short-term thinking among board members.

Although directors are normally given service contracts, these do not provide immunity against poor performance. Where a director has underperformed the board should be prepared to consider dismissal. The UK Code states that any compensation for loss of office should be reasonable and should be spread over time. To prevent the risk of overcompensation when contracts are terminated, they should not contain excessive notice periods. Normally the notice period should be no longer than one year.

Remuneration committee

The remuneration committee is the cornerstone of the UK Code's attempt to ensure that directors' rewards are appropriate. The UK Code states that this committee should be responsible for setting remuneration for executive directors and the chairman. The committee should consist entirely of independent non-executive directors. For larger businesses there should be at least three directors, and for smaller businesses at least two. The UK Code also states that no director should be allowed to determine his or her own level of rewards.

Although this committee is meant to prevent executive directors from being over-rewarded, critics point out that, in recent years, directors' pay and benefits have increased at a much faster rate than have corporate profits and sales (or the pay and benefits in other occupations). Furthermore, studies have shown that the relationship between directors' pay and performance is not a very clear one. (See reference 10 at the end of the chapter.) **Real World 12.8** gives some impression of recent pay increases for directors in the 100 largest UK listed companies.

Real World 12.8

It's tough at the top

FTSE 100 directors saw their total earnings rise by 49 per cent in the past financial year, taking the average to just under £2.7m, according to research by Incomes Data Services, the pay monitoring group. The increase will fuel controversy over executive pay as Vince Cable, business secretary, consults on proposals to clamp down on the 'escalation' of awards, including putting employees on remuneration committees and making shareholder votes binding.

FTSE directors' earnings have now soared for two years, according to IDS's data. The latest increase follows a 55 per cent rise in 2009–10 as profits bounced back from the recession.

For chief executives in the FTSE 100, the rise over the past year was 43 per cent, taking their average to £3.86m, while finance directors received 34 per cent, taking them to £2m.

IDS's figures are averages. If median figures are used – the halfway point between the largest and smallest rise – the increase is calculated at a more modest 16 per cent. Nonetheless, all these figures are way above the 2.3 per cent increase in average earnings across the economy in the year to April, as well as the 4.5 per cent rise in FTSE 100 shares over that period.

Steve Tatton, editor of the report, said 'Britain's economy may be struggling to return to pre-recession levels of output, but the same cannot be said of FTSE 100 directors' remuneration. 'At a time when employees are experiencing real wage cuts and risk losing their livelihoods, without further explanation it may be difficult for FTSE 100 companies to justify the significant increase in earnings awarded to their directors.'

An inherent problem of the remuneration committee is that non-executive directors are responsible for the rewards of executive directors. We have seen that non-executive directors are often executive directors of other companies and so there is a risk that they will be sympathetic to a high-reward culture. There may also, however, be problems with the way in which the committee goes about its business – as we shall now see.

Problems with the process

Various studies have pointed out problems in the way in which remuneration committees operate. One study by Main and others (see reference 11 at the end of the chapter) interviewed 22 independent non-executive directors with experience of remuneration committees and found that the businesses for which they served held, on average, 4.8 committee meetings per year. These meetings were tightly scheduled and often fairly brief (on average 1.5 hours). Despite the importance of their role, it seems that these committees do not devote much time to carrying it out. The study also found that it was quite common for the chief executive officer (CEO) and chairman to be present at remuneration committee meetings.

It seems that committee members are rarely selected on the basis of their experience in negotiating or developing reward packages or given training in these matters once appointed. (See reference 12 at the end of the chapter.) This can be a particular problem when hiring a new chief executive officer. The pool of talent for chief executives is small and it is a 'seller's market'. As a result, to recruit a suitable candidate, the committee may be tempted to offer more than is necessary. Incumbent chief executive officers may also be over-rewarded. They are often powerful personalities with considerable influence over other board members. There is a risk that committee members will be too deferential and will err on the side of generosity in contract negotiations.

A further problem arises from the process by which remuneration schemes for directors are developed. The committee is often not responsible for the initial development of these packages; the time spent by non-executive directors on committee meetings is simply not long enough. Instead, the human resource department will often gather data from within the business and commission market data from outside remuneration consultants. Proposals will be produced, which may then be sent to the chief executive officer and other senior directors for approval. After this has been done, they may be passed to the remuneration committee for consideration. Jenson and Murphy make the point that 'The fact that the committee only sees plans that have already been "blessed" by top managers creates an environment that invites abuse and bias.' (See reference 13 at the end of the chapter.)

The remuneration committee must be careful when using market data to formulate appropriate reward packages. Too great a focus on market trends and statistics has been held responsible, at least in part, for a ratcheting effect on directors' rewards. Such data can often be used to justify an increase in rewards: usually businesses do not want to be seen paying below-average rewards to directors. This can result in upward pressure on the average level of rewards without a corresponding increase in performance.

Improving the process

A strong chairman of the remuneration committee is vital for promoting its integrity and independence. The chairman should set the agenda and should attempt to ensure that the committee has the opportunity for open discussions without other directors being in attendance. The chairman should also try to ensure that the committee has access to appropriate information and expertise.

The remuneration committee should take direct responsibility for crafting reward packages for directors. To do this, committee members must invest time and effort in carrying out their role, and adequate training must be provided. To help to stiffen the resolve of committee members, regular meetings with shareholders should be arranged. It is inappropriate for the human resources department, in conjunction with outside consultants, to prepare reward packages for the remuneration committee simply to rubber stamp. It is also inappropriate for the chief executive officer and chairman to approve these packages before they are passed to the remuneration committee.

Non-executive directors

Setting up a remuneration committee does not deal with the problem of who determines the pay of the non-executive directors.

Activity 12.18

Who do you think should determine the pay of the non-executive directors?

The UK Corporate Governance Code states that the board of directors, or perhaps the shareholders, should take responsibility for doing this. Where the board sets their pay, the executive directors will have an influence over the pay of the non-executive directors (a point which may not be lost on those non-executive directors serving on the remuneration committee!).

Reporting directors' remuneration

The law requires that UK listed companies prepare an annual directors' remuneration report. This report must be submitted to shareholders for approval, which will normally take place at the annual general meeting. The report should set out the remuneration of each director with details of salaries and other benefits received. The chairman of the remuneration committee will normally attend the shareholders' meeting to deal with any issues that may arise.

Activity 12.19

How might these reporting requirements affect the level of directors' remuneration?

The requirement to report directors' remuneration may have a moderating effect on the amounts paid to them, particularly as shareholders are required to give their approval. (We saw in Real World 12.8, however, that directors' rewards have not been noticeably moderate in recent years.)

SETTING PERFORMANCE TARGETS

We saw earlier that a large proportion of the remuneration received by executive directors should be performance-related. There are various performance targets that can be used as a basis for rewarding directors and below we consider some of the more popular of these. Before we do so, however, it is useful to identify the characteristics, or qualities, a good performance target should possess. Perhaps the key characteristics are that it should:

- be in line with the goals of the company;
- lead to a convergence of directors' and shareholders' interests;
- reflect the achievement of the directors; and
- be robust and not easily distorted by particular policies, financing arrangements or manipulative practices.

No single performance target will perfectly encapsulate all of these qualities. Nevertheless, a number of potentially useful performance targets exist, as we shall now see.

Total shareholder return

A widely-used performance target is based on **total shareholder return (TSR)**. The total return from a share is made up of two elements: the increase (or decrease) in share value over a period plus any dividends paid during the period. To illustrate how total shareholder return is calculated, let us assume that a company commenced trading by issuing shares of £0.50 each at their nominal value (P_0) and by the end of the first year of trading the shares had increased in value to £0.55 (P_1). Furthermore, the company paid a dividend of £0.06 (D_1) per share during the period. We can calculate the total shareholder return as follows:

$$\text{Total shareholder return} = \frac{D_1 + (P_1 - P_0)}{P_0} \times 100\%$$

$$= \frac{0.06 + (0.55 - 0.50)}{0.50} \times 100\%$$

$$= 22\%$$

The figure calculated has little information value when taken alone. It can only really be used to assess performance when compared with some benchmark.

Activity 12.20

What benchmark would be most suitable?

Perhaps the best benchmark to use would be the returns from similar businesses operating in the same industry over the same period of time.

The reason that this benchmark is usually suitable is because it will compare the returns generated by the company with those generated from other investment opportunities that have the same level of risk. As a general rule, the level of return from an investment should be related to the level of risk that has to be taken.

Many large companies now publish total shareholder returns in their annual reports. **Real World 12.9** provides an example.

Tesco's TSR

Tesco plc publishes its total shareholder returns (TSR) for a five-year period, along with movements in the FTSE 100 index for the same period. The company uses this index as a benchmark as it reflects the performance of companies of similar size. However, when using TSR as a basis for rewarding directors, the company also uses other leading food retailers as a benchmark.

The TSR for the company is displayed graphically in Figure 12.7.

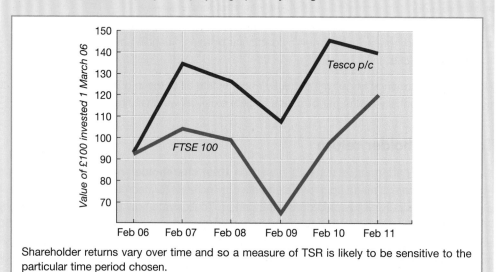

Shareholder returns vary over time and so a measure of TSR is likely to be sensitive to the particular time period chosen.

Figure 12.7 Tesco plc: total shareholder returns February 2006 to February 2011

Source: Tesco plc Annual Report and Financial Statements 2011, p. 81.

Real World 12.10 reveals how TSR is used by Unilever, a leading provider of food, beverages and household products, to reward directors.

Peer group pressure

Unilever awards shares in the company to executive directors under a share incentive plan. The number of shares awarded depends on performance over a three-year period. The maximum grant levels are 200 per cent of salary for the chief executive and 178 per cent of salary for other executive directors. The vesting range (that is the amount awarded) is from 0 per cent to 200 per cent of the maximum grant levels. This means that the chief executive could receive a maximum of 400 per cent of salary in the form of shares and other executive directors 356 per cent.

TSR is one of four measures used by the company to execute the incentive plan. The TSR of the company is compared against a peer group of 20 companies, which include Kraft, PepsiCo and Procter and Gamble. Shares are then vested according to how well the company performs in relation to its peer group over a three-year period.

The 2011 Directors' Remuneration Report of Unilever states that no awards of shares will be made if the company is ranked below 11th position in the peer group at the end of the three-year period. 50% of the shares will be vested if the company is ranked 11th, 100% if it is ranked 7th and 200% if it is ranked 3rd or above. Rewards are vested on a straight-line basis between these points.

Source: Unilever Annual Report and Accounts 2011, p. 53.

Problems with TSR

TSR measures changes in shareholder wealth and, therefore, has obvious appeal as a basis for rewarding executive directors. It is also a fairly robust measure which can accommodate different operating and financing arrangements. Nevertheless, care must be taken when using it. In particular, the issue of risk must be considered. Higher returns may be achieved by simply taking on higher-risk projects and directors should not necessarily be remunerated for increasing returns in this way.

To assess relative performance, TSR must be compared to that of similar companies. There may, however, be difficulties in finding similar companies as a suitable basis for comparison. (There is also a risk that unsuitable companies will be deliberately chosen to make the company's performance seem better than it is.) Other problems such as the inability to identify the contributions of individual directors to overall company performance, the inability to identify share price changes that are beyond the directors' control, and the fact that TSR can be manipulated over the short term (by, for example, the timing of announcements) all conspire to make this a less than perfect measure.

Economic value added (EVA®)

Performance targets based on **economic value added (EVA®)** offer another approach. This measure has been developed and trademarked by a US management consultancy firm, Stern Stewart. EVA®, however, is based on the idea of economic profit, which has been around for many years. The measure reflects the point made earlier that for a company to be profitable in an economic sense, it must generate returns that exceed the returns required by investors. It is not enough simply to make an accounting profit, because this measure does not take full account of the returns required by investors.

EVA® indicates whether the returns generated exceed the returns required by investors. The formula is

$$EVA^{®} = NOPAT - (R \times C)$$

where   NOPAT = Net operating profit after tax

R = Returns required by investors (that is, the weighted average cost of capital)

C = Capital invested (that is, the net assets of the company).

Dena plc has net assets of £250 million and the required return from investors is 10 per cent. The company made a net operating profit of £50m for the year and the appropriate tax rate is 20 per cent. What is the EVA® for the year?

EVA® will be

$$(\pounds50m - (20\% \times \pounds50m)) - (10\% \times \pounds250m) = \pounds15m$$

Only when EVA® is positive can we say that the company is increasing shareholder wealth. To maximise shareholder wealth, managers must increase EVA® by as much as possible.

What can managers do in order to increase EVA®? (*Hint*: use the formula shown above as your starting point.)

The formula suggests that in order to increase EVA®, managers may try to:

■ Increase NOPAT. This may be done either by reducing expenses or by increasing sales revenue.
■ Use capital invested more efficiently. This means selling off assets that are not generating returns that exceed their cost and investing in assets that do.
■ Reduce the required rates of return for investors. This may be achieved by changing the capital structure in favour of long-term borrowing (which is cheaper to service than share capital).

EVA® relies on conventional financial statements to measure the wealth created for shareholders. However, the NOPAT and capital figures shown on these statements are used only as a starting point. They have to be adjusted because of the problems and limitations of conventional measures. According to Stern Stewart, the major problem is that profit and capital are understated because of the conservative bias in accounting measurement. Profit may be understated as a result of arbitrary write-offs such as research and development expenditure written off and as a result of excessive provisions being created (such as allowances for trade receivables). Capital may also be understated because assets are reported at their original cost (less amounts written off), which can produce figures considerably below current market values. In addition, certain assets such as internally generated goodwill and brand names are normally omitted from the financial statements because no external transactions have occurred.

Stern Stewart has identified more than a hundred adjustments that could be made to the conventional financial statements to eliminate the conservative bias. However, it believes that, in practice, only a handful of adjustments to the accounting figures of any particular business tend to be needed. Unless an adjustment is going to have a significant effect on the calculation of EVA® it is really not worth making. The adjustments made should reflect the nature of the particular business. Each business is unique and so must customise the calculation of EVA® to its particular circumstances. (This aspect of EVA® can be seen as either indicating flexibility or as being open to manipulation depending on whether you support this measure!)

Under EVA®, managers can receive bonuses based on actual achievement during a particular period. If management rewards are linked to a single period, however, there is a danger that managers will give undue attention to increasing EVA® during this period rather than over the long term. This might be achieved in the short term, for example, by cutting back on necessary investment. The objective should be to maximise EVA® over the longer term. Where a business has a stable level of sales revenue, operating assets and borrowing, a current-period focus is likely to be less of a problem than where these elements are unstable over time. A stable pattern of operations minimises the risk that improvements in EVA® during the current period are achieved at the expense of future periods. Nevertheless, any reward system for managers must encourage a long-term perspective and so rewards should be based on the ability of managers to improve EVA® over a number of years rather than a single year.

The amount of EVA® generated during a period is rarely reported to shareholders. This means that shareholders will be unable to check whether rewards given to directors are appropriate.

Earnings per share

We may recall that the earnings per share (EPS) ratio (considered in Chapter 9) is calculated as follows:

$$\text{Earnings per share} = \frac{\text{Earnings available to ordinary shareholders}}{\text{Number of ordinary shares in issue}}$$

When used as a basis for directors' incentive plans, a particular level of growth in earnings per share is usually required in order to trigger rewards.

EPS poses problems when used as a performance target for rewarding directors. A major difficulty is that an increase in EPS does not necessarily lead to an increase in shareholder wealth. EPS may be increased by embarking on risky ventures, and an increased level of risk may be reflected in a decrease in share price. A further difficulty is that EPS can be increased in the short term by simply changing certain decisions and policies.

Activity 12.23

Can you think how EPS could be increased by changes in decisions and policies?

It may be done by restricting expenditure on discretionary items such as training, research and nurturing brands. Accounting policy changes, such as changing the point at which revenue is recognised, can also increase EPS.

An annual EPS target would be inappropriate where a company is suffering losses, caused perhaps by uncontrollable changes in economic conditions. It may take time to turn around the company's fortunes. The directors may have to make tough decisions and work hard over many years before there is any real prospect of generating a profit.

Real World 12.11 describes how one large listed company uses EPS and its own measure of economic profit (which is a variation of EVA®) to reward its managers.

Targeting a bonus

Kingfisher plc, the home improvement business which owns B&Q, has a long-term incentive plan that awarded shares in the company to certain executives. In 2011, a revised plan was introduced which awarded up to 500 per cent of annual base salary, subject to meeting performance targets based on EPS and economic profit. The plan covered the three-year period to January 2014.

Fifty per cent of the shares would be awarded subject to meeting EPS targets. The percentage of shares that would vest under this part would be as follows:

Compound annual growth in EPS*	Percentage of this part of the award that would vest
Below 8%	0%
8% (Threshold)	15%
10%	50%
15% (Maximum)	100%

* EPS in January 2014 would be compared to EPS in January 2011 (which was 20.5p) to measure the growth in EPS.

The remaining 50 per cent of shares would be awarded subject to meeting economic profit targets. The percentage of shares that would vest under this part would be as follows:

Aggregate Kingfisher economic profit* over the performance period	Percentage of this part of the award that would vest
Below £229 million	0%
£229 million (threshold)	15%
£257 million	50%
£386 million (maximum)	100%

* Economic profit is defined by the company as profit before interest and tax, lease adjusted – (capital employed, including capitalised leases, adjusted from pensions x WACC).

Source: Kingfisher plc Annual Report and Accounts 2011, Directors Remuneration Report, www.kingfisher.com.

Deciding on a target measure

In practice, other ratios based on profits, such as return on capital employed and return on shareholders' funds, may be used to reward executive directors. They suffer, however, from the same sort of problems that afflict EPS.

All of the target measures described have weaknesses. Reliance on a single measure as a basis for rewarding directors can therefore pose problems. Instead, a combination of measures may be used in an attempt to capture various aspects of performance and to overcome the weaknesses of a particular measure. We saw in Real World 12.11 how Kingfisher plc employs two measures for its long-term share incentive plan.

Directors' share options

One way in which long-term performance can be rewarded is through the granting of **directors' share options**. This type of reward, however, has provoked considerable controversy. For years a debate has raged over whether granting share options to directors is consistent with good corporate governance. Peter Drucker, an eminent management thinker, has been a vociferous critic of this practice and has referred to it as 'an encouragement to loot the corporation'. We shall now consider the main features of directors' share options and then go on to explore the case for and against using options to reward directors. We shall see that a company implementing a directors' share option scheme must grapple with a variety of issues and problems.

What are directors' share options?

A directors' share option scheme gives directors the right, but not the obligation, to buy equity shares in their company at an agreed price. The conditions of the scheme will usually stipulate that the option to buy must be exercised either on, or after, a specified future date. A final date for exercising the option will also usually be specified. Share options are normally awarded only to executive directors. The UK Corporate Governance Code states that non-executive directors should not be rewarded in this way.

Directors' share options will only be exercised if the market value of the shares exceeds the option price. Where the option is exercised, the company must issue the agreed number of shares to the director, who will make a profit from the transaction. The option differs from most financial options in that a director will not normally be required to pay for the option rights: they are granted at no cost to the directors concerned. Directors' share options, however, cannot be traded and will usually be forfeited if the person leaves the company before the option can be exercised.

In the UK, directors' share options are normally issued at the current market price of the underlying shares. In the past, share options were sometimes issued at a discount to the market price; however, the UK Corporate Governance Code has discouraged this practice. The terms of a share option scheme often allow the directors to exercise their option no earlier than three years, but no later than ten years, after the option has been granted. Tax rules and best practice guidelines from institutional investors limit the value of options to £100,000 or four times current salary (see reference 14 at the end of the chapter). The exercise of the option may be subject to certain performance targets, such as growth in earnings per share, being met (see reference 15 at the end of the chapter).

What are the benefits of granting options?

Directors' share option schemes have been a popular method of rewarding the directors of large listed companies and various arguments have been put forward to support their use. It is often suggested, for example, that a well-designed scheme will benefit shareholders as it will help to align the interests of directors with those of shareholders.

Activity 12.24

How might this alignment of interests occur?

It is argued that share options give directors an incentive to increase the value of the company's shares and, thereby, to increase the wealth of shareholders.

Some argue that share options may even help to strengthen the psychological bond that a director has with the company. Through exercising an option and acquiring shares, the directors may identify more closely with the company and feel a sense of shared purpose with other shareholders. This argument does depend, however, on the directors retaining, rather than selling, the shares acquired under the option agreement.

It has also been suggested that share options may help to retain board members. The fact that a director's share options are normally forfeited if a director leaves the company can provide a strong incentive to stay. Options can, therefore, provide a set of 'golden handcuffs' for talented directors who have other employment opportunities.

Unlike other forms of directors' remuneration, share options involve no financial outlay for the company at the time that they are granted. If the share price does not perform well over the option period, the option will be allowed to lapse and the company will incur no cost. If, on the other hand, the shares perform well and the options are exercised, they represent a form of deferred payment to the directors. This deferral of rewards may be particularly attractive to a growing company that is short of cash.

Where directors exercise their options and the company, therefore, issues shares at below their current market value, there is a very real cost to the company. Were the company to issue those same shares to an ordinary investor, it would receive the current market price for them.

What are the problems of options?

Many see share options as a poor means of rewarding directors. Warren Buffett, one of the world's shrewdest and most successful investors, has made clear his opposition to their use. One problem that concerns him is that share option schemes cannot differentiate between the performances achieved by individual directors. He argues:

> Of course stock [share] options often go to talented, value-adding managers and sometimes deliver them rewards that are perfectly appropriate. (Indeed, managers who are really exceptional almost always get far less than they should.) But when the result is equitable, it is accidental. Once granted, the option is blind to individual performance. Because it is irrevocable and unconditional (so long as a manager stays in the company), the sluggard receives rewards from his options precisely as does the star. A managerial Rip Van Winkle, ready to doze for ten years, could not wish for a better 'incentive' system. (See reference 16 at the end of the chapter.)

A further problem concerning the incentive value of share options, to which Buffett refers, is that, where the share price falls significantly below the exercise price, the prospects of receiving benefits from the share options may become remote and any incentive value will be lost.

Both rises and falls in share price may be beyond the control of the directors and may simply reflect changes in economy-wide or industry-wide factors. Any incentive scheme that is subject to the vagaries of the stock market is, therefore, likely to present problems. There is always a risk that directors will either be undercompensated or overcompensated for their achievements.

Buffett's criticism of share options is not confined to their dubious incentive value. He also challenges the view that share options place directors in the same position as that of shareholders. He argues:

> . . . the rhetoric about options frequently describes them as desirable because they put owners and managers in the same financial boat. In reality, the boats are far different. No owner has ever escaped the burden of capital costs, whereas a holder of a fixed-price option bears no capital costs at all. An owner must weigh upside potential against downside risk: an option holder has no downside. In fact, the business project in which you would wish to have an option frequently is a project in which you would reject ownership. (I'll be happy to accept a lottery ticket as a gift – but I'll never buy one.) (See reference 16 at the end of the chapter.)

This latter point, concerning the lack of 'downside' risk associated with the acquisition of options, may have an impact on the directors' risk-taking behaviour.

Activity 12.25

How might this affect the risk-taking behaviour of directors?

As options are granted to directors at no cost to them, the directors have an incentive to take risks when these options are 'underwater' (that is, when they cannot be exercised at a profit). By taking risks, there is a prospect of a rise in share prices and resulting benefits. If, on the other hand, by taking risks there is a fall in share prices, the directors will incur no financial loss.

Where share options are exercised, the directors may find themselves holding a large proportion of their total wealth in the form of company equity. The concentration of wealth in this form may have a number of unintended consequences. For example, it may lead to risk-averse behaviour as directors may be concerned with maintaining their wealth intact. This behaviour may not, however, find favour with the shareholders, who are likely to have a more diversified portfolio of investments and so may be more willing to take risks.

Share option schemes are based on the assumption that shareholders are concerned with share price increases and that directors' behaviour and incentives should reflect this concern. An excessive focus on share price, however, may not be in the best interests of shareholders. Share price represents only one part of the shareholders' total return from the company: the other part is dividend income.

Activity 12.26

How might directors behave as a result of this focus on share price increases rather than dividends?

There is a risk that this may lead the directors to restrict dividend payments so that profits are retained to fuel share price growth. Indeed, as directors are rewarded on the basis of share price growth rather than dividend growth, they have an incentive to act in this way. (This potential problem has led some companies to incorporate dividend protection conditions in the share option schemes offered to directors.)

Using similar reasoning, it can be argued that directors also have an incentive to have the company re-purchase its own shares as this too may lead to increases in share price.

In the UK, directors' share options have declined in popularity, which is partly due to the changes in the corporate governance environment. An influential report on directors' remuneration discouraged the use of share option schemes and a number of large institutional investors have voiced their concern over their cost and effectiveness. Furthermore, international accounting standards now require the 'fair value' of share option schemes to be included in the financial statements. Shareholders can now see more clearly the cost incurred by granting share options as it is shown as a charge against profits.

Share option schemes are open to abuse. The particular forms of abuse that have been identified usually relate to the conditions of the share option scheme and to the pricing of options. A share option scheme will often include a condition that certain performance targets, such as earnings per share, must be met before the directors can exercise their options. There have been allegations, however, that some companies have set performance targets too low for them to have any real incentive effect.

The pricing of options has often been a target for manipulation by unscrupulous individuals and, in the US, several scandals have been unearthed. Some high-profile US companies have been found to have reissued share options to directors at a lower price when the share price of the company fell below the option price. This practice effectively eliminates any risks for directors and may also eliminate any incentive effect that share options may have. (See reference 17 at the end of the chapter.)

Activity 12.27

Can you think of any circumstances under which reissuing share options to directors at a lower price might be justified?

It is sometimes argued that, by 're-pricing' options in this way, it may re-incentivise directors, particularly when stock market prices are falling.

Real World 12.12 describes one high-profile case concerning the re-pricing of options.

Real World 12.12

Buy now at Ebay

In a move likely to rekindle the debate over controversial pay practices in Silicon Valley, Ebay yesterday asked its shareholders for permission to reset the terms of its employee stock [share] options. The plan would allow employees whose options are 'underwater', or have exercise prices that are significantly higher than the current share price, to exchange them for restricted stock [share] units.

Re-pricing stock options is controversial because it benefits employees even as shareholders suffer from a depressed share price. Despite its unpopularity on Wall Street, it became common during the technology bust earlier this decade. Now, with the share prices of technology companies down because of the recession, options re-pricing may become common once again.

In January, Google unveiled a similar plan, responding to its own devalued share price. Sandeep Aggarwal, an analyst with Collins Stewart, said he believed additional companies would follow suit. 'I think there will be several more technology companies to do this,' he said. The window of opportunity to exchange under the Google plan ran out yesterday and the company said employees exchanged about 93 per cent for new options with a lower exercise price.

Stock options, a common part of Silicon Valley pay packages, are meant to encourage employees to work hard, stay with a company, and share in its profits. But when the market price of the share dips below the exercise price, the options lose their value.

In a filing with the US Securities Exchange Commission, Ebay said the plan would help boost morale in the company: 'Because of the continued challenging economic environment and the uncertain impact of our efforts to change our business, we believe these underwater stock options are no longer effective as incentives to motivate and retain our employees.'

 Source: 'Ebay seeks to alter terms of stock options', *Financial Times*, 11/03/2009 (Gelles, D),

An even more controversial practice is when directors benefit from the backdating of options. One study found that 1,400 directors of 460 US companies benefited from the backdating of share options to the lowest price in a monthly period. (See reference 18 at the end of the chapter.)

ASSESSING BOARD PERFORMANCE

It was mentioned earlier that the performance of the board should be subject to regular evaluation. This raises the question as to who should carry out the evaluation. The choice is effectively between the board members themselves or an external party, such as a firm of management consultants. In practice, it seems that boards prefer self-evaluation. The UK Code, however, states that, for larger companies, an external evaluation should be undertaken at least every three years.

Activity 12.28

What are the advantages and disadvantages of board members, rather than an external party, evaluating board performance?

The main advantage is that the board members have an intimate knowledge of the company's business and of board operations. They should therefore be in a position to ask more searching questions. A further advantage is that there is no risk that confidentiality will be breached.

A disadvantage is that shareholders might view this as being rather too cosy an arrangement. They may feel that an external party would provide a more objective and a more rigorous assessment of board performance. This may give more credibility to the process (although the cost is likely to be much higher).

A second question raised concerns the areas of performance that should be evaluated. As the evaluation of board performance is a fairly new process, there is still no consensus on this matter. However, some possible areas, based on the UK Corporate Governance Code and other sources of good practice are set out in Table 12.1.

Table 12.1 Evaluating board performance

Company objectives	• Are the objectives of the company clearly set out? • Is the board fully committed to these objectives? • Are the objectives used as a framework for board decisions? • Is there a regular board review of progress towards the achievement of the objectives?
Controlling the company	• Is the system of internal control and reporting regularly reviewed by the board? • Are the risk management and reporting systems regularly reviewed by the board?
Board structure and roles	• Are the roles and responsibilities of the board clearly defined? • Is the relationship between the board and key board committees appropriate and clear? • Are the roles of the chairman and non-executive directors appropriate and clear?
Board meetings	• Are board meetings called with sufficient frequency to permit timely decisions? • Is relevant material, including written agendas and minutes of previous meetings, sent to directors prior to a board meeting? • Are all directors required to attend board meetings and what is their attendance record? • Do the discussions at board meetings focus on strategic rather than operational issues? • Are urgent problems arising between board meetings properly managed and reported?
Board composition	• Is there a separation of the roles of chairman and chief executive? • Does the board reflect an appropriate balance between executive and non-executive directors? • Does the board membership reflect an appropriate mix of age, skills and experience? • Is the membership of important board committees, such as remuneration and audit committees, appropriate? • Do the tenure agreements of board members provide the opportunity to refresh the board over time?
Board discussions and decisions	• Does the board work together in an effective manner? • Do board discussions result in appropriate decisions being made? • Are board decisions implemented and monitored? • Are board members given the time and opportunity to express their views on key issues? • Is the contribution of all directors at board meetings satisfactory? • Are board discussions and decisions dominated by key individuals?
Board relations with shareholders	• Are there appropriate policies in place for communicating with shareholders? • Are the communication channels established between the board and institutional and private shareholders appropriate? • Are shareholders satisfied that their views are heard and considered by the board?
Board appointments and development	• Are rigorous procedures in place for the appointment of new directors? • Are there clearly defined and appropriate procedures in place for appraising the performance of individual directors? • Are appropriate training and development programmes (including induction programmes) available to board members? • Has the board developed clear succession plans?

IS IT WORTH IT?

Corporate governance rules and practices contribute further to the administrative burden imposed on large companies. To achieve high standards of corporate governance, additional management, training and disclosure costs will be incurred. The key issue, however, is whether these additional costs are outweighed by the benefits gained. Although potential benefits have been briefly mentioned at various points in the chapter, it may be useful to consider them in a little more detail.

We have seen that corporate governance rules and practices aim to provide greater transparency in the way in which a company conducts its business. This should help to reduce uncertainty in the minds of the various stakeholders, by providing a clearer picture of how a company is managed and how it has performed. We have also seen that corporate governance involves creating systems for monitoring and controlling the behaviour of directors. This should result in better-managed companies and a reduced risk that funds will be misapplied by the directors.

Corporate governance rules and practices should provide reassurance to the various stakeholders and should improve the reputation of the company. This should give providers of finance greater confidence to invest. Raising finance should become easier and the costs of finance may be reduced. Employees, customers, suppliers and the general public should also have greater trust and confidence in their dealings with companies. By strengthening relations with the various groups mentioned, the long-term sustainability of the company may be enhanced.

In practice, standards of corporate governance will vary between companies. This provides an opportunity for an individual company to use its commitment to high standards of corporate governance as a source of competitive advantage. Providers of finance and other stakeholders may differentiate companies according to the standards of corporate governance adopted.

THE RISE OF SHAREHOLDER ACTIVISM

Improving corporate governance has tended to focus on developing a framework of rules. Whilst rules are important, it is also important for shareholders to play their part by actively monitoring and controlling the behaviour of directors. In this section, we identify the main shareholders of listed companies and discuss their role in establishing good corporate governance. We also consider why there has been greater shareholder activism in recent years.

Who are the main shareholders?

Real World 12.13 provides some impression of the ownership of London Stock Exchange listed shares.

Going overseas

The breakdown of ownership of UK listed shares as at 31 December 2010 is as shown in Figure 12.8.

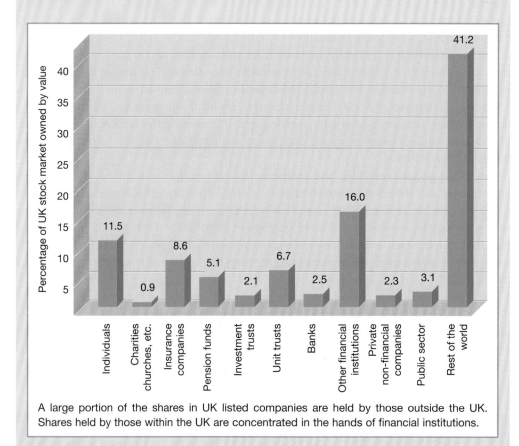

A large portion of the shares in UK listed companies are held by those outside the UK. Shares held by those within the UK are concentrated in the hands of financial institutions.

Figure 12.8 Beneficial ownership of UK shares by UK investors, 31 Dec 2010

Looking at the changes in the ownership of listed shares in recent years shows two striking features:

1 The value of listed shares owned by overseas residents has gone up progressively from 30.7 per cent in 1998 to 41.2 per cent in 2010; and
2 The value of listed shares held by UK individuals has fallen from 16.7 per cent in 1998 to 11.5 per cent in 2010. Share ownership is becoming increasingly concentrated in the hands of large financial institutions.

Source: Ownership of UK Quoted Shares 2010, Office for National Statistics.

The rise of the institutions does not mean that individuals have less investment in listed shares. It is simply that individuals are now tending to invest through the institutions, for example by making pension contributions, rather than by buying shares directly. Ultimately, all of the investment finance must come from individuals.

This concentration of ownership of listed shares means that financial institutions have enormous voting power and, as a result, the potential to exercise huge influence over the way in which Stock Exchange companies are directed and controlled. In the past, however, they have been reluctant to exercise this power and have been criticised for being too passive and for allowing the directors of companies too much independence.

Most financial institutions have chosen to take a non-interventionist approach and have preferred to confine their investment activities to determining whether to buy, hold or sell shares in particular companies. They appear to have taken the view that the costs of actively monitoring directors and trying to influence their decisions are too high in relation to the likely benefits. It is also worth pointing out that these costs are borne by the particular financial institution that chooses to undertake the monitoring whereas the benefits are spread across all of the company's shareholders. (This phenomenon is often referred to as the 'free-rider' problem.)

Waking the sleeping giants

In recent years, however, financial institutions have begun to play a more active role in corporate governance. More time is being devoted to monitoring the actions of directors and in engaging with the directors over key decisions. This change of heart has occurred for a variety of reasons. One important reason is that the increasing concentration of share ownership has made it more difficult for financial institutions simply to walk away from an investment in a poorly performing company by selling its shares.

Activity 12.29

Why might it be difficult for financial institutions to simply sell their shares?

A substantial number of shares may be held and so a decision to sell would have a significant impact on the market price, leading to heavy losses.

A further reason why it may be difficult to sell is that a company's shares may be included in a stock market index (such as the FTSE 100 or FTSE 250). Certain types of financial institutions, such as investment trusts or unit trusts, may offer investments that are designed to 'track' the particular index. They may, therefore, become locked into a particular company's shares in order to reflect the index. In both situations outlined, therefore, a financial institution may have little choice but to stick with the shares held and try to improve performance by trying to influence the actions and decisions of the directors.

It is also worth mentioning that financial institutions have experienced much greater competitive pressures in recent years. There have been increasing demands from clients for them to demonstrate their investment skills and, thereby, justify their fees, by either outperforming benchmarks or beating the performance of similar financial institutions. These increased competitive pressures may be due, at least in part, to the fact that economic conditions have not favoured investors in the recent past; they have experienced a period of relatively low stock market returns. Whatever the reason, the increased pressure to enhance the wealth of their clients has led financial institutions, in turn, to become less tolerant towards underperforming boards of directors.

The regulatory environment has also favoured greater activism on the part of financial institutions. The UK Corporate Governance Code, for example, urges institutional shareholders to use their votes and to enter into a dialogue with companies.

What might a financial institution wish to discuss with the directors of a company? Try to identify at least two financial and two non-financial aspects of the company.

Financial institutions are likely to take an interest in various aspects of a company. Some of the more important include:

- objectives and strategies adopted;
- trading and profit performance;
- internal controls;
- policies regarding mergers and acquisitions;
- major investments and disinvestments;
- adherence to the recommendations of the UK Corporate Governance Code;
- corporate social responsibilities; and
- directors' incentive schemes and remuneration.

This is not an exhaustive list. As shareholders of the company, anything that might have an impact on their wealth should be a matter of concern.

It is worth pointing out that listed companies have become more vulnerable to takeover, particularly by private equity funds. Takeovers very often lead to existing directors losing their positions. This makes the directors particularly sensitive to the views and aspirations of the large shareholders that have the power to resist a takeover by refusing to sell their shares.

Forms of activism

It is important to be clear as to what is meant by the term 'shareholder activism' as it can take various forms. In its simplest form it involves taking a more active role in voting for or against the resolutions put before the annual general meeting or any extraordinary general meeting of the company. This form of activism is seen by the government as being vital to good corporate governance. The government is keen to see a much higher level of participation than currently exists and expects institutional shareholders to exercise their right to vote. In the past, financial institutions have often indicated their dissent by abstaining from a vote rather than outright opposition to a resolution. There is some evidence, however, that they are now more prepared to use their vote to oppose resolutions of the board of directors. Much of the evidence, however, remains anecdotal rather than based on formal research.

A particularly rich source of contention between shareholders and directors concerns directors' remuneration and there have been several shareholder revolts over this issue. **Real World 12.14** provides an example of a fairly recent falling out.

Real World 12.14

Revolting shareholders

Sly Bailey, the chief executive of Trinity Mirror who was facing a shareholder revolt about her £1.7m pay package, unexpectedly handed in her notice to the board on Thursday. A statement from the company said that Ms Bailey, who has held the job for ten years, would leave by the end of the year.

Ms Bailey's departure followed a meeting of directors, who had held talks with investors earlier on Thursday. Aviva Global Investors, a top three shareholder with 11.9 per cent, had threatened to make public its opposition before the weekend. On Wednesday, the Financial Times reported that investors were unhappy about her pay package and were planning a revolt at the company's annual meeting next week.

One investor said the board had been involved in discussions for several weeks about concerns over her pay package, but talks broke down when it became clear that Ms Bailey was unhappy with any real changes proposed to her pay. One investor said 'she helped to bring everything to a head and wrote her own exit'. The next question is what exit terms she gets, he added.

Investors in the publisher of the Daily Mirror and The People have repeatedly demanded a substantial cut in Ms Bailey's pay in the light of the group's market capitalisation, which has dwindled from £1.1bn when she joined in 2003 to £83.7m currently. Trinity has paid no dividend since 2008.

The board has been in discussions with a number of leading institutions in recent weeks over limiting the size of Ms Bailey's potential bonus, ensuring it is reinvested in Trinity shares as well as aligning her long-term incentives more closely to the share price. However, the board's proposals have so far failed to appease angry shareholders.

Source: 'Sly Bailey to leave Trinity Mirror' (Fenton, B, Davoudi, S and Burgess, K) FT.com, 3 May 2012.

Although shareholder revolts are widely reported and catch the newspaper headlines, they do not happen very often. Nevertheless, the benefits for shareholders of flexing their muscles and voting against resolutions put forward by the directors may go beyond their immediate, intended objective: other boards of directors may take note of shareholder dissatisfaction and adjust their behaviour in order to avoid a similar fate. The cost of voting need not be high as there are specialist agencies which offer research and advice to financial institutions on how their votes should be cast.

Another form of activism involves meetings and discussions between representatives of a particular financial institution and the board of directors of a company. This requires a fairly high degree of involvement with the company and some of the larger financial institutions have dedicated teams for this purpose. This can be, therefore, a costly exercise. **Real World 12.15** reveals the approach taken by one major financial institution.

Real World 12.15

Getting active

Fidelity is one of the UK's largest investment fund managers. Its approach to engaging with investee companies is as follows:

> We hold regular meetings with companies to discuss specific results or events as well as a more informal dialogue incorporating site visits and other research initiatives. Regular access to executive management is a key part of FIL's investment process and we encourage managers to provide regular trading updates to the market in order to enhance this dialogue as much as possible.
>
> On occasion our views will differ from those of management and where this is accompanied by a failure to achieve our reasonable expectations for shareholder return we will consider promoting change. Our specific response will be determined on a case-by-case basis and we will weigh up the relative merit of intervention or a sale of the shares. Typically we will choose to intervene to promote change when the expected benefits of intervention (through increased returns to our investors) outweigh the anticipated cost.

Source: Extracts taken from Stewardship, Corporate Governance, Fidelity, www.fidelity.co.uk, accessed 12 May 2012.

Meetings between financial institutions and the managers of investee companies can be a useful mechanism for exchanging views and for gaining a greater understanding of the needs and motivations of each party. This may help to pre-empt public argument between the board of directors and financial institutions, which is rarely the best way to resolve issues.

The final form of activism involves intervention in the affairs of the company. This, however, can be very costly, depending on the nature of the problem. Where strategic and operational issues raise concerns, intervention can be very costly indeed. Identifying the weaknesses and problems relating to these issues requires a detailed understanding of the nature of the business. This implies close monitoring by relevant experts who are able to analyse the issues and then propose feasible solutions. The costs associated with such an exercise would normally be prohibitive, although the costs may be mitigated through some kind of collective action by financial institutions.

Not all forms of intervention in the affairs of a company, however, need be costly. Where, for example, there are corporate governance issues to be addressed, such as a failure to adhere to the recommendations of the UK Corporate Governance Code, a financial institution may nominate individuals for appointment as non-executive directors who can be relied upon to see that necessary changes are made. This should involve relatively little cost for the financial institution.

The main forms of shareholder activism are summarised in Figure 12.9.

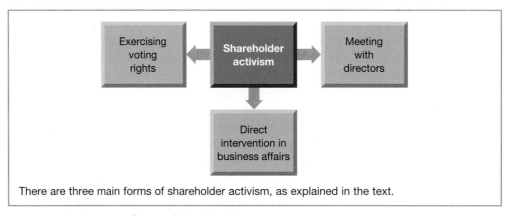

There are three main forms of shareholder activism, as explained in the text.

Figure 12.9 The main forms of shareholder activism

In July 2010 the Financial Reporting Council issued the UK Stewardship Code, which aims to improve the quality of engagement between financial institutions and investee businesses. **Real World 12.16** sets out the main elements of this code.

Real World 12.16

Active investing

The UK Stewardship Code sets out good practice concerning the dialogue between financial institutions and investee businesses. The code states that financial institutions should:

■ publicly disclose their policy on how they will discharge their stewardship responsibilities;
■ have a robust policy on managing conflicts of interest in relation to stewardship, and publicly disclose this policy;

- monitor their investee companies;
- establish clear guidelines on when and how they will escalate their activities, as a method of protecting and enhancing shareholder value;
- be willing to act collectively with other investors where appropriate;
- have a clear policy on voting and disclosure of voting activity;
- report periodically on their stewardship and voting activities.

Source: UK Stewardship Code, frc.org.uk, p. 4.

The future of shareholder activism

The rise of shareholder activism raises two important questions that have yet to be answered. First, is it simply a passing phenomenon? It is no coincidence that shareholder activism took root during a period when stock market returns were fairly low. There is a risk that financial institutions will become less active and less vigilant in monitoring companies when stock market returns improve. Secondly, does shareholder activism really make a difference to corporate performance? Early research in the US was not encouraging for those who urge financial institutions to take a more active approach. However, a recent study of one active fund in the UK suggests that abnormal returns may be made by institutions engaging with a company. (See reference 19 at the end of the chapter.) Further research is required and so we may have to wait some while for a clear picture to emerge.

Self-assessment question 12.1

The board of directors of Hexworthy Publishers plc recently endured a stormy annual general meeting of shareholders. During this meeting, the directors were subjected to intense scrutiny and criticism. Two of the non-executive directors were not re-elected for office by shareholders and all members of the remuneration committee resigned when a proposed new long-term share incentive plan for directors was comprehensively rejected.

At the meeting, shareholders expressed grave concerns over the way in which the company was being managed and felt that they were not being properly informed of key decisions. They were also concerned that the share price had fallen significantly over the past three years while directors' remuneration had increased significantly over the same period.

The board of directors met to decide how to respond to the anger of shareholders. At this meeting, it was decided to appoint Parix Consulting to carry out a thorough review of board performance. Parix Consulting would also be charged with advising the directors on the composition of the new Remuneration Committee and the ways in which communications between shareholders and the board could be improved.

Required:
Assume that you are a partner in Parix Consulting.

(a) Identify the sources of information that may be used to help evaluate the performance of the board of directors. (Use the checklist set out in Table 12.1 as the basis for carrying out this task.)
(b) Suggest a possible composition for the remuneration committee that may help to restrain excessive pay awards to executive directors.
(c) Set out recommended forms of communication with the shareholders, which incorporate corporate governance rules and good practice, for consideration by the board of directors.

A solution to this question can be found in Appendix C.

The main points of this chapter may be summarised as follows:

Corporate governance

- Corporate governance issues arise because of the separation of ownership from control of the company.

- Corporate governance rules are based around the principles of disclosure, accountability and fairness.

- The UK Corporate Governance Code, which applies to UK Stock Exchange listed companies, adopts a 'comply-or-explain' approach.

The board of directors

- The board governs the company on behalf of the shareholders.

- It is responsible for setting the strategic direction, exercising control and nurturing relations with shareholders and others.

- The chairman must lead and manage the board of directors.

- The chairman's role involves trying to ensure that the board operates effectively, providing advice and support to directors, communicating with shareholders and trying to ensure that the performance of the board and the directors is subject to regular scrutiny.

- The UK Corporate Governance Code states that the roles of chairman and chief executive should not be occupied by the same person. Furthermore, the chief executive should not go on to become chairman of the same company.

- The board is made up of executive and non-executive directors, all of which have the same legal obligation to the shareholders of the company.

Non-executive directors

- Non-executive directors are part-time and do not engage in the day-to-day running of the company.

- This more detached role allows them to take a more objective view of the issues confronting the company.

- Non-executive directors are meant to contribute to the main tasks of the board identified earlier and will play a key role in board committees concerned with the nomination of directors, the remuneration of executive directors and the integrity of financial statements.

- The role of non-executive directors contains the potential for conflict between the need to work with executive directors as part of a team and the need to monitor and assess the performance of executive directors on behalf of the shareholders.

The audit process

- An external audit is required by all but the smallest companies.

- External auditors are appointed by, and report to, the shareholders and their role is to examine the annual financial statements that have been prepared by the directors.

- Many large companies have an internal audit function, the main purpose of which is to provide the directors with reassurance concerning the reliability of the company's control and financial reporting systems.

- The UK Corporate Governance Code states that an audit committee should be created with delegated authority for ensuring that financial reporting and internal control principles are properly applied and for maintaining an appropriate relationship with the external auditors.

- The terms of reference of the committee will be determined by the board of directors.

- An audit committee report will be prepared for shareholders and presented at the AGM.

Remunerating directors

- The UK Corporate Governance Code states that directors' remuneration should be sufficient to recruit and retain directors of the right calibre and that a significant proportion of total remuneration should be linked to performance.

- The remuneration package of executive directors will usually have a fixed element and a variable element, with the latter being linked to the achievement of performance targets.

- The remuneration committee is the cornerstone of the UK Corporate Governance Code's attempt to ensure that directors' rewards are appropriate.

- Various problems in the way in which a remuneration committee functions may have contributed to excessive rewards being paid to directors.

- Performance targets should be consistent with the overall aims of the company, align the interests of directors with those of shareholders, reflect the achievement of the directors and be robust.

- TSR (total shareholder return) measures changes in shareholder wealth. To assess relative performance, similar companies must be used as a benchmark.

- EVA® (economic value added) indicates whether the returns generated exceed the returns required by investors. It relies on conventional financial statements to measure the wealth created but adjusts these to reflect the conservative bias in accounting measurement.

- EPS (earnings per share) can be used as a performance target by setting a particular level of growth required.

- Share options may be used to reward directors. However, these have been criticised for their failing to align the interests of directors with those of shareholders.

- Most listed public companies use a variety of measures and incentives to reward executive directors rather than relying on a single measure.

Assessing board performance

- The board should be subject to regular evaluation, which may be carried out by the board itself or by an external party, such as a firm of management consultants.

- Areas of performance to be evaluated may include achievement of company objectives, control exercised over the company's activities, board structure and roles, board meetings, board composition, board discussions and decisions, relations with shareholders and board appointments and development.

MyAccountingLab

Go to www.myaccountinglab.com to check your understanding of the chapter, create a personalised study plan, and maximise your revision time

KEY TERMS

chairman p. 422	**nomination committee** p. 427
executive directors p. 422	**remuneration committee** p. 427
non-executive directors p. 422	**external audit** p. 436
UK Corporate Governance Code p. 423	**internal audit** p. 437
executive committee p. 426	**earnings management** p. 443
chief executive officer p. 426	**total shareholder return (TSR)** p. 449
audit committee p. 427	**economic value added (EVA®)** p. 451
risk management committee p. 427	**directors' share options** p. 454

REFERENCES

1 OECD, *Corporate Governance: Improving Competitiveness and Access to Capital in Global Markets*, report by Business Sector Advisory Group on Corporate Governance, Organisation for Economic Co-operation and Development (OECD), 1998, p. 14

2 Kimbell, D. and Neff, T., 'Separating the roles of chairman and chief executive: Looking at both sides of the debate', *Spencer Stuart Research and Insight*, July 2006, p. 2

3 Stiles, P. and Taylor, B., *Boards at Work*, Oxford University Press, 2001, p. 108

4 Owen, G. and Kirchmaier, T., *The Changing Role of the Chairman: Impact of Corporate Governance Reform in the UK 1995–2005 on Role, Board Compensation and Appointment*, March 2006

5 Plender, J., 'Banks, bonuses and bad accountancy', FT.com, 25 March 2012

6 Haigney, N., 'Relationship between audit committee and internal audit', HM Treasury, www.nationalschools.gov.uk

7 Independent Audit Ltd, *Audit Committee Reporting in 2005*, www.boydeninterim.co.uk

8 Sulkowicz, K., 'New organisational and psychological challenges of the audit committee', *Audit Committee Quarterly*, Audit Committee Institute, Issue 8, 2003

9 Reported in Tucker, S., 'UK chiefs reluctant to take on audit role', FT.com, 30 January 2005

10 Girma, S., Thompson, S. and Wright, P., 'Corporate governance reforms and executive compensation determination: Evidence from the UK', *The Manchester School*, Vol. 75, 2007, pp. 65–81

11 Main, B., Jackson, C., Pymm, J. and Wright, V., 'Questioning the remuneration committee process', working paper, 21 February 2007

12 Lincoln, D., Young, D., Wilson, T. and Whiteley, P., *The Role of the Board Remuneration Committee*, PARC Research Report, March 2006

13 Jenson, M. and Murphy, K., *Remuneration: Where We've Been, How We Got Here, What Are the Problems and How to Fix Them*, European Corporate Governance Institute Working Papers in Finance, 2004, p. 22

14 Pope, P. and Young, S., 'Executive share options: An investor's guide', www.manifest.co.uk

15 Bender, R., 'Just rewards for a new approach to pay', *Financial Times*, 2 June 2005

16 Buffet, W., *Annual Report to Shareholders*, Berkshire Hathaway, Inc., 1985, p. 12

17 Monks, R. and Minow, N., *Corporate Governance*, 2nd edn, Blackwell, 2001, p. 226

18 Quoted in Guerrera, F., 'Study links directors to options scandal', *Financial Times*, 18 December 2006

19 Becht, M., Franks, J., Mayer, C. and Rossi, S., 'Returns to shareholder activism: Evidence from a Clinical Study of the Hermes UK Focus Fund', *The Review of Financial Studies*, Vol. 23, Issue 3, 2010, pp. 3093–3129

FURTHER READING

If you would like to explore the topics covered in this chapter in more depth, we recommend the following:

Elliott, B. and Elliott, J., *Financial Accounting and Reporting*, 15th edn, Financial Times Prentice Hall, 2011, Chapter 31

Mallin, C., *Corporate Governance*, 3rd edn, OUP, 2010, Chapters 3, 6, 8 and 9

Monks, R. and Minow, N., *Corporate Governance*, 5th edn, John Wiley and Sons Ltd, 2011, Chapters 2 to 4

Solomon, J., *Corporate Governance and Accountability*, 3rd edn, John Wiley and Sons Ltd, 2010, Chapters 3 to 6

REVIEW QUESTIONS

Solutions to these questions can be found in Appendix D.

12.1 What are the main tasks of the board of directors?

12.2 What are the benefits of separating the roles of chairman and chief executive?

12.3 A large public company wishes to improve its payroll accounting systems and is seeking outside help to do this. The external auditors of the company are a large firm of accountants that has a consultancy arm. What are the advantages and disadvantages of allowing the external auditors to undertake this task?

12.4 Why have institutional shareholders become more active in corporate governance issues in recent years?

EXERCISES

Exercises 12.4 and 12.5 are more advanced than 12.1 to 12.3. Solutions to the exercises with coloured numbers are given in Appendix E.

If you wish to try more exercises, visit the students' side of the Companion Website and MyAccountingLab.

12.1 Identify four ways in which the independence of an auditor of a large listed company may be strengthened.

12.2 Assume that the chairman of the board of directors of a large public listed company has asked you to develop a set of criteria against which the performance of a non-executive director could be appraised. Try to identify at least six criteria, based on the discussion of the role found in the chapter, which you might select.

12.3 Reviewing the risk management systems within a company goes beyond the traditional role of internal audit. What changes may have to be made to the internal audit function to enable it to carry out this enhanced role?

12.4 The board of directors of a listed company is likely to place considerable emphasis on maintaining good communications and strong relationships with its institutional shareholders. What are the main benefits and problems of doing this?

12.5 The newly appointed chairman of Vorak plc has been told that considerable tension and suspicion exists between the executive and non-executive directors on the board. The executive directors question the competence of the non-executive directors and the non-executive directors believe that important information is being withheld from them. Assuming that the concerns of each group are well founded, what advice would you give to the chairman concerning how to ease the tension and promote a better working relationship between the two groups?

INTRODUCTION

In Chapters 2 and 3, we saw how the financial transactions of a business may be recorded by making a series of entries on the statement of financial position (balance sheet) and/or the income statement. Each of these entries had its corresponding 'double', meaning that both sides of the transaction were recorded. However, adjusting the financial statements, by hand, for each transaction can be very messy and confusing. With a reasonably large number of transactions it is pretty certain to result in mistakes.

For businesses whose accounting systems are on a computer, this problem is overcome because suitable software can deal with a series of 'plus' and 'minus' entries very reliably. Where the accounting system is not computerised, however, it would be helpful to have some more practical way of keeping accounting records. Such a system not only exists but, before the advent of the computer, was the routine way of keeping accounting records. In fact, the system had been in constant use for recording business transactions since medieval times. It is this system that is explained below. We should be clear that the system we are going to consider follows exactly the same rules as those that we have already met. Its distinguishing feature is its ability to provide those keeping accounting records by hand with a methodical approach that allows each transaction to be clearly identified and errors to be minimised.

Learning outcomes

When you have completed this appendix, you should be able to:

- explain the basic principles of double-entry bookkeeping;
- write up a series of business transactions and balance the accounts;
- extract a trial balance and explain its purpose;
- prepare a set of financial statements from the underlying double-entry accounts.

THE BASICS OF DOUBLE-ENTRY BOOKKEEPING

When we record accounting transactions by hand, we use a recording system known as **double-entry bookkeeping**. This system does not use plus and minus entries on the face of a statement of financial position and income statement to record a particular transaction, in the way described in Chapters 2 and 3. Instead, these are recorded in accounts. An **account** is simply a record of one or more transactions relating to a particular item, such as:

- cash;
- property, plant and equipment;
- borrowings;
- sales revenue;
- rent payable; and
- equity.

A business may keep few or many accounts, depending on the size and complexity of its operations. Broadly, businesses tend to keep a separate account for each item that appears in either the income statement or the statement of financial position.

An example of an account, in this case the cash account, is as follows:

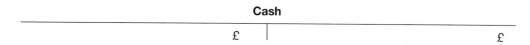

Cash

| £ | | £ |

We can see that an account has three main features:

- a title indicating the item to which it relates;
- a left-hand side, known as the **debit** side; and
- a right-hand side, known as the **credit** side.

One side of an account will record increases in the particular item and the other will record decreases. This, of course, is slightly different from the approach we used when adjusting the financial statements. When adjusting the statement of financial position, for example, we put a reduction in an asset or claim in the same column as any increases, but with a minus sign against it. However, when accounts are used, a reduction is shown on the opposite side of the account.

The side on which an increase or decrease is shown will depend on the nature of the item to which the account relates. For example, an account for an asset, such as cash, will show increases on the left-hand (debit) side of the account and decreases on the right-hand (credit) side. However, for claims (that is, equity and liabilities) it is the other way around. An increase in the account for equity or for a liability will be shown on the right-hand (credit) side and a decrease will be shown on the left-hand (debit) side.

To understand why this difference exists, we should recall (from Chapter 2) that the accounting equation is

Assets = Equity + Liabilities

We can see that assets appear on one side of the equation and equity and liabilities appear on the other. Recording transactions in accounts simply expresses this difference in the recording process. Increases in assets are shown on the left-hand side of an account and increases in equity and liabilities are shown on the right-hand side of the account. We should recall (the point made in Chapter 2) that each transaction has two aspects. Thus, when we record a particular transaction, two separate accounts will be affected. Recording transactions in this way is known as double-entry bookkeeping.

It is worth going through a simple example to see how transactions affecting items on the statement of financial position would be recorded under the double-entry bookkeeping system. Suppose a new business started on 1 January with the owner putting £5,000 into a newly opened business bank account, as initial equity. This entry would appear in the cash account as follows:

Cash

	£		£
1 January Equity	5,000		

The corresponding entry would be made in the equity account as follows:

Equity

	£		£
		1 January Cash	5,000

It is usual to show, in each account by way of note, where the other side of the entry will be found. Thus, someone looking at the equity account will know that the £5,000 arose from a receipt of cash. This provides potentially useful information, partly because it establishes a 'trail' that can be followed when checking for errors. Including the date of the transaction provides additional information to the reader of the accounts.

Now suppose that, on 2 January, £600 of the cash is used to buy some inventories. This would affect the cash account as follows:

Cash

	£		£
1 January Equity	5,000	2 January Inventories	600

This cash account, in effect, shows 'positive' cash of £5,000 and 'negative' cash of £600, a net amount of £4,400.

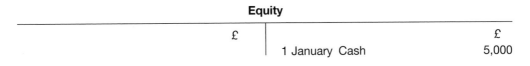

Activity A1.1

As you know, we must somehow record the other side of the transaction involving the acquisition of the inventories for £600. See if you can work out what to do in respect of the inventories.

We must open an account for inventories. Since inventories are assets, an increase in it will appear on the left-hand side of the account, as follows:

Inventories

	£		£
2 January Cash	600		

What we have seen so far highlights the key rule of double-entry bookkeeping: each left-hand entry must have a right-hand entry of equal size. Using the jargon, we can say that *every debit must have a credit*.

It might be helpful at this point to make clear that the words 'debit' and 'credit' are no more than accounting jargon for left and right, respectively. Generally, in English, (that is, when not referring to accounting), people tend to use credit to imply something good and debit something undesirable. Debit and credit have no such implication in accounting. Each transaction requires both a debit entry and a credit one. This is equally true whether the transaction is a 'good' one, like being paid by a credit customer, or a 'bad' one, like having to treat a credit customer's balance as worthless because that customer has gone bankrupt.

RECORDING TRADING TRANSACTIONS

The rules of double entry also extend to 'trading' transactions, that is, making revenue (sales and so on) and incurring expenses. To understand how these transactions are recorded, we should recall (from Chapter 3) that the accounting equation may be extended as follows:

Assets = Equity + (Revenues − Expenses) + Liabilities

This equation can be rearranged so that

Assets + Expenses = Equity + Revenues + Liabilities

We can see that increases in expenses are shown on the same side as assets and this means that they will be dealt with in the same way for recording purposes. Thus, an increase in an expense, such as wages, will be shown on the left-hand (debit) side of the wages account and a decrease will be shown on the right-hand (credit) side. Increases in revenues are shown on the same side as equity and liabilities and so will be dealt with in the same way as them. Thus, an increase in revenue, such as sales, will be shown on the right-hand (credit) side and a decrease will be shown on the left-hand (debit) side.

To summarise, therefore, we can say that

- Debits (left-hand entries) represent increases in assets and expenses and decreases in claims and revenues.
- Credits (right-hand entries) represent increases in claims and revenues and decreases in assets and expenses.

Let us continue with our example by assuming that, on 3 January, the business paid £900 to rent business premises for the three months to 31 March. To record this transaction, we should normally open a 'rent account' and make entries in this account and in the cash account as follows:

Rent

	£		£
3 January Cash	900		

Cash

	£		£
1 January Equity	5,000	2 January Inventories	600
		3 January Rent	900

The fact that assets and expenses are dealt with in the same way should not be altogether surprising since assets and expenses are closely linked. Assets transform into expenses as they are 'used up'. Rent, which, as here, is usually paid in advance, is an asset when it is first paid. It represents the value to the business of being entitled to occupy the premises for the forthcoming period (until 31 March in this case). As the three months progress, this asset becomes an expense; it is 'used up'. We need to remember that the debit entry in the rent account does not necessarily represent either an asset or an expense; it could be a mixture of the two. Strictly, by the end of the day on which it was paid (3 January), £30 would have represented an expense for the three days; the remaining £870 would have been an asset.

As each day passes, an additional £10 (that is, £900/90 (there are 90 days in January, February and March altogether)) will transform from an asset into an expense. As we have already seen, it is not necessary for us to make any adjustment to the rent account as the days pass.

Assume, now, that on 5 January the business sold inventories costing £200 for £300 on credit. As usual, when we are able to identify the cost of the inventories sold at the time of sale, we need to deal with the sale and the cost of sales as two separate issues, each having its own set of debits and credits.

First, let us deal with the sale. We now need to open accounts for both 'sales revenue' and 'trade receivables' – which do not, as yet, exist. The sale gives rise to an increase in revenue and so there is a credit entry in the sales revenue account. The sale also creates an asset of trade receivables and so there is debit entry in trade receivables:

Sales revenue

	£		£
		5 January Trade receivables	300

Trade receivables

	£		£
5 January Sales revenue	300		

Let us now deal with the inventories sold. Since the inventories sold have become the expense 'cost of sales', we need to reduce the figure on the inventories account by making a credit entry and to make the corresponding debit in a 'cost of sales' account, opened for the purpose:

Inventories

	£		£
2 January Cash	600	5 January Cost of sales	200

Cost of sales

	£		£
5 January Inventories	200		

We shall now look at the other transactions for our hypothetical business for the remainder of January. These can be taken to be as follows:

8 January	Bought some inventories on credit costing £800
11 January	Bought some office furniture for £600 cash
15 January	Sold inventories costing £600 for £900, on credit
18 January	Received £800 from trade receivables
21 January	Paid trade payables £500
24 January	Paid wages for the month £400
27 January	Bought inventories on credit for £800
31 January	Borrowed £2,000 from the Commercial Finance Company

Naturally, we shall have to open several additional accounts to enable us to record all of these transactions in any meaningful way. By the end of January, the set of accounts would appear as follows:

Cash

		£			£
1 January	Equity	5,000	2 January	Inventories	600
18 January	Trade receivables	800	3 January	Rent	900
31 January	Comm. Fin. Co.	2,000	11 January	Office furniture	600
			21 January	Trade payables	500
			24 January	Wages	400

Equity

		£			£
			1 January	Cash	5,000

Inventories

		£			£
2 January	Cash	600	5 January	Cost of sales	200
8 January	Trade payables	800	15 January	Cost of sales	600
27 January	Trade payables	800			

Rent

		£		£
3 January	Cash	900		

Sales revenue

	£			£
		5 January	Trade receivables	300
		15 January	Trade receivables	900

Trade receivables

		£			£
5 January	Sales revenue	300	18 January	Cash	800
15 January	Sales revenue	900			

Cost of sales

		£		£
5 January	Inventories	200		
15 January	Inventories	600		

Trade payables

		£			£
21 January	Cash	500	8 January	Inventories	800
			27 January	Inventories	800

Office furniture

		£		£
11 January	Cash	600		

Wages

		£		£
24 January	Cash	400		

Borrowings – Commercial Finance Company

	£			£
		31 January	Cash	2,000

All of the transactions from 8 January onwards are quite similar in nature to those up to that date, which we discussed in detail, and so we should be able to follow them using the date references as a guide.

BALANCING ACCOUNTS AND THE TRIAL BALANCE

Businesses keeping their accounts in the way shown would find it helpful to summarise their individual accounts periodically – perhaps weekly or monthly – for two reasons:

■ to be able to see at a glance how much is in each account (for example, to see how much cash the business has left), and
■ to help to check the accuracy of the bookkeeping so far.

Let us look at the cash account again.

Cash

		£			£
1 January	Equity	5,000	2 January	Inventories	600
18 January	Trade receivables	800	3 January	Rent	900
31 January	Comm. Fin. Co.	2,000	11 January	Office furniture	600
			21 January	Trade payables	500
			24 January	Wages	400

Does this account tell us how much cash the business has at 31 January? The answer is partly yes and partly no.

We do not have a single figure showing the cash **balance** but we can fairly easily deduce this by adding up the debit (receipts) column and deducting the sum of the credit (payments) column. However, it would be better if the current cash balance were provided for us.

To summarise or 'balance' this account, we add up the column with the largest amount (in this case, the debit side) and put this total on *both* sides of the account. We then put in, on the credit side, the figure that will make that side add up to the total that appears in the account. We cannot put in this balancing figure only once, as the double-entry rule would be broken. Thus, to preserve the double entry, we also put it in on the other side of the same account below the totals, as follows:

Cash

		£			£
1 January	Equity	5,000	2 January	Inventories	600
18 January	Trade receivables	800	3 January	Rent	900
31 January	Borrowings	2,000	11 January	Office furniture	600
			21 January	Trade payables	500
			24 January	Wages	400
			31 January	Balance carried down	4,800
		7,800			7,800
1 February	Balance brought down	4,800			

Note that the balance carried down (usually abbreviated to 'c/d') at the end of one period becomes the balance brought down ('b/d') at the beginning of the next. Now we can see at a glance what the present cash position is, without having to do any mental arithmetic.

Try balancing the inventories account and then say what we know about the inventories position at the end of January.

The inventories account will be balanced as follows:

Inventories

	£		£
2 January Cash	600	5 January Cost of sales	200
8 January Trade payables	800	15 January Cost of sales	600
27 January Trade payables	800	31 January Balance c/d	1,400
	2,200		2,200
1 February Balance b/d	1,400		

We can see at a glance that the business held inventories that had cost £1,400 at the end of January. We can also see quite easily how this situation arose.

We can balance all of the other accounts in a similar fashion. However, there is no point in formally balancing accounts that have only one entry at the moment (for example, the equity account) because we cannot summarise one figure; it is already in as summarised a form as it can be. After balancing, the remaining accounts will be as follows:

Equity

	£		£
		1 January Cash	5,000

Rent

	£		£
3 January Cash	900		

Sales revenue

	£		£
31 January Balance c/d	1,200	5 January Trade receivables	300
		15 January Trade receivables	900
	1,200		1,200
		1 February Balance b/d	1,200

Trade receivables

	£		£
5 January Sales revenue	300	18 January Cash	800
15 January Sales revenue	900	31 January Balance c/d	400
	1,200		1,200
1 February Balance b/d	400		

Cost of sales

	£		£
5 January Inventories	200	31 January Balance c/d	800
15 January Inventories	600		
	800		800
1 February Balance b/d	800		

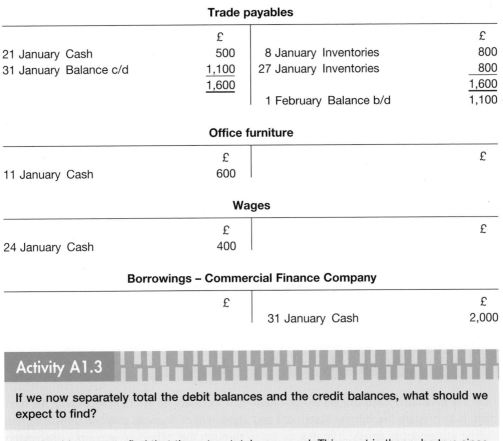

Trade payables

	£		£
21 January Cash	500	8 January Inventories	800
31 January Balance c/d	1,100	27 January Inventories	800
	1,600		1,600
		1 February Balance b/d	1,100

Office furniture

	£		£
11 January Cash	600		

Wages

	£		£
24 January Cash	400		

Borrowings – Commercial Finance Company

	£		£
		31 January Cash	2,000

Activity A1.3

If we now separately total the debit balances and the credit balances, what should we expect to find?

We should expect to find that these two totals are equal. This must in theory be true since every debit entry was matched by an equal-sized credit entry.

Let us see if our expectation in Activity A1.3 works in our example, by listing the debit and credit balances as follows:

	Debits	Credits
	£	£
Cash	4,800	
Inventories	1,400	
Equity		5,000
Rent	900	
Sales revenue		1,200
Trade receivables	400	
Cost of sales	800	
Trade payables		1,100
Office furniture	600	
Wages	400	
Borrowings		2,000
	9,300	9,300

This statement is known as a **trial balance**. The fact that it agrees gives us *some* indication that we have not made bookkeeping errors.

This does not, however, give us total confidence that no error could have occurred. Consider, for example, the transaction that took place on 3 January (paid rent for the month of £900). In each of the following cases, all of which would be a wrong treatment of the transaction, the trial balance would still have agreed:

■ The transaction was completely omitted from the accounts, that is, no entries were made at all.
■ The amount was misread as £9,000 but then (correctly) debited to the rent account and credited to cash.
■ The correct amount was (incorrectly) debited to cash and credited to rent.

Nevertheless, a trial balance that agrees does give some confidence that accounts have been correctly written up.

Activity A1.4

Why do you think the words 'debtor' and 'creditor' are used to describe those who owe money or are owed money by a business?

The answer simply is that debtors have a debit balance (that is, a balance brought down on the debit side) in the books of the business, whereas creditors have a credit balance.

PREPARING THE FINANCIAL STATEMENTS (FINAL ACCOUNTS)

If the trial balance agrees and we are confident that there are no errors in recording, the next stage is to prepare the income statement and statement of financial position. Preparing the income statement is simply a matter of going through the individual accounts, identifying those amounts that represent revenue and expenses of the period, and transferring them to the income statement, which is itself also part of the double-entry system.

We shall now do this for the example we have been using. The situation is complicated slightly for three reasons:

1 As we know, the £900 rent paid during January relates to the three months January, February and March.
2 The business's owner estimates that the electricity used during January is about £110. There is no bill yet from the electricity supply business because it normally bills customers only at the end of each three-month period.
3 The business's owner believes that the office furniture should be depreciated by 20% each year (using the straight-line method).

These three factors need to be taken into account. As we shall see, however, the end-of-period adjustments of these types are very easily handled in double-entry accounts. Let us deal with these three areas first.

The rent account will appear as follows, after we have completed the transfer to the income statement:

Rent

	£		£
3 January Cash	900	31 January Income statement	300
		Balance c/d	600
	900		900
1 February Balance b/d	600		

At 31 January, because two months' rent is still an asset, this is carried down as a debit balance. The remainder (representing January's rent) is credited to the rent account and debited to a newly opened income statement. As we shall see shortly, the £600 debit balance remaining will appear in the 31 January statement of financial position.

Now let us deal with the electricity. The electricity account will be as follows after the transfer to the income statement:

Electricity

	£		£
		31 January Income statement	110

Because there has been no cash payment or other transaction recorded so far for electricity, we do not already have an account for it. It is necessary to open one. We need to debit the income statement with the £110 of electricity used during January and credit the electricity account with the same amount. At 31 January, this credit balance reflects the amount owed by this business to the electricity supplier. Once again, we shall see shortly that this balance will appear on the statement of financial position.

Next we shall consider what is necessary regarding the office furniture. The depreciation for the month will be $20\% \times £600 \times \frac{1}{12}$, that is £10. Normal accounting practice is to charge (debit) this to the income statement, with the corresponding credit going to a 'provision for depreciation of office furniture' account. The latter entry will appear as follows:

Provision for depreciation of office furniture account

	£		£
		31 January Income statement	10

This £10 balance will be reflected in the statement of financial position at 31 January by being deducted from the office furniture itself, as we shall see shortly.

The balances on the following accounts represent straightforward revenue and expenses for the month of January:

- Sales revenue
- Cost of sales
- Wages.

The balances on these accounts will simply be transferred to the income statement.

To transfer balances to the income statement, we simply debit or credit the account concerned, such that any balance amount is eliminated, and make the corresponding credit or debit in the income statement. Take sales revenue, for example. This has a credit balance (because the balance represents a revenue). We must debit the sales revenue account with £1,200 and credit the income statement with the same amount. So a credit balance on the sales revenue account becomes a credit entry in the income statement. For the three accounts, then, we have the following:

Sales revenue

	£		£
31 January Balance c/d	1,200	5 January Trade receivables	300
		15 January Trade receivables	900
	1,200		1,200
31 January Income statement	1,200	1 February Balance b/d	1,200

Cost of sales

	£		£
5 January Inventories	200	31 January Balance c/d	800
15 January Inventories	600		
	800		800
1 February Balance b/d	800	31 January Income statement	800

Wages

	£		£
24 January Cash	400	31 January Income statement	400

The income statement will now look as follows:

Income statement

	£		£
31 January Cost of sales	800	31 January Sales revenue	1,200
31 January Rent	300		
31 January Wages	400		
31 January Electricity	110		
31 January Depreciation	10		

We must now transfer the balance on the income statement (a debit balance of £420).

Activity A1.5

What does the balance on the income statement represent, and where should it be transferred to?

The balance is either the profit or the loss for the period. In this case it is a loss as the total expenses exceed the total revenue. This loss must be borne by the owner, and it must therefore be transferred to the equity account.

The two accounts would now appear as follows:

Income statement

	£		£
31 January Cost of sales	800	31 January Sales revenue	1,200
31 January Rent	300		
31 January Wages	400		
31 January Electricity	110		
31 January Depreciation	10	31 January Equity (loss)	420
	1,620		1,620

Equity

	£		£
31 January Income statement (loss)	420	1 January Cash	5,000
31 January Balance c/d	4,580		
	5,000		5,000
		1 February Balance b/d	4,580

The last thing done was to balance the equity account.

Now all of the balances remaining on accounts represent either assets or claims as at 31 January. These balances can now be used to produce a statement of financial position, as follows:

Statement of financial position as at 31 January

	£
Assets	
Non-current assets	
Property, plant and equipment	
Office furniture: cost	600
depreciation	(10)
	590
Current assets	
Inventories	1,400
Prepaid expense	600
Trade receivables	400
Cash	4,800
	7,200
Total assets	7,790
Equity and liabilities	
Owners' equity	4,580
Non-current liability	
Borrowings	2,000
Current liabilities	
Accrued expense	110
Trade payables	1,100
	1,210
Total equity and liabilities	7,790

The income statement could be written in a more stylish manner, for reporting to users, as follows:

Income statement for the month ended 31 January

	£
Sales revenue	1,200
Cost of sales	(800)
Gross profit	400
Rent	(300)
Wages	(400)
Electricity	(110)
Depreciation	(10)
Loss for the month	(420)

THE LEDGER AND ITS DIVISION

The book in which the accounts are traditionally kept is known as the **ledger**, and 'accounts' are sometimes referred to as 'ledger accounts', even where they are computerised.

In a handwritten accounting system, the ledger is often divided into various sections. This tends to be for three main reasons:

1 Having all of the accounts in one book means that it is only possible for one person at a time to use the accounts, either to make entries or to extract useful information.

2 Dividing the ledger along logical grounds can allow specialisation, so that various individual members of the accounts staff can look after their own part of the system. This can lead to more efficient record-keeping.

3 It can lead to greater security, that is, less risk of error and fraud, by limiting an individual's access to only part of the entire set of accounts.

There are no clear, universal rules on the division of the ledger, but the following division is fairly common:

- *The cash book.* This tends to be all of the accounts relating to cash either loose (often known as *petty cash*) or in the bank.
- *The sales (or trade receivables) ledger.* This contains the accounts of all of the business's individual trade receivables.
- *The purchases (or trade payables) ledger.* This consists of the accounts of all of the business's individual trade payables.
- *The nominal ledger.* These accounts tend to be those of expenses and revenue, for example, sales revenue, wages, rent, and so on.
- *The general ledger.* This contains the remainder of the business's accounts, mainly those to do with non-current assets and long-term finance.

SUMMARY

The main points in this appendix may be summarised as follows:

Double-entry bookkeeping is a system for keeping accounting records by hand, such that a relatively large volume of transactions can be handled effectively and accurately.

- There is a separate account for each asset, claim, expense and revenue that needs to be separately identified.
- Each account looks like a letter T.
- The left-hand (debit) side of the account records increases in assets and expenses and decreases in revenues and claims.
- The right-hand (credit) side records increases in revenues and claims and decreases in assets and expenses.
- There is an equal credit entry in one account for a debit entry in another.
- Double-entry bookkeeping can be used to record day-to-day transactions.
- It can also follow through to generate the income statement.
- The statement of financial position is a list of the net figure (the 'balance') on each of the accounts after appropriate transfers have been made to the income statement.
- The accounts are traditionally kept in a 'ledger', a term that persists even with computerised accounting.
- The ledger is traditionally broken down into several sections, each containing particular types of account.

FURTHER READING

If you would like to explore the topics covered in this appendix in more depth, we recommend the following:

Bebbington, J., Gray, R. and Laughlin, R., *Financial Accounting*, 3rd edn, Thomson Learning, 2001, Chapters 2 to 7

Benedict, A. and Elliott, B., *Practical Accounting*, Financial Times Prentice Hall, 2008, Chapters 2 to 5

Thomas, A. and Ward, A. M., *Introduction to Financial Accounting*, 6th edn, McGraw-Hill, 2009, Chapters 3 to 8

Woof, F. and Sangster, A., *Business Accounting*, 12th edn, Financial Times Prentice Hall, 2011, Volume 1, Chapters 1 to 6

EXERCISES

Solutions to all three of these exercises are given in Appendix E.

A1.1 In respect of each of the following transactions, state in which two accounts an entry must be made and whether the entry is a debit or a credit. (For example, if the transaction were buying inventories for cash, the answer would be debit the inventories account and credit the cash account.)

(a) Bought inventories on credit.
(b) Owner made cash drawings.
(c) Paid interest on business borrowings.
(d) Bought inventories for cash.
(e) Received cash from a credit customer.
(f) Paid wages to employees.
(g) The owner received some cash from a credit customer, which was taken as drawings rather than being paid into the business's bank account.
(h) Paid a credit supplier.
(i) Paid electricity bill.
(j) Made cash sales.

A1.2 **(a)** Record the following transactions in a set of double-entry accounts:

1 February	Lee (the owner) put £6,000 into a newly-opened business bank account to start a new business
3 February	Bought inventories for £2,600 for cash
5 February	Bought some equipment (non-current asset) for cash for £800
6 February	Bought inventories costing £3,000 on credit
9 February	Paid rent for the month of £250
10 February	Paid £240 for electricity for the month
11 February	Paid general expenses of £200
15 February	Sold inventories for £4,000 in cash; the inventories had cost £2,400
19 February	Sold inventories for £3,800 on credit; the inventories had cost 2,300
21 February	Lee withdrew £1,000 in cash for personal use
25 February	Paid £2,000 to trade payables
28 February	Received £2,500 from trade receivables

(b) Balance the relevant accounts and prepare a trial balance (making sure that it agrees).

(c) Prepare an income statement for the month and a statement of financial position at the month end. Assume that there are no prepaid or accrued expenses at the end of the month and ignore any possible depreciation.

A1.3 The following is the statement of financial position of David's business at 1 January of last year.

	£	£
ASSETS		
Non-current assets		
Property, plant and equipment		
Buildings		25,000
Fittings: cost	10,000	
depreciation	(2,000)	8,000
		33,000
Current assets		
Inventories of stationery		140
Trading inventories		1,350
Prepaid rent		500
Trade receivables		1,840
Cash		2,180
		6,010
Total assets		39,010
EQUITY AND LIABILITIES		
Owners' equity		25,050
Non-current liability		
Borrowings		12,000
Current liabilities		
Trade payables		1,690
Accrued electricity		270
		1,960
Total equity and liabilities		39,010

The following is a summary of the transactions that took place during the year:

1 Inventories were bought on credit for £17,220.
2 Inventories were bought for £3,760 cash.
3 Credit sales revenue amounted to £33,100 (cost £15,220).
4 Cash sales revenue amounted to £10,360 (cost £4,900).
5 Wages of £3,770 were paid.
6 Rent of £3,000 was paid. The annual rental amounts to £3,000.
7 £1,070 was paid for electricity.
8 General expenses of £580 were paid.
9 Additional fittings were purchased on 1 January for £2,000. The cash for this was raised from additional borrowings of this amount. The interest rate is 10% a year, the same as for the existing borrowings.
10 £1,000 of the borrowing was repaid on 30 June.
11 Cash received from trade receivables amounted to £32,810.
12 Cash paid to trade payables amounted to £18,150.
13 The owner withdrew £10,400 cash and £560 worth of inventories for private use.

At the end of the year it was found that:

■ The electricity bill for the last quarter of the year for £290 had not been paid.
■ Trade receivables amounting to £260 were unlikely to be received.
■ The value of stationery remaining was estimated at £150. Stationery is included in general expenses.
■ The borrowings carried interest of 10% a year and were unpaid at the year end.

Depreciation is to be taken at 20% on the cost of the fittings owned at the year end. Buildings are not depreciated.

Required:
(a) Open ledger accounts and bring down all of the balances in the opening statement of financial position.
(b) Make entries to record the transactions 1 to 13 (above), opening any additional accounts as necessary.
(c) Open an income statement (part of the double entry, remember). Make the necessary entries for the bulleted list above and the appropriate transfers to the income statement.
(d) List the remaining balances in the same form as the opening statement of financial position (above).

Appendix B
GLOSSARY OF KEY TERMS

Account A section of a double-entry bookkeeping system that deals with one particular asset, claim, expense or revenue. *p. 473*

Accounting The process of identifying, measuring and communicating information to permit informed judgements and decisions by users of the information. *p. 1*

Accounting information system The system used within a business to identify, record, analyse and report accounting information. *p. 10*

Accruals accounting The system of accounting that follows the accruals convention. This is the system followed in drawing up the statement of financial position and income statement. *p. 81*

Accruals convention The convention of accounting that asserts that profit is the excess of revenue over expenses, not the excess of cash receipts over cash payments. *p. 81*

Accrued expenses Expenses that are outstanding at the end of a reporting period. *p. 77*

Acid test ratio A liquidity ratio that relates the liquid assets (usually defined as current assets less inventories) to the current liabilities. *p. 271*

Allotted share capital *See* Issued share capital. *p. 124*

Allowance for trade receivables An amount set aside out of profit to provide for anticipated losses arising from debts (trade receivables) that may prove irrecoverable. *p. 97*

Amortisation A measure of that portion of the cost (or fair value) of a non-current asset that has been consumed during a reporting period. The word 'amortisation' tends to be used where the particular non-current asset is an intangible one, whereas 'depreciation' is normally used with tangible assets. *p. 81*

Assets Resources held by a business that have certain characteristics, such as the ability to provide future benefits. *p. 33*

Associate company A company over which considerable influence, but not full control, may be exercised by another company. *p. 369*

Audit committee A committee of the board of directors whose task is to promote the reliability of the financial reporting systems. *p. 427*

Auditors Professionals whose main duty is to make a report to shareholders as to whether, in their opinion, the financial statements of a company show a true and fair view of performance and position and comply with statutory and financial reporting standard requirements. *p. 170*

AVCO *See* Weighted average cost. *p. 91*

Average inventories turnover period ratio An efficiency ratio that measures the average period for which inventories are held by a business. *p. 263*

Average settlement period for trade payables ratio An efficiency ratio that measures the average time taken for a business to pay its trade payables. *p. 264*

Average settlement period for trade receivables ratio An efficiency ratio that measures the average time taken for trade receivables to pay the amounts owing. *p. 264*

Bad debt An amount owed to the business that is considered to be irrecoverable. *p. 95*

Balance The net of the debit and credit totals in an account in a double-entry bookkeeping system. *p. 479*

Bonus shares Reserves that are converted into shares and issued 'free' to existing shareholders. *p. 122*

Business entity convention The convention that holds that, for accounting purposes, the business and its owner(s) are treated as quite separate and distinct. *p. 47*

Business review Part of the directors' report that helps shareholders to assess how well the directors have performed. It provides an analysis of financial performance, position and cash flows. It also sets out the principal risks and uncertainties facing the business. *p. 171*

Called-up share capital That part of a company's share capital for which the shareholders have been asked to pay the agreed amount. *p. 125*

Capital reserves Reserves that arise from unrealised 'capital' profits or gains rather than from normal realised trading activities. *p. 120*

Capitalisation Carrying forward expenditure as an asset as compared with writing it off as an expense. *p. 226*

Carrying amount The difference between the cost (or fair value) of a non-current asset and the accumulated depreciation relating to the asset. The carrying amount is also referred to as the written-down value (WDV) and the net book value (NBV). *p. 84*

Cash generated from operations (CGO) per ordinary share ratio An investment ratio that relates the cash generated from operations and available to ordinary shareholders to the number of ordinary shares. *p. 295*

Cash generated from operations to maturing obligations ratio A liquidity ratio that compares the cash generated from operations to the current liabilities of the business. *p. 271*

Chairman The person elected by the board of directors to lead the board so as to provide strategic direction for the business and to act in the best interests of shareholders. *p. 422*

Chief executive officer The senior executive director who leads the management team. *p. 426*

Claims Obligations on the part of a business to provide cash or some other benefit to outside parties. *p. 33*

Common-size financial statements Normal financial statements (such as the income statement, statement of financial position and statement of cash flows) that are expressed in terms of some base figure. *p. 303*

Comparability The quality that helps users to identify similarities and differences between items of information. It enhances the usefulness of accounting information. *p. 7*

Conceptual framework The main concepts, or principles, that underpin accounting, which can help in identifying best practice and in developing accounting rules. *p. 169*

Consistency convention The accounting convention that holds that, when a particular method of accounting is selected to deal with a transaction, this method should be applied consistently over time. *p. 95*

Consolidated financial statements *See* Group financial statements. *p. 338*

Consolidating Changing the nominal value of shares to a higher figure (from, say, £0.50 to £1.00) and then reducing the number of shares in issue so that each shareholder has the same total nominal value of shares as before. *p. 119*

Contingent asset A possible asset arising from past events, the existence of which will only be confirmed by future events not wholly within the control of the business. *p. 223*

Contingent liability A possible obligation arising from past events, the existence of which will be only be confirmed by future events not wholly within the control of the business; or a present obligation arising from past events, where either it is not probable that an outflow of resources is needed, or the amount of the obligation cannot be reliably measured. *p. 221*

Conventions of accounting A set of generally accepted rules that accountants tend to follow when preparing financial statements. They tend to have evolved over time in order to deal with practical problems rather than to reflect some theoretical ideal. *p. 14*

Corporate governance Matters concerned with directing and controlling a company. *p. 117*

Corporation tax Taxation that a limited company is liable to pay on its profits. *p. 114*

Cost of sales The cost of the goods sold during a period. Cost of sales can be derived by adding the opening inventories held to the inventories purchases for the period and then deducting the closing inventories held. *p. 70*

Creative accounting Adopting accounting policies to achieve a particular view of performance and position that preparers would like users to see rather than what is a true and fair view. *p. 172*

Credit An entry made in the right-hand side of an account in double-entry bookkeeping. *p. 474*

Current assets Assets that are held for the short term. They include cash itself and other assets that are held for sale or consumption in the normal course of a business's operating cycle. *p. 42*

Current cost accounting (CCA) accounting An approach to preparing financial statements that is concerned with ensuring that the business is able to maintain its scale of operations during a period of inflation. *p. 412*

Current liabilities Liabilities that are expected to be settled within the normal course of the business's operating cycle or within twelve months of the statement of financial position date, or which are held primarily for trading purposes, or for which the business does not have the right to defer settlement beyond twelve months of the statement of financial position date. *p. 44*

Current (or constant) purchasing power (CPP) accounting An approach to preparing financial statements this is concerned with ensuring that the general purchasing power of the owners' investment in the business is maintained during a period of inflation. *p. 410*

Current ratio A liquidity ratio that relates the current assets of the business to the current liabilities. *p. 270*

Debit An entry made in the left-hand side of an account in double-entry bookkeeping. *p. 474*

Depreciation A measure of that portion of the cost (or fair value) of a non-current asset that has been consumed during a reporting period. *p. 81*

Direct method An approach to deducing the cash flows from operating activities, in a statement of cash flows, by analysing the business's cash records. *p. 195*

Directors Individuals who are appointed (normally by being elected by the shareholders) to act as the most senior level of management of a company. *p. 117*

Directors' report A report containing information of a financial and non-financial nature that the directors must produce as part of the annual financial report to shareholders. *p. 171*

Directors' share options A directors' share option scheme gives directors the right, but not the obligation, to buy equity shares in their company at an agreed price. The conditions of the scheme will usually stipulate that the option to buy must be exercised either on, or after, a specified future date. *p. 454*

Discrete method An approach to interim profit measurement that treats the interim period as quite separate and distinct from the annual period. *p. 395*

Discriminate function A boundary line, produced by multiple discriminate analysis, which can be used to identify those businesses that are likely to suffer financial distress and those that are not. *p. 309*

Dividend The transfer of assets (usually cash) made by a company to its shareholders. *p. 118*

Dividend cover ratio An investment ratio that relates the earnings available for dividends to the dividend announced to indicate how many times the former covers the latter. *p. 293*

Dividend payout ratio An investment ratio that relates the dividends announced for the period to the earnings available for dividends that were generated in that period. *p. 293*

Dividend per share An investment ratio that relates the dividends announced for a period to the number of shares in issue. *p. 294*

Dividend yield ratio An investment ratio that relates the cash return from a share to its current market value. *p. 294*

Double-entry bookkeeping A system for recording financial transactions where each transaction is recorded twice, once as a debit and once as a credit. *p. 473*

Dual aspect convention The accounting convention that holds that each transaction has two aspects and that each aspect must be recorded in the financial statements. *p. 49*

Earnings management A term used to describe a situation where a misleading impression of profit performance is provided to external users, normally to benefit directors. *p. 443*

Earnings per share An investment ratio that relates the earnings generated by the business during a period, and available to shareholders, to the number of shares in issue. *p. 295*

Economic value added (EVA®) A measure of business performance that concentrates on wealth generation. It is based on economic profit rather than accounting profit and takes full account of the cost of financing. *p. 451*

Efficient capital market A capital market where prices always rationally reflect all that is known about the commodity (for example, shares) traded in that market. *p. 115*

Equity The owners' claim on the business. In the case of a limited company, it comprises the sum of shares and reserves. *p. 36*

Executive committee A committee of directors given delegated responsibility for developing strategic plans. *p. 426*

Executive directors Directors who are salaried employees with senior management responsibilities. *p. 422*

Expense A measure of the outflow of assets (or increase in liabilities) incurred as a result of generating revenue. *p. 68*

External audit A review by independent professionals, external to the company, to assess whether, in their opinion, the financial statements of a company show a true and fair view of performance and position and comply with statutory and financial reporting standard requirements. *p. 436*

Fair values The values ascribed to assets as an alternative to historic cost. They are usually the current market values (that is, the exchange values in an arm's-length transaction). *p. 54*

Faithful representation The ability of information to be relied on to represent what it purports to represent. This is regarded as a fundamental quality of useful accounting information. *p. 6*

Final accounts The income statement, statement of cash flows and statement of financial position taken together. *p. 33*

Finance lease A financial arrangement where the asset title remains with the owner (the lessor) but the lease agreement transfers virtually all the rewards and risks to the business (the lessee). *p. 229*

Financial accounting The identification, measurement and communication of accounting information for external users (those users other than the managers of the business). *p. 12*

Financial gearing The existence of fixed payment-bearing sources of finance (for example, borrowings) in the capital structure of a business. *p. 276*

First in, first out (FIFO) A method of inventories costing which assumes that the earliest acquired inventories are used (in production or sales) first. *p. 91*

Fully paid shares Shares on which the shareholders have paid the full issue price. *p. 125*

Gearing ratio A ratio that relates long-term fixed-return finance (such as borrowings) to the total long-term finance of the business. *p. 279*

Going concern convention The accounting convention that holds that a business is assumed to continue operations for the foreseeable future, unless there is reason to believe otherwise. In other words, it is assumed that there is no intention, or need, to liquidate the business. *p. 49*

Goodwill arising on consolidation Anything paid in excess of the underlying net asset value of the subsidiary's shares. *p. 345*

Gross profit The amount remaining (if positive) after the cost of sales has been deducted from trading revenue. *p. 70*

Gross profit margin ratio A profitability ratio that expresses the gross profit as a percentage of the sales revenue for a period. *p. 260*

Group (of companies) A situation that arises where one company is able to exercise control over another or others. *p. 328*

Group financial statements Financial accounting statements that combine the performance, position and cash flows of a group of companies under common control. Also known as consolidated financial statements. *p. 328*

Group income statement An income statement for a group of companies, prepared from the perspective of the parent company's shareholders. *p. 365*

Group statement of cash flows A cash flow statement for a group of companies, prepared from the perspective of the parent company's shareholders. *p. 368*

Group statement of financial position A statement of financial position for a group of companies, prepared from the perspective of the parent company's shareholders. *p. 337*

Historic cost convention The accounting convention that holds that assets should be recorded at their historic (acquisition) cost. *p. 47*

Holding company *See* Parent company. *p. 328*

Horizontal analysis An approach to common-size financial statements where all the figures in equivalent statements over time are expressed in relation to an equivalent figure for the base period (year, month and so on). So, for example, the sales revenue figure for each year will be expressed in terms of the sales revenue figure for the base year. *p. 306*

Impairment loss The amount by which the asset value is reduced as a result of having its value assessed as impaired. *p. 56*

Income statement A financial statement (also known as profit and loss account) that measures and reports the profit (or loss) the business has generated during a period. It is derived by deducting from total revenue for a period, the total expenses associated with that revenue. *p. 29*

Indirect method An approach to deducing the cash flows from operating activities, in a statement of cash flows, by analysing the business's other financial statements. *p. 195*

Intangible assets Assets that do not have a physical substance (for example, patents, goodwill and trade receivables). *p. 36*

Integral method An approach to interim profit measurement that regards the interim period as being simply part of the annual reporting period, whereby annual expenses are predicted and then a proportion of these are allocated to the interim based on the proportion of annual sales revenue generated in the interim period. *p. 395*

Interest cover ratio A gearing ratio that divides the operating profit (that is, profit before interest and taxation) by the interest payable for a period. *p. 280*

Internal audit A review by employees of the company to assess the strength of the company's internal control and reporting systems. *p. 437*

International Accounting Standards *See* International Financial Reporting Standards. *p. 152*

International Financial Reporting Standards Transnational accounting rules that have been adopted, or developed, by the International Accounting Standards Board and which should be followed in preparing the published financial statements of listed limited companies. *p. 152*

Issued share capital That part of the share capital that has been issued to shareholders. Also known as allotted share capital. *p. 124*

Key performance indicators (KPIs) Measures used by a business to evaluate the degree of success achieved in carrying out its operations. *p. 303*

Last in, first out (LIFO) A method of inventories costing which assumes that the most recently acquired inventories are used (in production or sales) first. *p. 91*

Ledger The book in which accounts are traditionally kept. *p. 485*

Liabilities Claims of individuals and organisations, apart from the owner(s), that have arisen from past transactions or events, such as supplying goods or lending money to the business. *p. 36*

Limited companies A form of business unit that is granted a separate legal existence from that of its owners. The owners of this type of business are liable for debts only up to the amount that they have agreed to invest. *p. 18*

Limited liability The restriction of the legal obligation of shareholders to meet all of the company's debts. *p. 111*

Loan notes Long-term borrowings usually made by limited companies. *p. 125*

London Stock Exchange The main stock market for the UK, where shares may be bought and sold. *p. 114*

Management accounting The identification, measurement and communication of accounting information for the managers of a business. *p. 12*

Matching convention The accounting convention that holds that, when measuring income, expenses should be matched to revenue, which they helped generate, in the same reporting period as that revenue was realised. *p. 76*

Materiality Accounting information is material where its omission or misrepresentation will alter the decisions that users make. The threshold of materiality will vary from one business to the next. *p. 6*

Materiality convention The accounting convention that states that, where the amounts involved are immaterial, only what is expedient should be considered. *p. 80*

Minimum lease payments Those payments the lessee can be required to make under the terms of a finance lease agreement. *p. 231*

Minority interests *See* Non-controlling interests. *p. 343*

Monetary items Items that appear on a statement of financial position that have a fixed monetary value assigned to them. *p. 409*

Multiple discriminate analysis (MDA) A statistical technique that can be used to predict financial distress; it involves using an index based on a combination of financial ratios. *p. 309*

Negative goodwill arising on consolidation The amount by which the underlying net asset value of the subsidiary's shares exceeds the amount paid for the shares. *p. 345*

Net book value *See* Carrying amount. *p. 84*

Nominal value The face value of a share in a company. Also called par value. *p. 118*

Nomination committee A committee of the board of directors whose task it is to recommend, to the board, potential new directors. *p. 427*

Non-controlling interests That part of the net assets of a subsidiary company that is financed by shareholders other than the parent company. Also known as minority interests. *p. 343*

Non-current assets Assets held that do not meet the criteria of current assets. They are held for the long-term operations of the business rather than continuously circulating within the business. Non-current assets can be seen as the tools of the business. They are also known as fixed assets. *p. 42*

Non-current liabilities Liabilities of the business that are not current liabilities. *p. 44*

Non-executive directors Directors who act purely as directors; they are not full-time employees of the company. *p. 422*

Offer for sale An issue of shares that involves a public limited company (or its shareholders) selling the shares to a financial institution that will, in turn, sell the shares to the public. *p. 130*

Operating cash cycle (OCC) The period between the outlay of cash to buy supplies and the ultimate receipt of cash from the sale of goods. *p. 273*

Operating lease An arrangement where a business hires an asset, usually for a short time. Hiring an asset under an operating lease tends to be seen as an operating, rather than a financing, decision. *p. 229*

Operating profit The profit achieved during a period after all operating expenses have been deducted from revenues from operations. Financing expenses are deducted after the calculation of operating profit. *p. 70*

Operating profit margin ratio A profitability ratio that expresses the operating profit as a percentage of the sales revenue for the period. *p. 259*

Ordinary shares Shares of a company owned by those who are due the benefits of the company's activities after all other stakeholders have been satisfied. *p. 118*

Overtrading The situation arising where a business is operating at a level of activity that cannot be supported by the amount of finance that has been committed. *p. 300*

Paid-up share capital That part of the share capital of a company that has been called and paid. *p. 125*

Par value *See* Nominal value. *p. 118*

Parent company A company that has a controlling interest in another company. *p. 328*

Partnership A form of business unit where there are at least two individuals, but usually no more than twenty, carrying on a business with the intention of making a profit. *p. 17*

Preference shares Shares of a company that entitle their owners to the first part of any dividend that the company may pay. *p. 120*

Prepaid expenses Expenses that have been paid in advance at the end of the reporting period. *p. 79*

Present value The immediate value of a stream of cash flows to be received at future times. *p. 231*

Price/earnings ratio An investment ratio that relates the market value of a share to the earnings per share. *p. 296*

Private limited company A limited company for which the directors can restrict the ownership of its shares. *p. 111*

Private placing An issue of shares that involves a limited company arranging for the shares to be sold to the clients of particular issuing houses or stockbrokers, rather than to the general investing public. *p. 130*

Profit The increase in wealth attributable to the owners of a business that arises through business operations. *p. 67*

Profit before taxation The result when all of the appropriately matched expenses of running a business have been deducted from the revenue for the year, but before the taxation charge is deducted. *p. 135*

Profit for the period The result when all of the appropriately matched expenses of running a business have been deducted from the revenue for the period and then, in the case of a limited company, the taxation charge deducted. *p. 70*

Property, plant and equipment Those non-current assets that have a physical substance (for example, machinery and motor vehicles). *p. 42*

Provision A liability where the timing or amount involved is uncertain. *p. 218*

Prudence convention The accounting convention that holds that caution should be exercised when making accounting judgements. It normally involves reporting actual and expected losses immediately but reporting profits when they arise. *p. 48*

Public issue An issue of shares that involves a public limited company (plc) making a direct invitation to the public to buy shares in the company. *p. 130*

Public limited company A limited company for which the directors cannot restrict the ownership of its shares. *p. 111*

Reducing-balance method A method of calculating depreciation that applies a fixed percentage rate of depreciation to the carrying amount of an asset in each period. *p. 84*

Relevance The ability of accounting information to influence decisions. Relevance is regarded as a fundamental characteristic of useful accounting information. *p. 6*

Remuneration committee A committee of the board of directors whose task it is to recommend to the board the amount of remuneration of the executive directors and the chairman. *p. 427*

Reporting period The time span for which a business prepares its financial statements. *p. 68*

Reserves Part of the owners' claim (equity) of a limited company that has arisen from profits and gains, to the extent that these have not been distributed to the shareholders or reduced by losses. *p. 117*

Residual value The amount for which a non-current asset is sold when the business has no further use for it. *p. 83*

Return on capital employed ratio (ROCE) A profitability ratio that expresses the operating profit (that is, profit before interest and taxation) as a percentage of the long-term funds (equity and borrowings) invested in the business. *p. 257*

Return on ordinary shareholders' funds ratio (ROSF) A profitability ratio that expresses the profit for the period available to ordinary shareholders as a percentage of the funds that they have invested. *p. 256*

Revenue A measure of the inflow of assets (for example, cash or amounts owed to a business by credit customers), or a reduction in liabilities, arising as a result of trading operations. *p. 67*

Revenue reserve Part of the owners' claim (equity) of a company that arises from realised profits and gains, including after-tax trading profits and gains from disposals of non-current assets. *p. 118*

Rights issues Issues of shares for cash to existing shareholders on the basis of the number of shares already held. *p. 127*

Risk management committee A committee of the board of directors whose task it is to evaluate and manage risk. *p. 427*

Sales revenue per employee ratio An efficiency ratio that relates the sales revenue generated during a period to the average number of employees of the business. *p. 267*

Sales revenue to capital employed ratio An efficiency ratio that relates the sales revenue generated during a period to the capital employed. *p. 266*

Segmental financial reports Financial reports that break down the overall results of a business according to its different types of business operations. *p. 385*

Shares Portions of the ownership, or equity, of a company. *p. 5*

Share premium account A capital reserve reflecting any amount, above the nominal value of shares, that is paid for those shares when they are issued by a company. *p. 122*

Sole proprietorship A form of business unit where an individual is operating a business on his or her own account. *p. 16*

Splitting Changing the nominal value of shares to a lower figure (from, say, £1.00 to £0.50) and then issuing sufficient shares so that each shareholder has the same total nominal value of shares as before. *p. 119*

Statement of cash flows A statement that shows a business's sources and uses of cash for a period. *p. 29*

Statement of changes in equity A financial statement, required by IAS 1, which shows the effect of gains/losses and capital injections/withdrawals on the equity base of a company. *p. 159*

Statement of comprehensive income A financial statement that extends the conventional income statement to include other gains and losses that affect shareholders' equity. *p. 157*

Statement of financial position A statement that shows the assets of a business and the claims on those assets. It is also known as a balance sheet. *p. 29*

Stock Exchange A market where 'second-hand' shares may be bought and sold and new capital raised. *p. 114*

Straight-line method A method of accounting for depreciation that allocates the amount to be depreciated evenly over the useful life of the asset. *p. 83*

Subsidiary company A company over which another (parent) company is able to exercise control, usually, but not necessarily, because a majority of its shares are owned by the parent company. *p. 328*

Sum of the digits method A means of allocating an amount over time, for example, to reflect the required pattern of financial charges under a finance lease. *p. 232*

Summary financial statements A summarised version of the complete annual financial statements, which shareholders may choose to receive as an alternative to the complete statements. *p. 172*

Takeover The acquisition of control of one company by another, usually as a result of acquiring a majority of the ordinary shares of the former. *p. 328*

Tangible assets Those assets that have a physical substance (for example, plant and machinery, motor vehicles). *p. 36*

Target company A company that has been identified by another company as a suitable target for a takeover. *p. 331*

Timeliness The provision of accounting information in time for users to make their decision. This quality enhances the usefulness of accounting information. *p. 7*

Total shareholder return (TSR) A measure of the total return from a share, which is made up of two elements: the increase (or decrease) in share value over a period plus any dividends paid during the period. *p. 449*

Transfer price The price at which goods or services are sold, or transferred, between divisions of the same business. *p. 388*

Trial balance A totalled list of the balances on each of the accounts in a double-entry book-keeping system. *p. 481*

UK Corporate Governance Code A code of practice for companies listed on the London Stock Exchange that deals with corporate governance matters. *p. 423*

Understandability The quality that enables accounting information to be understood by those for whom the information is primarily compiled. This quality enhances the usefulness of accounting information. *p. 7*

Univariate analysis A statistical technique that can be used to help predict financial distress, which involves the use of a single ratio as a predictor. *p. 309*

Value added statement (VAS) A financial statement that takes the revenue for a period and deducts the cost of external inputs to determine the value added by the business. *p. 398*

Verifiability The quality that provides assurance to users that the information provided faithfully represents what it is supposed to represent. It enhances the quality of accounting information. *p. 7*

Vertical analysis An approach to common-size financial statements where all of the figures in the particular statement are expressed in relation to one of the figures in that same statement, for example, sales revenue or total long-term funds. *p. 306*

Weighted average cost (AVCO) A method of inventories costing, which assumes that inventories entering the business lose their separate identity and any issues of inventories reflect the weighted average cost of the inventories held. *p. 91*

Working capital Current assets less current liabilities. *p. 197*

Written-down value (WDV) *See* Carrying amount. *p. 84*

Chapter 2

2.1 Simonson Engineering

(a) The statement of financial position should be set out as follows:

Statement of financial position as at 30 September 2012

	£
ASSETS	
Non-current assets	
Property, plant and equipment	
Property	72,000
Plant and machinery	25,000
Fixtures and fittings	9,000
Motor vehicles	15,000
	121,000
Current assets	
Inventories	45,000
Trade receivables	48,000
Cash in hand	1,500
	94,500
Total assets	215,500
EQUITY AND LIABILITIES	
Equity	
Closing balance	120,500
Non-current liabilities	
Long-term borrowings	51,000
Current liabilities	
Trade payables	18,000
Short-term borrowings	26,000
	44,000
Total equity and liabilities	215,500

* The equity is calculated as follows:	
Opening balance	117,500
Profit	18,000
	135,500
Drawings	(15,000)
Closing balance	120,500

(b) The statement of financial position shows:

- The biggest investment in assets is property, followed by trade receivables and inventories. These combined account for more than 76% of the value of assets held.
- The investment in current assets accounts for 44% of the total investment in assets.

- The total long-term finance is divided 70% equity and 30% long-term borrowings. There is not therefore, excessive reliance on long-term borrowings.
- The current assets (which are cash or near cash) cover the current liabilities (which are maturing obligations) by a ratio of more than 2:1.

(c) The revised statement of financial position will be as follows:

Statement of financial position as at 30 September 2012

	£
ASSETS	
Non-current assets	
Property, plant and equipment	
Property	115,000
Plant and machinery	25,000
Fixtures and fittings	9,000
Motor vehicles	15,000
	164,000
Current assets	
Inventories	38,000
Trade receivables	48,000
Cash in hand	1,500
	87,500
Total assets	251,500
EQUITY AND LIABILITIES	
Equity	
Closing balance (120,500 + 43,000 – 7,000)	156,500
Non-current liabilities	
Long-term borrowings	51,000
Current liabilities	
Trade payables	18,000
Short-term borrowings	26,000
	44,000
Total equity and liabilities	251,500

Chapter 3

3.1 TT and Co.

Statement of financial position as at 31 December 2011

	£
ASSETS	
Delivery van (12,000 – 2,500)	9,500
Inventories (143,000 + 12,000 – 74,000 – 16,000)	65,000
Trade receivables (152,000 – 132,000 – 400)	19,600
Cash at bank (50,000 – 25,000 – 500 – 1,200 – 12,000 – 33,500 – 1,650 – 12,000 + 35,000 + 132,000 – 121,000 – 9,400)	750
Prepaid expenses (5,000 + 300)	5,300
Total assets	100,150
EQUITY AND LIABILITIES	
Equity (50,000 + 26,900)	76,900
Trade payables (143,000 – 121,000)	22,000
Accrued expenses (630 + 620)	1,250
Total equity and liabilities	100,150

Income statement for the year ended 31 December 2011

	£
Sales revenue (152,000 + 35,000)	187,000
Cost of goods sold (74,000 + 16,000)	(90,000)
Gross profit	97,000
Rent	(20,000)
Rates (500 + 900)	(1,400)
Wages (33,500 + 630)	(34,130)
Electricity (1,650 + 620)	(2,270)
Bad debts	(400)
Van depreciation ((12,000 − 2,000)/4)	(2,500)
Van expenses	(9,400)
Profit for the year	26,900

The statement of financial position could now be rewritten in a more stylish form as follows:

Statement of financial position as at 31 December 2011

	£
ASSETS	
Non-current assets	
Property, plant and equipment	
Delivery van at cost	12,000
Depreciation	(2,500)
	9,500
Current assets	
Inventories	65,000
Trade receivables	19,600
Prepaid expenses	5,300
Cash	750
	90,650
Total assets	100,150
EQUITY AND LIABILITIES	
Equity	
Closing balance	76,900
Current liabilities	
Trade payables	22,000
Accrued expenses	1,250
	23,250
Total equity and liabilities	100,150

Chapter 4

4.1 Dev Ltd

(a) The summarised statement of financial position of Dev Ltd, immediately following the rights and bonus issue, is as follows:

Statement of financial position

	£000
Net assets (235 + 40 (cash from the rights issue))	275
Equity	
Share capital: 100,000 shares @ £1 ((100 + 20) + 60)	180
Share premium account (30 + 20 − 50)	–
Revaluation reserve (37 − 10)	27
Retained earnings	68
	275

Note that the bonus issue of £60,000 is taken from capital reserves (reserves unavailable for dividends) as follows:

	£000
Share premium account	50
Revaluation reserve	10
	60

More could have been taken from the revaluation reserve and less from the share premium account without making any difference to dividend payment possibilities.

(b) There may be pressure from a potential lender for the business to limit its ability to pay dividends. This would place lenders in a more secure position because the maximum buffer or safety margin between the value of the assets and the amount owed by the business is maintained. It is not unusual for potential lenders to insist on some measure to lock up shareholders' funds in this way as a condition of granting the loan.

(c) The summarised statement of financial position of Dev Ltd, immediately following the rights and bonus issue, assuming a minimum dividend potential objective, is as follows:

Statement of financial position

	£000
Net assets (235 + 40 (cash from the rights issue))	275
Equity	
Share capital: 100,000 shares @ £1 ((100 + 20) + 60)	180
Share premium account (30 + 20)	50
Revaluation reserve	37
Retained earnings (68 – 60)	8
	275

(d) Before the bonus issue, the maximum dividend was £68,000. Now it is £8,000. Thus the bonus issue has had the effect of locking up an additional £60,000 of the business's assets in terms of the business's ability to pay dividends.

(e) Before the issues, Lee had 100 shares worth £2.35 (£235,000/100,000) each or £235 in total. Lee would be offered 20 shares in the rights issue at £2 each or £40 in total. After the rights issue, Lee would have 120 shares worth £2.2917 (£275,000/120,000) each or £275 in total.

The bonus issue would give Lee 60 additional shares. After the bonus issue, Lee would have 180 shares worth £1.5278 (£275,000/180,000) each or £275 in total.

None of this affects Lee's wealth. Before the issues, Lee had £235 worth of shares and £40 more in cash. After the issues, Lee has the same total wealth but all £275 is in the value of the shares.

(f) The things that we know about the company are as follows:

- It is a private (as opposed to a public) limited company, for it has 'Ltd' (limited) as part of its name, rather than plc (public limited company).
- It has made an issue of shares at a premium, almost certainly after it had traded successfully for a period. (There is a share premium account. It would be very unlikely that the original shares, issued when the company was first formed, would have been issued at a premium.)
- Certain of the assets in the statement of financial position have been upwardly revalued by at least £37,000. (There is a revaluation reserve of £37,000. This may just be what is left after a previous bonus issue had taken part of the balance.)
- The company has traded at an aggregate profit (though there could have been losses in some years), net of tax and any dividends paid. (There is a positive balance on retained earnings.)

Chapter 5

5.1 Comments

(a) Dividends announced between the end of the reporting period and the date at which the financial reports are authorised for publication should *not* be treated as a liability in the statement of financial position at the end of that period. IAS 1 specifically precludes the treatment of such dividends as liabilities.

(b) IAS 1 provides support for three key accounting conventions – accruals, going concern and consistency. It does not specifically support the historic cost convention.

(c) IAS 1 does not permit bank overdrafts to be offset against positive bank balances when preparing the statement of financial position. For the sake of relevance they should be shown separately.

(d) IAS 8 states that accounting policies should be changed if it is required by a new financial reporting standard or if it leads to more relevant and reliable information being reported.

(e) IAS 10 states that *significant* non-adjusting events occurring between the end of the reporting period and the date at which the financial statements are authorised should be disclosed by way of note. The standard requires the nature of the event and its likely financial effect to be disclosed.

(f) The law only requires that London Stock Exchange listed companies publish an annual directors' remuneration report.

Chapter 6

6.1 Touchstone plc

Statement of cash flows for the year ended 31 December 2012

	£m
Cash flows from operating activities	
Profit before taxation (after interest) (see Note 1 below)	60
Adjustments for:	
Depreciation	16
Interest expense (Note 2)	4
	80
Increase in trade receivables (26 – 16)	(10)
Decrease in trade payables (38 – 37)	(1)
Decrease in inventories (25 – 24)	1
Cash generated from operations	70
Interest paid	(4)
Taxation paid (Note 3)	(12)
Dividend paid	(18)
Net cash from operating activities	36
Cash flows from investing activities	
Payments to acquire tangible non-current assets (Note 4)	(41)
Net cash used in investing activities	(41)
Cash flows from financing activities	
Issue of loan notes (40 – 20)	20
Net cash used in financing activities	20
Net increase in cash and cash equivalents	15
Cash and cash equivalents at 1 January 2012	
Cash	4
Cash and cash equivalents at 31 December 2012	
Cash	4
Treasury bills	15
	19

To see how this relates to the cash of the business at the beginning and end of the year it can be useful to provide a reconciliation as follows:

**Analysis of cash and cash equivalents
during the year ended 31 December 2012**

	£m
Cash and cash equivalents at 1 January 2012	4
Net cash inflow	15
Cash and cash equivalents at 31 December 2012	19

Notes:

1 This is simply taken from the income statement for the year.
2 Interest payable expense must be taken out, by adding it back to the profit before taxation figure. We subsequently deduct the cash paid for interest payable during the year. In this case the two figures are identical.
3 Companies pay 50% of their tax during their accounting year and the other 50% in the following year. Thus the 2012 payment would have been half the tax on the 2011 profit (that is, the figure that would have appeared in the current liabilities at the end of 2011), plus half of the 2012 tax charge (that is, $4 + (^1/_2 \times 16) = 12$).
4 Since there were no disposals, the depreciation charges must be the difference between the start and end of the year's non-current asset values, adjusted by the cost of any additions:

	£m
Carrying amount at 1 January 2012	147
Additions (balancing figure)	41
	188
Depreciation (6 + 10)	(16)
Carrying amount at 31 December 2012	172

Chapter 7

7.1 Prentaxia plc

	Note	£m
Draft profit before tax		87.2
Lease payment	1	3.0
Capitalisation of borrowing costs	2	2.0
Increase in existing provision	3	(2.6)
Reversal of provision	4	1.4
Recognition of a provision	5	(4.5)
Development expenditure	6	(1.3)
Revised profit before tax		85.2

Notes

1 Only the finance charge element of the lease payment should be treated as an expense. The total finance charge is calculated as follows:

	£m
Total lease payments (5 × £5m)	25.0
Cost of machine	19.0
Total finance charge	6.0

The finance charge for the current year, using the sum of the digits method, is calculated as follows:

Sum of the digits: 5 + 4 + 3 + 2 + 1 = 15

Finance charge: 5/15 × £6m = £2m

The lease payment charged to the income statement is £5m. This means that the net effect of replacing the lease payment with the finance charge will be a £3m (£5m − £2m) increase in profits.
2 Borrowing costs relating to the construction of an asset should be capitalised.
3 Any increase in the provision should be recognised by a charge to the income statement.
4 The provision should be reversed. There is no present obligation. The obligation to re-line the furnace can be avoided by selling it. The depreciation of the existing lining is appropriate. When the new lining is acquired, it should be capitalised and should be depreciated over time.

5 A provision should be recognised. On the basis of the evidence, there is a present obligation and it is probable that there will be an outflow of resources.

6 The search for new materials is cited in IAS 38 as an example of research expenditure, and should not be capitalised. It must therefore be treated as an expense.

7 There is no present obligation to fit smoke alarms and so there is no need to create a provision during the current year.

Chapter 8

8.1 Ali plc and Bhaskar plc

To answer this question, you may have used the following ratios:

	Ali plc	Bhaskar plc
Return on ordinary shareholders' funds ratio	$(99.9/687.6) \times 100 = 14.5\%$	$(104.6/874.6) \times 100 = 12.0\%$
Operating profit margin ratio	$(151.3/1,478.1) \times 100 = 10.2\%$	$(166.9/1,790.4) \times 100 = 9.3\%$
Inventories turnover period ratio	$(592.0/1,018.3) \times 12 = 7.0$ months	$(403.0/1,214.9) \times 12 = 4.0$ months
Settlement period for trade receivables ratio	$(176.4/1,478.1) \times 12 = 1.4$ months	$(321.9/1,790.4) \times 12 = 2.2$ months
Current ratio	$\dfrac{853.0}{422.4} = 2.0$	$\dfrac{816.5}{293.1} = 2.8$
Acid test ratio	$\dfrac{(853.0 - 592.0)}{422.4} = 0.6$	$\dfrac{(816.5 - 403.0)}{293.1} = 1.4$
Gearing ratio	$\dfrac{190}{(687.6 + 190)} \times 100 = 21.6\%$	$\dfrac{250}{(874.6 + 250)} \times 100 = 22.2\%$
Interest cover ratio	$\dfrac{151.3}{19.4} = 7.8$ times	$\dfrac{166.9}{27.5} = 6.1$ times

(Note: It is not possible to use any average ratios because only the end-of-year figures are provided for each business.)

Ali plc seems more effective than Bhaskar plc at generating returns for shareholders, as indicated by the higher ROSF ratio. This may be partly caused by Ali plc's higher operating profit margin.

Both businesses have a very high inventories turnover period; this probably needs to be investigated. This ratio is particularly high for Ali plc. Both may suffer from poor inventories management.

Ali plc has a lower settlement period for trade receivables than Bhaskar plc. This may suggest that Bhaskar plc needs to exert greater control over trade receivables.

Ali plc has a much lower current ratio and acid test ratio than Bhaskar plc. The acid test ratio of Ali plc is substantially below 1.0: this may suggest a liquidity problem.

The gearing ratios of the two businesses are quite similar. Neither business seems to have excessive borrowing. The interest cover ratios are also similar. The ratios indicate that both businesses have good profit coverage for their interest charges.

To draw better comparisons between the two businesses, it would be useful to calculate other ratios from the financial statements. It would also be helpful to calculate ratios for both businesses over (say) five years as well as key ratios of other businesses operating in the same industry.

Chapter 9

9.1 Achilles plc

(a)

Dividend payout ratio	$15/46 \times 100 = 32.6\%$
Dividend yield ratio	$((15/200)/(1 - 0.1)/3.49) \times 100 = 2.4\%$
Earnings per share	$46/200 = £0.23$
P/E ratio	$3.49/0.23 = 15.2$ Times

Without having some information about the business's past ratios, it is difficult to draw very many conclusions. What we can say is that a policy of distributing about a third of the profit for the year is well in line with what many businesses do in practice. Real World 9.2 showed that the average dividend yield and P/E ratios for all London Stock Exchange listed businesses were 3.27% and 10.62 times. On this basis, Achilles is somewhat lower than the average for dividend yield, but significantly higher for P/E. From a dividend yield perspective, this is not an attractive investment; it yields a return that is lower than can be earned from a savings account. The P/E ratio, however, suggests that the market views Achilles as having a bright future.

(b) The Altman-model Z-score is calculated as follows:

$$Z = 0.717a + 0.847b + 3.107c + 0.420d + 0.998e$$

where a = Working capital/Total assets
  b = Accumulated retained profits/Total assets
  c = Operating profit/Total assets
  d = Book (statement of financial position) value of ordinary and preference shares/ Total liabilities at book (statement of financial position) value
  e = Sales revenue/Total assets.

For Achilles plc, the Z-score is

$$0.717[(159 - 161)/812] + 0.847(151/812) + 3.107(97/812) + 0.420[351/(300 + 161)]$$
$$+ 0.998(701/812) = \underline{1.708}$$

According to Altman, those businesses with a Z-score of less than 1.23 tend to fail. The lower the score the greater is the probability of failure. Those with a Z-score greater than 4.14 tend not to fail. Those businesses with a Z-score between 1.23 and 4.14 occupied a 'zone of ignorance' and were difficult to classify. Thus Achilles finds itself in the zone of ignorance and uncomfortably close to the lower limit. It does not look a very healthy business. The problem probably lies with a negative working capital position, plus relatively low turnover and profit given the level of assets involved.

Chapter 10

10.1 Great plc

Group statement of financial position as at 31 December last year

ASSETS	£m
Non-current assets	
Property, plant and equipment (at cost less depreciation)	
Land	99
Plant	53
Vehicles	31
	183
Intangible assets	
Goodwill arising on consolidation (Note 1)	5
	188
Current assets	
Inventories	29
Trade receivables	27
Cash	22
	78
Total assets	266
EQUITY AND LIABILITIES	
Equity	
Called-up share capital: ordinary shares of £1 each, fully paid	100
Retained earnings (Note 2)	81
	181
Non-controlling interests (Note 3)	13
	194
Non-current liabilities	
Loan notes	50
Current liabilities	
Trade payables	22
Total equity and liabilities	266

Notes

1 Goodwill arising on consolidation: $53 - (80\% \times (20 + 35 + 5)) = 5$.

2	£m
Great plc's retained earnings balance	77
Great plc's share of Small plc's post-acquisition profits $(40 - 35) \times 80\%$	4
	81

3 Non-controlling interests: $(60 + 5) \times 20\% = 13$

Group income statement for last year

	£m
Revenue	118
Cost of sales	(59)
Gross profit	59
Administration expenses	(11)
Distribution expenses	(8)
Operating profit	40
Interest payable	(3)
Profit before taxation	37
Taxation	(16)
Profit for the year	21
Attributable to non-controlling interests $(20\% \times 5)$	(1)
Profit for the year attributable to Great plc shareholders	20

Chapter 11

11.1 The discussion should be along the following lines:

(a) A steward is someone who has custody and control of assets belonging to another or others. In a business context company directors are good examples of stewards. Stewardship accounting is concerned with reporting on how the owners' assets have been deployed and with what effect by the steward. Stewardship accounting may be concerned with bar profits, but is more likely not to be.

(b) The market model of financial reporting has nothing to do with street trading. It is, however, concerned with the theory (partly confirmed) that businesses that provide appropriate information to shareholders and others will be rewarded with a cheaper cost of capital. This is because appropriate disclosure can remove certain doubts and, therefore, risk. Individual businesses can then decide whether the cost of additional disclosure is likely to be adequately rewarded.

(c) IFRS 8 says that segmental information provided with the annual financial statements should be based on a 'management approach'. This means that, for the purposes of segmental external reporting, the business should be segmented along the same lines as it is managed. Thus, if the business is managed on a geographical basis, that basis will be used for segmental reporting. It is true that a segment with less than 10 per cent of the business's combined revenue can be aggregated with that of a similar segment.

(d) In a segmental report, inter-segment trading revenues should be included. Such revenues cannot be included in the revenue figure that appears in the business's income statement, however.

(e) The business review is a mainly narrative report that is intended to support and clarify the financial statements. It has nothing to do with auditing; it is not itself audited.

(f) Interim financial statements are not the first draft of the annual financial statements. They are financial statements for shorter periods than the normal one-year reporting period. Interims are usually for a six-month period, though they might be for three months or even some other period.

(g) A business's value added is not usually taken to be its sales revenue. It is usually taken to be the sales revenue less any bought-in goods or services used to generate that revenue.

(h) Current purchasing power financial statements are based on the historic cost ones. An adjustment is made for the movement in the relevant general price index from acquiring an asset and so on to the date of the end of the reporting period.

(i) Monetary items are those that are fixed in monetary terms, like a loan. Other items, say an item of plant, may have a monetary value next to it in the statement of financial position, but it is not a monetary item.

(j) CPP is particularly concerned with shareholders' spending power with reference to general goods and services. CCA is concerned with the business's ability to maintain its ability to continue to trade at the same level as it has recently been doing.

Chapter 12

12.1 (a) The sources of information that may be used could include the following:

- documents setting out the:
  - strategic plan of the company;
  - board structure and roles;
  - board appointments procedures;
  - operations of the board;
  - minutes of board meetings;
  - meeting agendas and background information;
  - criteria for directors' appraisal;
- interviews with board members;
- interviews with and/or questionnaires sent to senior management and shareholders;
- attendance and observation at board meetings;
- attendance and observation at meetings with shareholders, including the AGM;
- company website and published material, including the annual reports;
- CVs of board members;
- performance reports (such as monthly budget reports and sales reports) received by the board;
- information relating to training and development programmes carried out.

This is not an exhaustive list. You may have thought of other sources of information.

(b) The remuneration committee must be sensitive to the needs of shareholders and others with respect to directors' rewards. It may therefore be helpful to include an employee representative on the committee. It may also be helpful to exclude from membership of the committee any non-executive director who is also an executive director of a large listed company. Such changes may help to put a brake on the awarding of excessive payouts.

(c) Communication with shareholders can take various forms. The following are either required by law or are considered to be good practice:

- distribution of annual reports and interim reports to all shareholders as well as their publication on the company's website;
- timely releases throughout the year concerning major developments;
- a chairman's address at the annual general meeting;
- an address by the chairman of the audit committee and the chairman of the remuneration committee at the annual general meeting;
- an opportunity for shareholders to question the board of directors at the annual general meeting;
- publication of notice of all shareholder meetings on the website;
- dedicated staff to manage the company website and deal with shareholder queries;
- prompt publication of announcements and press releases on the company website;
- briefings for major shareholders and analysts and their publication on the company website;
- regular meetings between major shareholders and the chairman and chief executive;
- regular meetings between non-executive directors and major shareholders;
- email newsletters setting out new developments, financial results, announcements and so on to major shareholders and analysts.

Appendix D
SOLUTIONS TO REVIEW QUESTIONS

Chapter 1

1.1 The purpose of producing accounting information is to enable users to make more informed decisions and judgements about the organisation concerned. Unless it fulfils this purpose, there is no point in providing it.

1.2 The main users of financial information for a university and the way in which they are likely to use this information may be summed up as follows:

Students: Whether to enrol on a course of study. This would probably involve an assessment of the university's ability to continue to operate and to fulfil students' needs.

Other universities and colleges: How best to compete against the university. This might involve using the university's performance in various aspects as a 'benchmark' when evaluating their own performance.

Employees: Whether to take up or to continue in employment with the university. Employees might assess this by considering the ability of the university to continue to provide employment and to reward employees adequately for their labour.

Government/funding authority: How efficient and effective the university is in undertaking its various activities. Possible funding needs that the university may have.

Local community representatives: Whether to allow/encourage the university to expand its premises. To assess this, the university's ability to continue to provide employment for the community, to use community resources and to help fund environmental improvements might be considered.

Suppliers: Whether to continue to supply the university at all; also whether to supply on credit. This would involve an assessment of the university's ability to pay for any goods and services supplied.

Lenders: Whether to lend money to the university and/or whether to require repayment of any existing loans. To assess this, the university's ability to meet its obligations to pay interest and to repay the principal would be considered.

Board of governors and managers (faculty deans and so on): Whether the performance of the university requires improvement. Performance to date would be compared with earlier plans or some other 'benchmark' to decide whether action needs to be taken. Whether there should be a change in the university's future direction. In making such decisions, management will need to look at the university's ability to perform and at the opportunities available to it.

We can see that the users of accounting information and their needs are similar to those of a private-sector business.

1.3 The economic cost of providing accounting information should be less than the expected economic benefit from having the information available. In other words, there should be a net economic benefit from producing it. If this is not the case, it should not be produced. There are obvious problems, however, in determining the precise value of the benefit. There are also likely to be problems in determining the amount of the cost. Hence, making a judgement about whether to provide additional accounting information is not easy.

Economics is not the only issue to consider, particularly in the context of financial accounting. Social and other factors may well be involved. It can be argued, for example, that society has a right to certain information about a large business, even though this information may not have any direct economic value to society.

1.4 Since we can never be sure what is going to happen in the future, the best that we can often do is to make judgements on the basis of past experience. Thus information concerning flows of cash and of wealth in the recent past may well be a useful source on which to base judgements about possible future outcomes.

Chapter 2

2.1 The owner seems unaware of the business entity convention in accounting. This convention requires a separation of the business from the owner(s) of the business for accounting purposes. The business is regarded as a separate entity and the statement of financial position is prepared from the perspective of the business rather than that of the owner. As a result, funds invested in the business by the owner are regarded as a claim that the owner has on the business. In the standard layout of the statement of financial position, this claim will be shown alongside other claims on the business from outsiders.

2.2 A statement of financial position does not show what a business is worth, for two major reasons:

- Only those items that can be measured reliably in monetary terms are shown on the statement of financial position. Thus, things of value such as the reputation for product quality, skills of employees and so on will not normally appear in the statement of financial position.
- The historic cost convention results in assets often being recorded at their outlay cost rather than their current value. For certain assets, the difference between historic cost and current value may be significant.

2.3 The accounting equation expresses the relationship between a business's assets, liabilities and equity. For the standard layout, it is:

$$\text{Assets} = \text{Equity} + \text{Liabilities}$$

For the alternative layout mentioned in the text, the equation is:

$$\text{Assets} - \text{Liabilities} = \text{Equity}$$

2.4 Some object to the idea of humans being treated as assets for inclusion on the statement of financial position. It is seen as demeaning for humans to be listed alongside inventories, plant and machinery and other assets. Others argue, however, that humans are often the most valuable resource of a business and that placing a value on this resource will help bring to the attention of managers the importance of nurturing and developing this 'asset'.

Humans are likely to meet the criterion of an asset relating to future probable benefits, otherwise there would be little point in employing them. The criterion relating to exclusive right of control is, however, more problematic. A business cannot control humans in the same way as most other assets but it can have exclusive rights to their employment services. This makes it possible to argue that this criterion can be met.

Normally, humans sign a contract of employment and so the criterion relating to past transactions is normally met. The criterion concerning whether the value of humans (or their services) can be reliably measured poses the major difficulty. To date, none of the measurement methods proposed has achieved widespread support.

Chapter 3

3.1 When preparing the income statement, it is not always possible to determine accurately the expenses that need to be matched to the sales revenue for the period. It is perhaps only at some later point that the true position becomes clear. Nevertheless, we must try to include all relevant expenses and so estimates of the future have to be made. These estimates may include accrued expenses, depreciation charges and bad debts incurred. The income statement would lose much of its usefulness if we were to wait for all uncertainties to become clear.

3.2 Depreciation attempts to allocate the cost or fair value, less any residual value, of the asset over its useful life. Depreciation does not attempt to measure the fall in value of the asset during a particular accounting period. Thus, the carrying amount of the asset appearing on the statement of financial position normally represents the unexpired part of its cost, or fair value, rather than its current market value.

3.3 The convention of consistency aims to provide some uniformity in the application of accounting policies. In certain areas, there may be more than one method of accounting for an item, for example inventories. The convention of consistency states that, having decided on a particular accounting policy, a business should continue to apply the policy in successive periods. While this policy helps to ensure that more valid comparisons can be made of business performance *over time*, it does not ensure that valid comparisons can be made *between businesses*. Different businesses may consistently apply different accounting policies.

3.4 An expense is that element of the cost incurred that is used up during the accounting period. An asset is that element of cost which is carried forward on the statement of financial position and which will normally be used up in future periods. Thus, both assets and expenses arise from costs being incurred. The major difference between the two is the period over which the benefits (arising from the costs incurred) accrue.

Chapter 4

4.1 Both companies and individuals are required to meet their debts to the full extent of their available assets. Thus, their liability is limited only by the extent of their assets. It is the shareholders of a limited company that enjoy greater protection. Their liability for the unsatisfied debts of a company is limited to the amount that they paid or have pledged to pay for their shares.

This contrasts with the position of the owner or part owner of an unincorporated business. Here all of the individual's assets could be used to meet the unsatisfied debts of the business. Thus, while there is a difference between the position of a shareholder and that of a sole proprietor or partner, there is no difference between the position of the company itself and a sole proprietor or partner.

4.2 A private limited company may place restrictions on the transfer of its shares. (There is therefore an opportunity to control who becomes a shareholder.) A public company cannot have such restrictions.

A public limited company must have authorised share capital of at least £50,000. There is no minimum for a private limited company.

A public limited company may offer its shares and loan notes to the general public; a private company cannot make such an offer.

4.3 A reserve is that part of the equity (owners' claim) of a company that is not share capital. Reserves represent gains or surpluses that enhance the claim of the shareholders above the nominal value of their shares. Revenue reserves arise from realised profits and gains, such as ploughed-back trading profits. Capital reserves arise from issuing shares at a premium or from unrealised profits and gains (for example, the upward revaluation of non-current assets).

4.4 A preference share represents part of the ownership of the company. Holders of preference shares are entitled to the first part of any dividend paid by a company.

(a) Holders of preference shares are normally entitled to dividends up to a predetermined maximum value. Dividends to ordinary shareholders have no predetermined maximum. The priority awarded in receiving dividends means that preference shares are seen as less risky than ordinary shares. It is ordinary shareholders that are the primary risk-takers and who are given voting rights. Preference shareholders do not normally have voting rights.

(b) Loan notes represent borrowings for the company. Loan note holders normally have a contract that specifies the rate of interest, interest payment dates and redemption date. The loan notes are often secured on the company's assets. Preference shareholders have no such contract. The claims of preference shareholders are ranked below those of loan note holders in the event that the company is liquidated.

Chapter 5

5.1 The general rule is that the relevant figures for the earlier period(s) in which the error occurred should be restated for comparison purposes. The nature of the error and its effect on relevant items and on earnings per share for the current and the prior period should also be disclosed.

5.2 Accounting policies are the principles, rules and conventions used to prepare the financial statements. Individual policies define the approach taken to dealing with a particular type of transaction. Wherever possible, the policies should be determined by reference to an appropriate accounting standard. In the absence of an appropriate standard, managers must make suitable judgements to ensure that users receive relevant and reliable information.

5.3 Accounting rules help to ensure that unscrupulous directors do not exploit their position and portray an unrealistic view of financial health. They are also important for the purpose of comparability, both over time and between businesses.

5.4 The main methods of creative accounting are misstating revenues, massaging expenses, misstating assets, concealing 'bad news' and inadequate disclosure.

Chapter 6

6.1 Cash is normally required in the settlement of claims. Employees, contractors, lenders and suppliers expect to be paid in cash. When businesses fail, it is their inability to find the cash to pay claimants that actually drives them under. These factors lead to cash being the pre-eminent business asset. It is studied carefully to assess the ability of a business to survive and/or to take advantage of commercial opportunities.

6.2 With the direct method, the business's cash records are analysed for the period concerned. The analysis reveals the amounts of cash, in total, that have been paid and received in respect of each category of the statement of cash flows. This is not difficult in principle, or in practice if it is done as a matter of routine, or using a computer.

    The indirect method takes the approach that, while the profit (loss) for the reporting period is not equal to the net inflow (outflow) of cash from operations, they are fairly closely linked to the extent that appropriate adjustment of the figure for profit (loss) for the period will produce the correct figure for cash flow. The adjustment is concerned with the depreciation charge for, and movements in relevant working capital items over, the period.

6.3 **(a)** *Cash flows from operating activities*. This would normally be positive, even for a business with small profits or even losses. The fact that depreciation is not a cash flow tends to lead to positive cash flows in this area in most cases.

    (b) *Cash flows from investing activities*. Normally this would be negative in cash flow terms since many non-current assets wear out or become obsolete and need to be replaced in the normal course of business. This means that, typically, old non-current assets generate less cash on their disposal than must be paid to replace them.

    (c) *Cash flows from financing activities*. Businesses tend either to expand or to fail. In either case, this is likely to mean that, over the years, more finance will be raised than will be redeemed.

6.4 There are several possible reasons for this, including the following:

- Changes in inventories, trade receivables and trade payables. For example, an increase in trade receivables during a reporting period would mean that the cash received from credit sales would be less than the credit sales revenue for the same period.
- Cash may have been spent on new non-current assets or received from disposals of old ones; these would not directly affect profit.
- Cash may have been spent to redeem or repay a financial claim or received as a result of the creation or the increase of a claim. These would not directly affect profit.
- Tax charged in the income statement is not normally the same as the tax paid during the same reporting period.

Chapter 7

7.1 A contingent asset is a possible asset arising from past events, the existence of which will only be confirmed by future events not wholly within the control of the business.

The threshold for disclosure is higher for a contingent asset than for a contingent liability. A contingent asset is disclosed only when it is probable that there will be an inflow of resources, whereas a contingent liability will be disclosed unless the possibility of an outflow of resources is remote.

Where disclosure is required, the requirements for contingent assets and liabilities are similar in some respects. In both cases, a description of their nature and, where practicable, an estimate of their financial effect is required.

7.2 IAS 37 *Provisions, Contingent Liabilities and Contingent Assets* defines a contingent liability as:

1 a possible obligation arising from past events, the existence of which will only be confirmed by future events not wholly within the control of the business; or
2 a present obligation arising from past events, where either it is not probable that an outflow of resources is needed, or the amount of the obligation cannot be reliably measured.

The key differences between a provision and a contingent liability are:

1 The degree of uncertainty associated with each. Where a present obligation leads to a probable outflow of resources, a provision is recognised. Where a future outflow is possible, but not probable, a contingent liability arises.
2 Their presentation in the financial statements. A provision will be included in the financial statements. A contingent liability will normally be shown in the notes to the financial statements.

7.3 Research and development expenditure is incurred to generate future economic benefits. As a result, there is an argument for carrying this expenditure forward and charging it to the period(s) when the benefits are ultimately received. This would be in line with the accruals convention. A key problem, however, is that there is normally considerable uncertainty concerning future economic benefits. IAS 38 has therefore decreed that research expenditure should be charged to the period in which it is incurred and that development expenditure, which is incurred at a more advanced stage, can be carried forward to future periods, but only subject to tough conditions. These conditions include the need to demonstrate probable future economic benefits. The IASB has therefore taken a prudent approach to this type of expenditure.

7.4 A finance lease is, in essence, a form of borrowing. We saw that it gives rise to an obligation to make lease payments over time. When these lease payments are treated as an expense in the period incurred, the financial obligation is not recognised in the financial statements. It is possible, therefore, to conceal the true extent of borrowing by entering into finance lease agreements rather than entering into loan agreements (which are shown on the financial statements). Users of financial statements will not be able to make a proper assessment of the level of financial risk associated with the business if the obligation for future finance lease payments is not fully disclosed.

Chapter 8

8.1 The fact that a business operates on a low operating profit margin indicates that only a small operating profit is being produced for each £1 of sales revenue generated. However, this does not necessarily mean that the ROCE will be low. If the business is able to generate sufficient sales revenue during a period, the operating profit may be very high even though the operating profit per £1 of sales revenue is low. If the overall operating profit is high, this can lead, in turn, to a high ROCE, since it is the total operating profit that is used as the numerator (top part of the fraction) in this ratio. Many businesses (including supermarkets) pursue a strategy of 'low margin, high sales revenue'.

8.2 Factors that may affect the average settlement period for trade receivables include changes in:

- the credit terms offered
- the efficiency with which amounts due from credit customers are recorded and collected
- the economic environment within which the business operates
- the number of disputes concerning amounts due or goods/services provided
- the type of customer to whom credit is granted.

This is not an exhaustive list. You may have thought of others.

8.3 Three possible reasons for a long inventories turnover period are:

- poor inventories controls, leading to excessive investment in inventories;
- a desire to provide customers with greater choice or, perhaps, speedier supply;
- inventories building in anticipation of increased future sales.

A short inventories turnover period may be due to:

- tight inventories controls, reducing excessive investment in inventories and/or the amount of obsolete and slow-moving inventories;
- an inability to finance the required amount of inventories to meet sales demand;
- a difference in the mix of inventories carried by similar businesses (for example, greater investment in perishable goods which are held for a short period only).

These are not exhaustive lists; you may have thought of other reasons.

8.4 Size may well be an important factor when comparing businesses.

- Larger businesses may be able to generate economies of scale in production and distribution to an extent not available to smaller businesses.
- Larger businesses may be able to raise finance more cheaply, partly through economies of scale (for example, borrowing larger amounts) and partly through being seen as less of a risk to the lender.
- Smaller businesses may be able to be more flexible and 'lighter on their feet' than can the typical larger business.

These and other possible factors may lead to differences in performance and position between larger and smaller businesses.

Chapter 9

9.1 The statement of financial position is drawn up at a single point in time – usually the end of the financial period. As a result, the figures shown on the statement of financial position represent the position at that single point in time and may not be representative of the position during the period. When calculating ratios where one figure is for the period (say, taken from the income statement) and the other from the statement of financial position, wherever possible, average figures (perhaps based on monthly figures) should be used. However, an external user may only have access to the opening and closing statements of financial position for the year and so a simple average based on these figures may be all that is possible to calculate. Where a business is seasonal in nature or is subject to cyclical changes, this simple averaging may not be sufficient.

9.2 Factors that could affect a company's decision on the level of dividend to pay include the following:

- The level of profit for the period concerned. Businesses tend to be reluctant to pay dividends at a higher level than that of after-tax profits. They may be prepared to exceed this limit occasionally, when they have an abnormally poor year, but over a period of years dividends typically fall well below profit levels.
- The amount of cash available. Businesses tend not to borrow to pay dividends, though this would be perfectly legal. Only if they have sufficient liquidity will they normally pay dividends.

- Other demands on funds. This is linked to the liquidity point. Businesses may be constrained from paying dividends by the extent of other calls on their funds, particularly for investment. In theory businesses will pay out any cash remaining only after all profitable investments have been undertaken.
- Past practice. Businesses tend to adopt a fairly consistent dividend policy, from which they are often reluctant to vary. This is because it is believed that changes in dividend policy can send misleading 'signals' to investors. For example, cutting the level of dividends might signal that the business is in difficulties.

9.3 The P/E ratio may vary between businesses within the same industry for the following reasons:

- Accounting policies. Differences in the methods used to compute profit (for example inventories valuation and depreciation) can lead to different profit figures and, therefore, different P/E ratios.
- Different prospects. One business may be regarded as having a much brighter future due to factors such as the quality of management, the quality of products, or location. This will affect the market price investors are prepared to pay for the share, and hence it will also affect the P/E ratio.
- Different asset structures. One business's underlying asset base may be much higher than the other's, and this may affect the market price of the shares.

9.4 Three ratios that could be affected by overtrading are:

- Acid test ratio. This is likely to fall if overtrading is occurring, because the trade payables settlement period is likely to increase and overdraft finance is likely to exist. At the same time inventories and trade receivables levels could well fall.
- Cash generated from operations to maturing obligations ratio. This is likely to fall. Cash generated is likely to rise more slowly than maturing obligations if the business is overtrading.
- Interest cover ratio. This is likely to fall despite rising profits because interest, perhaps on short-term borrowing (for instance, overdrafts), is likely to rise more steeply.

Chapter 10

10.1 A group is said to exist when one company is in a position to exercise control over another company. This almost always means that the parent owns a majority of the voting shares of the subsidiary.

Where a group relationship exists, all companies in the group must prepare annual financial statements in the normal way, but, in addition, the parent company must prepare and publish a set of group financial statements.

10.2 The group statement of financial position shows the assets and external claims of all members of the group (including the parent company) as if they were those of the parent company. Where there are minority shareholders in any of the subsidiary companies, the fact that the parent company shareholders do not supply all of the equity finance of the group is recognised. This recognition takes the form of an item 'non-controlling interests' in the financing area of the group statement of financial position.

10.3 There are probably two reasons for this:

1 *Limited liability*. Each company has its own limited liability. Thus, one company's financial collapse will not affect the others directly. The group is a number of independent units as far as liability is concerned.
2 *Individual identity*. Operating a large business as a group of separate semi-autonomous departments is generally seen as good management. One means of emphasising the autonomy is to establish each department or division as a separate company. This arrangement may also be seen as a good marketing ploy since customers may prefer to deal with (what they see as) a smaller unit.

10.4 One company will be treated as an associate of another where another company or group has a long-term interest and can exercise significant influence over the operating and financial policies of that company. Influence is usually demonstrated through representation on the board of directors of the associated company and is supported by a substantial interest in the voting shares in that company. Usually ownership of 20% or more of the voting shares will represent a substantial interest in the voting shares.

The accounting consequences are that the group must include its share of the post-acquisition reserves of the associate, as well as the cost of the shares, in its own statement of financial position. It must also show its share of the operating profit, interest charges and tax charges relating to the associate in the income statement.

Chapter 11

11.1 This criticism may arise because of the problems mentioned in the text. It can be argued that the VAS promotes a view that the business is a coalition of interests. It can be seen as trying to foster a team spirit among key interest groups and trying to get employees 'on side' by treating them as team members. Critics argue that this is mere propaganda, which tries to obscure the underlying conflict between capital and labour. They argue that, as the main purpose of the statement is persuasive rather than informative, the integrity of the financial statements could be damaged in the eyes of users.

Problems relating to team membership and the classification of key items also undermine the usefulness of the statement and this may have a more general adverse effect on the credibility of the financial reports. Supporters of the VAS would dispute these claims. They would argue that value added offers an alternative measure of wealth creation that may provide new insights into business performance. Furthermore, most financial statements have to overcome theoretical or classification problems and the VAS is no exception.

11.2 Inflation may be defined as a general rise in prices or a fall in the general purchasing power of money. The level of inflation is measured by using a general price index, such as the Retail Price Index (RPI). The CPP approach is concerned with maintaining the general purchasing power of the owners' investment in the business and uses the RPI as the basis of making adjustments. It can, therefore, be described as a method of accounting for inflation.

The CCA approach is concerned with specific price changes rather than general price changes. It is concerned with ensuring that a business can maintain its scale of operations. Specific price increases, however, can occur even when there is no inflation. In a dynamic economy there will always be price movements. Thus, even during a period of zero inflation (and deflation) there will be price increases in certain goods and service, which will be offset by price decreases in others. Supporters of CCA, however, would argue that the key issue is not which method is the 'true' method of accounting for inflation, but rather which method is more helpful for decision-making purposes.

11.3 There are a number of possible drawbacks, which include the following:

- The reporting costs may be considerable.
- Reports covering a short period are more likely to be inaccurate because of estimation errors.
- Condensing complex information may result in a distorted portrayal of performance and position.
- It may encourage users to take a short-term perspective when evaluating performance.

11.4 There are various problems associated with the measurement of business segments. These include:

- the definition of a segment;
- the treatment of inter-segmental transactions, such as sales;
- the treatment of expenses and assets that are shared between segments.

There is no single correct method of dealing with these problems, and variations will arise in practice. This, in turn, will hinder comparisons between businesses.

Chapter 12

12.1 The main tasks of the board are to:

- set the strategic direction of the company;
- exercise control;
- maintain external relations.

12.2 The main benefits are that:

- it ensures that a single individual does not have too much power;
- the chairman can offer support and act as a mentor to the CEO;
- it can smooth the path of succession; and
- it can ensure that the responsibilities of both roles will be carried out more effectively than would be the case if a single individual occupied both roles.

12.3 The external auditors will have an intimate knowledge of the accounting and payroll systems that are currently in operation and should be well placed to suggest improvements that will suit the company's needs. There may therefore be a saving of time and cost if they are given the task. However, there is always a risk that the external auditors will receive too high a proportion of the total fees received from the company in the form of consultancy work. This runs the risk of compromising the auditors' independence.

12.4 Institutional investors have become more active for the following reasons:

- *Difficulties of disinvesting in a large public company*. Institutional shareholders tend to have significant shareholdings in companies and attempting to sell a large quantity of shares may provoke a fall in price. Furthermore, an institutional shareholder may be locked into a company's shares if it offers funds to investors which attempt to track the market.
- *Pressure to perform*. Poor stock market returns in recent years have increased pressures on institutional shareholders to provide good returns. One way in which this may be done is through intervention in a company's affairs.
- *Changed regulatory environment*. There is pressure on large institutional shareholders through the UK Corporate Governance Code and government exhortations to engage with companies over corporate-governance issues.

Appendix E
SOLUTIONS TO SELECTED EXERCISES

Chapter 2

2.1 Paul

Statement of cash flows for Thursday

	£
Opening balance (from Wednesday)	59
Cash from sale of wrapping paper	47
Cash paid to purchase wrapping paper	(53)
Closing balance	53

Income statement for Thursday

	£
Sales revenue	47
Cost of goods sold	(33)
Profit	14

Statement of financial position as at Thursday evening

	£
Cash	53
Inventories of goods for resale (23 + 53 − 33)	43
Total assets	96
Equity	96

2.2 Equity

	£
Cash introduced by Paul on Monday	40
Profit for Monday	15
Profit for Tuesday	18
Profit for Wednesday	9
Profit for Thursday	14
Total business wealth (total assets)	96

Thus the equity, all of which belongs to Paul as sole owner, consists of the cash he put in to start the business plus the profit earned each day.

2.3 Helen

Income statement for day 1

	£
Sales revenue (70 × £0.80)	56
Cost of sales (70 × £0.50)	(35)
Profit	21

Statement of cash flows for day 1

	£
Cash introduced by Helen	40
Cash from sales	56
Cash for purchases (80 × £0.50)	(40)
Closing balance	56

Statement of financial position as at end of day 1

	£
Cash balance	56
Inventories of unsold goods (10 × £0.50)	5
Total assets	61
Equity	61

Income statement for day 2

	£
Sales revenue (65 × £0.80)	52.0
Cost of sales (65 × £0.50)	(32.5)
Profit	19.5

Statement of cash flows for day 2

	£
Opening balance	56.0
Cash from sales	52.0
Cash for purchases (60 × £0.50)	(30.0)
Closing balance	78.0

Statement of financial position as at end of day 2

	£
Cash balance	78.0
Inventories of unsold goods (5 × £0.50)	2.5
Total assets	80.5
Equity	80.5

Income statement for day 3

	£
Sales revenue (20 × £0.80) + (45 × £0.40)	34.0
Cost of sales (65 × £0.50)	(32.5)
Profit	1.5

Statement of cash flows for day 3

	£
Opening balance	78.0
Cash from sales	34.0
Cash for purchases (60 × £0.50)	(30.0)
Closing balance	82.0

Statement of financial position as at end of day 3

	£
Cash balance	82.0
Inventories of unsold goods	–
Total assets	82.0
Equity	82.0

2.6 Conversation

(a) The income statement reveals the changes in wealth arising as a result of trading operations. It shows the increase in wealth (revenue) during the period, the decrease in wealth (expenses) in order to generate revenue and the resulting net increase (profit) or decrease (loss) in wealth for the period. While most businesses hold some of their wealth in the form of cash, wealth is also held in other forms, such as non-current assets, receivables and so on.

(b) To be included in a statement of financial position as an asset, an item must be expected to produce future economic benefits. These benefits may arise from selling the asset in the market, but they may also arise from its use – for example, in production.

There are other conditions that must be met in order for an item to be included in the statement of financial position. These are:

- the business must have an exclusive right to control the asset;
- the benefit must arise from some past transaction or event; and
- the asset must be measurable in monetary terms.

(c) The accounting equation is:

Assets = Equity + Liabilities

(d) Non-current assets are assets that do not meet the criteria for current assets. They are normally held for the long-term operations of the business. Some non-current assets may be immovable (for example, property) but others are not (for example, motor vans).

(e) Goodwill may or may not have an indefinite life – it will depend on the nature of the goodwill. There are no hard and fast rules that can be applied. Where this asset has a finite life, it should be amortised. Where it is considered to have an indefinite life, it should not be amortised but should be tested annually for impairment.

2.7 Crafty Engineering Ltd

(a)

Statement of financial position as at 30 June last year

	£000
ASSETS	
Non-current assets	
Property, plant and equipment	
Property	320
Equipment and tools	207
Motor vehicles	38
	565
Current assets	
Inventories	153
Trade receivables	185
	338
Total assets	903
EQUITY AND LIABILITIES	
Equity (which is the missing figure)	441
Non-current liabilities	
Long-term borrowings (Loan Industrial Finance Co.)	260
Current liabilities	
Trade payables	86
Short-term borrowings	116
	202
Total equity and liabilities	903

(b) The statement of financial position reveals a large investment in non-current assets. It represents more than 60% of the total investment in assets (565/903). The nature of the business may require a heavy investment in non-current assets. The current assets exceed the current liabilities by a large amount, being approximately 1.7 times as much as them. Hence, there is no obvious sign of a liquidity problem. However, the statement of financial position reveals that the business has no cash balance and is therefore dependent on the continuing support of short-term borrowing to meet maturing obligations. When considering the long-term financing of the business, we can see that about 37% (that is, 260/(260 + 441)) of total long-term finance is supplied by borrowings and about 63% (that is, 441/(260 + 441)) by the owners. This level of long-term borrowing seems high but not excessive. However, we need to know more about the ability of the business to service the borrowing (that is, make interest payments and repayments of the amount borrowed) before a full assessment can be made.

Chapter 3

3.1 Comments

(a) Equity does increase as a result of the owners introducing more cash into the business, but it will also increase as a result of introducing other assets (for example, a motor car) and by the business generating revenue by trading. Similarly, equity decreases not only as a result of withdrawals of cash by owners but also by withdrawals of other assets (for example, inventories for the owners' personal use) and through trading expenses being incurred. Generally speaking, equity will alter more as a result of trading activities than for any other reason.

(b) An accrued expense is not one that relates to next year. It is one that needs to be matched with the revenue of the accounting period under review, but that has yet to be met in terms of cash payment. As such, it will appear on the statement of financial position as a current liability.

(c) The purpose of depreciation is not to provide for asset replacement. It is an attempt to allocate the cost, or fair value, of the asset (less any residual value) over its useful life. Depreciation provides a measure of the amount that a non-current asset has been consumed during a period. This amount is then charged as an expense for the period. Depreciation is a book entry (the outlay of cash occurs when the asset is purchased) and does not normally entail setting aside a separate amount of cash for asset replacement. Even if this were done, there would be no guarantee that sufficient funds would be available at the end of the asset's life for its replacement. Factors such as inflation and technological change may mean that the replacement cost is higher than the original cost of the asset.

(d) In the short term, the current value of a non-current asset may exceed its original cost. However, nearly all non-current assets wear out over time through being used to generate wealth. This will be the case for buildings. Thus, some measure of depreciation is needed to reflect the fact that the asset is being consumed. Some businesses revalue their buildings upwards where the current value is significantly higher than the original cost. Where this occurs, the depreciation charge should be based on the revalued amount, which will lead to higher depreciation charges.

3.3 Business owner

The existence of profit and downward movement in cash may be for various reasons, which include the following:

- the purchase of assets for cash during the period (for example, motor cars and inventories), which were not all consumed during the period and are therefore not having as great an effect on expenses as they are on cash;
- the payment of an outstanding liability (for example, borrowings), which will have an effect on cash but not on expenses in the income statement;
- the withdrawal of cash by the owners from the equity invested, which will not have an effect on the expenses in the income statement;
- the generation of revenue on credit where the cash has yet to be received. This will increase the sales revenue for the period but will not have a beneficial effect on the cash balance until a later time.

3.4 Missing values

(a)	Rent payable – expense for period	£9,000
(b)	Rates and insurance – expense for period	£6,000
(c)	General expenses – paid in period	£7,000
(d)	Interest (on borrowings) payable – prepaid	£500
(e)	Salaries – paid in period	£6,000
(f)	Rent receivable – received during period	£3,000

3.7 WW Associates

Income statement for the year ended 31 December 2012

	£
Sales revenue (211,000 + 42,000)	253,000
Cost of goods sold (127,000 + 25,000)	(152,000)
Gross profit	101,000
Rent (20,000)	(20,000)
Rates (400 + 1,500)	(1,900)
Wages (−1,700 + 23,800 + 860)	(22,960)
Electricity (2,700)	(2,700)
Machinery depreciation (9,360)	(9,360)
Loss on disposal of the old machinery (13,000 − 3,900 − 9,000)	(100)
Van expenses (17,500)	(17,500)
Profit for the year	26,480

The loss on disposal of the old machinery is the carrying amount (cost less depreciation) less the disposal proceeds. Since the machinery had only been owned for one year, with a depreciation rate of 30%, the depreciation on it so far is £3,900 (that is, £13,000 × 30%). The effective disposal proceeds were £9,000 because, as a result of trading it in, the business saved £9,000 on the new asset.

The depreciation expense for 2012 is based on the cost less accumulated depreciation of the assets owned at the end of 2012.

Statement of financial position as at 31 December 2012

	£
ASSETS	
Machinery (25,300 + 6,000 + 9,000 − 13,000 + 3,900 − 9,360)	21,840*
Inventories (12,200 + 143,000 + 12,000 − 127,000 − 25,000)	15,200
Trade receivables (21,300 + 211,000 − 198,000)	34,300
Cash at bank (overdraft) (8,300 − 23,000 − 25,000 − 2,000 − 6,000 − 23,800 − 2,700 − 12,000 + 42,000 + 198,000 − 156,000 − 17,500)	(19,700)
Prepaid expenses (400 − 400 + 5,000 + 500)	5,500
Total assets	57,140
EQUITY AND LIABILITIES	
Equity (owner's capital) (48,900 − 23,000 + 26,480)	52,380
Trade payables (16,900 + 143,000 − 156,000)	3,900
Accrued expenses (1,700 − 1,700 + 860)	860
Total equity and liabilities	57,140

* Cost less accumulated depreciation at 31 December 2011	25,300
Carrying amount of machine disposed of (£13,000 − £3,900)	(9,100)
Cost of new machine	15,000
Depreciation for 2012 (£31,200 × 30%)	(9,360)
Carrying amount (written-down value) of machine at 31 December 2012	21,840

The statement of financial position could now be rewritten in a more stylish form as follows:

Statement of financial position as at 31 December 2012

	£
ASSETS	
Non-current assets	
Property, plant and equipment	
Machinery at cost less depreciation	21,840
Current assets	
Inventories	15,200
Trade receivables	34,300
Prepaid expenses	5,500
	55,000
Total assets	76,840
EQUITY AND LIABILITIES	
Equity	52,380
Current liabilities	
Trade payables	3,900
Accrued expenses	860
Borrowings – bank overdraft	19,700
	24,460
Total equity and liabilities	76,840

3.8 Nikov and Co

An examination of the income statements for the two years reveals a number of interesting points, which include:

- An increase in sales revenue and gross profit of 9.9% in 2012.
- The gross profit expressed as a percentage of sales revenue remaining at 70%.
- An increase in salaries of 7.2%.
- An increase in selling and distribution costs of 31.2%.
- An increase in bad debts of 392.5%.
- A decline in profit for the year of 39.3%.
- A decline in the profit for the year as a percentage of sales revenue from 13.3% to 7.4%.

Thus, the business has enjoyed an increase in sales revenue and gross profits, but this has failed to translate to an increase in profit for the year because of the significant rise in overheads. The increase in selling costs during 2012 suggests that the increase in sales revenue was achieved by greater marketing effort, and the huge increase in bad debts suggests that the increase in sales revenue may be attributable to selling to less creditworthy customers or that the debt-collection policy became weaker. There appears to have been a change of policy in 2012 towards sales, and this has not been successful overall as the profit for the year has shown a dramatic decline.

Chapter 4

4.1 Limited companies can no more set a limit on the amount of debts they will meet than can human beings. They must meet their debts up to the limit of their assets, just as we as individuals must. In the context of owners' claim, 'reserves' mean part of the owners' claim against the assets of the company. These assets may or may not include cash. The legal ability of the company to pay dividends is not related to the amount of cash that it has.

Preference shares do not carry a guaranteed dividend. They simply guarantee that the preference shareholders have a right to the first slice of any dividend that is paid. Shares of many companies can, in effect, be bought by one investor from another through the Stock Exchange. Such a transaction has no direct effect on the company, however. These are not new shares being offered by the company, but existing shares that are being sold 'second-hand'.

4.2 **(a)** The first part of the quote is incorrect. Bonus shares should not, of themselves, increase the value of the shareholders' wealth. This is because reserves, belonging to the shareholders, are used to create bonus shares. Thus, each shareholder's stake in the company has not increased.

(b) This statement is incorrect. Shares can be issued at any price, provided that it is not below the nominal value of the shares. Once the company has been trading profitably for a period, the shares will not be worth the same as they were (the nominal value) when the company was first formed. In such circumstances, issuing shares at above their nominal value would not only be legal, but essential to preserve the wealth of the existing shareholders relative to any new ones.

(c) This statement is incorrect. From a legal perspective, the company is limited to a maximum dividend of the current extent of its revenue reserves. This amounts to any after-tax profits or gains realised that have not been eroded through, for example, payments of previous dividends. Legally, cash is not an issue; it would be perfectly legal for a company to borrow the funds to pay a dividend – although whether such an action would be commercially prudent is another question.

(d) This statement is partly incorrect. Companies do indeed have to pay tax on their profits. Depending on their circumstances, shareholders might also have to pay tax on their dividends.

4.4 **Iqbal Ltd**

Year	Maximum dividend £	
2008	0	No profit exists out of which to pay a dividend.
2009	0	There remains a cumulative loss of £7,000. Since the revaluation represents a gain that has not been realised, it cannot be used to justify a dividend.
2010	13,000	The cumulative net realised gains are derived as (–£15,000 + £8,000 + £15,000 + £5,000).
2011	14,000	The realised profits and gains for the year.
2012	22,000	The realised profits and gains for the year.

4.6 **Pear Limited**

Income statement for the year ended 30 September 2012

	£000
Revenue (1,456 + 18)	1,474
Cost of sales	(768)
Gross profit	706
Salaries	(220)
Depreciation (249 + 12)	(261)
Other operating costs (131 + (2% × 200) + 2)	(137)
Operating profit	88
Interest payable (15 + 15)	(30)
Profit before taxation	58
Taxation (58 × 30%)	(17)
Profit for the year	41

Statement of financial position as at 30 September 2012

	£000
ASSETS	
Non-current assets	
Property, plant and equipment	
Cost (1,570 + 30)	1,600
Depreciation (690 + 12)	(702)
	898
Current assets	
Inventories	207
Trade receivables (182 + 18 − 4)	196
Cash at bank	21
	424
Total assets	1,322
EQUITY AND LIABILITIES	
Equity	
Share capital	300
Share premium account	300
Retained earnings (104 + 41 − 25)	120
	720
Non-current liabilities	
Borrowings − 10% loan (repayable 2015)	300
Current liabilities	
Trade payables	88
Other payables (20 + 30 + 15 + 2)	67
Taxation	17
Dividend approved	25
Borrowings − bank overdraft	105
	302
Total equity and liabilities	1,322

4.7 Chips Limited

Income statement for the year ended 30 June 2012

	£000
Revenue (1,850 − 16)	1,834
Cost of sales (1,040 + 23)	(1,063)
Gross profit	771
Depreciation (220 (−2 − 5 + 8) + (94 × 20%))	(240)
Other operating costs	(375)
Operating profit	156
Interest payable (35 + 35)	(70)
Profit before taxation	86
Taxation (86 × 30%)	(26)
Profit for the year	60

Statement of financial position as at 30 June 2012

ASSETS

	Cost £000	Depreciation £000	£000
Non-current assets			
Property, plant and equipment			
Buildings	800	(112)	688
Plant and equipment	650	(367)	283
Motor vehicles (102 − 8); (53 − 5 + 19)	94	(67)	27
	1,544	(546)	998
Current assets			
Inventories			950
Trade receivables (420 − 16)			404
Cash at bank (16 + 2)			18
			1,372
Total assets			2,370
EQUITY AND LIABILITIES			
Equity			
Ordinary shares of £1, fully paid			800
Reserves at beginning of the year			248
Retained profit for year			60
			1,108
Non-current liabilities			
Borrowings – secured 10% loan notes			700
Current liabilities			
Trade payables (361 + 23)			384
Other payables (117 + 35)			152
Taxation			26
			562
Total equity and liabilities			2,370

Chapter 5

5.1 Conceptual framework

Accounting is an evolving subject. It is not static and so the principles that are laid down at any particular point in time may become obsolete as a result of changes in our understanding of the nature of accounting information and its impact on users and changes in the economic environment within which accounting is employed. We must accept, therefore, that accounting principles will continue to evolve and that existing principles must be regularly reviewed.

5.2 Accountants' judgement

The quotation probably overstates the case. It is true that choice has been removed in some areas but there is still plenty of scope for accountants to make choices and to exercise judgement. Many decisions involving the valuation of assets and liabilities and the treatment of unusual items can involve difficult judgements. We have also seen that some accounting standards require judgements to be made (for example, those dealing with inventories and valuation).

5.5 I. Ching (Booksellers) plc

Statement of comprehensive income for the year ended 31 December 2012

	£000
Revenue	943
Cost of sales	(460)
Gross profit	483
Distribution expenses	(110)
Administrative expenses	(212)
Other expenses	(25)
Operating profit	136
Finance charges	(40)
Profit before tax	96
Taxation	(24)
Profit for the year	72
Other comprehensive income	
Revaluation of property, plant and equipment	20
Foreign currency translation differences for foreign operations	(15)
Tax on other comprehensive income	(1)
Other comprehensive income for the year, net of tax	4
Total comprehensive income for the year	76

5.6 Manet plc

Statement of changes in equity for the year ended 31 December 2012

	Share capital £m	Share premium £m	Revaluation reserve £m	Translation reserve £m	Retained earnings £m	Total £m
Balance as at 1 January 2012	250	50	120	15	380	815
Changes in equity for 2012						
Dividends (Note 1)	–	–	–	–	(80)	(80)
Total comprehensive income for the year (Note 2)	–	–	30	(5)	160	185
Balance at 31 December 2012	250	50	150	10	460	920

Notes:

1 Dividends have been shown in the statement rather than in the notes. Either approach, however, is acceptable.
2 The effect of each component of comprehensive income on each component of shareholder equity must be shown. The revaluation gain and loss on exchange translation are each transferred to a specific reserve and the profit for the year is transferred to retained earnings.

5.7 Accounting regulation

Here are some points that might be made concerning accounting regulation and accounting measurement:

For:

- It seems reasonable that companies, particularly given their limited liability, should be required to account to their members and to the general public and that rules should prescribe how this should be done – including how particular items should be measured. It also seems sensible that these rules should try to establish some uniformity of practice. Investors could be misled if the same item appeared in the financial statements of two separate companies but had been measured in different ways.
- Companies would find it difficult to attract finance, credit and possibly employees without publishing credible information about themselves. An important measure of performance is profit, and investors often need to make judgements concerning relative performance within an industry sector. Without clear benchmarks by which to judge performance, investors may not invest in a company.

Against:

- It could be argued that it is up to the companies to decide whether or not they can survive and prosper without publishing information about themselves. If they can, so much the better, as, by not doing so, they will save large amounts of money. If it is necessary for a company to provide financial information in order to be able to attract investment finance and other necessary factors, then the company can make the necessary judgement as to how much information is necessary and what forms of measurement are required.

- Not all company managements view matters in the same way. Allowing companies to select their own approaches to financial reporting enables them to reflect their particular personalities. Thus, a conservative management will adopt conservative accounting policies, such as writing off research and development expenditure quickly, whereas more adventurous management may adopt less conservative accounting policies, such as writing off research and development expenditure over several years. The impact of these different views will have an effect on profit and will give the reader an insight into the approach adopted by the management team.

Chapter 6

6.1 **(a)** An increase in the level of inventories would, ultimately, have an adverse effect on cash.

(b) A rights issue of ordinary shares will give rise to a positive cash flow, which will be included in the 'financing' section of the statement of cash flows.

(c) A bonus issue of ordinary shares has no cash flow effect.

(d) Writing off some of the value of the inventories has no cash flow effect.

(e) A disposal for cash of a large number of shares by a major shareholder has no cash flow effect as far as the business is concerned.

(f) Depreciation does not involve cash at all. Using the indirect method of deducing cash flows from operating activities involves the depreciation expense in the calculation, but this is simply because we are trying to find out, from the profit before taxation (after depreciation) figure, what the profit before taxation *and* depreciation must have been.

6.3 **Torrent plc**

Statement of cash flows for the year ended 31 December 2012

	£m
Cash flows from operating activities	
Profit before taxation (after interest) (see Note 1 below)	170
Adjustments for:	
Depreciation (Note 2)	78
Interest expense (Note 3)	26
	274
Decrease in inventories (41 − 35)	6
Increase in trade receivables (145 − 139)	(6)
Decrease in trade payables (54 − 41)	(13)
Cash generated from operations	261
Interest paid	(26)
Taxation paid (Note 4)	(41)
Dividend paid	(60)
Net cash from operating activities	134
Cash flows from investing activities	
Payments to acquire plant and machinery	(67)
Net cash used in investing activities	(67)
Cash flows from financing activities	
Redemption of loan notes (250 − 150) (Note 5)	(100)
Net cash used in financing activities	(100)
Net decrease in cash and cash equivalents	(33)
Cash and cash equivalents at 1 January 2012	
Bank overdraft	(56)
Cash and cash equivalents at 31 December 2012	
Bank overdraft	(89)

To see how this relates to the cash of the business at the beginning and end of the year it can be useful to provide a reconciliation as follows:

Analysis of cash and cash equivalents during the year ended 31 December 2012

	£m
Cash and cash equivalents at 1 January 2012	(56)
Net cash outflow	(33)
Cash and cash equivalents at 31 December 2012	(89)

Notes:

1 This is simply taken from the income statement for the year.
2 Since there were no disposals, the depreciation charges must be the difference between the start and end of the year's plant and machinery values, adjusted by the cost of any additions.

	£m
Carrying amount at 1 January 2012	325
Additions	67
Depreciation (balancing figure)	(78)
Carrying amount at 31 December 2012	314

3 Interest payable expense must be taken out, by adding it back to the profit before taxation figure. We subsequently deduct the cash paid for interest payable during the year. In this case the two figures are identical.
4 Companies pay 50% of their tax during their accounting year and 50% in the following year. Thus the 2012 payment would have been half the tax on the 2011 profit (that is, the figure that would have appeared in the current liabilities at the end of 2011), plus half of the 2012 tax charge (that is, $23 + (1/2 \times 36) = 41$).
5 It is assumed that the cash payment to redeem the loan notes was simply the difference between the figures on the two statements of financial position.

It seems that there was a bonus issue of ordinary shares during the year. These increased by £100m. At the same time, the share premium account balance reduced by £40m (to zero) and the revaluation reserve balance fell by £60m.

6.6 Blackstone plc

Statement of cash flows for the year ended 31 March 2012

	£m
Cash flows from operating activities	
Profit before taxation (after interest) (see Note 1 below)	1,853
Adjustments for:	
Depreciation (Note 2)	1,289
Interest expense (Note 3)	456
	3,598
Increase in inventories (2,410 – 1,209)	(1,201)
Increase in trade receivables (1,173 – 641)	(532)
Increase in trade payables (1,507 – 931)	576
Cash generated from operations	2,441
Interest paid (Note 3)	(456)
Taxation paid (Note 4)	(300)
Dividend paid	(400)
Net cash from operating activities	1,285
Cash flows from investing activities	
Proceeds of disposals	54
Payment to acquire intangible non-current asset	(700)
Payments to acquire property, plant and equipment	(4,578)
Net cash used in investing activities	(5,224)
Cash flows from financing activities	
Bank borrowings	2,000
Net cash from financing activities	2,000
Net decrease in cash and cash equivalents	(1,939)
Cash and cash equivalents at 1 April 2011	
Cash at bank	123
Cash and cash equivalents at 31 March 2012	
Bank overdraft	(1,816)

To see how this relates to the cash of the business at the beginning and end of the year it can be useful to provide a reconciliation as follows:

Analysis of cash and cash equivalents during the year ended 31 March 2012

	£m
Cash and cash equivalents at 1 April 2011	123
Net cash outflow	(1,939)
Cash and cash equivalents at 31 March 2012	1,816

Notes:

1 This is simply taken from the income statement for the year.

2 The full depreciation charge was that stated in Note 2 to the question (£1,251m), plus the deficit on disposal of the non-current assets. According to Note 2, these non-current assets had originally cost £581m and had been depreciated by £489m, so had a net carrying amount of £92m. They were sold for £54m, leading to a deficit on disposal of £38m. Thus the full depreciation expense for the year was £1,289m (that is, £1,251m + £38m).

3 Interest payable expense must be taken out, by adding it back to the profit before taxation figure. We subsequently deduct the cash paid for interest payable during the year. In this case the two figures are identical.

4 Companies pay tax at 50% during their accounting year and the other 50% in the following year. Thus the 2012 payment would have been half the tax on the 2011 profit (that is, the figure that would have appeared in the current liabilities at 31 March 2011), plus half of the 2012 tax charge (that is, $105 + (^1/_2 \times 390) = 300$).

6.7 York plc

Statement of cash flows for the year ended 30 September 2012

	£m
Cash flows from operating activities	
Profit before taxation (after interest) (see Note 1 below)	10.0
Adjustments for:	
Depreciation (Note 2)	9.8
Interest expense (Note 3)	3.0
	22.8
Increase in inventories and trade receivables (122.1 − 119.8)	(2.3)
Increase in trade payables (82.5 − 80.0)	2.5
Cash generated from operations	23.0
Interest paid (Note 3)	(3.0)
Taxation paid (Note 4)	(2.3)
Dividend paid	(3.5)
Net cash from operating activities	14.2
Cash flows from investing activities	
Proceeds of disposals (Note 2)	5.2
Payments to acquire non-current assets	(20.0)
Net cash used in investing activities	(14.8)
Cash flows from financing activities	
Increase in long-term borrowings	3.0
Share issue (Note 5)	5.0
Net cash from financing activities	8.0
Net increase in cash and cash equivalents	7.4
Cash and cash equivalents at 1 October 2011	
Cash at bank	9.2
Cash and cash equivalents at 30 September 2012	
Cash at bank	16.6

To see how this relates to the cash of the business at the beginning and end of the year it can be useful to provide a reconciliation as follows:

Analysis of cash and cash equivalents during the year ended 30 September 2012

	£m
Cash and cash equivalents at 1 October 2011	9.2
Net cash inflow	7.4
Cash and cash equivalents at 30 September 2012	16.6

Notes:

1 This is simply taken from the income statement for the year.

2 The full depreciation charge was the £13.0m, less the surplus on disposal (£3.2m), both stated in Note 1 to the question. (According to the table in Note 4 to the question, the non-current assets disposed of had a net carrying value of £2.0m. To produce a surplus of £3.2m, they must have been sold for £5.2m.)

3 Interest payable expense must be taken out, by adding it back to the profit before taxation figure. We subsequently deduct the cash paid for interest payable during the year. In this case the two figures are identical.

4 Companies pay 50% of their tax during their accounting year and the other 50% in the following year. Thus the 2012 payment would have been half the tax on the 2011 profit (that is, the figure that would have appeared in the current liabilities at 30 September 2011), plus half of the 2012 tax charge (that is, $1.0 + (^{1}/_{2} \times 2.6) = 2.3$).

5 This issue must have been for cash since it could not have been a bonus issue – the share premium account is untouched and 'Reserves' had altered over the year only by the amount of the 2012 retained earnings (profit for the year, less the dividend). The shares seem to have been issued at par (that is, at their nominal value). This is a little surprising since the business has assets that seem to be above that value. On the other hand, were this a rights issue, the low issue price would not have disadvantaged the existing shareholders since they were also the beneficiaries of the advantage of the low issue price.

6.8 Axis plc

Statement of cash flows for the year ended 31 December 2012

	£m
Cash flows from operating activities	
Profit before taxation (after interest) (see Note 1 below)	34
Adjustments for:	
Depreciation (Note 2)	19
Interest payable expense (Note 3)	2
Interest receivable (Note 4)	(2)
	53
Decrease in inventories (25 – 24)	1
Increase in trade receivables (26 – 16)	(10)
Increase in trade payables (36 – 31)	5
Cash generated from operations	49
Interest paid (Note 3)	(2)
Taxation paid (Note 5)	(15)
Dividend paid	(14)
Net cash from operating activities	18
Cash flows from investing activities	
Interest receivable	2
Proceeds of disposals (Note 2)	4
Payments to acquire non-current assets (Note 6)	(25)
Net cash used in investing activities	(19)
Cash flows from financing activities	
Issue of loan notes	20
Net cash from financing activities	20
Net increase in cash and cash equivalents	19
Cash and cash equivalents at 1 January 2012	
Cash at bank	nil
Short-term investments	nil
	nil
Cash and cash equivalents at 31 December 2012	
Cash at bank	7
Short-term investments	12
	19

To see how this relates to the cash of the business at the beginning and end of the year it can be useful to provide a reconciliation as follows:

Analysis of cash and cash equivalents during the year ended 31 December 2012

	£m
Cash and cash equivalents at 1 January 2012	nil
Net cash inflow	19
Cash and cash equivalents at 31 December 2012	19

Notes:

1 This is simply taken from the income statement for the year.

2 The full depreciation charge for the year is the sum of two figures labelled 'depreciation' and the deficit on disposal of non-current assets (that is, £2m + £16m + £1m = £19m). These were detailed in the income statement.

According to the note in the question, the non-current assets disposed of had a net carrying amount of £5.0m (that is, £15m – £10m). To produce a deficit of £1m, they must have been sold for £4m.

3 Interest payable expense must be taken out, by adding it back to the figure for profit before taxation. We subsequently deduct the cash paid for interest payable during the year. In this case the two figures are identical.

4 Interest receivable must be taken away to work towards the profit before crediting it, because it is not part of operations but of investing activities. The cash inflow from this source appears under the 'Cash flows from investing activities' heading.

5 Companies pay 50% of their tax during their accounting year and the other 50% in the following year. Thus the 2012 payment would have been half the tax on the 2011 profit (that is, the figure that would have appeared in the current liabilities at 31 December 2011), plus half the 2012 tax charge (that is, $7 + (^{1}/_{2} \times 16) = 15$).

6 The cost of the newly acquired non-current assets (plant and machinery) can be deduced as follows:

	£m
Cost of plant and machinery at 1 January 2012	70
Plant disposed of	(15)
Plant acquired	25
Cost of plant and machinery at 31 December 2012	80

Chapter 7

7.1 Provisions

1 A provision should be recognised because:

- the sale of the motor cars with a warranty gives rise to an obligation;
- it is probable (based on past experience) that there will be an outflow of resources arising from the warranty.

2 A provision should be recognised because:

- the evidence suggests that there is an obligation;
- an outflow of resources to compensate the victims is probable.

3 A provision should not be recognised because there is no present obligation. The business can avoid the future costs by selling the aircraft before the point at which the overhauls becomes due.

7.4 Darco Instruments plc

(a) The total finance charge is calculated as follows:

	£m
Total lease payments (4 × £3m)	12.0
Cost of plant	10.0
Total finance charge	2.0

The finance charge for each year, using the sum of the digits method, is as follows:

Year to 31 May	Allocation	£m
2013	4/10 × £2m	0.8
2014	3/10 × £2m	0.6
2015	2/10 × £2m	0.4
2016	1/10 × £2m	0.2
		2.0

Income statement extracts for each year of the lease will be as follows:

	2013 £m	2014 £m	2015 £m	2016 £m
Depreciation (£10.0m/4)*	2.5	2.5	2.5	2.5
Finance charge	0.8	0.6	0.4	0.2

* Depreciation is allocated over the lease period as it is shorter than the useful life of the machine.

Before showing the statement of financial position extracts, we must calculate the capital element of each lease payment as follows:

	2013 £m	2014 £m	2015 £m	2016 £m
Finance charge	0.8	0.6	0.4	0.2
Capital (balancing figure)	2.2	2.4	2.6	2.8
Total lease payment	3.0	3.0	3.0	3.0

The statement of financial position extracts are as follows:

	Inception of lease £m	2013 £m	2014 £m	2015 £m	2016 £m
Non-current assets					
Machine	10.0	10.0	10.0	10.0	10.0
Accumulated depreciation	0	2.5	5.0	7.5	10.0
Carrying value	10.0	7.5	5.0	2.5	0.0
Non-current liabilities					
Lease payments	7.8	5.4	2.8	0.0	0.0
Current liabilities					
Lease payments	2.2	2.4	2.6	2.8	0.0

(b) If the machine was acquired using an operating lease, the lease payments would be treated as an expense in each year.

Income statement extracts are as follows:

	2013 £m	2014 £m	2015 £m	2016 £m
Operating lease payments	3.0	3.0	3.0	3.0

Nothing concerning this will appear on the statement of financial position.

(c) This total finance charge must then be allocated between the relevant reporting periods so as to produce a constant rate of return on the outstanding lease payments. The finance charge will, therefore, be high at the beginning of the lease period, when the amount of outstanding lease payments is high, but will decrease over time as the liability for future lease payments decreases.

7.5 Barchester United Football Club plc

	Notes	£m
Draft profit before tax		48.8
Transfer to restructuring provision	1	5.4
Reversal of previous provision for unfair dismissal	2	2.2
Contingent asset	3	2.0
Research expenditure previously capitalised	4	(1.0)
Capitalisation of borrowing costs	5	3.3
Increase in finance charge	6	(0.3)
Revised profit before tax		60.4

Notes

1 Restructuring costs should be charged to the relevant provision.
2 As there is now no likelihood of an outflow of resources arising from the court case, the provision should be reversed.
3 As it is now virtually certain that the TV channel will pay the disputed amount, it should be recognised.
4 This research expenditure cannot demonstrate that future probable economic benefits exist. It should therefore be treated as an expense.
5 The borrowing costs should be capitalised as they are directly related to the construction of an asset.
6 The total finance charge is calculated as follows:

	£m
Total lease payments (4 × £1.5m)	6.0
Cost of turf	4.0
Total finance charge	2.0

The finance charge for the current year, using the sum of the digits method, is calculated as follows:

$$\text{Sum of the digits: } 4 + 3 + 2 + 1 = 10$$

$$\text{Finance charge } 4/10 \times £2m = £0.8m$$

The lease payment charged to the income statement is £0.5m (£2m/4). This means that the net effect of replacing the existing finance charge with the correct finance charge in the income statement will be a £0.3m (£0.8m – £0.5m) decrease in profits.

Chapter 8

8.1 Three businesses

A plc operates a supermarket chain. The grocery business is highly competitive and to generate high sales volumes it is usually necessary to accept low operating profit margins. Thus, we can see that the operating profit margin of A plc is the lowest of the three shown. The inventories turnover period of supermarket chains also tends to be quite low. They are often efficient in managing inventories and most supermarket chains have invested heavily in inventories control and logistical systems over the years. The average settlement period for receivables is very low as most sales are for cash (although, when a customer pays by credit card, there is usually a small delay before the supermarket receives the amount due). A low inventories turnover period and a low average settlement period for receivables usually mean that the investment in current assets is low. Hence, the current ratio (current assets/current liabilities) is also low.

B plc is the holiday tour operator. We can see that the sales to capital employed ratio is the highest of the three shown. This is because tour operators do not usually require a large investment of capital: they do not need a large asset base in order to conduct their operations. The inventories turnover period ratio does not apply to B plc. It is a service business, which does not hold inventories for resale. We can see that the average settlement period for receivables is low. This may be because customers are invoiced near to the holiday date for any amounts outstanding and must pay before going on holiday. The lack of inventories held and low average settlement period for receivables leads to a very low current ratio.

C plc is the food manufacturing business. We can see that the sales to capital employed ratio is the lowest of the three shown. This is because manufacturers tend to invest heavily in both current and non-current assets. The inventories turnover period is the highest of the three. Three different kinds of inventories – raw materials, work in progress and finished goods – are held by manufacturers. The average receivables settlement period is also the highest of the three given. Manufacturers tend to sell to other businesses rather than to the public and their customers will normally demand credit. A one-month credit period for customers is fairly common for manufacturing businesses, although customers may receive a discount for prompt payment. The relatively high investment in inventories and receivables usually results in a high current ratio.

8.2 I. Jiang (Western) Ltd

The effect of each of the changes on ROCE is not always easy to predict.

1 On the face of it, an increase in the gross profit margin would tend to lead to an increase in ROCE. An increase in the gross profit margin may, however, lead to a decrease in ROCE in particular circumstances. If the increase in the margin resulted from an increase in sales prices, which in turn led to a decrease in sales revenue, a fall in ROCE can occur. A fall in sales revenue can reduce the operating profit (the numerator (top part of the fraction) in ROCE) if the overheads of the business did not decrease correspondingly.

2 A reduction in sales revenue can reduce ROCE for the reasons mentioned above.

3 An increase in overhead expenses will reduce the operating profit and this in turn will result in a reduction in ROCE.

4 An increase in inventories held would increase the amount of capital employed by the business (the denominator (bottom part of the fraction) in ROCE) where long-term funds are employed to finance the inventories. This will, in turn, reduce ROCE.

5 Repayment of the borrowings at the year end will reduce the capital employed and this will increase the ROCE, assuming that the year-end capital employed figure has been used in the calculation. Since the operating profit was earned during a period in which the borrowings existed, there is a strong argument for basing the capital employed figure on what was the position during the year, rather than at the end of it.

6 An increase in the time taken for credit customers to pay will result in an increase in capital employed if long-term funds are employed to finance the trade receivables. This increase in long-term funds will, in turn, reduce ROCE.

8.3 Amsterdam Ltd and Berlin Ltd

The ratios for Amsterdam Ltd and Berlin Ltd reveal that the average settlement period for trade receivables for Amsterdam Ltd is three times that for Berlin Ltd. Berlin Ltd is therefore much quicker in collecting amounts outstanding from customers. On the other hand, there is not much difference between the two businesses in the time taken to pay trade payables.

It is interesting to compare the difference in the trade receivables and payables settlement periods for each business. As Amsterdam Ltd allows an average of 63 days' credit to its customers, yet pays suppliers within 50 days, it will require greater investment in working capital than Berlin Ltd, which allows an average of only 21 days to its customers but takes 45 days to pay its suppliers.

Amsterdam Ltd has a much higher gross profit margin than Berlin Ltd. However, the operating profit margin for the two businesses is identical. This suggests that Amsterdam Ltd has much higher overheads (as a percentage of sales revenue) than Berlin Ltd. The average inventories turnover period for Amsterdam Ltd is more than twice that of Berlin Ltd. This may be due to the fact that Amsterdam Ltd maintains a wider range of inventories in an attempt to meet customer requirements. The evidence therefore suggests that Amsterdam Ltd is the one that prides itself on personal service. The higher average settlement period for trade receivables is consistent with a more relaxed attitude to credit collection (thereby maintaining customer goodwill) and the high overheads are consistent with incurring the additional costs of satisfying customers' requirements. Amsterdam Ltd's high inventories levels are consistent with maintaining a wide range of inventories, with the aim of satisfying a range of customer needs.

Berlin Ltd has the characteristics of a more price-competitive business. Its gross profit margin is much lower than that of Amsterdam Ltd, that is, a much lower gross profit for each £1 of sales revenue. However, overheads have been kept low, the effect being that the operating profit margin is the same as Amsterdam Ltd's. The low average inventories turnover period and average settlement period for trade receivables are consistent with a business that wishes to minimise investment in current assets, thereby reducing costs.

8.7 Bradbury Ltd

(a)

	2011	2012
1 Operating profit margin	$\dfrac{914}{9,482} \times 100 = 9.6\%$	$\dfrac{1,042}{11,365} \times 100 = 9.2\%$
2 ROCE	$\dfrac{914}{11,033} \times 100 = 8.3\%$	$\dfrac{1,042}{13,943} \times 100 = 7.5\%$
3 Current ratio	$\dfrac{4,926}{1,508} = 3.3{:}1$	$\dfrac{7,700}{5,174} = 1.5{:}1$
4 Gearing ratio	$\dfrac{1,220}{11,033} \times 100 = 11.1\%$	$\dfrac{3,675}{13,943} \times 100 = 26.4\%$
5 Trade receivables settlement period	$\dfrac{2,540}{9,482} \times 365 = 98$ days	$\dfrac{4,280}{11,365} \times 365 = 137$ days
6 Sales revenue to capital employed	$\dfrac{9,482}{(9,813 + 1,220)} = 0.9$ times	$\dfrac{11,365}{(10,268 + 3,675)} = 0.8$ times

(b) The operating profit margin was slightly lower in 2012 than in 2011. Although there was an increase in sales revenue in 2012, this could not prevent a slight fall in ROCE in that year. The lower operating margin and increases in sales revenue may well be due to the new contract. The capital employed by the company increased in 2012 by a larger percentage than the increase in revenue. Hence, the sales revenue to capital employed ratio decreased over the period. The increase in capital employed during 2012 is largely due to an increase in borrowing. However, the gearing ratio is probably still low in comparison with other businesses. Comparison of the premises and borrowings figures indicates possible unused borrowing (debt) capacity.

The major cause for concern has been the dramatic decline in liquidity during 2012. The current ratio for that year is less than half that for 2011. There has also been a similar decrease in the acid test ratio, from 1.7:1 in 2011 to 0.8:1 in 2012. The statement of financial position shows that the business now has a large overdraft and the trade payables outstanding have nearly doubled in 2012.

The trade receivables outstanding and inventories have increased much more than appears to be warranted by the increase in sales revenue. This may be due to the terms of the contract that has been negotiated and may be difficult to influence. If this is the case, the business should consider whether it needs more longer-term finance. If the conclusion is that it does, acquiring more may be a sensible policy.

It would be difficult to conclude that the expansion programme has shown itself to be effective. ROCE has reduced and liquidity is substantially weakened. There may be greater benefits from the expansion in 2013, but this needs to be monitored closely.

8.8 Harridges Ltd

(a)

	2012	2013
ROCE	$\dfrac{310}{1,600} \times 100 = 19.4\%$	$\dfrac{350}{1,700} \times 100 = 20.6\%$
ROSF	$\dfrac{155}{1,100} \times 100 = 14.1\%$	$\dfrac{175}{1,200} \times 100 = 14.6\%$
Gross profit margin	$\dfrac{1,040}{2,600} \times 100 = 40\%$	$\dfrac{1,150}{3,500} \times 100 = 32.9\%$
Operating profit margin	$\dfrac{310}{2,600} \times 100 = 11.9\%$	$\dfrac{350}{3,500} \times 100 = 10\%$
Current ratio	$\dfrac{735}{400} = 1.8$	$\dfrac{660}{485} = 1.4$
Acid test ratio	$\dfrac{485}{400} = 1.2$	$\dfrac{260}{485} = 0.5$
Trade receivables settlement period	$\dfrac{105}{2,600} \times 365 = 15 \text{ days}$	$\dfrac{145}{3,500} \times 365 = 15 \text{ days}$
Trade payables settlement period	$\dfrac{300}{1,560^*} \times 365 = 70 \text{ days}$	$\dfrac{375}{2,350^*} \times 365 = 58 \text{ days}$
Inventories turnover period	$\dfrac{250}{1,560} \times 365 = 58 \text{ days}$	$\dfrac{400}{2,350} \times 365 = 62 \text{ days}$
Gearing ratio	$\dfrac{500}{1,600} \times 100 = 31.3\%$	$\dfrac{500}{1,700} \times 100 = 29.4\%$

* Used because the credit purchases figure is not available.

(b) There has been a considerable decline in the gross profit margin during 2013. This fact, combined with the increase in sales revenue by more than one-third, suggests that a price-cutting policy has been adopted in an attempt to stimulate sales. The resulting increase in sales revenue, however, has led to only a small improvement in ROCE and ROSF.

Despite a large cut in the gross profit margin, the operating profit margin has fallen by less than two percentage points. This suggests that overheads may have been more tightly controlled during 2013. Certainly, overheads have not risen in proportion to sales revenue.

The current ratio has fallen a little and the acid test ratio has fallen to less than half its previous value. Although liquidity ratios tend to be lower in retailing than in manufacturing, the liquidity of the business should now be a cause for concern. However, this may be a passing problem. The business is investing heavily in non-current assets and is relying on internal funds to finance this growth. When this investment ends, the liquidity position may improve quickly.

The trade receivables period has remained unchanged over the two years, and there has been no significant change in the inventories turnover period in 2013. The gearing ratio seems quite low and provides no cause for concern given the profitability of the business.

Overall, the business appears to be financially sound. Although there has been rapid growth during 2013, there is no real cause for alarm provided that the liquidity of the business can be improved in the near future. In the absence of information concerning share price, it is not possible to say whether an investment should be made.

Chapter 9

9.1 Next plc

The Next plc dividend yield is somewhat below that for the retailers section average. This might imply that Next pays lower dividends than other businesses in the sector. In fact this seems to be the case with Next paying out a substantially smaller proportion of its profit (cover of 3.2 times, compared with the 2.5 average). This implies that Next has a relatively high share price, compared to other retailers.

Compared to current (most recently reported) earnings, the current market price (P/E ratio) of Next is rather higher than the average for listed retailers. This implies that the investing public has more confidence in the future prospects of Next than in listed retailers generally. However, both dividend yield and P/E ratios can be difficult to interpret.

9.2 Telford Industrial Services plc

Common-size statement of financial position at 31 December

	2009	2010	2011	2012
	£m	£m	£m	£m
Non-current assets	100	83	106	102
Current assets				
Inventories	44	36	38	41
Trade receivables	71	69	56	46
Cash	–	5	–	–
	115	110	94	87
Total assets	215	193	200	189
EQUITY	100	100	100	100
Non-current liabilities	63	49	49	47
Current liabilities				
Trade payables	42	44	41	29
Short-term borrowings	10	–	10	13
	52	44	51	42
Total equity and liabilities	215	193	200	189

[The individual figures are calculated by dividing each of the original figures by the equity value for the year concerned and multiplying the result by 100. For example, the inventories figure for 2009 is 21/48 × 100 = 44. Since the revised values have been expressed in whole numbers (no decimal places), it was necessary to adjust to make the statement of financial position agree, despite rounding errors.]

Summary of income statements for years ended 31 December

	2009	2010	2011	2012
	£m	£m	£m	£m
Sales revenue	100	100	100	100
Operating profit	19	24	6	10
Interest payable	(3)	(2)	(4)	(3)
Profit before taxation	16	22	2	7
Taxation	(8)	(9)	–	(3)
Profit for the period	8	13	2	4

[The individual figures are calculated by dividing each of the original figures by the sales revenue value for the year concerned and multiplying the result by 100. For example, the operating profit figure for 2009 is 28/152 × 100 = 19.]

9.3 Ali plc and Bhaskar plc

(a) The Altman-model Z-score calculated is as follows:

$$Z = 0.717a + 0.847b + 3.107c + 0.420d + 0.998e$$

where a = Working capital/Total assets

b = Accumulated retained profits/Total assets

c = Operating profit/Total assets

d = Book (statement of financial position) value of ordinary and preference shares/ Total liabilities at book (statement of financial position) value

e = Sales revenue/Total assets

For Ali plc, the Z-score is

$$0.717[(853.0 - 422.4)/1,300.0] + 0.847(367.6/1,300.0) + 3.107(151.3/1,300.0)$$
$$+ 0.420[687.6/(190.0 + 422.4)] + 0.998(1,478.1/1,300.0) = \underline{2.445}$$

For Bhaskar plc, the Z-score is

$$0.717[(816.5 - 293.1)/1,417.7] + 0.847(624.6/1,417.7) + 3.107(166.9/1,417.7)$$
$$+ 0.420[874.6/(250.0 + 293.1)] + 0.998(1,790.4/1,417.7) = \underline{2.940}$$

(b) The Z-scores for these two businesses are quite close, with Bhaskar looking slightly safer. They are both in the category of businesses in the 'zone of ignorance' and, therefore, difficult to classify (a Z-score between 1.23 and 4.14). This is quite unusual in that the Altman model is able confidently to classify 91 per cent of businesses. Clearly, these two businesses fall into the remaining 9 per cent.

It is questionable whether the Altman model is strictly applicable to UK businesses, since it was derived from data relating to US businesses that had failed. On the other hand, it probably provides a useful insight.

9.5 Green Ltd

(a)

	2010		2011		2012	
(1) Return on capital employed ratio	(0.2)/(8.4 + 6.5) × 100	(1.3)%	(2.0)/(4.0 + 8.2) × 100	(16.4)%	1.9/(4.4 + 7.4) × 100	16.1%
(2) Acid test ratio	2.8/4.1	0.68:1	2.6/5.8	0.45:1	4.1/6.1	0.67:1
(3) Trade receivables settlement period ratio*	2.8/11.5 × 12	2.9 months	2.6/8.0 × 12	3.9 months	4.1/9.5 × 12	5.2 months
(4) Interest cover ratio		no cover		no cover	1.9/1.5	1.3 times
(5) Gearing ratio	6.5/(6.5 + 8.4) × 100	43.6%	8.2/(8.2 + 4.0) × 100	67.2%	7.4/(7.4 + 4.4) × 100	62.7%

* The year-end trade receivables figures were used because it would not have been possible, with the information provided in the question, to use the average for the years.

In terms of profitability, Green Ltd seems to have improved in 2012, relative to the previous two years, particularly 2011. This has probably been the main reason for the improvement in liquidity since 2011. The increase in the time taken to collect the cash from credit customers is a concern. This has almost doubled since 2010. Over 5 months seems a very long time.

Gearing, which increased in 2011, has dropped a little in 2012. Given the level of profit, gearing still looks high, with the interest obligations not being very well covered by operating profit.

(b) Possibly the most useful help that your business could offer Green Ltd is some advice on reducing its level of working capital (current assets less current liabilities). As mentioned in (a), the trade receivables level in 2012 seems very high. This seems also to be true of inventories. At the same time, trade payables seem quite low (only 50% of the level of inventories in 2012). It seems perfectly plausible that a combination of taking longer to pay suppliers, getting in cash from customers more quickly and reducing the level of inventories could generate sufficient funds to eliminate the bank overdraft.

Your business may be reluctant to involve itself in providing finance. It is not, presumably, in the business of doing so. It may prefer to suggest that Green Ltd looks for some bank or equity finance from a more traditional source. Given the already high level of gearing, even assuming that the overdraft can be eliminated, as suggested above, equity looks a better bet than loan financing. Given that it is your business's only source of certain products, you may feel that supplying finance, and gaining the influence that this may bring, is the best way to protect your business's interests.

If your business is able and willing to advance equity finance (buy new shares issued by Green Ltd), the following points need to be addressed:

- *Future profitability.* How profitable can Green Ltd be in the future, with the new machinery?
- *Influence.* If your business is to buy shares, it will need to be sure of some considerable influence over Green Ltd's management. A seat on Green Ltd's board of directors seems a minimum requirement.
- *Exit route.* How will your business be able to liquidate its investment, as and when it wishes to do so? Green Ltd is not a plc and cannot, therefore be Stock Exchange listed. This means that there is no ready and obvious market for the shares.

9.8 Genesis Ltd

(a) Current ratio $= \dfrac{232}{550} = 0.42:1$

Acid test ratio $= \dfrac{104}{550} = 0.19:1$

Inventories turnover period $= \dfrac{128}{1,248} \times 365 = 37$ days

Average settlement period for trade receivables $= \dfrac{104}{1,640} \times 365 = 23$ days

Average settlement period for trade payables $= \dfrac{184}{1,260} \times 365 = 53$ days

It is difficult to make a judgement about such matters with no equivalent ratios for past periods or for other businesses and without knowledge of the business's own plans, but there is some evidence that this business is, in fact, overtrading. Both of the liquidity ratios look weak. The acid test ratio should probably be around 1:1. Customers are paying more than twice as quickly as suppliers are being paid. This suggests that pressure may be being applied to the former to pay quickly, perhaps with adverse results. It may also imply that payments are being delayed to suppliers because of a lack of available finance.

(b) Overtrading must be dealt with either by increasing the level of funding to match the level of activity, or by reducing the level of activity to match the funds available. The latter option may result in a reduction in operating profit in the short term but may be necessary to ensure long-term survival.

Chapter 10

10.1 Toggles plc

(a) 1 'Non-controlling interests' represents the portion, either of net assets (statement of financial position) or profit for the year (income statement), which is attributable to minority shareholders. Minority shareholders exist where the parent company does not own all of the shares in its subsidiary. Since, by definition, the parent company is the major shareholder in each of its subsidiaries, any other shareholders must be a minority, in terms of number of shares owned.

2 'Goodwill arising on consolidation' is the difference, at the time that the parent acquires the subsidiary, between what is paid for the subsidiary company shares and what they are 'worth'. 'Worth' normally is based on the fair values of the underlying assets (net of liabilities) of the subsidiary. These are not necessarily, nor usually, the statement of financial position values. Goodwill, therefore, represents the excess of what was paid over the fair values of the (net) assets of the subsidiary. As such, goodwill arising on consolidation is an intangible asset that represents the amount that the parent was prepared to pay for the value of the fact that the subsidiary has a workforce in place and any possible synergies that will arise from the parent and the subsidiary having a close relationship.

3 The retained earnings of the parent company will be its own cumulative profits net of tax and dividends paid.

   When the results of the subsidiaries are consolidated with those of the parent, the parent's share of the post-acquisition retained earnings of its subsidiaries is added to its own retained earnings figure. In this way the parent is, in effect, credited with its share of the subsidiaries' after-tax profit that has arisen since the takeover.

(b) The objective of preparing consolidated financial statements is to reflect the underlying economic reality that the assets of the subsidiary companies are as much under the control of the shareholders of the parent, acting through their board of directors, as are the assets owned directly by the parent. This will be true despite the fact that the subsidiary is strictly a company separate from the parent. It is also despite the fact that the parent may not own all of the shares of the subsidiaries.

Consolidated financial statements provide an example where accounting tends to put 'content' before 'form'. That is to say, it tries to reflect economic reality rather than the strict legal position. This is done in an attempt to provide more useful information.

10.2 Arnold plc

Group income statement for the year ended 31 December

	£m
Revenue (83 + 47)	130
Cost of sales (36 + 19)	(55)
Gross profit	75
Administration expenses (14 + 7)	(21)
Distribution expenses (21 + 10)	(31)
Profit before taxation	23
Taxation (4 + 3)	(7)
Profit for the year	16
Attributable to non-controlling interests (25% × 8)	(2)
Profit for the year attributable to Arnold plc shareholders	14

10.3   **Giant group statement of financial position as at 31 March**

		£m
ASSETS		
Non-current assets (at cost less depreciation)		
Property, plant and equipment		
Land		39
Plant		63
Vehicles		25
		127
Current assets		
Inventories		46
Trade receivables		59
Cash		27
		132
Total assets		259
EQUITY AND LIABILITIES		
Equity		
Called-up share capital: ordinary shares of £1 each, fully paid		50
Share premium account		40
Retained earnings		46
		136
Non-current liabilities		
Loan notes		63
Current liabilities		
Trade payables		60
Total equity and liabilities		259

Note that the group statement of financial position is prepared by adding all like items together. The investment in 10 million shares of Jack Ltd (£30m), in the statement of financial position of Giant plc, is then compared with the equity (in total) in Jack Ltd's statement of financial position. Since Giant paid exactly the fair values of Jack's assets *and* bought all of Jack's shares, these two figures are equal and can be cancelled.

10.4 The statement of financial position of Jumbo plc and its subsidiary will be as follows:

Statement of financial position as at 31 March

		£m
ASSETS		
Non-current assets (at cost less depreciation)		
Property, plant and equipment		
Land		102
Plant		67
Vehicles		57
		226
Current assets		
Inventories		87
Trade receivables		70
Cash		24
		181
Total assets		407

EQUITY AND LIABILITIES	£m
Equity	
Called-up share capital: ordinary shares of £1 each, fully paid	100
Retained earnings	41
	141
Non-controlling interests	16
	157
Non-current liabilities	
Loan notes	170
Current liabilities	
Trade payables	80
Total equity and liabilities	407

Note that the normal approach is taken with various assets and external claims (that is, adding like items together). The 'non-controlling interests' figure represents the minorities' share (8 million of 20 million ordinary shares) in the equity of Nipper plc (40 per cent of £40 million).

10.5 The statement of financial position of Apple Ltd and its subsidiary will be as follows:

Statement of financial position as at 30 September

ASSETS	£000
Non-current assets (at cost less depreciation)	
Property, plant and equipment (950 + 320)	1,270
Goodwill arising on consolidation (see Note 2)	24
	1,294
Current assets	
Inventories (320 + 160)	480
Trade receivables (180 + 95)	275
Cash at bank (41 + 15)	56
	811
Total assets	2,105
EQUITY AND LIABILITIES	
Equity	
£1 fully paid ordinary shares	700
Reserves	307
	1,007
Non-controlling interests (see Note 3)	72
	1,079
Non-current liabilities	
Loan notes (500 + 160)	660
Current liabilities	
Trade payables (170 + 87)	257
Taxation (54 + 55)	109
	366
Total equity and liabilities	2,105

Notes

1 The normal approach is taken with various assets and external claims.

2 The goodwill arising on consolidation is the difference between what Apple Ltd paid for the shares in Pear Ltd (150,000 × £1.60 = £240,000), less the fair value of the net assets acquired (150,000/200,000 × £288,000 = £216,000), that is, £24,000.

3 The non-controlling interests figure is simply the minority shareholders' stake in the net assets of Pear Ltd. This is 50,000/200,000 × £288,000 = £72,000.

Chapter 11

11.1 Information

Some believe that the annual reports of companies are becoming too long and contain too much information. A few examples of the length of the 2011 reports of large companies are as follows:

Marks and Spencer plc	113 pages
Tesco plc	157 pages
Tate and Lyle plc	124 pages
Standard Life plc	271 pages

There is a danger that users will suffer from information overload if they are confronted with an excessive amount of information and that they will be unable to cope with it. This may, in turn, lead them to

- fail to distinguish between important and less important information;
- fail to approach the analysis of information in a logical and systematic manner;
- feel a sense of confusion and avoid the task of analysing the information.

Lengthy annual reports are likely to be a problem for the less sophisticated user. This problem has been recognised and many companies publish summarised accounts for private investors, which include only the key points. However, for sophisticated users the problem may be that the annual reports are still not long enough. They often wish to glean as much information as possible from the company in order to make investment decisions.

11.5 Dali plc

A striking feature of the segmental reports is that the car parts segment generates the highest revenue – more than the other two segments combined. Nevertheless, it is the aircraft parts segment that generates the highest profit. We can use some simple ratios at this point to help evaluate performance.

We can start by considering the profit generated in relation to the sales revenue for each operating segment. We can see from the table below that the boat parts segment generates the most profit in relation to sales revenue. Around 21 per cent, or £0.21 in every £1, of profit is derived from the sales revenue generated. The total revenue for this segment, however, is much lower than for the other two segments. Although the car parts segment generates the most revenue, less than 6 per cent, or £0.06 in every £1, of profit is derived from the sales revenue generated. It is worth noting that the aircraft parts segment suffered a large impairment charge during the year, which had a significant effect on profits. The reasons for this impairment charge should be investigated.

We can also compare the profit generated with the net assets employed (that is, total assets minus total liabilities) for each segment. We can see from the table below that the boat parts segment produces the best return on net assets employed by far: around 82 per cent, that is, £0.82 for every £1 invested. Once again, the car parts segment produces the worst results with a return of less than 24 per cent.

The relatively poor results from the car parts segment may simply reflect the nature of the market in which it operates. Compared with car parts segments of other businesses, it may be doing very well. Nevertheless, the business may still wish to consider whether future investment would not be better directed to those areas where greater profits can be found.

The investment in non-current assets during the period in relation to the total assets held is much higher for the boat parts segment. This may reflect the faith of the directors in the potential of this segment.

The depreciation charge as a percentage of segment assets seems to be high for all of the operating segments – but particularly for the car parts division. This should be investigated as it may suggest poor buying decisions.

Table of key results

	Car parts	Aircraft parts	Boat parts
Total revenue	£360m	£210m	£85m
Segment profit	£20m	£24m	£18m
Net assets (assets − liabilities)	£85m	£58m	£22m
Segment profit as a percentage of sales revenue	5.6%	11.4%	21.2%
Segment profit as a percentage of net assets employed	23.5%	41.4%	81.8%
Expenditure on non-current assets	£28m	£23m	£26m
Depreciation as a percentage of segment assets	51.6%	44.0%	34.1%

11.6 Alkrom plc

CPP income statement for the three-month period to 31 March

	CPP£m
Sales revenue (120/120 × £19.2m)	19.2
Cost of sales (120/115 × £16.0m)	16.7
Profit for the period	2.5

CPP statement of financial position as at 31 March

	CPP£m
ASSETS	
Non-current assets	
Property, plant and equipment	
Offices (£4m × 120/115)	4.2
Current assets	
Receivables	19.2
	23.4
EQUITY	
Equity (20.0 × 120/115)	20.9
Retained earnings	2.5
	23.4

11.7 Turner plc

We can see from the table below that the software segment generates the highest revenue, but also generates the lowest profit. We can use some simple ratios at this point to help evaluate segmental performance. We can start by considering the profit generated in relation to the sales revenue for each operating segment. We can see from the table that the engineering segment generates the most profit in relation to sales revenue. Around 23 per cent, or £0.23 in every £1, of profit is derived from the sales revenue generated. However, for the software segment, only 4 per cent, or £0.04 in every £1, of profit is derived from the sales revenue generated.

We can also compare the profit generated with the net assets employed (that is, total assets minus total liabilities) for each segment. We can see from the table that the electronics segment produces the best return on net assets employed: around £0.65 for every £1 invested. Once again, the software segment produces the worst results.

The reasons for the relatively poor results from the software segment need further investigation. There may be valid reasons; for example, it may be experiencing severe competitive pressures. The results for this segment, however, are not disastrous: it is making a profit. Nevertheless, the business may wish to re-evaluate its long-term presence in this market.

It is interesting to note that the software segment benefited most from the investment in non-current assets during the period – as much as the other two segments combined. The reason for such a large investment in such a relatively poorly performing segment needs to be justified. It is possible that the business will reap rewards for the investment in the future; however, we do not have enough information to understand the reasons for the investment decision.

Depreciation charges in the software segment are significantly higher than for the other operating segments. This may be because the segment has more non-current assets, although we do not have a figure for the non-current assets held. The depreciation charge as a percentage of segment assets is also higher and the reasons for this should be investigated.

Table of key results

	Software	Electronics	Engineering
Total revenue	£250m	£230m	£52m
Segment profit	£10m	£34m	£12m
Net assets (assets – liabilities)	£85m	£52m	£30m
Segment profit as a percentage of sales revenue	4.0%	14.8%	23.1%
Segment profit as a percentage of net assets employed	11.8%	65.4%	40.0%
Expenditure on non-current assets	£22m	£12m	£10m
Depreciation as a percentage of segment assets	42.9%	38.9%	29.4%

Chapter 12

12.1 Strengthening the independence of external auditors

Various suggestions have been made to strengthen auditor independence. They include:

- preventing auditing firms from undertaking non-audit work for a client company;
- rotating external auditors on a regular basis (say every five years);
- rotating the audit partner responsible for overseeing the audit (rather than the audit firm) on a regular basis;
- requiring peer group assessment (where another audit firm reviews the work that has been done for a client company). This type of assessment may be carried out every three years or so;
- establishing audit committees, which monitor and review the work carried out by the audit firm;
- preventing an audit firm from undertaking an audit where the audit fee would represent a large proportion (say 10 per cent or more) of the total annual fees generated by the audit firm.

12.2 Non-executive directors

The following criteria may be used to evaluate the performance of a non-executive director:

- willingness to spend time in understanding the business and in acquiring additional skills to improve effectiveness;
- contribution made to board discussions on key issues such as strategy development;
- effectiveness in challenging proposals made by identifying key weaknesses and assumptions;
- independence of mind and ability to resist undue pressure from other directors;
- perseverance in following up unresolved issues and in defending positions taken;
- ability to work as part of a team, when required, and to establish effective relations with key individuals, including other board members.

This is not an exhaustive list.

12.4 Institutional shareholders

The benefits that may accrue from close ties with institutional shareholders are as follows:

- It provides the board of directors with the opportunity to explain the future direction of the company, which may lead to a better understanding of board proposals and decisions that have been made. This may, in turn, make institutional shareholders more willing to offer support during difficult times.
- It may encourage institutional shareholders to take a long-term view. If the board can provide a clear vision and strategy for the company, the shareholders may become less concerned with any short-term setbacks and become more concerned with achieving long-term goals.

- It can provide an external discipline on the board. The directors will be subjected to considerable scrutiny when meeting institutional shareholders. They will have to justify their decisions and be prepared to answer tough questions. This can, however, improve the quality of decisions made.
- It can provide valuable feedback on board proposals. Institutional investors may be sounded out on particular ideas that are under review. Their views can then be taken into account when making a final decision.
- It can help in future funding. Where institutional shareholders have good relations with the board and have confidence in the future direction of the company, they are more likely to be sympathetic to requests for additional funding.

There are various problems that can arise from close links with institutional shareholders. For example, there is a risk that certain commercially sensitive information provided to them will not be treated in confidence. There is also a risk in upsetting small shareholders, who may feel that large institutional shareholders are given undue influence over decisions. Finally, there is a problem in determining what are the acceptable limits to the discussions and information that is offered.

Appendix A

A1.1 *Account to be debited*

(a)	Inventories
(b)	Equity (or a separate drawings account)
(c)	Interest on borrowings
(d)	Inventories
(e)	Cash
(f)	Wages
(g)	Equity (or a separate drawings account)
(h)	Trade payables
(i)	Electricity (or heat and light)
(j)	Cash

Account to be credited

Trade payables
Cash
Cash
Cash
Trade receivables
Cash
Trade receivables
Cash
Cash
Sales revenue

Note that the precise name given to an account is not crucial so long as it is clear to those who are using the information what each account deals with.

A1.2 (a) and **(b)**

Cash

		£			£
1 Feb	Equity	6,000	3 Feb	Inventories	2,600
15 Feb	Sales revenue	4,000	5 Feb	Equipment	800
28 Feb	Trade receivables	2,500	9 Feb	Rent	250
			10 Feb	Electricity	240
			11 Feb	General expenses	200
			21 Feb	Equity	1,000
			25 Feb	Trade payables	2,000
			28 Feb	Balance c/d	5,410
		12,500			12,500
1 Mar	Balance b/d	5,410			

Equity

		£			£
21 Feb	Cash	1,000	1 Feb	Cash	6,000
28 Feb	Balance c/d	5,000			
		6,000			6,000
			28 Feb	Balance b/d	5,000
28 Feb	Balance c/d	7,410	28 Feb	Income statement	2,410
		7,410			7,410
			1 Mar	Balance b/d	7,410

Inventories

		£			£
3 Feb	Cash	2,600	15 Feb	Cost of sales	2,400
6 Feb	Trade payables	3,000	19 Feb	Cost of sales	2,300
			28 Feb	Balance c/d	900
		5,600			5,600
1 Mar	Balance b/d	900			

Equipment

		£			£
5 Feb	Cash	800			

Trade payables

		£			£
25 Feb	Cash	2,000	6 Feb	Inventories	3,000
28 Feb	Balance c/d	1,000			
		3,000			3,000
			1 Mar	Balance b/d	1,000

Rent

		£			£
9 Feb	Cash	250	28 Feb	Income statement	250

Electricity

		£			£
10 Feb	Cash	240	28 Feb	Income statement	240

General expenses

		£			£
11 Feb	Cash	200	28 Feb	Income statement	200

Sales revenue

		£			£
28 Feb	Balance c/d	7,800	15 Feb	Cash	4,000
			19 Feb	Trade receivables	3,800
		7,800			7,800
28 Feb	Income statement	7,800	28 Feb	Balance b/d	7,800

Cost of sales

		£			£
15 Feb	Inventories	2,400	28 Feb	Balance c/d	4,700
19 Feb	Inventories	2,300			
		4,700			4,700
28 Feb	Balance b/d	4,700	28 Feb	Income statement	4,700

Trade receivables

		£			£
19 Feb	Sales revenue	3,800	28 Feb	Cash	2,500
			28 Feb	Balance c/d	1,300
		3,800			3,800
1 Mar	Balance b/d	1,300			

Trial balance as at 28 February

	Debits £	Credits £
Cash	5,410	
Equity		5,000
Inventories	900	
Equipment	800	
Trade payables		1,000
Rent	250	
Electricity	240	
General expenses	200	
Sales revenue		7,800
Cost of sales	4,700	
Trade receivables	1,300	
	13,800	13,800

(c)

Income statement

	£		£
28 Feb Cost of sales	4,700	28 February Sales revenue	7,800
28 Feb Rent	250		
28 Feb Electricity	240		
28 Feb General expenses	200		
28 Feb Equity (profit)	2,410		
	7,800		7,800

Statement of financial position as at 28 February

	£
ASSETS	
Non-current assets	
Equipment	800
Current assets	
Inventories	900
Trade receivables	1,300
Cash	5,410
	7,610
Total assets	8,410
EQUITY AND LIABILITIES	
Equity (owners' claim)	7,410
Current liabilities	
Trade payables	1,000
Total equity and liabilities	8,410

Income statement for the month ended 28 February

	£
Sales revenue	7,800
Cost of sales	(4,700)
Gross profit	3,100
Rent	(250)
Electricity	(240)
General expenses	(200)
Profit for the month	2,410

A1.3 (a) and **(b)**

Buildings

	£		£
1 Jan Balance brought down	25,000		

Fittings – cost

		£			£
1 Jan	Balance brought down	10,000	31 Dec	Balance carried down	12,000
	Cash	2,000			
		12,000			12,000
1 Jan	Balance brought down	12,000			

Fittings – depreciation

		£			£
31 Dec	Balance carried down	4,400	1 Jan	Balance brought down	2,000
			31 Dec	Income statement	
				(£12,000 × 20%)	2,400
		4,400			4,400
			1 Jan	Balance brought down	4,400

General expenses

		£			£
1 Jan	Balance brought down	140	31 Dec	Income statement	570
	Cash	580		Balance carried down	150
		720			720
1 Jan	Balance brought down	150			

Inventories

		£			£
1 Jan	Balance brought down	1,350	31 Dec	Cost of sales	15,220
31 Dec	Trade payables	17,220		Cost of sales	4,900
	Cash	3,760		Equity	560
				Balance carried down	1,650
		22,330			22,330
1 Jan	Balance brought down	1,650			

Cost of sales

		£			£
31 Dec	Inventories	15,220	31 Dec	Income statement	20,120
	Inventories	4,900			
		20,120			20,120

Rent

		£			£
1 Jan	Balance brought down	500	31 Dec	Income statement	3,000
31 Dec	Cash	3,000		Balance carried down	500
		3,500			3,500
1 Jan	Balance brought down	500			

Trade receivables

		£			£
1 Jan	Balance brought down	1,840	31 Dec	Cash	32,810
31 Dec	Sales revenue	33,100		Income statement	260
				(bad debt)	
				Balance carried down	1,870
		34,940			34,940
1 Jan	Balance brought down	1,870			

Cash

		£			£
1 Jan	Balance brought down	2,180	31 Dec	Inventories	3,760
31 Dec	Sales revenue	10,360		Wages	3,770
	Borrowings	2,000		Rent	3,000
	Trade receivables	32,810		Electricity	1,070
				General expenses	580
				Fittings	2,000
				Borrowings	1,000
				Trade payables	18,150
				Equity	10,400
				Balance carried down	3,620
		47,350			47,350
1 Jan	Balance brought down	3,620			

Equity

		£			£
31 Dec	Inventories	560	1 Jan	Balance brought down	25,050
	Cash	10,400		Income statement (profit)	10,900
	Balance carried down	24,990			
		35,950			35,950
			1 Jan	Balance brought down	24,990

Borrowings

		£			£
30 June	Cash	1,000	1 Jan	Balance brought down	12,000
31 Dec	Balance carried down	13,000		Cash	2,000
		14,000			14,000
			1 Jan	Balance brought down	13,000

Trade payables

		£			£
31 Dec	Cash	18,150	1 Jan	Balance brought down	1,690
	Balance carried down	760	31 Dec	Inventories	17,220
		18,910			18,910
			1 Jan	Balance brought down	760

Electricity

		£			£
31 Dec	Cash	1,070	1 Jan	Balance brought down	270
31 Dec	Balance carried down	290	31 Dec	Income statement	1,090
		1,360			1,360
			1 Jan	Balance brought down	290

Sales revenue

		£			£
31 Dec	Income statement	43,460	31 Dec	Trade receivables	33,100
				Cash	10,360
		43,460			43,460

Wages

		£			£
31 Dec	Cash	3,770	31 Dec	Income statement	3,770

Interest on borrowings

	£		£
		31 Dec Income statement	
		[(6/12 × 14,000) +	
		(6/12 × 13,000)] × 10%	1,350

(c) **Income statement for the year to 31 December**

	£		£
31 Dec Cost of sales	20,120	31 Dec Sales revenue	43,460
Depreciation	2,400		
General expenses	570		
Rent	3,000		
Bad debts (trade receivables)	260		
Electricity	1,090		
Wages	3,770		
Interest on borrowings	1,350		
Profit (equity)	10,900		
	43,460		43,460

(d) **Statement of financial position as at 31 December last year**

			£
ASSETS			
Non-current assets			
Property, plant and equipment			
Buildings			25,000
Fittings: cost		12,000	
depreciation		(4,400)	7,600
			32,600
Current assets			
Inventories of stationery			150
Inventories			1,650
Prepaid rent			500
Trade receivables			1,870
Cash			3,620
			7,790
Total assets			40,390
EQUITY AND LIABILITIES			
Equity (owners' claim)			24,990
Non-current liabilities			
Borrowings			13,000
Current liabilities			
Trade payables			760
Accrued electricity			290
Accrued interest on borrowings			1,350
			2,400
Total equity and liabilities			40,390

Index

Note: page numbers in **bold** refer to definitions in the Glossary

change, standards inhibiting 165
channel stuffing 173
charities 24
chief executive officers (CEO) 426, **491**
  audit committee communication with 441
  becoming chairmen 430–1
  chairmen and, separation of roles 428–30
  fees 435
churches 24
claims 33, **491**
  assets and relationship between 36–9
  bookkeeping entries 474
  classification of 44
  inter-company 364–5
  owners' 44, 117, 190–1
  statements of financial position 36–9, 44
clubs 24
common-size financial statements 303–7, **491**
community representatives 2, 3
Companies Acts 384
Companies House see Registrar of Companies
company law 153
company objectives 460
comparability, accounting information 7, 10, **491**
compensation for loss of office, directors 445
competitors 2, 3
completeness, accounting information 10
complexity of standards 166–7
compliance mentality 443
compound interest 244
comprehensive income, statements of see statements of comprehensive income
computers 43, 473
conceptual framework **491**
  IASB 169–70
  need for 168–69
confirmatory value, accounting information 10
conflicts
  non-executive directors' roles 433
  of interest 4, 421
conformity, false, standards imposing 166
consensus-seeking under standards 166
consistency convention 95, 161, **491**
consolidated financial statements see groups: financial statements
consolidating shares 119, **491**
constant purchasing power (CPP) see current purchasing power
construction contracts 75
constructive obligations 218, 219
contingent assets 223–4, **491**
contingent liabilities 221–2, **492**
continuous services 75–6
contracts, long-term 74–5
control
  accounting for less than controlling interests 368–71

boards of directors exercising 426–7, 460
directors' behaviour 421
goods passing to buyers 74
groups 328, 336
internal 441
conventions of accounting see accounting; conventions
copyrights 51
corporate governance 117, 420–2, **492**
  risk management 437–8
  shareholder activism 461–7
  statements 436
  UK Code 423–6, **499**
    assessing board performance 459–60
    audit committees 439–44
    chief executive officers becoming chairmen 430–1
    corporate governance statements 436
    directors' share options 455
    institutional shareholders 463
    non-executive directors 433
    remuneration policies 444–5
    separating chairman and chief executive officer roles 428
    service contracts 445
    shareholder activism 466
    tenure of directors 445
  value of 461
corporation tax 114, 135, **492**
cost-benefit analysis of accounting information 8–10
cost of goods sold see cost of sales
cost of sales 68, 70–1, 477–8, 480–1, 484–5, **492**
costs
  of assets 81–2
  borrowing, capitalisation 235–8
  finance leasing 230
  replacement 48
  of standards 166
  see also historic cost
CPP see current purchasing power
creative accounting 172–8, 220–1, 228, 313, **492**
credit 149
  sales 42, 74, 95
  see also debts; trade receivables
creditors 110
  trade see trade payables
credits, bookkeeping 474–86, **492**
current assets 42, 45–6, 270, **492**
current cost accounting (CCA) 412–14, **492**
current liabilities 44, 134, 270, 485, **492**
current purchasing power (CPP) 410–11, 413–14, **492**
current ratios 270, 272, 301, 302, 308–9, **492**
current value accounting 47–8
customer lists 228
customers 2, 3, 20